CONTENTS

Contents

Contents

ACKNOWLEDGMENTS

I am grateful to all the colleagues and friends who have encouraged this work over the years. The following list is surely incomplete, but let me do my best to remember them here.

Chapter 1 was originally presented as an address to the Hegel Society of Great Britain—I no longer remember precisely when, perhaps shortly before or shortly after I joined the Philosophy Department of the University of Essex in 1983. At all events, an enlarged version later appeared in *The Owl of Minerva* 17, no. 1 (Fall 1985): 5–19. I am grateful to the Society and to the editors and readers of the journal. The present version has expanded greatly, thanks to the assistance of Professor Christoph Jamme of the Universität Lüneburg.

Chapter 2 appears under the title "Three Ends of the Absolute: Schelling on Inhibition, Hölderlin on Separation, and Novalis on Density," in *Research in Phenomenology* 32 (2002): 60–85; and, under the title "Inhibition, Separation, Density: Ends of the Absolute in Schelling, Hölderlin, and Novalis," the piece will also appear in *Idealism without Absolutes: Philosophy at the Limits of Romanticism*, ed. Tilottama Rajan and Arkady Plotnitsky (Albany: State University of New York Press, 2004). My thanks to Jim Risser, John Sallis, Tilottama Rajan, and Arkady Plotnitsky. My thanks also to the students and faculty of the University of Western Ontario's Centre for the Study of Theory and Criticism, led at that time by Tilottama Rajan, and to David Clark, who heard an earlier version of this chapter and helped me to reconsider the matters discussed in its final part. The piece has been revised for its appearance here.

Chapter 3 began as a seminar at the Collegium Phaenomenologicum in Perugia, Italy, in the early 1980s. It was then published as "The Crisis of Reason in the Nineteenth Century: Schelling's Treatise on Human Freedom (1809)" in the volume *The Collegium Phaenomenologicum: The First Ten Years,* ed. John Sallis, Giuseppina Moneta, and Jacques Taminiaux (The Hague: M. Nijhoff, 1989), 13–32. My thanks to the editors and to all the colleagues of the Collegium over the years, especially John Sallis, Charles Scott, and Walter Brogan. A French version of the seminar was presented in Nice in early December of 1990 upon the invitation of Domique Janicaud, whose death in August of 2002 leaves so many of us bereft. And, while it may seem odd, I would like to express my thanks to Herman Melville, whose "The Bell-Tower" has given me so much—at the stroke of one. Someone asked me recently whether I was ashamed to be a U.S.-American and I replied that I was not—but that I was ashamed of George W. Bush because he clearly has read relatively little Melville.

Chapter 4 was written especially for this volume. It appears in a different form under the title "*Das Vergangene wird gewußt, das Gewußte [aber] wird erzählt*': Trauma, Forgetting, and Narrative in F. W. J. Schelling's *Die Weltalter*," in *Philosophy and the Discourses of Trauma*, ed. Linda Belau and Petar Ramadanovic, on-line in *Postmodern Culture* 11, no. 2 (January 2001), at http://www.iath.virginia.edu/pmc/. Book publication in *Topologies of Trauma: Essays on the Limit of Knowledge and Memory*, ed. Linda Belau and Petar Ramadanovic (New York: Other Press, 2002), 3–31. My thanks to Linda Belau and Petar Ramadanovic for their kind invitation to submit the chapter to them. And my thanks to my students over the years from 1992 to 2000 at DePaul University, where so much of the work gathered up into this book—including this chapter—was presented in graduate seminars.

Jason Wirth of Oglethorpe University asked me to contribute chapter 5, "God's Footstool," to a forthcoming edited volume on Schelling entitled *Schelling Now*, also to be published by Indiana University Press. In the present volume it is revised and expanded. Readers interested in Schelling owe a great deal to Jason Wirth's work as translator, commentator, and teacher. Unfortunately, his Schelling book, *The Conspiracy of Life* (Albany: State University of New York Press, 2003), appeared too late for me to make reference to it in the present volume—I intend to learn from it in the future.

Chapter 6, "Brazen Wheels," written especially for this volume, was also presented as a lecture at the conference "Elective Affinities: German Philosophy and Music," at the University of Wisconsin in October 2003, the proceedings of which are to be published. It appears here in greatly expanded form. My thanks to Jost Hermand and Gerhard Richter for the Madison Workshop on philosophy and music, and to Sabine Mödersheim, an essential member of the Wisconsin team.

"Voices of Empedocles," chapter 7, was originally a lecture course presented at the Collège International de Philosophie in November–December of 1990. I translated it into English during the summer of 2003, emending the lectures in accord with work done during the intervening years. My thanks to Michel Déguy, the late Jacques Derrida, and Françoise Dastur for their support of the original course.

Chapter 8 was written especially for this volume.

Chapter 9 has appeared in two different forms in two different places. It appeared first under the title "A Small Number of Houses in a Universe of Tragedy: Aristotle's περὶ ποιητικῆς and Hölderlin's *Anmerkungen*," in *Tragedy and Philosophy: A Collection of Contemporary Essays*, ed. Miguel de Bestegui and Simon Sparks (London: Routledge, 2000), 88–116. In a revised and expanded form it appeared under the title "A Small Number of Houses in the Tragic Universe: A Second Look at Aristotle's *Poetics* and Hölderlin's *Anmerkungen*," in *"Es bleibt aber eine Spur / Doch eines Wortes": Zur späten Hymnik und Tragödientheorie Friedrich Hölderlins*, ed. Christoph Jamme and Anja Lemke (Paderborn: Wilhelm Fink Verlag, 2003), 345–378. My thanks to Anja Lemke and Christoph Jamme, and to Miguel de Bestegui for first commissioning the essay. For the book I have once again revised and expanded the piece.

Chapter 10, written especially for this volume, was also the basis for the André Schuwer Memorial Lecture given at the Society for Phenomenology and Existential Philosophy in Chicago on October 12, 2002. My thanks to David L. Smith, C.S.Sp., for inviting me to give the lecture. I am grateful to the memories of André Schuwer and Father Ed Murray for what they achieved at Duquesne University in the 1960s and 1970s, for several generations of students. John Sallis, of course, was an essential member of that team. Whatever philosophical work I have done over the years, at least when it was at its best, was due to their teaching and encouragement.

"Antigone's Clout," chapter 11, written especially for this volume, provided the basis for a lecture given in the spring of 2003 at California State University at Stanislaus and the University of Oregon. My gratitude to Valerie Broin, Daniela Neu, Alejandro Vallega, Jena Jolissaint, and Peter Warnek. I first became interested in Lacan's reading of *Antigone*, in connection with Hölderlin's translation and commentary, as a result of Cecilia Sjöholm's lectures at DePaul University; conversations with Charles Shepherdson over the years have been invaluable.

Chapter 12, written especially for this volume, was also the basis for a lecture entitled "The Tragic Absolute: Hölderlin and Nietzsche." It was first a Studium Generale Invited Lecture at the Universiteit Nijmegen, Holland, on

September 26, 2000. Then, under the title "Hölderlin und Nietzsche zwischen Antike und Moderne," it was presented as a Studium Generale Invited Lecture at the Universität Tübingen on December 4, 2000. Finally, it was presented at the Universität Lüneburg on December 5, 2000. My thanks to colleagues at Nijmegen, Tübingen, and Lüneburg, especially Professors Iris Därmann and Christoph Jamme of Lüneburg, and Professor Günter Figal, at that time in Tübingen, now in Freiburg. A portion of the chapter appears under the title "Nietzschean Reminiscences of Schelling's *Philosophy of Mythology* (1842)," in *Epoché* 8:2 (Spring 2004), 181–193. My thanks to Walter Brogan.

At the moment I was ready to mail the final manuscript to the publisher, I received as a gift from Christoph Jamme the four volumes of his and Frank Völkel's *Hölderlin und der Deutsche Idealismus* (Stuttgart-Bad Canstatt: Frommann-Holzboog Verlag, 2003), over eighteen hundred closely printed pages of documents and interpretations of Hölderlin as a *philosopher*. The volumes also have much to tell us about Schelling, Fichte, Hegel, Novalis, and dozens of other figures in the history of German Idealism and Romanticism. These volumes were not so much a gift as an opportunity for me to pursue an entirely new education in the subject matter of my book. By rights I ought to have delayed publication of *The Tragic Absolute* for at least a year or two, in order to give myself the time to absorb the new information and the new insights granted by this publication. The delay would have changed many things about the present volume—for example, the way in which Hegel appears here, which is to say, scarcely at all; it would have turned me with heightened awareness to Hegel's earliest writings, long before *The Phenomenology of Spirit*. No doubt it would have altered many other things in the present book, expanding it immensely, but I have decided to go ahead and release it. I thank Christoph Jamme and pledge to him that I will continue my education; I apologize for the very few references I was able to incorporate into my work at the last minute. To younger scholars who are intrigued by the figures and texts of German Idealism and Romanticism I can say that there are scores of excellent topics for further research outlined in these volumes—a gold mine for those who wish to expand the kinds of inquiries we are currently making into this astonishing era of philosophy and letters.

I thank Angelica Nuzzo for our wonderful conversations over the years on Kant, Hegel, and German Idealism generally. Frequent conversations with Elizabeth Sikes over the past few years about Hölderlin and Schelling continue to challenge and inspire me. Dr. Marianne Schütz, of the Hölderlin-Archiv in the Landesbibliothek Baden-Württemberg, Stuttgart, has been the essence of hospitality and expertise, and I thank her for her generous assistance. Daw-Nay Evans and Andrew LaZella helped with the research for this book, as did the staff at the John T. Richardson Library at DePaul University, and I thank them. I am grateful to Dr. Kevin Thomas Miles for his calassol (yes, the spelling is perfect) friendship, and to Brigitte Bruns for the gift of solitude. Dee Mortensen and Janet Rabinowitch at Indiana University Press are publishers without parallel, and, like many others in the academic world, I owe them much thanks. Likewise, my thanks to Carol Kennedy, Miki Bird, and Jane Lyle for seeing the book through copyediting and production. Jason Wirth and Dennis Schmidt read the manuscript and made many valuable suggestions—I am most grateful to them. David Matthew Krell, my "roomie," designed the cover of the book, for which *muchisimas gracias*. Finally, to Anna Vaughn Clissold, Megan Cairns, David Thomas, and Memita, my thanks for their generous help with proofreading and the index.

The University Research Council at DePaul University and the German Academic Exchange Service supported the research, writing, and publication of this volume, and I am grateful to them. My thanks, finally, to the College of Liberal Arts and Sciences at DePaul University and its inspired dean, Dr. Michael Mezey, who for years now has generously supported my work with money, sympathy, patience, loyalty, and wit.

D. F. K.

Strobelhütte, St. Ulrich; Chicago

Note: Works that are clearly identified in the body of my text as the sources under discussion are not indicated by a code letter but are cited by page number alone. For example, chapter 3 discusses Schelling's *Weltalter Fragmente* at some length and in considerable detail, so that readers will not need any letter code in order to locate the volume cited. Readers should also note that the spelling in the German texts is often inconsistent: some editors modernize the German, others do not; some editors allow Schelling's and Hölderlin's Swabian dialect to stand, others spruce it up and turn it into *Hochdeutsch.* I have tried to cite each source faithfully, even at the risk of leaving readers baffled between *Sein* and *Seyn, Schicksal* and *Shiksaal, dies* and *diß.*

Works by G. W. F. Hegel

HW 1–20   Volumes 1 through 20 of G. W. F. Hegel, *Werke in zwanzig Bänden,* Theorie Werkausgabe, ed. Eva Moldenhauer and Karl Markus Michel. Frankfurt am Main: Suhrkamp, 1970 ff.

HB 1–4   Volumes 1 through 4 of G. W. F. Hegel, *Briefe von und an Hegel,* ed. Johannes Hoffmeister. Hamburg: Felix Meiner Verlag, 1952–1960.

PG   *Phänomenologie des Geistes,* ed. Johannes Hoffmeister. 6th ed. Hamburg: Felix Meiner Verlag, 1952.

Works by Friedrich Hölderlin

CHV 1, 2, 3   Volumes 1, 2, and 3 of *Friedrich Hölderlin Sämtliche Werke und Briefe,* ed. Michael Knaupp. Munich: Carl Hanser Verlag, 1992.

DKV 1, 2, 3   Volumes 1, 2, and 3 of *Friedrich Hölderlin Sämtliche Werke und Briefe in drei Bänden,* ed. Jochen Schmidt. Frankfurt am Main: Deutscher Klassiker Verlag, 1994.

I   *Hölderlin Werke und Briefe,* ed. Friedrich Beißner and Jochen Schmidt. Frankfurt am Main: Insel Verlag, 1969.

FHA 12–16   Volumes 12 through 16 of *Friedrich Hölderlin Sämtliche Werke,* ed. D. E. Sattler. Basel and Frankfurt: Stroemfeld and Roter Stern, 1988. This is the Frankfurter Historisch-Kritische Ausgabe, most often referred to in the literature as FHA.

StA 5   Volume 5 *(Übersetzungen)* of *Hölderlin Sämtliche Werke,* ed. Friedrich Beissner. Stuttgart: Verlag W. Kohlhammer, 1952. This is the Große Stuttgarter Hölderlin-Ausgabe, most often referred to as StA.

Works by Immanuel Kant

KrV   *Kritik der reinen Vernunft,* ed. Raymund Schmidt. Hamburg: Meiner Verlag, 1956. Cited according to the A and/or B editions of the Preußische Akademieausgabe.

KpV   *Kritik der praktischen Vernunft,* ed. Joachim Kopper. Stuttgart: Reclam Verlag, 1966. Cited according to the pagination of the Preußische Akademieausgabe.

KU   *Kritik der Urteilskraft,* ed. Gerhard Lehmann. Stuttgart: Reclam Verlag, 1966. Cited according to the pagination of the Preußische Akademieausgabe.

Works by Friedrich Nietzsche

KSA   *Kritische Studienausgabe der Werke,* ed. Giorgio Colli and Mazzino Montinari, 15 vols. Berlin and New York: Walter de Gruyter, 1980.

KSAB   *Kritische Studienausgabe der Briefe,* ed. Giorgio Colli and Mazzino Montinari, 8 vols. Berlin and Munich: Walter de Gruyter and Deutscher Taschenbuch Verlag, 1986.

Works by Novalis (Friedrich von Hardenberg)

Werke, Tagebücher und Briefe, ed. Hans-Joachim Mähl and Richard Samuel, 3 vols. Munich: Carl Hanser Verlag, 1987, cited without code by volume and page in the body of my text. Particular reference is made to vol. 2, *Das philosophisch-theoretische Werk.*

Works by F. W. J. Schelling

1   *Philosophische Briefe über Dogmatismus und Kriticismus,* ed. Karl Schelling for F. W. J. Schelling, *Sämmtliche Werke.* Stuttgart and Augsburg: J. G. Cotta'scher Verlag, 1859.

3   *Erster Entwurf eines Systems der Naturphilosophie,* ed. Karl Schelling for the *Sämmtliche Werke.*

5   *Philosophie der Kunst,* ed. Karl Schelling for the *Sämmtliche Werke* from his father's literary remains.

7   *Abhandlung über das Wesen der menschlichen Freiheit und die damit zusammenhängenden Gegenstände,* ed. Karl Schelling for the *Sämmtliche Werke.* See also the edition by Horst Fuhrmans. Stuttgart: Reclam Verlag, 1964.

8   *Die Weltalter, Erstes Buch,* ed. Karl Schelling for the *Sämmtliche Werke.* This volume also contains *Über die Gottheiten von Samothrake (1815).*

II/1   *Einleitung in die Philosophie der Mythologie* (1842), in the edition by Karl Schelling.

II/2   *Philosophie der Mythologie* (1842), in the edition by Karl Schelling.

II/3   *Einleitung in die Philosophie der Offenbarung; oder Begründung der positiven Philosophie* (the Berlin lectures, Winter Semester 1842–1843), in the edition by Karl Schelling.

System   *System der Weltalter: Münchener Vorlesung 1827/28 in einer Nachschrift von Ernst von Lasaulx,* ed. Siegbert Peetz. Frankfurt am Main: V. Klostermann, 1990, a later formulation of Schelling's never-completed, never-published magnum opus. *System des transzendentalen Idealismus,* Philosophische Bibliothek Band 254. Hamburg: Felix Meiner, 1957, cited without code by page number in the body of my text. *Die Weltalter Fragmente: In den Urfassungen von 1811 und 1813,* ed. Manfred Schröter. Nachlaßband to the Münchner Jubiläumsdruck. Munich: Biederstein Verlag und Leibniz Verlag, 1946. This volume presents the original versions of

Die Weltalter, set in print but not released for publication in 1811 and 1813; I cite it without code by page number in the body of my text.

Works by Sophocles

C   *Sophocles I: Oedipus the King, Oedipus at Colonus, Antigone,* in *The Complete Greek Tragedies,* ed. David Grene and Richmond Lattimore. Chicago: University of Chicago Press, 1954. In the 1991 edition, all three tragedies are translated by David Grene, but I have most often used the 1954 edition, in which *Oedipus the King* is translated by David Grene, *Oedipus at Colonus* by Robert Fitzgerald, and *Antigone* by Elizabeth Wyckoff.

L   *Sophocles,* tr. F. Storr. Loeb Classical Library, 2 vols. Cambridge, Mass., and London: Harvard University Press and William Heinemann, 1981, vol. 1. The Greek text is based on that of Dindorf (Oxford, 1860) and Jebb (Oxford, 1884–1896).

O   *Sophoclis Fabulae,* ed. H. Lloyd-Jones and N. G. Wilson, Oxford Classical Texts. Oxford: Oxford University Press, 1990.

T   *Sophokles Dramen: Griechisch und Deutsch,* tr. Wilhelm Willige and Karl Bayer, ed. Bernhard Zimmermann. 4th ed. Düsseldorf and Zurich: Artemis and Winkler, 2003. This "Tusculum" edition is based on the Greek text of A. C. Pearson (Oxford Classical Texts, 1957).

Other Works

DK   Hermann Diels and Walther Kranz, *Die Fragmente der Vorsokratiker,* 3 vols. 6th ed. Zürich: Weidmann, 1951. Cited by fragment number.

JS   Christoph Jamme and Helmut Schneider, ed., *Mythologie der Vernunft: Hegels "Ältestes Systemprogramm des deutschen Idealismus."* Frankfurt am Main: Suhrkamp, 1984.

RC   Roberto Calasso, *The Marriage of Cadmus and Harmony,* tr. Tim Parks. New York: Alfred A. Knopf, Borzoi Books, 1993.

VV   Jean-Pierre Vernant and Pierre Vidal-Naquet, *Myth and Tragedy in Ancient Greece*, tr. Janet Lloyd. New York: Zone Books, 1990.

JV   Christoph Jamme and Frank Völkel, ed., *Hölderlin und der Deutsche Idealismus*, 4 vols. "Specula 3." Stuttgart-Bad Canstatt: Frommann-Holzboog, 2003.

THE TRAGIC ABSOLUTE

INTRODUCTION

εἰ θεοί εἰσιν, ἵνα τί θρηνεῖτε
αὐτούς; εἰ δὲ θρηνεῖτε
αὐτούς, μηκέτι τούτους ,
ἡγεῖσθε θεούς.

If there are gods, why do you weep
for them? For, if you weep for them,
you no longer take them to be gods.

—*Attributed to Heraclitus
(DK B127)*

How am I to understand, how am I
to praise,
If, honoring divinity [τὰ θεῖ'
ἐπαινῶν],
I find the gods hateful [τοὺς θεοὺς
εὕρω κακούς;]?

SOPHOCLES, *Philoctetes, ll.
451–452*

"The tragic absolute," as a title, wants to
suggest a double movement in the work of
a number of German Romantic and Idealist thinkers and writers. On the one hand,
for many of them Greek tragedy occupies
a position of absolute importance, not only
for their theories of literature and aesthetics in general, but also for their metaphysics and moral philosophy; on the
other hand, the metaphysical or ontotheological absolute itself, traditionally defined
in terms of the predicates "groundlessness,
eternity, independence from time, self-
affirmation" (that is Schelling's definition
in the 1809 *Philosophical Investigations into
the Essence of Human Freedom* [7:350]), is
now seen as subject to a tragic reversal of
fortune. The twelve chapters of the present book focus on the views of Friedrich
Wilhelm Joseph Schelling (1775–1854)
and Friedrich Hölderlin (1770–1843) with
respect to this double movement—to repeat, the rise of tragedy in the aesthetics of
both thinkers and the tragic fall of the absolute in the metaphysics of both. For
what Schelling and Hölderlin call *das Absolute*, otherwise celebrated by Hegel, is
caught in catastrophe. The chapters of the

1

present book therefore stand at the crossroads of metaphysics and aesthetics, ontology and literary criticism.[1]

For the generation that came after Kant and read Kant's third *Critique*, which broached the theme of aesthetics merely in order to complete the Critical system by the addition of a certain type of judgment, and which therefore had no genuine interest or competence in the realm of the aesthetic as such, it became impossible nonetheless to pursue aesthetics and metaphysics along separate routes, impossible to leave the crossroads of ontology and literary criticism behind. The tragic absolute therefore also became the literary absolute.[2] As the importance of tragedy for literary and aesthetic reflection waxed, however, the fate of every metaphysics of the absolute became a tragic

---

1. Dennis J. Schmidt's recent book, *On Germans and Other Greeks*, which is subtitled *Tragedy and Ethical Life*, helps me to demarcate my own interests, which are less "ethical" than they are "metaphysical" or "ontological," and even "onto-*theo*-logical." True, where tragedy is concerned—tragedy and its "conflict of ultimates" (Schmidt, 18)—it would be foolhardy to try to draw a line between ethics and ontology, especially after "The Oldest Program toward a System in German Idealism" subsumes metaphysics under moral philosophy. If already for Kant the questions of knowledge, faith, and moral duty all point to the underlying question of human being—*Was ist der Mensch?*—we can hardly expect matters to be more clear-cut for us. In a sense, Schmidt's book has more future in it than my own, because it is consciously driven by questions posed by Nietzsche and Heidegger. My own effort here is far more modest, looking as it does back to the past and to questions of ontotheology that may not have much of a future. The moments of Schmidt's "Questions" (1–19) in which I find my own efforts most challenged are the following—though here it is merely a matter of a quick note, whereas I will return again and again to Schmidt's book in order to learn from it:

   1. Schmidt's principal thesis, that Greek tragedy is decisive for so many aspects of Occidental cultures (he cites "art and theater, death and grief, madness and self, law and family, fate and freedom" [3]), seems to me irrefutable.
   2. Schmidt notes that the principal German thinkers of the late eighteenth and early nineteenth centuries felt themselves "fated" to interrogate Greek tragedy, and that such a historical fatality "turns the question of tragedy back upon itself, squaring its significance, since the very notion of a fated question, of a destiny unfolding, is itself drawn from the idea of tragedy" (4); both points again strike me as undeniable.
   3. Schmidt argues that the above questions inevitably have to do with "the end of philosophy," conceived of as philosophy's having reached "the limits of its possibilities" (5); here once again he refers to our own destiny having become "exposed" at these limits (6). Tragedy reveals itself to be not merely one competing model for our thinking, but a realm that is "privileged, even mandated, by history itself" (ibid.).

   Schmidt himself is appropriately embarrassed about what such a mandate would look like, and he is perspicuous about the reflexivity and the redoubling of all his questions in our questionable time. Hölderlin, as we shall see, characterizes our age as having missed its fate, having passed right on by its destiny—our time, he says, is one of a dismal portion, δύσμορον. Schmidt writes: "it is our destiny to pose the question of destiny precisely at the historical juncture in which destiny seems lacking and the continuity of history appears to be broken, since in this discontinuity it has finally exposed the finitude of its own law. The time of crisis is then the crisis of time itself" (7). While my own efforts will not argue these points as positively as Schmidt has, it affirms them and doubtless depends on them. See Dennis J. Schmidt, *On Germans and Other Greeks: Tragedy and Ethical Life* (Bloomington: Indiana University Press, 2001).

   2. By referring to the literary absolute, I wish to salute the ground-breaking work by Philippe Lacoue-Labarthe and Jean-Luc Nancy, *L'Absolu littéraire: Théorie de la littérature du romantisme allemand* (Paris: Seuil, 1978).

fate. The last-ditch effort by Hegel, in this respect following Kant quite closely, to elevate comic over tragic poetry, and systematic-categorial philosophy over all poetry and art, was destined to founder. Neither Schelling nor Hölderlin was ever fooled by their friend's efforts to subordinate tragedy to either comedy or logic; their thinking as a whole, from start to finish, at least when it was at its adventurous best, may be called a tragic thinking—a thinking of the tragic absolute.

Herewith, by way of introduction, a brief itinerary of the present book. It begins by examining a much discussed, much disputed text, "The Oldest Program toward a System in German Idealism," attributed variously to Hegel, Schelling, and Hölderlin. Written in Hegel's hand in the spring of 1797 in Frankfurt, it announces the principal projects and passions of all three thinkers: to develop an *ethics* that would absorb into itself all metaphysics; to project a speculative *physics* for such an ethics as well, inasmuch as the relation of humankind to *nature* is vital for them all; to plan a massive theoretical attack on the *state* as currently constituted, including its churches, schools, and universities, inasmuch as the state treats its subjects like cogs in a machine; to sketch a *history of humanity*, tracing the gradual overcoming of the superstition and tyranny that inhere in governments and ecclesiastical hierarchies; to understand the supreme act of reason as an *aesthetic* act and *beauty* as the supreme idea of reason; to restore *poetry* to its rightful place as the instructress of humankind; and finally, to fabulate a *sensuous religion* for the masses of people as well as for the desiccated philosophers—a polytheism of the imagination conjoined with a monotheism of reason and the heart.

Yet where in this buoyant account of a new mythology of reason do we encounter any aspect of the tragic? Perhaps in two places: first, in the polemic against the current age, a time in which one witnesses the catastrophic passing of all hopes for a Golden Age, the default on a promise, as though all are condemned to suffer the fate of Empedocles, wandering on the plains of doom; second, in the gaping chasm between practical and theoretical reason, a chasm or an open wound that only a highly developed aesthetic sense—attuned to the beautiful and the sublime—might anneal. What more sublime and beautiful object could such a mythology of reason contemplate than Greek tragedy, however, which itself has recourse to ancient myths in order to challenge and reform the city and its citizens? Does not the urgent need for a new mythology mean that the current fables and superstitions have run their course and are in crisis and decline? Among those fables of power are all appeals to the absolute—the absolute right of kings, the absolute authority of churches, the absolute fraud of dogma. The *tragic* absolute will thus unsettle all the others.

3

Schelling, Hölderlin, and Novalis (Friedrich von Hardenberg, 1772–1801) are three of the many names (one should also have written extensively on Kleist, Goethe, and Schiller, the Schlegels, Tieck, and Hamann, among many others) that we associate with the end of traditional absolutes and the rise of the tragic. Chapter 2 examines Schelling's philosophy of nature, Hölderlin's theoretical essays on tragedy, and Novalis's scientific notebooks, in search of three exemplary ends of the absolute. For Schelling, the end of the absolute arrives with the notion of absolute *inhibition*, which he must posit in his account of freedom in nature, an inhibition in the free activity of the creative essence as such. For Hölderlin, it comes with the realization that consciousness is always and everywhere finite, that it inevitably undergoes radical *separation* from its most beloved objects. Judgment is by *ordeal*, and ordeal points to a primal division or sundering, *Ur-Teilung*, in being. The metaphor of intellectual intuition—which is the supreme act of reason in its aesthetic mode—is therefore neither successful synthesis of a manifold nor the free play of the imagination, but *tragedy*. Ours, says Hölderlin, is the time of "a frightful tragic muse." For Novalis, the end of the absolute hovers in the paradoxical notion of absolute *density*. Oxygen is the stuff of life; yet oxygen corrodes. One might therefore dream of an absolute as dense as gold, of a God that would be "infinitely compact metal." In other words, if life is "a sickness of spirit," then spirit itself is caught up in a contradiction that smacks of tragic necessity—of ἄτη and the μοῖρα. Spirit must undergo what Aristotle calls *peripety*, or sudden decline and fall, precipitous reversal of fortune. When dreams pass, one is left with the need voluntarily to surrender the absolute and accept the paradox—itself quite dense—that we can pursue "infinitely free activity" in ourselves, thus achieving a kind of absolute, "only through our incapacity to achieve and recognize an absolute." Infinitely free activity, whether in grandiose creation or in "the most motley life," is itself for Novalis a mourning-play, *Trauerspiel*.

Chapters 3 through 6 focus on Schelling, especially on two of his "middle period" texts, the 1809 *Philosophical Investigations into the Essence of Human Freedom and the Objects Pertaining to It* and the 1811–1815 *Ages of the World.* Among the objects pertaining to *human* freedom is the *divine* essence. Essence, however, is found to be *grounded*, and the ground of essence takes on a parlous life of its own. Chapter 3 pursues a "peripheral reading" of Schelling's images—he calls them *Ur-Bilder*, primal images—of the separations or "scissions" (*Scheidungen*) in the life of this essence. The two images that recur are those of birth and self-emasculation. Dominating the peripheral reading is the mood that prevails in the essence itself, whether it is in its contractive or expansive phase, namely, the mood of *languor*. Essence suffers yearning or longing (*die Sehnsucht*). Essence *languishes*. After this "peripheral reading," the chapter attempts an "indifferent reading," that is, a reading that follows Schelling's thinking back to a remote time prior to all opposition and difference, hence a time of *Indifferenz*. It tries to see whether the prospects for a divine essence ever improve, forward or back. However, languor never ceases to accompany the life of the absolute, and even though in 1809 Schelling still dreams of a total and perfect scission that would slough off all negativity, eliminating every ill and extirpating all evil, divine languishing continues unabated. A monistic essence proves to be impossible. At the stroke of one on the clock of "The Bell-Tower," where, as Melville writes, Una clasps the hand of Dua, the loving clasp is severed and time itself languishes. Near the end of his book, Schelling refers to the "pall of despondency" that is draped over the natural world that is God's ground, "the profound and indestructible melancholy of all life."

Chapter 4 takes the set of questions posed in and by Schelling's freedom essay to his remarkable *Ages of the World*. Schelling had this book set in print three times—in 1811, 1813, and 1815—and each time retracted it. To our astonishment, when we look at the three versions we see that they differ greatly from one another. Chapters 4 through 6 of the present book stress the first half of the 1811 printing, along with the 1815 lecture, "The Divinities of Samothrace." These two texts, among the richest in the German philosophical literature, explore what it was in the divine essence—back in some remote and elevated past, in the preworldly time of Chaos—that caused it to create the world, and to create it so tragically. In a word, Schelling uncovers the traumatic early history of divinity. Here the word *languor* is joined by an even more devastating word: Schelling writes of *die schmachtende Sehnsucht* and of *ein sehnsüchtiges Schmachten*, a languor that induces decrepitude and a decrepitude that entails languishment. The trauma in the life of the absolute arises from its discovery of the essentially bisexual and mortal character of divinity. The absolute is a mother, and he does not live forever. Essence, while majestic and manly in appearance, is needy and even squalid without its feminine counterpart. Yet no glory, not even that of the feminine, can save the tragic absolute. Finally, the dialectical method itself is not equal to this discovery: only fable, only the oldest stories, can recount it. *Narrative* proves to be essential. Thus the trauma of essence is traumatic for all the discourses of categorial philosophy.

One of the figures for the ground of God's essence, the ground that is the world of nature and earth, is the footstool—"the heavens are his throne and the earth is his footstool," says an Old Book of the absolute. Chapter 5 examines this item of essential furniture, only to discover that the relationship of footstool to footsole is more intimate than expected. The ground of essence is actually a matter of God's flesh, not furnishings. Schelling's pantheism, for which the philosopher is soundly chastised in his time, goes much farther than most doctrines of emanation and far beyond any sort of creationism. Schelling discovers resources for his pantheism in a painting by Raphael and in a monumental sculpture by Phidias. Yet no matter how glorious the prophet or regal the king of the gods—for the painting is of Ezekiel's vision of the Lord and the sculpture is of Olympian Zeus—these artistic resources expose divine sex and death. The footstool offers no rest for the weary absolute.

One of the most bizarre images of the preworldly time of Chaos, considered in chapter 6, is that of the Great Goddess in her chariot. The wheels of that chariot are rimmed with copper or iron, and the din they cause when the Goddess drives by is, says Schelling, the origin of *music*. And the music to which the Corybants dance their parts, then sacrifice them, gives birth to *tragedy*. No reader of Nietzsche will be surprised by this. No reader of the 1809 freedom essay will be surprised, either. Surprising nonetheless are Schelling's early accounts of music and tragedy, the former in his 1802–1803 *Philosophy of Art*, the latter in the tenth of his 1795 *Letters on Dogmatism and Criticism*. In the "Tenth Letter," freedom is experienced solely in and as perishing. The hero or heroine's demise in Greek tragedy—which is the subject of the letter—is double, involving what Jacques Lacan would call "a second death." For the hero or heroine, having struggled against necessity and lost, must also be punished by necessity. Punishment alone acknowledges the vanished, vanquished freedom of Oedipus and Antigone; punishment beyond death, as a kind of second death, alone honors their struggle, which is irremediably a vain struggle. Music, for its part, also possesses necessitous force—the force of *rhythm*, which is "the music in music." Whereas unadorned sound (*Klang*) expresses the depth and density of things, and is thus something like the self-consciousness and subjectivity in us, music's rhythms, tones, melodies, and harmonies articulate the coming-to-be of things in time. And while we know little about how the choral odes of Greek tragedies were actually danced, sung, and accompanied, we know that they constituted for the ancients the most exalted experience of music. What begins with simple repetition—two beats on a hollow log—finds its apotheosis in the βαρυβρόμων ὑπὸ τυμπάνων of enraptured Maenads and the πολλὰ τὰ δεινὰ of the elders of Thebes. Schelling therefore opens a question that Schopenhauer and

Nietzsche will not fail to pursue, namely, the question of the absolute *tragedy* that absolute *music* initiates—each, music and tragedy, in some sense giving birth to the other.

No one donated more of his time and considerable talent to Greek tragedy than the thinker and poet Friedrich Hölderlin. Chapters 7 through 11 focus on various aspects and phases of Hölderlin's preoccupation with tragedy and mourning-play, beginning with his own three versions of *The Death of Empedocles* and culminating in his translations of Sophocles' *Oedipus the Tyrant* and *Antigone* ("Oedipus the *Tyrant*" because of the way Oedipus's need to uncover his origins tyrannizes him and causes him to tyrannize others). Chapter 7 examines the three drafts of *Der Tod des Empedokles*, but only after considering a number of the fragments of Empedocles of Acragas. Diels-Kranz B137, from Empedocles' *Book of Purifications* (Καθαρμοί), along with B17, from his *Book on Nature* (Περὶ Φυσέως), seem to have been particularly influential for Hölderlin: in the one sphere of the cosmos—which ought to represent perfect unification—Love competes with Strife, and under the reign of Strife father slays son and child raises its hand against the mother. In the multiple voices of this great thinker of the tragic age of Greece Hölderlin seeks and finds his own poetic voice. By the time we reach the third of the three drafts of *The Death of Empedocles* we hear the sovereign language and the "hard rhythmic jointures" (Beda Allemann) of Hölderlin's late hymns. Among the themes and questions touched on in this chapter are the problem of the affirmation of life in a period of decline—put negatively, the problem of suicide, of Empedocles' leap into the crater of Etna, as an ostensible "ideal deed at the end"; the question of what is essential and what accidental to the composition of a tragedy or mourning-play, which in the present instance becomes the question of the female personages in the play, Rhea and Panthea; the problem of the ultimately undecidable impact of Empedocles' tragic flaw (*nefas*) on his fate or destiny (*Schicksal*) in the play; finally, the epochal problem of Empedocles' very identity in the face of Manes, his Egyptian Doppelgänger. The nagging question as to why these Empedoclean voices falter, why *The Death of Empedocles* is never brought to completion, is not so much answered as transformed: it becomes the question as to whether and how love and languor—and perhaps even languishment—can for a time successfully hold one back from the edge.

Chapter 8 initiates an extensive discussion of Hölderlin's "translations" of Sophocles. Hölderlin hoped that these texts, published in 1804, would serve as scripts for the ducal theater in Weimar, directed at that time by Goethe.

The plays were never produced during Hölderlin's lifetime. Indeed, their reception by the learned public was hostile: doubtless marred by an inadequate Greek text (Hölderlin used the 1555 Juntina edition of Sophocles' plays, which was riddled with errors) and by the slips due to Hölderlin's own imperfect mastery of Greek syntax, they were an easy target for ridicule. Only a few of Hölderlin's younger contemporaries—among them Bettina Brentano von Arnim—were disposed to hear the sublime poetry there. Sublime yet also occasionally harsh, and often utterly inscrutable. These remarkable works invite us to ask what translation in general ought to accomplish. Heidegger and Benjamin offer testimony in this regard. Finally, in the context of "translation," or μετάφρασις, the chapter examines the recent work of Philippe Lacoue-Labarthe on "theatrality."

Hölderlin appended to each of his translations a series of "Notes" or "Remarks," *Anmerkungen*. These few pages, which taken together are not nearly as long as the shortest of my chapters, have inspired endless commentary and considerable despair since their publication. Once again, contemporary critics heaped scorn. Since then, dedicated readers have heaped questions.

Chapter 9 begins with an Aristotelian paradox, trying to find an entry into Hölderlin's forbidding "Notes." The paradox is that even though the great Attic tragedians repeatedly turned to a very small number of households for their fables—the House of Atreus and the House of Oedipus (or Labdacus) were favorites—the resulting tragedies seemed to touch on something *absolute* about the human situation. Tragedy plays in the realm of universals, τὰ καθόλου, says Aristotle. Yet how should families where incest and murder abound grant instruction to the rest of us? And not mere instruction. For Aristotle's famous notion of catharsis seems to require the shocking character of the stories of these households for its effects. Cathartic effects are both salubrious and pleasureful, although the pleasure (ἡδονή), described in the nineteenth century by Jacob Bernays as a shattering ecstasy followed by the restoration of equanimity, is surely like no other. Like no other and yet exemplary, even *universal*. One might almost say *absolute*. The universe is tragic, even if tragedy reenacts the peculiar fates of a small number of particular houses.

It is not as though Hölderlin were an Aristotelian. Yet his "Notes" and other theoretical essays on tragedy often confirm or expand upon some of Aristotle's theses on tragedy. First, tragedy is in Hölderlin's view "ideational," so that what Aristotle calls διάνοια or "reasoning" pervades both a well-devised plot and the language of a tragedy. For Hölderlin, tragedy is the metaphor—in the literal sense of a carrier or vehicle—for an intellectual intuition. The latter involves apprehension of ever-expanding "unities of life," including, ultimately, the lives of mortals and immortals. What Aristotle calls *chance* and Schelling *necessity* bring these two groups of living beings together, almost always in wrath, fury, or passion (*Zorn,* ὀργή), before driving them asunder.

Second, the sequence of scenes in a tragedy must be ordered by a "lawful calculus." Not that one can apply a formulaic calculation to the content of any given play. Rather, the equilibrium of a play requires that the rush of its scenes toward the catastrophe be carefully regulated, properly "paced," as it were. The principal means of "pacing" is the introduction of a *caesura,* or "counterrhythmic interruption," designed to retard the sequence of representations at the crucial point. In both *Oedipus the Tyrant* and *Antigone* it is Tiresias the seer who effects the slowdown, though he does so at very different moments in the two plays. Because of his interventions, we are both engaged to the sweep of the play and enabled to see its representations *as* a representation. Our entire system of sensibility—from intuition through rational calculation—is caught up and exercised in the play.

Third, Hölderlin insists on the importance of *transport* in the tragic drama, perhaps in a double sense: (1) the *spectators* of a well-wrought play are transported to a prospect from which they can intuit the higher unities of life—even if gods and mortals appear to wrestle in irresolvable conflict; (2) the *protagonists* of the play may also be said to be transported from the familiar midpoint of their lives to what Hölderlin calls the "excentric realm of the dead" ("excentric" because elliptical, having at least two foci rather than one). Indeed, tragic transport conducts one and all to the realm in which the god himself must "appear in the figure of death." The peculiar pleasure of tragedy is therefore something like the unpleasure of the Kantian sublime: it hovers between pain and passion (*Leid/Leidenschaft*), as Novalis affirmed concerning life itself.

Fourth, the fate of Zeus is of special importance to Hölderlin, who (now quite far from the traditionally received Aristotle) sees the father of the gods turning decisively toward the earth, not away from it, and toward time, not eternity. The sky god is the "father of earth and of time." When Zeus enters the cell of Danaë as a golden shower, says Hölderlin, deliberately altering Sophocles' lines in the fifth choral ode of *Antigone,* the god takes on her mortality, inasmuch as it is now she who teaches him how to count the hours:

She counted off for the Father of Time
The strokes of the hours, the golden.

Fifth and finally, time itself is said to be experienced most elementally in pain. Pain and suffering seem to be shared by mortals and immortals alike: Hölderlin refers to the lines of dialogue and choral song in tragedy as "the *suffering organs* of a divinely wrestling body." Indeed, it is in suffering that mortals and immortals boundlessly unite—Hölderlin actually says that they couple—and then boundlessly separate in betrayal, blasphemy, and oblivion.

Yet this is merely the beginning. Things get complicated after that.

Among the scenes of *Oedipus the Tyrant* that call for special attention as a result of Hölderlin's translation and "Notes," the final scene between Oedipus and Jocasta is perhaps eminent. Chapter 9 identifies this scene as a "shadow caesura," that is, as a second counterrhythmic interruption of the forward sweep of the scenes. In *Antigone*, it is the fifth choral ode, which alludes to Danaë, that casts a long shadow. Chapter 10 picks up where 9 leaves off, by considering Hölderlin's tragic heroines. Jocasta, Antigone, Niobe, and Danaë are the four figures contemplated, two of them dramatic personages, two of them mythical figures. The questions put to them in chapter 10 are not difficult to pose: What do the gods—and, for that matter, the mortals—desire of these women? What do the women themselves desire? And how do these convergent or divergent desires drive tragedy? Informed by three particularly thought-provoking commentaries—those of Max Kommerell, Karl Reinhardt, and Nicole Loraux—this chapter tries to confront some of the most recalcitrant problems of Hölderlin's renderings of Sophocles' plays. Succinctly put, and only as a mere introduction: Jocasta's very long shadow (she is the sign that = 0, both as a mother who betrays her infant son Oedipus and as the victim of her husband Oedipus's wrath); Antigone's ἄτη, her infatuation or doom (her rushing to embrace her death as her peculiar eros, the eros that is celebrated in the fourth choral ode and problematized in the fifth); Niobe's tears (Niobe being both a universal figure of mourning and a potent threat to the reign of Zeus); and Danaë's gold (Danaë being less a victim of Zeus than an *antitheos*, as Hölderlin says of Antigone—that is to say, a threat to the father of time, the earth, and the gods).

Antigone, both the figure and the play, incites endless discussion. Chapter 11 takes up the astonishing interpretation of the figure and the tragedy as a whole by Jacques Lacan. It attempts a close reading of the final chapters of his seminar on the "ethics of psychoanalysis," precisely because these chapters often shed light on Hölderlin's translations and "Notes." And even when they shed darkness, which is the analyst's prerogative, the confluence of the two readings of Sophocles is uncanny—especially in view of the fact that (as far as I am aware) Lacan never mentions Hölderlin during the seminar. Lacan interprets the figure of Antigone as the most radiant incarnation of the death drives and as an image that purges the imaginary of all other images. His entire reading, focusing on what he calls the "in-between of two deaths," seems to remove us from the familiar midpoint of (conscious) life to the excentric realm of the dead. Yet there is nothing more beautiful or desirable than this splendid, erotic Antigone, who therefore incorporates what Freud calls the problem of *Triebvermischung*, the tangle of the erotic, reality, and death drives. For Lacan, Antigone, both the figure and the play, is the single most challenging inspiration for an ethics of psychoanalysis. It is above all the "divine use" of Antigone, that is, the use the gods would make of her, that brings Hölderlin and Lacan into proximity. That divine use draws Lacan out, extracts from him, in spite of all his own resistances, some of his most candid remarks on sublimation and the transference. If Zeus himself is under threat in Sophoclean tragedy, the analyst may not be far behind.

Finally, the confluence of Lacanian and Hölderlinian readings of *Antigone*, and even their agreement about some of the most disputed points of translation, sends us back to Sophocles' play once again. One may read *Antigone* as though Antigone herself were subject to the reign of Zeus and Kronos as portrayed in Plato's *Statesman* (296d 5–274e 3). For Antigone seems to grow ever younger and more tender as the rush of scenes takes her relentlessly to her womb-tomb. Like mother, like daughter.

What can be said of chapter 12, the conclusion of the book? It is clearly a phantasm, because it tries to imagine Schelling and Hölderlin remembering ahead to Nietzsche. However, if Nietzsche is a candidate for the authorship of "The Oldest Program," and he is, barring a few inconveniences of chronology, then why should not Schelling and Hölderlin be allowed to think ahead? They did anyway. The chapter opens with an account of Schelling's 1842 *Philosophy of Mythology* in its most radical moments—the moments that take mythology back behind the story of Kronos's sons—Hades, Poseidon, and Zeus—to the stories of Hestia, Demeter, Persephone, and Dionysos. With regard to the Kronide sons, Schelling remembers two lessons from antiquity: first, Zeus, Poseidon, and Hades all inherit their father's and grandfather's truculence—Aeschylus's *Prometheus Bound* (ll. 162–166) says that all three are marred by "bitterness and a harsh, unbending mind"; second, their truculence does not rescue them from the wiles of Kypris Aphrodite—the third choral ode of Sophocles' *Women of Trachis* notes that all three have succumbed to her influence, thus suggesting that even the Kronides must bow to the women and to their god, Dionysos. For Schelling, Dionysos is in a very real sense the central figure of mythology, insofar as he is the child of Semele. Semele hovers in mythology—somewhere between moon and earth—as a figure for Demeter. Hölderlin calls her "the impenetrable." Dionysos is her child. He is the god who is forever being born, forever in process of *coming* and *becoming*. There is much in Schelling's thought that looks forward to *The Birth of Tragedy from the Spirit of Music*—from the spirit of *absolute* music, one must say—and it is to the questions of absolute music and absolute rhythm that the final chapter ultimately turns.

Nietzsche, of course, has his own reminiscences, not so much of Schelling, whom he underestimates as just another Tübingen theologian beating the bushes for a god, but assuredly of Hölderlin. Nietzsche's secondary-school essay on "his favorite poet," Hölderlin, is both forward-looking and perspicuous in this regard. One must be especially fond of that essay because Nietzsche's teacher gave it a poor grade and its author the advice to stick to "healthier" and "more German" poets. Nietzsche disobeyed.

Obviously, this concluding chapter cannot undertake a study of Nietzsche's monumental *Birth of Tragedy*. It looks instead at some of the notes and lecture courses contemporary with that work, material that touches on the themes of the present book—a critique of Aristotelian catharsis, a self-critique of the genealogist, and, above all, a reprise of the theme of *absolute* music as the prime source of ἔκστασις. Whenever issues of music and rhythm are raised, however, Schelling is vindicated for Nietzsche, especially when Nietzsche's thoughts on the sexual nature of the Dionysian and "the pangs of the woman in childbirth" remind us of no one so much as Schelling's Demeter, Urania, and Kybele.

And Hölderlin? Is Hölderlin vindicated for Nietzsche? Hölderlin never needed vindication where Nietzsche was concerned. Sometimes one feels that Hölderlin remembered ahead for Nietzsche's sake alone.

Before proceeding on the itinerary only now outlined, one ought to revert for a moment to the matter of the title. "The tragic absolute"? Is the *tragic* absolute merely one more absolute in the long line of succession of absolutes—with multiple branchings, it is true—that constitutes the history of philosophy, especially in modernity? Surely not. Is it the *last possible* absolute? One very much wants to say *yes*, but is compelled to pause. The answer to that question—of the tragic absolute as the last possible absolute—has to remain ambiguous, precisely because tragedy celebrates the abyssal ambiguity of human existence, action, thought, and language.

Jean-Pierre Vernant and Pierre Vidal-Naquet take Heraclitus's famous fragment (Diels-Kranz B119), ἦθος ἀνθρώπῳ δαίμων, to be one of the grand instances of this ambiguity (VV 37–38, 43). Whereas philosophy has always preferred to hear the expression in one way, namely, "A human being's tutelary spirit is his or her character," tragedy, which certainly can hear it this way, also entertains a very different hearing: "A human being's character *is* a daimon," that is to say, human life is subject to monstrous forces (δεινά) outside its control, among them the forces of τύχη and ἄτη, inscrutable contingency and inescapable infatuation and doom. The tensions and ambiguities in Greek tragedy make it impossible for us to read Heraclitus's dictum as a speculative proposition; neither way of hearing it can be reduced to the other. The two senses of the expression (at least two, one must say) can be neither conflated nor sublated into some third synthetic proposition. Tragedy produces not proposition but tension. "And this tension that is never totally accepted nor entirely obliterated makes tragedy into a questioning to which there can be no answers. In a tragic perspective human beings and human action are seen, not as things that can be defined or described, but as problems. They are presented as riddles whose double meanings can never be pinned down or exhausted."[3]

"The tragic absolute" is therefore a catachresis beyond oxymoron. If it is ultimate, it is so only as the mixed metaphor—metaphor being understood as parlous transport, μεταφορά—by which all that lives bumps along until it reaches one or other terminal. Not even Athena knows where it will all end: she demands of the Erinyes, ποῦ τὸ τέρμα τῆς φυγῆς; "Where is there an end to this fugitive life?" (Aeschylus, *Eumenides*, l. 422). If the human being is possessed of language, that does not really help. Try reading the signs. Tragic ambiguity plays itself out precisely in language. Sometimes it seems as though the spectators are in on the game, insofar as they, observing the action from on high, can understand both sides of all those fatal malapropisms and lethal interpretations of Sibylline utterances declaimed down on the stage. As Vernant insists, however, neither playwright nor spectator is truly in on the game: what tragedy has to teach us is that there are "zones of opacity and incommunicability" in human life, action, and speech (VV 43). What becomes transparently clear is that matters are muddied down there, thinking muddled, talk confused, deeds frustrated, actions backfiring, all the while the personages depicted in the play are "tearing themselves apart" trying to get it right (ibid.).

---

3. VV 38. For a very similar wording of this central thesis of Vernant, see *Myth and Tragedy*, ch. 5, "Ambiguity and Reversal: On the Enigmatic Structure of *Oedipus Rex*," esp. 113–114. Vernant goes so far as to speak of "a purely operational schema of reversal" or "rule of ambiguous logic" in Sophocles; Oedipus is the outstanding embodiment of this Sophoclean schema, inasmuch as his "real greatness consists in the very thing that expresses his enigmatic nature: his questioning" (VV 139).

They fail. Their succeeding would make not a better play but a more mendacious one. The tragic discovery of the spectators and interpreters of tragedy is that "words, values, human beings themselves, are ambiguous, that the universe is one of conflict" (ibid.). Spectators and interpreters alike must relinquish their most prized presuppositions, must accept "a problematic vision of the world" (ibid.).

"The tragic absolute"? Not if that sounds like an answer. Only if it sounds like a questioning without answers, carried out in a world that consists of problems, in a universe that confronts us with enigmas that can never be resolved once and for all.

If the word *absolute* retains anything at all of its traditional ontotheological import, it is only in order to say that what philosophy has called "the Absolute," to wit, all gods and every God, including the God of faith and the Spirit of absolute knowing, is subject to the same ambiguity and is on the same bumpy ride as the rest of us. Suffering is written into the script. Languishing is of the essence.

Late in his life, between the years 1847 and 1852, Schelling composed and delivered a series of lectures at the University of Berlin designed to provide a "philosophical introduction to the philosophy of mythology, or the presentation of a purely rational philosophy." In the twentieth of these entirely rational lectures, Schelling wrote:

> The world's portion and the portion of humankind are *by nature* tragic portions. And every tragic event that unfolds in the world's course is but a variation on the one grand theme that renews itself continuously. The deed in accord with which all suffering is scripted did not happen once and for all; rather, that deed *is happening* always and eternally. For it is not, as one of our poets says, "something that never ever was"; it is what always and eternally is—"that alone which never grows old." (II/1:485–486)

Is the tragic portion restricted to the world of nature and humankind? Does the phantom limb of the absolute escape the tragic portion? Melville, *Moby-Dick*, chapter 106, "Ahab's Leg":

> To trail the genealogies of these high mortal miseries, carries us at last among the sourceless primogenitures of the gods; so that, in the face of all the glad, hay-making suns, and soft-cymballing, round harvest-moons, we must needs give in to this: that the gods themselves are not for ever glad. The ineffaceable, sad birth-mark in the brow of man, is but the stamp of sorrow in the signers.[4]

---

4. Herman Melville, *Moby-Dick; or, The Whale*, ed. Alfred Kazin (Boston: Houghton Mifflin, 1956 [1851]), 356.

If Aeschylus's Philoctetes finds the gods hateful, it is because he loves the languishing divinity in them. How can he not weep beyond his own woes? If pseudo-Heraclitus tells us that when we weep for divinities they are no longer divine, Heraclitus himself tells us that mortals and immortals, as well as immortals and mortals, die the life and live the death of the others, of each of the others, as if living one's own life and dying one's own death were not enough. How not shed tears of wonder and pain?

.

THE OLDEST PROGRAM
TOWARD A SYSTEM IN
GERMAN IDEALISM

1

I don't understand the least little
  smidgen
Of all this blab about old-time
  religion;
I don't want to brood over all this
  stuff—
If I can make them all peevish
  that'll be enough.
I won't let my intellect and won't let
  my gizzards
Be clogged up by all these high-
  flying wizards.
Rather, I assert that whatever duly
  is,
Whatever really and truly and
  indubitably is,
Is made for hands to touch and is
  built to last.
In order to grasp it one needn't go
  fast
Or beat down the body to total
  prostration
Or seek a violent out-of-body
  liberation.

—F. W. J. SCHELLING,
*Heinz Widerporst's
Profession of Faith (1799)*

The story of the tragic absolute begins not absolutely tragically but absolutely buoyantly. *Das älteste Systemprogramm des deutschen Idealismus* ("The Oldest Program toward a System in German Idealism") is the place where our inquiry begins, if only because the text itself, however recently discovered, and however fragmentary, is both ubiquitous and in almost every sense inaugural. Ubiquitous? Open any recent, reasonably complete edition of Hegel's works and you will find this two-page fragment. Examine any comparable edition of Schelling's works and you will find the same fragment under the same title. Finally, peruse any edition of the great poet Hölderlin and once again you will discover the identical piece. Nothing like it has ever happened before or since. What *is* this fragment that the editors of Hegel's, Schelling's, and Hölderlin's works are so keen to ascribe to their respective paragons—two of the greatest philosophers in the Western intellectual tradition and one of our very greatest poets and thinkers? And why are they so keen? Because virtually every project of German Idealism and Romanticism—in ethics, metaphysics, philosophy of nature, poetics and aesthetics, religion, education, and mythology—is *inaugurated,* that is, sketched out with uncanny prescience and boldness, in this document.

The fragment served as the basis of a discussion among friends. It grew out of their discussions and was intended to stimulate further discussion (JS 44, 11, 188).[1] The scope of a thoroughgoing discussion, one that would do justice to the entire fragment, would be vast: one could concentrate on this document as a source of information for the intellectual biographies of Hegel, Schelling, and Hölderlin; or one might read it as an elaboration of ideas shared by these three friends and their respective wider circles during the final years of the eighteenth century. The range of a *philosophical* discussion would be breathtaking, inasmuch as the seven or eight paragraphs of the program touch on matters of ethics and metaphysics, physics and philosophy of nature, politics and history, aesthetics and poetics, religion and mythology. What the fragment is *about*—the project in which it is engaged—is "mankind's ultimate and grandest accomplishment." No doubt, it will seem strange to find in such a grandiloquent birth certificate hints of tragic demise, indeed, the demise of the metaphysical absolute as such.

I will move quickly through an account of the philological dispute that the fragment has occasioned. I will then present the entire text of the *Systemprogramm,* in German and in an English translation, offering in what follows a series of comments on the sequence of the paragraphs and the stages of the argument. Finally, I will point to the first signs—as I read them—of the tragic demise of the absolute.[2]

1. I have used the critical edition of the *Systemprogramm* as presented in *Mythologie der Vernunft: Hegels "Ältestes Systemprogramm" des deutschen Idealismus,* edited by Christoph Jamme and Helmut Schneider. I am indebted to this work, not only for the text of the "Program," but also for the excellent commentary and presentation of sources. The *Systemprogramm* serves as the "clinching piece of evidence" (xxv) for H. S. Harris's account of the early Hegel, in *Hegel's Development: Toward the Sunlight, 1770–1801* (Oxford: Oxford University Press, 1972). Harris offers a detailed discussion of the fragment (249–257) and a translation of the text based on the edition by Horst Fuhrmans (510–512). Whether one can be so certain that Hegel is the author of the text, however, remains doubtful. *Das älteste Systemprogramm,* however ubiquitous, is nobody's "clincher." In any case, if Jamme and Schneider are right, the place and date of the text must be, not "Bern, 1796," but "Frankfurt, 1797." Harris's views on the "perfect logic" of the sequence of Hegel's early writings (255–256) thus need some minor alterations. For a recent discussion of the program, and an alternative translation, see Schmidt, 81–85.

2. When I first presented this text to the English-speaking public some fifteen years ago, I felt certain that I could attribute the text with certainty to a particular author—neither Hegel nor Schelling nor Hölderlin—but now I am not absolutely sure of my judgment. At that time I followed the hint offered many years ago by Ludwig Strauss, who argued that none of the three was the author, but an unknown fourth. I suggested that the author of the fragment was Friedrich Nietzsche, who, famously, claimed to have been born posthumously. Over the years, many colleagues and even perfect strangers have written to tell me that my attribution suffered from certain nuisances of chronology. And so, having grown in age and wisdom, I let my earlier thesis on authorship go. In the spring of 1999 Christoph Jamme, now at the Universität Lüneburg, kindly sent me a bibliography of twenty-

The Philological Dispute

In 1913 the Prussian State Library purchased at auction from the Liep-mannssohn firm of Berlin a single folio sheet covered recto-verso with a text written in the unmistakable hand of the young Hegel. In the mid-1970s, that folio sheet, long believed lost, was recovered (thanks to the scholarly sleuthing of Dieter Henrich) from the Jagiellonian Library in Kraków. On the basis of the watermark and a comparative study of Hegel's handwriting, stationery, and inks, editors at the Hegel Archive in Bochum in 1984 argued convinc-ingly that the text was written during the first weeks of 1797, that is to say, immediately after Hegel's journey from Bern to Frankfurt, where Hölderlin was engaged as a tutor in the household of Jacob and Susette Gontard. Hölderlin and Hegel were in constant contact during these months.[3] Franz Rosenzweig, later the author of *Der Stern der Erlösung*, published the text in 1917, supplying it with a long commentary and a title, *Das älteste Systempro-gramm des deutschen Idealismus: Ein handschriftlicher Fund* ("The Oldest Pro-gram toward a System in German Idealism: A Recently Discovered Holo-graph"). The folio sheet, measuring 21 x 33.5 centimeters, was apparently the second half of a *Bogen*, or vertically folded sheet of foolscap, so that its open-ing words, *eine Ethik*, were actually the concluding words of a sentence begun on the first (and missing) page of the foolscap. It was the final autograph frag-ment of the Hegel *Nachlaß* in the possession of Hegel's student Friedrich Förster to be offered for sale by Liepmannssohn. Where the first page of the folio was to be found—or whether for that matter there were any number of earlier folio sheets in the document—no one knew. Nor was it known whether Förster or Hegel himself tore the sheet in half. Friedrich Förster and Ludwig Boumann had ostensibly been reluctant to publish the fragment in their two-volume edition of Hegel's miscellany (1834–1835), because it did not "fit in well" with the remaining texts. (Such attributed unsuitability does not sit well with the judgment of H. S. Harris, Otto Pöggeler, Christoph Jamme, Helmut Schneider, and others that the text is indubitably by Hegel,

---

four post-1984 discussions of the *Systemprogramm*, evidence that the fragment continues to attract a great deal of scholarly attention. See especially Hans-Jürgen Gawoll, "Die Kontroverse um das soge-nannte 'älteste Systemprogramm des deutschen Idealismus': Ein Forschungsbericht," *Info Philo* 1 (1996): 46–51. Most instructive for my own purposes is Gawoll's account of the monograph by Frank-Peter Hansen, *'Das älteste Systemprogramm des deutschen Idealismus': Rezeptionsgeschichten und Interpre-tation,* Berlin, 1989, which stresses the importance of Schiller for Hegel's early formation, and Gawoll's own reply, 48–50.

3. JS 36–39. I permit myself a reference to the collection of Susette Gontard's letters to Hölder-lin, in Douglas F. Kenney and Sabine Menner-Bettscheid, tr. and ed., *The Recalcitrant Art: Diotima's Letters to Hölderlin and Related Missives* (Albany: State University of New York Press, 2000).

indeed as the "clinching piece of evidence.") At all events, the holograph lived a shadowy closet existence until Franz Rosenzweig's publication of it in 1917, at which point it disappeared again for another sixty years.

The claim that the contents of the text were not in accord with Hegel's other early writings preoccupied Rosenzweig as well. The fragment's assertive, even triumphant, tone seemed altogether foreign to the young Hegel, at least as Rosenzweig pictured him, toiling away at his theological and historico-political investigations. For years, Hegel's circle of friends had been referring to him as the Old Man, whereas, as anyone could see, the "System Program" was the work of someone quite young at heart. Rosenzweig concluded:

> Only one man in the philosophical Germany of year 1796 possessed this youthful, victorious tone; the very first fleeting glance we cast at the thoughts contained in the program informed us that it was he. This man alone employed the bold phrase "I shall" with such insouciance, employed it without cease to the end of his life when, an old man, he departed from a world that had changed, a world that had lost heart. So busy with programs he never got as far as a completed work; so busy with "ideas" and "projections," "presentations" and "reports," all of them promises only half-fulfilled, he never got as far as wholly accomplished deeds. "I shall" was to be his last word, as it was his first. (JS 87)

A new philosophy of nature, described in the program itself as a physics with "wings"; a new ethics, one that would span the Kantian and Fichtean chasms that had sundered theoretical and practical reason; a new politics, one that would in fact abolish the need for a state; plans for a philosophy and a practice of art and beauty, indeed, at the high point of the arc of the system—these clearly were the ideas of the twenty-one-year-old *Wunderkind* of German Idealism, the Hermes of the Tübingen triumvirate, Friedrich Wilhelm Joseph von Schelling. On January 22, 1796, Schelling had written to the philosopher and publicist Immanuel Niethammer in the tone Franz Rosenzweig was sure he was hearing in the *Systemprogramm:*

> I am resolved to devote myself for some time, at least for the most part, to philosophy. The first thing I shall undertake is a system of ethics (a counterpart to Spinoza, a work the idea of which has long excited me and which I have in fact already begun), a philosophy of the history of humanity—the Introduction to it is finished, and if you'd like to include it in your journal it is yours for the asking—and an interpretation of the *Critique of Judgment* in accordance with my own principles. (JS 111)

"A counterpart to Spinoza." Walter Schulz reminds us of a fact Rosenzweig knew well, namely, that Spinoza's declarations concerning a primordial, comprehensive One that embraces God and the world, especially the world of nature, became known to Schelling and his friends principally through Friedrich H. Jacobi's 1785 treatise, *On the Doctrine of Spinoza, in Letters to Moses Mendelssohn*.[4] No matter how much Jacobi may have been resisting the pantheism (= atheism) on which he was here reporting, the formula for Spinoza's comprehensive unity-in-diversity, Ἕν καὶ πᾶν, became the motto of the three Tübingen friends, Schelling, Hegel, and Hölderlin. Hölderlin wrote the phrase into Hegel's autograph album in 1791 as a symbol of the unity that bound them all, and Schelling deployed the phrase everywhere in his early treatises. Franz Rosenzweig's thesis concerning the authorship of the "System Program" seemed utterly convincing: the handwriting was Hegel's, the thoughts were Schelling's. What more could be said?

A great deal more, retorted Wilhelm Böhm, who wrote voluminously on the subject of the fragment's authorship in 1926. Böhm confirmed Rosenzweig's judgment that the text could not have stemmed from Hegel's stolid mind, but only from his hand. Anyone who had studied the first volume of Hölderlin's *Hyperion*, according to Böhm, and anyone who knew about Hölderlin's planned commentaries on Plato's *Symposium* and *Phaedrus*, anyone who appreciated the genuine radicality of the notion of *beauty* developed in the fragment, a notion so utterly at odds with the positings of a Fichtean transcendental ego and ultimately so subversive of the Kantian moral law—anyone who discerned these things would know that Friedrich Hölderlin alone was capable of authoring such a tract. Indeed, the foreword to the penultimate draft of *Hyperion*, specifically invoking Plato, had conjured up an idea of the "infinite unification" of humankind with nature, a unification that would transform the usual cognitive senses of intellectual intuition into a form of perfected *being:* "It [that is, such unification] is at hand—as beauty; to speak after the manner of Hyperion, a new realm awaits us, where beauty is queen" (I 558–559; DKV 2:257).

Böhm could uphold his thesis only by ignoring certain other aspects of this text, however. For even though Hölderlin puts all his store in "originality," identifying such originality as "intensity, depth of heart and spirit," he sees human life as radically decentered and dispersed: "We all run along an excentric orbit" (I 558; DKV 2:256). That orbit does not enable humanity to turn smoothly about the sun of ideal beauty; the journey is also about being lost, torn from nature by striving and strife—as Empedocles had so unforgettably lamented in his Καθαρμοί, or "Purifications." We are tossed between waves

---

4. Walther Schulz, in the Introduction to F. W. J. Schelling, *System des transzendentalen Idealismus*, Philosophische Bibliothek Band 254 (Hamburg: Felix Meiner, 1957), xi.

of mastery and servility; we are everything and nothing. And such striving, rather than ending in infinite unification, seems to go on and on. Ours is a life of infinite approximation—a life lived asymptotically:

> Whether we know it or not, the goal of all our striving is to put an end to that eternal conflict [*Widerstreit*] between our self and the world, to restore the ultimate peace, which is higher than all reason, so that we can unite with nature in one infinite whole.
>
> Yet neither our knowing nor our acting, in any period of our existence, takes us to the point where all conflict ceases, where all is one: the determinate line unites with the indeterminate line only in infinite approximation. (DKV 2:256)

Indeed, the more one studies Hölderlin's early work, the less convinced one can be that he ever dreamed the dream of infinite unification—unless as *tragic* unification, which one might have to think of as the tragic absolute. Yet most of these doubts remained foreign to Wilhelm Böhm. He continued to insist that Hölderlin was indubitably the author of *Das älteste Systemprogramm*—Hölderlin exercising the ultimate revenge of a fragile poet on the monumental philosopher-systematizers who were his erstwhile companions. Böhm allowed Schelling and Hegel to play a role in the drama, to be sure: Schelling was the messenger boy (the *Wunderkind*, Hermes, indeed!) who carried Hölderlin's original program to Hegel the Scrivener.

A year after Böhm's public defense of Hölderlin's authorship, in 1927, Ludwig Strauss sought to refute Böhm and to shore up Franz Rosenzweig's arguments on behalf of Schelling. Even though Strauss was astute enough to argue for a missing fourth as the genuine author of the *Systemprogramm*, he also recognized that Schelling's claim was stronger than Hölderlin's. True, the fragment's invocation of beauty was highly reminiscent of Hölderlin, but as for the rest, "To have the *Systemprogramm* in your head while reading Hölderlin is like playing Mozart while singing Brahms" (JS 65–66).

Only many decades later, in 1965, did Hegel find his champion—and a formidable champion—in Otto Pöggeler, supported in 1969 by Klaus Düsing and in 1972 by H. S. Harris. Pöggeler had begun by suspecting that the "Oldest Program toward a System," whoever its author, must have had a "powerful impact" on the young Hegel, inasmuch as so many of its ideas were found elsewhere in Hegel's Bern and Frankfurt writings. Pöggeler eventually concluded on the basis of internal evidence that Hegel was the likeliest of the three candidates. Yet Pöggeler himself remained aware of the precariousness of any such hypothesis: "The young Hegel—each year brings us a range of works about him, yet he still remains largely unknown: his work is overlaid with the various kinds of concealments that discoveries always bring in their train" (JS 138). Although the results of Dieter Henrich's philological detective work, published in 1976, tended to support Pöggeler's attribution of the *Systemprogramm* to Hegel, Henrich himself expressed doubts, plaguey doubts. Henrich certainly would not stand for any condescension or superciliousness on the part of the young assistants at the Hegel Archive who were working so assiduously and so convincingly on behalf of Hegel: the attribution to Hegel, Henrich insists, is still nothing more than a working hypothesis. Yet the hypothesis, one must say, has come to be accepted in most quarters, precisely as Martin Heidegger accepted it. In a letter to Pöggeler, Heidegger confessed, "I was never satisfied with the view that the text was by Schelling, the written copy by Hegel; but I didn't know where to turn" (JS 69). Let us set aside the question of authorship, however, and present the text, along with a translation.

Das älteste Systemprogramm des deutschen Idealismus: Text and Translation

eine Ethik. Da die ganze Metaphysik künftig in d[ie] *Moral* fällt—wovon Kant mit seinen beiden praktischen Postulaten nur ein *Beispiel* gegeben, nichts *erschöpft hat)* so wird diese Ethik nichts anders als ein vollständiges System aller Ideen, oder, was dasselbe ist, aller praktischen Postulate {enthalten}[5] seyn. die erste Idee ist natürlich d[ie] Vorst[ellung] *von mir selbst,* als einem absolut freien Wesen. Mit dem freyen, selbstbewußten Wesen tritt zugleich eine ganze *Welt*—aus dem Nichts hervor—die einzig wahre und gedenkbare *Schöpfung aus Nichts*—

an ethics. Inasmuch as the whole of metaphysics will in the future be subsumed under *moral philosophy*—a matter in which Kant, with his two practical postulates, has merely provided an *example,* and has *exhausted* nothing—this ethics will {contain} be nothing other than a complete system of all ideas, or, what comes to the same, of all practical postulates. The first idea is of course the representation *of me myself* as an absolutely free creature. At the same time, along with the free, self-conscious creature, a whole *world* comes to the fore—out of nothing—the

5. Fancy brackets indicate a word in the fragment that the author(s) crossed out, substituting the following word for it. Plain brackets are Jamme and Schneider's emendations, usually of the fragment's abbreviations into whole words. I have silently doubled the consonants where required. In general, though not always, I have made the English text more readable by not taking up all the errors and corrections into the text.

Hier werde ich auf die Felder der Physik herabsteigen; die Frage ist diese: Wie muß eine Welt für ein moralisches Wesen beschaffen seyn? Ich möchte unsrer langsamen an Experimenten mühsam schreitenden—Physik, einmal wieder Flügel geben. So—wenn die Philosophie die Ideen, die Erfahrung die Data angibt, können wir endlich die Physik im Großen bekommen, die ich von spätern Zeitaltern erwarte. Es scheint n[ich]t daß die jezige Physik einen schöpferischen Geist, wie der unsrige ist, od[er] seyn soll, befriedigen könne.[6]

Von der Natur komme ich aufs *Menschenwerk.* die Idee der Menschheit voran—will ich zeigen, daß es keine Idee vom *Staat* gibt, weil der Staat etwas *mechanisches* ist, so wenig als es eine Idee von einer *Maschine* gibt. Nur was Gegenstand der *Freiheit* ist, heist *Idee.* Wir müßen also auch über den Staat hinaus!—Denn jeder Staat muß freie Menschen als mechanisches Räderwerk behandeln; u[nd] das soll er nicht; also soll er *aufhören.* Ihr seht von selbst,[7] daß hier alle die Ideen, vom ewigen Frieden u.s.w. nur *untergeordnete* Ideen einer höhern Idee sind. Zugleich will ich hier d[ie] Principien für eine *Geschichte der*

sole true and conceivable *creation out of nothing.*—Here I shall alight on the fields of physics; the question is: How must a world be fashioned for a moral creature? To our sluggish physics, advancing laboriously with its experiments, I would like to lend wings once more. Thus—if philosophy provides the ideas, while experience supplies the data, we can finally get in general outline the physics I expect from later epochs. It does not seem as though our current physics could satisfy a creative spirit, such as ours is, or ought to be.

From nature I shall advance to the *works of mankind.* First of all, the idea of humanity—I want to show that there is no idea of the *state,* because the state is something *mechanical;* just as little is there an idea of a *machine.* Only that which is an object of *freedom* is called an *idea.* Thus we must also proceed beyond the state!—For every state has to treat free human beings like mechanical cogwheels; and it should not do so; hence it should *cease.* You yourselves see that here all ideas of eternal peace, etc. are only *subordinate* ideas with regard to a higher idea. At the same time, I want to lay down the principles here for a *history of hu-*

6. Note the word *unsrige.* Although the first person pronoun dominates the text, there are from time to time signs that a plurality or collective is involved in the authorship. True, in the present case it may simply be the spirit of the Tübingen community (part of which now resides in Frankfurt) that the "our" refers to.

7. Once again, the *Ihr seht* may refer specifically to the two other members of the authorial triumvirate.

Menschheit niederlegen, u[nd] das ganze elende Menschenwerk von Staat, Verfaßung, Regierung, Gesezgebung—bis auf die Haut entblösen. Endlich kommen d[ie] Ideen von einer moral[ischen] Welt, Gottheit, Unsterblichkeit—Umsturz alles {Aberglaubens} Afterglaubens, Verfolgung des Priesterthums, das neuerdings Vernunft heuchelt, durch d[ie] Vernunft selbst.—{die} absolute Freiheit der Geister, die d[ie] intellektuelle Welt in sich tragen u[nd] weder Gott noch Unsterblicheit *ausser sich* suchen dürfen.

Zulezt die Idee, die alle vereinigt, die Idee der *Schönheit*, das Wort in höherem platonischem Sinne genommen. Ich bin nun überzeugt, daß der höchste Akt der Vernunft, der, indem die alle Ideen umfast, ein ästhe{sti}tischer Akt ist, und daß *Wahrheit und Güte, nur in der Schönheit* verschwistert sind[.]— Der Philosoph muß eben so viel ästhetische Kraft besizen, als der Dichter, die Menschen ohne ästhetischen Sinn sind unsre Buchstaben Philosophen. Die Philosophie des Geistes ist eine ästhetische Philos[ophie] [.] {M} Man kann in nichts geistreich seyn{,} selbst über Geschichte kann man nicht geistreich raisonniren—ohne ästhetischen Sinn. Hier soll offenbar werden, woran es eigentlich den Menschen fehlt, die keine Ideen verstehen,— und treuherzig genug gestehen, daß ihnen alles dunkel ist, sobald es über

manity, and to strip down to the skin the whole wretched human apparatus of state, constitution, government, and legislation. Finally come the ideas of a moral world, divinity, immortality—the overthrow of all {superstition} belief in a hinterhaven, the prosecution by reason itself of that hypocritical priesthood that has recently begun to ape reason.—the absolute freedom of all spirits who bear the intellectual world within themselves and who dare not seek either God or immortality *outside themselves.*

And at the very end, the idea that unifies all, the idea of *beauty,* the word taken in its higher, Platonic sense. For I am convinced that the supreme act of reason, because it embraces all ideas, is an aesthetic act; and that only in beauty are *truth and goodness* akin.—The philosopher must possess as much aesthetic force as the poet. Those human beings who are devoid of aesthetic sense are our pedantic philosophers. The philosophy of spirit is an aesthetic philosophy. One can in no way be inspired—one cannot even ruminate on historical matters in an inspired way—without aesthetic sense. Here it should become obvious to us precisely what is defective in those human beings who understand no ideas,—and who concede forthrightly enough that everything becomes obscure to them the moment

Tabellen u[nd] Register hinaus geht.

Die Poësie bekömmt dadurch [ein]e höhere Würde, sie wird am Ende wieder, was sie am Anfang war—*Lehrerin der {Geschichte} Menschheit;* denn es gibt keine Philosophie, keine Geschichte mehr, die dichtkunst allein wird alle übrigen Wissenschaften u[nd] Künste überleben.

Zu gleicher Zeit hören wir so oft, der große Hauffen müße eine *sinnliche Religion* haben. Nicht nur d[e]r große Hauffen, auch der Phil[osoph] bedarf ihrer. Monotheismus der Vern[unft] u[nd] des Herzens, Polytheismus d[e]r Einbildungskraft u[nd] der Kunst, dis ists, was wir bedürfen!

Zuerst werde ich hier von einer Idee sprechen, die so viel ich weiß, noch in keines Menschen Sinn gekommen ist—wir müssen eine neue Mythologie haben, diese Mythologie aber muß im Dienste der Ideen stehen, sie mus [ein]e Mythologie der *Vernunft* werden.

Ehe wir die Ideen ästhetisch d.h. mythologisch machen, haben sie für das *Volk* kein Interesse u[nd] umgek[ehrt] ehe d[ie]Mythol[ogie] vernünftig ist, muß sich d[e]r Philos[oph] ihrer schämen. So müssen endlich aufgeklärte u[nd] Unaufgeklärte sich d[ie] Hand reichen, die Myth[ologie] muß philosophisch werden, und das Volk vernünftig, u[nd] d[ie]Phil[osophie] muß

it involves something more than tables and indices.

Poesy will thereby attain a higher dignity; in the end she will again become what she was in the beginning—*the instructress of {history} humanity;* for there will no longer be any philosophy, any history; the poetic art alone will survive all the other sciences and arts.

At the same time, we so often hear that the great mass of human beings must have a *sensuous religion.* Not only the masses but also the philosopher needs it. Monotheism of reason and of the heart, polytheism of the imagination and art, that is what we need!

First, I shall speak here of an idea that, as far as I know, no human mind has ever entertained—we must have a new mythology; but this mythology must remain in service to the ideas, must become a mythology of reason.

Until we make the ideas aesthetic, i.e., mythological, they will have no interest for the *people;* and conversely, until the mythology is rational, the philosopher will perforce be ashamed of it. Thus the enlightened and unenlightened must at long last clasp hands; mythology must become philosophical, and the people rational, while philosophy must become mythological, in order

25

mythologisch werden, um die
Philosophen sinnlich zu machen.
dann herrscht ewige Einheit under
uns. Nimmer der verachtende Blik,
nimmer das blinde Zittern des Volks
vor seinen Weisen u[nd] Priestern.
dann erst erwartet uns *gleiche* Ausbil-
dung *aller* Kräfte, des Einzelnen
sowohl als aller Individuen{,}. Keine
Kraft wird mehr unterdrükt werden,
dann herrscht allgemeine Freiheit und
Gleichheit der Geister!—Ein höherer
Geist vom Himmel gesandt, muß
diese neue Religion unter uns stiften,
sie wird das lezte, gröste Werk der
Menschheit seyn. (JS 11–14)

to make the philosophers sensuous.
Then eternal unity will prevail
among us. No more the contemptuous glance, no more the blind quak-
ing of the people before their sages
and priests. Only then can we expect
the *equal* formation of *all* forces, in
particular persons as well as in all individuals. No longer will any force
be suppressed; universal freedom and
equality of spirits will then prevail!—A higher spirit, sent from
heaven, will have to found this new
religion among us; it will be the very
last and the grandest of the works of
humanity.

Commentary

The fragment begins by announcing that metaphysics will be conflated
with moral philosophy. It thus expresses the desire to complete a tendency of
thought already well developed in Kant and fully in force with Fichte. Kant,
the author(s) contend(s), has not exhausted the postulates of practical reason.
Indeed, what one calls *ethics* will now be seen as subsuming under itself all
ideas, whether theoretical or practical. The first of such ideas, in true Fichtean
fashion, is "the representation *of me myself* as an absolutely free creature," that
is to say, as transcendental—indeed, absolute—ego. Along with the transcendental or absolute ego, however, an entire world of posited being comes to the
fore in a veritable creation out of nothing.

Four comments:

1. Commentators have rightly stressed the centrality of Kant's doctrine of
the postulates of practical reason (freedom, immortality, and God) for Hegel's
Bern theological writings of 1793–1794. Among the so-called "Fragments
Concerning a National Religion and Christianity," for example, Hegel explicitly refers to Kant's practical postulates; here too, however, as in the *Systemprogramm*, it is a question of *two* postulates, not three (HW 1:16–17). Surprisingly, the two postulates that Hegel attributes to religion (in contrast to

theology) are immortality of the soul and God—thus leaving freedom out of account. One would have expected the author of the *Systemprogramm* to include freedom first of all, and if there must be only two, to exclude God. Nevertheless, there are a number of references in Hegel's early writings on religion that point to Hegel as the author of the fragment: Hegel cites the importance of sensuality in human beings, in contrast to nonsensuous rationality (HW 1:10–11), refers to the normal active human being as a "machine" (HW 1:15, 22), criticizes the pedant, *den Buchstabenmensch* (HW 1:28), chastens the priestly and governing castes (HW 1:57), and so on. Most important, the role of a *Volksreligion* is emphasized throughout these early texts of Hegel, the popular religion that sounds the closing note of the *Systemprogramm*. Hegel's correspondence with Schelling also attests to the importance of Kant's practical postulates for him—now including the postulate of freedom. Hegel writes Schelling from Bern on April 16, 1795:

> As I was studying once again the postulates of practical reason I had a premonition of what you were explaining to me so clearly in your last letter: a number of gentlemen will be quite astonished by the consequences that arise from this. People will get dizzy when they achieve this highest height of all philosophy, a height to which humanity is so mightily raised. Yet why has it occurred to us only lately to set the dignity of man at a higher level, to acknowledge his capacity for freedom, which places him in the order of all other spirits? (HB 1:24)

On August 30, he once again refers to his speculations on religion, speculations "approaching God," and his belief that the practical postulates "command the world of appearances" (HB 1:29). Hegel confirms his belief that, whereas reason in its theoretical employ is denied all access to the absolute, the absolute nonetheless penetrates finite life in the free self-determinations of pure practical reason. Doubtless, Kant himself would never have sanctioned the program's proposed collapse of metaphysics into ethics, inasmuch as the Critical project as a whole would collapse along with it (JS 54). Yet Fichte had in the meantime declared that all philosophizing is rooted in practical philosophy; indeed, Kant himself had asserted the primacy of pure practical reason, "because all interest is ultimately practical" (KpV A219). Yet if this is so, then *all* ideas in philosophy are postulates. As Otto Pöggeler affirms, Kant's keystone and conclusion, namely, absolute freedom, would now have to become the *first* principle of philosophy (JS 131). If only two postulates of practical reason are cited in the system program, that may be because freedom is coterminous with the practical realm as such—less a postulate than an axiom, albeit an axiom that is lived rather than cognized.

2. Although the language of the *Systemprogramm* is predominantly Kantian, Hegel (or Schelling or Hölderlin) here formulates what will prove to be his (or their) persistent, systematic critique of Kantian reason: Kant splits reason into theory and practice, duty and inclination, law and self-determination, even though he knows that a rational system must be a single system, a monistic system. If a sys-tem does not "hold together," it is no system. The program is therefore to demonstrate the hold.

3. What the author of the *Systemprogramm* here establishes as his "first idea," that is to say, "my representation *of me myself*," he probably derives from Schelling's reading of Fichte in late 1794 and early 1795. Schelling has already published his first work on Fichte's philosophy, *On the Possibility of a Form of Philosophy in General*, undertaking to resolve the central problem of the transcendental ego as the basis of a deduction of the entire world of being. In early 1795 Schelling is preparing a second, more popular response to Fichte, *On the Ego as the Principle of Philosophy; or, On the Unconditioned in Human Knowledge*. Schelling writes to Hegel on February 4, 1795, "For me, the supreme principle of all philosophy is the pure, absolute ego, i.e., the ego insofar as it is naked ego, not yet conditioned by any object at all, but posited by *freedom*. The alpha and omega of all philosophy is freedom" (HB 1:22). Yet some earlier remarks in that letter show how difficult it will be for Schelling to sustain his Fichtean persuasion: he tells Hegel that he intends to go beyond the conception of God as a personality to the *Spinozist* conception of God as substance, being, or world. In both cases, with Spinozist pantheism and Kantian-Fichtean freedom, it is a matter of starting from what is *unconditioned*, that is, from the *absolute*. For the moment, Schelling seems to underestimate the difference it will make when he takes the world of nature, the not-I, as the absolute starting point.

4. By contrast, the reference to *creatio ex nihilo* seems, at least according to some, less likely to have stemmed from Schelling or Hölderlin and more likely to have come from the hand (and mind) of Hegel. That reference does bear the mark of Hegel's more orthodox or at least less Spinozist approach to the question of creation. Nevertheless, Schelling himself does refer to *eine Schöpfung aus Nichts*, in the very same language employed by the *Systemprogramm*: see his *Treatises toward an Elucidation of the Idealism of the Wissenschaftslehre* (composed in 1796–1797, hence contemporary with the "Program"), published in the *Sämmtliche Werke* of 1856–1857 at I/1:358.

The transition from questions of ethics and morality to physics is perhaps not easy to comprehend at first. The author of the program, after having touched on the high-flying question of creation out of nothing, immediately espies the "fields of physics," where he wishes to alight. His question is once again a Kantian question: How must a world be fashioned if it is to be the world of a moral (that is, free) creature? He promises to elaborate the question on the basis of the ideas of philosophy and the data of experience—including, presumably, the experience of natural science. In any case, this attempt to give wings to physics once again will not be accomplished overnight. All one can hope for is a "general outline," to be fleshed out by later generations. For the current generation can take no solace in the mechanistic physics of the times.

Three comments:

1. Although Franz Rosenzweig convincingly dates Schelling's descent onto the fields of physics, a descent that will occur (at the latest) between the years 1797 and 1799, most commentators once again attribute this descent to Hegel. (Ironically, the time is Easter 1796, precisely when the entire triumvirate ought to have been concerned to resurrect itself out of the physical field, as Hölderlin would have impishly reminded the others.) Otto Pöggeler notes that Hegel was preoccupied with the "Doctrine of Method" of Kant's *Critique of Judgment*, especially sections 85–86 on the alleged primacy of "ethicotheology" over "physicotheology" (JS 132–133; cf. 55). At the end of January 1795, two years before the *Systemprogramm* found its way to paper, Hegel wrote to Schelling of his desire to reverse the Kantian trajectory: Hegel would now try "to determine the extent to which we may—after securing moral belief—employ the legitimated idea of God in the opposite direction, for example, in explaining purposeful relationships, etc., taking the idea from ethicotheology back now toward physicotheology and letting it prevail along with the former" (HB 1:17).

2. However, physicotheology could never become for Hegel what it had quite readily become for the Tübingen theologians whom all three thinkers—Hölderlin, Hegel, and Schelling—so hotly despised. Nature could never be the paradisiacal setting for a traditional theodicy (JS 130). Hegel's *physis*, for example, was, and remained, jagged. Recall the unpropitious beginnings of sidereal Earth, as Hegel recounts them in the philosophy of nature of his mature system. Completely in accord with the later account, and with the darker side of Kant's Analytic of the Sublime, are the following lines from a journal Hegel kept while hiking in the Berner Oberland during the months of July

and August of 1796, six months before the *Systemprogramm* proposed to transform physics into a wingèd thing:

> After Guttanen the path gets wilder, more barren and monotonous. Always the same raw and dreary cliffs on either side. . . . The River Aar creates a number of tremendous waterfalls, plunging with frightful force. . . . Nowhere else does one get such a pure concept of the *has-to-be* [*das* Müssen] of nature than in viewing the eternally useless and eternally continuous crashing of waves of water against such rocks! . . . This family [seen gathering the roots of Gentian flowers for schnapps] lives all summer long here in complete isolation from other human beings; they have set up their distillery under towering granite boulders that nature has allowed to tumble there without purpose [*zwecklos*], yet out of whose accidental position these people know how to eke some advantage. *I doubt whether the most devout theologian would dare*, here in these mountains, to attribute to nature itself in any way *the aim of utility for man;* man, who has laboriously to rob nature of those few skimpy things he can use; who is never sure whether on account of his petty thefts, his tearing away a handful of grass, he will be crushed by rockslides or avalanches, whether the miserable labors of his hands, his squalid hut and cow stall will be ruined overnight. In these barren wildernesses, educated men would perhaps have invented every other theory and science, but they would scarcely have come up with that part of physicotheology that proves, much to man's pride, that nature arranged everything for his enjoyment and well-being; *a pride that characterizes our age*, inasmuch as it is more likely to find satisfaction in representing all the things some alien essence did for him than in the consciousness that it is actually he himself who has dictated all these aims to nature. (Hegel's emphases; HW 1:616–617)

A physics with wings? Perhaps. Yet, if Hegel is the aeronautical engineer in question, all physics will be as grounded and as slow-paced and cautious as any experimental science could ever be. Not everything about the *Systemprogramm* is translucent. Perhaps Hegel *did* copy it from some obscure and still unknown source?

3. That Schelling may be the principal architect of this physics with wings is suggested not only by his three great works in the philosophy of nature from 1797 to 1799 but also by his enduring fascination with nature. Even when Schelling is discussing art, for example, in his 1802–1803 aesthetics, he dreams of a speculative physics: "One has often heard in recent times that it would be possible to take from *physics*—as long as it is speculative physics, naturally—the material for a new mythology" (5:446). Both a speculative physics and the new mythology—contributions to the program principally by Schelling?

The program now turns to *das Menschenwerk*, the artifacts of human culture. It begins by asserting that the idea of humanity necessitates the elimination of the state, which treats human beings like cogs in a machine. Only objects of freedom can be ideas. All other social, political, and historical ideas—such as Kant's of eternal peace—must be subordinated to this idea of humanity. As it lays down the principles of a history of humanity, perhaps taking Herder as its model, the *Systemprogramm* unleashes a scathing critique of governments and churches. Indeed, the program seems to suggest that next on the list for such a critique are the very ideas of a moral world with which the fragment commences, namely, the practical postulates of God and immortality. The program now proclaims the overthrow of all *Afterglaube*, which is something like "superstition," and it dreams of rounding up the hypocritical priesthood that merely mimics reason. Finally, it affirms the absolute freedom that prevails *within*, rejecting all notions of God and immortality that are extrinsically derived, that is, derived from outside ourselves.

Three comments:

1. In an article entitled *"Das Menschenwerk des Staates,"* Otto Pöggeler comments in detail on these extraordinary lines of the *Systemprogramm* (JS 175–225). He discusses the machine metaphor at some length (JS 191–192), as do Christoph Jamme and Helmut Schneider (JS 55). The machine metaphor is universal in Enlightenment and Romantic discourses: it can be found in Herder, Mendelssohn, Schiller, Fichte, Hölderlin, and of course Kant himself. "An organized nature," Kant writes in his third *Critique*, "is thus not a mere machine" (KU B292). The radicality of the proposition concerning the cessation of the state clearly reflects disaffection not only from the petty princes of Germany and the burghers of the Swiss cantons but also from the Committees of Jacobin France. "Disaffection" is assuredly too weak a word. Indeed, if Hegel did write these lines, he appears in subsequent years—already by the Jena period—to have altered in the most topsy-turvy way his views on the state. Such radicality could be less easily ascribed to Schelling, and most readily to Hölderlin, for whom political community is a crucial stage in the "higher nexus of life" that is achieved through love alone. Yet Hölderlin can also be critical of his own utopian tendency: "What has turned the state into a hell," cries the narrator of Hölderlin's *Hyperion*, "is the fact that human beings wanted to make it their heaven" (DKV 2:40). He adds: "The state is nothing more than the rough husk wrapped around the kernel of life" (ibid.). Well, then, perhaps it should cease?

2. With regard to the hypocritical priesthood that abuses reason by aping it, we recall once again Hegel's, Hölderlin's, and Schelling's resentment of the Tübingen theologians Flatt, Storr, and, later on, their own Süskind (JV 1:169–258, 306–320). For, in the unforgiving eyes of their most gifted stu-

dents, these theologians arrogate to themselves Kant's doctrine of the practical postulates merely in order to justify all the traditional dogmas of their "positive" religion—founding an ostensibly Critical evangelical tradition that endures down to our own day (JS 131). Replying to a sardonic letter from Schelling, who at the end of January 1795 is still in Tübingen, Hegel writes that the two of them should stir up the theological "ant hill" as much as possible (HB 1:16–17). Their best tool will be nothing other than Kant's philosophy, pressed into radical service, and not used merely as a feint and a dodge. On April 16, 1795, Hegel replies to Schelling, "From the Kantian system and its supreme fulfillment I expect a revolution in Germany that will proceed on the basis of principles, principles that are already at hand and that will need only to be worked out in general, so that they can be applied to all prior knowledge" (HB 1:23–24). Hegel's letters too, argues Pöggeler, and not only Schelling's, thus betray the "victorious tone" that Rosenzweig attributes to Schelling alone. Such is the tone, add Jamme and Schneider, of a conspiratorial "revolutionary Spinozism" (JS 56). Perhaps we should not allow it to resound merely as an ironic indicator of how conservative Hegel was soon to become. Questions of authorship apart, these three thinkers would have welcomed the young Marx into their midst.[8]

3. Concerning the substitution of the word *Afterglaube* for *Aberglaube*, the following tidbit. *Afterglaube* is not merely an "improvement" on Kant's word *Aberglaube*, "superstition," as Jamme and Schneider suggest (JS 56), but an imitation of what Kant himself in Part IV of *Religion within the Limits of Mere Reason* calls *Afterdienst*. *Afterdienst* is Kant's word for the *Gottesdienst* of the churches—all the doings and the trappings of cult and liturgy, which he finds to be more sycophantic than hierophantic. Yet Kant is not merely asserting that cult must be supplemental to moral education, succeeding upon it in some sense. *Der After* is the anus, as both Kant and the generation after him knew full well, if only because it was a word much beloved of Martin Luther. In Middle High German there had been an adverbial-prepositional word *after*, possessing a meaning quite close to that of the modern English word. That word died out in the seventeenth century, presumably because of its discomfiting proximity to the noun *After*. Only in certain critical and even snide expressions (e.g., *Aftermuse*, *Afterweisheit*) was the word retained, now implying that its object was a merely second-rate supplement or cheap imitation, both inferior and posterior to the original, as it were. Thus liturgical bedazzle-

---

8. But, no, Karl Marx is *not* the author of *Das älteste Systemprogramm des deutschen Idealismus.* Unless he and Nietzsche met secretly at Pforta.

ments are inferior and posterior to moral education, and that does not merely mean that cult "comes after" moral education. When I first visited England, I saw Queen Elizabeth pass by on horseback—and in Her Majesty's train I observed an assiduous footman with broom and shovel performing what Kant and our three young authors alike would have called *Afterdienst*. It is clear to me that "belief in a hinterhaven" is not a very economical rendering of *Afterglaube*. Yet "anal compulsive religiosity" and "rectal rectitude" did seem to bend over backwards—indeed, one had difficulty keeping at a distance Lacan's designation of the projects of both Kant and Sade, in *"Kant avec Sade,"* as the rectification of ethics.[9]

"And at the very end," says the *Systemprogramm*, will come the idea of beauty. That idea will permeate not only poetic creativity but also religion—indeed, it will give birth to a new mythology. In the first of these final turns, the subject is poetry, or poesy. For beauty in the higher, Platonic sense unifies all, not as a theoretical or even practical postulate, but as an aesthetic sensibility engaged in an aesthetic act. "The philosopher must possess as much aesthetic force as the poet." Not the pedant but the poet will instruct humanity. "The poetic art alone will survive all the other sciences and arts."

Five brief comments:

1. In the remarks on beauty, aesthetic sense, aesthetic force, and poesy, we confront, in the words of Otto Pöggeler (JS 135), "a tension, if not a complete breach," with what has gone before in the *Systemprogramm*. Jamme and Schneider too (JS 56) see in this facet of the program "a complete shift in paradigm." Whereas the first half of the fragment expresses in a condensed form Hegel's interests of the Bern period, dominated by the Kantian conception of the postulates of pure practical reason and Hegel's own views on "subjective" religiosity and morality, as well as Schelling's interests of the Tübingen years, dominated by the Fichtean transcendental ego and the worlds of nature and history that he is trying to deduce from it, the second half adopts wholeheartedly Hölderlin's aesthetic Platonism (JS 53). To be sure, in our response to Wilhelm Böhm's attribution of the fragment to Hölderlin, we have already seen that such "aesthetic Platonism" has its darker side, one that neither Böhm nor the *Systemprogramm* itself appears to take into account. In any case, how to account for this shift in the direction of Hölderlin's passions and dreams, if not his nightmares? Jamme, Schneider, and Pöggeler argue that Hegel himself underwent an alteration in paradigm when he changed his em-

---

9. Jacques Lacan, "Kant avec Sade," in *Écrits* (Paris: Gallimard, 1966), 765: "Ici comme là, on prépare la science en rectifiant la position de l'éthique."

ployment and residence, moving from Bern to Hölderlin's proximity in Frankfurt. Indeed, they see in this move a long-awaited "liberation" (JS 128). Franz Rosenzweig offers perhaps the most lucid and convincing account of the necessity of such a paradigm shift, however, not only for Hegel and the *Systemprogramm* but also for German Idealism as a whole, so that we must now turn to Rosenzweig's analysis.

2. According to Rosenzweig (JS 98), Kant himself posed the problem of a "common root" for practical and theoretical philosophy. The two well-known Introductions to the third *Critique* thematize this problem. Further, many passages in that work, not only in the Doctrine of Method but also throughout, appear to be groping toward the grand Critical synthesis.[10] Consider these lines from section 76 of the Dialectic of Teleological Judgment: "Just as reason, in the theoretical observation of nature, must assume the idea of an unconditioned necessity in its primal ground [*Urgrund*], so does it, in its practical [application], presuppose its own causality as being unconditioned with regard to nature; that is, it presupposes its own freedom, insofar as it is conscious of its moral command" (KU B342). The assumed unconditioned necessity of nature's *Urgrund* and the presupposed unconditioned freedom of self-determining will—how are these *two* presumed "unconditionals," these *two* ostensible absolutes, related? That is what Schelling, Hegel, and Hölderlin wanted to know. They began by realizing that there cannot be two absolutes. For that would amount to saying that the absolute had suffered a stroke, that it had been sundered, bifurcated. They therefore went on to wonder whether the freedom of self-determining will was the same freedom as that experienced in the play of the faculties in aesthetic reflective judgments. The very fact that Kant's enigmatic book juxtaposed such apparently disparate items as judgments concerning self-organizing, self-reproducing organisms and judgments of aesthetic taste hinted that the link was to be sought in the reflective judgments that respond to the worlds of nature and culture alike. Schiller, in his correspondence with Christian Gottfried Körner, but also in his letters to Hölderlin, suggested that beauty alone—beauty conceived of as "freedom in appearance"—could bridge the gap between the reality of the sensuous world and the ideality of both practical and theoretical reason.[11]

10. I have offered my own brief account of Kant's attempt in a section of the Introduction to my *Contagion: Sexuality, Disease, and Death in German Idealism and Romanticism* (Bloomington: Indiana University Press, 1998), entitled "Hopes and Tangles," 6–15.

11. Friedrich Schiller, *Kallias oder über die Schönheit*, ed. Klaus L. Berghahn (Stuttgart: Reclam, 1971), 34–55: "Freiheit in der Erscheinung ist eins mit der Schönheit."

3. Thus the entire "Program toward a System" becomes a response to the challenge posed by Hölderlin's philosophy of unification, *Vereinigungsphiloso-phie*, as developed, for example, in the foreword to the penultimate draft of *Hyperion*, cited earlier (JS 45, 56, 128). If beauty is there crowned queen, her two daughters, truth and goodness, are also acclaimed in the *Systemprogramm*. Beauty, which is the object of the Eros of Plato's *Symposium* and *Phaedrus*, is the uppermost principle of unity, while intellect, theoretical reason, and the moral-ethical faculty are scions of the family tree. Whereas Schiller argues that beauty is "*in the family of reason*,"[12] Hölderlin reverses matters, making reason a child of beauty. "Judgment," *Urteil*, is the "ordeal," *Ur-teilung*, of reason, and it entails separation from the origin. "Being," *Seyn*, onto which the vision of beauty opens, is unification beyond identity. Theory and morality alike are alienations or departures from an original state of unity; that state can be restored only through intellectual intuition, which is aesthetic.[13]

4. One should not underestimate Schelling's celebration of art and poetry during these years, as though to suggest that Hölderlin alone could have been responsible for the paradigm shift. Three years after the "Program" is composed, Schelling's *System of Transcendental Idealism* appears.[14] In the very last section of his *System*, Schelling proclaims art "the sole eternal revelation" (3:618). When intellectual intuition becomes objective, it becomes aesthetic intuition—as in Hölderlin, so also here in Schelling. Hence, "art is the sole true and eternal organon and document of philosophy" (3:627). Art documents what philosophy cannot bring to external presentation, "namely, the unconscious [*das Bewußtlose*] in acting and producing" (3:627–628). What in the history of spirit eventually becomes the two separate realms of nature and history or culture "ignites in a single flame" as art (3:628). The most astonish-

---

12. Schiller, *Kallias*, 15.

13. I am grateful to Nick Walker for suggesting J. H. Stirling's inspired translation of *Urteil* as "ordeal." My more sober friend and colleague, Stephen Houlgate, assures me that the etymology of the two words will not support such a translation. And it is true that the prefix *ur-*for centuries meant no more than the verbal prefix *er-*. Yet from the seventeenth century on, the prefix seems to have regained its relation to things "primal" and "primordial." At all events, Hölderlin himself, and also Schelling, had (as we shall see) a genuine sense of spirit's life as one of ordeal—of trial and test, as well as of allotment. *The Oxford English Dictionary* offers an excellent portrait of the Teutonic *ordâl* that unites *Urteil* and *ordeal*: "An ancient mode of trial among the Teutonic peoples, retained in England till after the Norman Period, in which an accused or suspected person was subjected to some physical test fraught with danger, such as the plunging of the hand in boiling water, the carrying of hot iron, walking barefoot and blindfold between red-hot ploughshares, etc., the result being regarded as the immediate judgement of the Deity." When Hölderlin translates *Urteil* as *Ur-teilung*, he merely makes the judgment *of* the deity both a subjective and an objective genitive. To understand how the life of spirit requires the ordeal, however, requires that we understand something like a tragic absolute. For further discussion of intellectual intuition, see ch. 9 of this volume.

14. I shall use the "Philosophische Bibliothek" edition of the *System* (see note 4, above); this edition also refers to the *Sämmtliche Werke* volume number (3) and pagination, which I shall cite.

ing claim of Schelling's 1800 *System* is that philosophy as such, with all its discursive systematicity, flows back into the supreme art, namely, poesy. Schelling seems *per impossibile* to have studied sections 14–15 of Nietzsche's *Birth of Tragedy*, on the "Socratic supplement," that is, the transformation of all science and philosophy into art, before writing the following words: "Now, if it is art alone that is able to make objectively and universally valid what philosophy is able to present only subjectively, we may . . . expect that philosophy—which was born and nurtured by poesy in the childhood of science, and which accompanied all those sciences and brought them to maturity and completion in their sundry individual streams—flows back into the universal ocean of poesy, whence they all originated" (3:629). In the "General Remark on the Entire System," at the end of the treatise (3:630), Schelling notes that while philosophy achieves "what is supreme" (*das Höchste*) it brings "but a fragment" (*Bruchstück*) of the human being to the summit. Poetry and art do more. "Art brings *the whole human being*, as he or she is, to that point—namely, to the knowledge of the highest; on that rests the distinction and the miracle of art" (3:630). Is it not likely that Schelling entertained at least some of these radical ideas on art three years earlier, at the time of the "System Program"?

5. The words *tragic* and *tragedy* do not appear in the system fragment, and there is nothing that suggests that Sophocles will soon become the prophet of poesy. Of the three friends, Hölderlin will prove to have always dwelled closest to the tragic sensibility and to tragic insight, from 1792 until the end. Readers of Schelling will have to wait until the 1809 *Philosophical Investigations into the Essence of Human Freedom* and the three drafts of *The Ages of the World* (1811–1815) for the full force of the tragic to be felt, although we do have the remarkable "Tenth Letter" from his 1795 *Philosophical Letters on Dogmatism and Criticism* (see ch. 6 in this volume). Readers of *Hegel* will simply have to continue to fight about whether or not after the early theological writings Hegel does anything more than utilize tragedy for preconceived happy philosophical ends.[15]

15. One of the crucial texts here is, without doubt, the *Naturrecht* essay of 1802 (HW 2:434–530), which one must see as the culmination of a long development in Hegel's early thought. See the thorough treatment of the early Hegel and tragedy by Peter Wake, in "Tragedy, Speculation, and Ethicality in German Idealism" (Ph.D. dissertation, DePaul University, 2004). For a detailed, affirmative account of Hegel on tragedy, see Dennis J. Schmidt, *On Germans and Other Greeks* (cited in the Introduction to this volume), ch. 3, 89–121. Schmidt rightly sees that Hegel's confrontation with tragedy and the tragic occurs principally in the *Phenomenology of Spirit*. By contrast, the "systematic appropriation" of tragedy as a work of art in the *Lectures on Aesthetics* "blunts its force" (121). And even in the *Phenomenology*, Schmidt concedes, citing Hegel, a philosophy of spirit that is in search of "self-certainty" and "a state of spiritual well-being and of repose" (108) is in effect engaged to the *comic* absolute. Whereas I too would like to emphasize spirit's descent into risk and egress into conflict (see D. F. Krell, *Of Memory, Reminiscence, and Writing: On the Verge* [Bloomington: Indiana University

The final theme of the fragmentary *Systemprogramm* is that of a "sensuous religion." Not only the great masses of human beings require such a religion, but so also does the philosopher himself. For, as Hölderlin was to demonstrate throughout his 1792–1798 *Hyperion*, and as Schelling was to argue in his 1809 treatise on freedom, and as even the mature Hegel would suggest in his philosophy of nature, philosophy since Descartes is mutilated and unmanned by its divorce from the senses and from nature. In the *Systemprogramm*, which now invokes a monotheism of reason and heart, but a polytheism of the imagination and of art, we can imagine all three thinkers proposing their common solution to the pantheism-atheism scandal of the 1790s and early 1800s. The author(s) call(s) for a new mythology, one that will make ideas aesthetic and philosophers sensuous. This new mythology of reason, which we initially identify perhaps more with Schelling than with anyone else, has the political objective of eliminating the gap between the contemptible unenlightened and the contemptuous enlightened.[16] The program concludes by envisaging the equal development of all forces in all individuals, including the force of imagination, cultivated through poesy. At the end of the long history of human evolution, the *Systemprogramm* proclaims the instauration of a reign of "universal freedom and equality of spirits!" The program ends with both a cautionary note and a final burst of enthusiasm: "A higher spirit, sent from heaven, will have to found this new religion among us; it will be the very last and the grandest of the works of humanity."

Five brief comments on the final facets of the program:

1. The transition from poesy to a sensuous religion and a new mythology may seem abrupt and awkward to us, but it was an open road throughout the careers of Hölderlin and Schelling and—at least early on—also for Hegel. For all three thinkers, as also for Lessing, Herder, Goethe, and Schiller, that road was to lead the fragmented German lands to a national pedagogy, *eine Volkserziehung*, based on the School of Athens (JS 47, 57). In his discourse on

---

Press, 1990], 234–239), with absolute knowing placed in absolute suspension, it is clear that Hegel, in contrast to Schelling and Hölderlin, confronts the tragic only in order to pull back from all its consequences. "[T]he fault lines along which the tragic conflict develops are, according to Hegel, overcome" (Schmidt, 110). Yet fault lines are "overcome" only in the daydreams of bad seismographers. The *uses* Hegel believes he can make of tragedy in his ontotheological project—ethicality in the community and the establishment of the state—lead him to construct his system on what he takes to be solid ground. In the end, however, the Golgotha of spirit is utterly remote from the southern slope of the Acropolis.

16. Christoph Jamme, one of Hegel's most astute champions, taught a course at DePaul University in February of 1999 on "the new mythology," but focusing on texts of Goethe, Karl Philipp Moritz, and *Schelling* rather than Hegel. He was no doubt spurred on by Schelling's references to "a new mythology," for example, in his 1800 *System of Transcendental Idealism*, 3:629. On the new mythology of reason as the basis for a national religion, see JV 1:286–305; 3:245–272.

Athens at the end of the first volume of *Hyperion*, Hölderlin's hero says: "The first child of divine beauty is art. So it was with the Athenians. Beauty's second daughter is religion. Religion is love of beauty" (I 365; DKV 2:90). For Hölderlin, the poetic naming of the gods, poetic μύθειν, leaves behind the Kantian distinction between the "intellectual-universal" and the "historical-particular" elements of religion. Mythic remembrance, *Erinnerung*, achieves a synthesis more powerful than any Critical synthesis and more compelling than any (other) play of the imagination. By virtue of such a synthesis, Diotima tells Hyperion, "You will be the educator of our nation," *Erzieher unsers Volks* (I 375; DKV 2:100). Hölderlin thus adds his own voice to those of Herder, the Schlegel brothers, Novalis, and others. We have already heard Schelling connect the idea of a speculative physics to the "new mythology." And when we read the closing lines of the *Systemprogramm*, on the "very last and grandest of the works of humanity," we are reminded of a similar Schellingian formulation in 1795: in the tenth of his *Philosophical Letters on Dogmatism and Criticism*, he imagines a group of philosophers who would think of human freedom as the task of "bringing their final work to perfection" (1:340). Schelling often writes in this declamatory, programmatic style. Yet the proposed "mythology of reason," according to Jamme and Schneider (JS 58), seems to outbid and overreach all earlier formulations by all our authors. One must remember that throughout his Bern period Hegel too is profoundly interested in the problems of sensuous religiosity, that is, a religion of fantasy and heart as well as of morality and mind, along with a national education through a new mythology. In his text on "Enlightenment—Achieving an Impact by Means of Intellect," Hegel notes that for a national religion (*eine Volksreligion*) "it is of the greatest importance that fantasy and heart not be left dissatisfied, that fantasy be filled with grand and pure images and the heart awakened by the more benevolent sorts of feelings" (HW 1:30–31). Later, in the "Fragments on National Religion and Christianity," Hegel argues that the priestly and governing castes have all but destroyed the sense of freedom among the people (HW 1:57); the understandable reaction of the people is therefore hatred of the religion of love (HW 1:59). Indeed, Hegel concedes that any state that tries to practice the principles and commandments of original Christianity will soon collapse (HW 1:61). In the second addendum to "The Positivity of the Christian Religion," from the years 1795–1796, Hegel devotes himself to the development of a new mythology, one that could play the role that Greek mythology played in the national education of the Greeks; yet he remains skeptical about the possibility of such a development, which almost invariably becomes the grafting of a foreign limb onto an unreceptive stock, or the importing of anachronistic or alien elements into an inhospitable terrain (HW 1:197–202). No doubt, Hegel's radical interests and enthusiasms, no matter how soon they were to wither, brought him into conflict with the priestly and governing forces, precisely in the way that Kant's astringent religion of morality at least initially did.

2. It is noteworthy that sensuous religiosity is viewed in the *Systemprogramm* as essential not only for the masses but also for the philosopher. He himself (or, in our own time, she herself—unless the force of the "she herself" was already beginning to be felt by the generation of Early Romantic thinkers following immediately upon Kant) was to become, *mirabile dictu,* a sentient and sensuous creature. Sometimes one has the sense that Maurice Merleau-Ponty must have penned the *Systemprogramm,* especially if Schelling was its principal inspiration.[17]

3. A second philological tidbit or piece of *Afterweisheit:* according to Jamme and Schneider (JS 74 n. 82), the phrase *eine Idee, die noch in keines Menschen Sinn gekommen ist* is one that Hegel—if he is the author of the fragment—must have borrowed from Schelling. Indeed, in a note to the sixth of his *Philosophical Letters on Dogmatism and Criticism* (1795), Schelling makes a skeptical reference to his own era's inability to recognize the fact that the question of being (τὸ ὄν) is already raised in the systems of Descartes and especially Spinoza. (The note would surely have interested Heidegger, inasmuch as it is all about what Heidegger calls oblivion of being, *Seinsvergessenheit.*) Because Schelling's use of the phrase (to be precise, he writes [1:309], "*daß vorher nie etwas dergleichen in eines Menschen Sinn gekommen sey*") is a negative one, however, it becomes difficult to conceive of his using the phrase so positively in the *Systemprogramm,* or, for that matter, of Hegel's borrowing it from him so incautiously.

4. Observe in the peroration of the program the clear subordination of the goals of the French Revolution to those of a national religion and pedagogy. In the movement of thought that is visible in two fragments from Hegel's Frankfurt years, *Positiv wird ein Glaube genannt* and *Religion, eine Religion stiften* (HW 1:239–243), we can make out the lesson plan that such a pedagogy was to adopt, as it were, from the positings of the subject of pure practical reason to the higher unification of love. What sort of love? One that is situated—not altogether stably, and not very comfortably, one must say—

---

17. I invite skeptics to examine the remarkable work by Robert Vallier, "Institution: Nature, Life, and Meaning in Merleau-Ponty" (Ph.D. dissertation, DePaul University, 2001). See also his translation of Merleau-Ponty, *La nature* (Evanston, Ill.: Northwestern University Press, 2003).

between the Platonic Eros celebrated by both Schiller and Hölderlin and a charity more akin to the traditional Christian ἀγάπη. At all events, this new religion would have to be inspired by a revelation from heaven: it would be in the literal sense *apocalyptic* (JS 59).

5. A final comment, based on a thesis put forward by Annemarie Geth-mann-Siefert (JS 226–260) concerning the historical function of the "mythology of reason," as also of the work of art, in Hegel's later aesthetics. Gethmann-Siefert argues that although Hegel's views on art may have changed from the *Systemprogramm* to the *Lectures on Aesthetics*, one factor remains constant: Hegel's reception of Schiller never allows him to forget the historical perspective on art, as well as the political, religious, and cultural functions of the work of art (JS 227–228). Early on, from the Bern period, or even prior to it, until about 1803, Hegel's model for such functions is the Greek epic. Homer's gods and heroes found the polis; Homer is *staatstiftend.* Modern works of art, such as Schiller's own *Wallenstein* or Shakespeare's *Macbeth,* fail utterly to found a state, and they lose themselves in futile dreams and bad poetry when they try (JS 236). The shift in Hegel's view concerning the efficacy of art comes at Jena around the year 1803. At that point the parallel between the artwork and the political deed (*Kunstwerk/Staatwerk*) collapses; there is no Christian epic and hence no Christian mythology. There is only Revelation (*Offenbarung*), at least when it comes to expressions that are adequate to the Idea. The work of art therefore serves merely to illustrate the Idea in a foreign medium and is thus essentially inadequate to the Idea. From this point on in Hegel's work the meaning of art narrows significantly to mere *symbolism;* art is closer to the sensuous intuitions of mere representation (*Vorstellung*) than to the categories of thought. The *work* of art, that is, its function in the history of spirit, is at an end, whereas the meaning of the state expands and becomes coterminous with reason and the Idea as such.

Gethmann-Siefert insists that Hegel's development is consistent, inasmuch as Hegel always examines art in terms of its historical function; consistent, however, only to the extent that philosophy is now conceived of as knowledge of the absolute or as absolute knowing. Yet there is the rub. To conceive of philosophy as knowledge of the absolute begs the very questions that the *Älteste Systemprogramm des deutschen Idealismus* puts forward. For is not freedom the absolute—freedom as a postulate, axiom, or intellectual intuition of pure *practical* reason, or better, as an aesthetic act and a politico-pedagogical deed? Could mere knowing, even when conceived of as *das absolute Wissen,* comprehend such an absolute? Or would not all the absolutes of metaphysics have to be subsumed under an ethics—indeed, under an aesthetics and a poetic-political praxis? Would not such a praxis respond to the challenge of the unification of subject and object not in theoretical positings, whether phenomenological or logical, but in ecstasies of beauty and love, and in the chastened wisdom of a national education in myth and poesy? Surely, not even *absolutes Wissen*, and especially not it, would be adequate to such a response?

Such questions take us beyond mere commentary. They incite in us something like a *speculative interrogation,* if not a speculative proposition. One such interrogation, thinking of the role of the "System Program" in the history of philosophy, might raise the following question: What would be required of philosophy for it to have been able to carry out to the letter the oldest program toward a system in German Idealism? Another interrogation, more attuned to that branch of poesy that is tragedy, might raise the question: Are there any moments in this buoyant text, which seems to invest all its hopes in a future, that remember the highest form of poetry in antiquity, that is, Greek tragedy? Of the three thinkers, to repeat, Hölderlin is clearly the one who is already engaged in a life-long confrontation with tragedy; Schelling will come to such a confrontation later, and more traumatically. The chapters that follow will therefore focus on a series of Hölderlin's and Schelling's works. Yet is there anything that can be said now, whether with respect to Hölderlin or Schelling or Hegel, concerning an absolute that would be a *tragic* absolute?

The Tragic Absolute?

Allow me to revert to the question of authorship for a moment. From there we may be able to find our way to the unlikely question of tragedy. Contemporary philology and philosophy—and I along with them, even if kicking and screaming—are keen to determine the authorship of the fragment. Why? No one dare scorn the efforts of so many dedicated interpreters, editors, and commentators. Yet one may still wish to invite reflection on the demand for identifiable authorship in general. Why the *competition* among the disciples of Schelling, Hölderlin, and Hegel, when these three thinkers allowed their ambitions to be yoked to a common task, a shared historical-epochal vision and mission? More than authorship, this shared vision—this engaged friendship—intrigues me. Do we in the age of self-conscious collectives and universally espoused aspirations for community know anything like it? The oldest program toward a system in German Idealism develops out of an intense exchange of ideas and an interpenetration of styles: imagine in our own time a state of confusion as to whether a particular text had been written by one of the two leading philosophers of the century—or by that century's most remarkable poet! An idle fancy. Perhaps there is no confusion of styles nowadays because philosophers have been so thoroughly drubbed that we have no style? Perhaps we do not need style, do not want style, because we have cogency, or at least tenure and copyright? Things were certainly more precarious and less predictable in the Germany of the 1790s. Yet why in our own time, a time without style but with endless conversation and infinite nitpicking, is there so little *shared* thinking?

If we persist with the question of authorship, something strange begins to happen. It is certain that Hegel *wrote* the *Systemprogramm*, but who *authored* it? Whose is the dominant spirit, whose the tongue of the text? Much of it sounds like Schelling, as Franz Rosenzweig recognized. Even more of it sounds like Hegel. A paragraph or two, especially those on beauty and poesy, sound like Hölderlin on a dull day, when the poetry refused to come. Yet so much is strangely prescient and forward-looking in the text; so much appears to be far beyond anything Schelling and Hegel ever actually executed. Let us review some of the facets of the text one last time, with a look to the future:

• a metaphysics that becomes coterminous with ethics, such that the Kantian postulates are seen as permeating metaphysical thinking as such;

• an entire world springing from the nothing of human consciousness, as though in perspectival projection;

• a transformation of the question, "How must a world be furnished in order to suit a moral creature?" into the more radical question: "Not, how are synthetic judgments *a priori* possible, but: Why is belief—doubtless in the form of *Afterglaube*—in such judgments necessary?"

• a dismantling or destruction of all the current ideas concerning the state and culture; the construction of a history of humanity—perhaps by way of a genealogy—in order to lay bare the hypocrisies of society, to overthrow all anal-compulsive religion, and to round up the priests who have mastered only the empty gestures of reason, such a round-up to be conducted by untrammeled "free spirits," who seek no god or immortality outside themselves;

• a devotion to art and beauty, to the point where the philosopher, transformed into a sensuous creature, will require as much aesthetic force as the poet.

Seen in this futural light, the oldest fragment does suggest Nietzsche as its author, and my bad joke of fifteen years ago seems to have had a core of sense. At least, it may spur in us the question: If Nietzsche is the thinker of the birth of tragedy from the spirit of music, and also from Greek pessimism, which is a pessimism of strength, is there some sense in which the *Systempro-gramm* descries a tragic absolute? No doubt, the fragment is buoyantly optimistic, full of itself and full of faith in the future. Yet its stringent critique of the present, which represents a fallen state, the passing (forever?) of the Golden Age, shows that the author or authors know(s) about the dark side. The very split between the theoretical and practical sides of reason suggests that something is ailing the absolute. Absolute reason? Absolute freedom? Two absolutes are as good as none—indeed, to repeat, far worse than none. Two absolutes would raise the question not of the absolute but of the stroke that sundered the One before it could ever reach Two. Further, the split between philosophy and poetry reawakens all those questions about the ancient quarrel between philosophy and tragedy. Whereas Hölderlin may wish to write a commentary on *Phaedrus* and its notions of love and beauty, might he not also have to wonder why Plato felt it necessary to eject the tragic poets from the city and to rail against the enthusiastic rhetoricians and rhapsodes? Had tragedy seen something with absolute perspicacity, exposed something with absolute mastery, that philosophy would spend its entire career trying to cover up again?

Whereas the system fragment flaunts the representation of "me myself" as an "absolutely free creature," it everywhere feels the pressure of its chains. It senses in the philosophy and science of nature an unwillingness of the philosopher to "give over" to nature, to grant nature her due. Why that resistance? Why does the mechanist's view of nature flourish in a state where government too functions as an oppressive and repressive machine? Why has religion declined to the level of superstition, dogma, and tyranny? Why does it continue to be the inspiration for murder and the bloodthirsty genius of war? When we look at history, the history of humanity, through a perspective shaped by the *aesthetic* force, how are we to comprehend all the ugliness we see? If the philosopher is like the great mass of human beings, mutilated, desiccated, barely sentient, allergic to his or her sensuality and sensuousness, what good are all those libraries of learning? If the improvement of our portion waits upon an emissary from heaven—a heaven we have ceased to believe in, unless it light up inside ourselves by incandescence—then what has become of the very distinction between gods and mortals? Where shall we turn for lessons in such matters—if not to the Greek tragedians?

Could it be that the oldest program toward a system in German Idealism opens up a view on tragedy, or at least calls for such an opening? If so, that program may serve as the unlikely starting point for an inquiry into the tragic absolute. If not, one must wonder why Hölderlin and Schelling, very soon after they collaborated on the program, began to devote some of their best efforts to Greek tragedy, and why Hegel at least knew what he had most to fear, most to resist, most to subdue.

THREE ENDS OF
THE ABSOLUTE

2

The worst of criticizing Hegel is that the very arguments we use against him give forth strange and hollow sounds that make them seem almost as fantastic as the errors to which they are addressed. The sense of a universal mirage, of a ghostly unreality, steals over us, which is the very moonlit atmosphere of Hegelism itself. What wonder then if, instead of converting, our words do but rejoice and delight those already baptized in the faith of confusion? To their charmed senses we all seem children of Hegel together, only some of us have not the wit to know our own father.

—WILLIAM JAMES,
The Will to Believe

Even if one is not writing *about* Hegel, one is writing *of* and *from* Hegel, certainly insofar as one is invoking "the absolute."[1] That is the gist of William James's perceptive—and rather jaded, or at least weary—remark. James is weary and wary when it comes to "Hegelism" *and* the self-styled "refutations" of Hegelism. He would surely have affirmed the tendency of many twentieth-century readings of Hegel, however, which arise from the need to respect and pay heed to the larger legacy of German Idealism and Romanticism while at the same time eschewing all appeals to the absolute. "Dialectic" is only one of the words that capture something of this legacy. Indeed, German Idealism and Romanticism embrace a great deal more than dialectic. The present chapter reads three thinkers who were at best ambivalent about dialectic and who had grave prob-

1. My gratitude to Sonu Shamdasani of London for the epigraph by James on "Hegelism." To all appearances, the present book has little to do with Hegel, so that James's remarks may seem out of place. Yet the shadow of what in a book entitled *Contagion: Sexuality, Disease, and Death in German Idealism and Romanticism* (cited in note 10 of ch. 1, above) I have called Hegel's "triumphant idealism," the idealism of the absolute, is cast over the three figures I want to invoke in this chapter—Schelling, Hölderlin, and Novalis. None of them savored triumph, however, and each of them would have understood James's frustration. Yet one must in the end concede that Hegel's idealism in its earliest phases is not at all triumphant: much in our evaluation of Hegel would change if we were to study JV 1:12 and all the relevant documents of JV's four volumes. See, for example, JV 3:174–244.

lems with every discourse of the absolute, even when that discourse was coming out of their own mouths. The three in question are Novalis (Friedrich von Hardenberg, 1772–1801), Friedrich Hölderlin (1770–1843), and Friedrich Wilhelm Joseph von Schelling (1775–1854). It will be a matter of pursuing three different ends of the absolute in Schelling, Hölderlin, and Novalis, namely, their ideas of absolute inhibition, absolute separation, and absolute density, respectively.

One might well be struck by an initial skepticism with regard to the entire project. First of all, absolute inhibition, separation, and density appear to repeat and thus to reinstate the gestures of absolute knowing and absolute spirit, not to bring them to an end. By now we are familiar with conundrums of the "ends of metaphysics," "the end(s) of man," and so on. One might try to steer clear of these conundrums by insisting that with Novalis, Hölderlin, and Schelling a certain *materiality* and *elementality* come into play, something perhaps beyond or beneath (that is, subtending) the Heideggerian and even deconstructionist emphasis on history and historicity. Yet the skepticism will not be so readily quashed. To be sure, one can easily think of a number of *twentieth*-century adventures in idealism, from Whitehead to Merleau-Ponty, that have a highly developed relation to materiality and elementality. One might think, for example, of Luce Irigaray, who in books such as *Forgetting the Air* takes Gaston Bachelard's elemental thought in her own Empedoclean direction, or of Derrida's *Glas*, his remarkable response to Hegel's absolute knowing as absolute phantasm.[2] Yet is it truly conceivable that the thinkers and poets of German Idealism and Romanticism invoked here—Schelling, Hölderlin, and Novalis—could have been engaged in such an adventure? Did they not rather anticipate, or in some way participate in, the elevation of the absolute (as the absolute knowing of an absolute spirit) in Hegel's philosophy? *Ends* of the absolute in Schelling, Hölderlin, and Novalis? At first blush, nothing seems less likely.

Consider, for example, the case of Novalis, who confesses to August Wilhelm Schlegel on February 24, 1798, that in his study of chemistry the danger of getting lost in the details is greater than it is in his study of mathematics. "However," he continues, "my old inclination toward the absolute is once again rescuing me from the imbroglio of the empirical, and I am now and perhaps for ever hovering in loftier and altogether singular spheres [*ich schwebe*

---

2. Luce Irigaray, *L'Oubli de l'air chez Martin Heidegger* (Paris: Minuit, 1983); English translation, *The Forgetting of Air in Martin Heidegger*, by Mary Beth Mader (Austin: University of Texas Press, 1999); Jacques Derrida, *Glas* (Paris: Galilée, 1974); tr. John P. Leavey, Jr., and Richard Rand (Lincoln: University of Nebraska Press, 1986).

jezt und vielleicht auf immer in lichtern, eigenthümlichern Sfären]" (1:661). Many of Novalis's philosophical-scientific notes appear to confirm this self-description: his predilection for the absolute shapes his own tendency toward absolutization, which is his own definition of "the romantic" as such. Referring to Goethe's *Wilhelm Meister* and *Fairy Tale,* Novalis writes under the heading "romanticism": "Absolutizing—universalizing—classification of the individual moment, of the individual situation, etc., is the proper essence of *romanticizing"* (2:488).

Well, then, *absolutizing*—and not the *end* of the absolute, not an elemental or material idealism *without* absolutes. The third and last part of the chapter takes up Novalis's penchant for absolutization, arguing that this very penchant spells the end of the absolute. First, however, a word about Schelling and Hölderlin, about whom virtually the same objection could be raised, and in whom one will always find *traces* of a devotion to the absolute.

Absolute Inhibition: Schelling

The philosophy of organic nature, from Goethe and Kant onward, provides something like a theater in which we observe the failure of the absolute, and precisely in the imbrication of the phenomena of human sexuality, disease, and death. That, at least, is the thesis of the book *Contagion.* In what follows I will refer to several places in that book where the absolute is discussed, although I do not want to belabor the points made there. Allow me to begin with Schelling, and with what I am calling *absolute inhibition.* I will be referring principally to Schelling's major work in the philosophy of organic nature, his *First Projection of a System of Nature Philosophy* (1799), although the matters developed there continue to reverberate throughout the later stages of Schelling's career of thought, especially in his seminal *Philosophical Investigations into the Essence of Human Freedom* (1809) and monumental *Ages of the World* (1811–1815).[3]

3. See Friedrich Wilhelm Joseph von Schelling, *Erster Entwurf eines Systems der Naturphilosophie* (Jena and Leipzig: Gabler Verlag, 1799), reprinted in *Schriften von 1799–1801* (Darmstadt: Wissenschaftliche Buchgesellschaft, 1975), 1–268, cited henceforth in the body of my text as 3 (that is, vol. 3 of the *Sämmtliche Werke*) with page number. The new historical-critical edition headed by Hartmut Buchner is now under way, and the *Erster Entwurf* has recently appeared (too late, unfortunately, for my own work). See now the *Historisch-Kritische Ausgabe, Werke 7,* ed. Wilhelm G. Jacobs and Paul Ziche (Stuttgart: Frommann-Holzboog, 2001). A translation of this crucial text—the *First Projection of a System of Nature Philosophy* is regarded by most interpreters, myself included, as the most significant of Schelling's major texts on the philosophy of nature—has been prepared by Keith Peterson for SUNY Press. Two earlier works are also vital for Schelling's view of nature, namely, his 1798 *Von der Weltseele: Eine Hypothese der höheren Physik zur Erklärung des allgemeinen Organismus,* in *Schriften von 1794–1798* (Darmstadt: Wissenschaftliche Buchgesellschaft, 1980), 399–637, which presents the entire text, and *Ideen zu einer Philosophie der Natur als Einleitung in das Studium dieser Wissenschaft,* first

Many of the fundamental concepts and presuppositions of Schelling's philosophy of nature doubtless stem from Fichte, so that it is difficult if not impossible to begin without reference to Schelling's, Hölderlin's, and Novalis's great mentor. Yet Fichte's *Wissenschaftslehre* is its own bottomless pit. Let me therefore evade it, and with the guilty conscience of the skulker begin with the *First Projection* itself.

Schelling recognizes that the realms of freedom and nature are opposed to one another as being is opposed to becoming and as spirit is opposed to matter. Freedom, being, and spirit are "infinite activity"—that is, they are characterized by the absolutely active and unconditioned deed; nature, becoming, and matter, by contrast, are characterized by conditioned, compelled, necessitous activity. Yet Schelling will try to exhibit "the concealed trace of freedom" in nature (3:13). He will argue that the "formative drive" in nature as *natura naturans* is itself a path to freedom. Yet Schelling—at least at first—is clear about the limits of free activity in nature: "The essence of all organism is that it is not absolute activity. . . . For the subsistence of the organism is not a *being* [Seyn] but a perpetual *becoming reproduced* [*ein beständiges* Reproduciertwerden]" (3:222). The bedeviling problem for Schelling, as for the entire generation of thinkers after Kant, is how infinite activity could ever have submitted to such a compulsion to reproduction or to a condition or determination of any kind—above all, the compulsion of inhibition (*Hemmung*), which inheres in infinite activity as such and is therefore a particularly crippling condition, indeed a condition that neutralizes any and every sense of an unconditioned absolute.

Schelling would love to promote a monistic system of infinite activity as the sole possible system of reason, and yet he is compelled over and over again to posit a dualism. It is not a dualism of the traditional sort, nature vs. freedom, matter vs. spirit, becoming vs. being. For Schelling adopts the Fichtean notion of inhibition as a principle that is internal to and inherent in infinite activity. Schelling's difficulty is that he discerns both an "original dualism" in nature and an "infinite activity" in it. Absolute or infinite activity will therefore have to be inhibited absolutely or infinitely, in such a way that the distinction between free activity and necessitous inhibition becomes tenuous. Schelling himself emphasizes the following words: "*If nature is absolute*

---

published in 1797, with a second edition in 1803, in *Schriften von 1794–1798*, 333–397, which unfortunately contains only the introductions, not the main body of the text. An English translation of the entire work, *Ideas for a Philosophy of Nature,* has been done by Errol E. Harris and Peter Heath (Cambridge, England: Cambridge University Press, 1988). Schelling's *Von der Weltseele* has not yet been translated into English. For a discussion of the essay on human freedom and the incomplete treatise on the ages of the world, see chs. 3–6 of this volume.

*activity, such activity must appear as inhibited into infinity. (The original ground of this inhibition must, however, be sought in **nature itself** alone, inasmuch as nature is active **without qualification**)"* (3:16). Nature as becoming—not *being*, but a perpetual becoming reproduced—and yet as *absolute* activity? And again, absolute activity, active without reservation or qualification—yet also inhibited into infinity? Schelling is perfectly aware that he is here confronting "an insoluble difficulty" (3:17; cf. 151 n., 169, 219). For *inhibition* in the present instance means the presence in nature of "infinite negations" (3:20). Schelling's system of nature philosophy is in effect haunted and even hounded by the necessity of absolute inhibition, and one might designate his entire system of idealism as *tormented* idealism.

Whence this notion of *Hemmung*? How did it make its way into Fichte's *Wissenschaftslehre* and from thence into Schelling's philosophy of nature? We know how important the concept of inhibition will become for psychoanalytic discourse, as well as for various twentieth-century philosophies of biology. We know that Fichte and Schelling alike use it, and we know that it plays a role in Kant's third *Critique*. Indeed, inhibition is crucial to the argument of the Analytic of the Sublime, where, arguably, aesthetic and teleological forms of judgment meet—in "the feeling of a momentary inhibition of life forces."[4] Does it play a role in Kant's physiological and anthropological texts? Does it appear in Leibniz's account of *vis*? Can it be traced back through the grand systems and *summae* of medieval philosophy, or in various abstruse compendia in the history of medicine? Does it have its origin in Aristotle's βία, violent motion? Something like a *history of inhibition* is called for, very much in the sense of Heidegger's *history of being*. For it may well be that what Heidegger calls the mystery (*das Geheimnis*) of self-occluding, self-withdrawing being in the destiny or sending of being (*Geschick des Seins*) lies in an as yet untold *Hemmungsgeschichte*. Such a history would of course resist its own unfolding, frustrate its own recounting; its introversion and diffidence would characterize the history through and through—if indeed any characteristics could be ascribed to it at all. But to return to Schelling's *First Projection of a System of Nature Philosophy*.

The enigma of the dualism in nature, which is the product of an infinitely inhibited infinite activity, is stated in the boldest possible terms in the following passage:

> **Thus a common cause of universal and organic duplicity is postulated.** The most universal problem, the one that encompasses all nature, and therefore the

---

4. On this *Hemmung der Lebenskräfte*, see Kant, KU B75, 129.

supreme problem, without whose solution all we have said explains nothing, is this:

> **What is the universal source of activity in nature? What cause has brought about the first dynamic exteriority [*Außereinander*], with respect to which mechanical exteriority is a mere consequence? Or what cause first tossed the seed of motion into the universal repose of nature, duplicity into universal identity, the first sparks of heterogeneity into the universal homogeneity of nature?**[5]

Schelling is never able to answer these questions, each of which circles about the very problem he calls "insoluble."[6] What he learns repeatedly is that heterogeneity can never be merely "introduced" into homogeneity. In order for heterogeneity and duality to advene they must always already have been there—as disposition and latency, dormant yet potent—from the outset.

One example of the problem of "the seed of motion" is intussusception, the intake of liquid nourishment by a living entity by what used to be called *infection*, today *osmosis*. Schelling writes:

> Inasmuch as an intussusception between heterogeneous bodies is possible only insofar as the homogeneous is itself split *in itself*, no homogeneous state can be *absolute*; rather, it can only be a *state of indifference*. In order to explain this, we must suppose that there is in the universe a universal effect that replicates itself from product to product by means of (magnetic) distribution, which would be the universal determinant of all quality (and of all magnetism as universal). (3:260)

Although the role of magnetism will diminish in Schelling's later philosophy, without, however, disappearing from it altogether, the "state of indifference" to which he has only now referred will be a mainstay: it is, as we shall see, the crucial contrivance of the 1809 freedom essay, though no longer of the 1811–1815 *Ages of the World*. What we may say, making a very long and complex story short, is that Schelling discovers that the absolute is heterogeneous even before anything is "tossed" at it. He writes: "But to *bring* heterogeneity *forth* [hervorbringen] means to create duplicity in identity. . . . Thus identity must in turn proceed [*hervorgehen*] from duplicity" (3:250).

5. *Erster Entwurf,* 3:220; very similar wording appears at 240. Alan White, *Schelling: An Introduction to the System of Freedom* (New Haven: Yale University Press, 1983), has recognized the importance of this passage. He cites it in his brief discussion of Schelling's text, at 53–54.

6. For example, in the major division of his 1800 *System of Transcendental Idealism* (cited in note 4 of ch. 1) that deals with nature, Schelling applies the notion of inhibition to temporal succession: "Organization in general is succession that is inhibited in its course and, as it were, drawn to a halt [*erstarrte*]" (3:493). Yet what could "freeze" or "paralyze" infinite activity, so that it would be drawn—if only temporarily—to a halt? Walter Schulz, in his Introduction to the *System,* asserts twice, though with little fanfare, that Schelling's philosophy never succeeds in showing the transition from the infinite to the finite—which is all that his philosophy ever wanted to show. See Schulz, *System,* xiv–xv.

Schelling must, then, conceive of an original duplicity, a twofold or δυάς, in which infinite activity and infinite inhibition work together to produce the natural world. What rises to disturb his account of their interaction is the happenstance that the privileged site of inhibition is *sexual opposition*, and that sexual opposition shares many traits with *illness*. Sexuality and illness alike tend toward the universal and the infinite: it is as though infinite activity itself, the absolute as such, were both sexually active and subject to ultimate passivity and even inevitable sepsis and degeneration. It becomes difficult, if not impossible, for Schelling to locate the duplicitous source of life without colliding against the ultimate source of illness and demise—Hegel's notorious "seed of death."

True, there are places in the 1799 *Projection* where Schelling dreams of an "absolute organization," one that would dispense with duality and sexual opposition while also accounting for their eventual emergence on the scene. One such place is the following, in which he conjures up an *Urbild* or proto-image of a seamless or at least wholly annealed nature:

> This proto-image would be the absolute. It would be *sexless* and would no longer be either individual or species; rather, it would be *both at the same time;* in it, therefore, individual and species are conflated. For that reason, absolute organization could not be depicted by an individual product, but only through an infinity of particular products, which taken *individually* deviate into infinity from the ideal, but which when taken together as a *whole* are congruent with it. Thus the fact that nature expresses such an absolute original by means of all its organizations taken together is something that could be demonstrated simply by showing that all variation in the organizations is only a variation in the approximation of each to an absolute. We would then experience this absolute as though these organizations were nothing other than different developments of one and the same organization. (3:64)

Schelling's dream of a sexless absolute, while a *necessary* dream in and for every inheritor of the ontotheological tradition, soon turns into a nightmare. In the nightmare version, the absolute is an undeveloped simplex, a monotonous simpleton that has not yet developed in those "opposite" or "counterposed" directions (*die entgegengesetzte Richtungen*) that Schelling himself constantly invokes as the essential directions of the path of freedom. The one-and-the-same organization of all organizations in the graduated sequence of stages in nature would therefore have to be as complex as its most complex of stages, and if its most complex stages are always and everywhere stages for *duplex* organizations, a simplex god looks a little silly. No, not merely silly. For what is the unexpected force of Schelling's suggestion that the variants of infinite organization "deviate into infinity from the ideal"? The word *deviation* turns out to be the key word for Schelling's account of *illness*. Furthermore, deviation *of* infinity *into* infinity sounds a little bit like an infinite regress, or an infinite regression, which is to say, a regression *of* the infinite (*genitivus subiectivus et obiectivus*). The god of infinite organization should not be simpler than a sponge or polyp; he and she ought to be at least as complex, duplex, or multiplex as, let us say, naming one set of living creatures among others, women and men. However necessary and inevitable the dream of a sexless absolute may be, that is, the dream of a common origin for all the deviations and gradations to come, the compelling *necessity* of those variations and organic exfoliations rouses the deviant dreamer from his dogmatic slumber.

It is of course far too early to speak of the demise of the absolute in the Schelling of the 1799 *Erster Entwurf*. Yet the absolutely inhibited absolute will henceforth slip into an ever more remote past, a past that never was present and that never will have entertained a future—and that is a little bit like death, and very much like an end of the absolute. No doubt the two most important texts in this regard are the 1809 *Philosophical Investigations into the Essence of Human Freedom* and *The Ages of the World*, begun soon after the freedom essay but never completed. One might be justified in saying that in these two works Schelling encounters something like a traumatic experience early in the life of the absolute. The trauma has to do with sexuality and mortality—those two shadows of every philosophy of nature—and no amount of either inhibition or dialectic will relieve it. Indeed, one might rather say that absolute inhibition is another name for the trauma of the absolute, and that the trauma turns out to have absolutely lethal effects.

Absolute Separation: Hölderlin

The separation in question here—although in Hölderlin's view, at least early on in his career of thought, it could hardly be called absolute—is discussed in those famous lines of Hölderlin's "Seyn, Urtheil, Modalität" (CHV 2:49–50) concerning partition (*Theilung*) and separation (*Trennung*). Long before Schelling formulates his "identity philosophy" in the early 1800s, Hölderlin indicates his skepticism about the very notion of identity. Separation is essential to conscious identity, indeed, to consciousness of any kind. "Thus identity is not some sort of unification of object and subject that takes place in a straightforward manner, and thus identity does not = absolute being" (CHV 2:50). *Urtheil* Hölderlin takes to be *Ur-theilung*, the primordial sundering or dividing of consciousness and its object that he hopes an intellectual intuition will heal. To be sure, there is no thought here that the separation could itself possibly be absolute: that intimation comes later, in Frankfurt and in Bad Homburg, with the work on *The Death of Empedocles* and *The Mourning-Plays of Sophocles,* and it will come as a thought about *love,* if not sexual opposition as such.

One should of course trace the role of *intellectuale Anschauung* in Hölderlin's theoretical writings very carefully, from its appearance in "Being, Judgment, Modality" to later references in the poetological essays. Whereas, according to the first-named essay, subject and object are "most intensely united" in intellectual intuition (CHV 2:50; JV 2:136–140), the later poetological essay *"Wenn der Dichter einmal des Geistes mächtig . . ."* struggles to find that unity in "elongated" points, which nonetheless are points of "scission," *Scheidepunkte* (CHV 2:86–87). The *living* unity Hölderlin seeks, which he also calls "the larger nexus of life," will not be found in mere reflection; it will be "the hyperbole of all hyperboles, the boldest and the ultimate effort of the poetic spirit" (CHV 2:88). If intellectual intuition is no more than the harmony of subject and object, a subject-object whole that is doubtless "mythic" and "rich in images," the kind of intense unity of life that Hölderlin envisages surpasses all intuition. To be sure, such unity does remain a matter of intuition in the Kantian sense, insofar as it is bound up with sensibility and receptivity; yet what is "received" in such intuition is nothing like a manifold of sense data. Rather, the *Empfindung* in question, felt rather than known, Hölderlin calls *"beautiful, holy, divine"* (CHV 2:94–95).

According to another of the poetological essays, the proper bearer or "metaphor" of intellectual intuition is "the tragic poem," which is "ideational in its significance" (CHV 2:102). Hölderlin defines the intellectual intuition that undergirds tragic poetry as "that unity with everything that lives" which arises from "the impossibility of an absolute separation and individuation" (CHV 2:104). Yet the very impossibility of *absolute* separation seems to be what tragedy—and what Hölderlin calls *actual separation* and *tragic dissolution*—is all about:

> The unity that is at hand in intellectual intuition becomes sensuous [*versinnlicht sich*] to the precise extent that it egresses from itself and its parts are separated from one another, the parts separating only because they feel excessively unified [*zu einig*] whenever they are closer to the midpoint of the whole, or because they do not feel unified enough, with a view to completeness, whenever they are merely ancillary parts, lying farther removed from the midpoint, or, with a view to vitality, when they are neither ancillary nor essential parts in the designated

senses, because they are rather merely divisible parts, parts that have not yet come to be. And here, in spirit's excess of unity, and in its striving for materiality, in the striving of the divisible for the more infinite, more aorgic, in which everything that is more organic must be contained, inasmuch as everything determinate and necessarily existent makes something less determinate and more contingent necessary, in this striving of the divisible infinite for separation, a striving that communicates itself in the condition of the supreme unity of everything organic to the parts contained in it, in this necessary, arbitrary act of Zeus lies the genuine, ideal beginning of the actual separation. (CHV 2:106)

Hölderlin sees the arbitrary act of Zeus—the act of separation, caught up in a striving for the more infinite, the more untamed, and in search of the materiality and elementality of nature, an act having more to do with the ancillary parts of the whole than with the self-concentrating midpoint—at work in a particularly striking way in Sophocles' *Oedipus the Tyrant*. He does not elaborate on the matter at this point, yet one is reminded of the way in which the later *Anmerkungen* or "Notes" to his translation of *Antigone* will speak of both Zeus and the entire process of nature as being more decisively turned back to the earth.[7] While Hölderlin does not advance to a clear "doctrine" of the end of the absolute, there is something telling about the way in which the divine unity of intellectual intuition is brought to tragic separation and dissolution.[8] A late fragment on tragedy, apparently intended for an introduction to his translations of Sophocles' tragedies, does not declare the end of the absolute but does describe the "original," which is surely related to what has traditionally been called the absolute, as suffering from some sort of weakness or "debility":

> The significance of the tragedies is most readily grasped on the basis of paradox. For, inasmuch as all abundance is justly and equally apportioned, no original appears as actual in its original strength; rather, it genuinely appears in its debility alone, so that quite properly the light of life and the appearance of debility pertain to every whole.[9] Now, in the tragic, the sign is meaningless in itself, without

7. See the "Notes on Antigone," at CHV 2:372, ll. 15–17, and 374, ll. 1–2, in context. Hölderlin everywhere sees Zeus, the father of time and the earth, as the principal subject-object of epic and tragedy. The way in which tragedy brings the epic tradition to its fulfillment is suggested when Hölderlin remarks in a review that Homer's *Iliad* is "sung to honor Father Jupiter rather than Achilles or anyone else" (CHV 2:112).

8. On the issue of unification and dissolution in Hölderlin's interpretation of tragedy, see D. F. Krell, *Lunar Voices: Of Tragedy, Poetry, Fiction, and Thought* (Chicago: University of Chicago Press, 1995), ch. 2, "Stuff • Thread • Point • Fire: Hölderlin's Dissolution."

9. The notion of *Lebenslicht*, literally, "the light of life," is strange. Hölderlin refers to it in a number of late poems as well as in a letter to Böhlendorff, where he identifies it with a "savage martial" and "masculine" character, in which the "feeling of death" is experienced in "virtuoso" form (CHV 2:921). In short, the light of life is anything but debility in any usual sense, though it is shot through with a sense of mortality. See the additional references at CHV 3:402. Finally, one should recall that

effect; yet the original comes directly to the fore. For the original can appear in a genuine way only in its debility. Yet insofar as the sign in itself is meaningless and thus = 0, the original too, the concealed ground of every nature, can present itself. If nature presents itself genuinely in its weakest gift, then the sign that is given when it presents itself in its strongest gift = 0. (CHV 2:114; JV 4:46–48)

It is far from clear what the relation of original and sign in Hölderlin's reflections may be, yet the very proximity of debility to strength in the self-presentation of nature and the original bodes ill for the absolute, as does the genuine meaning that equals zero. Precisely what sort of ill becomes clearer when we examine in greater detail Hölderlin's lifelong preoccupation with the proper vehicle or metaphor of intellectual intuition in its most profound sense—to wit, tragedy.

In a secondary school essay, "History of the Fine Arts among the Greeks up to the End of the Age of Pericles" (CHV 2:11–27), young Hölderlin notes that the Greeks invented for their gods bodies of great beauty. Beauty was one of the "national traits" of the Greeks. Moreover, the Greeks implanted in their gods "a receptivity for the beautiful," and "caused them to descend to the Earth for the sake of beauty" (CHV 2:12). It is as though the pupil Hölderlin experiences the insight of the mature classicist Roberto Calasso, who opens *The Marriage of Cadmus and Harmony* by repeating the question "But how did it all begin?," answering that question, at least the first time, by affirming that a group of girls plucking flowers by the riverside again and again proved "irresistible to the gods" (RC 4). It is as though the pupil Hölderlin absorbs the lesson of Sophocles' *Women of Trachis:* Deianeira, the wife of Herakles, affirms that "Whoever wants to step into the ring against Eros / Will collapse into his arms like a fool. / For he rules the gods themselves at whim" (ll. 441–443). Herakles, who pummels everyone else into submission with his fists, is laid low by his love of a girl (ll. 488–489). The third choral song, echoing the famous fourth choral ode of *Antigone,* confirms that the power of Aphrodite is sufficient to defeat all other Olympians—μέγα τι σθένος ἁ Κύπρις ἐκφέρεται νίκας ἀεί: "Great is the might of Kypris, who always walks off with the victories" (l. 497). Lichas the herald sums up the play in three words: "Desire is overwhelming," ὁ δεινὸς ἵμερος (l. 476).

Decades later, in his "Notes" on Sophocles' *Antigone,* Hölderlin draws attention to the chorus's account of the descent of Zeus to the cell of the beautiful Danaë, who is celebrated in the fifth choral ode of the play (ll. 981ff.).

---

for the Schelling of the 1815 "Divinities of Samothrace" the original names for God designate not so much majesty and might as poverty and hunger. See notes 31, 36, and 47 (8:183–186 and 188–190), discussed in ch. 4 of this volume.

Hölderlin interprets the famous golden shower by which Zeus couples with Danaë as the golden hours that the father of earth and time spends with her. They are hours that *she* counts off for him—as though Zeus were learning from her nothing less than the time of his own earthy love and earthly mortality. In that same early school essay, Hölderlin also notes that the Greeks were particularly "receptive to tragedy" (CHV 2:23); he draws attention to Aeschylus's *Prometheus Bound,* the play in which the demise of Zeus on account of his liaisons is foretold. For even if, as he later writes in the "Fragment of Philosophical Letters," love and beauty are "happy to uncover tenderly," what they languish for is solace in the face of the "profound feeling of mortality, mutability, one's temporal limitations" (CHV 2:60).

Françoise Dastur argues convincingly that *time* is the consistent theme of Greek tragedy as Hölderlin conceives of it.[10] From early on, Hölderlin thinks of tragedy in terms of that ticking of the clock for immortals as well as mortals, a ticking that seems to begin when the immortals are drawn by desire to the earthbound mortals. As in Empedocles' account of the wandering δαίμονες who abandon the reign of Φιλία (Love) for the reign of Νεῖκος (Strife), surrendering their blessed abode for the blood-drenched plain of Ἄτη, Hölderlin sees the immortal gods drawn out of their (impossible) absolute separation into a fatal commingling with mortality. Like mortals, immortals eventually come to experience the passage of time as pain and suffering. Perhaps the most durable theme of Hölderlin's mature work is therefore that of the divine passion of time and temporality. Why passion? Because in time the gods themselves are absolutely separated from their absolution from all relations, all conditions.

Hölderlin already hears the ticking of the clock in his *Hyperion,* written and published between the years 1792 and 1798; in that novel he appeals to the figure of Empedocles, inasmuch as he is already beginning to sketch out *The Death of Empedocles* (1797–1800); Empedocles, like the namesake of Sophocles' *Antigone,* which Hölderlin is translating between the years 1800 and 1803, hears the ticking of the clock—precisely as Zeus hears it in Danaë's cell. Looking ahead to *Antigone* and to *The Death of Empedocles,* Hölderlin writes in *Hyperion:*

> And now tell me, is there any refuge left?—Yesterday I was up on Etna. I recalled the great Sicilian of old who, when he'd had enough of *ticking off the hours,* having become intimate with the soul of the world, in his bold lust for life plunged

10. Françoise Dastur, *Hölderlin: Le retournement natal* (La Versanne, France: Encre marine, 1997), which consists of two main parts, "Tragedy and Modernity" and "Nature and Poesy." See the discussion in Krell, *Lunar Voices,* 8–9 n. 9, 21–22 n. 21.

56

into the terrific flames. It was because—a mocker afterwards said of him—the frigid poet had to warm himself at the fire.

O how gladly I would precipitate such mockery over me! but one must think more highly of oneself than I do to fly unbidden to nature's heart—put it any way you like, for, truly, as I am now, I have no name for these things, and all is uncertain [*es ist mir alles ungewiß*].[11]

Hölderlin's *Hyperion* is also the text to which one may want to refer all the ideas discussed so far surrounding unity and separation, strength and debility, and the god's striving for materiality and elementality through sexuality and mortality. For in *Hyperion* and in the preliminary drafts of that novel the themes of unification, love, and beauty are brought into the greatest possible proximity with debility, dissolution, and death—including the death of all originals and all absolutes. Perhaps the greatest single advance in the conception and characterization of mortal love occurs in the metrical version of *Hyperion* (along with its draft in prose). Here Hyperion realizes that the "school of destiny and of the sages" has caused him to underestimate and even to scorn the world of the senses and the realm of nature, which is inevitably bound up with mortal love. The wizened sage, the stranger who now communicates the doctrine of Plato's Socrates in *Symposium* (for Diotima is not yet invoked by name), speaks with a more human voice—a more mortal voice—than the alternating angelic and strident voices one hears in the earlier drafts of the novel:

Allow me to speak in a human way. When our originally infinite essence first came to suffer something, and when the free and full force encountered its first barriers, when Poverty mated with Superfluity, Love came to be. Do you ask when that was? Plato says it was on the day when Aphrodite was born. At the moment, therefore, when the world of beauty commenced for us, when we became conscious, we became finite. Now we profoundly feel the confinement of our essence, and inhibited force strains impatiently against its fetters. Yet there is something in us that gladly preserves the fetters—for if the divine in us were bound to no resistance, we would know nothing outside ourselves and therefore nothing about ourselves either. And to know nothing of oneself, not to feel that we are in being, and to be annihilated—these are one and the same. (CHV 1:513)

"Inhibited force" strains against its fetters—shades of Schelling! Consciousness, love, and beauty—experienced solely in poverty and confinement! Perhaps it is not too much to say that the absolute—here called *infinite essence*

11. CHV 1:753; my emphasis. For the related passage in Hölderlin's translation of Sophocles' *Antigone* on Danaë's ticking or counting off the hours for Zeus, see 2:353.

and *free and full force*—faces a singular alternative: either it becomes conscious and thus finite, that is, bound for *eventual* annihilation, or it remains in absolute separation, catatonic isolation, and absolute autism, which is the equivalent of *immediate* annihilation. In effect, there is no alternative for conscious life—no alternative to living out the temporal unfolding of one's life as Danaë counts off the golden hours. The sole possible "absolute separation" would occur in the languor felt by the god when she stops counting. Absolute separation is the banishment of all absolution. Consciousness and finitude are reciprocally related, and not merely at the level of epistemology. The reciprocity of consciousness and finitude derives from the genealogy of ἔρως, born of Resourcefulness and Poverty, Πόρος and Πενία. Absolute separation, the active *absolvo* of a *solus ipse*, or absolute spirit, is impossible—unless spirit is either unconscious or dead.

Later on, from 1798 to 1800 in Bad Homburg, Hölderlin is working intensely on the first version of his tragic drama, *The Death of Empedocles*. (The first volume of *Hyperion* has already been published, and work on the second volume has already been completed.) During these days of reflection on the life and death of the great Greek thinker of Love and Strife, which are also the days in which he meets fleetingly with Susette Gontard in order to exchange letters and a few furtive touches,[12] Hölderlin's thinking advances as far as that of anyone in the era of German Idealism and Romanticism—including that of his teacher Fichte and his erstwhile friends Hegel and Schelling. At the farthest advance of his thought, Hölderlin envisages something like the end of the absolute—in the figure of an impossible "absolute monarchy." In a letter to Isaak von Sinclair, dated December 24, 1798, Hölderlin writes:

> The transience and mutability of human thoughts and systems strike me as wellnigh more tragic than the destinies one usually calls the only real destinies. And I believe this is natural, for if a human being in his or her ownmost and freest activity—in autonomous thought itself—depends on foreign influences, if even in such thought he or she is modified in some way by circumstance and climate, which has been shown irrefutably to be the case, where then does the human being rule supreme? It is also a good thing—indeed, it is the first condition of all life and all organization—that in heaven and on earth no force rules monarchically. Absolute monarchy cancels itself out everywhere, for it is without object; strictly speaking, there never was such a monarchy. Everything that is interpenetrates as soon as it becomes active. . . . Of course, *from every finite point of view some one of the autonomous forces must be the ruling force*, yet it must be observed to prevail only temporarily and only to a certain degree. (CHV 2:723)

12. See once again Kenney and Menner-Bettscheid, ed. and tr., *The Recalcitrant Art* (cited in note 3 of ch. 1, above).

Himself caught up in the daily, weekly, and monthly interpenetrations of Φιλία and Νεῖκος, Hölderlin, himself a child of Πόρος and Πενία, sees that every dream of solitary rule, every phantasm of absolution, every monism, is bound to dissolve. Nietzsche will experience the evanescence of the dream in his own way and will become famous for that experience; Heidegger will occupy that finite point of view in which time and the temporal announce themselves as the horizon of the only sense of being that gives itself to mortals. Yet Hölderlin arrives on that scene a century or more before them. Absolute separation is itself the end of the absolute.

Absolute Density: Novalis

No detailed account of Novalis's "magical idealism," or what one may prefer to call his "thaumaturgic idealism," retaining the reference to philosophy as beginning in wonder (θαυμάζειν), is possible here. Nor can Novalis's exponential and logarithmic methods or his own brand of logic, which he calls *Fantastik*, and which is quite beyond any familiar sense of dialectic, be presented in such a restricted space. Nor, finally, do I want to repeat very much of his extraordinary accounts of medicine and physiology, accounts with which the book *Contagion* is preoccupied. Yet the problem of the density of the absolute, an issue raised at the end of Novalis's "Fragments and Studies of 1799–1800" is a problem posed in *Contagion*, and so I will begin by restating the problem developed there as succinctly as I can.[13]

Here are the laconic lines—each constituting its own paragraph, each looming stonily and silently in the late notes of Novalis—that I most want to understand in the present undertaking:

> Gott ist von unendlich gediegenen Metall—das Körperlichste und Schwerste aller Wesen.
> Die Oxyd[ation] kommt vom Teufel.
> Leben ist eine Kranckheit des Geistes—ein leidenschaftliches Thun.
> Luftvernichtung ist Herstellung des Reich Gottes. (2:820)

---

13. In what follows, I will cite Novalis (Friedrich von Hardenberg), *Werke, Tagebücher und Briefe*, ed. Hans-Joachim Mähl and Richard Samuel, 3 vols. (Munich: Carl Hanser Verlag, 1987), by volume and page in the body of my text. I will make particular reference to vol. 2, *Das philosophisch-theoretische Werk*. The Hanser edition is a relatively inexpensive hardbound edition based on the historical-critical edition initiated by Paul Kluckhohn and Richard Samuel. The Hanser edition, while not complete, contains most of the material that is in vols. 2 and 3 of the larger, far more expensive edition. Readers should nevertheless check important passages in vols. 2 and 3 of the larger edition: Novalis, *Schriften*, ed. Richard Samuel et al., rev. Richard Samuel and Hans-Joachim Mähl, 5 vols. (Stuttgart: Kohlhammer Verlag, 1981). On the relation of Novalis's thought to that of Hölderlin, see JV 2:403–420.

> God is of infinitely compact metal—the most corporeal and the heaviest of all beings.
> Oxidation comes from the devil.
> Life is a sickness of spirit, an activity born to undergo *passio* [literally, "a passionate deed"].
> Annihilation of air establishes the Kingdom of God. (2:820)

What is this strange idolatry, this God or calf of solid gold, this compact, corporeal, massive, dense, unbreathing, rust-free divinity? Of what suffocating heaven is Novalis (who died at age twenty-nine of tuberculosis) dreaming? Does it not seem as though he has read Milan Kundera on the incredible lightness of being and wants to make reply, or that he has perused Hegel's mocking and cruel account of his (Novalis's) own consumption?

One may track the absolute through Novalis's brief career and astounding production. His early *Fichte-Studien* appear to make trouble for Fichte's positings concerning any and every sense of an absolute ego or subject. Whether it is the theme of feeling within intellectual intuition or of the hieroglyphic sign, of chaos, drives, or life itself, Novalis seems destined to resist Fichte's and his own predilection for the absolute, cited at the outset of the chapter: "Has not Fichte too arbitrarily deposited everything into the ego? With what legitimacy?" (2:12). And, several pages later, "Thus ego and not-ego, without absolute ego!" (2:15). Novalis continues to wrestle with the Fichtean hypothesis of an absolute ego (2:28–29), yet his way of resisting the absolute ego is to dilate and expand that notion exponentially. Alongside "systematics" in Novalis's notes stand "encyclopedics" and "prophetics," and the tendency of these last two is expansionist. Further, Novalis insists on the primacy of practice: "The practical is a longing [*Sehnen*]" (2:57), even if "praxis proper simply cannot be grasped conceptually" (ibid.). Early on, it seems, Novalis is clear about the goal of his studies: "Spinoza ascended to the point of nature, Fichte to the ego or the person, I to the thesis of God" (2:63).

Novalis's God, however, turns out to be exceedingly strange, absolutely dense. If at the outset of his theoretical work God appears to be the usual spiritual Creator, by the end of it creativity and spirituality are less comprehensible than they ever were. Early on, Novalis writes, "Matter and spirit correspond to one another quite precisely—one is like the other. Each has its pure causality in the other alone" (2:77). Yet as he continues with his encyclopedic studies, it is the causality at the heart of matter that comes to dominate his thought. If the grounding of God and world, of spirit and matter, is a "mutual grounding," as Novalis emphasizes, the traditional ways of understanding God and matter will have to change. "If only we could come to know the matter of spirit, and the spirit of matter" (2:167). Such a learning process would have implications especially for human beings, whom Kant pictures as hovering somewhere between the angelic and the bestial. By contrast, Novalis writes: "The sensuous must be presented spiritually, the spiritual must be presented sensuously" (2:194). At first these opposites seem to resist one another absolutely. Yet they must commingle. Novalis can write, without apparent discomfort, "Devil and God are the extremes from which the human being originates" (2:198). However, these very oppositions will soon, first, reverse their position in the hierarchy of values, and second, thoroughly contaminate one another, so that, third, the contamination will prove fatal to any straightforward opposition as such.

A growing respect for the mysteries of what the tradition has scorned as "passivity" characterizes Novalis's thought: passivity and receptivity—once again, shades of Kantian *Empfindung*. A growing respect for mixture and even fatal contamination is matched by a waxing suspicion concerning the "pure," which may be one of the most familiar attributes of the absolute: "Pure—that which is not related, not relatable. . . . The concept *pure* is thus an empty concept. . . . —Everything pure is therefore a deception produced by our imagination—a *necessary* fiction" (2:87). Among the mixtures, that of activity and inhibition—once again, shades of Fichte and Schelling—occupies a special place in the third group of handwritten *Fichte-Studies* (2:118, 124, 127). As we have seen, the necessary yet incomprehensible dialectic of absolute activity, that is, the activity of positing by an absolute ego and of absolute inhibition by that same ego, dominates the young Schelling's philosophy of nature. Novalis states it in the form of a paradox, tautology, or riddle: "Inhibited activity can be inhibited only by activity" (2:124; cf. 204). No doubt related to the theme of inhibition is what Novalis calls *Renitenz*, a kind of adversity or resistance that opposes action (2:130). Such adversity is essential to creativity. Novalis pictures a flutist: "Certain inhibitions may be compared to the fingerings of a Baroque recorder player who, in order to tease this or that tone from his instrument closes off this or that opening; to all appearances he makes the most arbitrary connections between the sounding and the mute openings" (2:217). In words quite reminiscent of Hölderlin's "Being, Judgment, Modality," Novalis writes: "Being [*Seyn*] does not express any absolute characteristic, but rather only a relation of the essence to a property in general—a capacity to be determined. It is an absolute relation. Nothing in the world *is merely*; being does not express identity" (2:156). If the vaunted absolute by definition stands alone, *solus ipse*, absolved of all relations with anything else, "absolute relation" is the oxymoron that explodes all discourse on the absolute. *Nichts in der Welt* ist blos." Nothing is merely, nakedly, what it is; every thing stands always in relation to an other, not accidentally but essentially. Yet that means that nothing stands as absolute, on its own, except perhaps the inflated and bemused human cogitator of the absolute. Novalis cites without comment a "derivation" of (the concept of) God from the German word for genus or species—or, understood as a verb, the word for mating: *Gott = Gattung* (2:145). Even if he later identifies the genus with the sphere, hence with a kind of monism, it is clear that the *monas* is a complete mystery: "We simply do not know what the genus consists of, what sort of a One" (2:161). Novalis is instead the thinker of the manifold. We may paraphrase his *Apprentices at Saïs* as saying, "*Mannigfache Wege gehet der Gott,*" the absolute walks manifold paths. And it may well be that every one of those paths, as Schelling believed, culminates in erotic, mortal embodiment.[14]

The upshot of all this is that Novalis's thaumaturgic idealism is condemned to a kind of *hovering* between extremes. Sometimes such hovering or oscillating seems to him a weakness: "I am too much on the superficies—not the tranquil inner life—not the kernel—working its effects from the inside out, from a midpoint—but rather on the surface—by way of zigzag—horizontally—without steadiness of character—play—accident—not lawful effect—the trace of autonomy—the externalizing of *one* essence" (2:167). And the despairing self-indictment, "Why must I always pursue things with painful insistence—nothing calm—leisurely—with releasement" (2:169). At its best, hovering (*Schweben*) promises a kind of harmony and integration of extremes; at its worst, it seems a form of self-deceptive vacillation suffered by a hyperactive imagination (2:177). Yet hovering is assuredly the best way to describe the thinking that produces the "genuine philosophical system," whose primary characteristic is "systemlessness": Novalis's directive to all who seek a monistic system is that "we must seek out the dichotomy everywhere" (2:200–201). In effect, this means the surrender of the philosophical search for ultimate or absolute grounds.[15]

14. Schelling notes in his *Ages of the World* at 8:325 that the culmination of God's every path, the *finis viarum Dei*, is embodiment. On Novalis's use of the *Mannigfach*, see his *Werke* 1:201, 205, 218–221, 229, 347.

15. On the entire question of "hovering," let me once again (as I did in *Contagion*) warmly recommend the study by Lore Hühn, "Das Schweben der Einbildungskraft: Zur Frühromantischen Überbietung Fichtes," *Deutsche Vierteljahrsschrift für Literaturwissenschaft und Geistesgeschichte* 70, no. 4 (Dec. 1996): 569–599. Hühn investigates the metaphor of the "hovering imagination," *schwebende Einbildungskraft*, in Fichte, Novalis, and other early Romantics. She argues convincingly that Novalis and others, such as Friedrich Schlegel, follow and even surpass Fichte in establishing the imagination as the faculty that more than any other engages actuality. Moreover, the actuality engaged by the imagination, which hovers between being and nonbeing, is precisely "life" (593).

And so we arrive at one of the most telling of Novalis's notes on the absolute: "By means of a voluntary renunciation of the absolute, an infinitely free activity originates in us—the sole possible absolute that can be granted to us, and the one we can find solely by means of our incapacity to achieve and recognize an absolute. This absolute, the one granted to us, can be known only negatively, by our acting, and by our discovering that no action ever achieves what we were searching for" (2:180–181). The absolute is our absolute inability to think or act in conformity with an absolute. Whence in all the world, then, our drive to think and act on the horizon of such impossible absolutes?

Perhaps the most detailed observation by Novalis concerning the drive to universals and absolutes comes in the first group of handwritten notes for *Das allgemeine Brouillon* (The Universal Sketchbook):

> ENCYCLOPEDICS. Every science has its God, which is at the same time its goal. Thus mechanics actually thrives on the *perpetuum mobile*—and at the same time it seeks to construct a *perpetuum mobile*, which is its supreme problem. Thus chemistry thrives on the *menstruum universale*—and on *spiritual* matter, or the Philosophers' Stone. Philosophy seeks its first and its sole principle. The mathematician seeks the squaring of the circle and a principal equation [*eine Principalgleichung*]. The *human being—God.* The physician seeks an elixir of life—a rejuvenating tonic, a complete feeling about the body and a complete method of dealing with it [*Gefühl und Handhabung*]. The politician seeks a perfect republic—eternal peace—a free state. (2:530)

Novalis now inserts a parenthetical remark, centering it on the page, as he often does in his notebooks, apparently for emphasis:

> (Every disappointed expectation and every renewed expectation, over and over again, gestures toward a chapter in the lore of the future. See my first fragment in *Blüthenstaub*.) (Ibid.)

The familiar first fragment of *Pollen* reads: "*Wir suchen überall das Unbedingte, und finden immer nur Dinge*," "We seek something unconditioned in every nook and cranny, and all we ever find are [conditioned] things" (2:227). In *The Universal Sketchbook*, Novalis formulates what he himself calls his principle of approximation, his asymptotic principle. It is as though he were declaring himself a disciple of Heraclitus, whose one-word fragment ἀγχιβασίη (DK B122) suggests unending approach: "On the obstacles that block the accomplishment of every one of these tasks. (The principle of approximation. Belonging to it is also the *absolute ego*)" (ibid.). If there is an absolute obstacle to the absolute ego, neither the obstacle nor the ego appears to be absolutely absolute—although, granted the cruel nature of paradox, it may well be that the only true absolute is precisely the absolute obstacle, absolute ἀπορία. And if ἀπορία is the negation of Πόρος, it must be absolute Πενία. That is to say, poverty is *Ausweglosigkeit, huit clos,* resourcelessness, impenetrability—absolute density. Yet we approach the tantalizing and tantalized character of Novalis's thought as we complete our reading of his observations on asymptotic approximation:

> That these tasks are not successfully completed lies solely in the flawed nature of the objects of these tasks, in the imperfect relations of the chosen constructive *elements* of these objects. (Elements are *accidents.*) The tasks are theoretically true and are identity propositions, pleonastic statements, as, for example, *perpetuum mobile, eternal life—measured circle.* The philosophy of these tasks. (Ibid.)

It seems as though Novalis is committing himself to the impossible task of the absolute (his old familiar predilection), to be carried out through infinite approximation, in the hope that if the elements of construction are more wisely chosen a lifetime spent in search of a pleonasm might be a life well lived. Such a life would contribute, as we have already heard, to the lore of the future: "LORE OF THE FUTURE OF HUMANITY. (THEOLOGY.) Everything that is predicated of God contains the human lore of the future. Every machine that now thrives on the grand *perpetuum mobile* is itself to become the *perpetuum mobile*—every human being that now thrives on God, through God, is himself or herself to become God" (2:531). A cheerful prospect: the lore and lure of the future in the lives of mortals is the promise or dream that they will become God—waiting only for Jean-Paul Sartre to remark on the human quest as *une passion inutile.*[16] Yet Novalis does not have to wait for Sartre. In a note under the misleading rubric "psychology" Novalis writes:

> All passions come to an end, as does a mourning-play. Everything that is one-sided comes to an end in death—thus the philosophy of sensation—the philosophy of fantasy—the philosophy of the thought. All life comes to an end in old age and death. All poesy manifests a tragic trait. (Real pain underlies seriousness. The tragic impact of farce, of puppet theater—of the most motley life—of the common, of the trivial.) (2:541)

There is something tragic too about the philosopher's search for a system. Under the rubric "philosophy" Novalis notes somewhat laconically, "1. Supposition: there is a philosophical system—2. *Description* of this ideal—of this phantasm . . ." (2:611). Novalis's Copernican Revolution is therefore quite

---

16. Jean-Paul Sartre, *L'Etre et le néant* (Paris: Gallimard, 1943), 678; English translation by Hazel Barnes, *Being and Nothingness* (New York: Philosophical Library, 1956), 615.

different from Kant's and Fichte's: "*Die Philosophie macht alles* los." "Philosophy sets everything in *motion*—relativizes the universe. Like the Copernican system, it cancels all *fixed* points—and makes of everything at rest something hovering [*ein Schwebendes*]" (2:616). Setting in motion, oscillating, vacillating, hovering, and finally, "crooked rules": "At the basis of every ideal lies a deviation from the common rule, or a *higher rule* (a crooked rule)" (2:653). Among these crooked rules at the foundation of every ideal is of course the moral law, which claims to propound maxims for praxis (ibid.).

If we think back to the discussion in *Contagion* of Novalis's "theory of voluptuosity," which hovers at the core of his thaumaturgic idealism, we can say that, in accord with his theory of approximation, Novalis's theories of love and illness arrive at nothing more than an approximation to the absolute, to the "well-nigh" absolute:

Theory of Voluptuosity

It is *Amor* that presses us together. The basis of all the functions mentioned above [i.e., dancing, eating, speaking, communal experience and work, companionship, as well as hearing, seeing, and feeling oneself] is voluptuosity (*sympathy*). The genuinely voluptuous function is the one that is most mystical—well-nigh absolute—or the one that compels us toward the *totality* of unification (mixture)—the *chemical.* (2:666)

If one insists on pursuing such a theory of voluptuosity into the neighborhood of chemistry, a chemistry that once seemed an imbroglio from which only an absolute could rescue Novalis, one runs the risk of absolute contagion. Novalis accepts the inevitably ambiguous diagnosis of the absolute drive to perfection and completeness. He writes:

An absolute drive to perfection and completeness is illness as soon as it exhibits its destructive attitude, its disinclination with respect to the *imperfect*, the incomplete.
   If one wants to act in such a way as to achieve something in particular, one must stake out boundaries that are determinate, even if provisional. Whoever cannot bring himself to do this is the perfectionist, one who refuses to swim until he knows precisely how to do so. —
   He is a magical idealist, just as there are magical realists. The former seek a miraculous motion, a miraculous subject; the latter seek a miraculous object, a miraculous configuration. Both are caught up in *logical illnesses,* forms of delusion, in which, to be sure, the ideal reveals or mirrors itself in a twofold way—[both are] holy—[both are] isolated creatures—that refract the higher light miraculously—true prophets. (2:623; cf. 481–482, 499, 624)

The line in Novalis's *Fantastik* between true prophecy and logical illness is, at best, a crooked line, and Novalis never knows which side of that line he is standing or falling on. Novalis straddles. Novalis hovers. Not because he lacks resolve, but because he is not a charlatan. Ambiguity concerning the illness or well-being of the magical idealist extends to the very limits of life itself. Novalis argues that life is "phlogistical process," that is, the process of oxidation and combustion. All illness, accordingly, is "antiphlogistical" process, that is, anything that inhibits oxidation (2:818–819). As we heard at the outset, however, there is something about combustion itself that is destructive. Oxidation is corrosive. Moreover, the corrosion is *of spirit*, not of material nature. "Transience, vulnerability is the character of a nature that is bound up with spirit. It testifies to the activity, the universality, and the sublime personality of spirit" (ibid.). Not to flee a transient world and a vulnerable corporeality to a disembodied spirit, but to recognize that transience and vulnerability are the very earmarks of spirit, as it were: that is Novalis's insight, the insight that condemns him to a kind of underground—a limbo at the heart of the Western tradition in which he must be seen as hovering, oscillating, vacillating.

Novalis pursues that insight. On the same page of his notebook he indicates, first, that "all dead matter is *phlogiston*," and second, that "*Phlogiston* = spirit," thus leading himself and his readers to the conclusion that, third, spirit is dead matter. At all events, a kind of stasis and inertia, or heaviness (*Schwere*), is attributed to divinity, and the following propositions (from which we began and toward which we have been heading all along) ensue, one after the other, isolated and terrible in their impact and import:

> God is of infinitely compact metal—the most corporeal and the heaviest of all beings.
> Oxidation comes from the devil.
> Life is a sickness of spirit, an activity born to undergo *passio*.
> Annihilation of air establishes the Kingdom of God. (2:820)

Whither such a breathless thought? Novalis is perhaps heading toward that bizarre conception of divinity projected by Georg Simmel early in the twentieth century—projected, it is true, in remembrance of Schelling rather than Novalis. Simmel recognizes that the only way to escape from the consequences of "the death of God" is to think, in a cogent and coherent way, the fact that God always was dead, that the attribution of life and breath to the divine is the original error and the original sin. Simmel calls the assumption that God lives a "vulgar stupidity," *eine Borniertheit*. He urges his readers to return to Schelling's metaphysics of "indifference," to Spinoza's radically ungraspable "infinite attributes," and, above all, to medieval German mysticism, which is "freer and deeper than all earlier or later dogmatics and philosophies of religion."[17]

Whether Meister Eckhart or Richard of Saint-Victor or Spinoza or Schelling ever conceived of their pantheisms as a festival of death, however, is a question that should give us pause. Perhaps now we can understand why the "religious task," in Novalis's view, is to show compassion toward divinity: "*Mitleid* mit der *Gottheit zu haben*" (2:759). Compassion for the dead is possible, at least as mourning, but compassion for what was never alive? That the absolute should end as absolutely dead—as having never, absolutely never, been alive—is a thought to which we may still be entirely unaccustomed. Novalis was clearly on his way to it. So were Hölderlin and Schelling, the two thinkers who dominate the remaining chapters of this book.

A Note on Absolute and Relative Death

Remarkably, the first reference to the absolute in the book *Contagion* is not to absolute knowing or absolute spirit but to absolute death.[18] It is a reference to the way in which Goethe resists the possibility of absolute death, a resistance expressed in his concept of "relative death." Only the individual dies, not the species, so that any given death is always "relative." Yet what about the mortal individual, who, "in each case," is at least under the illusion that his or her death is his or her "own"? Is there not something absolutely cruel about relative death? An early aphoristic work on nature, perhaps merely copied into a notebook by Goethe (*Die Natur,* ca. 1780), expresses in its antiphonal form—in the intense, unresolved, unrelieved countermanding of its every confident assertion by a stubborn counterassertion—the ambivalence Goethe feels toward nature:

> Nature! We are surrounded and embraced by her—without being able to exit from her or to enter into her more deeply. Unasked and unwarned, we are taken up into the circuitry of her dance; she has her way with us, until we grow weary and sink from her arms. . . .
>
> We live in the midst of her and are foreign to her. She speaks to us ceaselessly and does not betray her secret to us. We work our endless effects on her, yet have no dominion over her.

17. Georg Simmel, *Lebensanschauung: Vier metaphysische Kapitel* (Munich and Leipzig: Duncker und Humblot, 1918), 109. See the discussion in D. F. Krell, *Daimon Life: Heidegger and Life-Philosophy* (Bloomington: Indiana University Press, 1992), 94–95.

18. Krell, *Contagion* (cited in note 10 of ch. 1, above), 5.

> She seems to have invested all her hopes in individuality, and she cares nothing for the individuals. Always she builds, always she destroys, and we have no access to her workshop.
>
> She lives in a profusion of children, and their mother, where is she? —
>
> She squirts her creatures out of nothingness, and does not tell them where they came from and where they are going. Their task is to run; hers is to know the orbit.[19]

In an essay of his own from the year 1824, Goethe has much to say about "relative death," and the absolute absence of "absolute death" in nature (1:424). Yet it is the constant hovering of this dire relative of relative death—absolute demise—that shadows and haunts Goethe's otherwise inspiring and inspired philosophy and science of nature. For is not death always *absolute* for the *individual* that is absolved of life, whether wildflower or human being or god? Are not all of nature's hopes invested in the individuals she invariably consigns to demise? And is not absolute death somehow coiled at the very heart of life and love, whether in a rose or in a rose by any other name? "She seems to have invested all her hopes in individuality, and she cares nothing for the individuals." "And their mother—where is she?" She appears to have a heart of stone? Well, then, let us go all the way with such a mother. Let us adore compact metal.

Now we know why Hegel rejects the individual and goes for the genus—the *Gattung* that is God. He finds it in logic, however, rather than in unruly crowds of the living. And we also understand the courage of Schelling, Hölderlin, and Novalis, who never let their logics distract them from the weak-voiced plea of the dying individual, for whom even a relative death is absolutely absolute. Yet there may well be a fitting time for this thought of relative death—if it be a time before absolute death advenes. Novalis takes up the notion in what he calls "inoculation with death"—*nota bene*, not inoculation *against* death, but *with* it. "Death is the romanticizing principle of our life" (2:756), he says, even if death is "minus," and life "plus." Negativity invigorates life: "Life is strengthened by means of death" (ibid.).

Well, then, *life*—and not absolute density. A life of oxidation and combustion, a life dancing through the mix of air, even if oxygen is of the devil, especially for a man whose lungs are being consumed. For a brief moment in his work, Novalis entertains the metallic God of immortality, who is undying only to the extent that he is death itself. Hölderlin, in his "Notes" to Sophocles' *Antigone,* declares that the god now comes on the scene solely and in-

19. Johann Wolfgang von Goethe, *Naturwissenschaftliche Schriften*, ed. Rudolf Steiner, vol. 2 (Dornach, Switzerland: R. Steiner Verlag, 1982), 5–7.

evitably—and that means absolutely—"in the figure of death," *in der Gestalt des Todes* (CHV 2:373). Yet in the end Schelling, Hölderlin, and Novalis always take the part of life, and that means of mortality and mixture. Novalis is anything but oblivious of the air. For absolute purity, absolute density, is absolute asphyxiation and death. Novalis—like his brothers Hölderlin and Schelling—prefers the death of all absolutes to the absolute of death.

AT THE STROKE OF ONE

3

—"Well, Bannadonna," said the chief, "how long ere you are ready to set the clock going, so that the hour shall be sounded?" . . .

—"To-morrow, Excellenza, if you listen for it,—or should you not, all the same—strange music will be heard. The stroke of one shall be the first from yonder bell," pointing to the bell, adorned with girls and garlands, "that stroke shall fall there, where the hand of Una clasps Dua's. The stroke of one shall sever that loved clasp."

—HERMAN MELVILLE,
"The Bell-Tower"

The tragic absolute is in multiple senses the stroke of one—the stroke *of* one *by* one. That stroke instigates critique, judgment, crisis, separation, severance, and divorce; it also initiates the more languid moments of love and desire that we call *languor* and *languishment*. The stroke severs one not into two, that is, not into two clearly definable units, but into a manifold that resists synthesis. The stroke of one severs "that loved clasp" of Una and Dua, severs all singular identities and all binary oppositions. The stroke of one in the philosophy of Schelling introduces us to a realm that will be most aptly described (centuries later) by Maurice Merleau-Ponty's "philosophy of ambiguity" and Jacques Derrida's notion of "undecidability"; in the mid–nineteenth century it will be portrayed in a novel by Herman Melville called *Pierre: or, The Ambiguities*, as well as in the short story cited above, "The Bell-Tower." The stroke of one marks the end of all philosophies of eternity and the instauration of a new understanding of time and temporality. It sounds a knell, initiating a period of progressive paralysis and ultimate decrepitude for all absolutes; yet it also rings the bell, at least to Schelling's ear, at the birth of a finite human freedom.

Schelling's treatise on human freedom, *Philosophische Untersuchungen über das Wesen der menschlichen Freiheit und die damit zusammenhängenden Gegenstände* ("Philosophical Investigations into the Essence of Human Freedom and the Objects Pertaining to It") was written and published in 1809. With it, Schelling took a new turn in his thinking, beyond his early works in the philosophy of nature (beyond them, yet never abandoning them—indeed, always returning to them) and beyond the system of his "transcendental idealism" (1800) and his "identity philosophy" of the years immediately subsequent.

The present chapter pursues what one might call a *peripheral reading* of the 1809 text, rather than a well-centered one. A well-centered reading of Schelling's investigations into human freedom would elaborate in a straightforward way the philosophical problem of the origin and existence of evil, a problem that bedeviled Schelling from the time of his master's thesis on.[1] By contrast, a peripheral reading, remaining as it does on the outskirts of the text, *performs* something with regard to the problem of evil, though that does not mean that the reading can be perspicuous about its own performance. A well-centered reading would involve itself passionately in Schelling's own quest for the origin of evil in human and divine existence, in nature and in life itself, and it would find itself plagued by the selfsame doubt that assailed Schelling. For Schelling doubts whether any system of reason (*Vernunftsystem*) past or present, whether monistic or dualistic, even if it is dialectical in its method and presuppositions, can resolve the aporias that go variously under the rubrics of "freedom and determinism," "pantheism and atheistic fatalism," "divine omniscience and divine beneficence," and so on.

From Plotinus and Augustine through Leibniz and Spinoza, the question concerning the origin of evil in existence has in Schelling's view been obfuscated rather than exhibited. Schelling wonders whether the systems of reason that are competing for the attention of his own generation, no matter how *critical* and transcendentally self-aware those systems may appear to be, might be merely displacing the difficulty "one point farther down the line," while not

---

1. See Schelling's 1792 *Antiquissimi de prima malorum humanorum origine philosophematis Genes. III explicandi tentamen criticum et philosophicum* [A critical and philosophical explication of the oldest philosopheme of the third book of Genesis concerning the first origin of human evil], in the new historical-critical edition, *Werke 1*, ed. Wilhelm G. Jacobs, Jörg Jantzen, Walter Schieche, et al. (Stuttgart: Frommann-Holzboog, 1976), 47–181. See also Schelling's 1794 treatise, *Über Mythen, historische Sagen und Philosopheme der ältesten Welt*, 1:195–246, which deserves a separate treatment. See the discussion and the extensive excerpts in JV 1:262–286.

relieving it. (Schelling's trenchant phrase, by which he indicts all systems of reason, including the Kantian, reads: ... *die Schwierigkeit nur um einen Punkt weiter hinausgerückt, aber nicht aufgehoben wäre;* see 7:355.)[2] A well-centered reading of Schelling's text would duly note each of the philosopher's attempts to anneal traditional dualisms and complexify traditional monisms. These attempts become increasingly frantic, in my judgment, as the scalpel of difference, separation, divorce, and what we henceforth will render as scission (*Scheidung*) cuts deeper and deeper into the flesh of God and the life—and love—of the absolute. The hemorrhaging that occurs as a result of Schelling's deftest strokes, in spite of everything his surgical science can do, ceases only when his patient has become a bloodless shade. Many decades later, Nietzsche will discover this shade hovering in a cavern, deprived utterly of its life, though not yet entirely divested of its power to haunt (KSA 3:467).

Another way of putting all this—a way more in keeping with the Melvillean figure of the "severed clasp" of Una and Dua at the stroke of one—is that no complex monism can stop at two. Dualism, while an inevitable *development* of monism (or, better, an unavoidable *presupposition* of monism), invariably proliferates. The One to which every dualism secretly appeals, as to its Third, begins to dissolve. *Progress* in Schelling's meditation therefore always entails *infinite regression.*

After pursuing a peripheral reading of Schelling's treatise, that is, a reading that circulates among the *images* of Schelling's problem rather than penetrating to the heart of it, we will take up an *indifferent* reading. "Indifferent," not in the sense that we will not care, but in the sense that we, along with Schelling, will try to move back behind the reign of difference to the double eternity of the not-yet-different, not-yet-divergent. Even that indifferent reading, however, will discover that Schelling is always a thinker of scission and crisis: crisis of reason, crisis of Criticism, crisis of divinity, crisis of ontotheology, crisis of love and languor.

The peripheral reading that precedes the indifferent one will seem arbitrary and headstrong, blind to the consequences of crisis, even as it tries to envisage what Schelling means when he writes κρίσις as such. According to the strictures of Schelling's own treatise, a peripheral reading strays from the center of divine logos and love, and also from the center of human freedom. Such

---

2. That is, F. W. J. Schelling, *Sämmtliche Werke*, vol. 7 (Stuttgart: J. G. Cotta'scher Verlag, 1859ff.), 355. I shall cite this edition throughout the book. Yet the text that I have used in my day-to-day work on the treatise is the handy edition by Horst Fuhrmans (Stuttgart: Reclam, 1964). The currently available English translations are unfortunately either out of print or difficult of access; all translations here are my own.

a reading is therefore evil, and it will have to be supplanted by a reading that at least has the virtue of being indifferent.

A Peripheral Reading of Schelling's Treatise on Human Freedom

On the final page of his *Philosophical Investigations into the Essence of Human Freedom* Schelling invokes the "unwritten revelation" that is nature. Nature is always the point of departure and return for Schelling's thinking. Nature, he now writes, contains prototypes or paradigms, proto-images (*Vorbilder*), which he urges his readers to contemplate. The present peripheral reading will follow Schelling's urging, though with a slight alteration: it will contemplate what one might call a series of proto-images that are preeminently images of scission and crisis in the landscape of Schelling's text.[3] "Crisis" (*Krise*, κρίσις) and "scission" (*Scheidung*) are the key words for this peripheral pursuit of images. Further, *Scheidung*, the root of *Entscheidung*, "decision," and *Unterschied*, "distinction," conjures up images of separation, divorce, discrimination, apportionment, allotment, expulsion, elimination, and virtually all forms of cutting or sundering. *Scheiden*, related to the English word "to shed," derives from the Greek σχίζω, to split or sunder. *Die Scheide* may be a limit or boundary, a watershed or a sheathe. At the end of the seventeenth century it becomes the principal translation of the Latin word *vagina*.

On the metaphoric perimeter of Schelling's text, as it were, the peripheral reading will pay heed to two varieties of the proto-image of *Scheidung* or κρίσις, namely, those of (1) self-mutilation, emasculation, and castration, and (2) conception, gestation, and birth. For these images are not entirely remote from the divine center—the heart or sun, the logos—of Schelling's *Philosophical Investigations*.

Yet one cannot begin without citing Schelling's own most striking simile for the very move from center to periphery or perimeter, the move to which the peripheral reading must commit itself. It is a move that in Schelling's view is not only evil but also sick. Schelling writes:

> Illness here offers the most apt simile [*Gleichnis*]. As the disorder that comes into nature through the misuse of freedom, illness is the true replica of evil or sin. Universal illness never occurs without the emergence of the concealed forces of

---

3. See, for example, 7:366, 380, 404. Compare the *Stuttgarter Privatvorlesungen* of 1810 (7:483), which presents a similar passage on *Krisis* and *Scheidung* in nature. In both texts *Krisis* means a series of decisive cuts and separations, *Scheidungen*.

> the ground [*des Grundes*]. Illness originates when the irritable principle, which should reign in the tranquil depths as the innermost cincture [*Band*] of forces, actuates itself; or when Archaeus, suddenly disturbed, quits his tranquil dwelling in the center and moves to the circumference. In the same way, contrariwise, all original healing consists in the restoration of the relation of periphery to center; and the transition from illness to health can really happen only by virtue of the opposite, to wit, the reabsorption of separate and singularized life into the inner beam of light in the essence [*die Wiederaufnahme des getrennten und einzelnen Lebens in den innern Lichtblick des Wesens*], after which reabsorption the scission (crisis) again occurs. (7:366)

Illness and health—and presumably evil and good—are in some sense cyclical and are therefore as much on the periphery, the selfsame periphery, as at the center. A theory of illness and evil would therefore have to be a theory of contagion or contamination.

In this brief chapter it cannot be a matter of elucidating the sources of Schelling's ruling image, the image of a cyclical or periodic movement from center to periphery and back to the center. Some of those sources would no doubt surprise us: one would do well, for example, to search the pages of Kant's *Religion within the Limits of Mere Reason* (1793) for instances of such movement from center to periphery and back again, movements often signaled by the word *Eigendünkel*, which is a kind of egotism of thinking and willing. Schelling himself, in the pages of his *Philosophical Investigations*, cites Franz Baader, who, through Jacob Böhme, would take us back to Plato's *Timaeus*, the Pythagorean Brotherhood, the Cabala, and all the hermetic doctrines of the Middle Ages and early modernity, so that in the end we could neither pinpoint a particular center for such sources nor circumscribe their circumference. Baader himself (cited at 7:366–367 n.) invokes the "center (*mysterium*)" of primal fire, and the "periphery" of the primal moisture within fire, noting their cyclical economy of peaceful coexistence and discord (*Zwietracht*). When the center (ego) shifts to the periphery (egotism) and seeks to occupy the entire circle, evil reigns. And Baader, with his mélange of theosophy, psychology, and chemistry, so foreign to the contemporary mind, continues:

> Where there was once ☉ we now have ◯. That is, at one particular place in the planetary system that dark center of nature is closed, latent; precisely for that reason it serves luciferously [*als Lichtträger*] to grant entry into the higher system (a shaft of light—or revelation of the ideal). Precisely for that reason this place is the open point (sun—heart—eye) in the system—and if the dark center of na-

ture would rise or open there, <u>then *eo ipso* the point of light would occlude, light</u> <u>would become darkness in the system, or the sun be extinguished!</u>

Baader's ⊙ and ○ grant us a first glimpse at the radical undecidability of the center/periphery movement: the dark center of nature is marked not, as one might think, by ⊙ but by ○. <u>For when the center disappears in the pe-</u> <u>riphery, as it were, there is closure</u>: <u>the dark spot in the middle does not</u> <u>merely disappear at one point on the periphery but expands to the periphery</u> <u>at each point, spreading the dark in its flight as the curtain of night. Yet clo-</u> <u>sure is itself an opening onto the point as such; it is the solar center writ large,</u> as it were. Or, to alter the metaphor, yet remaining within Baader's symbol- ism, the ocular ⊙ is most radically open to light at its black center •, which it- self appears without center, or as mere center, center alone, center ostensibly absolute. <u>Yet the heart of the essence throbs with all space, which invades it</u> <u>from every point on the periphery. Accordingly, if the heart of darkness is also</u> <u>the bearer of light, it is not clear—to say the least—how any scission, decision,</u> <u>distinction, or divorce could ever separate periphery and center in a definitive</u> <u>way. Indeed, both Baader and Schelling appear to insist that interrupting the</u> <u>cycle is impossible</u>. The marks of health and illness, good and evil, would therefore no longer be distinguishable in principle. Such marks, taken by themselves, would signify nothing, would not be signs or symbols at all. There would be no identifiable periodicity, no period, period ⊙. Period ○. And so on and on.

If, like Archaeus, we suddenly quit our tranquil dwelling at the center, it is only because, again like Archaeus, we are disturbed—and from the origin. Which means that we are utterly unlike Archaeus, or that Archaeus is ec- static, or at the end of his tether. And it may not be a matter of illness or evil. One of the senses of the move from center to periphery that we have not yet mentioned may have to do with what a very late text—the 1842 *Philosophy of Mythology*—calls the development of god in the direction of femininity: Schelling explicitly relates the δυάς of duality with the female (Una clasping the hand of Dua), and the female as the movement from a self-centered, cen- tripetal existence to the more generous, centrifugal, outward-bound τὸ περ- ιφερές (II/2:142). Yet let us put all these preliminaries aside and begin to as- semble the proto-images of Schelling's text.

1. Scheidung *as castration, emasculation, and self-mutilation.* Three pas- sages from various segments of Schelling's *Philosophical Investigations into the Essence of Human Freedom* solicit our attention. First, a passage from what one

might call the "historical introduction" to the problem of evil in philosophy as such: here Schelling pinpoints the principal flaw in *modern* philosophy, that is, philosophy since Descartes. Modern *idealistic* philosophy, which is one of the two strands of post-Cartesian philosophy, has mutilated itself or emasculated itself, inasmuch as it contains no *realistic* philosophy of nature. It may strike us as odd that philosophy, which since medieval times is always represented as a woman (one thinks of the delightful "Filosofia" carved into the pulpit of the cathedral at Pisa), is here made to suffer emasculation. And we will also have to leave in suspense the curious fact that precisely when the (masculine) modern philosopher ignores (feminine) nature he obliterates his own (masculine) nature. Or is there anything at all curious about this? How else does emasculation occur, except as ignorance, insult, and hurt with regard to the feminine in both man and woman? As we shall see, the feminine in Schelling's text appears under two guises: first, as the plenitude of fecund nature, as the Mother; second, as lack and debility, affectation and hysteria, effeminacy and flaw. No one will be surprised by such an ambivalence in the imagery, although virtually everyone will be chagrined. Yet if we endure the peripheral reading a bit longer we will discover that the second, negative guise of the feminine brings us back precisely to the problematically masculine modern idealist: modern philosophy becomes effeminate precisely insofar as it spurns the feminine. Yet how are we to distinguish or separate, divorce or divide, these two (affirmative/negative) proto-images of the feminine? We should not be surprised if the image of the crisis in modern philosophy becomes itself the crisis of such imagery. For the moment, we should take comfort in the fact that Schelling is by no means promoting emasculation as some sort of approximation to the feminine; nature is not for him a lack or flaw, nor a hysteric whom the idealist successfully emulates. Yet all these remarks—too hurried, too harried—anticipate the following passage:

> Modern European philosophy as a whole, from its beginning (in Descartes), has this common flaw: nature does not exist for it; it lacks a living ground. Spinoza's realism is in this regard as abstract as Leibniz's idealism. Idealism is the soul of philosophy, realism its body; only the two together constitute a living whole. Never can the latter [i.e., realism, as *der Leib* of philosophy] provide the principle, but it must be the ground and the medium [*Grund und Mittel*] in which the former actualizes itself, assuming flesh and blood. If a philosophy lacks this living fundament—which is usually a sign that the ideal principle too was only feebly at work in it from the outset—it loses itself in the kind of system whose attenuated concepts of aseity, modifications, etc. stand in sharpest contrast to the vital force and fullness of actuality. Yet wherever the ideal principle actually works its effects to a high degree, while failing to find the reconciling and medi-

ating basis, it generates a turbid, wild enthusiasm [*da erzeugt es einen trüben und wilden Enthusiasmus*] that irrupts in self-mutilation [*Selbstzerfleischung*] or—as with the priests of the Phrygian goddess [i.e., Kybele]—self-emasculation [*Selbstentmannung*]. This in fact transpires in philosophy when reason and science are surrendered. (7:356–357)

When idealism fails to take on flesh and blood in the womb of realism, its high spirits and presumed high-mindedness culminate in a *Selbstzerfleischung* that the idealist wanted to rule out in the first place—as though there were already in idealism, quite in spite of its conception of itself, a *Fleisch* susceptible of mutilation. Kant's almost frenzied resistance to "enthusiasm" in the third *Critique* and elsewhere, his resistance to music and mysticism alike, here receives its explanation. Self-mutilation is a self-castration after the manner of the husbands of Kybele, that is, the Corybants, or a self-emasculation after the manner of the hero of Ernest Hemingway's "God Rest You Merry, Gentlemen."[4]

We recall that castration was precisely what Augustine in his *Confessions* prayed for; it is what the Church Father Origen, heeding the advice of Paul, actually achieved for himself. Perhaps a reminder about the Corybants, however, is called for. They were the priests of Kybele, the Great Goddess of Asia, and Schelling refers specifically to them when he mentions the priests of the Phrygian goddess. The Corybants were well known for their frenzied dancing, and are often held to be the distant forebears of the Whirling Dervishes of Anatolia. They were also well known, since antiquity, for their initiation rite of self-castration. The Corybants were also called Γάλλοι, Latin *Galli*, not to be confused with the Celtic Gauls. (We will see Johann Georg Hamann refer to the *Gallier* in a moment.) The singular form of the noun, *Gallus*, is often written in the feminine form *Galla*, "humorously," the dictionaries tell us, inasmuch as *gallus* is the cock. One might also recall, in anatomy, the designation of the *crista galli* in the penis, whose significant role is discussed by none other than Hegel in his Jena lectures on the philosophy of nature.[5]

Yet to turn now from these peripheral figures back to Schelling's own text—as though periphery and center were not already imbricated and even coextensive. Precisely how does such castration or emasculation occur in modern European philosophy? First of all, it does not occur at all where the

---

4. Ernest Hemingway, *The First Forty-Nine Short Stories* (London: Jonathan Cape, 1972), 322–326.
5. G. W. F. Hegel, *Gesammelte Werke*, ed. Rolf-Peter Horstmann, vol. 8 (Hamburg: F. Meiner Verlag, 1987), 173. For further discussion, see Krell, *Contagion*, chs. 9–12, with endnotes.

ideal principle is weak, but only where it "works its effects to a high degree, while failing to find the reconciling and mediating basis." When a philosopher in whom the ideal principle is effective abnegates the reconciling and mediating basis (*Grund*) of that principle, he or she abjures reason and science, which constitute the potency of philosophy. However, philosophic science itself, initially in the form of a philosophy of nature, initiates the distinction "between essence insofar as it exists and essence insofar as it is merely the ground of existence" (7:357). Indeed, this distinction in the divine essence between *existence* and *ground of existence*, with the latter (*der Grund*) taken to be the source of all *life*, will be the mainstay of Schelling's philosophy to the very end. The problem, as we shall see, is how to prevent this distinction (*Unterschied* as an *Unter*-scheidung, within essence) from degenerating into a scission that will unman science as definitively as every idealism heretofore. In other words, beyond the separation and divorce of scission, there must be some reconciling and mediating basis or *ground* for mind and body, spirit and matter, existence and *ground* of existence. A scientific philosophy must at some point stop wielding its keen-edged distinctions, locate those protean, redoubled, proliferating *grounds*, and dwell there.

The second passage on scission as castration in Schelling's text is actually an extended quotation from a text by Johann Georg Hamann (1730–1788), along with Schelling's commentary on that text. This second passage will justify the seemingly capricious reference a moment ago to Origen and to the Corybants. Hamann's topic is the human passions:

"If the passions are the members of dishonor, do they thereby cease to be weapons of manhood? Do you understand the letter of reason more discerningly than that allegorical chamberlain of the Alexandrian Church understood Scriptures when he made himself a eunuch for the sake of the kingdom of heaven?— The prince of this eon adopts as his favorites those who are perfect little demons toward themselves—his (the devil's) jesters are the harshest enemies of beauteous nature, which has Corybants and Galli as its renegade monks but vigorous spirits as its true worshippers." [Schelling cites Hamann's *Cloverleaf of Hellenistic Letters*, 2:196, and comments as follows:] It is only that those whose philosophy is made more for women's rooms [*Gynäceum*, from ἡ γυναικεία, that part of a house in ancient Greece that was reserved for the women, most often on the second floor of the house; cf., however, τὰ γυναικεία, defined by Liddell-Scott as the *partes muliebres*] than for the Academy or the Palaestra of the Lyceum do not wish to bring those dialectical propositions [i.e., those that assert the identity of good and evil: cf. 7:400] before a public which, misunderstanding both them and itself, sees in them a cancellation of all distinction between justice and injustice, good and evil; before a public where they belong just as little as do the statements of the ancient dialecticians, Zeno and the other Eleatics, before the forum of shallow, effete spirits [*seichter Schöngeister*]. (7:401)

It is difficult to separate out here the various levels of polemic and their respective targets. Suffice it for the moment to note once again the curious deployment and recoil of the castration/emasculation imagery: the male member, dishonorable though it may be precisely because of its susceptibility to the elements of the *Gynäceum*, and perhaps to those of the forum of effete spirits as well, is acknowledged as manhood's weapon par excellence. (Schelling himself often refers to the body in general as the "tool" or "imple- ment" of spirit, *das Werkzeug des Geistes*, rather than as spirit's weapon; Hegel too, as we know, consistently employs the "tool" image, and precisely in the present context.) Only a "womanish" philosopher, a philosopher of the kitchen and the loom (forgetting for the moment Herakles' labors at the loom, and not breathing a word about the bedroom), would hesitate to assert the dialectical identity of good and evil because an effete and shallow public fears such identification. The public in fact prefers a sterile dualism—for ex- ample, the Axis of Good vs. the Axis of Evil—to a fructifying monism that would be capable of sustaining profound *Scheidungen* and surviving severe *crises*. Such a monism (and Schelling writes for the moment as though he were such a monist) would have to gird its loins. As we will see, however, it would have to gird itself with a sheathe rather than a sword: if there is a flam- ing sword at work in Schelling's system—not yet here in his *Philosophical In- vestigations* but later in his sketches toward *The Ages of the World*, and even there only incipiently, only tentatively, never with full confidence—it is a sword that executes in one fell stroke the invagination of God. Yet some, per- haps themselves members of a timorous and effete public, would take such in- vagination to be the decapitation of God and the end of the absolute.[6]

It would be possible to show that Schelling's *Weltalter* sketches lead him beyond the merely abstract assertion of God's embodiment—which, to be sure, is something altogether different from orthodox phallic Incarnation—to

6. Roberto Calasso has an excellent account of the ambivalence vis-à-vis femininity that we are confronting here, making explicit reference to the *gynaeceum* or women's rooms of the house. Calasso takes this ambivalence to be typical of Greek antiquity—in which misogyny proves to be rooted in a deep-seated fear that feminine sexuality conceals "a mocking power that eludes male control" (RC 80). Fear of the "erotic self-sufficiency" of the female is figured in the seer Tiresias's blinding by Hera, inasmuch as the seer has insight into (and betrays the secret of) the following possibility: "Perhaps woman, that creature shut away in the gynaeceum, where [according to Pseudo-Lucian] 'not a single particle of true eros penetrates,' knew a great deal more than her master, who was always cruising about gymnasiums and porticoes" (RC 81).

a realization of the essential bisexuality (indeed, a multiple sexuality beyond even hermaphroditism) of divinity. For the moment, trying not to move too quickly ahead, we may be satisfied to cite Horst Fuhrmans's reference (see Schelling's *Sämmtliche Werke*, 8:16) to an unpublished text by Schelling, dated 1812, which intensifies his polemic against modern idealist philosophy. The polemic against idealism will always be stronger than the charges laid against Spinoza, to whom Schelling feels a growing affinity. To the idealists Schelling cries: "You have maligned nature for deploying the senses, for failing to create man on the model of your own abstractions. You have abused and maimed [*geschändet und verstümmelt*] his nature to suit yourselves; in insolent fury you have raged against her, like those who in earlier times castrated themselves for the sake of heavenly bliss [*verschnitten um der Seligkeit willen*]." Not until Nietzsche will there again be such an urgent polemic against the spirit of asceticism, mortification, and self-mutilation.

One final passage on the scission of castration—particularly revealing as regards the ambiguous plight of modern philosophy, which becomes womanish ("womanish," to be sure, only if one remains within the phallocratic equation of woman and castration/emasculation) precisely in its recoil from womanly nature—appears in a footnote quite late in Schelling's text (7:409–410). Here Schelling is eager to add his voice to those that object to "the unmanly pantheistic swindle" in contemporary German philosophy, religion, and letters. Eager, because it is he who is being accused of pantheism and swindle, and precisely by his brother-in-law-once-removed, Friedrich Schlegel. If modern philosophic idealism from Descartes to Leibniz is unmanned, modern pantheism in Spinoza and his epigones is unmanly. Schelling thus finds himself caught between two eminently vulnerable positions: too little devotion to a philosophy of nature and he joins the ranks of the gelded Kybeline priesthood; too much devotion and he capitulates to a simpering pantheism. In either case the result is the same—the unkindest cut of all.

And yet. However much pantheism may imply both vertigo and fraud (*Schwindel* here, as in Hegel's *Phenomenology of Spirit*, where the word is predicated of historical skepticism, suggesting both dizziness and the will to deceive, that is, to swindle), Schelling is ultimately willing to dally with pantheism. Indeed, a year later he will conclude his *Stuttgarter Privatvorlesungen* (7:484) by saying, "Then God is actually all in all, and pantheism true." For the moment, in his *Philosophical Investigations*, he cuts himself off from pantheism, abjures it at the decisive moment, the moment of absolute indifference—which is to say, precisely when One clasps the hand of Two. Schelling and his God, by insisting on divorce (*Scheidung*) from illness and evil, and ultimately from nature itself, cut themselves off by the stroke of One.

2. Scheidung *as conception, gestation, and birth.* Of the many references to reproduction and birth in the treatise on human freedom, I will refer to only three. Quite early in his text (7:346–347), Schelling tries to express the relation of ground and existence in the divine essence without recourse to pantheistic excess. The passage begins cautiously enough and is delicate to the point of ambiguity:

> Consideration of the divine essence itself offers a much higher standpoint. The idea of that essence is of a sequence that would not fully contradict generation, that is, the positing of something self-sufficient [*eine Folge, die nicht Zeugung, d.h. Setzen eines Selbständigen ist, völlig widersprechen würde:* the subjunctive mood and the periphrasis indicate Schelling's caution; the confusing parataxis of *nicht* and *Zeugung* is well-nigh equivocal in its effects, as though canceling the word "generation" or "procreation" before writing it]. God is not a God of the dead, but of the living. It is utterly incomprehensible how the most perfect essence of all [*das allervollkommenste Wesen*] could take its pleasure in even the most perfect machine [*auch an der möglich vollkommensten Maschine seine Lust fände*]. However one might think of the manner of procession of essences from God, it can never be a mechanical one, no mere effecting or putting in place, whereby what is effected is nothing for itself; just as little can it be emanation, whereby the efflux would remain the same as that from which it has flowed, and thus would be nothing of its own, nothing self-sufficient [*Eignes, Selbstständiges*]. The procession of things from God is a self-revelation of God. However, God can be revealed to himself only in what is similar to him, in essences that act freely from out of themselves; for there is no ground for their being other than God; but they are in the way that God is. He speaks, and they are there.

If the procession of essences or creatures (and *Wesen* means both essence and creature, both *ens increatum* and *ens creatum*) from the primal essence (or creature) cannot be mechanical—and we recall from chapter 1 that for German Idealism and Romanticism as a whole the machine is sheer oppression and death—then it must be a matter of *Zeugung,* that is, procreation and generation. Since Aristotle, there has been but one set of alternatives: a being is either produced by τέχνη or reproduced in the process of generation that is proper to nature (τίκτειν, γένεσις, φύσις). If the Demiurge of Plato's *Timaeus* is declared without much fanfare to be both the "father" and the "maker" of the cosmos, the mysterious apposition of paternity and technicity continues to plague Western metaphysics and theology from beginning to end. Yet if mere technicity and mechanism seem utterly unworthy modes of divine existence and action, paternity has its own attendant indignities, and

Schelling is reluctant to bless anything as liquorous as emanation. He tries to displace the indignities and the liquidity onto a second scene, to wit, the scene of humanity. The displacement, however, is unsuccessful, if only because of the ambiguity in *Wesen*. The displacement onto the human scene merely pushes the problem one point farther down the line, without resolving it. The indignities of paternity cling to divine creation all the more stubbornly as Schelling hopes that some ultimate divorce will sunder them. What are these indignities? The entire wake of mortality: time, finitude, illness, and evil. Soon after the passage with which this chapter began, the passage on the self-emasculation of modern philosophy, Schelling writes the following concerning the scission between ground and existence in God:

> In order to be separated [*geschieden*] from God, they [i.e., *die Dinge*, the things of created nature] must come to be in a ground that is different [*verschieden*] from him. Yet because nothing can be outside God [*außer Gott*], this contradiction can be resolved only thus: the things have their ground in whatever in God himself is not *He Himself*, that is, in that which is ground of his existence [*daß die Dinge ihren Grund in dem haben, was in Gott selbst nicht E r S e l b s t ist, d.h. in dem was Grund seiner Existenz ist*]. (7:359–360)

In a note to this passage, marked for insertion after the phrase *was in Gott selbst nicht E r S e l b s t ist*, Schelling declares this "the sole correct dualism," namely, a dualism that simultaneously "admits of a unity" by virtue of the fact that it "subordinates" the "evil principle" to the good. How that subordination (*Unterordnung*) is to occur is, of course, the capital question. At this point we are confronted with the conundrum that there is something in God himself that is not he himself. That something is his ground, the source of his, and all, life.

The divine *selbst* is written twice here, once without a capital and without emphasis, and then a second time capitalized and in spaced type.[7] Mediating between these two invocations of the divine self are the negative word *nicht* and the masculine pronoun, also capitalized and set in spaced type: *E r.* The passage continues, after a paragraph break:

> If we wish to make this essence more accessible in human terms [*menschlich näherbringen*], we can say that it is the yearning [*die Sehnsucht:* languor, languishing, longing] felt by the eternal One to give birth to itself [*sich selbst zu gebären*]. It [i.e., *Sie*, this languor] is not the One itself, yet it is still co-eternal with it. It wants to give birth to God, that is, to the ungroundable unity [*Sie will Gott, d.h.*

7. In two works written during 1810, the *Stuttgarter Privatvorlesungen* (see, e.g., 7:434, 458, 475) and the dialogue on the nexus of nature and the spirit-world, *Clara* (9:75), Schelling writes *Er Selber.*

die unergründliche Einheit gebären]; but to that extent unity is not yet in it itself
[*in ihr selbst*].

The translation inevitably obfuscates the curious pronominal play of
Schelling's text, which therefore needs to be reconstituted—even though
everything that is written here ostensibly has merely heuristic value, designed
to bring the divine essence a bit closer to the human. When the third-person
masculine pronoun *Er* is opened up by spaced type there is suddenly room for
the feminine word *Sehnsucht*, longing, languor, and languishment. One might
go so far as to say that when the eternal One opens itself to the desire to give
birth to itself it experiences something like gyneceal room, or space. The feminine word for "longing," "languor," "languishing," *die Sehnsucht*, commands
the feminine pronoun in the following line: *Sie*, "she." "She," languid longing,
is not the One itself, *das Eine* being neuter, that is, neither the one nor the
other, neither masculine nor feminine. Even so, she is coeval with the One.
"She," this languishing longing, wants to become pregnant with God, wants
to conceive, bear, and give birth to him. Or to "it," the One. *Gebären* derives
from the Greek φέρω, to bear or carry, and the prefix *ge-*, expressing the result
of the pregnancy, that is to say, looking forward to the Son—for surely in the
present case it can be a matter only of sons, not of daughters—that will eventually be *ge-boren* from this longing. Unity is not yet in her, not yet in her self,
in ihr selbst, presuming that one can speak of ground and languor as possessing selfhood, which of course they do not.

Juxtaposed to the phrase *Er Selbst* we now have the phrase *in ihr selbst*.
No, not merely juxtaposed. For she, languid longing, is *in* the One itself, *in*
him or it, *in* God. How did she get there? She got there because in God himself there arises—or has always already arisen, from all eternity—a languor, a
yearning or longing (expressed in terms of the human scene) to engender
himself, *to make himself his own mother*. Are we, then, quite sure that it will not
be a matter of daughters?

Is all this fuss concerning the human, all-too-human playground of
pronominal language to be discounted? Perhaps the points we are making now
have nothing to do with God but only with a contingency of German grammar, with its three genders of nouns and pronouns. Furthermore, does not
Schelling himself explicitly invoke the second scene, the scene of humanity,
precisely in order to speak heuristically, in parables or fables, and merely by way
of analogy, in order to bring the (divine) essence (or creature) nearer to us foolish humans? Presumably, the divine essence itself will suffer no such division?
And yet. The essence *as such* is divided into ground and existence: such is

the initial and the final insight of Schelling's science of nature and of freedom. "Divided" here cannot mean the empty, formal, abstract *Unterscheidungen* of prior idealisms. Here it is not a matter of making confident and clever distinctions, or even pious and lugubrious ones. Here it is not a matter of the Scholastic solution to every possible embarrassment, to wit, "X must be taken as referring to two possible cases, the first, etc. etc., the second, etc. etc.," such distinctions opening the convenient yet always transparent loophole for escape and flight. Rather, division in the essence must be *real*. And, being real, such division, the result of real scission, inevitably refers to a kind of *suffering*. What is this divine passion? What is languor?

Excursus on *Sehnsucht:* Languor, the Languid, and Languishment

Languor is hardly a common word in spoken or written English and American parlance these days. A word or two on that word, and on the related words *languid* and *languishment,* may therefore be in order. For *Sehnsucht* will prove to be the central notion of Schelling's account of the primal and originary divine essence; moreover, that notion will not pass, will not be absorbed into some more edifying and less troubling notion of love, neither in the freedom essay nor in *The Ages of the World.*

The Oxford English Dictionary cites the original, archaic sense of *languor,* here closer to the modern sense of *languishment,* as "disease, sickness, illness"; Spenser, in the *Faerie Queene,* writes, "From thenceforth a wretched life they ladd, In wilfull languor and consuming smart" (III, xii, 16). This archaic sense of *languor* captures the meaning of *Sehnsucht* perfectly, however, inasmuch as the suffix *-sucht* refers not to a "search" but to *Seuche,* an epidemic, addiction, or infestation. A second obsolete meaning, as old as the first, is "distressed condition, sad case, woeful plight"; again, Spenser: "Whiles thus thy Britons doe in languour pine." Of equal antiquity is a third obsolete meaning, "mental suffering or distress, pining, sorrow, affliction of spirit," with the phrase "to make languor" meaning to mourn or to cause lamentation. In *Titus Andronicus* (III, I, 13), Shakespeare writes, "My harts deepe languor, and my soules sad teares." In Scotland the word *languor,* perhaps because of a perceived relation to the verb and the adjective *long,* has traditionally meant *ennui,* profound boredom, the German *Lange-weile.* From here it is not far to the fourth sense of the word, the first sense not marked "obsolete," to wit, "faintness, weariness, lassitude, fatigue (of the body or the faculties)." Goldsmith, in 1762, notes, "All the senses seem so combined, as to soon be tired into languor by the gratification of any one of them." The articulation of this last sense—the faintness and weariness consequent upon gratification—is as follows: "Expression or indication of lassitude, in the voice, features, etc.; ... Habitual lassitude and inertia in one's movements and behaviour, want of energy and alertness (whether as a natural quality or an affectation); ... Tenderness or softness (of mood, feeling, etc.); lassitude of spirit caused by sorrow, amorous longing, or the like." And, finally, a fifth sense: "Of immaterial things: Depressed or drooping condition; want of activity or interest; slackness, dullness; ... Of the air, sky, etc.: Heaviness, absence of life and motion, oppressive stillness." As though all the world were suffering in the heat of the dog days, with its cosmic tongue (*lingua, langue, ling-*) drooping.

The adjective *languid*, still commonly used in English, the *OED* defines as "faint, weak; inert from fatigue or weakness; wanting in vigour or vitality." The medicinal *Pulse-Watch* of 1707 warns, "A languid Pulse depends upon languid Spirits," while Goldsmith encourages, "Unknown to them when sensual pleasures cloy, To fill the languid pause with finer joy." Pope's *Dunciad* espies the approach of persons "With mincing step, small voice, and languid eye." Macauley's *History of England* refers to "an appeal which might have moved the most languid and effeminate natures to heroic action." Languid may be said of persons who are spiritless and apathetic, affected and effete, and it may also be attributed to a writing style that lacks vividness. Similarly, when trade is not brisk, business grows languid.

As for the English word *languish*, best used, I believe, to translate Schelling's verb *schmachten*, discussed in greater detail in the following chapter, the meanings that seem most relevant are the following: "Of living beings (also of plants or vegetation): To grow weak, faint, or feeble; to lose health, to have one's vitality impaired; to continue in a state of feebleness and suffering." More generally, "to live under conditions which lower the vitality or depress the spirits." Attributed to appetites or activities, languishment is slackness, loss of vigor or intensity; to languish is "To droop in spirits; to pine with love, grief, or the like." Dryden writes, "With two fair Eyes his Mistress burns his Breast; He looks, and languishes, and leaves his Rest." To languish is "To waste away with desire or longing *for*, to pine *for*," the *for* here stressing a kind of intentionality (to use a phenomenological term) or objective correlative for languor and languishment. De Quincey expresses compassion, surely not feigned, for "The poor nuns, who ... were languishing for some amusement."

Finally, the *OED* cites *languishment* as referring "especially" to: "Sorrow caused by love or by longing of any kind; amorous grief or pain." Spenser hopes to confine that sorrow within a limited though lengthy cycle of years,

years conterminous with the reign of sexual love: "The Spheare of Cupid fourty yeares containes: Which I have wasted in long languishment." Mrs. Oliphant refers to "Love-agonies and languishments beyond the reach of words," and presumably also beyond the reach of forty years. George Eliot witnesses or imagines "adorers who might hover around her with languishment."

Why detail all these senses of the English words *languor, languid,* and *languish?* Simply because Schelling employs *die Sehnsucht* to translate the Latin word of which *languor* is the precise cognate, namely, *languor,* from *langueo,* related to the Greek λήγω, "I cease and desist, I refrain from." *Langueo* means to be without tension and force, to be inert and inactive, even benumbed. Its inchoative, *languesco,* means to suffer a diminution in strength of body and mind, to become indifferent and lukewarm about vital matters. Such a state is associated with the negative influence of the new moon and of Aphrodite—Ovid refers to the *Veneris languescere motu.*

Perhaps one may be forgiven the anachronism of referring to a contemporary French discourse on *langueur,* or *languor,* inasmuch as the phenomenon under discussion and the sources cited do seem to stretch from antiquity into postmodernity. Roland Barthes's *A Lover's Discourse: Fragments* contains an entire section on "Love's Languor," which it defines as a "subtle state of amorous desire, experienced in its dearth, outside of any will-to-possess." The section merits extended quotation:

1. The Satyr says: I want my desire to be satisfied *immediately.* If I see a sleeping face, parted lips, an open hand, I want to be able *to hurl myself upon them.* This Satyr—figure of the Immediate—is the very contrary of the Languorous. In languor, I merely wait: "I knew no end to desiring you." (Desire is everywhere, but in the amorous state it becomes something very special: languor.)

2. "and you tell me my other self will you answer me at last I am tired of you I want you I dream of you for you against you answer me your name is a perfume about me your color bursts among the thorns bring back my heart with cool wine make me a coverlet of the morning I suffocate beneath this mask withered shrunken skin nothing exists save desire." [Philippe Sollers, *Paradis*]

3. "for when I glance at you even for an instant, I can no longer utter a word: my tongue thickens to a lump, and beneath my skin a subtle fire breaks out: my eyes are blind, my ears are filled with humming, and sweat streams down my body, I am seized by a sudden shuddering; I turn greener than grass, and in a moment more, I feel I shall die." [Sappho]

4. "My soul, when I embraced Agathon, came to my lips, as if the wretch would leave me and go elsewhere." In amorous languor, something keeps going away; it

is as if desire were nothing but this hemorrhage. Such is amorous fatigue: a hunger not to be satisfied, a gaping love. Or again: my entire self is drawn, transferred to the loved object which takes its place: languor would be that exhausting transition from narcissistic libido to object libido. (Desire for the absent being and desire for the present being: languor superimposes the two desires, putting absence within presence. Whence a state of contradiction: this is the "subtle fire.") [Plato, Goethe, Ruysbroeck, Freud, de Rougemont][8]

Four final references—to Descartes, Goethe, Sade, and Euripides. These references, one should note, respect not chronology but expertise.

Descartes, in his *Treatise on the Passions of the Soul,* is not ignorant of the action—or inaction—of *langueur.*[9] The word signifies for him a relaxation of tension in all the limbs of the body, which relaxation or slackening results from the insufficiency of animal spirits in the nerve tubes of the muscles. What makes languor notable, however, is that the insufficiency occurs not in the limbs themselves but in the pineal gland, that is, in the seat of the soul itself, which fails to dispatch the animal spirits to any of the muscles. Why this failure? Descartes neglects to say. Yet it is surely because the gland, acting as the hapless homunculus it always is in Descartes's system whenever descriptions encounter difficulties, so that the gland merely mimics the behavior it is supposed to cause, is suddenly struck by apathy—in other words, by *langueur.* Love and desire usually cause this apathy of the gland when the soul imagines that the acquisition of its loved and desired object is at present impossible. The soul is so obsessed with its absent object that it instructs the animal spirits to ignore everything else in the universe and focus on the image of this one impossible presence. With all the animal spirits frenetic in the brain, circling the elevated image of the desired one in the way that the male chorus in Ballanchine's choreography of Ravel's *Bolero* circles about the elevated woman, only the *idea* of the desired object is "fortified," while the rest of the body is "left languishing" (751). Finally, although Descartes concedes that languor might also result from the violent action of other emotions, such as hatred, sadness, "and even joy" (ibid.), languor arises in cases of *amour* more than anywhere else. Love's labor, once lost, does not like surprises: it remains rapt to the familiar yet unobtainable object.

Young Werther, who perhaps has encountered Descartes in his studies, bemoans his "sluggishness," which he knows is due to the impact of an unlucky love. His "active forces" dwindle to the oxymoron that perhaps best

8. Roland Barthes, *A Lover's Discourse: Fragments,* tr. Richard Howard (New York: Hill and Wang, 1978), 155–156; translation slightly modified.

9. I cite, by page number in parentheses, Descartes, *Œuvres et Lettres,* ed. André Bridoux (Paris: Gallimard/Pléiade, 1953), 750–751, which contains articles 119–121 (in Part II of the *Treatise*).

characterizes languor, namely, "restless lassitude," *unruhige Lässigkeit*. "I cannot find leisure and yet I cannot undertake anything," he complains.[10] Werther's malaise is like a chronic, crippling disease, one that deprives him of the power to intervene in events. Eventually, of course, he does intervene—if suicide is an intervention. Yet one must try to place young Werther's words in the mouth of the absolute (or Schelling's *Wesen*) in order to get an inkling of the problem of infinite freedom and infinite inhibition: "And can you demand of the unfortunate one whose life is gradually, relentlessly ebbing away under the influence of a consumptive illness [*einer schleichenden Krankheit*], can you demand of him that he put an end to his pain once and for all by means of a dagger thrust? And does not the ill that eats away at his forces also at the same time rob him of the courage to liberate himself?"

One mocks at one's own peril the lengths to which that "sage and serious doctor of the Sorbonne" in Sade's *One Hundred and Twenty Days of Sodom* must go—or, rather, the lengths to which he must beg young Aurora to take him—in order to escape from *cet état de langueur* into which he has fallen. Weary of witnessing "the sheer loss of God's existence in the schools," the old rhetorician visits the bordello, "in order to convince himself of the existence of God's creatures."[11] One mocks at one's own peril because the languor in question—whether the Sorbonne sage or the Parisian prostitute happens to embody it at the moment (in other words, whether that languor is laughable or lascivious)—is the suffering of divinity, perhaps of that very divinity that has gone missing in the schools.

One final reference to the *languid*, therefore, must be noted—here in the words of William Arrowsmith, the well-known classicist and translator of Euripides' *The Bacchae*. Arrowsmith is introducing his readers to the particular quality of the god Dionysos in Euripides' masterpiece:

> Dramatically, the core of the play is an exquisitely constructed confrontation between the two major opponents, the young god Dionysus and the young man Pentheus. The contrasting itself seems almost schematic: the athletic Pentheus pitted against the languid god; traditional Greek dress contrasted with the outlandish Asiatic livery of the Bacchante; the angry, impetuous, heavy-handed young man as against the smiling, soft-spoken, feline effortlessness of Dionysus; the self-ignorant man confronted with the humanized shape of his necessity.

10. Johann Wolfgang von Goethe, *Die Leiden des jungen Werther* (Frankfurt am Main: Insel, 1997 [written and published in 1774]), 74 ("Am 22. August"). For the following quotation, see 59 ("Am 8. August").

11. D. A. F. Sade, *Oeuvres complètes du Marquis de Sade*, vol. 1: *Les cent vingt journées de Sodome*, ed. Annie Le Brun and Jean-Jacques Pauvert (Paris: Pauvert, 1986), 156–157.

Below the contrasts run the resemblances, for these young rivals, we need to remember, are first cousins and they share a family likeness.[12]

Euripides' play depicts the violence that the languid, languorous, languishing god exacts on his mother's sisters and on Agave's son, his own cousin. That violence is a measure of the languishment, the sickness, that Dionysos himself has suffered vicariously on behalf of his slandered mother, Semele. Pentheus is merely Dionysos in the ascendant, on his way to the mountains and his ordeal. And Schelling is the thinker who more than any other in our tradition (with the possible exception of Hölderlin) understands the price of divinity—the human cost of immortality, as it were—dictated by the word *Sehnsucht*, languor and languishment.

The Peripheral Reading (continued)

It is no accident that precisely at this point—the point of languor and languishing, yearning and craving, hysteria and the divine compulsion to conceive—Schelling feels compelled to defend himself against the (mis)understandings of his contemporaries Eschenmayer and Georgii.[13]

Misunderstandings do arise here, Schelling assures us, on account of the obduracy (*Eigendünkel*) that, as Kant taught, is the root of evil itself. Such misunderstandings not only betray obduracy but are also accompanied by "womanish wailing" (*die weibischen Klagen*), namely, the loud lament of philosophers who are afraid of the dark (7:360). It is not Schelling's God but Schelling's critics who show themselves to be womanish.

One may object to Schelling's polemical and even sardonic sally against modern idealist philosophy by posing the question: Why *womanish*, when it is longing herself, *die Sehnsucht*, from which the effete philosopher-critics shrink? It is already clear that Schelling wants to retain the (negative) feminine as a pillory and a polemic, while the deepest insights of his own critique of modern philosophy *and* his nascent pantheism need the (positive) feminine as their most profound resource. This objection stands—until we reach *The Ages of the World*, and perhaps even after that. But let us return to the freedom essay, which now advances beyond polemic to Schelling's positive account of the ground of the divine essence.

12. William Arrowsmith, in the introduction to his translation of *The Bacchae*, in *Euripides V* (Chicago: University of Chicago Press, 1968), 146.
13. For the Schelling-Eschenmayer correspondence, see 8:137–189; see also Horst Fuhrmans's note, 147.

For if misunderstandings do arise here, more than obduracy lies behind them. Indeed, Schelling concedes that it is extremely difficult to think back beyond the realm of the ordered universe, where all is rule and measure, to the remote past of Chaos. The word *Sehnsucht*, Schelling explains, designates a reality that we can no longer observe in and of itself; the reality it represents has long been repressed (*verdrängt*) by something "higher" (7:359). Our will to know "intimates" this remote past, says Schelling, here employing the word that in *The Ages of the World* will refer to our relation to the future, to wit, *Ahndung*. Yet the contradiction is only apparent. For the remote past, having been repressed, can only be our future. Nevertheless, something about languor exceeds all the dimensions of time: *Sehnsucht* designates "the ungraspable basis of reality, the remnant that is never wholly absorbed [*die unergreifliche Basis der Realität, der nie aufgehende Rest*]" and that "remains eternally in the ground" (7:360).

The primal will, as yet unconscious and devoid of intellect, wants to give birth to itself as intellect and will proper. Concerning this birth—for we have not by any means left behind the figure of *Scheidung* as gestation and birth—Schelling writes:

> All birth is birth from darkness into light; the kernel of seed must be implanted in the earth, dying in gloom, in order that the more beautiful configuration of light [*Lichtgestalt*] arise and unfold along the beams of the sun. The human being is formed in the mother's womb;[14] and from the darkness of what is without understanding (from feeling, languor, the magnificent mother of knowledge) first burgeon buoyant thoughts.[15] Thus we must represent to ourselves the original languor [*die ursprüngliche Sehnsucht*], which indeed orients itself toward the understanding that it does not yet grasp, just as in longing we yearn for some unknown and nameless good; and, moving on an intimation, languor bestirs itself as does a swelling, seething sea, like Platonic matter, according to an obscure and uncertain law, unable to form for itself something lasting. (Ibid.)

Languor longs for the intellect, of which it is only vaguely aware. It bestirs itself and orients itself in the direction of the understanding. Yet it heaves and subsides, *wogend wallend*, like the sea, presumably without goal, purpose, or end. Thus Schelling reads Plato's *Timaeus*, a text to which he had devoted

---

14. In the first edition, the edition Schelling himself saw through the press, the phrase reads *wird in Mutterleibe gebildet*, almost suggesting that "the human being is formed *into* the mother's womb." Schelling's son, seeing the dative ending of *Mutterleibe*, quite rightly altered the father's preposition *in* to *im*, thus rescuing the sense, thus rescuing sense, thus sensing rescue, etc.

15. "Light" is of course the opposite of darkness, *Dunkel*. The "configuration of light" (perhaps to be thought preeminently in terms of Goethe's *Metamorphosis of Plants*) rises and unfolds along the beams of the sun. Yet this means that *die lichten Gedanken* are not only luminous but also buoyant and ascensional. The original pendant to "light" in Schelling's text (see 7:358) is not darkness but gravity, mass, or weight, *Schwerkraft*.

an unpublished commentary some fifteen years earlier.[16] In 1809 he still confronts the irresolvable enigma of the conjunction of Logos and Ananke in a world where "female parts" subsist solely as supplements, that is, as essential yet essentially extraneous components of the system.[17] In order to rescue the divine essence from the all-engulfing duplicity of Logos-Ananke, as though from what Melville calls "the shroud of the sea," Schelling now endeavors to neutralize the metaphors (if that is what they are) of languor, procreation, fecundation, and birth: "However, in accord with the languor which, as the still obscure ground, is the first stirring of divine existence, there is generated in God himself [*erzeugt sich in Gott selbst*] an inner reflexive representation through which, because it can have no other object than God, God envisages himself in a likeness [*durch welche . . . Gott sich selbst in einem Ebenbilde erblickt*]" (7:360–361). The icon or eidolon that God espies in his inner reflexive representation appears to transmogrify itself, Proteus-like, from scene to scene in Schelling's *Philosophical Investigations*. At times that representation, or *Vorstellung*, appears to be the Word itself, the full presence of the eye and voice of the Father; at other times it appears as the Son, as Christology, or as the union of Son and Father in the (Holy) Spirit; finally, it appears at the center of the circle of humankind, also made in the image and likeness of the Father—although one is compelled to ask, in this story of fathers and sons, what has happened to the woman who produces them in all their differences. Be

16. See now F. W. J. Schelling, *"Timaeus" (1794)*, ed. Hartmut Buchner (Stuttgart-Bad Cannstadt: Frommann-Holzboog, 1994). On "preexistent primal matter" and its lawlessness (*Regellosigkeit*, the selfsame word Schelling uses in 1809 [7:359–360]), see the *Timaeus* commentary, 27. The question of ἀνάγκη becomes particularly pressing from 50 onward, where Schelling investigates the sort of "necessity," as opposed to intellect, that is at work in matter, and poses the question concerning the possibility of "persuasion" as the intellect's way of negotiating necessity. Schelling himself has not yet in 1794 made the discovery of *die Sehnsucht*, the languorous yearning that inheres in matter itself. Only on the final two pages of his commentary does he broach the famous question of the Platonic χώρα, without using this term explicitly. Yet Schelling is clearly aware that the perduring substance, which for Plato hovers somewhere between matter and space, is the central and as yet unresolved puzzle of *Timaeus*. More than a puzzle, it is the baffling aporia (*Verlegenheit*) from which philosophy never escapes, the aporia that can be broached only by a bastard reasoning and as though in a dream. For an insightful analysis of Schelling's commentary on Plato's *Timaeus* (and on other Platonic writings), see Anna Vaughn Clissold, "Schelling's Commentary on Plato's *Timaeus*" (Ph.D. dissertation, DePaul University, 1998). See also John Sallis, *Chorology: On Plato's* Timaeus (Bloomington: Indiana University Press, 2000), and Jacques Derrida, *Khôra* (Paris: Galilée, 1993). Finally, see JV 1:134–168.

17. In the freedom essay (7:390), Plato's "bastard reasoning," λογισμῷ τινι νόθῳ, becomes "false imagination," which ponders in vain the irresolvable enigma of Necessity, or Ananke. The Zwiebrücken (Bipontus) edition, which he cites (7:349), offers Ficino's translation of the phrase as *adulterina ratione*. The deleterious *falsche Imagination* has as its opposite *wahre Ein-Bildung*, "true informing imagination" in the womb of knowledge (7:362). Such in-forming imagination, however, and the "necessity" to which it would appeal are not easily detached from bastard reasoning or false imagination, inasmuch as all the ancient names for necessity are female. Roberto Calasso: "Adrasteia, Moira, Tyche, Ananke, Atē, Aisa, Dikē, Nemesis, Erinyes, Heimarmene: such are the names that embody necessity. And they are all women" (RC 124).

that as it may, Schelling for the most part successfully resists the shape of Proteus that both Goethe and Nietzsche perceive as the fruit of the original separation in God's essence—the shape of Lucifer.[18]

A peripheral reading cannot thematize or even summarize in any detail *die Scheidung der Kräfte*, the "scission" or "sundering" of forces, that now occupies Schelling's *Investigations*. It can merely observe that such scission conducts us back to the point where we began—with the metaphor of illness and with Archaeus's abandonment of the serene center. The essence or original principle abandons the center and, in crisis, loses itself on the periphery. One final glimpse of this crisis on the human scene, a glimpse we are granted during the course of Schelling's description of "the formal essence of freedom," awaits us. Schelling is discussing "the eternal deed," *die ewige Tat*, by which humanity—in some time prior to all times, in some ineffable coeval eternity—freely performs the deed that determines its troubled nature:

> This universal judgment of a proclivity to evil, which in terms of its origins is entirely unconscious and indeed irresistible, as an act of freedom points to a deed and thus to a life prior to this life; except that it may not be thought of as preceding in terms of time, inasmuch as the intelligible is altogether outside of time.[19] Because supreme consonance prevails in creation, and because nothing occurs in separation and sequence [*nichts so getrennt und nacheinander*], which is the way we are constrained to represent it, but where the later is also at work in the earlier and everything happens simultaneously in one magic stroke [*alles in Einem magischen Schlage*], because of this, humanity, which appears here decisively and determinately, is captured in a determinate shape in the first creation and is born as what it was from all eternity, inasmuch as, by means of that deed, the very type and particular quality of its corporization [*die Art und Beschaffenheit seiner Korporisation*] is determined. (7:387)

The passage has to do with determinations, *Bestimmungen*, essential determinations that are difficult to visualize.[20] These determinations arise "in one magic stroke," at a single *coup*, falling at the stroke of one, from all eternity. Not only the human proclivity to evil, its obdurate inclination to things peripheral, is explained by this deed, but presumably also the peculiar nature of the human being's embodiment, *die Art und Beschaffenheit seiner Korporisation*. The word

---

18. See Nietzsche's various accounts of his rediscovery, at age twelve, of Goethe's insight into the likelihood that Lucifer is the second person of the Trinity: KSA 5:249, 8:505, and 11:253, 616.

19. Compare Schelling's earlier remarks (7:358) on the "circle" of time and eternity, a circle that precludes both priority in time and priority of essence.

20. There can be no doubt that the eternal deed of which Schelling writes here has to do with the problem of the "intelligible character" posed by Kant's Critical project. I cannot enter into this difficult and fascinating area of questions, but recommend to my readers the excellent treatment by Don Kelly Coble, "Inscrutable Intelligibility: Intelligible Character and Deed in Kant, Schelling, Mach, and Musil" (Ph.D. dissertation, DePaul University, 1999).

Art, in Schelling's German, means (among other things) "species," and it is usually taken as including both sexes. Yet in Hegel's philosophy of nature the word for "species" is *Gattung,* where the *Arten* designate distinct male and female genders (HW 9:500–519; §§368–369). It is therefore difficult to know what precisely Schelling is thinking of when he writes *Art und Beschaffenheit.* The intriguing phrase could refer to any specific or intraspecific property of human embodiment, to head, hands, or feet. It may be excessive or merely eccentric to read it as sexual difference and opposition. Yet can a peripheral reading such as ours, here, preoccupied as it is with the metaphorics of center and circumference, fecundity and sterility, wholeness and mutilation, the languor of God and the draw of the magnificent mother (as opposed to womanish wailing), read the phrase any other way? To be sure, the proclivity to read the phrase this way, while no doubt evil, does not seem to bring us one flea-hop closer to our problem (as Marx would say). For why should there be any connection between sexual difference and the deed that ushered evil into the world? Is the ancient mytheme of Eve and Adam, or of Lilith and Adam, guiding Schelling's thought at this point? Is the magic stroke of embodiment—the genitally bifurcated body of the human animal—the curse and plague of evil as such? Would such bifurcation go some way toward accounting for at least the negative guise of the female in Schelling's text? Is bifurcated embodiment, at the stroke of one, in essence female? That is to say, are we witnessing here the force of the traditional hierarchy of intellect over coarse matter, *der Verstand* (masculine) in opposition to *die Materie* (feminine)? Furthermore, if the human and divine centers tend to elide in Schelling's text, elide and coalesce, so that the "likeness" of God, whether as Self, Christ, Spirit, or Son of Man, is radically undecidable, would not the eternal deed of humankind recoil on the divine essence as such? If during the years 1810 to 1815 Schelling remains fascinated by the consequences of his insight that the terminal point of God's every path—the *finis viarum Dei* (8:325)—is embodiment, does not the opening of an ineluctable duality in the divine essence itself both promise to advance science and threaten to annihilate it? If the ground of existence is that which in God himself is not he himself, must not Schelling cross out *Selbst* and write (if only in dialect) *Gott anderst?* Must not Schelling cross out the masculine pronoun and introduce the feminine? Not God himself, but God himother? God herself? And would that, in Schelling's view, imply anything less than God's self-emasculation, the magic stroke of evil incarnate, so that the eunuchs of ancient Christendom and modern Western philosophy will prove to have been right all along? "The appearance of the world came about with the copulation of a god with that which was not god, with the laceration and dispersion of a god's body; it was the expulsion into space of a cloud of infected matter, infested by the sacred" (RC 293).

An Indifferent Reading of Schelling's Treatise on Human Freedom

Even if we persist on the periphery of Schelling's *Philosophical Investigations*, advancing along the perimeter of his metaphorics of *Scheidung*, we will find our way to a point of absolute indifference. Schelling calls it "the supreme point of the entire investigation" (7:406). It is presumably the point at which existence and ground in the essence undergo ultimate scission, the point at which judgment, as κρίσις, putatively expels every ill and all evil and proclaims the rule of love—a love ostensibly beyond the ravages of languishment. Even though our circling about the periphery has hardly prepared us to occupy this supreme point, let us try to follow Schelling's text quite closely here—if only, for the most part, by way of paraphrase.[21]

Schelling returns to his starting point, which is the insight achieved by the philosophy and science of nature. What purpose does that first differentiation within essence—insofar as it is *ground* and insofar as it *exists*—serve? If ground and existence never interpenetrate and share no midpoint, the inevitable result is dualism and the collapse of every system of reason. Science must therefore strive to find that *Mittelpunkt*. It cannot be found in the absolute identity of opposites (light and dark, buoyant and heavy, good and evil), inasmuch as absolute identity would mean stasis, the dull decrepitude of all such systems. Science must therefore insist that at the very stroke of one there is but *one* essence, *one* essence *prior to* every ground and *prior to* everything else that exists—although, presumably, such priority can be thought in terms of neither time nor causality nor ontological eminence. What else can we call it, Schelling asks, than the *primal ground*, or, rather, the *nonground*? In Schelling's text (". . . *wie können wir es anders nennen als den Urgrund oder vielmehr* Ungrund?"), the primal, primordial, incipient, originary ground and the nonground are brought into the closest possible proximity: only a single letter distinguishes them, and not even an entire letter, inasmuch as here it is merely a matter of expanding a single stroke of one letter, extending the arc of the *r* in *Urgrund* to the *n* of *Ungrund*. That one downward stroke of the pen, performed at the stroke of one, alters origins to nihilations. The (original) nonground, which is the nonorigin of all grounds, precedes both opposition and identity, all binary sets and straightforwardly oppositional units, every dualism

---

21. For the following analyses, paraphrases, and quotations, see 7:406–408.

and every monism. It is insufficient to call it a *coincidentia oppositorum*, after the manner of certain well-known systems from Cusa to Böhme and Baader. In the case of the individual members of every eventual oppositional pair, *der Ungrund* can only be "the absolute *indifference* [Indifferenz] of both."[22]

It is as though the primal essence has always already passed through *Scheidung* and so has become *ein geschiedenes Wesen*, a thing apart, whose development lies far behind it. To be sure, that would urge the question as to why such an essence would need to develop at all, why its trajectory would be futural, inasmuch as what is essential to it would already have been accomplished for it in the remote past. Schelling does not put that question, at least not yet; his approach to the realm of the "indifferent" is tenuous, to say the least. No predicates adhere to the undifferentiated essence, especially not those of "good" or "evil." The essence in its nonground is, if we may say so, quite beyond good and evil—or, if not beyond, then well on the hither side of them. Yet Schelling shrinks from the consequences of such indifference; he quickly calls for a restoration of sorts. "Nothing can stop us," he declares, from predicating *both* opposites *in disjunction*, not as opposites but as a sheer *duality*. "Nothing can hinder us [*aber es hindert nichts*]," inasmuch as the original nonground is careless of both good and evil: *gleichgültig*, indifferent, not in the sense of "insouciant," but in the sense that the two members of the disjunction are equally valid, literally *gleich-gültig*. Nonground is a neither-nor, a neutral *ne-uter* from which all duality (and all eventual opposition) can proceed. "*Without* indifference, that is, *without* a nonground, there would be no twofold of principles."

It may astonish us to learn that Schelling's speculation on the nonground derives from none other than Kant. In the "Critique of All Speculative Theology" in the *Critique of Pure Reason*, Kant tries to show that the ideas of pure reason in and of themselves can no longer be viewed as dialectical; only their "misuse" by the "rabble of rationalizers" distorts these ideas, which are originally granted to reason "by the nature of our reason," and which therefore *cannot* be

---

22. Compare the crucial role of "absolute indifference" in Hegel's Logic, as the "Becoming of Essence," the culmination of the doctrine of being, which I can only note here, without commenting on it. See Wissenschaft der Logik, Part I, "Objective Logic," Division 3, "Measure," ch. 3. Perhaps it is also worth noting that in his account of human genitality, in the 1805–1806 Jena Realphilosophie, Hegel designates the uterus as das Indifferente. For the sources and discussion of them, see Krell, Contagion, 133–140, along with the corresponding notes. As for thinking through the consequences of the *Ungrund*, I agree entirely with David L. Clark that to plumb the *Ungrund* "would be the most difficult thing to do," and that "we cannot be sure that Schelling does it." See David L. Clark, "The Necessary Heritage of Darkness: Tropics of Negativity in Schelling, Derrida, and de Man," in Tilottama Rajan and David L. Clark, ed., *Intersections: Nineteenth-Century Philosophy and Contemporary Theory* (Albany: State University Press of New York, 1995), 137; cited in Martin Wallen, *City of Health, Fields of Disease: Revolutions in the Poetry, Medicine, and Philosophy of Romanticism* (Aldershot, Hampshire, England: Ashgate, 2004), 188n. 13.

naturally dialectical (KrV B697ff.). Thus what earlier on in the *Critique,* indeed, from the outset, appeared to be the natural proclivity of reason (to pose questions it cannot answer) and a fate or fatality (to try to expand its knowledge where it can only interpret and purify it) turns out to be a mere blooper committed by a "lazy" or "perverted" reason. We industrious and upright critics can permit ourselves to employ "certain anthropomorphisms," writes Kant (B725), inasmuch as these anthropomorphisms are placed in the ἄνθρωπος by "the wise intention" of the Demiurge himself. Eminent among these anthropomorphisms is the presupposition concerning the "regulative principle of the systematic unity of the world." In the first edition of the *Critique* Kant calls the systematic unity of the world "this *'primal ground' [dieser* 'Urgrund'] of cosmic unity in itself" (A697); in the second edition (B725) he alters *"Urgrund"* to *"Ungrund,"* primal ground to nonground, even though many editors and commentators even today take the alteration to be, ironically, not a correction but a blooper on Kant's part. To have made such a blooper, with the stroke of one, and precisely when one wanted to regulate others! But to return once again to sobriety and Schelling.

Sensing that his own "dialectical discussion" of duality resembles all too closely the logical legerdemain he elsewhere derides, Schelling proceeds as follows (7:407–408): "The essence of the ground, like the essence of what exists, can only be what *precedes* every ground, hence the absolute considered purely and simply, the nonground." Formula: essence = the absolute = nonground. Whereas Schelling's text has heretofore interpreted the ground of essence, a ground that is *in* the essence but not *of* it, in terms of a compelling and spontaneous languor, *die Sehnsucht,* the danger of that *Scheidung* in essence now prods the text to conjure an absolute that is prior to ("prior to" in "scare quotes," since it is impossible to say or think this "prior to") all scission. So far, the absolute has received only a negative name, a name Schelling prefers over the invocation of origins: the proper name of the absolute is not *Urgrund* but *Ungrund.* "Yet the nonground can be the absolute (as demonstrated) in no other way than by diverging into two equally eternal commencements [*zwei gleich ewige Anfänge*]; not that it is both commencements *simultaneously* [zugleich], but that in each of them it *is in the same way* [gleicherweise]; it is thus the whole in each, or an essence all its own [*in jedem das Ganze, oder ein eignes Wesen*]."

Somehow—inexplicably—the divergence into *two* commencements, *two* eternities (one thinks of the "two eternities" that "affront one another" in the gateway called "blink of an eye," *Augenblick,* in *Thus Spoke Zarathustra,* Part III, "On the Vision and the Riddle" [KSA 4:199–200]), leaves the wholeness and ipseity of the absolute untouched. By itself alone, ab-solute, One becomes Two. Una clasps the hand of Dua—at least before (until? after?) the stroke of One.

Schelling must now explain (or explain away) the bifurcation of nonground as both essential and transient, both eternal and temporal/temporary. He must explain (or explain away) the very possibility of a second, nonsimultaneous eternal commencement. He must explain (or explain away) how the initial commencement leaves the wholeness and propriety of essence without a trace, so that the second commencement *can be* a commencement. The κρίσις of the absolute, *die Scheidung*, will conform utterly to what Derrida (in a different yet related context) has elaborated as "the logic of the supplement."[23] Schelling continues:

> Yet the nonground divides itself into the two equally eternal commencements solely in order that the two which are in it as nonground, and which could not be simultaneous or be one, become one through love. That is to say, the nonground sunders itself merely in order that there be life and love and personal existence. For love is neither in indifference nor there where opposites are joined, opposites that need joining in order to be; rather (to repeat a phrase already invoked), this is the mystery of love, that it joins beings that could be each for itself alone and yet are not and cannot be without the other. (7:408)

Love requires an initial divergence, an incipient sundering, as do life and personal existence. Schelling will later (7:425) call this divergence a "doubling" (*Doublierung*) of essence, "thus an enhancement of unity." The mystery and enigma of love is that it freely fuses the duality that it itself inaugurates; or, to put it the other way around, love initially severs that which it is destined to anneal. Original violence, nihilation, is the secret life of love. Hegel carries over Schelling's insight into his *Philosophy of Right* when he observes that love is "the most monstrous contradiction, one that the intellect cannot resolve," inasmuch as "love is the introduction and the resolution of the contradiction at one and the same time" (HW 7:308). Each fragment of the resulting duality *could* be for itself alone (*sein könnte*, a hypothetical subjunctive that is disquietingly close to a subjunctive contrary-to-fact, *Irreales*), and yet each *is not* and *cannot* be (*nicht ist, und nicht sein kann:* indicative) without its other. Original violence, in the indicative, is real. "Therefore, just as duality comes to be in the nonground, so also does love come to be, a love that joins what exists (the ideal) with the ground of existence. However, the ground remains free and independent of the Word up to the final total scission [*bis zur endlichen gänzlichen Scheidung*]."[24]

"Up to," "until": *bis zur*. The nonground is in process, as we have been as-

---

23. Jacques Derrida, *De la grammatologie* (Paris: Minuit, 1967), 207–234 and 441–445; English translation by Gayatri Chakravorty Spivak, *Of Grammatology* (Baltimore: Johns Hopkins University Press, 1976), 144–164 and 313–316.

24. Compare the phrase *der notwendige Weg zur endlichen wirklichen Differenzierung*, from the *Stuttgarter Privatvorlesungen* (7:426).

sured from the beginning, even though we are uncertain about what *process* can mean for the two coeval yet nonsimultaneous commencements, the two eternities, that the essence always already has behind it, as it were, in its remote past. The remote past, *die Vergangenheit*, will itself become the principal problem for Schelling in the ensuing years, as he contemplates *The Ages of the World*. Yet even in these later years Schelling will insist that the nonground is unfolding, is in development: something always awaits it and draws it on. What awaits it? What draws it? The moment (of eternity, or of two eternities) that awaits the essence and that opens up a future for it is the moment when nothing will remain independent of its Word. Yet that moment is now envisaged not as one of conjunction (*Verbindung*) but as one of divorce (*Scheidung*). And not just any divorce: the essence waits upon the advent of a scission that will be *endlich* and *gänzlich*. Presumably, *endlich* here means "final" and not "finite," inasmuch as the primal (non)ground could hardly be expected to suffer finite division—that would surely spell the *end* of its life, its love, and its personal existence. *Final*, then, in the sense of *ultimate*. Ultimate in the sense of a *culminating, consummating, apocalyptic* sundering. Apocalyptic and *gänzlich*, "total." At long last (*endlich!*), a total sundering, a scission of the whole (*das Ganze*), the whole that each of the two eternal commencements sustains. At long last, the end of languor and languishment. Yet if the nonground initially diverges (*auseinandergeht*), solely in order to allow the doubling or the fold of love, why and how should its process culminate in *Scheidung*, total divorce? Love, the end of all languor? Love, without languishing? Love as divorce?

Both predicates of scission (*endlich, gänzlich*) prove to be troublesome. *Endlich*, we said, cannot refer to finitude, and yet Schelling's text now suddenly shifts to the scene of finite humanity. *Gänzlich*, we said, should refer to the restoration of wholeness by love and life, not by divorce and death, and yet Schelling's text now suddenly shifts to the scene of mortality. But to continue, now presenting the German text first, in order to allow the pronoun *er* to implicate the words (the words *and* the things designated by the words) *der Grund, der Ungrund, der Gott*, and *der Mensch* in the tangled syntax of scission:

> Dann [d.h. in der endlichen gänzlichen Scheidung] löst er [d.h. der Grund] sich auf, wie im Menschen, wenn er [d.h. der Mensch] zur Klarheit übergeht und als bleibendes Wesen sich gründet, die anfängliche Sehnsucht sich löst, indem alles Wahre und Gute in ihr ins lichte Bewußtsein erhoben wird, alles andre aber, das Falsche nämlich und Unreine, auf ewig in die Finsternis beschlossen, um als ewig dunkler Grund der Selbstheit, als *Caput mortuum* seines Lebensprozesses und als Potenz zurückzubleiben, die nie zum Aktus hervorgehen kann. (7:408)

Then [that is, in the final, total scission] it [that is, the ground] is dissolved, as in
the human being, when it is transfigured and is established as perdurant essence,
when the incipient languor dissipates, inasmuch as everything true and good in
it is elevated to buoyant consciousness, but everything else, namely, the false and
impure, is sealed off eternally in gloom, in order to remain back behind as the
eternally dark ground of selfhood, as the dross of its life-process and as a potency
that can never proceed to act.

Schelling's dream (a dream from which, as we shall see in our account of
The Ages of the World, he must awaken) is that a final divorce will sever, at the
stroke of one, the languor and the languishing that have defined the very life
of essence from the outset. In humans, "incipient languor" ceases only in
death and transfiguration. The term *caput mortuum* refers to the lifeless, value-
less residue of an alchemical or industrial process—the dross of a metal casting, for example, destined to be sloughed off and discarded. Another name for
the *caput mortuum* in alchemy is *earth.*

It ought to give us pause if the ultimate insight of the philosophy and science of nature is that earth, the stuff of nature, is the waste product of divine
elimination or the unabsorbed yet ineliminable residue of consciousness.
Where would essence find the space to bury such excreta? For if its waste perdures back behind it (*zurückbleibt*), will it not contaminate the perdurant
essence (*das bleibende Wesen*), even and especially if the "dead-head" should
appear to be lifeless? Can it be lifeless? A potency with no latency, no dor-
mancy, no deferral, no subterranean life? Was it not a "kernel of seed" that
earlier was said to have been "implanted in the gloom"? Must not the ground
be a living germ rather than a dead-head? Finally, what would be the difference between the two sorts of *bleiben* or *Bleibe,* that of the transfigured essence
and that of the eternally turbid ground? The final, finite, whole and total reduction of living seed to dead waste, of semen and egg to lifeless effluvia—
would not such a separation be a fatal stroke to the (divine) personality?

None of these questions receives a convincing answer—at least until the
earliest sketches toward *The Ages of the World,* to be examined in chapters 4
through 6 of this volume. However, let us continue the quotation, bringing
both it and our own indifferent reading to a close:

Then all will be subordinate to spirit. In spirit whatever exists is one with the
ground of existence; in spirit both are actually simultaneous; in other words, spirit
is the absolute identity of both. However, above spirit [*über dem Geist*] is the incipient nonground. It is no longer indifference (equal validity [*Gleichgültigkeit*]),

nor is it the identity of both principles; rather, it is unity in general, which is equal to all things while captive to none of them, the beneficence that is free from all things while pervading them all—in one word, love, which is all in all. (7:408)

Much is left hanging here, suspended in utter ambiguity. And all of it has to do with the loving, languorous way in which Una grips the hand of Dua before the stroke of One severs that loved clasp. Existence and ground are said to be one for spirit—immediately after ground has been said to have been subjected to final, total scission. The two coeval commencements were earlier said to be *not* simultaneous; now existence and ground are said to be simultaneous in spirit. Spirit is said to be the absolute identity of existence and ground, with everything else *subordinate to* it; yet the nonground is also said to be *superior to* spirit. Moreover, all that is incipient (*anfänglich*), namely, all that the ground contains, is said to be transfigured by the scission; yet the nonground that is superior to spirit is itself also said to be *anfänglich*. Indifference is said to be left behind, albeit not in absolute identity. Rather, love is to be that all-unifying force that is captive to nothing it unifies. In the final, total scission, languor and longing, the languid and languishment, appear to submit forever to beneficence or altruism, *Wohltun*. The secret of human (and divine?) freedom is said to be all-pervasive love, achieved at one stroke.

An indifferent reading, such as the present one, cannot resolve the most troubling questions that Schelling's text raises. If one has difficulty accepting the traditional phantasm and sophism of a love that is absolutely disinterested, a love that is not in the least captivated by what it captures, is "the will of love" at all distinguishable from the incipient languor and languishment that permeate and animate the ground of essence? Is it simply a matter of differentiating the "central essence," namely, humankind, from the divine essence? Can beneficence be attributed to the latter, and evil to the former, without collapsing back into the most supine of dogmatic positions? Or must not the realm of evil that humankind inhabits be seen as utterly coextensive with the kingdom of God? When Schelling writes of evil that "it is not an essence but a non-essence," *ein Unwesen*, even if *Unwesen* might have the sense of "sinister doings," is not he too merely aping Augustine? Is he not merely displacing the problem of evil "one point farther down the line," without resolving it? Can the phantasmatic hope of a final, total scission be understood in any other way than as a seduction by the most banal of traditional stratagems, a quick trip through Purgatory on the highway to Paradise, a quick slash of the knife? Banal, inasmuch as "the stroke of one" has to be taken also in the sense of the *genitivus obiectivus*, that is, as the One that severs itself. Una, at the stroke of One, is already Two, which explains why she is always at sixes and sevens.

Does not Schelling himself see, if only darkly, that the divine essence—become life, love, personality, and process—proceeds unswervingly toward the abyss of its own womanhood, its own manhood, its own languishment, and its own death, so that the apocalypse of an *endlichen gänzlichen Scheidung* is either the feverish self-mutilation or the progressive paralysis of God? Does he not see that the ultimate scission within essence would be a crisis of reason with which no system of reason could possibly cope? Does he not in fact see that there is something traumatic about both divine and human existence—perhaps the very trauma of animal existence?[25]

25. On this system that is "no longer a system," destroyed by the scission of ground and existence and by a cut no *Seynsfüge* can mend, see Martin Heidegger, *Schellings Abhandlung über das Wesen der menschlichen Freiheit (1809)* (Tübingen: M. Niemeyer, 1971), esp. 194. Heidegger too sees that the breakdown of the system has everything to do with languor and languishment. He does not neglect the issue of *Sehnsucht* in Schelling; on the contrary, that issue lies at the center of the 1936 Schelling course. Heidegger tries to avoid every conception of creation in terms of fabrication and of "the gigantic," *des Riesenhaften*. That is the term he chooses to designate the totality of being as conceived by National Socialism. In brief, Heidegger argues that Schelling succeeds in interrupting the fatal tie that binds ontotheology from Plato—through the metaphysical subjectivity of modernity since Descartes and Leibniz—to the technology of gigantism. The difficulty with his reading is that his analysis of *Sehnsucht* remains too rigid, too "hard and heavy," too militant and even bellicose: to languor and even love Heidegger attaches the predicates of "grandest struggle" (*größter Kampf*), "most profound strife" (*tiefster Streit*), and "self-mastery" ([*Selbst-*]*Bewältigung*) (195). At the same time—and it is a time when all the world wants to expose and banish Heidegger once and for all as a philosopher of the selfsame, and the worst of the selfsame—one must confront the fact that Heidegger makes himself indispensable precisely in the question of otherness and the Other. Not only Lévinas and Derrida but Heidegger too writes remarkably of such an "otherwise," and nowhere more passionately than in the case of Schelling: "The essence of the ground in God is languor? Here we can scarcely restrain the objection that this statement projects a human condition onto God—. Quite right. Yet matters could also be otherwise. For who has ever demonstrated that languor is something purely human? And who has been able to refute conclusively, with sufficient reasons, the possibility that what we call *Sehnsucht*, which is the condition in which we stand, ultimately is something other than we ourselves? Does there not lie concealed in languor something that gives us *no right* to limit it to human being, something that would sooner give us cause to grasp it as that in which we humans *are liberated out beyond our limits* [*über uns weg* entschränkt werden]? Is not precisely such languor proof of the fact that human being is something other than mere human being [*daß der Mensch ein Anderes ist als nur so ein Mensch*]?" (150). Derrida has commented insightfully on Heidegger's Schelling course in this respect. See Jacques Derrida, *De l'esprit: Heidegger et la question* (Paris: Galilée, 1987), esp. 122–124; English translation by Geoffrey Bennington and Rachel Bowlby, *Of Spirit: Heidegger and the Question* (Chicago: University of Chicago Press, 1989), 79–82. Finally, at the risk of repeating material I analyzed in *Daimon Life* (especially the section of ch. 9 that is entitled "Stirrings of Languorous Divinity," 296–300), I want to add a word on the limitations of Heidegger's reading of Schelling. "Bestirring," *Regung*, is the word Heidegger chooses to characterize the languor (*Sehnsucht*) in the essence of the divine ground. Significantly, it is the word he will use in his language essays of the 1950s to designate the action of the words of language. The stirring, or bestirring, of divinity in languor has nothing to do with sentimentality, he assures us in the Schelling lectures. In his discussion of languor, Heidegger is trying to designate "the *essence* of the *ruling metaphysical animatedness*" in the divine as such. After stressing the relationship of *Sehnsucht* to *Sucht* and *Seuche*, that is, to addiction and disease, he argues that divine

The two readings ventured here, the peripheral and the indifferent—are they indeed two? If circulating on the periphery leads us willy-nilly to the point of indifference, if on the circumference of Schelling's system we are always already at the point of indifference, how can we hope to maintain the distinction between these two presumed modes of reading? The centrifugal force that casts us from the center to the periphery does not simply abandon us there. Our intention to remain on the outer perimeter of the system, far from its central claims, and to rest content with metaphors and images of scission, whether of self-mutilation or of birth, finds itself suddenly reversed: the reader of Schelling enters *volens nolens* into the labyrinth of indifference, that undifferentiated state anterior to all the binary oppositions that enable our logical and technological systems to function. The reader enters into the center, but finds that the center is itself eternally displaced, askew, eccentric, elliptical. The reader begins to move, hesitates, ill-assured, longing to resolve once and for all and at a single stroke all the problems over which Schelling himself languishes. To read Schelling is to learn to lament the loss of the center of meaning, which has become a cinder, and to lament that loss forever. To read Schelling is to feel, perhaps in perpetuity, a sense of languishment, languishment to the point of melancholy, and melancholy to the point of tragic peripety.

Neither a peripheral reading nor an indifferent one can fully appreciate the enormity of Schelling's undertaking. Recalling William Faulkner's own estimation of his early masterwork, *The Sound and the Fury*, we may be content to acclaim Schelling's *Philosophical Investigations into the Essence of Human Freedom* "the most splendid failure" in the history of metaphysics— the most splendid failure *of* metaphysics. It is a failure, to repeat, that will lead to Schelling's never-completed magnum opus, *The Ages of the World.* If the latter is a book about Αἰών, Heraclitus's child at play, tossing the dice with a

---

languor and languishment resist the Word; indeed, *Sehnsucht* is essentially *nameless;* wherever languor prevails, "*the possibility of the word* is missing" (151). Oddly, what Heidegger fails to note is that it is this absence of words and the Word—the absence of both language and the Christological interpretation of the Word as disembodied Love—that brings the divine essence into the greatest possible proximity to *animal life* as such. The essentially nameless bestirring of languor in the essence of God is "the absolute beginning of an egress-from-self" (ibid.). Schelling himself calls languor "the first stirring of divine existence," *die erste Regung göttlichen Daseins* (7:360–361). That stirring bestirs divinity to Creation: the animatedness of becoming (*Werdebewegtheit*) has its source in the incipient stirring and excitation in the dark ground of *Sehnsucht* (159). Yet the secret of the divine ecstasy, or egress, plays no role in Heidegger's own fundamental ontology and only the most minor role in his "other commencement." Heidegger's inadequate response to just-plain-life in *Being and Time,* whether it be the life of Dasein or of other animals, will return to haunt his later thought when it is *language* that bestirs presencing. Heidegger never returns to the reign of Chaos, which is prior to the reigns of humankind *and* divinity. That was the eon in which we could hear, understand, and speak to the other animals (Plato, *Statesman,* 272b–c). Because he never made the return, however, his history of being as truth, and of truth as unconcealment, collapses back into classic metaphysical distinctions.

laugh (DK B52), its thought is nonetheless the weightiest thought of metaphysics. Indeed, in the three drafts of *The Ages of the World*, Schelling's weightiest thought reaches back behind metaphysics to the tragic sensibility of our oldest narratives, tales from Sumer, Neith, Palestine, Phoenicia, Samothrace, and ancient Attica—stories from Gilgamesh to Ecclesiastes to Aeschylus. One sees unmistakable signs of this tragic sensibility in Schelling, certainly by the 1809 treatise on human freedom, where at the stroke of one his nocturnal thoughts turn about the languishing absolute. Beyond the polemical sallies of his *Philosophical Investigations*, beyond the bravado of all the ontotheological maneuvers, and beyond the daylight dream of a redemptive Word, a "source of sadness" (*ein Quell der Traurigkeit*) permeates Schelling's writings during these years and flows freely into the troubled future that is our own. From that source of sadness and mourning, spreading like a veil of waterfall, "comes the pall of despondency [*der Schleier der Schwermut*] that is draped over the whole of nature—the profound and indestructible melancholy of all life [*die tiefe unzerstörliche Melancholie alles Lebens*]" (7:399).

GOD'S TRAUMA

4

Perhaps there hovers over all things a magnificent maternity, a collective languor.

—RAINER MARIA RILKE, *Letters to a Young Poet*

Here is the primal source of the bitterness that is intrinsic in all life. Indeed, there must be bitterness. Bitterness must irrupt immediately, as soon as life is no longer sweetened. For love itself is compelled toward hate. In hate, the tranquil, gentle spirit can achieve no effects, but is oppressed by the enmity into which the exigency of life transposes all our forces. From this comes the deep despondency concealed in all life; without such despondency there can be no actuality—it is life's poison, which wants to be overcome, yet without which life would drift in endless slumber.

—SCHELLING, *The Ages of the World*

I begin.

That is to say, I *am* beginning.

And yet I am *always* beginning; I *will always have begun* this way.

Enough. I *shall* begin, and right now. I shall begin immediately with a series of questions about trauma and about the relationship between philosophy and trauma studies.

It is clear at the outset that trauma studies have much to teach philosophers, but is there reason to believe that trauma studies have anything to learn from philosophy? The happenstance that philosophy today, whether of the analytical or hermeneutical persuasion, is itself traumatized—having both run out of problems and bored even its most dedicated audiences to death—is no guarantee. It seems incredible that a never-completed work of romantic-idealist metaphysics, namely, Schelling's *Ages of the World* (1811–1815) could have much to tell the contemporary student of trauma. What could the absolute—the omnipotent divinity that is celebrated in ontotheology and heralded by ethics as its ultimate instance of authority—have to say to victims of violence?

What would the God of traditional metaphysics and morals know about *igno-minious* suffering—about a *passio* deprived of the safety nets of sacrifice and salvation? I am not sure. In the present chapter I am operating on the (naive?) assumption that several aspects of Schelling's account of God's difficulties—those recounted in narratives about the remote past—are perforce related to the traumas that human beings have undergone in the recent past and are undergoing in our own time. While I am not prepared to declare that Schelling's God is suffering from PTSD (posttraumatic stress disorder), there do seem to be grounds for saying that God's memories, like those of his or her creatures in our time, are "stored in a state-dependent fashion, which may render them inaccessible to verbal recall for prolonged periods of time."[1] As we shall see, the inability to recall memories over prolonged periods of time is precisely what Schelling understands to be the principal trait of time past and present. Further, if experiencing trauma is "an essential part of being human," and if human history "is written in blood," then being human is an essential part of divinity: the blood spilled in human history, we are assured, is the blood of the lamb.[2] The memory of God surely runs deep, but it is also anguished, humiliated, tainted, and unheroic.[3] If human memories are "highly condensed symbols of hidden preoccupations," and are thus very much like dreams, and if the memories that are "worth remembering" are memories of trauma, then it is arguable that a memorious God could be nothing other than a suffering godhead.[4] Indeed, if psychic trauma involves not only intense personal suffering but also "recognition of realities that most of us have not begun to face," no God worthy of the λόγος would want to be without it.[5] No Creator worthy of the name

1. Bessel A. Van der Kolk, A. C. McFarlane, and L. Weisaeth, eds., *Traumatic Stress: The Effects of Overwhelming Experience on Mind, Body, and Society* (New York: Guilford Press, 1996), xix–xx.

2. Bessel A. Van der Kolk and A. C. McFarlane, "The Black Hole of Trauma," in *Traumatic Stress*, 3.

3. Lawrence L. Langer, *Holocaust Testimonies: The Ruins of Memory* (New Haven: Yale University Press, 1991). It may be perverse or blasphemous to suggest that the Judeo-Christian God of Schelling's philosophy has been traumatized; worse, it may seem to be some sort of "revisionist" trick. Yet if the traumatic suffering of the Jewish people in the twentieth century bears no relation to the suffering of Yahweh, that very fact bodes ill for the chances of divinity. See in this regard Pierre Vidal-Naquet, *Assassins of Memory: Essays on the Denial of the Holocaust*, tr. Jeffrey Mehlman (New York: Columbia University Press, 1992), throughout. On the difficulty of remembering and memorializing what dare not be forgotten, see James E. Young, *The Texture of Memory: Holocaust Memorials and Meaning* (New Haven: Yale University Press, 1993), esp. part 2, "The Ruins of Memory." It is unfortunate that Young's wonderful book was produced prior to Daniel Libeskind's "Between the Lines," his addition of a Jewish Museum to the Berlin Museum, the most remarkable of nonmemorializing monuments that I have seen. See Daniel Libeskind, "Between the Lines: The Addition of a Jewish Museum to the Berlin Museum," *Archithese* 19 (Sept.–Oct. 1989): 62–67.

4. Michael Lambek and Paul Antze, "Introduction: Forecasting Memory," in Antze and Lambek, eds., *Tense Past: Cultural Essays in Trauma and Memory* (New York: Routledge, 1996), xii.

5. Cathy Caruth, in Caruth, ed., *Trauma: Explorations in Memory* (Baltimore: Johns Hopkins University Press, 1995), vii.

would be willing to forgo the test of his or her creative powers against radical loss—the terrible test of survival and eventual mortality.[6] Finally, such a suffering God would also have to become his or her own historian, exercising a craft in which both memory and narrative are crucial—and disenchantment inevitable.[7] The suffering godhead would have to advance—or regress—from trauma to melancholia, living a life "that is unlivable, heavy with daily sorrows, tears held back or shed, a total despair, scorching at times, then wan and empty," under the dismal light of a black sun.[8] In the light—and dark—of all these recent inquiries into traumatized memory, the question is not whether trauma studies have anything to learn from philosophy but whether philosophy is capable of thinking its traumas.

Having spoken of narrative, trauma, forgetting, the past, and time in general, let me try to situate Schelling in some recent philosophical discussions about the possibility of recuperating the past. Is the past essentially available for recovery and inspection, or is it ruined by radical passage and radical loss? Is the past so absolutely past that we must say that it was never present? More pointedly, is trauma itself the source of repression—of all that bars or distorts every possible memory of the past? Would trauma then be the nonorigin of origins?

In Heidegger's view, the temporal dimension of the past (*die Vergangenheit*) is the only dimension that needs to receive a new name for both the fundamental-ontological analysis of ecstatic temporality and the "other thinking" of the "propriative event": from hence, according to Heidegger, we will think not the *past* but the *present perfect*, "what-has-been," *die Gewesenheit*. Yet, before Heidegger, Hegel too had preferred *das Ge-Wesene* to *das Vergangene*, as though the absolute finality of the past—which a number of contemporary French thinkers write and think as *le passé absolu*—would absolutely resist positive speculative dialectic. There appears to be a split between Hegel and Heidegger, on the one hand, and Merleau-Ponty, Lévinas, and Derrida, on

---

6. David Aberbach, *Surviving Trauma: Loss, Literature and Psychoanalysis* (New Haven: Yale University Press, 1989). See esp. ch. 6, "Loss and Philosophical Ideas," although there is little in Schelling's biography that would lend itself to a biographical reduction of his ideas concerning the traumatic difficulties of divinity.

7. Jacques Le Goff, *History and Memory*, tr. S. Rendall and E. Claman (New York: Columbia University Press, 1992). On the return of narrative to the historian's craft, see ix. On disenchantment, see 215: "The crisis in the world of historians results from the limits and uncertainties of the new history, from people's disenchantment when confronted by the painful character of lived history. Every effort to rationalize history, to make it offer a better purchase on its development, collides with the fragmentation and tragedy of events, situations, and apparent evolutions."

8. Julia Kristeva, *Black Sun: Depression and Melancholia*, tr. Leon S. Roudiez (New York: Columbia University Press, 1989), 4.

the other, a split between conceptions of the past as either essentially recoverable or absolutely bygone. (The case of Heidegger is, of course, much more intricate than I have made out here.) How old and how wide is this split? Does the split itself testify to something like a trauma of absolute spirit? For if the past is irrecoverable, spirit can be absolute only in the sense that it is tragically cut off from its own life, hence absolutely destitute.

The present chapter will approach these questions only indirectly by offering an account of Schelling's earliest notes on *Die Weltalter*, notes not yet dated with certainty but probably from the year 1811. These notes focus on the words *Vergangenheit, gewußt, erzählt* ("the past," "known," "narrated"), and they culminate in the famous opening sentences and paragraphs of the introductions to all the printed yet unpublished versions of *The Ages of the World*: "*Das Vergangene wird gewußt, das Gegenwärtige wird erkannt, das Zukünftige wird geahndet. / Das Gewußte wird erzählt, das Erkannte wird dargestellt, das Geahndete wird geweissagt.*" In translation: "The past is known, the present is cognized, the future is intimated. / The known is narrated, the cognized is depicted, the intimated is foretold." Why the *known* past must be *recounted* or *narrated* rather than depicted or presented dialectically is a crucial question—it is Schelling's question, and right from the start. One may surmise that Schelling speaks to *us* about *our own* fundamentally split experience of the past, which seems to be both absolutely irrecoverable and absolutely inescapable.

This chapter does three things. First, it looks closely at the oldest of Schelling's sketches toward *The Ages of the World*, trying to see how these first steps on Schelling's path determine the rest of the endless journey toward that book. Naturally, that is too large an undertaking for a single chapter. One may therefore restrict the investigation to the first half of the 1811—that is, the first—printing of *The Ages of the World*. (The only two exceptions will be brief sallies into the second half of the 1811 draft, where Schelling's "genealogy of time" receives its most concise treatment, and into the 1815 lecture, "The Divinities of Samothrace," where Schelling's account of the "oldest" religious system is developed.) Second, the chapter pays particular attention to the emergence of several figures of *woman* in Schelling's account of the past, woman as the night of Earth, the wrath of God, and the giver of life, inasmuch as she seems to be at the epicenter of trauma, repression, and forgetting in the divine life. Third, it poses some general questions about the nature of the trauma that Schelling seems to descry in the life of the divine, namely, in the mechanism of repression that he finds at work both in our own time and in the divine consciousness that began to stir in the most remote past.

The Earliest Notes toward Schelling's *The Ages of the World*

Karl Schelling, serving as the editor of his father's never-completed magnum opus, identifies the first recorded plan of *The Ages of the World* as "The Thought of *The Ages of the World* [*Gedanke der Weltalter*]."[9] Of the three original *Bogen* of the plan—that is, of the three folded sheets of foolscap—only two (A and C) are preserved. On the left-hand side of the first page of fascicle A we find a margin extending over a third of the width of the page. In it are nine numbered notes and two unnumbered ones; these notes consist of key words, many of them abbreviated and therefore difficult to decipher. Across from these notes, covering two-thirds of the page, appears the exposition of the plan itself.

Why bother with such a problematic sheet of notes, especially before the Schelling-Kommission has prepared it in its historical-critical form? The answer lies in Schelling's own preoccupation with the art of beginning and with the languor and longing attached to all beginnings. Virtually all the *Weltalter* sketches, plans, and drafts thematize in a reflexive and reflective way the problem of beginning.[10] More strictly, they deal with the impossibility of beginning at the beginning, since the beginning is in a radical sense *bygone*. Not only is the beginning past, but its past also pertains to a time before time, a time that in the current age of the world (namely, the present) never was present. Schelling will eventually say that the beginning is an *eternal beginning*—that in a sense the beginning has neither end nor beginning (78). We therefore cannot simply assume that our own present and future flow from this distant or "elevated" past—Schelling always calls it *die hohe Vergangenheit*—for which we are searching. True, he is driven by the belief that we must stand in some sort of *rapport* with the elevated past; yet he is disquieted by the suspicion that the elevated past is closed off to us, encapsulated, isolated, cut off from us. Sometimes it seems to him that the past is all by itself, *solus ipse*, absolutely solitary, well-nigh *un passé absolu*. If we do experience some sort of

9. Friedrich Wilhelm Joseph von Schelling, *Die Weltalter Fragmente: In den Urfassungen von 1811 und 1813*, ed. Manfred Schröter, Nachlaßband to the Münchner Jubiläumsdruck (Munich: Biederstein Verlag and Leibniz Verlag, 1946), 187, cited henceforth by page number in the body of my text. This volume presents the original versions of *Die Weltalter*, set in print (but not released for publication) in 1811 and 1813, along with the earliest sketches and plans for the project. The first half of the 1811 version is, I believe, of special interest, and my chapters are devoted especially to it. Only the 1815 version of *The Ages of the World* is available in English: see the translation by Jason Wirth (Albany: State University of New York Press, 2000).

10. Slavoj Žižek, *The Indivisible Remainder: An Essay on Schelling and Related Matters* (London: Verso, 1996), 13. Žižek rightly recognizes the force of the unconscious in Schelling's *Ages of the World*, yet because of his desire to develop a political philosophy based on the idea of freedom he does not grant "the unconscious act" that occurs "before the beginning" its full traumatic power. That said, Žižek's is a stimulating interpretation, one that deserves a more careful reading than I can give it here.

rapport with it, all the critical apparatus of science and philosophy must be brought to bear on this presumed relation, and from the very beginning. Yet something more than science and philosophy will have to be brought to bear: we will need to appeal to something like the art of *fable* or *narrative* in general.

Let us therefore begin with the very beginning of the *Früheste Conzeptblatt,* reprinting its text as it stands, in all its enigmatic form, and introducing some necessarily conjectural comments on it, as we proceed—with trepidation—to translate it.[11]

1. Ich beginne.
2. alles an Verg.
3. Die wahre Vergang. d. Urzust. d. Welt . . vorhand. unentfaltet eine Zeit . .
4. Philos.-Wiss. Verg.
5. Was gewußt wird, wird erzählt.

"Number one. I begin." Or, in the progressive form, "I am beginning." One might wish to use this progressive form in order to avoid the sense "I *always* begin," which would mean as much as "This is the way I *have* always *begun.*" Finally, there is nothing that prevents us from reading the present tense as an elliptical future tense, "I shall begin." Perhaps the first thing that is odd about the beginning of this earliest sketch is that its apparently straightforward, candid, self-referential, self-indexing "I begin" (look at me start, you can see me getting under way at this very instant) can yield a number of different tenses and aspects—simple and continuous present, present perfect, and future. It is perhaps important to notice, however, that the simple past, which other languages call *the imperfect,* is *not* among the tenses into which we can translate *Ich beginne.* The past seems to resist both Schelling's beginning and our own. And yet everything hangs on the question of a possible access to the elevated past.

"Number two. Everything in the past [or: everything *concerning* the past]." Is the sense here that all that is, all being, reverts and pertains to the past? Or is Schelling making a distinction, as he is wont to do, between *things past*—in the mundane sense of the history of our present world—and the past in itself, the past in some more lofty sense?

---

11. My own commentary should not be confused with Schelling's exposition, which does not always seem to be in tandem with these notes in the left-hand margin. Although I will reprint the whole of Schelling's left-hand margin, I will take up his exposition only in part. Whether or not such intense focus on the margin of this earliest sketch will help us with a more general reading of *Die Weltalter* remains to be seen.

"Number three. The true past. The primal state of the world .. at hand, undeveloped, a time [or: an age] .." The past properly speaking is a time or an age unto itself. In that former time the world was at hand in its undeveloped state, whereas now, in the present time (the eon of the present), the worlds of both nature and history are constantly unfolding. Yet could the elevated past—with which we presumably stand in some sort of *rapport*—be truly undeveloped? If developed, however, then when and how could its developmental dynamism have been introduced? This, we recall, is the very conundrum that stymied Schelling's philosophy of nature: his *First Projection toward a System of Nature Philosophy* (1799) was unable to imagine what might have initiated movement and life in a static universe. If dynamism and dualism pervade nature now, in the eon of the present, they must always have done so, and right from the start. For omnipresent life and ubiquitous animation are contagion.

"Number four. Philosophical-scientific past." The past is the proper object of dialectic, which is the method best suited to speculative knowledge. However,

"Number five. Whatever is known is narrated." If knowledge is the goal of philosophy as science, it is difficult to understand why the known must be recounted, narrated, or told as a story. The suggestion is that even though the past, considered philosophically-scientifically, is the proper object of knowledge, the proper medium of knowledge concerning the elevated past is not argumentation, deduction, presentation, depiction, or portrayal, all of which pertain to the present, but some other form of communication. Schelling will often call it "the fable." Perhaps he is thinking of the astonishing figure of *Fabel* in the Klingsohr fairy tale of Novalis's *Heinrich von Ofterdingen* (1798–1801). In any case, a hidden reference to Novalis's *Lehrlinge zu Saïs* (1798) seems to lie in the opening of Schelling's more detailed exposition.

Let us therefore return now to the top of the front side of A, back to the beginning, or to the *second* beginning, in order to take up Schelling's exposition—which one may here, for simplicity's sake, translate without reference to the many corrections in Schelling's text: "I am what then was, what is, and what shall be; no mortal has lifted my veil.' Thus, once upon a time, according to several types of narrative [*nach einiger Erzählung*], from under the veil of the image of Isis, spoke the intimated primal essence in the temple at Saïs to the wanderer" (187). It is unclear why this traditional narrative—a fable in Novalis's if not in Aesop's sense—begins the exposition. Nor is the import of the fable unequivocal. For Schiller's poem, Novalis's prose text, and Hegel's account of the myth in his philosophy of nature, the goddess's words are sometimes heard as a warning, sometimes taken as an invitation. Lifting the veil sometimes grants immortality, sometimes instantaneous mortality. If Schiller's wanderer is struck dead because he dares to lift the veil, Hegel has the written inscription on the hem of the goddess's dress dissolve under the penetrating gaze of spirit, while the far more gentle Novalis declares that only those who dare to lift the veil—with respect, but without remorse—deserve to be called *apprentices* at Saïs. Schelling's exposition offers us no clue as to how the old fable is to be heard. Yet it does affirm the tripartite division of the ages of the world for philosophical science: past, present, and future are not mere dimensions of the present time but independent ἀρχαί, ages, eras, eons, or times of the world.

If reams of questions begin to pile up for readers of Schelling's exposition, the numbered remarks in the left-hand margin seem to anticipate some of the difficulties. Let us return again to the margin:

6. Warum unmöglich
7. da ich mir nur vorges. in dem ersten Buch d . . dieser Verg. zu behandeln, so wird es nicht ohne Dial.
8. D. Vergang. folgt die Gegenwart. Was alles zu ihr gehört—Natur Gesch. Geisterwelt, Erkentn.-Darstellung—Nothw. wenn wir die ganze Gesch. d. Gegenwart schreib. wollten, so d. univ. unter aber nur d. Wesentl. denn . . nur d. Syst. d. Zeiten kein Ganzes d. Nat.n.

"Number six. Why [it—the narrative—is] impossible." The exposition tells us that it is not enough to know the One. We must also know the three divisions of the One, namely, what was, what is, and what will be. And after we *know* these three, we must *narrate* them, even if something about such narrated knowledge is "impossible." Yet the nature of this impossibility—which has to do with both the supremacy of narrative over dialectic and the repression of narrative in our own time—is not clear to us.

"Number seven. Because I have proposed [reading *vorges.* as *vorgesehen* or *vorgestellt*] to treat only what pertains to this past, it will not be without dialectic [*Dial.*]." It is not yet clear why dialectic is called for at all in our scientific-philosophical pursuit of the past; indeed, we can be rather more assured of Schelling's troubled relation to dialectic. In the various plans and drafts of *Die Weltalter,* Schelling employs dialectic—and yet almost always he expresses his worry that dialectic may be no more than manipulation of concepts without the requisite seriousness of purpose or thoughtfulness. Schelling often seems to trust images and fables more than he does dialectic, which he faults for being a kind of intellectual sleight of hand, a conceptual juggling act. "The

Past" will be about that time before (the present) time when the intellect was unclear about everything that was, when dialectic was more strife and suffering than controlled negation and confident synthesis. Perhaps the very fact that the first book of *The Ages of the World* will need dialectic is the mark of a flaw or an incapacity? That is an interesting possibility, if only because the editor of these early drafts, Manfred Schröter, consistently denigrates the first half of the 1811 draft as being too "naive," too suggestive, too full of images— in a word, insufficiently dialectical. We will have to come back to the question of dialectic, because the narrative or recounting that Schelling has in mind can be understood only in (nondialectical) opposition to dialectic, only in some sort of distance and releasement with regard to dialectic.

"Number eight. The present follows the past. All that belongs to it—nature, history, the world of spirits, knowledge-presentation—Necessary if we wished to write the entire history of the present, thus of the universe [reading *so des universums*], but only in its essential aspects; for [this is] only the system of the times, not the entirety of all their natures." Here the decoding is particularly hazardous. The first word, "D." must be *Der*, the feminine dative, since *folgen* takes the dative: *Der Vergangenheit folgt die Gegenwart*, the past is followed by the present, the present follows the past. Now, it is clear that Schelling intends to provide no more than a "system of the times," not a detailed inventory of everything in nature and history. What is entirely unclear, however, is why and how the present can be said to follow the past. Might *folgen* here mean to obey, or even to comprehend? Yet does the present obey the past? Does it ever comprehend the past? For what has been emphasized so far is that the past is not only essentially prior to or earlier than but also cut off from the present time of the world. If past, present, and future are not to be taken as measures or dimensions of the current time (namely, the present), but as "three times that are actually different from one another," as the exposition says (188), then it is not at all clear that the present should follow upon the past. The problem is blurred when one translates the plural of *Zeit*, namely, *die Zeiten*, as "ages" or "eras"; when one translates them and tries to think of them as three distinct *times*, the problem becomes recalcitrant. Indeed, that *rapport* on which Schelling stakes everything, the relation that ostensibly links the present to the past, remains entirely problematic: everything that Schelling does to elevate the past to its "true" and "genuine" status vitiates the *rapport* that those of us who live in the present (that is, all human beings, past, present, and to come) might have with it; everything that Schelling does to expose the efficacy of the present in repressing the true past debilitates our faith in his or anyone's ability to accede to it. In a time of *désoeuvrement*, a time of debility and demise, we may have to doubt whether the present follows the past in any sense—such a past could only be the future of our inchoate desires, our nostalgia, and our repression.

Let us now turn to the ninth of Schelling's marginal notes on the left-hand side of the page:

> 9. Die Zukunft so d. Besch. d. Welt nur .. D. hier bg. Werk wird in 3 Bücher abgeth. seyn, nach Verg. Gegenw. u. Zuk. welche hier .. in d. hier beg. Werk nicht als bloße Abm. d. Z. sond. als wirkl. Zeiten vers. wäre d.— Welt—allein. Ein Altes Buch—

"Number nine. The future. It is thus [usually taken to mean] the way the world turns out [reading *Besch.*, very uncertainly, as *Bescheidung*] .. The work presented here will be divided into 3 books, according to Past, Present, and Future, which here in the work that we have begun are not mere dimensions [*Abm.* = *Abmessungen*] of time, but are to be understood as actual times—the world—alone. [¶] An Old Book—" Much in these final lines resists our reading, especially the relation of "—the world—alone" to the three "actual times." Why does Schelling insist that there are three distinct ages or times? He does so, he says, because of "an Old Book." The book is *Ecclesiastes*, and to its own question, "What is it that has been?" the book replies, "Precisely what will come to be afterwards." And to the further question, "What is it that will come to be afterwards?" the book replies, "Precisely what also has been before." Because it is not speaking of the essence, says Schelling, and because it evades the problem of the *past* by speaking in the *perfect*, the Old Book can equate past, present, and future and declare that there is nothing new under the sun. Yet the sun of that Old Book shines on the things of *this* world alone, the *present* world, says Schelling, so that *Ecclesiastes* is actually pointing in the direction of something else. "The time of this world is but one vast time, which in itself possesses neither true past nor genuine future; because the time of this world does not possess them, it must presuppose that these times belonging to the whole of time are outside itself" (188).

In Schelling's view, the true or genuine past, that is, the remote and elevated past, is clearly privileged. At least he will say throughout his work on *The Ages of the World*—which never gets *out of* the past precisely because it never gets *into* it—that as much soothsaying skill is needed to discern the past as to augur the future. Two final unnumbered notes on the left-hand margin now try to distinguish the elevated past from the present eon:

Wenn es die Abs. ist dieß Syst. d. Zeit. zu entw. s. steht d . . doch Verg. u. Gegenw. nicht gleichs . . . D. Verg. gewußt.

Woher nun Wiss. d. Verg. in jenem hohen, Sinn philos. verstanden? Wenn aber warum nicht erzählt?

"If the intention [of this work] is to develop this system of the times, then past and present are not posited as identical . . . The past is known. [¶] Now, whence our knowledge of the past, understood in that elevated philosophical sense? Yet if [it is known], why [is it] not narrated?"

Here the left-hand margin comes to an end, whereas the exposition continues to elaborate the questions posed. And the principal question seems to revolve about the apparent contradiction that, whereas the known is narrated, the past, though indeed known, is *not* narrated—but then *why* not? Schelling argues that "the true past time is the one that came to be before the time of the world; the true future is the one that will be after the time of the world," and the present time—with its own epiphenomenal past, present, and future—is but one "member" of time. Yet no one has as yet lifted the veil: what was, is, and will be—considered as three distinct times—remains concealed.

Schelling's exposition now finds the statement that will serve as the opening for the introduction to *The Ages of the World* in all its drafts: "The past is known, the present is cognized, the future is intimated. The known is narrated, the cognized is depicted, the intimated is foretold" (189). Yet this refrain—both more and less than an assertion or the thesis of a dialectic—merely underscores the severity of the double question posed in the margin. If the past is known, where does that knowledge come from? How can we in the present time of the world know anything of the remote, elevated past? The second question is more confusing, and Schelling's marginal formulation of it is quite condensed: "But if [the past is known], why [is it] not narrated?" Up to now Schelling has made use of an ancient myth, to wit, the myth of Saïs, reported to his contemporaries by Herder and recapitulated in very different ways by Schiller and Novalis—and an Old Book that is part of the Good Book. Apparently, therefore, *something* of the past has indeed been recounted. Yet Schelling wants to know why it is recounted in such cryptic, Sibylline forms:

Science would thus be the content of our first part [on the past]; its form would have to be narrative [*erzählend*], because it has the past as its object. The first part, namely, a science of the preworldly time, would speak to everyone who philosophizes, i.e., everyone who strives to cognize [*erkennen*] the provenance and the first causes of things; but why is that which we know not narrated with the candor and simplicity with which everything else we know is narrated; what holds back the Golden Age, when science will be story [or history: *Geschichte*] and the fable will be truth? (189)

We cannot read Schelling's words without thinking ahead to Nietzsche's account, in *Twilight of the Idols*, of "how the true world finally became a fable" (KSA 6:80–81). Schelling's account would alter only slightly the sense of the *endlich*, "finally." For what Schelling envisages is a recurrence of that time, that Golden Age, in which truth and fable were coextensive, the time when inquiry (Aristotle's ἱστορία) was—and will be—indistinguishable from story and poesy (ποίησις). The gold of that Golden Age will prove to be both the densest of metals and the fabulous metal that feels as though it has an oily skin.

After two false starts, themselves quite significant ("There still slumbers in human beings a consciousness of the past time . . . ," and "It is undeniable that human beings are capable of cognizing only that with which they stand in living relation . . ."), Schelling avers that human beings today still retain a "principle" from the primordial time, or preworldly time, of the world. The elevated past still serves as a kind of matrix or foundation (*Grundlage*) of the present eon. Yet that matrix or foundation has been "repressed" or in some way "covered over" (*verdrungen oder doch zugedeckt*), "relegated" to, or "set back" into, the dark (*ins Dunkel zurückgesetzt*) (189–190). Schelling believes that the principle of the proto-time continues to prevail in the human "heart of hearts," *das Gemüth*. Yet a genealogy of *Gemüth* would surely have to trace the human heart back to its divine ancestor. A word about this difficult word *Gemüth* is therefore called for.

We would need to trace the history—or the story—of *Gemüth* from Kant's third *Critique* to Heidegger's *Being and Time* in order to feel the full weight (past and future) of Schelling's asseveration. For Schelling, the *rapport* we sustain with the earlier time, the time before our own worldly time, arises within the human *Gemüth*, which is not a *faculty* but a *principle* ruling from the beginning. His genealogy of time(s), carried out in the second half of the 1811 printing, will be a genealogy of *Gemüth*—and here it is almost as though Schelling were quoting *Being and Time*, if one can quote from a future that can only be intimated.[12] At all events, it will be a genealogy designed to elaborate and sustain a *rapport* in the face of the most powerful resistance and repression. For even when the past is repressed or covered over in the present, there is something in the human heart of hearts that under-

12. See the *Urfassungen*, 74–88, discussed in the following section of the chapter.

goes the experience of *déjà vu;* even when the past is "set back" into the dark, it preserves its treasures.

One is reminded—if one may take yet another leap into the future—of the way in which Husserl insists that even at the zero-point of internal time consciousness, where retention fades away into absolute nothingness, something of the past is preserved. For Husserl, such preservation will constitute the secret font of *Evidenz.* It is perhaps not out of place for us to note here that Husserl is also implicated in Schelling's more dialectical deduction of the three times of the world, inasmuch as that deduction has to do with the problem of what Husserl calls *die lebendige Gegenwart,* the living present. Yet Schelling's problem, as we shall see, is the obverse of Husserl's: whereas Husserl needs the living present in order to explain our retention of the past, Schelling fears that the living present will expand excessively and thus occlude all passage to the genuine, elevated, remote past. Those who live in the present age, eon, or time are all like the Greeks of the classical age, as the priests of the war-goddess Neith at the temple of Saïs, according to the story in Plato's *Timaeus,* saw them: we are all like children who have no memory, especially no memory for the beginnings of things. And if we have a vague presentiment of an ancient memory, we cannot find the words to tell it. Thus Plato's Socrates, whenever he is confronted by an irascible problem in his argument, will always call upon the higher power that is represented in myth; he will invariably perform or undergo some recollection, so that by collection and division—that is, by the dialectical dissection and analysis of old stories—he can struggle to remember what we all have forgotten. We are all like Faust: two souls dwell in our breast, and it is the art of interior discourse—the dialogue of self and soul—that enables philosophy to search for what it has forgotten and then to give birth to dialectic. If candor and simplicity (*Geradheit und Einfalt*) are the virtues of philosophical reasoning and dialectic, it is nevertheless the case that something prevents our heart of hearts from hearing and understanding in the same way the *stories* of the remote past. The present seems to have repressed the past. It is as though some undiscovered trauma had consigned the past to the inner darkness of *un for intérieur,* encysting it in our interior life and causing it to be inaccessible to us. What could have been the motive or the trigger of such repression? Why are the treasures of the past locked away in an interior vault? What accident, contingency, or shock could have induced such repression? And what kind of narrative will release the effects of the obfuscation and give us back our *rapport* with our own provenance, restore to us our own past, and thus promise us a future?

One recognizes the astonishing parallel with, or anticipation of, the trauma analyses carried out by psychoanalysis. One could understand the parallel as a straightforward historical inheritance, from Schelling to Schopenhauer to Freud to Lacan. Or one could problematize (or at least leave open) the very meaning of "inheritance" and historical succession. One would thereby show greater respect for both psychoanalysis and Schelling, precisely by setting out in quest of the undiscovered source of primal repression. That source lies hidden in a time so remote that it appears—to both Schelling and Freud—as timeless.[13]

The Genealogy of Time, and the Golden Age

Nothing but the occasional double paragraph break demarcates the divisions or subsections of *The Ages of the World* in all three of its versions—no numbering system, no titles or subtitles. When one examines these breaks in the 1811 and 1813 printings, one finds the earlier version to be far more complex than the later one: the 1811 printing has ten double paragraph breaks (hence ten sections), as opposed to four. The designations "first half," "second half," with regard to the 1811 printing are usages introduced by Manfred Schröter, the editor of *Die Weltalter Fragmente*. One inevitably falls into the habit of using them, even though they are based on a highly problematic comparison of the 1811 and 1813 printings, one that privileges the later version. If one accepts these usages at all, one may say that the "first half" of the 1811 printing contains four sections, the "second half" six. Almost all the material treated in this and the following two chapters of the present book derives from the four sections that constitute the "first half." Yet for the moment we are leaping ahead into the third section of the "second half" (73–87: *Wir haben uns schon* . . . ["We have already . . ."]), inasmuch as Schelling at least promises there to offer his most detailed treatment of the succession of times, eons, or ages.

Because the section on the genealogy of time is notoriously difficult, let us begin with a summary statement. The birth of each moment of time, that is, of time as a whole and of the times that one may call "ages," occurs in the "polar holding-apart" of the entire mass of past and future (75). These births of the moments of time are in each case scissions (*Scheidungen*) compelled by love, which is both a seeking (*das Suchen*) and an experience of languor (*die Sehnsucht*). Such births are always a matter of the father's contractive force and the son's expansive force; they are also a matter of overcoming the passing of

---

13. For more on repression (*Verdrängung*), see the second half of the 1811 printing, 99–100.

the past by means of a hold granted by the present perfect, "as absolute having-been" (79). The present perfect provides "that gentle constancy" (80)
which tends toward the *future* as toward the promise of love. On its way to the
future, love creates time, space, and the natural world. However, as we shall
see, such creations alter forever our sense of who or what the creator—or cre-
ators—may have been.

The genealogy of time opens with an account of the Christian trinity: the
father is the contractive, centripetal principle, the son is the expansive, centrifugal force, and spirit the union of the two. Most remarkable about these
opening lines of the genealogy is Schelling's retraction of a point he had insisted on in his *Philosophical Investigations*. There he envisaged a final, total
scission of the forces or principles of the divine essence and its ground, "as it
were, in one magic stroke," *in Einem magischen Schlag*. Here, in the 1811
printing of *The Ages of the World*, he denies that the son can separate himself
off from the father and achieve luminous self-consciousness "in one stroke,"
nicht gleichsam mit Einem Schlag (73). In the unfolding of the divine essence it
is always a matter of subordination and reduction to latency rather than outright overcoming through divorce. But now to begin.

Being, *das Sein,* which is the father, meets resistance (*Widerstand*) and so
cannot remain in undeveloped eternity. Past and present now differentiate
themselves in divine existence, which existence is *das Seiende,* as opposed to
das Sein, or being. Schelling characterizes this initial differentiation as a "complete dualizing" (ibid.). Yet the dualizing into past and present does not restrict itself to two; it heads toward a future. "Thus time originates in every
moment [*Augenblick*], indeed as the *whole* of time—as time in which past,
present, and future are dynamically held asunder, yet at the same time are
thereby held together" (74). Because the dynamic relationship produced by
such dualization is unstable, however, inasmuch as being is overcome only
gradually, and never in one fell swoop, one time follows upon another. Thus
the ages—better, the times, *Zeiten*—come to be. The beginning of the process
depends upon the bipolarity expressed in the two principles: time opens up in
the middle, as it were, between contraction and expansion, rather than at one
end of the timeline. Always a future stretches out ahead, always a past streams
away behind (75).

Schelling now proposes to delineate "the principal moments of the entire
genealogy of time" (ibid.). The "proper force" of time lies in eternity. Past,
present, and future advene by virtue of being, existence, and their ultimate
unity. Yet they are closed off, or occluded, in eternity—enfolded there, as

Schelling likes to say, *eingewickelter Weise*. To be sure, the actual beginning of time can arise only as a result of God's absolute freedom—regardless of that earlier talk about resistance. Absolute freedom is nothing other than love: "It is love that in the first occluded unity urges toward scission [*auf Scheidung dringt*]" (ibid.). Initially, the urge results in confusion, the befuddlement that every search entails—in this case "the beginning's seeking and not being able to find itself [*aus dem Suchen und Nichtfindenkönnen des Anfangs*]" (ibid.). Little is said here about the manner in which this primeval confusion is overcome, other than that it finds the Word: "The found beginning is the found Word, by which all conflict is resolved" (74–75).

It is clear to Schelling that the primal compulsion or urge to love, which is the urge toward emancipation from the closed unity of eternity, remains the central mystery. All he can do is insist that "the first impact of love," or love's first "working of effects," *Wirken*, constitutes "the absolute beginning" (75). Nothing prior to love can stand in relation to being—so that even the notion of resistance is difficult for us to comprehend. Indeed, Schelling now concedes that the primal condition of the divine essence presupposes a fully unfolded existence, inasmuch as being (the father) can never be a mere "foundering in total self-absorption" (ibid.). Thus Schelling finds himself on the verge of an infinite regress: the search for the beginning is an eternal search.

He tries a new tack. The will that wills nothing may well be the highest form of will, but no transition follows from it. Hence the will must will *something*. We might expect Schelling to invoke "the will of love" here, yet he does not, at least not directly. He writes: "Thus the beginning of languor [*Sehnsucht*] too must be the absolute beginning in the will" (77). Presumably because the word *Suchen* has already fallen—in the "search" for a beginning—the word *Sehnsucht* can now follow. Yet once the word *languor* has fallen, there will be no way to modify the urgent love and the mysterious resistance that disturb the cloister of eternity.

Chronos, in the form of the Titan Kronos, resists the truth of successive time by swallowing the moments that would polarize his forces. Such swallowing of progeny, Schelling says, produces the *simultaneity* of the moments in eternity as traditionally conceived. Only when the son is truly produced by the paternal force, however, can there be a real relationship for the divine essence. Instead of simultaneity, there are now *periods* of time (78). Such periods share a common characteristic: "At each moment, as in the first, the stringency and taciturnity of the father are overcome" (ibid.). The result is not the time in which we intuit things in the world (which is Kant's fundamental error), but the time which is *intrinsic in* all things. Intrinsic in varying degrees, of course, inasmuch as this is the time that causes each entity to be separated off from every other (79).

Because time originates in a dualizing process, that is, in the midpoint between two rotating fluxes, the contractive and the expansive, one should not ask how much time has elapsed (*schon verflossen*) since the beginning; one must rather ask how many times have already come to be (*wie viele Zeiten sind schon gewesen*) (80). What earlier seemed to be an infinite regress of commencements now appears as "absolute having-been," *absolute Gewesenheit* (79). Because the moment reproduces the whole of time in each birth, so that it is never a question of the mere succession of the parts of time, as *partes extra partes*, we have the sense of time as a continuum, "that gentle constancy of time," *jene sanfte Stetigkeit* (80). Because the moment reproduces the whole of time in each birth, we can speak of absolute time, *die absolute Zeit* (81). This would be the time that Aeschylus calls "all-accomplishing time," παντελὴς χρόνος (*Choephoroi*, 1. 965), Sophocles' "all-governing time," παγκρατὴς χρόνος (*Oedipus at Colonus*, l. 609), the "vast, all-embracing, and uncountable time," ἅπανθ' ὁ μακρὸς κἀναρίθμητος χρόνος, in which the visible vanishes and the invisible advenes (*Ajax*, ll. 646–647; cf. 714). The relationship of part and whole in absolute time, according to Schelling, is essentially organic rather than mechanical (ibid.). "Without such an organism, all of history would be a chaos full of anomalies" (82). Organic time organizes its periods in such a way that they point toward the whole of time. "But the whole of time is the future" (ibid.). As the past belongs to the father, and the present to the son, so the future belongs to spirit. "Spirit thus unifies and orders the times" (ibid.). As the source of order in the ages of the world, spirit is also the source of the science that Schelling would practice: "Spirit alone seeks everything out, even the depths of divinity" (ibid.). What do these depths reveal? Schelling reaffirms that the depths of divinity reveal nothing other than freedom (83). Yet in this respect the difference between God and humanity dwindles to insignificance. Schelling writes:

> As with God, so with humanity: only by means of scission from his being can he rise to supreme self-presence [*Selbstgegenwärtigkeit*] and spirituality. He alone is free whose entire being has become for him a tool. Everything that still lives in nonseparation [*Ungeschiedenheit*], to the extent that it still lives there, lives in the past. Whoever resists scission in himself will find that time appears to him as stringent and earnest necessity. For those who are gripped in perpetual self-overcoming, however, and who do not look back to see what is behind them but for-

ward to see what lies ahead, their power will not be felt. [The text reads: . . . *wird ihre Macht unfühlbar.* The meaning seems to be that those who are gripped by self-overcoming will not be overpowered by those who resist scission in themselves.] Love urges toward the future, for only on account of love will the past be surrendered. Languor clings to the past, languishes after the first unity, is lack of active love [*Sehnsucht hängt an der Vergangenheit fest, ist Schmachten nach dem ersten Einsseyn und Mangel an thätiger Liebe*]. Joy is in the present; time disrupts both [i.e., presumably, both joy—or pleasure—and its present; or, alternatively, both present and past], and befriends love alone. (84–85)

Once again Schelling expresses the hope that active love will overcome languor and that the future will be liberated from the past.

The genealogy of time now exhibits the genesis of space from time, on the model of organic turgescence. While the genealogy of space has its attendant attractions—and its own problems—we ought to pause in order to take stock of the genealogy of time thus far. It seems to be marred by two principal failings. First, the generation of all time out of the midpoint of the moment makes it impossible for us to isolate any given period of the past as such; worse, it makes it impossible for us to gain access to the remote, elevated, preworldly time that the first book of *The Ages of the World* promises to open up and articulate for us: the past. Second, whereas the first use of *Sehnsucht* in the genealogy (77, l. 8) has to do with the search (*Suchen*) for a beginning, and is thus allied to absolute commencement and thereby to the son (as the present and as love), the second use (85, l. 9) ties languor to languishment and a hungering for the past, to a "lack of active love," and even to closure and taciturnity. In other words, it seems impossible to distinguish the loving urge that produces the son from the resistance (*Widerstand*) that compels the father— however inexplicably—to cling to the past. Resistance? The German word is masculine in gender, but the reality of resistance seems to compel the question *Who is she?* The expansive, dilating, opening force of love, which Schelling no longer calls the will of love (as in his 1809 *Philosophical Investigations,* where he confidently counterposes it to the will of the ground), remains unexplained, even after Kronos stops swallowing his sons. The surviving sons, Zeus, Poseidon, and Hades, languish as much as the father ever did. All the other sons were consumed by the father; the survivors will always be the ones who are not yet destroyed; the past holds no future for them, and their future is in some uncanny sense all past. The intransigence of the father is thus passed on to the son, and the spirit that unites them can only look back to ask what sort of storm it was that blew them all out of paradise.

The genealogy of time must account for the genesis of "active love," that effulgence of love which Schelling identifies with what the ancients called the Golden Age. The Golden Age? Was there ever such an age? Does it lie in our future? What is holding it back?

Schelling saw the 1811 text of *The Ages of the World* into print, then retracted it. After revising the text, rewriting much of it, he had it typeset, then retracted it once again, in 1813. After going through the same ritual in 1815, he set aside the third and final draft forever. Different commentators highlight different parts of these three drafts, which comprise some three hundred pages of text; in my view, to repeat, it is the earliest part of the 1811 draft that seems most remarkable, most memorable, and most repressed. For it is the "first half" of the 1811 printing of "The Past" that presses back to the most recalcitrant materials—including the material of matter itself. Indeed, much of the material in the opening pages of the 1811 draft appears in the *final* pages of the 1815 draft, as though Schelling, in his final version, wanted to leave his readers with these powerful *initial* insights and impressions. Whereas the second half of the 1811 text, in which we find the genealogy of time, takes familiar solace in the Christological story, the story of the jealous solar father and his loving mirror-image son, and a spirit who finds the Word of reconciliation, the first half finds itself forced to introduce the themes of darkness, wrath, and the mother. Whereas the second half expresses confidence in the expansive force of active love, the first half cannot escape the lineage of love that is longing, languor, and languishing (*die Sehnsucht*), as well as craving and tumult (*Begierde, Taumel*). Whereas the second half of the 1811 printing is happy to fall back on the reiterated story of the spiritualization of all matter, the first half tarries with the matter and the materials—gold, oil, balsam, and flesh—that seem themselves to invite and incite divinity.

Having only now mentioned gold, we must add that Schelling's "Golden Age" is unlike that of any other thinker except perhaps Novalis. For both Schelling and Novalis think of gold materially, elementally, metallically—that is to say, in terms of flesh. Schelling refers to gold, oil, and balsam as first or primordial materials (perhaps the Aristotelian-Scholastic prime matter), in which spirituality and materiality coexist in harmony. Such materials are "points of transfiguration" at which the lines of spirit and matter cross (32). The malleability of gold, its "tenderness," which is so like flesh, the ethereal oil of plants, which accounts for their verdure and for their kinship with healthy animal life, the "balsam of life," which glows in healthy eyes and flesh—these are the privileged moments of materiality, in which matter is still permeated by the spiritual mother (33). Oddly, it is in the second half of the

1811 printing that *Sehnsucht*—the languor and languishing of God—is most discussed (57, 77, and 85), even though the mother by that time seems to have disappeared altogether from the father-son axis. But let us back up a bit.

The 1811 printing is marked by many revisions and corrections, and is therefore difficult to read and cite. The narrative always seems to be fighting against a strong current, or against two powerful currents, one wanting to sweep it up and away into the remote past, the other threatening shipwreck on the familiar shores of Christological consolation and salvationist delights. These cross-currents make the going rough, both for the reader and (presumably) for the writer; the waters are choppy, the interruptions irregular but quite frequent. The text is filled with what the trained logician will gleefully expose as blatant contradictions: the first words of "The Past" tell us, "How sweet is the tone of the narratives that come from the holy dawn of the world," whereas seven lines later we hear, "No saying reverberates to us from that time" (10). It is true that the contradiction may be resolved if "that time," the eon that produces "no saying," refers to an elevated past that precedes the "holy dawn of the world" and all its sweet stories. Yet what is our access to "that time"? What narrative could have been written or read in the darkness before dawn?

Among the many topics pursued by Schelling in the first half of the 1811 printing (10–53), one may single out three: first, the problem of the living present and the negative deduction of the times of the world; second, the problem of the natural basis or birthplace of the world; third, the wrath, strength, and tenderness of God. All three topics should contribute to the overriding methodological question that haunts *The Ages of the World*, reappearing in every draft in virtually the same words, words we have already heard from the "earliest conception," but now taken from the introduction to the 1811 printing: "Why cannot what is known to supreme science also be narrated like everything else that is *known*, namely, with candor [or straightforwardly, *mit der Geradheit*] and simplicity [*Einfalt*]? What holds back the Golden Age, of which we have a presentiment [*Was hält sie zurück die geahndete goldne Zeit*], in which truth again becomes fable, and fable truth?" (4).

Clearly, the Golden Age is as much of the future as of the past. It is intimated or anticipated more than known, and yet is the proper object of the scientific-philosophical pursuit of the elevated past. It surely remains the proper object of contemplation for the duration of Schelling's own future: in his 1842 "Introduction" to the philosophy of mythology (II/1:175), Schelling invokes *das goldene Weltalter*, "the Golden Age of the World," perhaps in recollection of his attempts thirty years earlier to write *The Ages of the World*, and perhaps even in recollection of his master's thesis of 1792 (fifty years earlier!), which interprets the Fall of Man entirely in terms of the end of the Golden Age. In both the master's thesis and the 1842 lecture course he refers to the *Statesman* myth of Plato, and specifically to the reign of Zeus and Kronos in that fable. However, the fabled past, anticipated as the hallowed future for us all, poses problems for the truth of the present. Science, which is to say, dialectical philosophy, will have to tell stories about the past as well as deduce the principles of its genealogy; it will have to listen to narratives as well as to arguments. Not only its enemies but also its friends will ridicule it for its fascination with that night in which all cows are black—and in which they are telling tales that Farmer Brown very much needs to hear. Yet if ridicule will not quash Schelling, it also will not quell the disquiet in all who mock, will not dispel the suspicion that something is *holding back* the recurrence of the harmonious Golden Age. Some as yet nameless trauma or suffering is still causing the past to be *repressed,* covered over and buried. Freud will use Schelling's word *Verdrängung,* perhaps not knowing that it is Schelling's word, although he will quite consciously use Schelling's definition of the "uncanny," in his essay of that name.|[4] The methodological question—the question as to whether and how we can ever resist the force of repression—is what invites us to ask about (1) the negative deduction of the times of the world from the enigma of the living present, (2) the birthplace of the world, which is a site and situation of trauma and suffering, and (3) the sundry qualities and contradictions of divinity. As we shall see, all three of these topics (but most notably the second and third) have to do with figures of the female and the feminine in Schelling's text.

1. If the past is a taciturn time, in that no saying comes to us from it—no matter how sweet the tone of our inherited narratives may be—how will we approach it? How broach an object of silence rather than science? Nothing is more difficult. For we live in a living present, a present that seems to dilate and stretch its envelope forward into the infinite future and backward into the infinite past, such that these two dimensions are never truly released by the present. "Most human beings seem to know nothing at all of the past, except for the one which expands in every fleeting instant [*in jedem verfließenden Augenblick*], precisely through that instant, and which itself is manifestly not yet past, that is, separated from the present" (11). Schelling's problem, the obverse

14. Sigmund Freud, "Das Unheimliche," in *Studienausgabe,* ed. Alexander Mitscherlich, Angela Richards, and James Strachey, 12 vols. (Frankfurt am Main: S. Fischer Verlag, 1982), 4:241–274; for the references to Schelling, see 4:248, 250, and 264. For further discussion, see ch. 12 of this volume.

of Husserl's, is perhaps closer to Aristotle's. Whereas Husserl will deploy the dragnet of retentions and the antennae of protentions as a *solution,* one that prevents past and future from vanishing beyond the zero-point, a prevention that is necessary if internal time-consciousness is to provide the matrix for all evidence, Schelling, like Aristotle, sees the contiguity of the dimensions of time as a *problem.* Access to the past is closed if the past is still (of the) present, so that Husserl's solution is but a restatement of the problem of continuum. What Schelling seems to yearn for is passage back beyond the zero-point into the territory that both he and Husserl will populate with figures of night and death, the funereal figures of the spirit world.[15] Schelling has recourse to that Old Book, *Ecclesiastes,* which he reads in an admittedly bizarre way: if, as the Old Book avers, there is nothing new under the sun, then we must ascend beyond the solar system, or at least beyond the system of the present world, in order to encounter something new—a system of remote times or ages in an expanded world. Within such an extended system, "the genuine past, the past without qualification, is the preworldly past [*die vorweltliche*]" (ibid.). Schelling realizes that he is trying to sound the seas of time, and that abyss after abyss may bottom out, in such a way that the appropriate response is horror (13). Only the discovery of a "basis" or "true ground" of the past that sustains the present world will banish the sense of horror.

2. Schelling realizes also that he is speaking in an all-too-human or anthropocentric way when he asks about the basis. "Who can describe with precision the stirrings of a nature in its primal beginnings, who can unveil this secret birthplace of essence [*diese geheime Geburtsstätte des Wesens*]?" (17). Schelling has already called *The Ages of the World* the companion science to Creation (*Mitwissenschaft der Schöpfung*) (4), and he acknowledges that— whatever the impossibilities of working with a loner like God—the search for pristine beginnings can be nothing less than that. If the essence of all essence is divine, and if divinity is purest love and love infinite outflow and communicability (*unendliche Ausfließlichkeit und Mittheilsamkeit*) (19), we can expect the essence of essence to be the expansive force. Yet if divinity is in being, if it *is,* then it must be *on* its own and *as* its own; to *be* is to come to the fore as a precipitate that resists total outflow or absolute dissolution. Divinity must be

15. For Husserl's figures and metaphors, see Edmund Husserl, *Analysen zur passiven Synthesis,* Husserliana 11, ed. Margot Fleischer from lecture and research manuscripts dating from 1918 to 1926 (The Hague: M. Nijhoff, 1966), esp. 172–222 and 364–385; see also the discussion in D. F. Krell, *The Purest of Bastards: Works of Mourning, Art, and Affirmation in the Thought of Jacques Derrida* (University Park: Penn State Press, 2000), ch. 6, 130–133.

what Walt Whitman in "Crossing Brooklyn Ferry" calls the human being, namely, a "float forever held in solution."[16] Divinity must have a ground (*einen Grund*); otherwise it would dissolve, disintegrate, evaporate. Such a ground would be "what eternally closes itself off, the occluded [*das ewig sich Verschließende und Verschlossene*]" (ibid.). Such occlusion would be unfriendly to the very idea of outsiders; it would spell the death—death by fire—of any creature that sought love from it. Self-closing would be the very figure of a wrathful God, the figure of eternal fury (*ewiger Zorn*), which, as we shall see, is an unexpected figure of *woman*. Even in his 1842 *Philosophy of Mythology*, Schelling relates self-centered, allophobic wrath, *Zorn*, to the feminine figure of Nemesis (II/2:143–148). *Le nom (le* non!) *du Père, c'est la Mère.*

3. Schelling begins to deduce the two opposed forces that constitute the divine essence—the expansive, dilating, centrifugal force of love, and the contractive, centripetal force of the ground. For Schelling, these two forces constitute what one might call the ontological difference: in God one finds both a to-be (*Sein*), as the basis, and a be-ing, or existing (*das Seiende*); one finds both contraction and expansion. Presumably, the birthplace of the world would manifest both the infinitival to-be and participial being, both ground and love, inasmuch as lovemaking—and prior to it, craving, desire, languor, and languishing—leads to the conception that in turn leads to gestation and birth, the birth that is itself to serve as the birth*place* of the natural world. As Schelling pushes back into the remote past that belongs to love and ground, dilation and contraction, he confronts his first three images of the lordly mother—first, the image of living animals, second, the image of the once-proud Niobe, whose children are being slaughtered by Apollo and Artemis, and third, the image of the Amazons. The strength of God, the very pith of his essence and the starch of his character (*die Stärke Gottes*), is what makes him himself—himself alone, sole and solitary, "cut off" from everything else (*von allem abgeschnitten*). Yet if there is something *living* in divinity, that something must be superior to God's mere to-be (*über seinem Sein*), or beneath it, serving as the deeper ground of ground.

In the following chapter we will examine the source of these images of the divine ground, that source being God's footstool, or perhaps God's foot-sole. Yet for the moment let us hasten to the conclusion Schelling draws from the images themselves. All three images—living animals, Niobe's children,

---

16. Walt Whitman, "Crossing Brooklyn Ferry," in *Leaves of Grass*, ed. Sculley Bradley and Harold W. Blodgett (New York: Norton, 1973), 162, ll. 62–64: "I too had been struck from the float forever held in solution, / I too had receiv'd identity by my body, / That I was I knew was of my body, and what I should be I knew I should be of my body."

and the Amazons—are meant to evoke the effulgent force of *life* that subtends the infinite being of God. Yet at least two of the three are images of woman, and they are images that evoke violence and death. The Amazons are devoted to Artemis and Ares, and are remembered for the bloody battles they fought against Herakles and Theseus. Niobe's seven sons and seven daughters were killed by the Olympian twins, Artemis and Apollo, after Niobe had mocked the twins' mother, Leto. According to ancient interpreters, the slaughter of Niobe's children may in fact be a cryptic retelling of the battle of the Olympian gods against the seven Titans and Titanesses. In any case, Niobe's children and the Amazons alike are images of wrath and of the night. They are joined by an image of elevated, animated animality—which is precisely where Schelling himself will locate the birthplace of the natural world. Niobe, Penthesilea, and the animal: that is where the father (the mother?) contracts.[17]

To be sure, Schelling devotes himself to "the tender godhead which in God himself is above God" (21), not to the God of wrath. This tender divinity he clearly associates with the expansive will of love—even though there is but one meager reference to the will of love by the time we reach the final (1815) version of *The Ages of the World* (8:305, l. 5)—and he counterposes it to the God of wrath who closes in on herself. "Herself," because the age of wrath, the time of the night, will repeatedly be identified with womankind and even with the mother, in spite of the fact that it is difficult (impossible?) to interpret the contraction that gives birth to the natural world as anything other than an anticipation or even perfect realization of expansion and dilation—what Schelling in the treatise on human freedom calls the will of love. If God "herself" is shut off in the night, closing in on "herself" and furious toward everything that might be external to her, wrathful toward every creature, she is also *abgeschnitten*, "cut off." She hovers in the selfsame relation to her self that obtains between us and our own elevated past, which has been cut off from us. And yet, hovering in the night, she also dilates and flowers—and not first of all when giving birth. She seems to embody the two fundamental

---

17. One should note here—although I will take up these issues in detail later in the book—the importance of Phrygian Niobe also for Friedrich Hölderlin's understanding of tragedy: in the *Anmerkungen zur Antigonä*, Hölderlin identifies her as the "more aorgic realm," the realm of savage, untamed nature, which (in the figure of Danaë in the fifth choral song of *Antigone*) counts or ticks off the hours for the father of time, Zeus. (Recall too that this "ticking off" of the hours characterizes the malaise of Empedocles—in the Frankfurt plan to Hölderlin's drama, drawn up in the summer of 1797.) Niobe, Melville would have said, stands where Una joins hands with Dua on the clock of "The Bell-Tower," or, rather, as we saw in the foregoing chapter, where their loving clasp is severed. On Hölderlin's Niobe, see CHV 2:372, and chs. 9–10 of this volume.

principles, both infinitival to-be and participial being, both existence and ground of existence.

Matters of the divine birthplace are indeed more complicated than the images of castration and emasculation might suggest. Schelling refers to an "active occlusion, an engaged stepping back into the depths and into concealment," a description that is reminiscent of *earth* in Heidegger's "Origin of the Work of Art."[18] For Schelling, such an occlusive force is also a force that suffers (*Leiden*). The folding in upon itself, or contraction, of the essence is prelude to the expansiveness of love. Yet it is unclear to Schelling whether love—the tender will—can ever leave behind its capacity for passion and passivity, pain and suffering. Everything about this "beginning" is obscure: "Darkness and occlusion make out the character of primal time. All life is at first night; it gives itself shape in the night. Therefore the ancients called Night the fecund mother of things; indeed, alongside Chaos, she was called the most ancient of essences" (24). If light is taken to be superior to darkness and to Hesiodic Night, it is nonetheless true that the superior presupposes the inferior, rests on it and is upheld by it (*trage und emporhalte*) (25). Living divinity requires a ground so nocturnal and so abyssal that in the 1809 treatise Schelling called it the *Ungrund*, the "nonground." In his address to the Bavarian Academy of Sciences on October 12, 1815, entitled "The Divinities of Samothrace," which Schelling hoped would provide the very ground of his *The Ages of the World*, which was so difficult of birth, he explicitly related the rigors of wrathful, primal fire—the source of all light—to the magic of Persephone.[19]

In *The Ages of the World* Schelling writes: "Thus too wrath must be earlier than love, rigor earlier than mildness, strength earlier than gentleness [*Sanftmuth*]" (25–26). And, perhaps exhibiting that dialectical legerdemain he has warned us about, he quickly adds: "Priority stands in inverse relation to superiority" (ibid.). For a project that seeks the beginning, however, in the *a priori* prior, and seeks the *a priori* prior in the *elevated* past, it is surely odd to say that its object is *not* superior. Indeed, one of the cross-currents alluded to above is the force of "the early" as such: Schelling will always feel swept away by the phantasm of the earlier and the earliest, and he will release himself to its at-

18. Martin Heidegger, "The Origin of the Work of Art," in *Holzwege* (Frankfurt am Main: V. Klostermann, 1950), 36–37.
19. F. W. J. Schelling, "Über die Gottheiten von Samothrake," discussed below. Schelling's lecture is published in *Sämmtliche Werke*, vol. 8. See also the long endnote 64 of "Samothrace." Perhaps this relatively brief and compact text—voluminously documented in its notes, however—offers the best testing-ground for the theses contained in the present chapter. Note that Schelling also refers to the abyss or nonground (*Ungrund*) in the second half of the 1811 printing of *The Ages of the World*, at 93.

tractive force because he is convinced that there can be no superior goal for science. He can never be certain whether he is being drawn upward to the expansive will of love or downward toward the center. Indeed, he can never be certain that he is not being displaced from the center to the periphery—which was Franz von Baader's and his own description of *evil* in the 1809 *Philosophical Investigations*. Schelling's essential indecision about these forces induces a call for their *existentielle Gleichheit*, "existential equality" (27). He notes that although the south pole exerts a weaker magnetic pull than the north, and although the female sex is reputedly "weaker than the male," even so, the one must for a time bow to the other (ibid.). What is odd, however, is that in the beginning for which he is searching nothing can be less certain than the putative weakness of the female—an imputation that sounds more like a prejudice of Schelling's (and perhaps our own) age, which admittedly has no sense of the true, elevated, superior past.

In the remote, elevated, superior past, the first existent is in fact a double essence (*ein Doppelwesen*) (29). When it comes to the primal images of the world, which our tradition calls *ideas*, the principle of existential equality and of doubling prevails. Further, such ideas cannot be thought "in the absence of everything physical" (31). The spiritual cannot be thought without its being bound up with "the first, most tender corporeality [*mit der ersten, zartesten Leiblichkeit verbunden*]"; the highest form of purity (*Lauterkeit*) takes on "the first qualities of suffering [*die ersten leidenden Eigenschaften*]" (ibid.). "The spiritual and the corporeal find themselves to be the two sides of the same existence so early on that we may say that the present moment of their supreme intimacy [*Innigkeit*] is the communal birthplace of what later come to stand in decisive opposition to one another as matter and spirit" (32). If these opposites were not identical twins, they could never partake of one another: "If there were no such point where the spiritual and the physical entirely interpenetrated, matter would not be capable of being elevated once again back into the spiritual, which is undeniably the case" (ibid.). Schelling begins to look for this "point of transfiguration" in which spirit and matter are one, and he believes he espies it in the very place where Novalis too, in his final notes (discussed above, in chapter 2), saw it: spirit looms in the most dense and compact metals—gold, for example. For the density of gold makes it soft to the touch: gold seems to have a skin, as we noted earlier, and its skin seems to have a smooth, almost oily texture. Gold has the softness, viscosity, and tenderness that make it similar to flesh (*die Weichheit und fleischähnliche Zartheit*), which is why men and women crave to feel gold right up against their skin. Gold also combines density and viscosity with malleability (*Gediegenheit*)

(33). Gold is not only metal but also mettle. Not only Novalis but also Hegel praises the *Gediegenheit* of gold. Hegel too finds it in the skin of human beings—specifically, in the skin of the black African.[20]

The Golden Age is therefore the time in which matter and spirit—and presumably also female and male—are in perfect harmony. Schelling finds the principle at work in organic nature in particular. The ethereal oils mentioned above, which nourish the green in plants, "the balsam of life, in which health has its origin," make the flesh and the eye of animals and human beings transparently healthy (33). Health is a physical emanation (Schelling again uses the word *Ausfluß*, which earlier described the expansive force of love) that irradiates everything pure, liberating, beneficent, and lovely. The most spiritual form of this radiance is what Schiller identifies as *Anmuth*, the grace, gracefulness, and graciousness that transcend the merely charming. Yet no matter how transfigured or spiritualized the physical may seem to be in *Anmuth*, which may be related more than etymologically to *Gemüth*, the very heart of the mind, the physical or corporeal is undeniably palpable in it: *Anmuth* astonishes us precisely because it "brings matter before our very eyes in its divine state, its primal state, as it were" (ibid.). Perhaps that is why artists who sculpt or paint the divine are drawn to Amazons and Niobes and other living beings. Perhaps that is also why—as Hölderlin shows in his *Antigone* translation—Zeus begs Danaë in her prison cell to count off for him, who is the Father of Time, the golden strokes of the hours.

Trauma, Repression, and the Absolute Past

Yet gracious and graceful life is not without its fatality, its passion and suffering. As Schelling is swept back to the beginnings, to the distant and elevated past, suffering and fatality become ever more central to his own narrative. It is as though the way up were the way down. For the centripetal essence of the to-be (*Sein*) feels the centrifugal, affirmative force of love as suffering, even as a kind of dying. If contraction is embodiment, and expansion spiritualization, pain and suffering are bound up with both: contraction cramps, expansion distends. There is a principle of gloom that does not cease to strive against spirit, light, and love—indeed, light and love themselves participate in that gloom. The farthest reaches of the past are reaches of strife and supreme enmity or revulsion (*Streit, höchste Widerwärtigkeit*) (37). Schelling finds himself propelled back to the era of Chaos, the yawning abyss in which matter is

20. See D. F. Krell, "The Bodies of Black Folk: From Kant and Hegel to Du Bois and Baldwin," *boundary 2: an international journal of literature and culture* 27, no. 3 (Fall 2000): 103–134.

fragmented into the smallest particles, only to be refigured in sundry Anaxagorean mixed births. In the inner life of the essence, such Chaos can be experienced only as suffering and pain. Which essence? The essence of all essence, whereby *Wesen* can mean—and, as we said in chapter 3, perhaps must mean—both creature and creator. If there is confusion here, it derives from the stamp of sorrow in the signers. "Suffering is universal, not only with a view to human beings, but also with a view to the Creator—it is the path to glory [*der Weg zur Herrlichkeit*]" (40).

The age of the Titans, which for both Hölderlin and Nietzsche is the tragic age, is the era of "monstrous births." During this preworldly, protocosmic time, wild visions and phantasms beset the essence. "In this period of conflict, the existent essence broods as though caught up in oppressive dreams that loom out of the past: in the waxing strife, wild fantasies soon pass through its inner life, fantasies in which it experiences all the terrors of its own essence. . . . Its corresponding sensation is the feeling of anxiety" (41). Even the primal time of Chaos—out of which, according to the myth of Plato's *Statesman*, both the Titanic-Olympian age (dominated by Kronos and Zeus) and the anthropological age (in which no god or titan guides humankind) arise—is haunted by a still more primordial past. So many crises and separations (both words translate the word *Scheidung*, which, we recall, is the second key word of Schelling's 1809 *Philosophical Investigations*, the first being *Sehnsucht*) are experienced, that the centripetal force fears it will be pulled apart; being trembles (*zittert*) like a dog before the storm or a bomb before it explodes.[21] The essence is anything but free. The lightning bolt of freedom, wielded by Zeus (or by Prometheus the Titan? or by some essence earlier than both the Olympian and Titanic?), cannot be grasped. Spirit and

---

21. When Schelling writes here of the essence of trembling (*Zittern*) it reminds us of Heidegger's assertion in the *Beiträge zur Philosophie* that precisely "the last God" *erzittert*. See the expression *die Erzitterung des Götterns* in Heidegger, *Beiträge zur Philosophie: Vom Ereignis*, Gesamtausgabe vol. 65 (Frankfurt am Main: V. Klostermann, 1989), 239. For Schelling, the last God came first. One further shiver: Nietzsche, in *The Birth of Tragedy* (KSA 1:63), refers to the tragic drama as a shivering or trembling image of Dionysos in the soul of the spectator/participant—the magic of drama itself being a ". . . *magisch vor seiner Seele zitternden Bild des Gottes.*" (My thanks to Dr. Iris Därmann for this last reference.) As we have seen, in the second half of the 1811 printing (at 61) Schelling concedes that *Scheidung* is never complete: there can never be an absolute rupture with the effects of the past. What the 1809 *Philosophical Investigations* had called *die ewige gänzliche Scheidung* is therefore still eternal but never total. Heidegger, of course, read the freedom essay with considerable attention. What he apparently never read—even though Manfred Schröter was an admired colleague and friend—was *The Ages of the World*. I am grateful to Otto Pöggeler for this last observation. In a personal communication, Pöggeler asked me to speculate as to *why* Heidegger might have avoided *Die Weltalter*. Neither he nor I came up with a telling answer, yet we suspected that there is something *subversive* about the latter text, subversive perhaps also of Heidegger's own confidence in a *Gewesenheit*—a present perfect—that putatively enables him to appropriate the past for an "other" beginning. Subversive if only because Schelling's gesture fails so conspicuously to achieve what it wants to achieve.

consciousness suffer "a kind of madness," and even if it is the divine μανία envisaged in Plato's *Phaedrus*, the essence that suffers it does not *feel* divine. Even if, as we shall learn in chapter 6, its tumult proves to be the origin of music and dance, the essence that suffers it feels like the helpless prey of voracious animals, perhaps the voracious animals that forever accompany Dionysos—but also the Great Goddess, Kybele.

No one assists at the birth of essence. Human beings help one another at birth, and so do gods. "Yet nothing can assist the primal essence in its terrifying loneliness; it must fight its way through this chaotic state alone, all by itself" (ibid.). "The spinning wheel of birth," discussed also in the second half of the 1811 printing (68–69, once again in the context of the genealogy of time), represents the overwhelming force of nature; as it spins, both Schelling and his readers are confused about whether the force it represents is centripetal and contractive or centrifugal and expansive or both at once. What is certain is that this spinning wheel of fortune—as the opening song of Carl Orff's *Carmina burana* emphatically tells us—points sometimes up, sometimes down, *statu variabilis*.

Schelling's concluding discussion yields two further points of interest. The second has to do with the greatest of the Titans, namely, Prometheus— the Titan without whose craftiness and foresight Zeus would never have defeated the other Titans, thus instituting the reign of the Olympians, and the Titan without whom humanity would have perished utterly. The first point has to do with that transfigurative point in the beginning of the beginning, when spirit and matter interpenetrated with grace—the grace of gracefulness or beauty in motion. Schelling knows that many of his readers will be shocked by this apparent elevation of matter to equiprimordiality with spirit, and so he tries to absorb some of the shock:

> By the bye, what is it about matter that most people consider an insult, such that they would grant it an inferior provenance? In the end it is only the humility [*Demuth*] of matter that so repels them. Yet precisely this equanimity [*Gelassen-heit*] in the essence of matter shows that something of the primeval essence dwells in it, something that inwardly is purest spirituality and yet outwardly is complete *passio* [*Leidenheit*]. As highly as we honor the capacity for timely action [*Aktuosität*], we nevertheless doubt that in itself action is supreme. For even though the essence out of which God himself emerges glistens with purity, such glistening can only stream outward, can achieve no effects. On all sides, gentle suffering and conceiving seem to be prior to achieving and being active. For many reasons, I do not doubt that in organic nature the female sex is there before the male, and that in part at least this accounts for the presumed sexlessness of the lowest levels of plant and animal life. (46–47; cf. 150, in the 1813 printing)

Suffering is here called "gentle." It is the suffering of love. Yet the gentle suffering of love remains indistinguishable from *Sehnsucht,* languor, languidness, and languishing—the chronic illness of a passionate divinity and mortality alike.

No doubt, many will find Schelling's association of women with suffering, passivity, and the lowest levels of life as troubling as they find women's association with wrath reassuring—or at least refreshingly different. Yet perhaps it is a mistake to translate *Leiden* too quickly as "suffering": it is the root of *Leidenschaft,* "passion," so that the "passivity" of equanimity (*Gelassenheit*) may be something quite animated and vital. Indeed, as we shall now see, Schelling wishes to upset the usual ways we (of the present age) think of activity and passivity. Let us not underestimate the impact of Schelling's words. For here the traditional metaphysical priority of activity over passivity falls away entirely. In Schelling's view, Meister Eckhart's releasement or "letting-be," *Gelassenheit,* prevails over the "actuosity" that our tradition has always preferred—and which it has always identified with the logos and the masculine.[22] Schelling coins a new word or two here, the most telling one being *Leidenheit,* the quality of suffering and passion, or perhaps the capacity to undergo or to experience in general. True, he celebrates *passio* and identifies it with the principle of matter. He does not break with the traditional association of *materia* with the mother, or of the mother with woman, or of woman with sensuality and sexuality, but Schelling does break with the long-standing tradition inaugurated by Plato's *Timaeus* when he suggests that the female sex comes first—*in* the beginning, *at* the beginning, *as* the beginning *of* the beginning.[23] Even a sparkling God, radiant and unalloyed, is a flash in the pan until he can achieve effects. And "he" can achieve effects only when "he" achieves for "himself" a gentle passivity, a passionate tenderness, a release by virtue of which alone he may become pregnant with a future. In the second half of the 1811 printing, Schelling describes God's past and future as bound up with nature: "Nature is nothing other than divine egoism softened and gently broken

---

22. It is important to note, however, that *Gelassenheit* in Schelling's text sometimes has consequences that would perhaps have surprised Eckhart, or at least driven him to his own most radical conclusions. For one of the things that Schelling eventually feels compelled to let go and release is God. Schelling concludes the second of two "preliminary projections" of the *Weltalter* by asserting that "to leave God is also *Gelassenheit*" (200).

23. In a personal communication, John Sallis reminds me that in *Timaeus* woman "comes second" only in the final lines of the dialogue, lines that can only appear as *comic* in the light of the dialogue's earlier insistence on the eminence of χώρα, "the mother and nurse of becoming." See Sallis, *Chorology* (cited in note 15 of ch. 3, above). See also the first chapter of D. F. Krell, *Archeticture: Ecstasies of Space, Time, and the Human Body* (Albany: State University of New York Press, 1997). See also finally, or in the first place, Jacques Derrida, *Khôra* (cited in note 15 of ch. 3, above). I look forward to the doctoral dissertation of Jena Jolissaint, of the University of Oregon, on this topic.

by love [*der durch Liebe gemilderte, sanftgebrochne göttliche Egoismus*]" (85). Perhaps that gentle breaking, that loving acceptance of a humble yet passionate passivity which is rooted in the body, will also make her a better storyteller? And him a more languorous narratrix?

One final passage, the Promethean, seems as ungentle as any passage might be. For Prometheus is the epitome of titanic strength, light, and power. Yet the Prometheus that Schelling has in mind is the Prometheus of Aeschylus—Prometheus passionate, Prometheus *philathropos,* Prometheus *bound.* Bound by what, to what, for what? Schelling's answer is surprising:

> There is something irrational in the first actuality, something that resists confrontation. Thus there is also a principle that repels the creaturely, the principle that is the proper strength in God: in the high seriousness of tragedy, Force and Violence, the servants of Zeus, are depicted as those who fetter Prometheus—who loves human beings—to the cliffs above the surging sea. It is thus necessary to acknowledge that this principle [i.e., the violent principle that repels creatures] is the personality of God. In the language of traditional philosophy, that personality is explained as the ultimate act or the final potency by which an intelligent essence immediately subsists. It is the principle by which God, instead of mixing with creatures—which surely was the intention—separates himself from creatures eternally. Everything can be communicated to the creature except one thing, namely, its possessing in itself the immortal ground of life, that is, its being itself, that is, its being by and on the basis of itself. (52)

Would such incommunicability and lack of generosity be unworthy of God? Not at all, says Schelling, if it were essential to his to-be. Yet both Zeus and Yahweh turn to violence in order to repress that past in which they *were* the very woman they *loved,* or in which they were unable to make the distinction between themselves and Demeter. Whether the Christological story—which is always the story of fathers and sons—can help us to confront the mother, feminine and masculine sexuality, and mortality is to be doubted, unless the Magdalene is invited to join the panoply. The only rescue for us groundless, orphaned mortals of the present, Schelling suggests, is pantheism—beyond both idealism and realism, and also beyond dualism. For pantheism, which is the oldest of the old stories, embraces every form of life, whether divine or creaturely. The problem is that the narratives of pantheism have been proscribed by more recent history, so that the all-encompassing unity of life that pantheism celebrates lies beyond our reach. Precisely this system of the primal time, writes Schelling (and here the first half of the 1811 printing ends), "comes to be increasingly repressed by subsequent ages [*durch die folgende Zeit immer mehr verdrungen*] and posited as past [*und als Vergang-*

enheit gesetzt werden soll]" (53). We will always already have forgotten what the old stories told us to remember above all.

An Excursion to Samothrace

Schelling addressed the Bavarian Academy of Sciences on October 12, 1815, on the subject of "The Divinities of Samothrace." He published the lecture as a supplement (*Beilage*) to *The Ages of the World*, so that *The Ages* is perhaps the only philosophical work whose sole published part is a supplement to the unpublished main work. Actually, in an "Afterword" to the lecture, he called it a supplement "to a series of works that have the ages of the world as their common center" (8:423).

What does he mean by "a series of works"? Presumably, he means more than the 1811, 1813, and 1815 drafts of *Die Vergangenheit*. Because of the Allied bombing raid on Munich toward the end of World War II, however, we may never find out what he meant; we certainly will be in the dark until the Schelling-Kommission culls all the surviving materials for the historical-critical edition. If he is referring solely to the extant 1811, 1813, and 1815 drafts, he may be hinting at that compositional drama mentioned in passing above—the fact that in the final (1815) version Schelling saves the striking materials sketched out in the *opening* pages of the 1811 version till last, for the very culmination or *chute* of his work. In any case, we can be certain about Schelling's own high estimation of "The Divinities of Samothrace." For in his "Afterword" he says that the lecture is less an appendix to a completed work than "a commencement and transition" to other works, all of them designed to provide a historical analysis of "the proper primal system of humanity," meaning "the system of Samothrace," which is to say, "the doctrine of the Cabiri." Our brief excursion to Samothrace cannot do justice to Schelling's seminal lecture, and certainly not to its extensive notes, but it can at least suggest something of the perdurant legacy of the *Weltalter* project.

Samothrace does not have the reputation of an Eleusis, a Delphi, or a Dodona. It is veiled in the mists of archaic time. Yet its fabled rites play a role early on in the heroic age and in the even earlier age of the Pelasgians (RC 316). Jason leads his Argonauts to the island, where they are all initiated into the cult, already ancient by that time. (Phoenician sailors were the first to settle the island, it is said.) When he is caught in a storm after having set sail from Kalypso's Ogygia, Odysseus sees a white seagull perched on the mast, a purple sash in its beak. He remembers that it is the κρήδεμνον, the sash that is tied around an initiate's waist at Samothrace. It is the sash or veil of

Leukothea, the "Shining Goddess," who saves sailors from drowning. The Cabiri of Samothrace are themselves veiled in the most ancient of concealments.[24] Leukothea is actually Ino, herself a victim of drowning, one of the four ill-fated daughters of Cadmus and Harmony (RC 366–367). Harmony, Cadmus's queen, is a native of Samothrace. Cadmus discovers her, the love child of Aphrodite and Ares, while he is scouring the seas for his sister Europa, carried off by Zeus. Reluctant at first to accept Cadmus's suit, Harmony relents only after she is comforted by the myths of Orion and Selene, the east and the west. Harmony is in a sense the first mythographer (RC 381–383). The marriage of Cadmus and Harmony in Thebes turns out to be the very last time that gods and mortals are convivial and share the same table—with Harmony, in harmony (RC 387). Samothrace is, in Schelling's view, that convivial past, that promising future.

It remains astonishing that Schelling should have found his way to Samothrace, when the other religious centers of Greece were so much more accessible in the literature. Yet he finds his way there—like Cadmus, Jason, and Odysseus—because of a search or quest in which he is already long engaged. He is searching, as we have seen, for the matrix of all languor. Readers of the *Philosophical Investigations into the Essence of Human Freedom* may have hoped that languor and languishing, *die Sehnsucht*, would be but a temporary inconvenience for the absolute, that the more edifying "will of love" would somehow absorb all the disturbing references to epidemic infestation and illness in that word. Yet "the will of love" does not appear in "The Divinities of Samothrace." *Sehnsucht* does, both in the main text and even more imperiously in the "Notes." And it does not merely appear in these places; rather, it provides the key to the "primal system" of humanity.

As a preparation for our excursion, let us inquire into the language of Samothrace—a language that Schelling translates into two key terms: *die Sehnsucht* and *das Schmachten*. Schelling writes, *die schmachtende Sehnsucht*, then inverts the phrase to *das sehnsüchtige Schmachten*. *Schmachten* does not appear in the 1809 treatise on human freedom, whereas the word *Sehnsucht*, as we have seen, is central to that text. *Sehnsucht* continues to speak in *The Ages*

---

24. "The veil, or something that encloses, that wraps around, or belts on, a ribbon, a sash, a band, is the last object we meet in Greece. Beyond the veil, there is no other thing. The veil is the other. It tells us that the existing world, alone, cannot hold, that at the very least it needs to be continually covered and discovered, to appear and to disappear. That which is accomplished, be it initiation, or marriage, or sacrifice, requires a veil, precisely because that which is accomplished is perfect, and the perfect stands for everything, and everything includes the veil, that surplus which is the fragrance of things" (RC 368). On sails and veils in Homer, see D. F. Krell, "Καλυψώ: Homeric Concealments after Nietzsche, Heidegger, Derrida, and Lacan," in *The Presocratics after Heidegger*, ed. David C. Jacobs (Albany: State University of New York Press, 1999), 101–134.

of the World and in "The Divinities of Samothrace." Defined as "intense, painful yearning or longing," *Sehnsucht* derives from the Middle High German *sensuht*, an intensification of the noun *sene* and the verb *senen*, "to yearn for love; to suffer the cares and troubles of love," or, more generally, the condition of having lost one's strength, "to droop, grow weak." The word *Sehnsucht* is a conjunction of the verb *sehnen* and the noun *Sucht*. The former, as a reflexive verb, *sich sehnen*, means that intense, painful yearning only now mentioned; a synonym is the rarely used *sich härmen*, to worry excessively, to be plagued or pained by something. The two most common usages of *sich sehnen* relate to either homesickness or erotic love; hence the occasional translation of *Sehnsucht* as "nostalgia," literally, pain associated with (absence from) home, as well as the more common sense of lovesick languishment. It is difficult to say whether *sich sehnen* has anything to do with *die Sehne*, "sinew," or, more generally, cord or bowstring: although a connection with *sich sehnen* at first seems preposterous, and although two very different etymons seem to be involved here, the tendons and ligaments are in fact known for their ability to stretch—in German, *sich dehnen*—and it is such stretching and reaching out that *sich sehnen*, for its part, appears to suggest. The latter half of the word *Sehnsucht*, *die Sucht*, "a pathologically exaggerated need," is related by folk wisdom to *die Suche*, "search." That folk wisdom—challenged by both etymological dictionaries and learned folk in general—is based on the insight that the ill often hanker after what does them the gravest harm: hence the German words *Fallsucht*, epilepsy, *Wassersucht*, the build-up of excessive fluid, *Mondsucht*, lunacy, *Fettsucht*, obesity, and so on. Hermann Paul more specifically associates *Sehnsucht* with words such as *Tobsucht*, "raving madness, frenzy," and *Trunksucht*, "alcoholism, dipsomania."[25] The modern use of the word accordingly suggests "addiction." Yet the Old High German form of *Sucht*, namely, *suht*, suggests "illness" of any kind: it is a phonological transformation of the word *siechen*, "to wither away with sickness," and *Seuche*, "epidemic or infestation," from the Old Germanic word *seuka*, "sick." *Siech* is perhaps related to *saugen*, according to Paul: to be attacked by a succubus, to be "sucked dry" by sickness-demons. In short, and to put an end to this unpleasant portion of our language lesson, to be *sehnsüchtig* is to be sick with longing, to languish.

We may treat the word *schmachten* more quickly. *Schmachten* is to suffer thirst or hunger, or, more figuratively, to hunger or thirst after a beloved person. It is related to words that are cognate with the English "small," in the

25. For this entire discussion, see Hermann Paul, *Deutsches Wörterbuch*, 6th ed., ed. Werner Betz (Tübingen: M. Niemeyer, 1966), and Gerhard Wahrig, *Deutsches Wörterbuch* (Gütersloh: Bertelsmann Lexikon-Verlag, 1975).

sense of diminishing or wasting away. It is also related to *schmähen,* "to despise, to express contempt," and *Schmach,* "shame, dishonor, humiliation," perhaps in the sense that when we are humbled and belittled in love, and are feeling slighted, we may well become petty. Yet there is also a certain delicacy about this diminution: *schmächtig* often means "slender," "delicate." Thus in their multiple senses, both positive and negative, *schmachten* and *schmächtig* seem to lend themselves to *Sehnsucht.* Georg Trakl, in his "Song of the Hours," the second poem of *Sebastian im Traum,* puts these words—so important in his vocabulary generally—into the greatest possible proximity:

> . . . In starrender Finsternis
> Umschlingen schmächtig sich die sehnenden Arme.[26]

> . . . In paralyzing gloom
> Their languorous arms delicately entwine.

Delicately, yes, but also hungrily. Hence the proximity of the delicate *schmächtig* to the reach and stretch of *sehnen.*

So much, then, for *Sehnsucht* and *schmachten.* With this excessively Nordic language training under our belts we are, like Goethe's homunculus, ready to travel to the Thracian shore of ancient Greece and the island of Samothrace—although we may wonder what sort of divinities could ever be related to either *der schmachtenden Sehnsucht* or *dem sehnsüchtigen Schmachten*—a yearning that causes us to languish and wither.

Samothrace: the volcanic island to the west of the Dardanelles and the Sea of Marmora, frequented by Phoenician sailors, the perch from which Poseidon observes his Trojans going down in defeat; the place where—as on ancient Thera, the lost Atlantis, today's Santorini, where the cult of the Cabiri survives down to the Hellenistic age—subterranean fire and oceanic water intermix, and the site of the most important cult of the Cabiri, those chthonic deities who promise rebirth and a future life to mortals. The doctrine of the Cabiri, or rather, the mystery cult devoted to these gods, is thus related to the teachings of the most famous philosopher of the more famous cognate island, Samos, in the Dodecanese, namely, Pythagoras; it is also bound up with those mysteries associated with Eleusis and with the names Demeter, Kore (Persephone), Triptolemos, Dionysos, and Orpheus. Schelling is drawn to the cult of the Κάβειροι precisely because it reflects the "oldest faith," its antiquity pertaining to an "indeterminable prehistory"; it is the "primal system" of the

---

26. Georg Trakl, *Dichtungen und Briefe,* 3rd ed., ed. Walther Killy and Hans Szklenar (Salzburg: Otto Müller Verlag, 1974), 45.

most hoary human past, though we know it only darkly (8:347, 349, 423, and elsewhere).

It is important at this juncture to observe that the myth and cult discussed by Schelling in 1815 are taken to be much more than allegory. In his 1842 lectures "introducing" the philosophy of mythology—introducing it for over 570 pages of book text—Schelling expresses his pleasure with an assertion by Samuel Taylor Coleridge in the *Transactions of the Royal Society of Literature*. Mythology as a whole, says Coleridge, is not allegorical but *tautegorical*—it means precisely what it says (II/1:195–196). In a long note, Schelling reports with evident delight the use that Coleridge has made of his 1815 "Divinities of Samothrace" in order to come to that conclusion. Let the following account of the cult of the Cabiri therefore be taken not allegorically but tautegorically.[27]

Schelling's account relies on ancient historians such as Strabo and Mnaseas, who identify the four Cabiri as Axieros, Axiokersa, Axiokersos, and Kasmilos—Phoenician-Semitic-Hebrew names that may be translated respectively as Demeter, Persephone, Hades, and Hermes. In addition, Zeus and Dionysos, along with Athena and Hephaistos, are at various moments drawn into the Cabirian fourfold. Yet the "ascending sequence" of these gods, with—perhaps surprisingly—Hermes in the uppermost position, seems to slip and slide in the manner of all syncretisms. Nothing about the identity of these gods, including their gender identity, is settled. Nothing, that is, except the fact of their *squalor*. The very name Axieros, or Demeter, suggests "hunger, poverty, and, as a consequence of this, decrepitude, sickness [*Hunger, die Armuth, und in weiterer Folge das Schmachten, die Sucht*]" (8:353). Thus the root *Sucht* appears in Schelling's lecture even before the word *Sehnsucht*, which is so often translated into English as the seemingly harmless "longing" or "nostalgia," or even "wistfulness." Schelling adds a long note on the Hebrew, Farsi, and Arabic words that induce him to translate Axieros–Demeter by the words *Schmachten* and *Sucht*. Perhaps the most striking thing about this note is the fact that it follows two notes concerning the dignity and majesty of the goddess (in this case, Demeter, the Earth Mother) who can say "Mine is the Earth" (8:376). From worthiness and dignity, however, we immediately take a plunge to *paupertas* and *egestas*, bitter poverty and need. And even if the corresponding god in question is father and lord, he is characterized in the first

---

27. In the *Philosophie der Mythologie* proper, Schelling does not mention Samothrace until quite late in the course. See II/2:647. Yet even there he speaks of the Cabirian mysteries as causing one to shudder whenever they are mentioned. Why? Because those mysteries are *uncanny*. See the discussion in ch. 12 of this volume.

place by ravishing hunger for both food and sex (*concupivit, avidus fuit, avide voravit aliquid de cibo*) (8:378).

Precisely in this context Schelling notes "the ambiguity in the sex of all gods" (ibid.). Divinity is both female and male, *femina et mas*, even if *coelum* should be the prototypical masculine divinity, *terra* the female (8:412). Parmenides and Empedocles alike see Aphrodite at the center of the sphere, but there is also a Kyprian Aphrodit*os*, an *Almus Venus*, a *Deus Lunus*—even an *Astartus*. In short, there is "a gender-duplicity [*Geschlechts-Doppelheit*] in all the ancient gods," not in the sense that they are androgynous, but in the sense that "every stage in the sequence of gods was designated simultaneously by a masculine and a feminine deity" (8:367). It is as though Schelling had drawn lessons from Himalayan art, that is, from the depictions of the divinities in Hindu and Buddhist art of the Himalayan region. It is as though he had seen smiling Vishnu holding the breast of Lakshmi, or Chakrasamvara embracing Vajravarahi to the point of perfect conflation, achieving *yabyum*, the ecstatic copulation of compassion (identified with the father) and insight (identified with the mother). Be that as it may, languishing and languor—at least in the Cabirian system—belong inextricably to the constellation of doubles. One might think that a dual gender would guarantee satiety and plenitude, but the reverse appears to be the case. The Hebrew word for father and productive power (*die väterliche, urhebende Kraft*) immediately suggests desire, "concupiscence," and concomitant poverty. Schelling now introduces the word *Sehnsucht*, relating it to *Schmachten*, hunger and thirst (8:378–379). Even if "superabundant plenitude" seems to characterize the primal essence, it is nonetheless true that such an essence "possesses **nothing**"—nothing and no one with which or with whom it can share or to which or to whom it can communicate itself; such an essence "must appear to itself as utter poverty and supreme neediness" (8:352). Schelling now invokes Πενία, the mother of Eros, precisely in the way that Hölderlin will introduce her, not simply as the comic figure of Plato's *Symposium*, but as the divine mother of Love, who in turn is the first god to emerge from the cosmic egg. In Hesiodic and Orphic terms, all the early gods are children of the Night. "Yet what is the essence of Night, if not lack, neediness, and languor?" (ibid.).

Schelling, however, tries once again to retreat from the consequences of his own insights. He seeks to deny that the primal essence is uppermost in value, a ploy he attempts several times, as we have seen, in both *The Ages of the World* and "The Divinities of Samothrace." A marginal note to the latter reads: "The first is at the same time the lowest" (8:353). Such denials, to repeat, are in tension with his own desire to seek the most ancient, the primal and primary, the absolute commencement—precisely as a desire for the most valid and valuable system of belief, the very origin and seedbed of science. The languor of the night that wants to conceive and the languishing of Demeter (and even of Hestia) inevitably bring devaluation and derogation in their train: "But just as the very femininity of this polynomial essence, along with the names of the first nature, point either obscurely or quite clearly to the concepts of languor and of a languishing yearning [*die Begriffe der Sehnsucht und des schmachtenden Verlangens*], just so, the essence of Ceres . . . is entirely absorbed in languor. 'I am Deo,' she says to the daughters of Celeus, announcing herself first of all as the one who is sick with longing and languishing . . ." (8:353).[28]

The hunger of Axieros–Demeter is unlike any other, and it has its own dignity: that burning hunger has something to do with the genealogy of time and with "the first number," which is a "languishing longing" or a "longing languishing" (8:354). In a note, Schelling relates this notion of time to the indifferent (*als das an sich Gleichgültige* [*Indifferente*]), in the identical way the treatise on human freedom related it, but here citing the Zend-Avesta: "The true Creator is Time, which knows no limits, has nothing above it, no root, which was eternally and shall be eternally" (8:381). Schelling asserts that neither time nor eternity as usually conceived is an adequate concept here. The most he can say about these concepts positively is that "unity and difference itself are posited as One" (ibid.). Yet the One is bound up with πόθος, the very languishing that is under discussion. More specifically, note 47 informs us that languor involves something like a temporal system: "Πόθος [longing, yearning, regret] is a languishing [*Sehnsucht*] after a lost or now absent good. As Πόθος is related to the past, Ἵμερος [longing, yearning after] is related to what is present in the present [*das Gegenwärtige, Anwesende*] . . . ; Ἔρως is the first enkindling, desire, which precedes possession, and which thus strives toward what is still futural" (8:382). Pursuing this train of thought, Schelling is led to the conclusion that Axieros–Demeter–Ceres alone, who has lost both her daughter and the god for whom, like Isis, she pines, can be the divinity who relates most strongly to the past (8:383). As Plato's Aristophanes sug-

---

28. Schelling clearly belongs among those philologists for whom δέω means "I am lacking," rather than "I tie a knot" (RC 97–98). Yet if Anankē binds in nets and knots, may one not say that the tie that binds always involves a lack, a discontinuity, a gap in being—so that languor and the search are bound up with the knot of Necessity? Schelling goes on to discuss the nature of *Sehnsucht* as a seeking, *Suchen*, thinking preeminently of Demeter or Ceres in search of her missing daughter, Persephone or Proserpina. (Elsewhere he will assure us that the search actually has the god, her consort, and not her daughter, as its goal.) Nonetheless, the search in question is passionate and needy, is a *Schmachten* and a *Sucht*.

gests, however, in order to understand the nature of the forlorn we must presuppose a prior union with what is now lost (*ein vormaliges Einsgewesenseyn*). Thus Schelling is driven to conclude that a sundering or separation somehow precedes what is said to be initially unified (*eine vorhergegangene Scheidung*). Prior to the One in the beginning is a traumatic divorce that begins all. And prior to the divorce is a union remembered only in languor and languishing. In the beginning things were perfect, and divinity is sick about it. Yet if that is the case, we need hardly be surprised that all ἔρως implies ἵμερος, and all ἵμερος a πόθος, that is to say, that all futural, erotic love implies craving here and now, and all craving a languishing for what is bygone. The Persian women under the reign of Xerxes languish for want of news of their husbands, who once again have undertaken to conquer Greece (Aeschylus, *The Persian Women*, l. 62); Electra yearns for the reappearance of Orestes, longs for that homecoming to the point where she craves nothing further in her life (Sophocles, *Electra*, ll. 171–172, 822); Deianeira withers during Herakles' absence, because she does not know whether the hero still longs for her (Sophocles, *Women of Trachis*, ll. 631–632). And the word πόθος is used to evoke each of these situations, in which future, present, and past are hopelessly entangled. If in Schelling's view πόθος must be thought of as female, *weiblich*, then we need hardly be surprised that Poverty, Πενία, passes on her traits to the present and future of all time, all times, and all loves. Ceres, or Demeter, "lies at the ground of all, is the fundament" (8:395). Her Corybants and Curetes oversee the birth of Zeus on Ida (8:398). As the most august of all the chthonic divinities, θεοὶ χθόνιοι, Demeter or Ceres, in the figure of the lost daughter Persephone, oversees the realm of the dead (8:418). If the most ascendant of the Cabiri, Hermes, is the god of paths and byways, it remains true that at the beginning of god's journey stands *Sehnsucht* (8:394). The fundament suffers a lesion; the ground bottoms out. Eros, "the perennial, ruthless youthfulness of the world" (RC 326), is constantly called back to its checkered past. Drawn back by Himeros and Pothos, "Eros is the helplessness of that which is sovereign: it is strength abandoning itself to something elusive, something that stings" (RC 377). What stings is Oistrus, the gadfly of love, "that small, malicious creature" (RC 328) who gives us no peace.

The note that Schelling attaches to Ceres' announcement that she is Deo, that is to say, sick with longing and languishing, relates the corresponding sacred Hebrew words referring to the ostensible lordship of the gods over the earth precisely to *languit*, "he or she languishes," adding, *languor, praesertim muliebris* ("I am languishing; especially predicated of women"), and *languor ex morbo* ("languishing on account of illness") (8:379). Such meanings are "altogether in conformity" with the Greek word πόθος and, as we have already heard, with the German word *Sucht*, as in *Mondsucht* or *Tobsucht*. Schelling's source defines *Sucht* as a morbidity that afflicts the entire health of the human being; such—that source adds—*sunt omnes cupiditates*. Languishing is a being consumed, a withering away or melting, as though from a failure to eat or from thirst, or from a desire (*desiderio*) that will not let us drink or eat, unless it be of the vanished beloved. The derivation of god from "good," *bonus*, is therefore "altogether improbable," concludes Schelling (8:380), as though he has been studying or remembering ahead to the first treatise of Nietzsche's *Genealogy of Morals*.

In the main body of his lecture text, Schelling paraphrases an ancient Phoenician cosmogony to the following effect: "At first there was a veil of gloomy air and a turbid Chaos, all of it without bounds. But when the spirit of love burned with desire [*entbrannte*] for his own beginnings, and a contraction [*Zusammenziehung*] came about, this cincture was called languor [*Sehnsucht*], and this was the beginning of the creation of all things" (8:354). Schelling comments:

> Here the beginning is posited in a burning desire for oneself, a seeking oneself; the cincture that thereby originates is once again languor, except that it is now, as it were, embodied [*wieder, nur die gleichsam verkörperte, Sehnsucht*] and is the occasion for the creation of all things. Native to Phoenician cosmogonies therefore was the notion of languor as commencement, as the first ground of creation. Yet was this also believed in Samothrace? A passage in Pliny replies to this question, when it says that the works of Skopas designate Venus and Phaethon, that is, Languor and Pothos as divinities that (as he adds) were honored in Samothrace with the holiest usages. Thus it is certain that among the divinities of Samothrace there was one that was bound up with the concept of languor. (Ibid.)

Demeter-Ceres is of course that goddess of languor, as the names Axieros, Axiokersa, and Axiokersos suggest; she is mother and daughter in one, one in languor. It would surely be worthwhile to follow the career of Ceres-Proserpina, which is bound up with fire and magic, especially the magic of the hearth and the forge, the magic of Maja and Hephaistos. Yet we must be satisfied for the moment with Schelling's summary of the ascending row of Cabirian divinities:

> The ascending sequence therefore appears in the following way: at the deepest level we find Ceres, whose essence is hunger and malaise [*Sucht*], Ceres, who is the first and most remote commencement of all actual, revealed being. Next is Proserpina, essence or fundamental beginning of the entirety of visible [external] nature; then Dionysos, lord of the spirit world. Above nature and the spirit

143

world, the one who mediates the two, both between themselves and with the transcosmic gods, namely, Kadmilos, or Hermes. And, above all these, the god who is free with regard to the world, to wit, the Demiurge. Thus the doctrine of the Cabiri is an ascending system, from subordinate personalities or nature gods to a supreme personality who rules them all, an ultramundane God. (8:361)

One can see quite readily the grand syncretism of which Schelling is dreaming, one that would encompass the mystery doctrine of the Cabiri and Judeo-Christian doctrine, ascending from Demeter and Dionysos to Christ and the Father. Yet the oldest system, and the most ancient rung of its ancient ladder, is the mother-maid, the keeper of the night. And if she is marked by languor and languishing, one can expect that her descendants will inherit that mark, no matter how much their *dignitas* and *majestas* will seem to suffer. One is left wondering what an ascending series means in any case when wasting away, *Schmachten*, sets the seal of trauma on the commencement—*at* the commencement, *as* the commencement.

Why pursue the repressed past? Why pursue the matter of God's trauma? In order to discover a living divinity who in the end, after initial revulsion, will not keep her distance from mortals, will not accept violence, not even her own, and who will embrace human beings as the children to whom she gave birth. What would it take for such a God to embrace her children? She would have to overcome the trauma, the shock, and the suffering that initially caused her to cut herself off from her children. She would have to accept the full implications of what Schelling in the second half of the 1811 printing calls *Zeugungslust*, the desire to procreate, as the only possible form of creation and the only possible mode of divine life. The castration and emasculation suffered by her male worshipers is therefore not an *imitatio matris*, inasmuch as her sex is not elaborated by a cut, but an effect of the men's enthusiasm and memory, ecstasy and mourning. It is elaborated as an unfolding and infolding—*Entwicklung* and *Einwicklung* being Schelling's favorite words for the expansive and contractive forces at work in her. Yet neither will it do for us, here, to dream endlessly of *das ewige Weibliche* dragging us onward, whether enthused or kicking and screaming. For the sobering fate of the Amazons and of Niobe's children—seven males, seven females—is portrayed, as we shall presently see, on the pedestal of divinity. When God learns of his femininity as well as her masculinity, when God learns *longing*, he and she alike will learn that *languishing* is indigenous to passion. When God learns what love entails, she and he will discover that they are forever dying, even if their death is coming to meet them out of a past so distant, so elevated, so remote, that it seemed it would never arrive.

It will.

Such a death could be announced only in a story, a narrative that would itself be an *arrêt de mort*.

I begin. I am beginning. Always. Until the end.

Not enough—indeed, nothing at all—has been said here about the question this chapter set out to discuss, namely, the necessity that makes the known past an object of narrative or recounting, an object of saga or fable. It is a necessity that prevails beyond all dialectic—and my own dialectical foray does not seem to be up to telling the tale. What can be said affirmatively, rather than negatively, about the necessity of narrative? Narrative recounts creation, is itself creation. Better, it is that *telling moment* prior to creation in which memory and desire mix and words are spilled. In such a mix, creation is procreative, both centripetal and centrifugal at once. Creation recounts the itinerary followed by the gods to mortals—to mortal women and men on this earth—without return. Narratives as such, as Novalis says, are essentially tragic, inasmuch as they recount passions. Even if the exhibition of those passions—as in the puppet plays of *Being John Malkovich*—should make us laugh hysterically, narrativity as such—whether in philosophy or poesy, puppet theater or farce, no matter how trivial or motley—is tragic. The ancient myths, with their endless variations and repetitions, are the tragic narratives Schelling is seeking.

In our time, no one has evoked the narrative quality of myth with greater poetic force than Roberto Calasso. In *The Marriage of Cadmus and Harmony,* Calasso says the following about mythic repetition and variation: "The repetition of a mythical event, with its play of variations, tells us that something remote is beckoning to us. There is no such thing as the isolated mythical event, just as there is no such thing as the isolated word. Myth, like language, gives all of itself in each of its fragments" (RC 136). Several pages later he elaborates:

> No sooner have you grabbed hold of it than myth opens out into a fan of a thousand segments. Here the variant is the origin. Everything that happens, happens this way, or that way, or this other way. And in each of these diverging stories all the others are reflected, all brush by us like folds of the same cloth. If, out of some perversity of tradition, only one version of some mythical event has come down to us, it is like a body without a shadow, and we must do our best to trace out that invisible shadow in our minds. Apollo slays the monster, he is the first

slayer of monsters. But what is this monster? It is Python's skin, camouflaging itself among bushes and rock, and it is the soft skin of Daphne, already turning into laurel and marble. (RC 147–148)

In Calasso's view, it is precisely the way in which myth escapes ritual, rather than points back to it (as it does, for example, for all modern ethnography), that is decisive for narrative. Once again one must quote *The Marriage of Cadmus and Harmony* at length:

> In Greece, myth escapes from ritual like a genie from a bottle. Ritual is tied to gesture, and gestures are limited: what else can you do once you've burned your offerings, poured your libations, bowed, greased yourself, competed in races, eaten, copulated? But if the stories start to become independent, to develop names and relationships, then one day you realize that they have taken on a life of their own. The Greeks were unique among the peoples of the Mediterranean in not passing on their stories via a priestly authority. They were rambling stories, which is partly why they so easily got mixed up. And the Greeks became so used to hearing the same stories told with different plots that it got to be a perfectly normal thing for them. Nor was there any final authority to turn to for a correct version. Homer was the ultimate name one could evoke: but Homer hadn't told all the stories. (RC 279)

The poetic license of mythic narrative recapitulates the principal theme of the myths themselves, namely, the amorous license of the gods, especially Zeus. "Divine incursions" into the human realm represent an "unexpected overflowing of reality," leaving in their tumultuous wake a whole series of names—which become the *characters* of stories (ibid.). The contingencies and oblique relationships of such characters defeat logic. No dialectic can account for Apollo's Python or Daphne, for the scaly skin of the snake, the smooth skin of the girl, the alternately smooth and scaly bark of the tree, no matter how one adds them up—even if, or precisely because, logic and dialectic are gifts of this same Apollo. Calasso compares the mythical gesture to an ocean wave "which, as it breaks, assumes a shape": the narrative shape whelms us with the full force of its characters and twists of plot, and yet, as the wave recedes, "the unvanquished complications swell in the undertow, and likewise the muddle and the disorder from which the next mythical gesture will be formed" (RC 281). The result is that myth precludes system, refuses to be ordered into some dialectical sequence. "Indeed, when it first came into being, system itself was no more than a flap on a god's cloak, a minor bequest of Apollo" (ibid.). Narrative, by contrast, responds to the rhythm of mythic repetitions and variations, an irregular cadence of unstoppable tales.

Schelling, along with his friend Hölderlin, had been attentive to such tales since the days of their youth. Both knew why Zeus could not keep his distance from Europa, Io, Niobe, Semele, Danaë, Ganymede, and the countless other mortals for whom the father longed and languished. And they knew that the deepest secret of Zeus, passed on to his son Dionysos Zagreus alone, was that in that cave on Cretan Ida or Dikte he had indeed died at the hands of the Titans. These two friends, Schelling and Hölderlin, knew why Pindar sang of "primeval grief," why Plutarch remembered "primeval contaminations," and why the mysteries commanded silence: "For those not initiated in the mysteries, they seem to have to do with the immortality of men; for the initiates, the mysteries are a moment when the gods become entangled with death" (RC 315–316). Hölderlin sang uninhibitedly of this encrypted secret, this divine riddle, in many different places in his work, as far back as the earliest drafts of *Hyperion*. The most famous of his recountings is in *Der Rhein*. That hymn recounts a story he would have related to his friend Schelling as the two young enthusiasts wandered through the thick woods that border the Neckar River near Tübingen, the woods and the riverbank that smack sweetly of pantheism:

A riddle wells up pure. Even
Song can scarcely veil it. For
As you begin, so you shall remain.
Much is achieved by necessity
And also by discipline, but most
Can be achieved by birth....

Who was it that first
Ruined the cincture of love,
Tearing it to shreds?
After that they made their own law
And surely these spiteful ones
Mocked the fire of heaven, only then
Spurning mortal paths,
Choosing overbold
And striving to be equal to the gods.

Yet they have enough of their own
Immortality, the gods, and if they need
One thing, the celestial ones,
Then it is heroes and human beings
And whatever else is mortal. For if
The most blessed ones of themselves feel nothing,
Then it must be, if to say such a thing

> Is allowed, that in the name of the gods
> Another feels for them, takes their part;
> This other they need.[29]

One should remember, however, that the final words of this hymn recall the feverish days and nights of the eon of the present, in which we flit about and fret away our frenetic lives. We are agitated by a hectic and forgetful time. Trauma and oblivion seem to accompany us every step of the way; indeed, they are the troubling themes of our very best narratives. The present in which we tell these stories to one another is itself a Chaos linked—by its repressed memories of suffering and its longing for a caress—to a remote past and a distant future. Ours is thus an inevitably traumatized present, struggling as much to remember as to look ahead,

> In the night, when all's a jumble,
> Devoid of order, and all that recurs is
> Primeval confusion.

---

29. Hölderlin, CHV 1:342–348, ll. 46–51, 96–114, and, for the lines appearing below, 219–221.

GOD'S FOOTSTOOL

5

Schelling never saw God's footstool, and
neither have we seen it. Melville's Pip, at
the bottom of the coral-building sea, saw
God's *foot* on the treadle of the loom, but
neither Pip nor Schelling nor we have ever
seen God's footstool. No one has seen it
since the day the pious and avaricious em-
peror Theodosius II removed the cult
statue of Zeus from Olympia, in the
Western Peloponnese, to the Eastern im-
perial capital of Constantinople. Theodosius laid waste to the temples of Olympia
in the Year of Our Lord 426, thirty-two
years after his father put a stop to the
Olympic games. Theodosius II "rescued"
the gold and ivory statue—which, however, was destroyed in a fire only fifty years
later. God's footstool vanished, gone up in
smoke, for all the later ages.
    It is this vanished statue that
Schelling is describing when in the 1811
printing of *The Ages of the World* he writes
about God's footstool, *der Fußschemel
Gottes* (20–21; 250). How does he give an
account of something he has never seen?
This, I believe, is the problem of "The
Past" *in nuce,* that is to say, the problem of
The Ages of the World whole and entire.

Schelling "sees" the footstool when he reads the account of Olympia that Pausanias gives in the *Guide to Greece*. Schelling cites Pausanias more than once (see, for example, the "Notes" to *The Divinities of Samothrace*, 8:383), yet he is silent about his source for the footstool image. I call it an "image," and thereby miss the point of "The Past," as of Schelling's entire "middle period" production. For at least since the 1809 *Philosophical Investigations into the Essence of Human Freedom* Schelling is on the lookout for the primal images (*Ur-Bilder*) that are the very ideas espied by the Demiurge.[1] In other words, and in other worlds, the "image" of God's footstool is the prime reality, the proto-real; it is less an image of anything else than the original of everything else.

Every thing that is—a footstool? Or reposing *on* God's footstool? The world should be so comfortable!

In the three versions of *The Ages of the World* that we possess, all of them versions of Part 1, "The Past," Schelling refers to God's footstool only once. Indeed, he does so early on in the first (1811) draft. He then drops the image. That is to say, he lets go of the prime reality and the proto-real. Why? Is there something wrong with the "image"?

Winckelmann apparently thinks so. In his *Thoughts on the Imitation of Greek Works in Painting and Sculpture* (1755) he urges his readers to look at the works of the great artists in the way Lukian looked at Phidias's Olympian Jupiter: one must focus on Jupiter himself, "not at the stool for his feet."[2] Yet this is only half the story. For what Winckelmann is trying to indicate with the Phidian example is the exact opposite of what Lukian appears to be suggesting. Winckelmann wants to say that the "great artists" are wise "even in what they neglect" (ibid.); that is to say, great artists "cannot err without at the same time instructing us" (ibid.), so that even if the god's footstool were only the obverse of the coin, as it were, the crudely drawn "tails" to a more finely wrought "heads," that obverse of the coin still merits close examination.

Manfred Schröter, one of the most important editors of Schelling's works during the twentieth century, and the scholar who edited *Die Weltalter Fragmente*, does not agree about the value of such images, especially of the cruder sort. Schröter believes that, generally speaking, the first half of the first draft of *The Ages of the World* is excessive in its imagery; he finds the second (1813) version philosophically superior, less picturesque and more dialectical-con-

---

1. "... *in ewigen Ur-Bildern*," says the 1811 version of *Die Weltalter* (31). See also the conclusion to the *Philosophical Investigations* (7:415), cited in ch. 3, above, which says of nature that she "contains primal images [*Vorbilder*] that no human being has as yet interpreted."

2. J. J. Winckelmann, *Gedanken über die Nachahmung der griechischen Werke in der Malerei und Bildhauerkunst*, ed. Ludwig Uhlig (Stuttgart: Reclam, 1995 [orig. publ. 1755; 2nd, expanded ed., 1756]), 5.

ceptual. Of the images that disappear in the second and third versions, none is perhaps more worthy of obsolescence in Schröter's view than God's footstool. Schröter locates quite precisely the very page in the second version (p. 42, folios 62–64) where the footstool *might have* appeared but *did not*. In the Editor's Introduction (p. xxx) to *Die Weltalter Fragmente,* in the context of a discussion of nonbeing in relation to the divine, Schröter argues that the absence of the footstool in the 1813 draft is a particularly apt demonstration of the philosophical acuity of the second version vis-à-vis the first.[3] The footstool metaphor is meant merely as a heuristic device to make more palpable or "intuitable" (*veranschaulichen*) the highly abstract problem of God's contracting, negating will. Schröter notes that Schelling had used the image in his 1810 *Stuttgarter Privatvorlesungen,* preserving it for the 1811 version of *Die Weltalter* but then (wisely, in Schröter's view) discarding it. By 1813, according to Schröter, Schelling's abstract concept of nature has progressed (*fortgebildet*) to the point where such "accompanying representations from the realm of myth" are no longer necessary. The image of God's footstool in particular, which offers the eye a panoply of representations "bursting with life" (*lebenstrotzend*), needs to be subdued and sublimated into the "filigree work" of the concept— even if the footstool image is, as Schröter assures us, one of Schelling's favorites (*eine Lieblingsvorstellung Schellings*).

How shall one decide whether Schröter's desire to turn Schelling into Hegel is justified?

Or is Schelling a writer and thinker of a kind that Hegel never was and never could be?

Against Schröter, one could well argue that from 1809 through the 1815 printing of *The Ages of the World,* as well as both prior to this period and well after it, Schelling becomes increasingly suspicious of the dialectical-conceptual sophistication that philosophers then as now so much admire. Indeed, against Schröter's portrait of a Schelling at first befuddled by images and only belatedly making his way toward the concept, one could readily reply that the very earliest sketches toward *The Ages of the World* (185–275) show the greatest possible methodological sophistication and philosophical maturity: as the foregoing chapter showed, in these earliest sketches Schelling lucidly and decisively demonstrates the limitations of dialectical-conceptual presentation, insisting as he does on the superiority of narrative (*Erzählung*) in the science

---

3. It is perhaps revealing that in our own day Slavoj Žižek prefers this second version to the others. Like Manfred Frank, however, I prefer to draw attention to the first. See Manfred Frank's selection of Schelling's writings, *Ausgewählte Schriften,* vol. 4 (Frankfurt am Main: Suhrkamp, 1985), 213–320.

of preworldly time—indeed, the superiority of fable (*Fabel*) in the search for the thoroughly repressed truth of the past. The doubling of self in dianoetic dialectic (which *Theaetetus* and *Sophist* define as the soul's conversation with itself), while essential to philosophy, does not obviate the necessity of a remembrance within solitude, that is to say, the necessity of the struggle to recollect preworldly time and to recount what is remembered "with candor and simplicity" (192–193). Schelling does not seek to burn off concepts and essences from the mash of crude images in the distillery of dialectic—Hegel as "Old Granddad." He tries to recapture a memory of the proto-real, itself captured in the stuff of stone and paint and verse, seeking such recapture without shame. Although the "image" of the footstool also disappears from the 1815 Samothrace lecture and notes, the recognition that simple narrative (*einfache Erzählung*) is superior to dialectical legerdemain perdures in Schelling's work. With it perdures Schelling's refusal to disdain the eidolon, his determination to resist the perennial philosophic dream that sensuous images can or should be left behind by conceptual logistics. If nature can no longer be saved in the image of the divine footstool, that can only be because nature becomes the very foot that would love to seek repose on some sort of support. God's are busy feet, as we shall see. Busy feet with divinely delicate soles. And all of this is simply too pedestrian for dialectic.

So much by way of preliminaries. Let us now read the "footstool" passage in the 1811 draft of *The Ages of the World*, comparing it with the relevant passages in the 1810 *Stuttgarter Privatvorlesungen* and the 1827–1828 Munich lectures on the "system" of the "ages of the world." We will then present a passage in which the footstool reappears, a passage, according to Schröter's own edition of the *Fragmente*, from folio 32, intended for the introduction to the never-completed *second* volume of *The Ages of the World*, namely, "The Present." Finally, we will examine an extended passage from Pausanias's *Guide to Greece*, the probable source for Schelling's God's footstool, insofar as that God is as much Hellenic Zeus as Hebrew Yahweh.

From the 1811 Draft of *Die Weltalter*, with Variants from the 1810 *Stuttgarter Privatvorlesungen* and the 1827–1828 *System der Weltalter*

The context is Schelling's argument concerning the special status of the nonbeing or nothingness, μὴ ὄν, out of which the created world putatively arises:

Das Nichtseyende ist nicht absoluter Mangel an Wesen, es ist nur das dem eigentlichen Wesen entgegengesetzte, aber darum in seiner Art nicht minder positive Wesen; es ist, wenn jenes die Einheit ist, der Gegensatz und zwar der Gegensatz schlechthin oder an sich. Schon darum ist [es] eine ewige Kraft, ja wir würden richtiger sagen es sey die ewige Kraft schlechthin, die Stärke Gottes, wodurch vor allem andern Er Selbst als Er Selbst ist, der einzige, von allem abgeschnittene, der zuerst und allein seyn muß, damit anderes seyn könne. Ohne dieses wirkende Princip wäre der Begriff der Einzigkeit Gottes ein leerer, ein gemeinverneinender Begriff. Wenn auch Gott gewollt hat, daß dieses Princip dem Wesen als der eigentlichen Gottheit in ihm unterworfen sey: so ist es darum doch in sich nicht weniger ein Lebendiges. Gott der eigentlich seyende ist über seinem Seyn; der Himmel ist sein Thron und die Erde sein Fußschemel; aber auch das in Bezug auf sein höchstes Wesen Nichtseyende ist so voll von Kraft, daß es in ein eignes Leben ausbricht. So erscheint in der Vision des Propheten, wie sie Raphael dargestellt hat, der Ewige nicht von dem Nichts, sondern von lebendigen Thiergestalten getragen. Nicht minder groß hat der hellenische Künstler das Aeußerste menschlicher Schicksale, den Tod der Kinder der Niobe am Fuße des Thrones gebildet, auf welchem sein olympischer Zeus ruht, und selbst den Schemel des Gottes durch die Vorstellung der Amazonenkämpfe mit kräftigem Leben geschmückt. (20–21)

Nonbeing is not absolute lack of essence; it is merely what is opposed to the essence proper. Yet for all that, it is not any the less positive essence. If being is unity, nonbeing is the contrary—it is the opposite without qualification, or in itself. For that very reason it is an eternal force; indeed, it would be more correct to say that it is eternal force without qualification, God's strength, by means of which, above all else, he himself is as he himself, the solitary one, cut off from everything, the one that must be first of all and all alone if anything else is to be. Without this efficacious principle, the concept of God's singularity would be a vacuous, all-negating concept. Even if God willed that this principle be subordinate to the essence that is divinity proper in him, it is nonetheless in itself something living. God, as what properly is, surpasses his being. Heaven is his throne and earth his footstool. Yet even that which in relation to his supreme essence is nonbeing is so full of force that it irrupts into a life of its own. Thus in the vision of the prophet, as Raphael depicts it, the eternal is sustained not by nothingness but by forms of living animals. No less grand is the manner in which the Hellenic artist portrays the extremity of human fate, to wit, the death of Niobe's children, on the foot of the throne on which his Olympian Zeus reposes; and, representing there as he did the battles of the Amazons, he decorated the very footstool of the god with energetic life.

Nonbeing is eternal force and energy, opposed to the divine essence proper yet somehow conjoined with it and essential to it. Energetic nonbeing is the very *Stärke* of God—his strength, his starch, his *pith*, as one says of the moist interior fibers of woody-stemmed plants. If life is energy, then the energetic life of God rests on nonbeing. Without the energetic source, God could not reign as solitary and majestic—he himself, by himself, cut off from everything else, *abgeschnitten*. In a word, there is a nonbeing that is efficacious, working effects in and as the divine life. God is doubtless superior; he subordinates all else to himself. "Heaven is his throne and earth his footstool." This sounds like a quotation from or an allusion to what Schelling always calls "an Old Book," meaning of course the Bible, and it is. For this is the syncretic footstool of Isaiah's and Ezekiel's Yahweh—but also of Phidias's Zeus.

An odd footstool, in any and all cases. It ought to sit there in God's parlor and grow faded and lumpy, ragged from the scratchings of the house cat and dusty from the motes in sunbeams and the passing of the hours. Yet this particular footstool, like Melville's "Apple-Tree Table," with its "Original Spiritual Manifestations," bursts into life. Indeed, the footstool takes on a life of its own, turning the parlor into a greenhouse—though not into God's Green Acres, which is a military cemetery, Niobe's children to the contrary notwithstanding. One word more, therefore, about what sort of footstool this is *not*. Schelling never refers to the most polemical biblical passage on God's footstool, from Hebrews 1:10–13. The context is Paul's effort to convince the Hebrews that Jesus, as the Son of God, is much more powerful than any angel:

> And, Thou, Lord, in the beginning hast laid the foundation of the earth; and the heavens are the works of thine hands. They shall perish; but thou remainest; and they all shall wax old as doth a garment; and as a vesture shalt thou fold them up, and they shall be changed: but thou art the same, and thy years shall not fail. But to which of the angels said he at any time, Sit on my right hand, until I make thine enemies thy footstool?[4]

Luther translates: *Bis ich lege deine Feinde zum schemel deiner füsse.* Paul's Hebrew God is less about weak Messianic voices, the voices of the defeated and defunct to which the *angelus novus* of Walter Benjamin turns, than it is about turning one's enemies into upholstery. To repeat, this ignominious footstool is not the footstool to which Schelling will refer.

Yet first things first. To which painting of Raphael is Schelling alluding? Siegbert Peetz, the editor of Schelling's inaugural lecture course at the Uni-

---

4. I am grateful to my colleague and friend Peter Steeves, who brought this Pauline footstool to my attention in a personal communication, adding the following apt depiction of Creation in one of its more jaded aspects: "He makes not only the Earth and the Heavens, but also footstools—dirty things constructed out of bad people." Dr. Peter Wake reminds me of one of Hegel's favorite passages from the Sermon of the Mount (Matthew 5:34–35; HW 1:330), a passage that refers to the celestial throne and earthly footstool—namely, the admonishment against oath-taking by the heavens or by the earth.

Lukas Cranach the Younger created this full-page illustration for the 1541 edition of
Luther's Bible, which contained a new interpretation (and a retranslation) of Ezekiel
1:6–14. Luther sees the numerous depictions of the number four in Ezekiel's vision—with
the animals' faces, hands, and feet, as well as with the four wheels and hubs—as indications
that Christianity will conquer all four corners of the globe. Note that the platform on
which Christ's throne is placed has been cut away—perhaps in order to allow the earth to
serve as his footstool. Note too the brazen wheels (to be discussed in the following chapter) that seem to want to roll the footstool in all four directions at once. Finally, Luther is
fascinated by the "rounded feet" of the four figures: what Cranach illustrates as hooves are
actually feet that can roll angel and beast as though they were portable footstools.

versity of Munich in 1827–1828, *System of the Ages of the World*, argues that Schelling is "obviously thinking of such paintings as the 'Sistine Madonna' in the Dresden Art Gallery or the 'Disputa del Sacramento' in the Stanza della Segnatura in the Vatican."[5] The 1811 *Weltalter* draft, as we have seen, clearly refers to the "Vision" of "the Prophet," albeit without the quotation marks, that is, without citing a specific work.

Before pursuing the question of Raphael's painting any farther, however, we need to present this second (Munich 1827–1828) variant of God's footstool in greater detail. The context in the present case is slightly altered: it is not so much the question of nonbeing, but the issue of freedom and necessity in God's essence, that is under discussion. It is especially difficult here to cut into the flow of Schelling's lecture course in order to make a selection, but let the following lines suffice for our purposes:

> Gott kann nicht mit dem Sein befangen sein, welches immer nur ein anderswerdendes ist. Gott ist das Wesen in seiner Lauterkeit, aber nur der bei sich bleibende Geist ist der als Geist-seiende Geist. Also konnte Gott kein sich Entfremdendes werden. Zwar könnte man das Verhältniß der sich gleich bleibenden und sich entfremdenden Substanz so bestimmen, daß man diese als nur zur Form der Existenz Gottes, nicht zum Wesen gehörend betrachtete, so daß nur dieses ewig in sich seiende Wesen von dieser Form der Endlichkeit getragen würde; wie der göttliche Raphael in jener Vision an die Fußsohlen und Füße die höchsten lebendigen Gestalten als ihre Träger malte—; allein dieses, eine Form der Existenz Gottes[,] konnte es nur sein, wenn es eine freiwillige Selbstoffenbarung war. Nun frägt es sich: Ob diese Existenz eine freiwillige sich-selbst-Offenbarung war: dann wäre diese Existenz eine gewordene. Allein diese Offenbarung seiner selbst war nicht als freiwillig gedacht, sie war als nothwendig angenommen. (*System* 52)

> God cannot be fettered by being, which is always only a becoming-other. God is the essence in its purity, but only spirit that abides with itself is spirit that exists spiritually. Hence God could not become self-alienating. To be sure, one might define the relation of a substance that remains the same and yet is self-alienating in such a way that one takes the alienation as pertaining merely to the form of God's existence, not to the essence, so that the essence that exists eternally in itself is merely borne by this form of finitude; in the way that the divine Raphael in his vision painted those supremely vital figures onto the footsoles and feet as their carriers—; except for the fact that it could be a form for the existence of God only if it was a voluntary self-revelation. Now, the question arises whether this existence was a freely willed revelation of self: in that case, this existence

---

5. *System* 52–54. I have not been able to see the *Sistine Madonna*, housed in Dresden. However, none of the many other madonnas by Raphael shows the kind of animal vitality, especially around the feet, that Schelling is referring to; the *Disputa del Sacramento* I *have* seen recently, and there is nothing in the painting—other than clouds—to suggest the kind of vitality we are seeking. I will return to this question in a moment.

would be something that came to be. Yet this revelation of self was not thought of as being *voluntary*, it was accepted as being *necessary*.

As we shall see, the reference to Raphael here conflates something that in the *Stuttgarter Privatvorlesungen* pertained to the Hellenic image alone. However, before proceeding with the commentary, and at the risk of confusing the 1811 text now with *earlier* rather than *later* material, let us examine the variant we find in Schelling's 1810 *Stuttgarter Vorlesungen*, itself too a text gleaned from Schelling's literary remains and never published during his lifetime. The context is quite similar to that of the 1811 *Weltalter* draft, involving as it does a particular kind of nothingness that possesses "a terrifying reality" (7:437), a nothingness that is not οὐκ ὄν but μὴ φαινόμενα (7:436), that is to say, a nothingness that is not simply nonbeing but a potency that refrains from appearing. Schelling elaborates:

Auch das bloße *Seyn* in Gott ist kein todtes Seyn, sondern auch in sich wieder ein lebendiges, das auch selber wieder ein Seyendes und ein Seyn in sich schließt. Gott selbst ist *über* der Natur, die Natur sein Thron, sein Untergeordnetes, aber alles in ihm ist so voll Leben, daß auch dieses Untergeordnete wieder in ein eignes Leben ausbricht, das rein für sich betrachtet ein ganz vollkommenes Leben ist, obgleich in Bezug auf das göttliche Leben ein Nichtleben. So hat Phidias an der Fußsohle seines Jupiters die Kämpfe der Lapithen und Centauren abgebildet. Wie hier—vielleicht nur durch jenen wunderbaren Instinkt geleitet, der in allen griechischen Werken ist—der Künstler auch noch die Fußsohle des Gottes mit kräftigem Leben erfüllt, so ist gleichsam das Aeußerste und Entfernteste von Gott noch volles, kräftiges Leben in sich selbst. (7:437–438)

Even mere *being* in God is not dead being; in itself, it too is a living being, one that embraces in itself in turn something existent and a being. God himself is *above* nature; nature is his throne, his subordinate; yet everything in him is so full of life that even what is subordinate irrupts once again into a life of its own. Observed purely in and of itself, such life is altogether perfect, even though in relation to the divine life it is a nonlife. Thus Phidias depicted on the footsole of his Jupiter the battles of the Lapiths and Centaurs. Perhaps in this he was merely guided by that wonderful instinct we find in all Greek works. Yet just as the artist fills the very footsole of the god with energetic life, precisely so is the very extremity, the most remote facet of God, as it were, in itself full and energetic life.

In both the late 1827–1828 course and the early 1810 *Stuttgarter Privatvorlesungen* there is suddenly talk of footsoles rather than footstools. In the Munich lecture course, Raphael is said to have painted something at or on the footsoles and feet of the main figure in the painting. Schelling does seem to say *onto* the footsoles and feet, as though the footsoles of the prophet's God were a kind of stretched canvas. (Perhaps in that case he ought to have written *auf den Fußsohlen*, choosing the dative of place, with the accusative object—namely, the figures that were painted there—clearly indicated as such; yet if the painted figures were mere supports for or carriers of the feet, would not those figures be *unter*, that is, subordinate to, the feet? Would they not at least be *bei* or *neben* the feet?) The longer we read and try to decipher the text, the more it seems that Raphael must have painted something on the footsoles of the Lord. We will have to look at the painting.

Which painting? The most likely choice is Raphael's "Vision of Ezekiel."[6] The Glory of the Lord, according to the Book of Ezekiel, appears in the midst of four bizarre winged animals. After the establishment of the Christian church, these animals come to represent the four evangelists, Matthew, Mark, Luke, and John. In Raphael's rendition of the vision, the Lord appears to be sitting on the back of an eagle (John), which is bearing him aloft or bringing him down to earth—it is impossible to tell which, although the flow of hair and beard suggests downward motion. The Johannine eagle is the living throne, the heaven and nature, of God. A central visual element in the painting is the Lord's outstretched right foot—the footsole, with the big toe slightly splayed, is clearly visible, and indeed is in the eye of the

---

6. Raphael (1483–1520), *The Vision of Ezekiel*, executed between 1514 and 1518, now in the Pitti Palace, Florence. Did Schelling ever see this painting? Did he know of it only through Wilhelm Heinse's account of it in *Ardinghello*? I have not found evidence of an *Italienreise* in Schelling's life—and yet in the 1802–1803 *Philosophy of Art* Schelling speaks of having seen a number of works in St. Peter's Basilica in Rome, so that one wonders whether the Florentine Raphael may also have been familiar to him. See 5:552. Johann Heinrich Meyer's three articles in Goethe's journal, *Propyläen*, published at the turn of the nineteenth century, could have inspired Schelling's remarks, although I see no explicit discussion there of "the vision" of a "prophet." See "Raffaels Werke besonders im Vatikan," *Propyläen* 1, 1:101–127; 1, 2:82–163; and 3, 2:75–96. The journal has been photomechanically reproduced by the Cotta Verlag (Stuttgart, 1965) and by the Wissenschaftliche Buchgesellschaft (Darmstadt, 1965); see in these modern reproductions the following pages: 153–179, 268–349, and 973–994. Yet to revert now to the Schelling lectures on art: it is also clear from the lecture course how much Schelling esteemed Raphael. For example, he praises the symbolic-historical paintings of Raphael, especially "the calm and tranquillity of the main figures" represented there (5:559). Indeed, if Michelangelo is the master of drawing, Correggio of chiaroscuro, and Titian of color, it is Raphael who holds all these aspects in balance, so that he is "the truly divine priest of modern art" (5:560). Raphael possesses all the requisite technique to invent freely, and he paints after the manner of the essence itself: "He scorns the superfluous, achieving the greatest effects with the simplest of means, thereby breathing into his works such objective life that they seem to subsist entirely on their own, developing out of themselves and producing themselves with necessity" (ibid.). Who else, then, is fit to paint images of the ground of essence? No one—other than Phidias. For Phidias and Raphael are mentioned in tandem throughout the *Philosophy of Art*. Each is an avatar—one in antiquity, the other in modernity—of "the grand style" in art. (No, Nietzsche does not invent the term *der große Stil*.) Such a style is pure, highly rhythmical, yet measured, harmonious and well proportioned. See 5:610–611. I am grateful to Anna Vaughn Clissold, of DePaul University's Humanities Center, for first bringing Raphael's *The Vision of Ezekiel* to my attention.

Wilhelm Heinse, *Ardinghello*, Part V (1787): "Florence, January. . . . Among the paintings, of which there are many, I want to tell you about just a few by Raphael. . . . The second one is quite small, only a little more than a foot in height and breadth, altogether rare among his paintings, even though it was completed during his finest period. [¶] God the Father sits on an eagle in the upper air . . . supported lightly by two angels; below him are the four Evangelists with their animals; then clouds, then the earth with trees. . . . The head is all sublimity. . . . The figure, naked from chest to upper thighs, is as exquisite in its detail as a statue from antiquity. He rests his feet on the winged bull and lion and gazes like Jove—benevolent and strong and mighty—at beast and man. Hair and beard are swept back by the wind. A heavenly little portrait; charmingly apocalyptic mood!"

Raphael, *The Vision of Ezekiel*. Oil on panel 40.5 x 30 cm. Reproduced with the generous permission of the Superintendent of Florentine Museums.

beholder. There are no tattoos or markings of any kind on the sole. (There is of course no circular *chakra,* indicating a center of consciousness in the body, nor a diamond-shaped figure—perhaps a *vajra*—cupped in the arch of the foot, as there is so often in Himalayan art, where ostentation of the footsole seems essential to sacred and meditative postures.) The right foot of the Lord is reposing on one of the pinions of the winged ox or bull (Luke), an image that conflates heaven and earth, throne and footstool. Below the Lord's left hand we see a winged lion (Mark) and a winged human or quasi-human being, presumably an angel (Matthew). One may in fact wonder whether all these animals are Cherubim, as Luther believes, inasmuch as the Cherubim are carriers. Whatever the case, the evangelical animals are appreciably larger than the *puttos* of the painting. The animals gaze upward, their mouths gaping. They are cawing, bellowing, roaring out the Gospel. Even the human being or angel—and she appears to be a woman, her hands crossed over her breasts—seems to be singing or declaiming. Only the attendant *puttos* seem to be taking the divine afflatus or descent in stride. The Glory of the Lord is itself stern and sober; some might describe the facial expression as anxious. Schelling is right: the vitality of the painting rests on the winged and noisy creatures that support the Lord, animals that are galloping on air. But to return to the Munich lectures, and their fundamental, unresolved problem.

For the problem of the *necessity* of nature as the ground of God's existence, along with that of *freedom* in the self-revelation of divinity, remains. Schelling now introduces into his Munich lectures the essential aspect of historicity (*Geschichtlichkeit*), as the site of the further development of this question, and he refers to both the *Phenomenology of Spirit* and the concept of "absolute spirit" in the system of one of his "opponents," indeed, the most famous of his opponents. For the moment, at least, the problem is whether the succession of configurations in the self-revelation of God proffers freely assumed forms or unfolds in accord with necessary presuppositions. Can the totality of such forms be thought of as freely willed, or is it merely posited as necessitous? We pick up the text of the lecture after a gap of about a page:

> Das Vorausgesezte ist nicht das Höhere zugleich, wol aber das Obere, es ist ein superius. Die vorausgesezte Totalität ist deswegen nicht das Höhere so wenig der Stein das Höhere ist aus dem der Künstler eine Figur gestaltet. Gott ist nun zwar allerdings das von einzenlnen Formen getragene, wie es in jener Vision so schön heißt: "Der Himmel ist sein Thron und die Erde seiner Füße Schemel." Diese blos scheinbare Priorität aber hebt sich im lezten Begriffe auf. Der absolute Geist existiert, sowie er die Form voraussezt. Die Formen sind Emanationen seines nothwendigen Seins. (*System* 53–54)

What is presupposed is not forthwith the higher, although it is what is above, something superior. The presupposed totality is thus not the higher, just as little as is the stone out of which the artist shapes a figure. Now, to be sure, God is that which is borne by individual forms, as it is so beautifully phrased in that vision: "The heaven is his throne and the earth the stool for his feet." This merely apparent priority, however, is relieved in the final concept. Absolute spirit exists, just as it presupposes form. The forms are emanations of its necessary being.

Thus ends the thirteenth lecture of the course. Yet it ends unfortunately. For emanation and necessity are what Schelling has all along resisted, inasmuch as they are the death of freedom. The course ends doubly unfortunately. For the concept (*der Begriff*) that should relieve—or dialectically cancel, sublate, relieve, and surpass—the forms that bear and carry the divine is precisely that Hegelian logistical device that Schelling has all along abjured. These larger issues—of freedom, necessity, images, the proto-real, the ground, and the concept, issues on which Schelling's entire philosophy hangs—are too much for us to decide here, here or perhaps anywhere else.

Let us try to find our feet. Siegbert Peetz locates the biblical source(s) of Schelling's footstool image, finding it at the very end of the Book of Isaiah (66:1), and inviting us to compare Deuteronomy 10:14. Isaiah 66:1, in Luther's translation, reads: "*So spricht der HERR / Der Himel ist mein Stuel / und die Erde meine fusbanck.*" (The verse from Deuteronomy cites heaven and earth as being "of the LORD God," but makes no reference to throne or footstool.) Perhaps all we need to note about the Book of Isaiah is that it is the iconoclastic book par excellence, that is, the book that warns the children of God not to worship images. It is no doubt also important to note that the 1810–1811 allusions to Phidias are dropped in the 1827–1828 lecture course. The references to Jupiter Zeus in general are rare here, although one reference deserves mention. In the course of a discussion of contingency and accident with regard to the divine, indeed the *Urzufall,* or primal accident, which Schelling calls "blindly necessary existence," Schelling notes: "Mythology therefore represents the potency of the beginning as *Fatum,* as *Fortuna primigenia,* in whose arms Jupiter lay" (*System* 135, 135 n. 87). Cicero refers to Fortune as the one who accompanies her favorites from the moment of their birth. Yet if Fortune must accompany the boy Zeus, or, rather, the infant Zeus, sequestered in a cave on Mount Ida or Mount Dikte, *Fortuna primigenia* becomes a name for the fatal accidents that may befall even the king of the gods. Schelling adds: "At all events, Fortuna = the Dyas, the περιφερές, because it can be inverted [*weil es sich herumdrehen läßt*]" (ibid.). Chance, fate, or fortune are peripheral, not in the sense that they are remote from the center, but because they determine the strange circle in which center and circumference are coextensive, the circle that spins.

What in the 1810 *Stuttgarter Privatvorlesungen* variant merits further commentary? We should say something about a divine being and divine existent (*Seyn, Seyendes*) that are essentially *living*, even though God sits on celestial nature (and puts his feet up on earthly nature) as something subordinate, notwithstanding the fact that such subordination "irrupts into a life of its own." And, above all, we should say something about the apparently unwarranted reference to Zeus's footsole (about which, as we shall soon see, Pausanias says nothing). For, according to the Schelling of 1810, an energetic life prevails even on the god's footsole, the sole of the foot being as far from the soul of the god and as far from the head of the godhead as anything could be. Here the primal image becomes a tattoo, inscribed and incised on the flesh of the god. What sort of flesh is that? And how is it related to human flesh?

In his 1802–1803 aesthetics, Schelling stresses the difficulty of mastering fleshtones in painting. The difficulties in painting prove to be quite parallel to difficulties in the initial creation of flesh. Indeed, Schelling compares the mix of colors in fleshtones to the mix that occurred during the reign of Χάος, described in Plato's *Statesman* and Hesiod's *Theogony* as the eon in which the flesh of the human body itself originated. From the start, and on through the age of modern painting, flesh is heir to a sea of emotions: "The supreme marriage of light with matter, such that the essence becomes wholly matter and wholly light, occurs in the [painterly] production of *flesh*. Flesh is the true Chaos of all colors. . . . The inner stirrings [in the faces of painted portraits], of anger, shame, languor, and so on, set that sea of colors in motion, as it were, and cause the waves to beat sometimes mildly, sometimes wildly" (5:540). To be sure, Schelling is writing here about the flesh of the painted face, not the flesh of the feet. Yet how are face and foot disposed with regard to languorous flesh, whether palpable or painted? Once again the 1802–1803 lectures on the philosophy of art provide insight. In his account of Greek sculpture, which he regards as an "immediate expression of reason," Schelling, following a hint in Kant's third *Critique*, finds the principal ideas of plastic art to be expressed in representations of the human body (5:602). The "symbolic significance" of the human body is outlined in four points. First, the erect posture of the body suggests that the body has always already torn itself free from the earth— Schelling speaks of nothing less than a complete emancipation and violent disjunction, *eine gänzliche Losgerissenheit* (5:604). Plants have this same vertical posture, yet are bound to the earth. Animals, because they have a horizontal posture, represent a partial inversion of the plant world, an inversion by half, as it were. Both the vertical plant and the horizontal animal worlds cohere with the earth. As for the human body, which unites vertical directionality with horizontal mobility, a superior destination is indicated. Nevertheless, a great part of the weight of the human body resides in organs of the alimentary system. These exert a downward pull on the body, all the way down to its feet, which have to bear the burden—at least when they are not flying. Ovid expresses the true purpose of the body when he speaks of our turning our faces up to the stars. Second, the human body is symmetrical across a vertical line—made famous in Leonardo's drawing. This vertical line represents the annihilation of the east-west polarity in human beings as opposed to plants (5:605). The eye in particular expresses this indifference to east and west, inasmuch as it pivots in every direction through every dimension. Third, the human body is characterized by a "decisive subordination" of the systems of nourishment, reproduction, and locomotion to the "uppermost" system, "whose seat is the head," adds Schelling in disarming yet classic catachresis (ibid.). Notably, it is the human body that serves as the primal image of other animal bodies, which are derivative of it and unequal to it. Schelling says nothing here about divine flesh, but the erstwhile divinity of human flesh is already clearly indicated.

The lectures on aesthetics go on to offer a complete portrait of the body, with Plato's *Timaeus* serving as the model. The human body is a "middling creature," *ein Mittelwesen,* stretching between sky and earth, not only in the sense of Kantian anthropology, for which man is half angel and half beast, but also in the sense that the body is half liquid and half solid. Other creatures crawl "on the *ground* of the sea of air," whereas the human being "elevates itself most freely in that sea" (ibid.). Again a disarming catachresis—yet one that is common to the time, with Hölderlin too thinking of the ethereal air as a sea—mixing the elements of earth, water, and air, so that the birdlike human, if not the winged ox, is the most buoyant fish in the sea. The human head represents the sky, and in the sky the sun. As all the planets orbit about the sun, so all the parts of the body turn about the head. The chest, on the line of descent toward the feet, represents the sea of air between sky and earth. The chest rises and falls, swells and subsides, as it takes in and releases air. The heart dilates—and thus dissolves the hardness of the heart that is so stubbornly directed toward itself and its own interests. When it heats in passion, inclining toward and desiring another, heart becomes hearth (*Herz/Herd*). The ribcage is stretched like a vault over the earth, marking an essential divide. For the lower belly contains the reproductive forces that are at work in the interior of the earth, pushing toward the surface to get a view of the sun. Greek art suitably reduces the size of everything in the body that is related to the alimentary and reproductive systems: statues of the gods are flat-bellied—indeed, the gods have no bellies to speak of—and statues of the goddesses reduce "the superfluity of the female breasts," thus encouraging Greek women in real life to do the same "by artificial means" (5:615).

At long last Schelling descends to the "auxiliary organs," that is, the extremities. The hands wield tools, as we expect them to. And the feet? Contrary to what we might expect, the feet "express our disjunction from the earth," that is to say, our being torn free from the fixed vertical and even mobile horizontal positions (5:606). Because the feet unite near and far, "they designate the human being as the visible image of divinity, for which nothing is near, nothing far" (ibid.). Human feet are divine; they do fairly fly. The feet are nothing more than the vehicles of motion *across* the earth, a motion that symbolizes independence *from* the earth. On flying feet, the human being prances and runs like a god: "Homer describes Juno's stride as being as fast as a human being's thought whenever that thought traverses in an instant's time the many countries once visited: 'I was here, and then I went there.' The speed of Atalanta is described thus: when she ran, her feet left no prints at all in the sand over which they dashed" (ibid.). *Atalanta fugiens*, an important alchemical text from the early seventeenth century, serves as the model: all the dross, the entire *caput mortuum* of the feet, has been sloughed off—no prints, no gravity, no east-west orientation, no flesh, no ferment, no footsoles, and no footstools. No rest for the weary or the wicked—or rather, for the blessed, who would run, or soar, like a god. The fourth and final characterization of the configuration of the human body is that it represents even at rest "a completely balanced system of motions" (ibid.). "Perfect harmony," says Schelling, taking up the musical metaphor that pervades his aesthetics (see the following chapter). Perfect harmony—expressed in "the rhythm of its motions" (5:607). One senses in the 1802–1803 aesthetics the distance that Schelling will have to run in his later texts in order to catch up with the flesh of god.

However, after this long digression on face, feet, and flesh, let us return to the passage cited earlier from the *Stuttgarter Privatvorlesungen*, again raising a series of questions concerning its inclusions and exclusions. Why the reference to the battles between the Lapiths and Centaurs, ostensibly on the footsoles of Zeus, a reference that does not survive in any of the three drafts of *The Ages of the World* or in the 1827–1828 lecture course? Why, if one can ask such a thing, the absence of Niobe and the Amazons, once the subordination of nature is in place? *Is* it in place? What *is* this irruption of the ground into a life of its own? Would not such a life *of its own* be the divine life *proper*, the sole life and existence of God?

If the Centaurs are indistinguishable from satyrs, at least in the prehistory of Greece, they effectively represent the forceful, irrepressible life of which Schelling speaks. Their shameless behavior at the wedding of Perithous and Hippodameia, depicted on the gable of the temple of Zeus at Olympia, certainly suggests their satyric roots: after drinking excessively—they were unaccustomed to wine—they attempted to rape the bride. Centaurs and Lapiths, horse-people from the plains of Thessaly and the mountains of Pelion, themselves incarnate the central problem of Schelling's text, to wit, the "mixed form" of divinity and natural life. These horse-people run faster than people-people, and they hold their heads higher. Excessive life is not so readily tamed.

In order to conclude this first stage in the analysis, let us return to the 1811 draft of *The Ages of the World*. Here the reference to Niobe is particularly striking, inasmuch as the positive tone of "a life of its own" is suddenly reversed to the extremity of suffering. One is reminded once again of the importance of Niobe in Sophocles' *Antigone* as a figure for Antigone herself; Hölderlin, in his 1803 "Notes" on the tragedy, makes much of this figure. Niobe's relation to Zeus is that highly ambivalent familial relation of sympathy, eros, and conflict: a granddaughter of Zeus, she is nonetheless his first mortal (or semi-mortal) conquest. Like Io, Europa, Semele, and Danaë, she causes Zeus considerable anxiety: it has been foretold that one of her progeny somewhere down the line will take the life of Zeus. In this respect she is like the figure of Io in Aeschylus's *Prometheus Bound,* and like so many others among Zeus's paramours; she is also like Danaë, who, at least according to Hölderlin's translation of *Antigone,* ticks off the golden hours of time for the very father of time and the earth. Zeus is both in a panic to engender a hero that will protect him and anxious about giving life to the force that will kill him. Niobe is ultimately a figure of that *Fortuna primigenia* by virtue of which the fortunes of both mortals and immortals may spin and suffer reversal. Whereas the God of the prophets is putatively borne safely aloft on pinioned animals, Zeus is uneasily enthroned, easily unthroned, his feet twitching nervously on a footstool that has suddenly burst into uncontrollable life.

From the Sketches toward the *Second* Proposed Volume of *Die Weltalter,* "The Present"

Manfred Schröter introduces the following sketches of the second proposed part of Schelling's grand *Weltalter* scheme with the demur that they betray "fundamental flaws in the speculative approach to a philosophy of nature" (186). Predictably, he singles out the sketches toward volume two for special mention, precisely because of their "unmediated naiveté" (ibid.). What he doubtless has in mind, though he does not say so, is the very footstool over which he stumbles—even though the 1813 and 1815 versions of *Die Weltalter* had cleared away this embarrassing bit of parlor furniture and had long since banished the footsole that meant to rest on it. Folio 32 of the sketches and plans for *The Ages of the World*, replete with excisions (in angle brackets: <>), begins as follows:

> Daß die Natur nicht ursprünglich in diesem Verhältnis [d.h. als Grundlage und Werkzeug der Offenbarung] sich befunden, davon würde uns schon ihr ganzer Anblick überzeugen; denn überall erscheint sie ja als eine gebeugte u. gebrochene Kraft, die aber auch zugleich einer höheren Verklärung entgegenharrt. Wäre dieses Verhältniß ihr ursprüngliches <nothwendiges, wie vermöchte sie> woher käme ihr die Freyheit, auch aus diesem Verhältniß herauszutreten, sich gegen das höhere zu erheben, welches ihr nicht <abzuläugnen> abgesprochen werden kann? Denn es ist jene Unterordnung nicht als ein gänzliches Unabhängigwerden zu denken, Gott der eigentlich Seyende ist über dem Seyn, der Himmel ist sein Thron und die Erde sein Fußschemel; aber auch dieß in Bezug auf sein höchstes Wesen Untergeordnete ist so voll von <Licht u.> Leben, daß es nach allen Seiten in Lebendiges ausbricht. So erscheint der Ewige im Gesicht der Propheten, wie es Raphael dargestellt <hat>, nicht von dem Nichts sondern von lebendigen Thiergestalten getragen. So hat jener hellenische Künstler das äußerste menschliche Schicksal, den Tod der Kinder der Niobe, am Fuße des Thrones gebildet, auf welchem sein olympischer Zeus ruhte u. selbst den Schemel des Gottes durch die Vorstellung der Amazonenkämpfe mit kräftigem Leben geschmückt. (250)

> The view we have of nature in its entirety would suffice to convince us that nature is not found originally in such a state [i.e., in the relation of foundation and as a tool of divine revelation]. For nature everywhere appears as a subordinate and broken force, one which, it is true, at the same time looks forward to a higher transfiguration. Were this its original relation <its necessary relation, how would it be able>, whence would arise its freedom to emerge from the relation, to elevate itself toward what is higher, which is something that cannot be <denied> refused nature? For the subordination is not to be thought of as God's total independence. God, as what properly exists, surpasses his being; heaven is his throne and earth his footstool. Yet that which is subordinate in relation to his supreme essence is so full of <light and> life that it irrupts on all sides into living things. Thus the eternal appears in the vision of the prophet, as Raphael <depicted> depicts it, sustained not by nothingness but by forms of living animals. Thus the Hellenic artist portrays the extremity of human fate, to wit, the death of Niobe's children, at the foot of the throne on which his Olympian Zeus reposes; and he decorated the very footstool of the god with energetic life, representing there as he did the battles of the Amazons.

Here Schelling returns to his earliest formulation of the primal image (earliest for the *Weltalter* drafts, though not as early as the *Stuttgarter Privatvorlesungen*). What is most worthy of comment is perhaps Schelling's response to critics who say that pantheists deify nature. To these critics Schelling replies, "Well, it is surely the case that God himself deifies nature"; God puts on nature, invests himself in it, "as a covering or a body" (ibid.). The distance between footstool and footsole can be measured in the disjunction "covering *or* body," although once that distance is closed we are no longer in God's parlor but on his flesh. The story of the present eon, *die Gegenwart*, which will be the story of nature and the spirit-world, will never again be about the mere elevation of the latter out of the former, never again about the suppression of flesh for the sake of fire. Yet unending incarnation of God in "The Present" exposes him to the extremity of human fate: one lives to see one's children die—as Schelling himself lived to see Caroline's daughter Auguste die in July of 1800, in spite of all his science and doctoring. Energetic life is a battle in which the winner takes nothing. If the Amazons are images of energetic life, they must shear off a breast when their weaponry demands it, and when it is Achilles who pierces Penthesilea's breast, she expires. Nature, "energetic life," appears in "the present" as a "broken force." It looks forward to a second birth, looks longingly toward its transfiguration. Schelling, like Heidegger after him, refers to Paul in this regard. In the 1815 version of *The Ages of the World*, Schelling cites Romans 8:20 in the following way:

> So sollte denn nichts auf bloßer Nothwendigkeit ruhen und die höchste Freiwilligkeit schon in den ersten Anfängen des Lebens die unumschränkte Freiheit Gottes beurkunden.
>
> Gleich uranfänglich hat sich also die Natur unterworfen, nicht vermöge ihres eignen oder natürlichen Willens, sondern genöthigt durch die Noth (dieß ist der Sinn des οὐχ ἑκοῦσα, Röm. 8, 20, wo indeß von einer späteren Unterwerfung die Rede ist), wohl aber um deß willen, der sie unterworfen, und auf Hoffnung, daß auch sie dadurch frei werden und von der Knechtschaft (blinden Nothwendigkeit) jenes ewig vergänglichen, sich selbst verzehrenden Wesens in eine unvergängliche Herrlichkeit erhoben werden soll. (8:266; cf. *Fragmente*, 99–100)

Thus nothing was to rest on mere necessity; in the first beginnings of life, supremely free volition was to document the unbounded freedom of God.

Just as primordially, nature subordinated itself, not by virtue of its own natural will, but compelled by need (this is the sense of the "involuntarily," Romans 8:20, where, it is true, what is referred to is a *later* subordination); to be sure, nature subordinated itself for the sake of that which subordinated it and in hopes of becoming in this way free, elevated from the servitude (blind necessity) of that eternally transient, self-consuming essence to immutable glory.

The reference to the transient, indeed, to the "eternally transient," is the first such reference to *Vergänglichkeit* in the third draft of *"Die Vergangenheit"* ("The Past"); it is noteworthy not only because of the title of Part 1 of *Die Weltalter* but also because of the theme of dying and death, which the text begins to discuss at that juncture (8:260, 262). It is quite remarkable that Heidegger, in his 1929–1930 lecture course on theoretical biology, cites that same Pauline epistle, and in a similar vein. Heidegger cites verse 19, rather than 20, but to the same effect. Verse 19 refers to *das engstliche harren der Creatur*, a surprising reference when one remembers that for Heidegger *Angst* is supposedly the earmark of Dasein or human existence alone. He is speaking of the "poverty in world" and general "deprivation" that putatively characterizes animal—as opposed to human—life:

> If deprivation [*das Entbehren*], in certain of its transformations, is a suffering [*ein Leiden*]; and if a being deprived of world, as well as poverty, belong to the animal's being; then a suffering and a sorrow [*ein Leiden und ein Leid*] would have to permeate the entire animal kingdom and the realm of life in general. Biology knows absolutely nothing about this. To fabulate on such things is perhaps the poets' privilege. . . . The fact that biology knows nothing of this is no counterproof against metaphysics. That perhaps only poets occasionally speak of it is an argument that dare not be taken as allowing us to cast metaphysics to the winds. In the end, one does not really need Christian faith in order to understand something of those words that Paul (in Romans 8:19) writes concerning the ἀποκαραδοκία τῆς κτίσεως, the creatures' and all creation's languorous gaze [*von dem sehnsüchtigen Ausspähen der Geschöpfe und der Schöpfung*]; for the ways of creation, as the Book of Esra (IV, 7, 12) also says, have in this eon become narrow, mournful, and arduous [*schmal, traurig und mühselig*].[7]

Whereas Schelling focuses on the involuntary subordination (*Unterwerfung*) of creatures, Heidegger focuses on that "anxious waiting" that the creatures' "languorous gaze" betrays. Schelling, however, is also interested in the Pauline promise that with the arrival of the "children of God," that is, human beings, creatures too will be freed from their "servitude to transient being" (in Luther's words, *von dem Dienst des vergenglichen wesens*). All creatures will be

7. Martin Heidegger, *Die Grundbegriffe der Metaphysik: Welt—Endlichkeit—Einsamkeit*, Gesamtausgabe vol. 29/30 (Frankfurt am Main: V. Klostermann, 1983), 393, 396; English translation by William McNeill and Nick Walker as *The Fundamental Concepts of Metaphysics: World, Finitude, Solitude* (Bloomington: Indiana University Press, 1995), 271, 272–273. See also Krell, *Daimon Life* (cited in note 17 of ch. 2, above), Introduction and ch. 3, esp. 130–131. Interestingly, the poet Hölderlin, both early and late in his career, seems to have been aware of this passage from Paul. In the "Thalia Fragment" of *Hyperion*, from the summer of 1794, he refers to "the sobs of creatures, the feeling of a lost paradise," *das Seufzen der Kreatur, das Gefühl des verlornen Paradieses* (CHV 1:491). In the late hymn, *Germanien*, contained in the *Homburger Folioheft*, he refers once again to this sobbing of the forest creatures, *Seufzen der Creatur* (CHV 1:406).

elevated to human status and acknowledged as children of God (Luther: *zu der herrlichen Freiheit der kinder Gottes*). On this side of salvation, however, Heidegger wants to barricade the animals in their worldless world, in order to save the notion of "world" for human beings alone. Yet he too comes very close—not as close as Schelling, but still very close—to expanding the notion of anxiety to include animal life, which, like human life, is invaded by death. Paul writes (Romans 8:22, in Luther's translation), *"Denn wir wissen / das alle Creatur sehnet sich mit uns / und engstet sich noch jmer dar."* "For we know that all creatures languish with us, and that they are constantly beset by anxiety." Such languishing is apparently a familiar theme in the Christian tradition, familiar enough for Stephen Dedalus to reflect on it as he gazes languorously at the languid fronds swaying in the late-morning tide on Sandymount Strand:

> Under the upswelling tide he saw the writhing weeds lift languidly and sway reluctant arms, hising up their petticoats, in whispering water swaying and upturning coy silver fronds. Day by day: night by night: lifted, flooded and let fall. Lord, they are weary: and, whispered to, they sigh. Saint Ambrose heard it, sigh of leaves and waves, waiting, awaiting the fullness of their times, *diebus ac noctibus inurias patiens ingemiscit.* To no end gathered: vainly then released, forth flowing, wending back: loom of the moon.[8]

The tendency shared by Schelling and Heidegger is to break down the barriers between human beings and other living beings—precisely with regard to the essential moments of languor and anxiety unto death. If both pull back from their own most radical insights, with Heidegger pulling back more nervously than Schelling, it is surely out of something we might call *animal*—and after Dedalus's Ambrose even *vegetable—anxiety.*[9]

It is one thing, of course, to be anxious in the way an animal is anxious, another to be anxious about *becoming* an animal, which is to say, coming to be alive. This is perhaps closer to the situation of Schelling's god or goddess of the night. A note of Nietzsche's concurs that precisely the process of becoming an animal is divine. Moreover, it is the path of knowledge as such. Number 249 of the "Tautenburg Sketches for Lou von Salomé," dated July–August 1882 (KSA 10:83), reads: *Der Erkennende fühlt sich als die Thierwerdung Gottes* ("The knower feels himself to be God's becoming an animal"). With regard to such divine *Thierwerdung*, consider two possibilities for the etymology of the word *Tier.* The first is the accepted derivation of the word from a Germanic root that also grants us the English word *deer: ein Tier* is a four-footed wild

---

8. James Joyce, *Ulysses* (London: Bodley Head, 1969), 62.
9. See Krell, *Daimon Life,* 67–70, "The Anxious Animal."

animal, a denizen of the forest. Yet one must wonder whether the entry in the Brockhaus encyclopedia under *Tyr* is germane to the etymology of *Tier*. Tyr was an ancient Germanic god, originally named *Teiwas* or *Tiwas*, in Old High German *Ziu* or *Tiu*. (To this, of course, one can compare the Latin words *deus*, *divinus*, and the Greek words Ζεύς, ζάω, ζα-.) The god Tyr occupied a high place in ancient Germanic religion: human sacrifice was made to him. In compound words, *Tyr* means as much as "God" pure and simple. The Swabian word *Zeistag* and the English *Tuesday* derive from *Tyr*. If one understands Nietzsche's phrase *Thierwerdung* as the *Tyr-werdung* of God, the very becoming-god of god, then the distinction between God and animal dissolves altogether, long before anything like theriomorphism, and long before any human sacrifice is offered. Whether or not the second etymology holds, the present chapter is predicated on the possibility of an animated and knowledgeable God, which is the possibility that drives Schelling's philosophy from beginning to end.

The Olympian Zeus of Pausanias's *Guide to Greece*

When Schelling refers to the "Olympian Zeus" he does not merely mean the Zeus who dwells on Mount Olympus; he is alluding to the statue of Zeus sculpted and erected by Phidias at Olympia. Pausanias, in his *Guide to Greece*, describes the splendid statue, which was still standing when he visited Elea in the second century C.E. To be sure, he mentions decorative themes and motifs on the statue other than those of the Centaurs and Lapiths in battle, Niobe's children, and the battles of the Amazons. One would have to speculate as to why Schelling selects the details he does for his sundry accounts of the image. (Recall that it was the battles of the Lapiths and Centaurs that first drew his attention, then Niobe and the Amazons, until in 1827–1828 Phidias capitulated totally to Raphael.) Presumably, those themes and motifs are especially germane to the *Ur-Bilder* of nature that Schelling is seeking. The following passage from the second-century *Guide* is edited down from several pages, but even this pared-down version offers many more details than Schelling's brief allusions do. Pausanias's *Guide to Greece*, Book V, "Elea," describes Phidias's statue of Zeus at Olympia as follows:

> The god is sitting on a throne; he is made of gold and ivory. There is a wreath on his head like twigs and leaves of olive; in his right hand he is holding a Victory of gold and ivory with a ribbon and a wreath on her head; in the god's left hand is a staff in blossom with every kind of precious metal, and the bird perching on

this staff is Zeus's eagle. The god's sandals are gold and so is his cloak, and the cloak is inlaid with animals and flowering lilies. The throne is finely worked with gold and gems, ebony and ivory. There are animals painted on it and figures worked on it: four Victories dance on the four feet of the throne, with two more at the bottom of each of the four feet. On the two forward feet the children of Thebes are being carried off by sphinxes, and beneath the sphinxes Apollo and Artemis are shooting down Niobe's children. Between the feet of the throne there are four bars stretching right across from one foot to another; the first begins with seven figures, but the eighth, no one knows how, has become indecipherable: they could be representations of the contests of antiquity, as in Phidias's time the boys' contests had not been instituted. They say the one tying the ribbon round his head looks like Pantarkes, an Elean adolescent who was Phidias's boyfriend, and who in fact won in the boys' wrestling at the eighty-sixth Olympics. On the other bars is Herakles' regiment fighting the Amazons. The number of figures on both sides is twenty-nine, and Theseus is serving with Herakles' allies. The throne rests not only on its feet but also on four columns standing between them. It is impossible to get underneath the throne.... On the topmost part of the throne above the statue's head Phidias has carved three Graces and three Seasons. Epic poetry tells us they were among Zeus's daughters, and Homer has written in the *Iliad* that the Seasons were given charge of heaven like some kind of royal palace guards. [Translator's note: *Iliad*, 5:749f. The gates of heaven and heaven itself and the peak of Mount Olympus belonged to the Seasons, who could open and shut the barriers of clouds.] The stool under Zeus's feet, which in Attica they call τὸ θρανίον, has golden lions worked on it and Theseus fighting the Amazons, the first Athenian act of valour outside of civil war. On the platform that holds up Zeus and all the decoration that goes with him there are golden figures of the Sun mounting his chariot, and Zeus and Hera and [indecipherable name] with a Grace, followed by Hermes, who in turn is followed by the Hearth goddess, and then Eros welcoming Aphrodite as she rises from the sea, and Persuasion crowning Aphrodite with a wreath; Apollo and Artemis are worked on it, Athena and Herakles, and right at the end of the platform Amphitrite and Poseidon, and the Moon, who I think is driving a horse; some people have said the goddess rides on a mule and not a horse and they tell some silly story about the mule.

I know the recorded measurements of the height and breadth of Zeus at Olympia, but I find myself unable to commend the measurers since the measurements they give fall a long way short of the impression this statue has created in those who see it, who say even the god himself bore witness to the art of Phidias: when the statue was completely finished, Phidias prayed to the god to make a sign if the work pleased him, and immediately a flash of lightning struck the pavement at the place where the bronze urn was still standing in my time.[10]

---

10. Pausanias, *Guide to Greece*, tr. Peter Levi, S.J., vol. 2 (Harmondsworth: Penguin Books, 1971), 226–229; translation slightly altered. Levi notes: "The famous masterpiece is represented on the coinage of Elis. . . . Quintilian says this statue added something to human religion. Paulus Aemilius when he saw it said it was the Zeus of Homer. It perished in a burning palace in the fifth century A.D. in Constantinople" (2:226 n. 97). Schelling himself, in his 1842 *Philosophie der Mythologie*, refers to Quintilian's praise of the statue's beauty and religious power (II/2:660).

Of the many rich details in Pausanias's description, perhaps only two should detain us here. First, it seems strange that Zeus is wearing sandals ("The god's sandals are gold"), strange insofar as the god's shod footsoles could never have been seen. Perhaps, after all, when Schelling writes *Fuß-sohlen*, he means—in the case of the Olympian Zeus, though not Raphael's vision of the prophet—*shoe* soles. Second, and by way of compensation, Zeus's cloak seems to perform the work that otherwise either footstool or footsole would have had to perform ("the cloak is inlaid with animals and flowering lilies"). So much more could be said or written about God's footstool, as of the cloak, and of the god himself—a "seated giant encrusted with creatures," Roberto Calasso calls him (RC 170). Indeed, Calasso's description of the statue of Olympian Zeus, recounting Pausanias, comes to the identical conclusion that Schelling came to, without knowing or acknowledging it:

> The gold and ivory seethed like an ants' nest. Zeus didn't exist except as a support for animals and lilies, arches and drapes, old scenes forever repeated. But Zeus was more than just the motionless guardian seated on his throne: Zeus was all those scenes, those deeds, muddled and shuffled about, rippling his body and throne in tiny shivers. Without meaning to, Phidias had illustrated that Zeus cannot live alone: without meaning to, he had represented the essence of polytheism. (RC 171)

Yet the longer we go on about it the more the suspicion obtrudes that perhaps Schelling was right to drop the footstool and the footsole. God's feet might cause the same sort of embarrassment to him that "the big toe," according to Georges Bataille, causes human beings.[11]

The Forlorn Foot of Divinity

It now behooves us to note three places where the footstool/footsole image does *not* appear in Schelling's texts, namely, in the two later drafts of *The Ages of the World* and in "The Divinities of Samothrace." For in each of these places Schelling discusses God's pith or strength in relation to nature, being and nonbeing, freedom and necessity—places that formerly called forth the image in question. We will see that there is something about God's sometime strength and reputed repose that may require a withdrawal—or a transfiguration—of the primal image.

11. For the reference to Bataille, and a discussion of the feet of God, see Krell, *The Purest of Bastards* (cited in note 15 of ch. 4, above), 157–168. See also ch. 4 of my *Archeticture* (cited in note 23 of ch. 4, above).

1. At the very place in the second (1813) printing where the footstool ought to appear (140–141; folios 61–63) Schelling once again, as in the 1827–1828 *System,* appears to offer grist for Manfred Schröter's mill. For here, in the course of defining the pith of God in terms of the father's negating will, that is, a will that contracts as an aboriginal centripetal force, Schelling explicitly rejects images. He does so, in accord with an ancient and revered rhetorical ruse, condemning images by appealing to images in sentences replete with images:

> A counterstriving obtrudes everywhere. Everyone senses this Other, which, so to speak, ought not to be and yet is; this *no* that counterposes itself to the *yes,* this penumbra that counterposes itself to the light, the crooked to the straight, the left to the right, and however else one has tried to express this eternal opposition in images. Yet one is not readily in a position to express it, much less to conceptualize it scientifically. (140)

Schelling's best effort to avoid images in this second draft of *Die Weltalter* finds him simply declaring the paradox that God *"posits himself* as nonbeing," and that such posited nonbeing is in fact God's force, "his very strength [*als die Stärke selber*]" (141).

2. There are two places in the third and final (1815) version of *The Ages of the World* where God's footstool might well have appeared, one fairly early in the text, the other at its very end. The primal image of nonbeing as living force, as the very vitality and pith of the divine life, could have appeared in this passage:

> This is the eternal force and strength of God, that he negates himself, closes off his essence, and withdraws into himself. In this act, the negating force is all that is revealed of God, whereas his proper essence lies concealed. . . . This is therefore the beginning, or, as we have already otherwise expressed it, the first potency.
>
> According to the most ancient doctrines, the night is generally not considered to be the uppermost essence (as we today tend to misunderstand those doctrines); rather, it is the first, which precisely for that reason, as the movement progresses, will prove to be nethermost. Precisely that which negates all revelation has to be made the ground of revelation. (8:223)

What sort of image could there be—whether primal or derivative—of that which is never revealed? And if "night" is never revealed as such, what narrative will broach it? Would it not invariably prove to be the "other night," which Blanchot defines as the neutral time of narration as such?[12] And would not such a night belong to a past that has never been present, an absolute past? Finally, would not such an absolute past imply the passing of the absolute as such?

On the penultimate page of the third and last draft, Schelling allows these questions, which are anachronistic in the form presented here but which have their more fitting formulations in Schelling's own text, to take him to the genre of tragedy. Specifically, these questions take Schelling to Aeschylus's *Prometheus Bound.* Schelling begins by declaring his own time to be a time of images (*Bilder*), of "dreams of shadows"; a victorious idealism has successfully intellectualized the world and God, thereby losing all sense of darkness, covert strength or pith, and "that barbaric principle . . . which has been overcome but not annihilated" (8:342–343). The shadowy idealists, from Fichte through Hegel, have lost sight of "the foundation of all grandeur and beauty" (8:343). They have lost touch with the very nonbeing that constitutes God's life and grants him his force:

> In the first existence [*in dem ersten Daseyn*] there must be a principle that strives against revelation. For only such a principle can become the ground of revelation. . . . How otherwise could there be freedom. At work in the first existence is an irrational principle that opposes confrontation and thus also repulses creatures; this principle is the proper strength in God, as the supreme seriousness of tragedy shows us. Strength and Violence, the servants of Zeus, are the ones who fasten philanthropic Prometheus to the sea-battered cliffs. (8:343; cf. the 1811 draft, 52)

Zeus is no longer in repose, with his feet on a footstool or even a pedestal. He is instead the god who requires Titanic thugs—his father's henchmen—to do his work for him and to save his life. He is the god who is threatened by a philanthropist. What sort of "strength" is this? What sort of piteous pith? The entire *Weltalter* project, and especially "The Past," is in search of God's peculiar pith—his energetic ground, strength, and force. That force must be older than the Titans. For in his 1842 *Philosophy of Mythology* Schelling identifies the Titans as those who are *tense,* or *tensed* (from τείνω, τιταίνω), in the way that Kronos tenses his arm in order to emasculate his father Uranos (II/2:618). Yet if that kind of tension produces a Zeus who is every bit as much in fear of his manhood, his reign, and his life as any Titan prior to him, the search for the primordial ground must go on. Perhaps the most com-

---

12. Maurice Blanchot, *L'Espace littéraire* (Paris: Gallimard, 1955), ch. 5, sec. 1, 215–226. See also Krell, *Lunar Voices: Of Tragedy, Poetry, Fiction, and Thought* (Chicago: University of Chicago Press, 1995), ch. 5, 145–148.

pelling and even shocking answer to the question of God's strength lies hidden in the "Notes" to Schelling's 1815 address to the Bavarian Academy of Sciences, "The Divinities of Samothrace," which we examined at the end of the preceding chapter. Let us conclude the present chapter as well with a brief reminder of what transpired on Samothrace.

3. Neither God's footstool nor his footsole appears in "The Divinities of Samothrace." This astonishing lecture, we recall, does not so much summarize the *Weltalter* project as proffer a new beginning, a "commencement and transition" to "several new works" that will have as their goal an elaboration of "the proper primal system of humanity [*zugleich Anfang und Übergang zu mehreren andern, deren Absicht ist, das eigentliche Ursystem der Menschheit ... ans Licht zu bringen*]" (8:423). Schelling identifies that primal system with the cult of the Cabiri on the ancient isle of Samothrace. One of the most fascinating paradoxes of the Cabirian system is that in it Zeus Pater is consistently identified with the "new Zeus," Dionysos, and Dionysos with Zagreus—the vulnerable and fragmented infant god. The Zeus who comes to the fore in this text and these "Notes" is not the enthroned, majestic, Phidian-Olympian Zeus but the Cretan Zeus, that is to say, the newborn Zeus huddling in a cave of Mount Dikte or Mount Ida, the Zeus whom the Curetes, Corybants, and Dactyls promise to protect from the all-devouring father. This is Zeus, as W. K. C. Guthrie puts it, "not on the plane of power but on the plane of weakness." Guthrie cites Strabo (who is also one of Schelling's principal sources) as follows:

> What is known about them [i.e., the Curetes, or Kouretes] suggests rather the Satyrs and Sileni and Bacchi and Tityri. For according to writers on Cretan and Phrygian lore, the Kouretes are similar daemons or attendants upon gods, and are mixed up with certain sacred rites, both mystic and other, concerned with the rearing of the child Zeus in Crete and the orgiastic worship of the Mother of the Gods in Phrygia and around Mount Ida in the Troad. There is much confusion in these accounts. Some declare that the Korybantes and Kabiri and Idaean Daktyls and Telchines are the same as the Kouretes, others pronounce them related and distinguish certain small differences between them, but agree that in general terms, and to name their prevailing characteristics, all alike are enthusiastic and Bacchic types, who in the guise of acolytes, by dances in arms, with tumult, noise, cymbals, tympana and weapons, also with the music of flutes and shouting, arouse the passions in the course of religious ceremonies. Thus the rites also become common property, both those of the Kouretes and those performed in Samothrace and in Lemnos and many others, because the attendant daemons were identified.[13]

13. W. K. C. Guthrie, *The Greeks and Their Gods* (London: Methuen, 1968), 43–44. Roberto Calasso writes: "In the solitude of the primordial world, the affairs of the gods took place on an empty

Guthrie adds that according to Strabo the main intention of such noise is to deceive Kronos—the threatening father, who seeks to preserve his rule at all costs—by distracting him from the cries of the infant son who is destined to unseat him.

Cretan Zeus remains under the sway of the mother, whether she be called Demeter, Ge-meter, or Persephone. "Ceres," notes Schelling, "is the fundament" (8:395). Even if Zeus is Malki-Gedek, "Heaven and Earth," himself "the supreme god" of both throne and footstool, the one truth that wisdom can affirm (as Heraclitus noted) is that the name *Zeus* is both wanted and found wanting when we are naming the god (8:401). Even if the ancient names of the Cabirian deities all mean "mighty, strong" (8:409), the concealed history of those names points to the vulnerability of the son and the languishing (*Sehnsucht, Schmachten*) of the mother. Indeed, the god is inevitably the destitute twofold of masculinity and femininity; (s)he is the chthonic divinity long before he becomes the lord of the vaulted sky (8:414–418).

Accordingly, as we have seen over the course of the last three chapters, figures of the feminine come to play an extraordinary role in the three drafts of *Die Weltalter* and in *Über die Gottheiten von Samothrake*. It would take pages and pages of analysis to do these figures justice. Allow me here simply to catalogue a few of them. Woman, in Schelling's texts, is both Isis (the goddess of Saïs, who was, is, and will be) and Πενία, the "Poverty" of Plato's *Symposium*.[14] She is mother and nurse, Ἑστία, τιθήνη, and thus, as we heard in chapter 3, is related to the night: "Darkness and occlusion constitute the character of primal time. All life first comes to be and shapes itself in the night; that is why the night is called by the ancients the fertile mother of things; indeed, along with Chaos, she is called the oldest of essences."[15] The second reference in the "Notes" to Pausanias's *Guide to Greece* (8:383–384), a reference

---

stage, with no eyes to mirror them. There was a rustling, but no clamor of voices. Then, from a certain point on (but at what point? and why?), the backdrop began to flicker, the air was invaded by a golden sprinkling of new beings, the shrill, high-pitched cry of scores of raised voices. Dactyls, Curetes, Corybants, Telchines, Silens, Cabiri, Satyrs, Maenads, Bacchants, Lenaeans, Thyiads, Bassarides, Mimallones, Naiads, Nymphs, Titires: who were all these beings? To evoke one of their names is to evoke them all. They were helpers, ministers, guardians, nurses, tutors, and spectators of the gods" (RC 302). However, as Calasso himself soon notes, they are also the assassins of the god: the deepest and darkest secret of Zeus is that the Curetes and Corybants betray the god, killing and devouring him, just as the Maenads—devouring the raw flesh of the fawn they have only now suckled—consume the god they worship" (RC 304–305, 307–308).

14. For Isis, see *Die Weltalter Fragmente*, 9, 187; 8:206, 263, 382; for Πενία, 8:244, 259, 352.

15. *Fragmente*, 24; cf. 181, 240; in the third (1815) version of *Die Weltalter*, see 8:243–244, 260, 269, 278, 283–284, 286, 296, 325, 331, 337; in *Samothrake*, see 8:349, 351, 378, 391, 395, 412, 414, 418.

alluded to earlier, proposes a remarkable identification (in the doctrine of the Cabiri) of erotic languor (*Sehnsucht*) with Πόθος, a mournfulness and languishing directed toward the past. Yet such mournfulness is embodied in the figure of Samothracian Venus, "the divinity worshipped in Samothrace as languor" (8:384). Woman is also the daughter or maid, Kore, Persephone, or Proserpina, the queen of the dead, an amalgam of tenderness ("like the tenderness of flesh," 8:283) and wrath (*Zorn*, 19–21), joy and terror, grace and anxiety, playfulness and suffering (*spielende Lust, Leid,* 8:296). She embodies what both father and son were missing.

Whereas Achsi-Eres (= Axieros = Demeter) means "Mine-is-the-Earth," the dignity and majesty of this primal divinity are rooted in "the opposite of satiety" (8:378). In other words, the etymon of god as such is not "strength" or "pith" but, as we have seen, *paupertas et egestas*, poverty and squalor. Whether the god be designated in feminine or masculine forms, as Aphrodite or Aphroditos, as Dea Luna or Deus Lunus, the majesty of its divinity is grounded in hunger and desire: "(s)he desired, grew avid, and avariciously devoured whatever food (s)he could find" (ibid.). From Titanic power and celestial majesty it is but one quick primal step (or stumble) to a desperate languor and languishing (*schmachtende Sehnsucht*), to morbidity, mourning, and mortality (8:379–380, 384, 418). God himself, as Hölderlin writes in 1803, appears in the figure of death, *in der Gestalt des Todes*. "For even God," writes Schelling in 1811, "is but the husk of divinity" (33).

The present catalogue is by no means complete; it is but an initial attempt. Yet as one begins to draw it up, one already sees the end to which such a catalogue of divine origins inevitably points: if the end of God's every path (*finis viarum dei*) is embodiment, as we have heard Schelling affirm (8:325), the way toward that embodiment and "the secret birthplace of essence" (17) is the bipolar route of languor and crisis.[16] If one remembers that *Sehnsucht* and *Scheidung* alike are central to both the 1809 *Philosophical Investigations into the Essence of Human Freedom* and the 1811–1815 *Ages of the World*, the continuity of their unifying-sundering strife in Schelling's thought becomes quite striking—as striking as the fact that languor and crisis sustain a special relation to the feminine, to sexuality, and to death. These three facets of the primal image emerge again and again in Schelling's texts, even when Schelling wishes to tell tales of fathers and sons and spirits alone. An exclusively masculine Trinity?

16. *Fragmente,* 55, 77, 85; 8:147, 241, 274; *Samothrake,* 8:351, 377–378, 352–354, 379–380, 382, 384.

An abstract Greek absurdity has crazed the man—
Recall that masculine Trinity. Man, woman, child (a daughter or a son),
That's how all natural or supernatural stories run.[17]

By this time we are far from footstools, unless they be decorated by scenes of death and mourning, which is to say, by the extremity of mortal suffering—Niobe. We are far from footsoles, unless they be marked and marred by the signs of passage and passing. Callused, as it were. Schelling sees the decoration of these footstools and footsoles not as a *memento mori* for us but as a message to the god. God will need all the strength (s)he can muster to confront a dual sexuality and a singular mortality. For these are two of the blessings or curses to which mortal divinity is heir. Whether there are further ills in God's life—such as radical evil, the pendant to illness—is also a question that exercises Schelling from beginning to end. Yet let us be satisfied for the moment to have witnessed him descrying in an overdetermined image, an image that is not an image at all but the primal real, divine sex and death.

17. William Butler Yeats, "Ribh Denounces Patrick," in *The Collected Poems of W. B. Yeats* (New York: Macmillan, 1956), 283.

BRAZEN WHEELS

6

"You, Kant, always get what you want."

—HEDWIG, *in Hedwig and the Angry Inch*

Who that has heard a strain of music feared then lest he should speak extravagantly any more forever?

—HENRY DAVID THOREAU, *Walden*

The present chapter will take up one of the most striking passages of the 1811 printing of *The Ages of the World*, a passage reminiscent of Hegel's famous remarks on "Bacchic tumult" in his analysis of "the religion of art" in the *Phenomenology of Spirit*.[1] Schelling's 1811 text exhibits more corrections and emendations in this passage than anywhere else, and one feels compelled to reproduce them (the excisions in angle brackets, the additions in square brackets), inasmuch as they show how diligently he worked on these lines, trying to get them right. The context here is the same as that in the case of God's footstool, to wit, the burgeoning life that springs from the ground of the divine essence. Even what seems to lie outside or beneath that essence, verging on nonbeing, is bursting with autonomous life. The ground is riotous with life, insane with life:

> Nicht umsonst haben die Alten von einem göttlichen Wahnsinn gespro-

---

1. G. W. F. Hegel, *Phänomenologie des Geistes*, ed. Johannes Hoffmeister, 6th ed. (Hamburg: Felix Meiner Verlag, 1952), 504. The Schelling passage in question appears in a slightly altered form in the 1815 draft of *The Ages of the World*, 8:337–338. (My thanks to Jason Wirth for reminding me of this 1815 version.)

chen. [, den sie dem Dichter und jedem andern zuschreiben, in dem eine Kraft sich zeigt, die mehr wirkt als sie begreift. So] <Denn so> sehen auch wir noch die sichtbare [schon beruhigte] Natur, <welche nur das äußerlich gewordne Bild der innern ist,> in dem Verhältniß, als sie dem Geist sich annähert, gleichsam immer taumelnder werden. Denn es befinden sich zwar alle Dinge der Natur in einem besinnungslosen Zustande; jene Geschöpfe aber, die der letzten Zeit des Kampfes zwischen Scheidung und Einung, Bewußtseyn und Bewußtlosigkeit, angehören sehen wir in einem der Trunkenheit ähnlichen Zustand und <gleichsam> [wie] von [zerreißendem] Wahnsinn getrieben dahinwandeln. Nicht umsonst wird der Wagen des Dionysos von Löwen, Panthern, Tigern gezogen; denn es war dieser wilde Taumel von Begeisterung, in welchem die Natur <über dem> [vom] innerm Anblick des Wesens geräth, den der uralte Naturdienst ahndender Völker in den trunkenen Festen bacchischer Orgien gefeyert [gleichsam den Untergang d. alten reinen Naturd. zu beklagen]. Wogegen [der schreckliche Druck der zusammenziehenden Kraft,] jenes wie wahnsinnig in sich selbst laufende Rad der anfänglichen <Natur> [Geburt], und die <mächtigen> [darinn wirkenden] furchtbaren Kräfte des Umtriebs in anderem schrecklichem Gepränge uralter götterdienstlicher Gebräuche durch besinnungslose, rasende Tänze, durch den erschütternden Zug der Mutter aller Dinge auf dem Wagen mit ehernen Rädern, begleitet von dem Getöse einer rauhen, theils betäubenden theils zerreißenden Musik abgebildet wurde. (42–43)

Not for nothing did the ancients speak of a divine madness. [, which they attribute to the poet and to every other person in whom a power becomes manifest that works more effects than it can grasp. Thus] <For thus> we also see the visible [already becalmed] nature, <which is but the extrinsic image of the inner nature,> in such a way that when nature approaches spirit it becomes increasingly tumultuous. For it is true that all things of nature find themselves in a state that is devoid of contemplation; yet those creatures that pertain to the final period of struggle between scission and unification, consciousness and consciouslessness, we see wandering about in a state similar to that of drunkenness, and <as it were> [as though] driven by [devastating] madness. Not for nothing is it said that the chariot of Dionysos is drawn by lions, panthers, tigers. For it was this wild tumult of inspiration into which nature was plunged <by virtue of> [by] the inner view into its essence that was celebrated in the primeval cult of nature among intuitive peoples, with their drunken festivals of Bacchic orgies [as though thereby to lament the demise of the old and pure things of nature]. In contrast to that we find [the terrific pressure of the contractive force,] that wheel of incipient <nature> [birth] turning crazily on itself, and the <powerful> frightful forces of circular motion [working from within], symbolized in that other terrifying display of primitive ritual custom, to wit, insensate, frenzied dancing, which accompanied the terrifying procession of the mother of all things, seated on the chariot whose brazen wheels resounded with the deafening clamor of an unrefined music, in part hypnotic, in part devastating.

Divine madness and the madness of the things of nature—these two related forms of devastating madness—are the themes of the passage: madness, enthusiasm, and intoxication, or, more literally, the *inspiriting* or *spiriting away* of the divine essence in and by matter, in a nature in which spirit and matter struggle somewhere between unification and separation. Dionysos appears in the text as the god of green life, of ivy and vine, of sap and serum and wine. Yet his companion animals—panther, tiger, and lion, the great cats—lend the reference a foreboding quality. Excessive life is dangerous. Schelling is no doubt thinking of the Corybantic dancers, the subject, as we saw in chapter 3, of that long quotation from Hamann cited in the 1809 *Philosophical Investigations into the Essence of Human Freedom*. However, whereas their rites of self-emasculation served Schelling in 1809 as a parallel for his polemic against modern Cartesian philosophy, which with its mind-body split mutilates science and philosophy, here the allusion occurs in the context of a discussion of essence itself and as such. The Corybants, of which the Whirling Dervishes are distant descendants, dance the inner strife of essence. Their terrifying rites, which require them to throw their severed organs against the statue of the Great Mother as her brazen car clatters by, suggest something quite specific about the celestial father's suffering and pain, to which Schelling's 1811 printing of *The Ages of the World* is most sensitive.

Schelling adds several dramatic details to the passage in the 1815 version, referring to *Handlungen einer sich selbst zerfleischenden Wuth*, "enraged deeds that lacerate the flesh," specifically, self-emasculation, "whether to express the unbearable degree of the oppressive force or the cessation of that force as reproductive potency"; he also refers to the Corybants' *Herumtragen der zerstückelten Glieder eines zerrissenen Gottes*, "carrying about the lacerated members of a fragmented god" (8:337–338). If later, for Nietzsche, music gives birth to Greek tragedy, the most savage of Greek (or Oriental) cults will, prior to that, in Schelling's philosophy, give birth to music. Schelling's 1811 text continues:

Denn weil Klang und Ton allein in eben jenem Kampf zwischen Geistigkeit und Körperlichkeit zu entstehen scheinen: so kann die Tonkunst allein ein Bild jener uranfänglichen Natur und ihrer Bewegung seyn, wie denn auch ihr ganzes Wesen im Umlauf besteht, da sie von einem Grundton ausgehend, durch noch so viele Ausschweifungen zuletzt immer in den Anfang zurückkehrt. (43)

For sound and tone appear to originate solely in that struggle between spirituality and corporeality. Thus the art of music alone can provide an image of that primeval, incipient nature and its motion. For its entire essence consists of a cycle, taking its departure from a founding tone and, after an incredible number of extravagant sallies, returning to that beginning-point.

"For nothing is more similar to that inner madness than music," adds the 1815 version (8:338). Here music is characterized by "the tones' perpetual excentric evasion" of their tonal center—a center back to which, however, the tones are inevitably drawn (ibid.). *Klang und Ton*, sounds and tones, played an important role, as we shall see, in Schelling's lectures on the philosophy of art, held at Jena in 1802–1803 and repeated in Würzburg in 1804–1805. Yet before we turn to those lectures, a general remark is in order. For there has been very little specific talk of tragedy in these chapters up to this moment. True, everywhere in Schelling's texts between 1809 and 1815 the Titans loom large—those pre-Olympian gods who are identified with the overwhelming forces of nature, such as lightning, windstorm, earthquake, and tidal wave. Likewise, one often sees the shadows of the earliest Greek thinkers playing about the pages of the treatises Schelling composed between 1809 and 1815, the thinkers Nietzsche located in "the tragic age of the Greeks," among them, Heraclitus, Pythagoras, Anaxagoras, Empedocles, and the Parmenides who wanders on "the way of seeming." Moreover, as Schelling moves ever farther back into "The Past" in search of essence and the *ground* of its existence, he uncovers conditions that can only spell tragedy for that essence. In the passage presented above, Schelling unites the thought of tragedy with a recollection of the Great Goddess, and the thought of her chariot with the origins of music. The present chapter will therefore proceed archaeologically, working its way back from the years dedicated to the themes of human freedom and the ages of the world to two much earlier texts in which music and tragedy are discussed at some length: first, the famous "Tenth Letter" of the *Philosophical Letters on Dogmatism and Criticism*, from the year 1795, and second, the 1802–1803 lectures on aesthetics, published as *Philosophy of Art*.[2]

Yet archaeology will have to cede to teleology as we approach the end of the chapter. For halfway through a very late text, the 1842 *Philosophy of Mythology*, the wagon of the Great Goddess clatters onto the scene once again. We will have to advance to the very end of Schelling's career before coming to any conclusions about the origins of music and tragedy.[3]

2. The "Tenth Letter" appears in F. W. J. Schelling, *Philosophische Briefe über Dogmatismus und Kriticismus*, in vol. 1 of the *Sämmtliche Werke*; the lectures on aesthetics appear as *Philosophie der Kunst*, discussed in the foregoing chapter, appearing in vol. 5 of the *Sämmtliche Werke*. The former work appears now in *Werke 3* of the *Historisch-Kritische Ausgabe*, ed. Hartmut Büchner, Wilhelm G. Jacobs, and Annemarie Pieper (Stuttgart: Frommann-Holzboog, 1982), the "Tenth Letter" at 106–112.

3. F. W. J. Schelling, *Philosophie der Mythologie*, II/2:1–674. For the passages on the Great Goddess, see 351–362. It is worth noting that in a separate work, the *Einleitung* to a philosophy of mythology, Schelling pledges that he will take up the theme of "the *first feminine deity*," but in this text does not do so (II/1:153). In the *Philosophie der Mythologie* proper, he does fulfill his pledge. Here in the "Introduction" he merely says that the first feminine divinity "is communicated to us everywhere as the

Freedom to Burn: Schelling's Tenth Letter

With a view to the tragic absolute, one must begin with the *context* of the *Philosophical Letters on Dogmatism and Criticism*. For the topic of these letters is everywhere the absolute. The "Ninth Letter" (1:326–335), for example, counterposes the Kantian-Fichtean "Critical" philosophy to traditional dogmatic philosophy precisely in terms of the claim made by both to achieve the absolute—that is, the presuppositionless beginnings and perfect ends—of philosophy. "Absolute thesis," absolute positing, or absolute unity is the aim and the proclaimed accomplishment of each (1:327). In the "Ninth Letter," Schelling moves through a comparison of Critical and dogmatic philosophy with a view to (1) the absolute synthesis of subject and object in epistemology and metaphysics, (2) the ultimate identity of Stoic and Epicurean ethics from the vantage point of absolute felicity, (3) the ultimate imbrication of modern philosophical idealism and realism, and (4) the perfect identity of freedom and necessity within the absolute. Let us pause over this fourth area of comparison, inasmuch as it leads directly to the "Tenth Letter." Schelling begins:

> Whoever has reflected on freedom and necessity has automatically discovered that these principles must be *united* in the absolute—*freedom*, because the absolute acts on the basis of unconditioned self-empowerment, *necessity*, because precisely for the same reason it acts always in accord with the laws of its being, the inner necessity of its essence. There is no longer any sort of will in it that could deviate from a law, but there is no longer any sort of law that it does not impose on itself by its actions alone, no law that would have reality independently of the actions of the absolute. Absolute freedom and absolute necessity are identical. (1:330–331)

Significantly, Schelling cites Spinoza at this juncture—Spinoza, whose *Ethics* will become so important for the entire generation after Kant, and to no one more so than to Schelling, who by 1795 is already studying physics and chemistry with a view to a proposed philosophy of nature.

By the time one ascends to the absolute, notes Schelling, all conflicting principles and systems appear to be united. The problem is that if all systems take us to the same end, why should anyone bother to go the arduous Critical route rather than remain contentedly dogmatic? Schelling's uncompromising reply is that Critical philosophy never truly reaches the absolute. Its activity is

---

transition from the first to the second god, i.e., to genuine polytheism" (ibid.). With regard to the 1802–1803 lectures on aesthetics, we should note that the "Introduction" to the philosophy of mythology also comments on the importance of mythology for a philosophy of art (241).

endless and can only "approach" the ultimate goal (1:331). A finite subject would have to annihilate itself in order to do more. Indeed, the very dream of doing more exposes philosophy to "all the terrors of enthusiasm," whereby *Schwärmerei* seems to be referring to Hamann's complaint concerning the Corybants. "Endless striving" to realize the absolute in oneself, "by means of *unlimited activity*," is therefore what Schelling proposes. That comes close to saying what we will later hear Hölderlin assert, which is that all thinking is and must be *asymptotic*, approaching infinitesimally but never touching the desired goal.[4]

Schelling's "Ninth Letter" concludes with a brave peroration: "My *determination* in Criticism is—*to strive toward unchangeable selfhood* [unveränderliche Selbstheit], *unconditioned freedom, unbounded activity*. [¶] Be! that is the

4. Walter Schulz, in his Introduction to Schelling's *System of Transcendental Idealism*, confirms that in Schelling's philosophical development from 1794 to 1797—and I would advance the latter date well into the first decade of the 1800s, with the *System of Transcendental Idealism* and Schelling's subsequent "identity philosophy"—the golden thread running through the entire tapestry is "the *question* of the absolute and its relation to the world" (xviii). The *answers* that Schelling comes up with differ during these early years. "Whereas in the beginning, in the text *On the Ego*, the absolute is proclaimed unity without distinction, a unity that is simply counterposed to the finite sphere, Schelling attempts already in the *Letters* to bridge the gap by announcing that the absolute is 'of use' only as a guiding determination for our unlimited freedom and autonomy" (ibid.). Dennis Schmidt, in *On Germans and Other Greeks* (73–83), offers an excellent discussion of Schelling's *Philosophical Letters*. The following passage from Schmidt (77–78) suggests the importance of the "Tenth Letter" for the present project, that is, for what I am calling *the tragic absolute:* "[Peter] Szondi is quite right when he writes that 'after Aristotle there is a poetics of tragedy, only after Schelling is there a philosophy of the tragic.' [Peter Szondi, *Versuch über das Tragische* (1956, 1963), in *Schriften I*, ed. Jean Bollack et al. (Frankfurt am Main: Suhrkamp Verlag, 1978), 151.] That is the essential shift effected by the modern form of the question derived from the philosophical encounter with Greek tragedy. But one could argue that this way of characterizing the shift does not exhaust its significance; even more, . . . it is important to bear in mind both that there is a peculiar necessity driving this move—that is, Schelling's decision to single out Greek tragic art is not an arbitrary one, but very much a response to the needs of history at that moment—and . . . that *this renewal of the questions of Greek tragedy is equally its reinvention*. The philosophical question of tragedy that reappears at the very end of the eighteenth century is marked by such a profound shift away from the terms and concerns that characterized Plato's and Aristotle's treatment of it that its reappearance coincides, not by chance, with the claim that the very same tradition inaugurated by Plato and Aristotle had reached the point of its own closure. *The reappearance of the topic of tragedy—now posed as a matter of the tragic—is contemporaneous with the arrival of the end of metaphysics as a possibility.* In this regard the arrival of the topic of the tragic in philosophy must be understood as marking a double event: the reinvention of the question of tragedy and the closure of the possibility of metaphysics." The only alteration of emphasis I would make in Dennis Schmidt's perceptive account is the following: what concerns me in the *closure of ontotheology* that is commencing in Schelling, Hölderlin, Novalis, and others at the end of the eighteenth century is not so much the "reinvention" of tragedy, or the shift from tragedy to "the tragic," but the need to interpret anew virtually everything we have assumed to be "Platonic" or "Aristotelian" in and about the tradition—and this by reading the texts of Plato and Aristotle in a manner that can only trouble interpreters who accept without disquiet their own Platonistic or Scholastic formation. Likewise, we should anticipate that the *end(s) of metaphysics as possibility* will enable us to experience the tragedies of Aeschylus, Sophocles, and Euripides in utterly new ways. The tragic absolute may not reinvent Plato, Aristotle, and the tragedians, but it will open the texts of antiquity to unanticipated and compelling readings—after which we will be less certain than ever about the very distinction between antiquity and modernity, the Greek and the Hesperian, the "ancient narratives" and our contemporary predicaments.

supreme command of Criticism" (1:335). We can have no idea what Schelling's fictional correspondent might have replied to what looks like the emphatic end of the *Philosophical Letters*. Whatever that reply, it apparently calls on Schelling to think further about freedom and necessity, and to do so in the context not of Kantian philosophy but of Greek tragedy. The tenth and final "Letter" begins:

> You are right, one thing is left for us to do—to *know* that there is an objective power that threatens to annihilate our freedom. And with this firm and secure conviction in our hearts—to struggle *against* it, to challenge it with all one's freedom, and thus to perish. You are doubly right, my friend, because this possibility, even if it has disappeared under the light of reason, must be preserved for art— for what is supreme in art. (1:336)

Schelling immediately turns to the art of Greek tragedy, as both the highest kind of art and the supreme test for freedom. His question is: How could Greek reason bear the contradictions that are played out in the Greek tragedies? Oedipus, without being named as such, provides the model of the Greek hero. He suffers the most unbearable contradictions: a mortal fated to commit a crime, he himself struggles against his fate, and yet is punished terribly, as though he were responsible for the deeds of destiny. At the bottom of this contradiction lies precisely what makes it supportable, namely, the striving of freedom against the power of the objective world. The latter is the superior power, so that the mortal is bound to be defeated; yet because he is defeated not without struggle he must be punished for his defeat. The fact that the unwitting criminal is punished is the sole acknowledgment of human freedom, the single honor that is due freedom. As Nietzsche will later say quite pointedly, "The hero is victorious because he perishes" (KSA 7:219). Schelling writes:

> Greek tragedy honored human freedom by allowing its heroes to *struggle* against the superior power of destiny: in order not to leap over the barriers of art, tragedy had to let the hero be defeated; yet also, in order to compensate for this humiliation of human freedom, it had to let him pay—even for a crime committed by destiny. As long as he is still *free*, he stands tall over against the power of fate. As soon as he is defeated, he also ceases to be free. As he goes into defeat, he condemns destiny for the loss of his freedom. Even Greek tragedy could not rhyme freedom with perishing. Only an essence that was *robbed* of its freedom could be defeated by destiny.—It was a *grandiose* thought, willingly to bear the punishment for an *unavoidable* crime, in order thus to demonstrate precisely this freedom in the loss of it and to go down with a declaration of free will on one's lips. (1:336–337)

As long as the free human being represents and conceptualizes nature, he or she freely masters it. Yet when human beings venture out into the unimaginable, unrepresentable, and unthinkable, they are lost. The Greeks found it natural to remain within the bounds of nature; whenever they did transgress those bounds, says Schelling, no nation was were more terrifying. These are the people who invented tragedy. Better, these are the people whom tragedy invented.

At this point, Schelling introduces a note on the Greek gods into his account. The note is worth reproducing in its entirety:

> The Greek gods still remained within nature. Their power was not invisible, not unreachable, for human freedom. Often human cleverness carried the day, overcoming the physical power of the gods. The courage of their heroes caused even the Olympians to be terrified. Yet what is properly supernatural for the Greeks begins with *fate*, the invisible power that no force of nature can touch, and about which the immortal gods themselves can do nothing.—The more terrifying the Greeks are in the realm of the supernatural, the more natural they themselves are. And the more sweetly a people dreams of the supersensible world, the more contemptible and unnatural they themselves are. (1:337 n. 1)

Schelling's dreams about the supersensible realm are never sweet. Indeed, as we have seen in previous chapters, he will eventually cause the gods to face the selfsame terrors that once seemed to have been reserved for human freedom alone. After the note, Schelling's text continues: "The invisible power is too sublime to be bribed by flattery; its heroes are too noble to find rescue in cowardice. Here there is no choice but—struggle and perishing" (1:337–338).

The "Tenth Letter" now turns briefly to the theme of the Titanic age—shifting, as it were, from the Sophocles of the Theban plays back to the Aeschylus of *Prometheus Bound*.[5] Tragedy presupposes a race of Titans, inasmuch as human beings would simply tremble in the face of such a superior power as Zeus or Fate. Schelling now unleashes a polemic against his own remarkably un-Promethean age, which tries to bargain with the terrors of the next world by offering—in exchange for safe conduct to that world—a whole series of abstentions, renunciations, and discomfitures in the present world.

---

5. The latter is the only tragedy on which the philosopher of spirit, Hegel, never comments, even though he assures his students that he knows "just about everything concerning the splendid works of antiquity and modernity" (HW 15:550). *Prometheus Bound* is arguably the single most significant tragedy for a philosophy of spirit. At the same time, the revelations by both Prometheus and Io in the play make *Prometheus Bound* the tragedy that most challenges—and perhaps even subverts—every philosophy of spirit. Perhaps Hegel did well to ignore it. For his two most extensive observations on Prometheus, themselves embarrassingly thin, see HW 14:67–68 and 17:107–108.

The polemic expands to the point where the subject of the "Tenth Letter," namely, Greek tragedy, appears to be forgotten, obliterated by the dogmatism, superstition, and "moral inertia" of Schelling's own age. We are left with that one insight into human freedom with which the letter opens: freedom asserts itself in downgoing, welcoming the punishment that honors the hero with an uncanny obsequy: *You were destined to fail in the face of a higher power, but even so you struggled—in vain! in freedom!* For the hero and the heroine there is only an imperfect freedom, a freedom that can reply only thus: *By this you see that I, the defeated one, was free. I had freedom . . . to burn!*

Let us now turn to the 1802–1803 *Philosophy of Art*, where tragedy occupies a most important place—the place of culmination. Once again the tragic conflict will be interpreted in terms of freedom versus necessity: the core of the 1795 "Tenth Letter" is taken up almost verbatim into the lectures on aesthetics. What is new in that course, however, is the extensive treatment of music. Our main task in what follows is to determine how music and tragedy are structurally related as particular art forms, and to ask why each of these two, music and tragedy, occupies a place of absolute significance—being the alpha and omega of the absolute as such—in Schelling's aesthetics. Schelling introduces his discussion of both music and tragedy by means of a kind of speculative polytheology, that is, an account of the gods in ancient Greek myth and mythology.

Absolute Mythology: The 1802–1803 *Philosophy of Art*

Nothing could be more surprising than the importance of music in the 1802–1803 aesthetics, inasmuch as *language* and *light* are as omnipresent there as they will be many years later in Hegel's aesthetics. Both the preeminence of the eye among the other sense organs, including the ears, and the preeminence of speech among all possible objects for the hearing ears make us wonder whether music can truly occupy a position of importance. Is there not too much necessity—rather than freedom—at work within the porches of our ears, which funnel into us all the tocsins of the world? In a text that begins by asserting the importance of *absolute freedom* for the system—the freedom of the all-dominating eye, as it were, assisted by the all-dominating logos—one is surprised by Schelling's acknowledgment of the invasive power of sound and tone, the necessitous pulsions of musical rhythm, melody, and harmony.

Schelling's lectures on art and mythology continue to celebrate the identity philosophy—the philosophy of the absolute—that followed directly in the wake of the 1800 *System of Transcendental Idealism*.[6] For identity philosophy, philosophy as such is the science of the absolute, that is, of the totality of ideal determinations and levels of potency in the universe, taking as its point of departure the absolute identity or absolute indifference of opposites (5:366–367). Philosophy has to do with particulars—particulars such as art— only "to the extent that the particular takes up the whole of the absolute into itself and presents it in itself" (5:367). Yet philosophy also and above all has to do with primal images, *Urbilder*, and one of these primal images is music. Music appears already in the introduction to the lecture course as "nothing other than the primal image of rhythm in nature and in the universe itself" (5:369). Also appearing early on in the introduction is the art of tragedy. Among the particulars of poesy, the introduction tells us, is tragic drama: "Drama = synthesis of the universal and the particular" (5:371). The primal images of music and tragic drama are about to converge.

Schelling's lecture course unfolds in two main stages: first, a "general" part, which considers the construction of art as matter and as form; second, a "particular" part, which treats of various art forms in terms of their ideality and reality. The general part, proceeding through a series of seventy-five theses (marked as §§), seeks to establish that "the absolute, or God," is the beginning and end of the philosophy of art. God, as absolute, is infinite affirmation of self, absolute identity and totality, perfect eternity, absolute freedom and necessity, as well as absolute indifference of opposites (§§13–14; 5:380). The relation to the absolute of so particular a matter as art may seem strange, and Schelling's "preliminary determination" of art is anything but clear: "Philosophy is immediate presentation of the divine; art is immediately the mere presentation of indifference as such (this, the fact that indifference alone constitutes the counterimage [*das Gegenbildliche*]. Absolute identity = primal image)" (5:381). Even when we recall that *Indifferenz* is not carelessness but a prior point of nondistinction among eventual oppositions and dualities, it is hard to imagine that indifference could be anything other than tone-deaf and iconoclastic. Yet in a telling synthesis of the two halves of Kant's third *Critique*, Schelling declares that "in the ideal world philosophy comports itself to art as in the real world reason comports itself to the organism" (§17; 5:383). Matters nevertheless take an unexpected turn when the unification of the uni-

6. F. W. J. Schelling, *System des transzendentalen Idealismus* (cited in note 4 of ch. 1, above). Schelling's fascination with Greek mythology—and even with a "new mythology" for his own time— in the lectures on art is completely continuous with both "The Oldest Program toward a System in German Idealism," discussed in ch. 1, and the 1800 *System*. See 3:619, 629.

versal and the particular is described as the production of *images* of divinity—in real terms, the production of *gods* (§28; 5:390). Art is essentially polytheistic, and mythology comprises its essential stuff.

What is most divine about the gods of myth is their charming imperfection. Not surprisingly, Schelling's favorite example of charming imperfection is Venus Aphrodite. She is never more divine than when she satisfies Paris's lust for Helen and so, quite demurely, precipitates a war. No doubt we wish her a bit more circumspection. "But then she wouldn't be the goddess of love anymore; no longer would she be an object of our fancy, for which the universal and the absolute in the particular—in the bounded—is supreme" (5:393). We do not reason with Aphrodite; we fancy her. Precisely when Aphrodite is least herself—for instance, when she enters the fray as an incompetent warrior whom Diomedes handily wounds, so that Athena can mock her by saying that she must have pricked herself with a golden brooch as she was slipping out of her clothes and Zeus can tell her to stick to what she's good at, namely, lovemaking—she is most divine. In other words, precisely as a source of jokes and playful laughter, Venus exhibits to the fancy of humankind what it means to be god (5:394). The fundamental lesson bears repeating several times: primal images answer to fancy, *Phantasie,* alone. And to Xenophanes' complaint that the Homeric gods are often unethical, Schelling replies that whereas human beings need ethicality, gods do not. For they are "absolutely blessed" (§32; 5:396). Indeed, later in the course (5:420), he will say that ethicality, "like sickness and death," is something that "befalls mortals alone." How Hegel must have scolded his younger yet professionally more advanced colleague!

To be sure, less charming limitations of the gods are displayed in mythology, and Schelling does not shy from them. The relatively perfect images of the Olympians can appear "only after what is purely formless, dark, and monstrous is repressed [*verdrungen ist*]" (5:394). For the formless dark is precisely that which causes us "to remember eternity, the first ground of existence [*den ersten Grund des Daseyns*]" (ibid.). These words are familiar to us from the treatises of 1809 through 1815, although we may be surprised to find them in such an early text. Mythology, which recounts the oldest fables, tales that had intrigued Schelling since his school days, would be nothing without Hesiodic χάος, nothing without the Titans and their mother, gloomy Night:

As the common seed of gods and human beings, absolute Chaos is Night, or Gloom. The first figures that the fancy causes to be born of Night are also shapeless. A world of unformed and monstrous figures must founder before the milder realm of blessed and lasting gods can enter on the scene. In this respect too the Greek poems remain true to the law of all fancy. The first births that result from the embraces of Ouranos and Gaia are still monstrous—they are hundred-armed Giants, mighty Cyclops, and savage Titans. These are births in the face of which the begetter himself is horrified: he banishes them to the concealment of Tartaros. Chaos must once again swallow its own births. Ouranos, who keeps his progeny in hiding, has to be suppressed [*verdrungen*]. The dominion of Kronos begins. Yet Kronos too swallows his own children. Finally, the kingdom of Zeus commences, but here too not without antecedent destruction. Jupiter has to free the Cyclops and the hundred-armed Giants so that they can help him battle Saturn and the Titans. And only after he has conquered all these monsters and the final progeny of Gaia, the mother who is angered by the wretchedness of her own children—that is, only after he has defeated the heaven-storming Giants and the monster on whom Gaia squanders the final ounces of her strength, namely, the Typhon—do the heavens clear: Zeus takes unchallenged possession of a cheerful Olympus. In place of all these indeterminate and formless divinities arise determinate, well-wrought figures—in place of old Okeanos, Neptune, in place of Tartaros, Pluto, in place of Helios the Titan, the eternally youthful Apollo. Even the oldest of all the gods, Eros, whom our archaic poems allow to originate simultaneously with Chaos, is born once again as the son of Venus and Mars, thus becoming a well-outlined, perdurant figure. (5:394–395)

Once again Schelling refers to "the law of fancy," *die Phantasie*, or active imagination, as the faculty of primal images. Thesis 31 asserts: "The world of the gods is an object of neither mere intellect nor reason; rather, it is to be grasped solely by fancy" (5:395). Fancy "is thus intellectual intuition in art" (ibid.). Fancy's primal images are beautiful, Schelling assures his listeners, even if the particulars depicted in them incite revulsion or invite ridicule. Limping Hephaistos, hirsute Pan, obese Silenos, the not-so-heavenly host of frolicking fauns and satyrs, even if they are "inverted ideals" and serve as a source of unconquerable laughter, are beautiful (5:398–399). The Parcae too, who spin and cut the thread of our lives, are beautiful. It is as though Schelling were already thinking of what Nietzsche will argue in *The Birth of Tragedy from the Spirit of Music*, namely, that *schön* and *Schein* are the same word. Primal images shine, even in the night: "—Night and Fate, the latter holding sway *over* the gods, just as the former is the mother of the gods, are the dark background, the concealed and mysterious identity from which they all have proceeded" (5:400). These are words that once again remind us of a later Schelling, a less confident Schelling, the Schelling of the tragic absolute.

Although Dionysos plays no role in the 1802–1803 course, Eros certainly does. For the gods are absolutely procreative. Thesis 36 reads: "The relation of dependence among the gods can be represented in no other way than as reproduction [*Zeugung*]" (5:405). Speculative polytheology pursues theo*gony*, and theogony is truly divine. It is absolute, in spite of the talk of dependence. Indeed, sexual reproduction "is the sole kind of dependence in which the dependent remains none the less absolute in itself [*bei welcher das Abhängige gleichwohl in sich absolut bleibt*]" (ibid.). For the future philosophy of scission and languor, such an assertion is essential—even if it expresses a mystery rather than explains a state of being.

Schelling has little to say about Orphism and other mystery religions (though see 5:421), which will become important for his later work, for example, in "The Divinities of Samothrace." His passing remarks on Persian and Hindu myths, the latter exuding "an atmosphere of languor and lust" (5:423), lead all too quickly to a more detailed treatment of Christian mythology—if that is not a misnomer. For, in a sense, mythology founders altogether with the advent of Christianity, inasmuch as the Christ enters on the scene in order to bring antiquity to a close.[7]

Schelling will return to the theme of mythology when tragedy is the art form under discussion. Meanwhile, we need only note that the kind of artistic *genius* that conforms to a philosophy of the absolute is one that seeks to inform the finite by means of the infinite—the art of sublimity (§§63–65; 5:460–461). The return to mythology is in a sense already prescribed when Schelling defines Chaos as "the grounding intuition of the sublime," an intuition that is essential to "the intuition of the absolute" as such (5:465). In transition to the second half of the lecture course, where particular art forms are to be delineated, speech and language are once again emphasized (5:482). We hear once again the voice intoning its soulful plaint, the voice that resounds in Rousseau's *Essay on the Origin of Languages* (5:485). We suspect once again that any discussion of music will quickly deteriorate, becoming what it usually is for philosophers, namely, an opportunity to get the logos going—a conceptual logos whose logic will banish music to one of the lower rungs on the ladder of the arts and trump tragedy with comedy and categories. Kant and Hegel will always have fomented this suspicion on our part. Yet with Schelling things are different. In the final lines of the theoretical part of the

---

7. Schelling refers to the Christ in a phrase that will become vital for Heidegger's *Contributions to Philosophy*. Earlier we referred to Heidegger's Schellingian conception of the "shivering" (*Zittern*) of the godhead, and here we note a possible source of the title of one of the most mysterious sections of the *Beiträge*—Schelling refers to the Christ as "the last god" (*der letzte Gott*). See Heidegger, *Beiträge zur Philosophie* (cited in note 21 of ch. 4, above).

course, Schelling criticizes Kant's treatment of music as "subjective" and "vague" (5:487). Hegel he has no need to mention, at least not yet.

The *Klang* of Music, the Fine Arts, and Tragedy

Music begins with sound, *der Klang*, which Schelling defines as the informing of the finite by the infinite as indifferent—*mere* sound (§76; 5:488). Such informing both occurs *in time* and expresses through sonority the cohesion and density of bodies *in space* (5:489). Sound is ultimately produced by the magnetism that constitutes, in Schelling's view, the very substance or in-itself of the spatio-temporal universe (ibid.). Further, in every tone we hear concordant tones—octaves and dominants—and even sympathetic tones at the very limits of audition (5:490). Schelling is clearly the original thinker of that thought which Hegel makes so famous—that sonority expresses the first interiority of nature as spirit: Schelling calls *Klang* "nothing other than intuition of the soul of the physical body [*Körper*]" (ibid.).

Music expresses the real unity of objects in the world, yet it does so in successive time, which itself is the principle of self-consciousness in the subject (5:491). In other words, music has the enormous synthesizing power that Western philosophy normally reserves for cognition. Music binds unity and uniformity with multiplicity and the manifold, and does so precisely as rhythm: "Rhythm belongs among the most remarkable mysteries of nature and art; no discovery seems to have been more immediately inspired in humankind by nature itself" (5:492). One beat on a hollow log or gourd means nothing. Repeat that beat and you get regularity, periodicity, and eventual *Takt*. Following the beat, human beings count unconsciously, and the work of an entire group of laborers gets done in cooperation and with pleasure; rhythm liberates human beings from their subjugation to successive time by making fortuitous time *necessary* time—and this, as it were, merely by *keeping* time (5:493). Rhythm is therefore not merely the initial aspect of music to be discussed. It is what transforms mere sound into music, beyond all mere noise and reverberation. "*Rhythm is the music in music,*" Schelling declares, allowing the mere repetition of the word in this tautology to be the distant drummer for all synthesizing thought (5:494).

Modulation of tones (not merely in the modern sense of a shift in key signature, but in the sense of any recognized change in pitch) constitutes the next step. Modulation of tones adds *qualitative* difference to the *quantitative* difference of rhythm. When one thinks of tones as themselves products of a rhythm of pitched sounds—and Schelling here seems quite close to the later concept of sound waves—modulation is of course no more than an elaboration of the music in music (5:495). Melody is the third unity, harmony the fourth. Yet before engaging in a discussion of harmony Schelling describes in broad strokes the dimensions opened up by the unities of rhythm, tone, and melody: music as rhythm is "reflexion and self-consciousness"; music as modulation of tones is "sensibility and judgment"; music as melody is "intuition and the imagination" (5:496). Harmony will prove to be the coexistence of all of these, a kind of "breadth" expressed vertically on the musical staff. Because the three fundamental art forms are music, painting, and the plastic arts, and because rhythm is the music in music, we may anticipate that modulation of tones is a painterly quality, while melody is a kind of plastic art—and Schelling's thought does double back on itself (or double *forward* on itself) in this way throughout the lectures. Already we hear echoes of his famous pronouncement concerning architecture, namely, that it is "frozen" or "concrete" music (5:577, 593).

Because rhythm is the music in music, it is, when thought "in absoluteness," the "whole of music" (5:495). It is this that makes the music of the ancients so powerful. A sublime simplicity characterizes it—at least in our surmise of it, inasmuch as no one living has ever heard it. Carefully avoiding taking sides in the most famous dispute of modern music, that between melody (Rousseau) and harmony (Rameau), Schelling turns to the sublimity of ancient Greek choral odes, the pulsating odes that Aeschylus and Sophocles composed for their plays. We know little about how they were performed, although we can be sure that later Christian choral hymns, with their plodding beat, are a bloodless shade of the ancient chorals (5:497). Although Schelling's discussion is truncated here, he returns to the choral ode when taking up the art of Greek tragedy.

Schelling continues to discuss melody and the transformation of unity into a multiplicity and harmony as the arrangement in breadth, so to speak, of multiplicity into a unity—melody being a succession of tones, harmony their coexistence (5:498). Yet he is careful not to allow harmony to appear as merely the latest and most refined of musical dimensions. For, to repeat, even in a single sound there is a harmony of concordant and sympathetic tones. Nevertheless, Schelling is prepared to identify strongly rhythmic music as music that satisfies "hearty affects," whereas harmony better expresses "striving and languor" (5:500). Sophocles produces plays of pure, necessitous, driving rhythm, whereas Shakespeare, with his complex plots and subplots, is a master of counterpoint and harmony—including that *dissonance* on which striving and languor presumably thrive.

Finally, Schelling is unable to abandon the subject of music without referring to Pythagoras, Kepler, and the entire hallowed tradition of the "music of the spheres." Anyone who ever wanted to lend physics wings would know to take up the theme of music as the expression of pure motion (5:502), and pure motion is precisely what music is:

> Now for the first time we can establish firmly the supreme meaning of rhythm, harmony, and melody. They are the first and the purest forms of motion in the universe, and, intuited as real, they are the manner in which material things can be equal to ideas. On wings of harmony and rhythm, celestial bodies hover. What we call centripetal and centrifugal forces are nothing but that—this rhythm, that harmony. Elevated by those same wings, music hovers in space in order to weave an audible universe out of the transparent body of sound and tone. (5:503)

Looking back, or ahead, to the contractive and expansive forces of essence in the preworldly past, we may say that God, or the absolute, undergoes the push and pull of primal rhythm and primal harmony as such. The beat of his own heart pulls him inward and causes him to turn on his own axis and focus on his own sphere of interest; meanwhile, harmony exerts the pull of other spheres, other axes, and the primal rhythm is interrupted by a sometimes melodious, sometimes dissonant languor. That, at least, is one image. A different image, as we have seen, is that of the *mother* of all things, transported on the rhythmic clatter of her rimmed wheels. Those wheels, and their well-centered axle, appear to be what the entire modern world yearns for: Schelling says that in our time we are generally in need of the centripetal force, suffering as we do from dispersion, so that we long to find the center—*Sehnsucht nach dem Centrum* is his phrase (5:504). Perhaps there is some truth in both images. Perhaps music is this maddening interplay of centripetal rhythms and centrifugal harmonies, to which both female and male are summoned to dance. Music appears as both the most closed of all the arts, as though grasping at the still shapeless figures of Chaos, and the most unbounded art, as though soaring in and as pure motion itself (ibid.). Music is the first potency of nature, and, depending on how we hear it, the highest and most universal or the deepest and most earthbound of the arts.

We must now pass by many theses and many pages of the lecture course—on painting and the plastic arts—in order eventually to take up one genre of poetry, to wit, tragic drama. We are doing so upon the urging of the brazen wheels. Even so, however, there are moments when we have to pause, as at the moment when Schelling compares light with sound and the movement of physical bodies with developed sound, that is, music. Sound continues to be thought here as *Indifferenz*, nondifferentiation, a unifying quality:

> Sound [*Der Klang*] is nothing other than the indifference of soul and body. Yet it is this indifference only to the extent that it lies in the first dimension. Wherever the infinite concept is absolutely bound up with the thing, such as in a celestial body, which even as finite is still infinite, there originates the inner music of the movements of the stars; wherever it is merely relatively bound up with the thing, sound originates, sound being nothing other than the act of reinstantiating the ideal in the real; thus sound is the appearance of indifference after both have been torn out of this indifference. (5:508)

Though much in this comparison of visible light to audible sound resists our understanding, even after repeated reading and study, Schelling's conclusion is clear: "Sound is thus the indwelling or finite light of corporeal things; light is the infinite soul of all corporeal things" (ibid.). Presumably, even though light prevails, when mere sound becomes music the objects that reflect or radiate light are already in motion.

Echoes of sound and music—however finite they may appear to be at first—continue to resound in Schelling's account of visibility, as when he calls drawing "the rhythm of painting" (5:520), or when he compares chiaroscuro—itself the painting in painting—first to harmony (5:538), then to rhythm (5:540). If the limitation of music seems to be that it merely expresses the formal coming-to-be of things, *das Werden*, whereas painting, for example, represents those things as having already become (5:542), one must wonder whether insight into the *process* of becoming should ever be made to stand in the shadow of any given represented thing. In other words, whereas music, painting, the plastic arts, and poetry seem to take their places in a hierarchically ordered system, the very *becoming* of the system seems to occupy Schelling's attention first and foremost. Hence all the fore- and back-shadowings. To the extent that Schelling is an archaeological thinker, rather than a teleological one, and to the extent that he will always prefer a good story to an apparently sound argument, he remains a musical thinker.

The special relation of architecture to music has already been mentioned. Architecture, like music, strives to return to the anorganic realm of pure elements (§107; 5:572). Hegel for that reason thinks it crude; Schelling thinks it high art. Yet the parallel between the arts of music and architecture is sometimes disconcertingly detailed: Schelling compares the three classical columns of architecture—the Doric, the Ionic, and the Corinthian—to, respectively, rhythm, harmony, and melody (§117; 5:591). He suggests, or at least implies, that the "architecture" of the ancient Greek lyre, the tetrachord, reflects the fact (which he has learned, presumably, from Rousseau's *Dictionnaire de musique*, cited at 5:497) that the oldest musical system of the Greeks knew only four tones in an octave, the base tone, the *tonus major*, the fifth, and the octave. So far, so good. Yet he also speculates that this in turn has an influence on the dominance of *triglyphs* in monumental architecture (5:393–394). At all events, plastic art is taken to be "the accomplished in-formation [*Einbildung*] of the infinite into the finite" (§125; 5:617), so that plastic art at its best embodies the *sublimity* that is also characteristic of music. Strangely—and Schelling leaves this without much comment—the informing of infinity into finitude confronts human mortality, as though every bas-relief and every free-standing sculpture were a funerary monument: "plastic art represents the supreme touching of life by death" (5:618).

The word for "touching" here, *Berührung*, suggests a contact and contiguity of unknown intimacy. Two objects can "touch" one another; so also can one hand "touch" an object, or two hands "touch" one another. How does death "touch" life in plastic art? Schelling observes what he calls the "mix" of life and death in the universe—the mix of music and tragedy, as it were—but he passes quickly by; he will be reminded of the mix once again when discussing an ancient sculptural group devoted to the subject of Niobe and her slaughtered children, a story we heard in the previous chapter, where it was a question of the Olympian Zeus's pedestal. Schelling does not cite a specific work here, but he seems to be talking about another work ostensibly by Phidias. At all events, an ancient statue of Niobe and her dying children, a sculptural group that apparently also shows the figure of Death, elicits from Schelling one of the very few references to death and dying in his lectures on the philosophy of art. Schelling writes, in words vaguely reminiscent of what Hölderlin is writing (in his "Notes" to Sophocles' plays, discussed in chapters 9 through 11 of this volume) precisely in that same year, 1803:

All life rests on the connection of something in itself infinite with something finite; life as such appears only in the juxtaposition of these two. Wherever their supreme or absolute unity prevails we find, viewed relatively, death—yet precisely for that reason once again we find supreme life. It is, generally speaking, the work of plastic art to present that supreme unity; for that reason, absolute life appears—when art shows it in derivative images, already in and of itself, and also when compared with the appearance—as death. [The sentence is difficult to unravel: *Da es nun überhaupt Werk der plastischen Kunst ist, jene höchste Einheit darzustellen, so erscheint das absolute Leben, von dem sie die Abbilder zeigt, an und für sich schon, und verglichen mit der Erscheinung, als Tod.*] In the "Niobe," however, art itself has betrayed this secret by presenting supreme beauty in death, and the calm that pertains to divine nature alone, but is unattainable for mortals, is achieved only in death, as though to suggest that the transition to the supreme life of beauty has to appear, in relation to the mortal, as death. (5:625)

The passage raises a number of questions without answering them. How can the connection of infinite and finite ever appear in "supreme or absolute unity"? How can it be precisely *death* that appears in that *absolute* unity, viewed *relatively*? And how, even when viewed relatively, as death, do we "for that reason once again find supreme life"? What has "Niobe" to do with this juggling of undefined concepts—the sort of dialectic that Schelling, when he is at his best, spurns? Finally, one must wonder whether it is to this figure of death, or perhaps to the various figures of the dying children, in the (as yet unidentified) "Niobe" group that *Hölderlin* is referring when he writes in his "Notes" that the god has to appear "in the figure of death," *in der Gestalt des Todes*?[8]

8. Schelling appears to be describing an actual sculptural group depicting Niobe and her slaughtered children, one in which either an allegorical figure of Death or a stunning representation of a dead child appears. (To repeat: perhaps when Schelling refers to the "supreme beauty in death" he merely means to characterize the beauty of the child who is no longer struggling but is sculpted in the perfection and finality of death.) Dr. Carlo Petzold, late professor emeritus of ancient history at the Universität Tübingen, informed me that the group Schelling appears to be describing is reminiscent of ancient *vase* decorations, which were often used as inspirations for sculptural groups in late antiquity and the Renaissance. (Professor Petzold refers us to the article on "Niobe" in *Realenzyklopädie* 17, no. 1: 698.) The Uffizi Gallery in Florence (Sala 42, "The Niobe Room") possesses such a sculptural group, which represents Niobe and her children along with a Psyche ("Psyche Tormented") and a number of other figures—and it may well be to this group that Schelling is referring. The Niobe group in the Uffizi, attributed to Scopas and dated from the second half of the fourth century B.C.E., was unearthed in a vineyard near the Lateran Hill in Rome in 1583; the sensational discovery was brought to Tuscany in 1770, where from 1790 to the present day it has been on display. As for Psyche, "Psyche Tormented," with her hand outstretched in an effort to resist the oncoming threat, she stands as a symbol for the entire room. Psyche, we recall, appears as a winged sprite or "butterfly" figure in ancient vase decorations; recall, for example, the figures represented in Jane Ellen Harrison's *Prolegomena to the Study of Greek Religion* (Cleveland: Meridian Books, 1966), esp. chs. 2 and 5, but also throughout. Such a "soul" in flight from the body could readily be taken as an allegorical depiction of Death. In the journal edited by Goethe at the turn of the nineteenth century, *Propyläen*, cited in note 6 of ch. 5, above, we find a detailed discussion by Johann Heinrich Meyer of Scopas's Niobe and her children. See "Niobe mit ihren Kindern," *Propyläen* 2, no. 1 (1799): 48–91. (In the reproductions by J. G. Cotta in Stuttgart and the Wissenschaftliche Buchgesellschaft in Darmstadt, both in 1965, see 410–453. I am grateful to Dr. Lydia Goehr of Columbia University for this reference to Meyer and Goethe's *Propyläen*.) Meyer also refers to Psyche, and to the butterfly image of the soul (445). Yet Meyer is clearly struck above all by the sculpture of the youngest son of Niobe, a figure of death that Meyer praises as particularly beautiful (432). "The Dying Niobean" (Uffizi catalogue number 298) is supine, his trunk and torso supported by the sculpted pedestal, his legs extended and slowly coming to rest on the (imagined) earth. The youth's head is stretched back and down, his right arm obscuring the face. There is doubtless still tension in the figure: death has not yet supervened. And yet the tension produces no effects of struggle. Properly speaking, then, the boy is not yet sculpted in death, as we asserted above; he has not yet expired, is not yet an allegory of Death. It is the *process* of dying, which is

For the moment, at least, Schelling prefers to gaze on the statues of the immortal gods, the Olympians. He praises "the supreme equilibrium and the profound and utter calm" in their facial expressions (5:622). Only two emotions show through: the activity of thought, which in human beings at least furrows the brow, and "pleasure and desire, which draw the gods out of themselves" (5:623). Again, Schelling passes quickly by, failing to note that the conflict of centripetal and centrifugal forces represented in furrowed brow and inflated nostril is quite sufficient to shatter equanimity. The word *Indifferenz* (§131; 5:623) now takes on a strangely modern, psychological sense: the sculpted god is said to be indifferent to pain and suffering. Even Prometheus, "the primal image of all tragic art" (ibid.), suffers not pain but righteous indignation. "Thus in the figures of the gods no expression can be seen which, in and of itself, would show that their inner equanimity has been canceled [*aufgehoben*]" (ibid.). Zeus does not grimace in pain, at least not in statuary. Which leaves unexplained only that statuette of a grinning, lascivious, and temporarily triumphant Zeus carrying off the boy Ganymede—one of the prize possessions of the Archaeological Museum of Olympia, not mentioned by, and probably unknown to, Schelling. It is assuredly not an image of "indwelling indifference" or "contentment," much less "inner equanimity" (5:624). In short, Schelling's own analyses of plastic art often do not ring true; they fail to harmonize with his own absolute mythology. Schelling still has a way to go.[9]

We ourselves are trying to move on to the theme of tragedy, but we will pause one last time in order to make a general remark about dialectic and narrative in Schelling's 1802–1803 lecture course. The theses themselves are always formulated with dialectical conciseness and precision. These axiomatic propositions of absolute philosophy are interrupted, however, by addenda or remarks that often go on for pages. These more discursive pages, however, contain the heart of what Schelling's aesthetics is about. They are the pages on mythology, music, and tragic poetry. As the theses become more dispersed

---

to say, the terminal *life*-process, that is depicted in such a godlike way here. The Uffizi's "Sala Niobe" is designed in such a way that "The Dying Niobean" is the first object one sees upon entering the room, and it is the image around which visitors to the Gallery even today linger for the longest time.

9. It is intriguing that Ganymede is the figure cited by Jacques Lacan when it is a question of an eros that conquers gods as well as mortals. Lacan writes: "Ἵμερος [desire] is the same term that in the *Phaedrus* points to what I am trying to grasp here as the reflection of the kind of desire that binds even the gods. It is the term used by Jupiter to designate his relations with Ganymede. Ἵμερος ἐναργής is literally desire rendered visible." Jacques Lacan, *Le Séminaire, livre VII: L'éthique de la psychanalyse, 1959–1960*, ed. Jacques-Alain Miller (Paris: Seuil, 1986), 311; in English, *The Seminar of Jacques Lacan, Book VII: The Ethics of Psychoanalysis, 1959–1960*, tr. with notes by Dennis Potter (New York: W. W. Norton, 1992), 268. See ch. 11 for further discussion of Lacan's reading of Sophocles' *Antigone*.

and the addenda expand, we begin to see what by 1811 Schelling himself will thematize, namely, the superiority of narrative and even fable over dialectic. In 1802–1803 there are hints of this. One is struck, for example, by Schelling's enthusiastic description of Goethe's *Wilhelm Meisters Lehrjahre* (1795) as a manifold of narrations, each strongly rhythmic in its prose, the whole being a compendium of epic, lyric, dramatic, and even mythic forms (5:674–675; 681–682). In short, in the 1802–1803 aesthetics we witness the subtle victory of discursive thought over axiomatics, even if discursive thought risks dispersion. Wherever dialectic remains victorious, it is merely a sign that an issue cannot yet be faced—an issue such as human mortality or divine desire. Only the old stories spur Schelling's thinking, the oldest fables arising from the pre-worldly time of Chaos. Tragedy proves to be the genre that presents the ancient μύθοι most tellingly.

In preparation for his account of the arts of speech and language (*Rede, Sprache*), among which tragedy will hold pride of place, Schelling reminds us of the "principal propositions" of his philosophy of the absolute:

> The universe . . . is divided into two sides, which correspond to the two unities in the absolute. In the one, observed *for itself*, the absolute appears merely as *ground* of existence, for it is that in which the absolute configures its eternal unity into difference. In the other, the absolute appears as *essence*, which is to say, *as* absolute. For, just as there (in the first unity) the essence is shaped into form, here, by contrast, form is shaped into essence. There form is dominant, here the essence. (5:630)

Even though the terms will shift slightly by 1809, the problem will not budge—the problem as to how the two unities are themselves united in what must be, after all, one absolute. Always at the stroke of one, One becomes Two, and that loved clasp is severed. There is something about the ground of existence that resists total absorption and assimilation into the essence. As long as that resistance prevails in the ground, there is no absolute but tragedy.

In the turn to speech and language, Schelling stresses ποίησις, the creation (*Erschaffung*) of things. The ancient Romans called this *natura rerum*, which Schelling translates as "the birth [*Geburt*] of things" (5:631). The reminiscence of Lucretius, and from Lucretius back to Empedocles (not Epicurus), is essential here, and we will continue to take it up in the following chapter, on Hölderlin's *Death of Empedocles*. For the moment, we will move quickly through Schelling's account of poesy as lyric, epic, and dramatic poetry, in order to reach the summit—tragedy. Schelling begins by recalling the importance of absolute sound (*Klang*) in his system. "Sound = pure in-forming of the infinite into the finite" (5:635). Language completes the long development of sound by becoming the "stuff" of the infinite as such. "Matter is the Word of God gone into the finite. This Word, which still announces itself in sound through an entire range of differences (in variation of tone), and which is still anorgic, in the sense that it has not yet found the body that corresponds to it, finds that body now in language" (ibid.). In the identical way that flesh-tones reflect all the different colors of the spectrum, speech is the "stuff" that restores all the differential tones and sounds to their original indifference. Speech is the glorified flesh of the Word, luminous and transparent matter. When rhythm informs such matter, rhythm being "the talking art" (5:636), poetry is born. If poetry is not sung, that is, if its spoken word falls back upon the "elementary tones" of natural speech, its syllables can nevertheless be stressed (5:637). Lyric poetry arises. All that needs to be observed concerning lyric poetry in the present context is that it expresses passion, *Leidenschaft*. Schelling appears to forget for the moment the role that the passions play in mythology, and also later in tragedy; he seems to forget the disruption of the equanimity of the gods in passion. He offers the following definition: "Passion in general is of the character of the finite, or of particularity, as opposed to universality" (5:641). Schelling's later philosophy will remember the short-sightedness of that definition. (And, apropos of forgetting, it is interesting to note that the divine Sappho is missing altogether from Schelling's account of lyric poetry.) Schelling does note that *modern* lyric poetry almost universally has love as its theme; he also notes that *elegiac* poetry, whether ancient or modern, "sings of languor satisfied no less than of the stings of unrequited love" (5:660). Among modern elegies, Schelling singles out Goethe's *Roman Elegies* for praise: "These elegies sing of the supreme stimulation of life and pleasure" (5:661), as though languor, life, and pleasure were more than merely finite matters.

The fundamental characteristic of epic poetry is that it is indifferent to time. Because the eventual outcome of every epic adventure is guaranteed—no matter how toilsome it may have been, for instance, to build the walls of Rome—time passes episodically and without genuine tension (5:650). Necessity and freedom never enter into real opposition in epic: even if Odysseus and Aeneus are buffeted and bumped about, they will wend their way home for sure, whether that home is old (Ithaca) or new (Rome). Epic hexameter—six of one, half a dozen of another—is the representative meter: its iambs are ultimately indifferent to time and can linger or move on as the rhythm of the episodes dictates (5:653). Epic is unthinkable without the mythic background (5:654), yet epic poems themselves do not develop in any way the mysteries concealed in mythology. Drama, and in particular tragic drama, differs profoundly from epic in this respect. Drama reflects "a higher identity" than either epic or lyric; it embraces both of these and is the "supreme appearance" of art, arriving last also in the order of historical time (5:687). In dramatic poetry, and especially in tragedy, the conflict between necessity and freedom takes shape. Conflict alone enables necessity and freedom to show themselves as they are (5:689).

Much of Schelling's analysis here duplicates that of the "Tenth Letter," which we considered earlier; we need not rehearse these matters again. Let us indicate what seems new, if only in emphasis. Here we find full recognition of the fact that necessity, in Greek tragedy, always enforces ill (*das Ueble verhängt*), and that freedom must voluntarily take on this dire necessity (*das Uebel übernimmt*) (5:691). *Das Üble, das Übel,* the origins of our "ill" and "evil," means both physical and moral evil (see chapter 3 of this volume). *Übelkeit* is nausea, *verübeln* is to take amiss, to blame, *verüben* to commit a crime. Tragedy deals with fateful necessity, and fate deals out ill. Also new here is the emphasis on victory as opposed to defeat—Pyrrhic victory, to be sure. The "essential aspect" of tragedy is that the actual strife between freedom and necessity ends in a double victory: freedom and necessity "appear as both victorious and defeated at the same time, in perfect indifference" (5:693). Also new is Schelling's grasp of a point made by Aristotle in his *Poetics,* a point that will occupy us in chapter 9. Aristotle insists twice in his treatise that even though tragedy touches on what is universal about humankind, its stories derive from a very few households. In Schelling's words: "Aristotle adds . . . that ages ago poets had brought all sorts of fables onto the stage, although now, by *his* time, the best tragedies limited themselves to very few families, such as those of Oedipus, Orestes, Thyestes, Telephos, and those others to whom it befell either to suffer or to commit overwhelming things [*denen überhaupt begegnet wäre Großes zu leiden oder zu verüben*]" (5:695). A small number of houses—the House of Labdacus, the House of Atreus, the latter being what Sophocles' *Electra* (l. 10) refers to as πολύφθορόν τε δῶμα, a house of extreme corruption and repeated calamity—disclose a universe that is essentially tragic.

We are already familiar with the role of punishment in tragedy—the punishment that heroes and heroines take on willingly even though the crime itself is ordained by an overpowering destiny—as that which honors the heroic victim and acknowledges his or her freedom. Yet Schelling now offers a strange formulation of the struggle: "Thus we see that the strife between freedom and necessity is truly present only when necessity subverts the will itself, and freedom engages in a battle on its own turf" (5:696). One must ask whether this is not a formulation for Schelling's own future: the essence of human and divine freedom will ultimately be forced to surrender the discourse of voluntarism, taking up instead an unheard-of discourse on the *Boden* or *Grund*, the soil, turf, or ground on which the struggle takes place. No philosophy will have prepared Schelling or anyone else for such a task. Schelling can reiterate that tragedy is the sublime art (5:699), but that now seems to mean not that freedom is lifted up and purified of all dross (*erhoben/erhaben*), but that the *ground of necessity* will have to become the object for thought—not empirical necessity, Schelling insists, but *absolute* necessity, which cannot be grasped empirically (5:700). The gods themselves, in a world that appears to be divided between gods and mortals, stand under the sway of such necessity. Mythology already tells us that. Yet the question as to how the gods themselves are to be engaged in tragedy baffles Schelling. They cannot be mere heroes, nor can they rescue the hero or heroine from a necessity to which the gods themselves are subject (5:702). However, Schelling ends his meditation on absolute necessity long before entertaining the possibilities that will drive his own later thinking, along with the thinking of Hölderlin and Nietzsche. He remains for the moment far from the thought that tragedy implicates the gods themselves in downgoing and death, and that every hero and heroine from that small number of houses relates a part of the story of the sufferings of Dionysos.

Among the formal aspects of tragedy that Schelling discusses, we must pause to note only three, since they will prove to be important for the development of his and others' thoughts about tragedy. First, tragedy is presentation of the necessitous, and as such is dominated by a constancy (*Stetigkeit*) of plot itself deriving from the "pure rhythm" of its scenes (5:704–705). One must wonder whether Schelling's lucubrations on necessitous rhythm here have something to do with what Hölderlin—again, precisely during these years 1802–1803—calls "counterrhythmic interruption," the famous caesura. Nothing in Schelling's treatment of constancy suggests it, yet the attribution of the musical essence (rhythm) to the form of tragic drama is an attribution that Schelling and Hölderlin may have shared, no matter how far apart they had drifted in their personal lives. Second, Schelling notes the importance of the *chorus* in tragedy, as had Schiller before him. To the chorus falls "the determination of anticipating what would be going on even in the spectator, the movement within his deepest soul [*Gemüth*], both his being caught up and his being able to reflect [*die Theilnahme, die Reflexion*], not allowing the spectator to be free even in this respect, and thereby captivating him utterly by means of the art" (5:706). Once again, one is reminded of what Hölderlin will see as the very purpose of caesura, namely, a simultaneous *engagement in* the entire sweep of the play and a *reflection upon* the play's representations *as* representation. Third, and last, Schelling affirms the importance of Aristotelian catharsis, taking it in a more refined sense than usual. At least in the plays of Aeschylus and Sophocles, catharsis is not the purgation of pity and fear; rather, catharsis works on the soul of the spectator by purifying the passions (5:709). Tragedy seeks "to perfect the passions in themselves and to make them whole, not to eradicate and disperse them" (ibid.).

So much for the 1802–1803 *Philosophy of Art* and the 1795 "Tenth Letter" on tragedy. Let us now advance forty years, to the end of Schelling's career, with the Berlin lectures on the *Philosophy of Mythology*, 1842–1843. We will then return to our original passage from the 1811 printing of *The Ages of the World*, obeying in all this the rhythm propounded by the brazen wheels of the Great Goddess. Let us see whether our archaeology has dug up any useful artifacts.

Ironclad Necessity

Midway through his 1842–1843 lectures at Berlin in the *Philosophy of Mythology*, Schelling begins to discuss the orgiastic cults. He needs to refer to them inasmuch as mythology is under way to the mystery religions (II/1:351–352). He traces the multiple senses of *Orgiasmus*, referring back to the Greek word ὀργή, meaning anger, rage, wrath (*die Wut, der Zorn;* see, for example, Sophocles' *Electra*, ll. 628, 1011, 1282, and *Oedipus at Colonus*, l. 905), as well as to the original word for reaching out in desire, ὀρέγω. Thus begins his final confrontation with the Phrygian Mother, Kybele. She is the middle figure among the three great Goddesses, Urania coming before her and Demeter after her.

She descends from the mountain, is herself a καταβολή, in order thereby to become the very ground of the heretofore efficacious god (II/1:353). It is possible, on the basis of a reference that Schelling makes here, that Lucretius—whom we have seen Schelling place in the company of Empedocles—is the source for Schelling's entire description of the Great Goddess in her chariot.[10] It is not actually a chariot but a large wagon with iron wheels.

---

10. II/2:361. Lucretius interrupts his discussion in Book II of the original kinds contained within Mother Earth, a discussion heavily influenced by Anaxagoras and Empedocles (though not, Schelling says, Epicurus), with an account of the goddess herself: "Therefore she alone is called Great Mother of the gods, and Mother of the wild beasts, and genetrix of our bodies [*et nostri genetrix haec dicte est corporis una*]. She it is of whom the ancient and learned poets of the Greeks have sung, that seated in a chariot she drives a pair of lions, thus teaching that the great world is poised in the spacious air, and that earth cannot rest on earth. They have yoked wild beasts because any offspring, however

The Goddess is seated, but there are many empty seats around her in the wagon. It is as though she has come down from the mountain in order to prepare places for the other gods, the gods to whom she will give birth. Her pomp—again the word *Gepränge*—is replete with sacred shuddering (*voll heiligen Schauers*). As she drives through the city, her route is strewn with roses, as well as with the ores of iron and silver. She says nothing: *Munificat tacita mortalis muta salute* (II/2:362, citing Lucretius, 2:625). If there is music here, it is *absolute* music. Schelling writes:

> Also sie selbst ist stumm, als die dem Gotte stille, ganz hingegeben ist, indeß, den heiligen Wahnsinn zu erhöhen, oder die letzte Angst vor dem Polytheismus in dieser Agonie des Bewußtseyns zu übertäuben, das Getöse einer wilden, zerreißenden Musik sie umstürmt, erregt durch donnernde Pauken, gellende Becken, rauh klingende Hörner und die stachelnden Töne der phrygischen Pfeife, dieselben Mittel, deren man auch jetzt sich bedient, den Krieger, der in den grausamen Todeskampf geht, in einen besinnungslosen Zustand zu versetzen. (Ibid.)

Thus she herself is silent whenever she surrenders herself entirely, quietly, to the god; meanwhile, in order to enhance the sacred madness, or to anesthetize his final anxiety in the face of polytheism in this agony of consciousness, the tumult of a wild, lacerating music surrounds her as a whirlwind, excited by thundering kettledrums, shrilling cymbals, grating horns, and the piercing tones of Phrygian pipes, the identical means that we employ nowadays in order to transpose into a state of torpor the warrior who is about to go off to his cruel death-struggle.

---

wild, ought to be softened and vanquished by the kindly acts of the parents. And they have surrounded the top of her head with a mural crown, because embattled in excellent positions she sustains cities; which emblem now adorns the divine Mother's image as she is carried over the great earth in awful estate. She it is whom different nations in their ancient ritual acclaim as the Idaean Mother, and give her troops of Phrygians to escort her, because men declare that first from that realm came the grains [*fruges*], which they spread over the round world. They give her eunuchs, as wishing to indicate that those who have violated the majesty of the mother, and have been found to be ungrateful to their parents, should be thought unworthy to bring living offspring into the regions of light. The taut tomtoms thunder under the open palm, the concave cymbals sound around, horns with hoarse-echoing blare affright [*tympana tenta tonant palmis et cymbala circum / concava, raucisonoque minantur cornua cantu*], hollow pipes prick up the spirits with their Phrygian cadences, martial arms show a front of violent fury, that they may amaze the ungrateful minds and impious hearts of the vulgar with fear through the goddess's majesty. Therefore, as soon as she rides through mighty cities, silently blessing mankind with unspoken benediction [*munificat tacita mortalis muta salute*], they bestrew the whole path of her progress with silver and copper, enriching it with bounteous largesse, and snow down roseflowers in a shower, overshadowing the Mother and her escorting troop. Here an armed group, whom the Greeks name the Curetes, whenever they sport among the Phrygian bands and leap up rhythmically, joyful with blood [*exultant sanguine laeti*], shaking their awful crests with the nodding of their heads, recall the Dictaean Curetes, who are said once upon a time to have concealed that infant wailing of Jupiter in Crete; when, boys round a boy in rapid dance, clad in armor, they clashed bronze upon bronze in rhythmic measure, that Saturn might not catch him and cast him into his jaws and plant an everlasting wound in the Mother's heart." Lucretius, *De rerum natura*, tr. W. H. D. Rouse, rev. M. F. Smith, Loeb Classical Library (Cambridge, Mass.: Harvard University Press, 1992), Book II, ll. 598–643.

New here is the soldier in his death struggle—no longer the mother in her birth struggle. His appearance is surprising at first, since 1842 is not 1848, nor 1871, nor 1914. Yet we recall that the original Curetes, associated with the Corybants, were armed, and that it was their swords and shields that provided the first percussion section. New too are the horns, rough sounding, raw, grating. New, finally, is the initial fantasy of the passage, in which the Great Goddess silently surrenders to the old, stern star god. The last time we saw her, she was requiring the god to surrender something to her. Yet now too the *Galli* are not absent—those emasculated priests, who "in the tumult of fanatical frenzy mutilate themselves, merely in order to repeat on themselves the god's emasculation" (II/2363). Such self-mutilation and emasculation, Schelling insists, perhaps to our surprise, is the typically Greek way of saying what the Phrygians think of as a less violent transition to the feminine Urania—although, as Schelling concedes, the Phrygians too have their Attis. However, let us move back several decades to Schelling's first draft of *The Ages of the World*, in order then to come to a conclusion.

At the end of the 1811 passage, repeated with variations in the final, 1815 printing, the passage that so strikingly invokes the brazen wheels of the goddess and identifies them as the source of divine tragedy and of a music that both anesthetizes and devastates, Schelling makes the remark we heard earlier concerning the helplessness of essence. If we think of the essence as the father, there is no surgeon present to cauterize the wound; if we think of the essence as the mother, there is no midwife to assist her in her "terrifying loneliness"; in either case, there is no one there to help (43).[11] Schelling finds corroboration for the truth of his drastic description of the primordial epoch of Chaos in the following happenstance—and with this he closes the section (the third of four in the 1811 printing). The figure of the "spinning wheel of birth," which is the very madness that "wildly lacerates itself," makes it seem as though the cutting of the mother in episiotomy or of the infant's cord at birth were indistinguishable from emasculation, and as though the two images of *Scheidung* that occupied us in chapter 3 were really only one. "Even now," says Schelling, the wheel grinding away on its axis "is what is innermost in all things," *das innerste aller Dinge* (ibid.). The innermost essence of things "can be mastered and, as it were, indemnified by the light of a higher intellect," which, however, is but one product of "the proper force of nature and all its production" (ibid.). The only thing that remains mysterious—and it remains mysterious throughout Schelling's philosophy from beginning to

---

11. We are once again back in *Die Weltalter Fragmente*, cited by page number alone in my text.

end—is how anything like intellect and reason could ever have been spun off by such a brazen wheel, spinning with ironclad necessity.

The problem of "The Past," thought as the remote, elevated past, is the problem of the preworldly time of Chaos. *Jenes göttliche Chaos*, "that divine Chaos," Schelling calls it (38). Chaos is godly in the sense that it is the ground of divine essence as such, the turf on which ironclad necessity and a nonvoluntaristic freedom struggle. Our initial passage begins with an allusion to "divine madness" in Plato's *Phaedrus*. Yet whereas Plato is thinking of poetic and mantic inspiration, Schelling is thinking of manic and even maniac divinity itself. For on its way to glory the absolute suffers every sort of monstrous birth—if only in its head. It could account itself king of infinite space, were it not that it has bad dreams—"heavy dreams, welling up from the past" (41). *Angst* is its entire sensibility as it goes to confront "all the terrors of its own essence" (ibid.). It suffers scission after scission, like an onion that feels its outer layers being peeled away, and fears for the nonexistent center. Essence "trembles for its very existence" (ibid.).

There is nothing cheering or cheerful in the Bacchic tumult that nature undergoes. The dipsomania of those creatures that are caught in the final toils and coils of scission and unification produces not visions of sugarplums but *delirium tremens*. Like Io, stung by the gadfly, or Pentheus, dazzled by the god, spirit suffers delusions. Dionysos, excluded from the panoply of Olympians in 1802–1803, returns with a vengeance to claim his or her rights. (His or her? King Pentheus is unsure: he sees Aphrodite smiling out of the eyes of the stranger, and when the young king goes to spy on the revels of the women in the mountains he goes in drag.) The great cats, the felines, pull the chariot of Dionysos, which is the first chariot we see in the passage, though it will not be the last.

Traffic thickens. The tumult of nature is also called a *Begeisterung*, which Schelling would want us to understand inspirationally as a kind of enthusiasm that produces spirit. Yet in the context of "The Past" it is more like the Classical Walpurgisnacht of Goethe's *Faust II*, the saturnalia of all hundred-armed Giants and craggy Cyclops. The ancient peoples, intimating (*ahndend*) the secret heart of nature in Chaos, celebrate Bacchic orgies. These are not suburban adventures in sex but lamentations of the destruction of the old order. The word *Wogegen*, difficult to translate and to assess, now falls. Does it mean that the centripetal force about to be described *opposes* the turmoil? What sense would that make? For it is the closure of essence in its own bad dreams that causes the turmoil in the first place. Chaos is of the essence. For the wheel that is spinning on its own axis is itself called *wahnsinnig*, repeating once again the "divine madness" (*Wahnsinn*) of the opening line and the "drivenness" of the things in "madness" (*Wahnsinn*) from a later line. It is the wheel of incipient . . . Schelling first writes *nature*, then, remembering the lesson of the *rerum natura* in Lucretius and Empedocles, and perhaps also Jacob Böhme, *birth*. (In his *Introduction to the Philosophy of Revelation* [II/3:123], Schelling tells us that he has this expression, *das Rad der Natur oder der Geburt*, from Böhme—that "truly theogonic nature," who is so important to Schelling from 1809 onward.) These scissions of nature or birth are parturings, cuttings of the cord, the sort of thing that fathers seldom suffer, or suffer only once. The intimating peoples, sensing the frightful forces that impel them, invent a form of pomp and circumstance (*Gepränge*) that imitates the cycle of births and, presumably, deaths: they spin in rhythmic dance to the point of entrancement. Or, alternatively, they call for a procession (*Zug*), the shattering or agitating procession "of the mother of all things."

Like Dionysos, the mother too rides in a chariot or wagon, drawn by cats. The chariot's wheels turn as the cycles of birth and death in incipient nature—for death is part of the "mix." One might think that those wheels will roll on forever, but it would probably be safer to think of them as the last Aureliano does in Gabriel García Márquez's *One Hundred Years of Solitude* when he tells Pilar Ternera—herself a great goddess—of his love for Amaranta Úrsula and she replies by noting the gradual wearing away of the axle of recurrence:

> When Aureliano told her, Pilar Ternera let out a deep laugh, the old expansive laugh that ended up as a cooing of doves. There was no mystery in the heart of a Buendía that was impenetrable for her because a century of cards and experience had taught her that the history of the family was a machine with unavoidable repetitions, a turning wheel that would have gone on spilling into eternity [*dando vueltas hasta la eternidad*] were it not for the progressive and irremediable wearing of the axle [*por el desgaste progresivo e irremediable del eje*].[12]

Pilar Ternera knows, as Aureliano comes to know, that lineages born on this earth receive no second chance, precisely because of the wearing away of that axle.

The wheels of the chariot are *ehern*, perhaps ironclad, or hooped in bronze—inasmuch as the German translations of Homeric Greek often translate copper and iron indiscriminately, as some sort of unspecified ore or metal. Whatever the metal, it produces a rough sort of music, partly anes-

---

12. Gabriel García Márquez, *Cien años de soledad* (Buenos Aires: Editorial Sudamericana, 1967); tr. Gregory Rabassa as *One Hundred Years of Solitude* (New York: Harper and Row; London: Jonathan Cape, 1970), 334/402.

thetizing, partly lacerating—*zerreissend*, which is exactly what those great cats would do if they caught us. The essence of this overwhelming music is the *rhythm* of that clangor, the raw sound of metal on cobblestone or marble pavement, a rhythm obeyed necessitously by the throwing arms of the Corybants. One would certainly prefer another sort of image and another form of cult, less drastic, but, as Schelling says, there is no one there to help.

Klang and *Ton* alike appear in the struggle between spirituality and corporeality. Modulation of tone supplies all the differences—the spokes of the wheel joining circumference to hub—in the incipient world of nature. Modulation is sensibility and judgment, and these would be of enormous help to the shivering essence in its present position. Intuition, imagination, and breadth would also help. For melody and harmony alone can supply the constancy (*Stetigkeit*) and synthetic power that the cycles of nature need in order to survive the reign of Chaos. Harmony would also provide the fleshtones, melody the architecture and the sculpted bodily frame, the two of them together guaranteeing coexistence and succession. With succession we are back at the hearty affects of rhythm, though the striving and languor of harmony are not far. *Tonkunst*, the art of rhythms and tones, is alone adequate to the savage dance of essence in the time of Chaos. One might prefer a pure Word, or pure Reason, but Kant does not always get what he wants. When it comes to music, Kant's nettlesome neighbors, the prisoners of Königsberg, raising their raucous voices heavenward in hymns of praise, prevail.[13] Kant doesn't know whether to hold his ears or some other part. *Tonkunst* alone supplies an image—not by way of programmatic music, but in *absolute* music—of the motions of primeval, incipient nature. *Tonkunst* alone elaborates an intuition of that cycle of births in which death is part of the mix.

The mother of all things could of course be the Great Goddess, angry with her wretched children and collecting her tribute of severed members, as though by way of dismal compensation. Turn in your badges, boys, you're through. Indeed, that is Schelling's image in the 1811 printing of *The Ages of*

13. "Over and above all this, music has a certain lack of urbanity about it. For owing chiefly to the character of its instruments, it scatters its influence abroad to an uncalled-for extent (through the neighborhood), and thus, as it were, becomes obtrusive and deprives others, outside the musical circle, of their freedom. This is a thing that the arts that address themselves to the eye do not do, for if one is not disposed to give admittance to their impressions, one has only to look the other way. The case [of music] is almost on a par with the practice of regaling oneself with a perfume that exhales its odors far and wide. The man who pulls his perfumed handkerchief from his pocket gives a treat to all around whether they like it or not, and compels them, if they want to breathe at all, to be parties to the enjoyment, and so the habit has gone out of fashion." Alas, if only the singing of hymns in prisons would go out of fashion, so that a man could open the windows of his house and not be molested! See this selection from the Analytic of the Sublime of the *Critique of Judgment* in Jost Hermand and Michael Gilbert, eds., *German Essays on Music*, The German Library (New York: Continuum, 1994), 24–25.

the World, an image not only the editors of his works would like to suppress—or repress. It is the moment when the self-absorbed father, spurning all creatures and swallowing his children, is forced to remember who she is. Trauma enough for anyone. Yet the mother could also be Niobe, mourning those wretched children, her pride and contumely finally purged in the snowmelt of tears. "Niobe," the most rhythmic of sculptures, in which the most musical figure is Death.

However, if only in order not to end this way, speaking so brazenly of Death, we should invoke the melismatic image with which the 1811 (and the 1815) passage closes. Melisma: a sequence of higher tones, taking their departure from, and returning to, the *Grundton.* Should night be descending, one may hear these melismas of birth and death in the second movement of Brahms's First Piano Concerto, which strikes the grounding tone deep in the double bass, allowing the piano to meander through a series of melismatic tones on high—Brahms always allows his musical ideas as much time as they want, telling them *You* can *always get what you want*—until, finally, they cascade to their source in the ground, whereupon they cease. Or, should it be in the brilliant light of midmorning, one may hear them in the final thirty measures of Bach's extraordinary *Fantasy in G* (BWV 572), perhaps the wildest melismatic venture of Occidental music. Although Bach's *Grundton* is always shifting—as though proclaiming "the law of *Phantasie*" in absolute mythology and creating the churning ground of essence as such—the melismas bubble with life, are insane with life. *Phantasie,* we remember, fancies Venus Aphrodite above all: the Venus who commands not mutilation but laughter and languor.

VOICES OF EMPEDOCLES

7

Is it an accident that the two great solitaries whose work continues to shape our own future—Hölderlin and Nietzsche—confronted the figure of Empedocles, and that both conversed with this figure, seeking in that way to comprehend the task they had been assigned?

—Martin Heidegger, 75:337 (1944)

Among the didactic poems of the earliest Greek thinkers and their Roman epigones—the poems of Parmenides, Xenophanes, Empedocles, Lucretius, and others—we have seen Schelling single out those of Lucretius and Empedocles for special mention. Empedocles combines "the seriousness of Pythagorean wisdom" with Anaxagorean physics, attaining in his didactic poem on nature "the greatest rhythmic energy and a truly Homeric force" (5:665). About this the ancient critics are unanimous. Lucretius is therefore to be considered a disciple of Empedocles. Both Lucretius and Empedocles, says Schelling, call upon Aphrodite as their muse. Both express rage against the limits of human knowledge and struggle against the shackles of brittle piety and rigid ethicality that inhibit their times. Finally, both Lucretius and Empedocles are poetic thinkers of languor and languishment: if for them nature dissolves into a play of inscrutable forces of love and enmity, they emerge from their study of it with a sense of yearning (*Sehnsucht*) that carries over into their accounts of ethical life—elaborated, in Empedocles' case, in the book of

"Purifications," Καθαρμοί. "Nothing more true or more fitting can ever be said about the bootlessness of languor [*das Fruchtlose der Sehnsucht*], the insatiability of desire, the vacuity of both fear and hope in life" (5:666). Yet are languor and desire to be found at the heart of nature, or are they merely the marks of a bootless humanity? Or merely the marks of struggling poets?

In the autumn of 1799 Hölderlin writes to Schiller:

> The valuable advice you gave me some time ago, and which your last letter repeats, I have not allowed to remain altogether unheeded; I am earnestly trying to cultivate in myself that tone which, without being capricious, seemed to lie closest to my natural, untrammeled way of thinking. I have now made it a maxim of mine to develop myself solidly in a single form of poetic creation and to attain character before I strive to be versatile. Versatility can only be the property of one who has *achieved* a secure standpoint. I believed I could execute most completely and most naturally the tone I wished to make peculiarly my own in the tragic form, and I have taken up the challenge of a mourning-play [*Trauerspiel*], *The Death of Empedocles*. (I 916; CHV 2:819)[1]

Searching for his proper tone and his own voice, so to speak, in the effort to identify his own character and the poetic form that is suitable to it, seeking something that he could declare his own (*Eigentum*) and occupy as a standpoint (*Standpunkt*), Hölderlin chooses the tragic tone that resounds in the legendary figure of ancient philosophy, Empedocles of Acragas. Why are tragedy and philosophy conjoined in this way? Why try to find one's own in what is antique and foreign? Why search for one's own voice in the throat of another, and why this particular other? Finally, why the imperfect tense among those verbs dispatched to Schiller that tell of a project in which he is currently engaged? Why *zu liegen schien* ("seemed to lie"), *ich glaubte* ("I believed"), *ich wünschte* ("I wanted")? The imperfect troubles the confidence expressed otherwise in the present and perfect: *ich suche mich* ("I am trying"), *habe mich an ein Trauerspiel gewagt* ("I have taken up the challenge of a mourning-play").[2] As we know very well, *The Death of Empedocles* is all about a failure, three times the failure to find the voice, three truncations of the same *Trauerspiel*, three sets of ruins.

---

1. Each of the four principal editions of Hölderlin's works available today has its advantages and disadvantages, so that no single one can be recommended to readers above all the others without various qualifications and reservations. In this and the following chapters I will refer to the four editions of Hölderlin's works cited according to the code found in "Key to Works Cited."

2. The German word *Trauerspiel* may most often be taken as synonymous with *Tragödie*. Yet because mourning, *die Trauer*, constitutes such an important motif for Hölderlin's late hymns, his drama *Der Tod des Empedokles*, and his novel *Hyperion*, it seems best to use the English word *tragedy* only when its German cognate appears. I accept the risk of offending the English ear with the more literal *mourning-play* for *Trauerspiel*.

In the present chapter it will not be a matter of subsuming the three versions of Hölderlin's *Der Tod des Empedokles,* composed between 1797 and 1800, under any sort of philosophical program, whether of Hölderlin's time or our own, whether that subsumption wants to close Hölderlin within or liberate him from the supposed confines of German Romanticism and Idealism.[3] As chapter 1 suggested, Hölderlin could readily have affirmed the entire "Oldest Program toward a System in German Idealism." His desire for a new physics finds voice in Empedocles' *On Nature* (Περὶ Φυσέως), even if that should be a generic title for a text attributed to virtually all the thinkers of the tragic age. Hölderlin is as susceptible to that voice as Hegel and Schelling are: like them, Hölderlin surely wishes to reverse the order of the Kantian ethicotheology and physicotheology. Furthermore, the critique of the state and the church in the "Program" is one that Hölderlin subscribes to; indeed, his *Hyperion* has things to say in this regard that are as harsh as anything produced by his two roommates. As is universally affirmed, the final paragraphs of the "Program," on the all-unifying idea of beauty, the restoration of poetry as the instructress of humankind, and the call for a new mythology, have most to do with Hölderlin: when the "Program" insists that beauty is to be taken "in the higher, Platonic sense," we think of Hölderlin's proposed commentary on *Phaedrus,* envisaged in a letter to Neuffer in the autumn of 1794:

> Maybe I can send you an essay on *aesthetic ideas* . . . , which can be taken as a commentary on Plato's *Phaedrus,* since a passage from it serves as my explicit text. . . . Basically, it is to contain an analysis of the beautiful and the sublime, according to which the Kantian analysis can be both simplified and expanded, as Schiller has already shown in part in his treatise *On Charm and Dignity* [*Über Anmut und Würde*], even though Schiller fails to step far enough across the Kantian boundary, in my opinion at least. Wipe that smirk off your face! I may be wrong, but I've been studying the matter, studying it long and hard. (I 830; CHV 2:550–551)

Schiller's notion of "charm," *Anmut,* better translated by a combination of gracefulness, graciousness, and grace, is important to Hölderlin: we will soon see it in the mouth of Empedocles—this attractive, seductive, sublime, and even uncanny force of nature and rhetorical art—and we will not be able to suppress the memory that on one of Hölderlin's report cards a teacher wrote of him, *venusta, liebreizend,* "completely charming."

---

3. For an extensive discussion of Hölderlin's relation to Empedocles and a generous selection of documents, see JV 3:352–395. Jamme and Völkel emphasize the political aspects of that relation as well as the affinity of Hölderlin's mourning-play with the early political and theological essays of Hegel.

Nevertheless, the unification achieved by beauty becomes, in the course of the three versions of *The Death of Empedocles,* a *tragic* unification. This may mean that Hölderlin by this time is taking some distance from the buoyant optimism of the "Program," precisely in the way that his 1795 essay "Being, Judgment, Modality" takes its distance from Fichte—a distance measured by Hölderlin's flight from Jena in May of that year (JV 2:1–51). Whereas Hölderlin may still affirm that the highest act of reason is an aesthetic act, and that the philosopher must possess as much aesthetic force as the poet, inasmuch as all the sciences and arts are to be absorbed by *Dichtkunst,* and whereas no one other than Hölderlin himself could have written so eloquently of that "higher spirit sent from heaven," it remains true that the three versions of Hölderlin's mourning-play take distance on all of this—uncanny distance.

"Dame Philosophy Is a Tyrant"

We know from his letter to Sinclair of December 24, 1798, that Hölderlin read Diogenes Laertius's famous *Lives of the Philosophers* only after having commenced work on his mourning-play. Yet a certain number of details in Diogenes' account must have impressed the poet and stayed with him for the remainder of his project. The opening lines of the first version of *The Death of Empedocles,* for example, refer to Empedocles' fame in the chariot races at the Olympic games; this may have resulted from a confusion between the philosopher and his grandfather of the same name. Empedocles' illustrious family would have been important to the twice-fatherless Hölderlin, Jean Laplanche would insist.[4] Even more important for Hölderlin would have been Empedocles' association with the great masters of philosophy prior to him: a disciple of Pythagoras (even if he is excommunicated from the Pythagorean Brotherhood, reputedly for having betrayed one of the hermetic doctrines, an important detail for the *second* of the three versions of Hölderlin's play), he is a disciple also of Parmenides, the thinker who writes of "the well-rounded sphere of truth," so important for Empedocles' own cosmology, and the poet of hexameters, the form adopted by Empedocles for his poems; an admirer of Xenophanes of Colophon, the acerbic critic of Homer and Hesiod, and the poet of a Zeus whose power resides in his "unmoving thought," Empedocles

---

4. Jean Laplanche, *Hölderlin et la question du père* (Paris: Presses Universitaires de France, 1961), *passim.* Compare the treatment by Pierre Bertaux, *Friedrich Hölderlin: Eine Biographie* (Frankfurt am Main: Insel Verlag, 2000), 599–600, which says virtually nothing about Hölderlin's reaction to the deaths of his "two fathers."

is, finally, a rival of Zeno, the inventor of dialectic—inasmuch as Empedocles will invent rhetoric. If Empedocles is a master of rhetoric, however, he is also a great poet. Diogenes says that Empedocles is ὁμηρικός, which is the superlative encomium. He elaborates in a strange way by averring that Empedocles is μεταφορητικός, "well-versed in all the poetic devices," and even "powerful in versification to an uncanny degree," καὶ δεινὸς περὶ τὴν φράσιν.[5]

Empedocles' skills extended to all the sciences and arts: according to several of Diogenes' sources, he wrote both tragedies and philosophical discourses, was both rhetorician and physician, both dramaturge and thaumaturge, an expert in all the φάρμακα affecting body and mind. Hölderlin would perhaps have been most struck by a reference Diogenes makes twice to a certain woman Empedocles reputedly healed. There may have been several such cases, but the name Pantheia (Hölderlin will write her name as *Panthea*) is associated with one of them. Pantheia in turn is associated with a certain Pausanias, who is said to have been the favorite (ἐρώμενος) of Empedocles. Pantheia, a victim perhaps of the plague, was considered by her father and by all the citizens to be dead. Empedocles the doctor and pharmacologist, discovering a source of warmth in her belly, managed to preserve her life. Empedocles the thaumaturge preserved her body for thirty days without a pulse and without respiration. After having been restored to health, Pantheia presumably became a disciple, and was particularly associated with Empedocles at the time of his death. It was reportedly during the sacrifice offered for her recuperation that her doctor and savior took his life by leaping into the crater of Etna. During the night, Diogenes reports, the crowd heard a woman's voice cry out the name Ἐμπεδοκλέα. Nietzsche will decide that this woman in fact joined Empedocles in his death; whether Hölderlin ever entertained the idea of such a *Liebestod*, even for a moment, we do not know. It did not become a part of his play.

There is significant controversy surrounding Empedocles' political life. According to Diogenes, Aristotle assures us that Empedocles became a radical democrat, almost an anarchist, ἐλεύθερον γεγονέναι καὶ πάσης ἀρχῆς ἀλλότριον, that he refused to accept the people's wish that he become τύραννος, and that he thought only of the welfare of the people, τῶν τὰ δημοτικὰ φρονούντων. Yet others dispute this, saying that he was arrogant

---

5. See Diogenes Laertius, *Lives of Eminent Philosophers*, tr. R. D. Hicks, vol. 2, Loeb Classical Library (Cambridge, Mass.: Harvard University Press, 1972), 366–391, which comprises Book VIII, sections 51–77, for this and the following. See also JV 3:354 n. 5, 358–359.

and self-seeking, ἀλαζόνα καὶ φίλαυτον.[6] Diogenes twice refers to Empedocles' mantic pretensions and places these words in Empedocles' mouth: "As for me, I am immortal god, no longer a mortal," ἐγὼ δ' ὑμῖν θεὸς ἄμβροτος, οὐκέτι θνητός. The ultimate hubris, one must say, the most nefarious *nefas* that one can imagine—unless Empedocles' self-willed death outstrips the claim to divinity and is itself the ultimate hubris. Diogenes delights in the multiple reports concerning that death: a fraud perpetrated by the crafty thaumaturge and desperate dramaturge, who sets the scene for the launching of his own legend, plays the τραγικός up to the very end, yet in that end is finally unmasked, or unshod; or, on the contrary, the hierophant, γεγόνι θεός, "become god," having mixed his flesh and blood with the elements of fire, water vapor, volcanic gases, and liquefied earth in Etna, home of the defeated Typhon.

Among the fragments of Empedocles to which Hölderlin had access, there are a number that must have fascinated him—although this is a matter of speculation.[7] Diels-Kranz B27–28, on the σφαῖρος κυκλοτερής, would surely have struck Hölderlin as the perfect symbol of unification, albeit tragic unification, inasmuch as the one sphere is riven by the opposing forces of Love and Strife, Φιλία καὶ Νεῖκος. Diels-Kranz B17, transmitted by Simplicius, opens the tale of crisis in the sphere by pronouncing these words: δίπλ' ἐρέω, "I shall tell a double tale," as though the cosmic cycle itself were duplex and duplicitous. For "there is a double becoming of things mortal, and a double disappearance," δοιὴ δε θνητῶν γένεσις, δοιὴ δ' πόλειψις. If love, Κύπρις 'Αφροδίτη herself, occupies the center of the sphere, all-present yet invisible, her reign is nonetheless troubled and troubling. The trouble lies in the duplicity of doubles and doublings that we find throughout the tragic age of the Greeks, from Aeschylus's *Agamemnon* to Euripides' *The Bacchae*. One recalls in the latter all the duplicities of Dionysos, masked as a priest of the god yet present as the god himself; one also recalls his first cousin and eventual double, Pentheus, who, doubling as a woman worshiper of the god, goes to meet his Dionysian fate. The words δίπλ' ἐρέω could easily have opened and closed this play—in a sense, they do, in every word spoken by the god. Similarly, Aeschylus's *Agamemnon* is replete with references to the twofold and duplicitous, especially touching the two-edged sword that is called Clytaimestra (ll. 325, 642–643). She herself is a "double-edged doom," δίλογ-

---

6. As the source of the allusion to Aristotle in Diogenes, JV cites Aristotle's fragment 66 (Rose); see JV 3:356, *Erläuterung*.

7. JV 3:346 n. 35 notes the availability to Hölderlin of the fragments of Empedocles (including the fragments on nature) in the edition by Henricus Stephanus, *Poesis Philosophica*, published in 1573, 11–13, 17–31.

χον ἄτην, a double-barreled infatuation and fatality for Agamemnon, an all-encompassing tangle of doom, ἄτης παναλώτου (l. 361). Her rancor against her husband, swallowed over and over again during the years of his—and Iphigeneia's—absence, is itself a "redoubled sickness," διπλοίζει ... νόσον (l. 835). Finally, one thinks of the duplex nature and duplicity of Oedipus's sons, the belligerent brothers, Polyneices and Eteocles, in Aeschylus's *Seven against Thebes*. After their double fratricide, Ismene and Antigone (ll. 971–973) cry out in rapid stichomythia:

> ANTIGONE: You were slain by your own blood!
> ISMENE: You slew your own blood!
> ANTIGONE: Duplicitous speech [διπλόα λέγειν]!
> ISMENE: Duplicitous sight [διπλόα δ' ὁρᾶν]!

The trouble—double trouble—is pervasive, and is of the Empedoclean sphere itself. And yet fragment B17 gives Hölderlin and us encouragement:

> Fire and water and earth and air up above,
> Off to the side, Strife, the whole well harmonized,
> And in the center, Love, equal in breadth and in height;
> Look at her with your mind's eye, do not be astonished.
> You know her, she surges in the limbs of mortals;
> Thanks to her, they think of love and do unifying deeds,
> Calling out her name: O Delight! Aphrodite!
> As she turns there among the other elements
> No mortal male [θνητὸς ἀνήρ] can recognize her.
> But you must follow my footsteps, the pace of my words.
> They will not disappoint you.

How could Hölderlin, himself mad for unifying deeds, himself the victim of strife "off to the side," have resisted the Empedoclean seduction—even if it is duplicitous, and in multiple senses? Empedocles is said to have written two books, and commentators have never been sure about how they can be aligned with one another. *On Nature* is joined by *Purifications*, Καθαρμοί. The extant fragments of the latter must have astonished Hölderlin. For if the one sphere of the cosmos is itself separated absolutely into reigns of love and strife, the human world feels the effects of that separation with particular force: the human world is unrelievedly ruined by murder and omophagy, the cannibalism that humans commit against their own and against other living beings, the crime committed by the Titans against the god Dionysos and by Tantalos against his own son. (The first version of *The Death of Empedocles* will mention Tantalos by name.) One of the most gripping of the ancient Empedoclean fragments, Diels-Kranz B137, envisages the father snatching up his son—his form altered—as a sacrificial victim, the father ("the fool!") laying out a spread for his people; the mother, in turn, is seized by her children, killed, and eaten.[8] Hölderlin, who lost his fathers early on, was spared at least one form of murder. Yet the world of absolute separation is his world. In "The Ground to Empedocles," Hölderlin will call Empedocles "a son of his sky and of his period, a son of his fatherland, a son of the violent oppositions between nature and art in which the world appeared before his eyes" (FHA 13:362). The "son" in each case is to be understood as a sacrificial victim whose blood will be shed. Hölderlin therefore would have found Empedocles' two books entirely commensurate: if the sphere is divided against itself in alternating reigns of love and strife, and if self-division derives from strife, then the rule of strife in the sphere never ends. Strife, "off to the side," contaminates the sphere to the point where love cannot be identified as such: love has no identity apart from languor and languishment. This would be a radicalization of what Hölderlin himself was thinking in "Being, Judgment, Modality," namely, separation. If identity does not equal absolute being, if I am set into opposition with myself, and not simply after the manner of Fichtean positings, then am I not a fugitive and a vagabond? Does not the soul "wander and flee" (φεύγει καὶ πλανᾶται) on the "plains of doom" (B121: Ἄτης ἀν λειμῶνα)? One cannot help but think of a line written by Georg Trakl a century or more later, Trakl being the poet who picked up the lyre when it slipped from Hölderlin's hands: *Es ist die Seele ein Fremdes auf Erden,* "A foreign thing is the soul on earth."

The foreignness and duplicity that mark Empedocles are precisely the qualities that attract Hölderlin and give him his unsteady voice. Already in *Hyperion* he invokes those "plains of doom," or "the field of curse" (CHV 1:616: *Feld des Fluchs*) that is the Empedoclean equivalent of banishment from Paradise. Hölderlin surely would also have noticed the word ἔμπεδος in Empedocles' fragment B17, inasmuch as it indicates the ultimate duplicity of a signature. On the one hand, it refers to the immutability of things forever within the sphere, αἰέν ἔασιν ἀκίνητοι κατὰ κύκλον. Yet the tale is duplicitous—δίπλ' ἐρέω—and has fatal consequences for all that lives: for, on the other hand, that which does not cease to be within the sphere is forever

---

8. Roberto Calasso writes: "The primordial crime is the action that makes something in existence disappear: the act of eating. Guilt is thus obligatory and inextinguishable" (RC 311).

caught in the separation of lovehate and is therefore never at rest, οὔ σφισιν ἔμπεδος αἰών. "Not lasting," "not steadfast," οὔ . . . ἔμπεδος. That sounds like a question in French: Where *is* Empedocles? Where *is* the steadfast one? Where can one find a foothold in destitute times, whether the epoch in question be that of Empedocles, Hölderlin, or ourselves? Steadfast? When Agamemnon returns victorious from Troy to Argos he prays that victory, νίκη, will remain steadfast in his life, ἐμπέδως μένοι. This is immediately before he steps into the bath and the net that Clytaimestra and Aegisthus have drawn for him. The chorus assures him that the only thing in Argos that is ἐμπέδως is the anxiety of a terrified heart (Aeschylus, *Agamemnon*, ll. 854, 975).

We know that the period Hölderlin spent at Bad Homburg vor der Höhe (1798–1800, the years of *The Death of Empedocles*) was one of retreat, rest, and recuperation. Without rest, without recuperation. Hölderlin had been fired from his tutorship and expelled from the Gontard household in Frankfurt after a terrible scene with Jacob Gontard, Susette's husband and the father of her children, and Susette herself, who did not intervene to save the tutor. Suddenly he was deprived of his job, his chargelings, whom he loved, and Diotima herself. Now there were only letters, exchanged during clandestine meetings.[9] Yet it was also a period of retreat from philosophy. Not that Hölderlin was ever a stranger to philosophy. We recall the letter to Neuffer of December 10, 1794, in which Hölderlin envisaged a tragedy "on the death of Socrates." However, it would no longer be a commentary on Plato's *Phaedrus* or a discourse of "aesthetic ideas" that drew Hölderlin, nor would it be Fichte's lectures at Jena (see his letter to Hegel, dated January 26, 1795). Hölderlin's ambivalent attitude toward theoretical work in general is expressed in a letter to Schiller dated September 4, 1795:

> My displeasure with myself and with what surrounds me has driven me into abstraction. I am trying to develop for myself the idea of an infinite progression in philosophy. I am trying to show that the relentless demand that must be made on every system, namely, the unification of subject and object in an absolute—in an ego or in whatever one wants to call it—is possible, albeit aesthetically, in intellectual intuition. It is possible theoretically only through an infinite approximation, as in the squaring of the circle. I am thus trying to show that in order to realize a system of thought an immortality is necessary—every bit as necessary as

9. See Kenney and Menner-Bettscheid, trs. and eds., *The Recalcitrant Art* (cited in note 3 of ch. 1).

it is for a system of action. I believe that I can prove in this way to what extent
the skeptics are right, and to what extent not. (I 846–847; CHV 2:595–596)

The ambivalence felt toward theoretical systems is most strongly manifested
in a letter to Immanuel Niethammer dated February 24, 1796: Hölderlin confesses that philosophy is "once again" his "only preoccupation," as he reads
Kant and Reinhold and hears Fichte reverberating in his brain: "Dame Philosophy is a tyrant, and it is more the case that I put up with her compelling
me than that I voluntarily submit to it" (I 851; CHV 2:614). Finally, in a long
letter dated November 12, 1798, addressed to Neuffer, we hear this ambivalence in the context of the *Trauerspiel* in which Hölderlin is now engaged:

I have been here [in Bad Homburg vor der Höhe] for a bit more than a month.
I've been working quietly on my mourning-play, in the company of Sinclair, en-
joying the beautiful autumn days. I was so torn apart by suffering that I have to
thank the gods for the good fortune of this calm. . . . What most occupies my
thoughts and my senses now is vitality in poetry [*das Lebendige in der Poesie*]. I
feel so deeply how far removed I am from achieving it, even though my entire
soul is wrestling to attain it, and this realization overcomes me so often that I
have to weep like a child. The presentations of my drama are lacking in this or
that respect, and yet I cannot twist free from the poetic errancy in which I wander. Oh, the world has frightened my spirit back into itself, from my youth onward. And I still suffer from that. There is one sanctuary, it is true, to which a
botched poet like me can honorably flee—philosophy. Yet I cannot give up the
hopes of my youth; I would rather go down with honor than alienate myself
from the sweet homeland of my muses, from which mere accident has banished
me. If you can give me some good advice, so that I can get to the truth of all this
as quickly as possible, do not fail to give it to me. I am not lacking in force, but in
agility; I don't lack ideas, but nuances; I'm not missing the main tone, but all the
other tones of the scale; I've got light, but not the shadows. And all for one reason: I shy away much too much from the common and the ordinary in real life.
I'm nothing but a pedant, if you will. Yet, if I'm right, pedants are usually cold
and loveless, whereas my heart is overanxious to be a brother to every person and
every thing under the moon. I almost think I am pedantic for no other reason
than love. . . . I'm afraid that the warm life in me will catch cold in the frigid history of our times. . . . And, just so you know everything about this moody brood-
ing of mine, I confess to you that for the past few days my work has ground to a
halt, so that I have to fall back on ratiocination. (I 879–881; CHV 2:710–712)

Hölderlin's mourning-play offers him the chance to escape from the tyranny
of *Philosophia*, even if the play itself is a site of ideas. He finds his way to those
ideas only gradually.

One of the most remarkable anticipations of *The Death of Empedocles* occurs in a passage that appears late in the second volume of *Hyperion*, written presumably in 1798. It depicts the ancient Sicilian magus "ticking off the hours" of his banishment from the city, weary of time and life. Hyperion writes to Notara: "And now tell me, where can I find sanctuary?—Yesterday I was up on Etna. There I thought of the great Sicilian who, once he had had enough of ticking off the hours, intimate with the soul of the world, in his bold lust for life threw himself down into the splendid flames, because the chilly poet had to warm himself at the fire—that's what the mockers said of him" (CHV 1:753). A still more intense identification with Empedocles had already been expressed in Hölderlin's lyric poem, "Empedocles," first sketched out in the summer of 1797, achieving its final form in 1800, and published in 1801:

Empedokles

Das Leben suchst du, suchst, und es quillt und glänzt
    Ein göttlich Feuer tief aus der Erde dir,
        Und du in schauderndem Verlangen
            Wirfst dich hinab, in des Aetna Flammen.

So schmelzt' im Weine Perlen der Übermut
    Der Königin; und mochte sie doch! hättst du
        Nur deinen Reichtum nicht, o Dichter,
            Hin in den gärenden Kelch geopfert!

Doch heilig bist du mir, wie der Erde Macht,
    Die dich hinwegnahm, kühner Getöteter!
        Und folgen möcht ich in die Tiefe,
            Hielte die Liebe mich nicht, dem Helden. (DKV 1:241)

Empedocles

You seek life. You seek, and out of the earth
    Flows and blazes forth a godly fire to you,
        And you, in shuddering yearning,
            Cast yourself down into Etna's flames.

Thus the queen's haughtiness melted pearls
    In wine; let them melt! if only you
        Had not sacrificed your riches, O poet,
            In the bubbling chalice!

Yet you are holy to me, as is the power of the earth,
    That took you away, bold victim!
        And gladly would I follow into the depths,
            If love did not hold me back, this hero.

The words "shuddering yearning" (*schauderndes Verlangen*) are repeated in the first version of the mourning-play, where they have quite a different impact. For there Empedocles utters them sarcastically, in a moment of hesitation and self-contempt. Empedocles has been hearing the pleas of his favorites, Pausanias and Panthea, from the beginning of the play—their worry that his planned suicide may simply be an effect of melancholy or punctured pride, not some grandiose "ideal deed." Such doubts plague Empedocles increasingly as the three versions of the play succeed upon one another; the worries of the others gradually become Empedocles' own doubts, doubts that can only cripple action. In act II, scene 6 of the first version, Empedocles soliloquizes: "Shuddering yearning! What! Is it death alone / That kindles life in me at the end . . . ?" (FHA 12:237). Queen Cleopatra melts her pearls in a chalice of wine, but she does so out of insolence or haughtiness, *Übermut*. If it is not melancholy, is it haughty ambition that tempts Empedocles with his "one full deed at the end"? In the lyric poem, love holds the singer back; the singer's voice is closest to that of Pausanias or Panthea in the play. Why does the love of Pausanias, or that of Panthea, fail to hold the dramatic hero Empedocles back? If it is neither melancholy nor pride nor haughtiness, is it a failure of love that destroys the thinker?

Several other details in the lyric poem deserve our attention. First, the irony of Empedocles' situation: seeking life, he throws himself into the crater. The power of the earth, which is holy to the singer, both gives life and takes it away. Second, the manner in which the earth takes life is violent: Empedocles may be bold, but he is the one who is boldly "killed," *kühner Getöteter*. Much later, in his "Notes on Antigone," Hölderlin will write about the murderous force of the word in ancient Greek tragedy: even though words merely mediate action, they can nonetheless be deadly. Hölderlin will distinguish between "factically deadly" (*tödlichfaktisch*) and "factically deadening" (*tödtendfaktisch*) words. Something of each in this difficult distinction seems germane to the bold death of Empedocles, although the suicide—the self-imposed sacrifice of riches—is fundamentally a matter of regret for the singer. Empedocles is here apostrophized as "poet," even though the action of the later play might cause us to think of him more as "politician." As we shall see, that confusion is at the heart of the conflict of the play. Born to be a poet, Empedocles will become a sacrifice of his city and his times. Finally, the ultimate paradox: what holds the singer back from following Empedocles into the crater is the very force that invites Empedocles into it—that simple word which caused so much centrifugal force to be exerted on Schelling's "essence," which at first only wanted its own centripetal force, namely, love. Or the far less simple word *Verlangen*, longing, Schelling's *Sehnsucht*, "languor." For, as we shall see, the words *sehnen* and *Sehnsucht* appear in *The Death of Empedocles* as well.

Essence or Accidents?

Before proceeding with a discussion of the three versions of *Der Tod des Empedokles*, we might do well to remind ourselves of the movement of plot and incident in them. (Those readers who are unfamiliar with the three versions of the play might want to consult the appendix at the end of the book, "Plot Summaries of *The Death of Empedocles*.") And we might summarize the import of the chapter thus far by saying that if Dame Philosophy is a tyrant from whom Hölderlin is seeking release, it is nonetheless the case that many of his extraordinary poetological and theoretical works are written during the periods of such desired release. Even if Hölderlin is seeking release from the Fichtean absolute ego, and thus taking his distance from much of what we call German Idealism, he is never seeking release from *thinking*. When he listens for the voice that will be his own, he hears one of the greatest thinkers of antiquity. If this is a doubling of voices, it is no accident that the thinker who fascinates Hölderlin is the one who begins with the words δίπλ᾽ ἐρέω, the thinker who may have confused himself with the gods, the thinker who tells of lovehate in the sphere, the thinker who tells of an eon without ἔμπεδος. Empedocles—without foothold, but with anxiety.

The so-called "Frankfurt Plan" of the tragedy, sketched in September of 1797, precedes the work on the first draft by an entire year. Only in October or November of 1798, in Homburg vor der Höhe, in that sanctuary arranged by Isaak von Sinclair, does work on the play itself commence. D. E. Sattler suggests that during that year of latency the Etna scene of *Hyperion* (volume two) and the lyric poem "Empedocles," which we only now examined, were probably composed. Work on the *first* draft of the mourning-play stops probably in spring or early summer of 1799; work on the *second* version stops soon after that, in late June or July of 1799. Sattler imagines Hölderlin working on both the first and the second versions simultaneously, though the vast difference in versification argues against this. At all events, work on both is interrupted by Hölderlin's need to devote his time to a planned mensual review of poetry and criticism, *Iduna*, designed to reach a female audience, as well as the need to work on a narrative-epistolary poem entitled "Emily on the Eve of Her Wedding." Hölderlin discusses the latter in a letter to Neuffer dated July 3, 1799, and we will examine it in a moment. It is useful to juxtapose "Emily" with "Empedocles" for insight into the difference between tragic and sentimental poetry, as Hölderlin practices them, inasmuch as the difference between essence and accident is expressed in that juxtaposition. Finally, in order to complete the chronology, Hölderlin composes his theoretical text, "The Ground to Empedocles," in October or November of 1799. He thereupon begins the *third* and final attempt in December—even if the September letter to Schiller, cited at the outset, uses those verbs in the imperfect tense, as though the final failure has already been anticipated.

Luckily, a number of ideas expressed in the "Frankfurt Plan" are dropped in the execution of the play, such as the idea of having the central conflict of the play revolve about a quarrel between Empedocles and his wife. Yet some aspects of the plan remain relevant, especially its famous opening paragraph:

> Empedocles, by temperament and through his philosophy long since destined to despise his culture, to scorn all neatly circumscribed affairs, every interest directed to sundry objects; an enemy to the death of all one-sided existence, and therefore also in truly beautiful relations unsatisfied, restive, suffering, simply because they are special kinds of relations, relations that fill him utterly only when they are felt in magnificent accord with all living things; simply because he cannot live in them and love them intimately [*innig*], with omnipresent heart, like a god, and freely and expansively, like a god; simply because as soon as his heart and his thought embrace anything at hand he finds himself bound to the law of succession—[.] (I 567; FHA 12:20, 26)

In the manuscript of Hölderlin's very first effort to write this sketch, Sattler notes the name "Empedocles" and then eight empty lines, the phrase next appearing being, "an enemy to the death of all one-sided existence" (FHA 12:20). Existence viewed in only one of its facets, exclusively from one side—that would naturally be the enemy of one who begins, "A twofold tale I shall tell." A line of filiation connects the thoughts of one-sidedness, omnipresence, and succession—connects them by disjunction. The thought of temporal succession, of course, would require us to review Kant's "Transcendental Exposition of the Concept of Time" in the Transcendental Aesthetic of the *Critique of Pure Reason,* along with the Deduction in the second edition, where succession is treated as the result of a movement or action, in addition to the Schematism and the first two Analogies of Experience. We may assume that Hölderlin studied all of these. Without going into excessive detail, we may isolate a few Kantian propositions from these sections of the first *Critique.* First, only in time can two opposite and contradictory predicates be conjoined in one and the same object, that is, one after the other—indeed, this is a mere repetition of Aristotle's law of noncontradiction. Second, time is nothing other than the form of our inner sensibility, that is, our intuition of ourselves and of our interior condition. Third, this intuition has no form of its own, hence the analogy of the line; the analogy is essentially faulty, however, inasmuch as the points of a line are simultaneous, whereas the parts of time are always successive.

The relation of succession to one-sidedness is expressed in a text written perhaps during the period of the "Frankfurt Plan," a text Friedrich Beißner's edition calls "Reflexion," Sattler's "Seven Maxims" (I 604–605; FHA 14:43–45, 47–48). The penultimate aphorism tells us that we come to know all matters and relations only successively; hence the need for repetition before an intuition can become truly "lively." Even so, when we merely grasp things in the intellect, our knowledge is "one-sidedly askew." Hölderlin opposes such intellectual grasping to love, which "is pleased to uncover tenderly" (*Da hingegen die Liebe gerne zart entdeckt*). Love intuits the whole nexus of relations more intensely and more intimately (*inniger*) than intellect can. Again we see the word *innig*, which appears in the Frankfurt Plan, considered above. Intensity is of the essence for Hölderlin, as it is for the Greeks: every "sudden heightening of intensity," according to Roberto Calasso, brings one "into a god's sphere of influence" (RC 95; cf. 283–284), which of course may be a blessing or a curse. Often enough, the conflict between knowledge through love and knowledge through understanding produces *Trauer*, the mournfulness of the mourning-play. Hölderlin writes here of "the profound feeling of mortality, of change, of life's temporal limits" (I 604; FHA 14:44, 48). A mournful sense of separation and loss always accompanies hopes for unification. Hölderlin's Empedocles, who grew up within such a loving unification of nature and art, spoiled by the gods, undergoes this mourning process. His challenge is not to let chagrin destroy his life. "For he has attained much who can understand life without mourning," says the maxim (ibid.). Not to try to attain too much, not to hope for too intense a unity, not to blast away at the pervasive horizon of *Trauer*, not to try to escape the inevitable season of mourning with hopes for too much—that is perhaps Empedocles' challenge. The profound feeling of mortality may spur us to exercise all our forces, but it may also cause us to conjure up "some sort of phantom" and to "close our eyes" (ibid.). How, then, to keep our eyes open to the law of succession without losing heart? Is the hope for *omnipresence* a stimulant to our forces or a soporific phantasm?

Two appearances of this omnipresence in the first draft of *The Death of Empedocles* may shed light on the problem. In act II, scene 4, Empedocles tells Critias that it is not Empedocles himself that the people need. What should speak to them are "The flowers of the sky, the blossoming stars, / And those myriad blooms of the earth, / For divinely present nature / Needs no speech" (I 513; FHA 12:143, 228–229). *Göttlichgegenwärtig* is Empedocles' word here. Presence as such is the recurrence of gods in nature. In the previous scene, immediately after his "transformation" into an essentially affirmative spirit, Empedocles tells Pausanias the same:

> Siehest du denn nicht? Es kehrt
> Die schöne Zeit von meinem Leben heute
> Noch einmal wieder und das Größre steht
> Bevor; hinauf, o Sohn, zum Gipfel
> Des alten heilgen Aetna wollen wir.
> Denn gegenwärtger sind die Götter auf den Höhn.
> (FHA 12:114–116, 217).

> For do you not see? Today recurs
> The beautiful time of my life
> Once again and something still more grand
> Awaits; upward, my son, to the peak
> Of ancient holy Etna. That is where we shall go.
> For the gods are more present on the heights.

Yet for all the emphasis on presence and recurrence, it is the past that haunts Empedocles. His unity with the gods is, at present, only a memory. Whether that memory can be affirmed, that is, experienced affirmatively, or whether it must be suffered in bitterness and regret during the time of dreary succession, is Empedocles' problem. The question of memory may be raised with regard to "Emily on the Eve of Her Wedding," the poem that interrupts work on both the first and second versions of *Empedokles*. The poem itself, a narrative-epistolary poem rather than a dramatic one, is full of contingencies and accidents, actually quite bizarre ones.[10] The tale is told by Emily in a series of letters to Clara. Emily recounts her brother Eduard's death in the Corsican wars and her encounter with Armenion—who is the exact double of her brother, a sort of fraternal Doppelgänger. She tells of her father's initial opposition to their marriage and the eventual reconciliation. The duplicity of the simulacrum brother-lover, Eduard-Armenion, remains disconcerting. In the forest with her father, Emily sees—quite close by—her dead brother. Even though it is indiscreet to mention accidents of biography in a literary or philosophical context, it is perhaps worth noting that Hölderlin himself was, for Susette Gontard, the exact image of her brother Henry—on whom she doted and after whom she named her only son. It is not a matter of incest, neither in

---

10. For what follows, see I 278, 280, 282–283; DKV 2:585–586, 587–588, 589–590.

life nor in the work, nor yet a reference forward or back to Antigone, who unites her brother and lover in death. Here it is simply a matter of the question of accidents—of the accidental and contingent. The final section of the "Frankfurt Plan," which we have ignored until now, confronts the issue of contingency and accident when it outlines Empedocles' ripening resolve to unite himself with infinite nature by means of a voluntary death. The plan for act V reads:

> Empedocles prepares himself for his death. The accidental occasions [*zufälligen Veranlassungen*] of his resolve now fall entirely away from him, and he regards this resolve as a necessity that follows from his innermost essence. In the brief scenes he has here and there among the dwellers in the region, he everywhere finds his mode of thinking and his resolve confirmed. His favorite comes after him, intimating the truth, but is so overwhelmed by the spirit and the grandiose movements in his master that he blindly heeds his command and leaves. Soon after that, Empedocles casts himself into glowing Etna. His favorite, wandering aimlessly through the region, restless and troubled, soon after that finds the iron shoe of the master, which the lava has catapulted out of the abyss; he recognizes the shoe, shows it to Empedocles' family and his disciples among the people, and gathers with them on the volcano in order to express their collective grief and to celebrate the death of the great man. (FHA 12:24–25, 28)

The question of course is what these "accidental occasions" in the drama will have been, and how they can be separated off from Empedocles' "innermost essence." One does not want the incidents leading to an "ideal deed at the end" to turn up like bronzed shoes. Camus says somewhere that a person commits suicide because while he or she is in a phone booth making a call another person waiting to get into the booth scowls. A stranger's curse is enough. Even in ultimate situations, and especially there, it is difficult to know—and to portray dramatically—what is essence and what accident. In his letter to Neuffer dated July 3, 1799, about the time when work on the first two drafts ceases, we read that the material for "Emily" is not at all heroic, but sentimental. Yet the identical problem arises here as well as in his work on the mourning-play, namely, how to avoid both mere "submission to old forms" and sheer "rulelessness." If one tries to write a love story in the heroic style of the ancients, the lovers always sound as if they are quarreling. For a mourning-play, what seems fitting is a tone of grandeur, in which each scene follows upon the last without any sort of embellishment, in "alternating harmony." One who writes a mourning-play must avoid the temptation of inserting something brilliant or tender (*Glänzendes oder Zärtliches*), and must practice a "proud renunciation of everything accidental." A love story, by contrast, needs to affirm *this tender awe in the face of the accidental* [zarte Scheue des Akzidentellen]." The problem with *The Death of Empedocles* is that Empedocles' heroism is a heroism of love—love of nature and the earth, but also of Pausanias and Panthea. Or are these two characters mere accidents? And is love of the earth too a mere accident?

If it is true that the doubts entertained by the two "favorites" of Empedocles eventually become the hero's own doubts, then it is difficult to regard either these personages or their words as mere accidents. Delia, called Rhea in the first draft, in the opening moments asks the crucial question: *Wie lebt er mit andern?* "How does he live with others?" Panthea is the one who best recognizes Empedocles' suffering and his longing—*Sehnen* is her word. Even though she shies away from him ("A frightening, all-transforming essence is in him"), she is nonetheless "a tender reflection" of him: . . . *und ich war der zarte / Widerschein von ihm.* Panthea is tender awe personified; yet she is essential, and not accidental, to the play. Moreover, the second draft of the play ends with words spoken by Panthea yet taken from the very mouth of Empedocles' "innermost essence," perhaps the most famous of all the dactyls of this second version:

So will es der Geist
Und die reifende Zeit
Denn Einmal bedurften
Wir Blinden des Wunders.
(FHA 13:299, 327)

Thus the spirit wills it
And the ripening time
For if it be but once
We blind needed a miracle.

In the third version, Panthea is to be no longer the woman who has been cured by Empedocles, no longer his "tender reflection," but his sister. To be sure, siblings too may be reflections, as "Emily" demonstrates and as Antigone will prove. *Schwester naiv. idealisch,* say the plans. Are we to regard this as a reduction of Panthea's role? What speaks against any such reduction is that her brother, Empedocles himself, is also designated as naive and idealizing, *Empedokles naiv. idealisch.* If the tender reflection is an accident, the hero is himself that accident: *zart* and *zärtlich,* "tender, tenderly," no matter how much our tradition wants us to relegate the words (and the things) to the sentimental, are among the most important words for both Hölderlin and Hölderlin's Empedocles.[11]

Nefas or Destiny?

The question of Empedocles' blasphemy or sacrilege, his *nefas*, is of the essence in all three versions of the play. Hölderlin uses the word *nefas* in the "General Ground," which is the second part of his "Ground to Empedocles," and he continues to use it later in the 1803 "Notes on Oedipus." Normally, one would translate *nefas* as sacrilege, sin, or evil, or as the tragic flaw in the hero, ἁμαρτία. Yet Hölderlin never ceases to ask himself the question, What is the hero? Who may become a hero? Hovering somewhere between the celestial ones and the mortals, the hero is a demi-god, or a δαίμων in Plato's sense. How then can one, from a more lowly perspective, determine the hero's "flaw" or "sin"? If Tantalos (cited in the first version of the play as well as much later, in Hölderlin's first letter to Casimir von Böhlendorff, dated December 4, 1801) is a paradigm of the hero, that paradigm is difficult to understand—even and precisely in its most horrific acts. The earlier reference, in act I, scene 3 of the first draft, arises in the context of Empedocles' accusation against

11. In the first chapter of *Lunar Voices*, I argued that the importance of the female characters of Hölderlin's drama *The Death of Empedocles* did not—whatever appeared to be the case—diminish but grew as the three versions of the play succeeded upon one another. Although Hölderlin's Empedocles is more than willing to soliloquize for himself, and out of his own mouth, so to speak, the poet needed the women Panthea and Delia (originally called Rhea) to express his deepest insights. As Max Kommerell argues (337), Panthea is the only one who understands Empedocles' suffering. She is the one who is determined by nature and by love to be, again in Kommerell's words, "the woman who interprets the world" and "the woman who interprets the interpreter" (ibid.). Panthea is therefore the new Diotima, replacing the character of that name in Hölderlin's novel *Hyperion*, until Panthea's place in turn is taken—if it ever is taken—by Manes in the third and final version of *Empedocles*. If the seer Manes *can* take Panthea's, Delia's, and Diotima's place at all, however, it is because Manes, like Tiresias, is somehow double-natured and is a woman-man. Both are remnants or remainders of Rhea, the daughter of Gaia; we will have to return to these remnants in the course of the chapter. The questions I wish to pose here with regard to Hölderlin's *Der Tod des Empedokles* have not changed much since the first two chapters of *Lunar Voices*. Yet I would formulate them now in the following way. First, the question of time as decline, the downfall of an individual within a native land and an entire culture that are themselves in decline. Such individual and universal catastrophe appears in and as the eternal return of the tragic—the tragic absolute, if you will. Can one say *yes* to such an absolute? Second, the question of tragic unification (*die tragische Vereinigung*) as languor and languishment, and the relation of sensuality and sexuality—the remnants of Rhea, as it were—to tragedy. Third, the question of the omnipresence of Empedocles throughout the epochs of Western philosophical and poetic history, from the tragic age of the Greeks to Irigaray's *The Forgetting of Air*. Why do the multiple voices of Empedocles suggest something like the suspension of all suspension—the end of the epochal and of the absolute—as such? See Max Kommerell, *Geist und Buchstabe der Dichtung: Goethe, Schiller, Kleist, Hölderlin*, 6th ed. (Frankfurt am Main: V. Klostermann, 1991 [originally published in 1940]), cited in my text by page number. See also the first two chapters in my *Lunar Voices* (cited in note 8 of ch. 2, above), 3–51. See, finally, Françoise Dastur's wonderful book, *Tragédie et modernité*, reissued under the title *Hölderlin: le retournement natal* (cited in note 10 of ch. 2, above), 25–96.

himself in the antistrophe to his grand soliloquy, "Into my tranquillity you came":

> O Schattenbild, verbirg dirs nicht! du hast
> Es selbst verschuldet, armer Tantalus
> Das Heiligtum hast du geschändet, hast
> Mit frechem Stolz den schönen Bund entzweit
> Elender! (FHA 12:51–52, 188–189)
>
> O mirage, do not hide it from yourself! you
> Yourself are to blame, miserable Tantalos
> You have sullied the sacred precinct, have
> With insolent pride severed the sweet bond
> Wretched one!

The letter to Böhlendorff (I 941; CHV 2:914) speaks of "old Tantalos, who became more of gods than he could digest" (*dem alten Tantalus, der mehr von Göttern ward, als er verdauen konnte*). We recall the myth: Tantalos served up his own son to the gods, who of course refused to partake—refused to be "tantalized." (Perhaps it is precisely of Tantalos that Empedocles of Acragas is thinking when, in the Καθαρμοί, fragment B137, he portrays in ghastly hues the father, the fool, sacrificing his son.) Yet in Hölderlin's account, it is not Tantalos who offers something to the gods, but the gods who offer something to him, something excessive, more than *he* can digest. Uncanny reversal! A key question for the very idea of the heroic would be, Who tantalizes whom? Who is *capable* of tantalizing whom? When it comes to gods and heroes, where perfection and excess meet in an economy of sacrifice, the victim and the victimizer are never clearly identifiable. Calasso writes: "The perfect brings death upon itself, since one can't have fullness without spillage, and what spills out is the excess that sacrifice claims for itself" (RC 111).

With Empedocles, therefore, it is precisely a question as to how and why he tantalizes the gods, how he is capable of tantalizing them. Is it his destiny to tantalize them? In that case, it would be they who are tantalizing him, as they once tantalized Oedipus. Four textual references, two on the side of *nefas*, or Empedocles' guilt, and two on the side of fate or destiny, set this dilemma in sharp relief. In act I, scene 2, of the first version, Hermocrates says that Empedocles is "soulless" and "in the dark" ever since the day "the drunken man / In front of all the people named himself a god." At this point (FHA 12:40–41, 184) Hölderlin enters a marginal note on the difference between modernity and antiquity with regard to this blasphemy. For us moderns, Empedocles' sin is a sin against the intellect. To proclaim oneself a god is a very stupid mistake. For the ancients, by contrast, it was not a nonsensical thing to do, but a crime, a crime they will not forgive because it offends their "tender sense of freedom" (*ihr zarter Freiheitssinn*). Because they esteemed the genius more than we do, says Hölderlin, they were more profoundly afraid of his insolence or excessive pride (*Übermuth*). In the same scene, Hermocrates (called the "old man," as Manes too will be called in the *third* draft) says that the secret of Empedocles' crime is that he has "too much forgotten the difference" between himself and the gods. Compare now two textual references that suggest that tantalization is Empedocles' destiny, not the sign of his guilt. In the very scene in which Hermocrates condemns Empedocles, he compares the thinker to those mad women of Asia who carry the thyrsus. Yet this puts the old priest in the position of Euripides' Pentheus and Empedocles in the position of the god Dionysos. *Übermüthig*, the word that was applied to the haughty Cleopatra in 1797, is now a word applied to both Empedocles and the Bacchants. (Pentheus too, however, will soon occupy the position of the god—as fragmented—when he becomes the surrogate victim, Dionysos Zagreus.) In scene 5, when Critias incites the people against Empedocles, Empedocles compares himself to the son of Tantalos: "Go ahead! flay and butcher your prey, and may / The priest bless the meal you enjoy, and his old friends, the gods of revenge, be invited to partake!" (FHA 12:200). This puts Empedocles in the position of the sacrificed son, not the foolish father. In short, it is virtually impossible to say whether Empedocles' words are those of an insane hubris or a measured knowledge of the lot that has fallen to him. In act II, scene 4, Empedocles replies to Hermocrates, who has come (in bad faith) to invite Empedocles back into the city, "You die your common death, which is fitting, / With the soulless sensibility of the knave, / Another portion is mine, another path / Has been prophesied by those gods / Who were present to me when I was born" (FHA 12:127, 221).

A marginal note by Hölderlin to act I, scene 4, seems to say it all. The context is Empedocles' admission to Pausanias that he has committed a grave sin: "I alone / Was god, and said so with insolent pride [*im frechen Stolz*]." Into the right-hand margin of the manuscript Hölderlin jots the following note: "His sin is the original sin and for that reason is nothing less than an abstraction, just as supreme joy is nothing less than an abstraction. The only thing to do is to represent it in genesis and in a lively fashion" (FHA 12:60, 192). The *drama* requires that Empedocles' misdeed be brought forcefully onto the stage. Yet if there is something fateful or fated about that misdeed, how can one prevent its seeming to be generic and abstract? Pausanias's exclamation at the end of the first draft is infinitely abstract: "How can the son of gods help it? / The infinite one is struck infinitely" (FHA 12:240). How is the playwright to portray on the stage the particularity of Empedocles' "insolent pride"?

The opposition between *nefas* and destiny is posed with even greater force in the *second* version of the play. Already the opposition seems beyond resolution, the conflict beyond remedy. It may be that this conflict destroys the drama as such, inasmuch as it is fatally interwoven with the problem of Empedocles' melancholy and bitterness. For *ressentiment* might readily stir in one who is destined to become more of the gods than he can digest. Does Empedocles contemplate the leap into Mount Etna in order to embrace and affirm Mother Earth? Or does he mean to join forces with Typhon, Zeus's final enemy, who lies coiled in impotence and rancor at the base of the volcano (Aeschylus, *Prometheus Bound*, ll. 363–365)? We notice in the second draft a proliferation of explanations surrounding Empedocles' supposed *nefas*, the ostensible fault or sin of Empedocles. He is identified (in scene 1) as Prometheus the Titan, the one who stole fire from heaven and gave it to mortals. Hermocrates says that Empedocles is a spoiled child of the gods, one who was excessively happy in his youth, so that he is bound to be disappointed in later life. Finally, Hermocrates chides Empedocles for having loved mortals excessively—again, like Prometheus—and for having been ultimately betrayed by the very ones he loved, in this case, the citizens of Agrigent. Finally, Empedocles has betrayed a sworn secret—Hölderlin here picking up on Diogenes Laertius's report that the philosopher was accused by some of having betrayed Pythagorean mysteries. Mekades (formerly Critias) is reluctant to affirm these accusations and to join in Empedocles' persecution; his reluctance mirrors that of the spectator or reader who is aware that Empedocles has been *destined* or *fated* to this exceptional position. If the gods have spoiled him—then the *gods* have spoiled him. Perhaps the most *philosophical* facet of Empedocles' possible *nefas* appears in the magus's strange speech to Pausanias in scene 3. Pausanias feels that the speech is out of character, and so takes it as mere sarcasm. Yet Empedocles seems to be speaking of his own past—which is actually the future of Kantian-Fichtean subjectivity—in what follows (FHA 13:283–284, 321):

> Right! I know everything, I can master all.
> Like my own handiwork, I know it all
> Through and through, and I steer as I like[.]
> A lord of the spirits, the living one,
> Mine is the world, and subservient to me
> Are all its forces, she has become but a maid to me

This nature who needs a master.
And if she is still honored, then it is by me.
For what would be the sky and the sea
And isles and stars, and whatever looms
Before human eyes, what would this
Lifeless thrum of strings be if I did not give it
Sound and speech and soul? What are
You gods and you spirit, if I do not
Bear witness to you—now! say, who am I?

Here *nefas* is the subjective idealism of Fichte run amok—the Faustian confidence in technique and mastery that troubles every thoughtful mind down to our own times. Yet the question that troubles us in our own times is whether Faust may be held accountable for the mess we are in, or whether something like a "destining of being" has brought us to this impasse. "Now! say, who am I?"

Formal Aspects of the Three Drafts of Hölderlin's Mourning-Play

I have neither the competence nor the desire to analyze the style of the three drafts of *The Death of Empedocles*, their versification, diction, and poetic form. Nor can I present a literary-historical account of these things from, let us say, Klopstock to Schiller. I wish merely to interrupt the thematic treatment I have offered so far in order to point out some aspects of Hölderlin's language that are particularly pertinent to the themes I am developing, and to improve my own sense of hearing when it comes to these voices of Empedocles. Which themes? Without imposing a hierarchical order, they are: the conflict between the supposition of a tragic flaw in Empedocles' character and the realization that in the case of Empedocles all is destiny; the problem of Empedocles' time as a time of inevitable downgoing and decline, which raises the problem of any possible affirmation of a sacrifice made to that time; and the role of those characters in the play who may seem "accidental," but whose accident has to do with love—hence with Empedocles' innermost essence.

Certain formal aspects of the three drafts—their poetic form, their versification, diction, and meter—can be identified and stated succinctly. Hölderlin initially chose for his play the then current form of *Trauerspiel*, that is, a piece in five acts, each divided into multiple scenes, the whole presented in elevated diction and set in iambic pentameter—that is, five feet of one short and one long syllable each, or one each of unaccented and accented syllables—in a word, blank verse, what Charles Olson calls "iambic five," the French, delightfully, va-VOOM-cinq. What has to be said at the outset is that whereas Hölderlin strives to remain true to some formal structures, such as the five-act requirement, he never adheres strictly to any given meter, not in any of the drafts. Here there is little va-VOOM. Friedrich Beißner remarks on the transformation of style across the three versions. The *second* version cuts the line after three iambs (the antistrophe of "Into my tranquillity . . ." offers an apt example of this), and is otherwise full of metric variation. We noted above the particularly effective use of dactyls ("*So will es der Geist / Und die reifende Zeit*"). The *third* version returns to blank verse, yet differs from the first in a way that is difficult to explain though easy to hear: it is the more compressed, compact, trenchant, mature style—the late style of the famous hymns.

A comparison of the three initial soliloquies spoken by Empedocles in the three drafts may make the formal comparison more concrete. The second draft reprints the opening strophe of *In meine Stille* almost verbatim, which is quite surprising in view of the alteration of meter from the first to the second drafts. Yet the antistrophe is greatly changed: in the second draft, the antistrophe is prolonged, the tone intensified, the change in mood from despair to defiance more brusque, more trenchant, as are the lines themselves:

> Weit will ichs um mich machen, tagen solls
> Von eigner Flamme mir! du sollst
> Zufrieden werden, armer Geist,
> Gefangener! (FHA 13:273, 316)

> I will have space about me, day should dawn
> From my own flame! you should
> Be at peace, wretched spirit,
> Prisoner!

The final strophe in the second draft achieves greater calm, as the first part of "The Ground to Empedocles" says it must. In keeping with the ultimate undecidability of *nefas* and destiny, it borrows and yet transforms some of the concluding lines from the soliloquy in the first version:

> Ist nirgend ein Rächer, und muß ich allein
> Den Hohn und Fluch in meine Seele sagen?
> Muß einsam seyn auch so? (FHA 13:274, 317; cf. 12:189)

> Is there no avenger, and must I alone
> Tell my soul of contempt and curse?
> Must I be lonely even so?

The principal soliloquy of Empedocles in the *third* version is remarkably different. It opens the drama and therefore has to recount everything that the earlier versions dramatized. The tone of the soliloquy resists description—one is tempted to say simply that its tone and style are "sovereign." Note in this soliloquy the altered diction, word selection, assonances, and alliterations:

> Euch ruf ich über das Gefild herein
> Vom langsamen Gewölk, ihr heißen Stralen
> Des Mittags, ihr Gereiftesten, daß ich
> An euch den neuen Lebenstag erkenne.
> (FHA 13:374–375, 421)

> I call to you across the fields
> From slow-moving clouds, you radiant beams
> Of midday, you beams most ripe, so that in you
> I may know this new day of my life.

The "sovereign" flow of the words is of course deceptive: in the manuscript, between the second and third lines, a dozen tentative lines are sketched, then scratched out. Sattler's composite (variorum) text is nowhere as nightmarishly difficult as it is here. Yet in the end, the words are gathered as parts of a composite whole, suggested by the three *Ge*-words that are themselves collective nouns: *Gefild, Gewölk, Gereiftesten.*

Earlier on we heard the lines from the first version involving Tantalos. In the second version the name Tantalos disappears, yet the diction and versification of *nefas* seem to intensify. Empedocles is addressing nature, whom he now says must despise him, since he is the one who has betrayed her:

> Dein Geächteter! weh! hab ich doch auch
> Dein nicht geachtet, dein
> Mich überhoben, hast du
> Umfangend doch mit den warmen Fittigen einst
> Du Zärtliche! mich vom Schlafe gerettet?
> (FHA 13:273, 317)

> Despised by you! alas! Nor did I
> Respect you, boosted myself
> Above you, but did you not
> Embrace me once in your warm plumage,
> You tender one! rescuing me from sleep?

The three broken lines here, filled with monosyllabic words and hard consonants, are suddenly softened by the fourth and fifth lines, which stretch their wings and introduce the memory of a more harmonious and tender relation with nature and her gods.

In the strophe of the first soliloquy (of drafts one and two), *In meine Stille kamst du leise wandelnd*, one notes the liquidity of the *l*'s, the elegiac tone suited to the images of plant life, rivulet, and light. In the antistrophe (in both drafts, in spite of the many alterations) the tone is suddenly cold, even brittle; the lines are broken by rhetorical questions and cries of grief, all in a super-abundance of harsh consonants:

> —vertrocknet bin
> Ich nun, und nimmer freun die Sterblichen
> Sich meiner—bin ich ganz allein? und ist
> Es Nacht hier oben auch am Tage? weh!
> (FHA 12:48, 188; cf. 13:316)

> —desiccated I
> Am now, and no mortal will ever take joy
> In me—am I all alone? and is
> It night up here even in the day? alas!

The final strophe of the soliloquy in the *second* version adds something new, however: a lamentation, without any sign of aggression or resentment—what Whitman, in "Out of the Cradle Endlessly Rocking," calls a threnody:

> Weh! einsam! einsam! einsam!
> Und nimmer find' ich
> Euch, meine Götter,
> Und nimmer kehr ich
> Zu deinem Leben, Natur!
> (FHA 13:273, 317)

> Alas! lonely! lonely! lonely!
> And never will I find
> You, my gods,
> And never will I return
> To your life, O nature!

Perhaps it is an extension of this threnodic style that will help us to introduce one of the most important themes of all three versions of *The Death of Empedocles*, even though I have so far left it almost entirely out of account. It may be no accident that only closer attention to the *language* of the poems enables us to descry this theme. That theme is *fidelity to the earth*, and it is expressed by the *elemental* thinker Empedocles, whom one might easily take to be—in Hölderlin's version at least—excessively ethereal, solar, celestial. In act I, scene 4, of the first draft, Empedocles speaks to Pausanias, while apostrophizing nature and the earth:

> So ward auch mir das Leben zum Gedicht.
> Denn deine Seele war in mir und offen gab
> Mein Herz wie du der ernsten Erde sich
> Der Leidenden und oft in heilger Nacht
> Gelobt ichs   ihr, bis in den Tod
> Die schiksaalvolle furchtlos treu zu lieben.
> (FHA 12:54–55, 190)

> Thus my life became even to me a poem.
> For your soul was in me and openly
> My heart gave itself to the earnest earth
> The long-suffering and often in holy night
> I swore   to her, the fateful one,
> That unto death I would love her truly, fearlessly.

The allusions to the second choral ode of Sophocles' *Antigone* are surely no accident here: the long-suffering earth, earnest and fateful, scarified by the machines of men, is the object of the hero's love. "All-patient nature!" exclaims the third version, and continues:

> Du hast mich, und es dämmert zwischen dir
> Und mir die alte Liebe wieder auf.
> Du rufst, du ziehst mich nah und näher an—
> Und wenn die Wooge wächst, und ihren Arm
> Die Mutter um mich breitet, o was möcht'
> Ich auch, was möcht' ich fürchten. Andre mag
> Es freilich schröken. Denn es ist ihr Tod.
> (FHA 13:377–379, 422)

> You have me, and the glow of day between you
> And me, our old love, begins to rise again.
> You call, you draw me close and closer still—
> And when the wave waxes high, and her arm
> My mother's arm wraps me round, oh, what should
> I want, what should I fear? Others may
> Be terrified by this. For it is their death.

Again, the sovereign style—what Beda Allemann once called the hard rhythmic jointures—is not so easily won: between the first and second lines quoted here, the manuscript shows a full page of false starts, continuations, emendations, returns. Other lines seem to come quite readily, for example, those final lapidary phrases, almost an imitation of what is spoken in the streets: "Sure, others may be terrified by this. It's going to kill them." Preceding this direct language, which, incidentally, the late hymns always manage to insert when we are least expecting it, preceding these pure words, is an elegiac style that celebrates mother-love and sexual love in the same embrace—the sweet assonances and alliterations of *wenn die Wooge wächst*, the softness of the murmured *m*'s, *Mutter um mich . . . möcht' . . . möcht'*. The sweetness and softness are suddenly broken by the intrusion of the reality from which Empedocles has for the moment concealed himself: for the others, the crater means death; for him, the embrace of the mother. The challenge is not to allow that embrace to obscure the destiny of one's own death, not to allow the thought of eternal return to betray the earth with thoughts of a Typhon's rage. For such a betrayal would mean the surrender of tragic intensity.[12]

Other characters in the play, especially Panthea, often appropriate the voice of Empedocles, speaking from out of his "spirit and mouth," nowhere more so than when expressing fidelity to the earth. In the very first scene of the first version, Panthea says to Delia, "Here he feels like a god / In his element, and his joy / Is celestial song" (FHA 12:35, 181). And again: "O eternal mystery! what we are / And seek, we cannot find; what / We find, we are not" (FHA 12:39, 183). When Delia (that is, Rhea) asks her how she knows so much about Empedocles, Panthea replies, "To be him, that is / Life and we others are the dream of it" (FHA 12:36, 182). Yet this invocation of Rhea reminds us of one more formal matter, which may prove to be not entirely formal. It may be material, and have to do with the mother's embrace and with fidelity to the earth.

Rhea's Disappearance and the Rise of the Doppelgänger

The name *Rhea* disappears entirely from all three drafts of the Beißner text. In his manuscript, however, Hölderlin replaces it with the name *Delia* only in the final scene of the first version's first act, and he does so without comment (FHA 12:95, 208). A detail perhaps without importance, an accident. Yet when one looks at the first page of the manuscript of the first draft, what one sees are the names: *Panthea. Rhea.* Panthea, a variant of the ancient Pantheia, means "all the goddesses," or "all the divinities." Rhea, as we know, means flow, flux, or flight. The two names together seem to play with the

---

12. Roberto Calasso writes of "the acceptance of a life without redemption, without salvation, without hope of repetition, circumscribed by the precarious wonder of its brief apparition. . . . It is only because life is irretrievable and irrepeatable that the glory of appearance can reach such intensity" (RC 117).

apocryphal Heraclitean phrase, ascribed to Heraclitus by Plato, πάντα ῥεῖ.[13] "Everything flows." Or, more tragically, "All divinity has flown." All is in the course of evanescence, swept away by that river into which, as Nietzsche remarks, one cannot step even once. Rhea, as we know, is the spouse of Kronos, the Titan who comes to be associated with time, χρόνος. Rhea is the daughter of Gaia, the earth, and the mother of the Olympian brothers Zeus, Poseidon, and Hades. She is also the mother of Tantalos. Perhaps Rhea, coupled with Panthea, can serve as a symbol of fidelity to the long-suffering, ever-changing divine earth—the theme introduced only a moment ago.

In his 1842 "Introduction" to the philosophy of mythology, and in the *Philosophy of Mythology* itself, Schelling notes that Rhea, the wife of Kronos, derives from ῥέειν, ῥεῖν, "to flow," "to move" (II/2:578). In general, Schelling takes such flow or motion in the feminine to be a movement from the center to the periphery of essence. In his "Introduction" (II/1:39), he associates the name Rhea with that of Theia—not Panthea, but close to it. He suggests that "the common concept of the two is *being driven out* [Fortgetriebenwerden], the distinction between the two being that something of its substance is retained (Theia), while something of it is also lost (Rheia, from ῥέω, to flow)." One is tempted to say that if Rhea vanishes from Hölderlin's tragedy, that is precisely what she is supposed to do, inasmuch as she is the flight of the gods. Yet before she disappears, she speaks. Perhaps she speaks for all the Titans, as much an embodiment of the Titanic age as is her consort, Kronos. The Titanic in general is something outside the opposition of gods and mortals. It is therefore essentially closer to the heroic. Sometimes—for example, in Aeschylus's *Prometheus Bound*—the Titanic seems more divine than the Olympian gods themselves. For the Titanic is a theogonic and cosmogonic force, a force productive of sites, of space and time, of scenes in which gods and mortals play. Sometimes that force seems to be nothing less than the force of fate—the Μοῖρα, whom, as Schelling notes, no god can touch.

Are there any remains of Rhea in *The Death of Empedocles*? If the name Delia signifies the isle that is sacred to Apollo, Delos—which is one of the places to which Panthea is to be sent for her protection, according to Empedocles' instruction to her father, Critias—is that to say that the grand Titaness is to be replaced by Apollo? Who is Delia? She is the incarnation of tenderness. Does she not seem to speak with the voice of Ismene, the sister of

---

13. It was Andrea Rehberg who first pointed this out to me many years ago at the University of Essex, and I thank her again for it.

Antigone, whom Delia invokes? If Ismene is the voice of timidity in the face of the law, fear in the face of the king, is Delia a name for the docility of the little woman in the face of the man? Is she, in other words, the sort of *accident* that expresses and experiences nothing of the tragic conflict of an Empedocles? In the first version we see Empedocles in his garden, almost as one of the plants there, one of the immovable oaks in his sacred grove. He is Empedocles-Pharmakeus in his *Pflanzenwelt*. Priest of nature, he is faithful to the earth. The opening words of the play are Panthea's: "This is his garden." She adds that the plants seem to notice when he passes and that the subterranean streams begin to flow wherever his staff touches the earth. Later she says that the plants "with all their forces" are open secrets to Empedocles. Yet this vegetative Empedocles is also the self-proclaimed son of Ouranos, like Zeus himself. His most common apostrophe is *O Vater Aether!*

If we pose the question of Empedocles' genealogy, we have to wonder whether there is a conflict between his maternal and paternal sides, between matriarchy and patriarchy. One might also think of this in terms of the vertical and horizontal axes discussed by Schelling in his *Philosophy of Art* (see chapter 5 of this volume), axes that are still influential in Georges Bataille's philosophical anthropology. If the horizontal axis is the axis of the earth, and the vertical that of the sky, one might ask whether Empedocles—this son of the earth who nightly pledges an oath of loyalty to her—is not always craning his neck to scan the heavens. Does he not, like Oedipus, have an eye too many perhaps, a pineal eye located at the top of his skull? This would not be a Cyclopian or Titanic eye, the eye of Rhea, which looks to the horizon, but a Typhon's eye directed at the sun. Empedocles' nostalgia for the gods who have fled—does it not seem an ascensional nostalgia, *aerienne*, as Bachelard would say, always anxious to quit the earth? The leap into the crater—is it profound fidelity to the earth or a chance to evaporate into the sky?

Let us take up the question of the vanished Rhea and the figure of Delia once again. We find in the second draft two passages that touch on the matter of the Titanic conflict between earth and sky. First, in the dialogue between Pausanias and Empedocles, Pausanias insists on the powerful divinity of his master, whom he calls "heaven's favorite," *der Liebling des Himmels*, whom grief is now "bending down to earth." Empedocles reaffirms his fidelity to the earth, but only after effusively praising the sun, and he finishes with a vision of *Aether*. If Empedocles is elemental, his genealogy is clearly both tellurian and celestial. In the second passage, Panthea and Delia come as close as they ever do to an argument, in which Delia (formerly Rhea) takes the side of the

239

earth, Panthea the side of heaven. The *first* draft breaks off at the point where Delia complains that Empedocles thinks "more like the gods" than a mortal—almost a reminiscence of Hermocrates' words concerning Empedocles' oblivion of the distinction. Hölderlin enters a marginal note into his manuscript at this point: "because Empedocles held the temporal [*die Zeitlichkeit*] in such low esteem" (FHA 12:177, 240). In the *second* draft the identical conflict appears. Why should the honor of mortals detain Empedocles, asks Panthea, "when Aether opens his arms to him?" (FHA 13:289, 323). Delia replies with words we have heard before, declaring the splendor and amiability of the earth (ibid.). In the closing exchanges of the second draft, Panthea and Pausanias loyally uphold Empedocles' status as a hero, that is to say, one whose downgoing is holy, while Delia demurs: "You are only too glad, Empedocles / Only too glad to sacrifice yourself" (FHA 13:294, 326). Delia incorporates the tiny remainder of Rhea in the play. And yet there is nothing "accidental" about the exchanges between these personages, who are themselves no "accidents." The theme of fidelity to the earth, and the question of the vanished Rhea, will not disappear from Hölderlin's third and final attempt, even if the seer should now be called a brother.

When we turn to the third and final draft of *The Death of Empedocles*, we are struck by the differences between it and the earlier versions. We may well want to exclaim with Pausanias, "I no longer recognize you," and to reply with Empedocles, "I am not the one who I am." The difference may well be due to the theoretical text that Hölderlin writes between the second and third drafts, *Der Grund zum Empedokles*. The essay that begins with the words *Das untergehende Vaterland* . . . , given the title *Das Werden im Vergehen* by Beißner, is also found in the margins, so to speak, of the final sketches for *Empedokles*. It is undeniable that lucubrations of the sort represented in these essays have had an impact on this third version of the play. One need not enter into those essays here, except when the impact on the third version seems most clearly and powerfully felt.[14] For the moment, one may set aside these rich texts, in order to read the third draft of the play, begun probably in December of 1799.

The issue of the Titanic, raised by Pausanias in the second scene of the third version, grows in importance. Empedocles, despite his name, has little about him that is steadfast, ἔμπεδος. He admires the trees of the grove, the oaks that are sturdy and well grounded, precisely because this is what he lacks. He is not one of them. Even in the first two versions, one hears the question

14. Again, the first two chapters of *Lunar Voices* treat these theoretical essays in some detail.

over and over again, "Who are you?" Hermocrates to the citizens, in act I, scene 5 of the first version: "Just ask him yourselves / Who he may be?" In the same scene, Empedocles to the others: "Am I not that? (. . .) Do you know me?" Act II, scene 4, a citizen to Empedocles: "Who are you, man?" In act II, scene 3, Pausanias to his master: "And so regret [*Gram*] can bend down to the earth / Heaven's favorites? or are you / Not one of them?" We have already heard the Empedocles of version three: "I am not the one who I am." Which may be Hölderlin's answer to Yahweh.

Hölderlin now transforms the character Hermocrates into Manes, a priest of the Egyptian war-goddess Neith, from the temple at Saïs. Manes is one of "our brothers in Egypt," to whom Empedocles has already referred. Manes is still Empedocles' opponent, but he is more than ever an *intrinsic* opponent, the enemy on the inside. His name may be a pun on ἔμπεδος, if *manes* can be heard as a form of *maneo*, "I remain." The Latin *manes, manium*, ambiguously masculine and feminine in gender, is apparently related to words meaning "the good," "the early," "the dawn." The *manes* are souls of the departed, especially deceased ancestors, revered as divine. By metonymy, *manes* refers to the gods or powers of the dead and the underworld itself, and more rarely, the corpse; important in the present instance is that the word can mean the tutelary genius or δαίμων of a human being. An expression from Virgil's *Aeneid* reads: *quisquis suos patimus manes*, everyone must make amends "as their *manes* command." Before the name of the deceased on the tombstones of Roman graveyards often appear the letters DM: *Dis Manibus*—sacred to the gods (or the souls) of the dead. The assertion that *Manes* might have something to do with *maneo, manēre*, is therefore probably indefensible in strict philological terms, even if *bleiben* is assuredly a theme of Hölderlin's tragedy. Whether there is some relationship between *manes*, the Old Latin *manus*, meaning "good," and *manus* as "hand," especially in the sense of power, governance, or rule, is difficult to say. It is clear, however, that Hölderlin is aware of the *manes*: early on in the first volume of *Hyperion* the narrator refers to himself and Adamas as "*manes* from times past," *wie Manen aus vergangner Zeit* (CHV 1:620). He is no doubt also aware that the Di Manes are the δαίμόνες, and that the realm of the tutelary spirits is τὸ δαιμόνιον. Hölderlin's early, inchoate plan to write a tragedy on *Socrates* surely would have involved Socrates' δαίμων. And, no doubt, Hölderlin's hymns on the demigods, the river Titans, invoke the earth itself as τὸ δαιμόνιον. Finally, one should note that Schelling's *Philosophy of Mythology* proposes *Manes* as a variant spelling of the Mani, that is, the Persian Manichean sect; he declares that their name means "the dividers," those who sunder life into two fundamentally opposed principles (II/2:505). At all events, Manes rises as the alter ego of Empedocles, a figure out of the Oriental past—and the Greek present.

That Manes is not simply an opponent of Empedocles is indicated by the plan to continue the third version, literally the final page of the *Empedocles* materials. For the third scene of act IV, Hölderlin envisages the final exchange between Empedocles and the Egyptian priest. He characterizes Manes as follows: "Manes, who has experienced all, the seer, is astounded by Empedocles' speeches and by his spirit; he says that Empedocles is the one who has been called [*der Berufene*], who can take life and give it, in and through whom a world will dissolve and be renewed" (FHA 13:419, 438). After Empedocles has committed his one final deed at the end, presumably in scene 4, the fifth and final scene gathers Manes and all the other personages of the play. Hölderlin's description of the action: "On the following day, at the festival of Saturn, he [Manes] wants to proclaim to them the nature of Empedocles' last will" (ibid.). The festival of Saturn is of course in honor of the "son of Ouranos," Empedocles himself. However, if this is Hölderlin's final plan for the play, the last pages that he actually sketches out work against it. In the manuscript of the play itself, Manes is called simply *Der Greis*, "the old man." His exchanges with Empedocles have the effect of displacing Empedocles to an impossible remove and spoiling every ideal deed and every celebration. The entire third version is filled with displacements of time, day, and even epoch, displacements of scene, and displacements of character. Pausanias is advised to go on an anachronistic voyage to Plato's Athens, where Empedocles says he has already been ("where once upon a time, / Drunk with light, I often walked with my Plato"), but which lies a century and a half ahead, and to Aeneas's Rome, "the land of promises," which lies many hundreds of years in the past. (The first draft had already ventured into anachrony, with Rhea invoking Sophocles, and an Agrigentian citizen the Romans.) Empedocles himself, as we will see, is displaced from his very identity. The third version begins with the radiant beams of midday, not the dawn, and it ends with Pausanias being sent off to "my brothers in Egypt" as though he were Solon or Critias's grandfather, in the story recounted at the outset of Plato's *Timaeus*. In the meantime, Empedocles and Pausanias are both displaced to the heights of Mount Etna, far from Agrigent.

The effect of these displacements is to dissolve the question of *nefas* versus destiny. Manes too will accuse Empedocles of a "dark sin" and will announce himself as sent by God (here in the singular) to prevent Empedocles from proclaiming himself "the one who is called." Yet because the identities of Empedocles and Manes slip into and out of each other, it is difficult to know who is sent by whom and for what. As for the remains of Rhea, and the all-important question of fidelity to the earth, this too slips into indeterminacy, undecidability. The final lines that Hölderlin actually writes for the play are lines for a choral ode to be sung by a group of citizens of Agrigent—those citizens who have proved to be so ambivalent toward Empedocles in the first two drafts. The choral ode that closes the first—and only—act of version three is itself a sign of the end of all fidelity, even if it begins with the promise of a "future," a "new world":

Chor.

Neue Welt

    und es hängt, ein ehern Gewölbe
der Himmel über uns, es lähmt Fluch
die Glieder den Menschen, und ihre stärkende, die erfreuenden
Gaaben der Erde sind, wie Spreu, es
spottet unser, mit ihren Geschenken die Mutter
und alles ist Schein —

O wann, wann öffnet sie sich
    die Fluth über die Dürre.

Aber wo ist er?
Daß er beschwöre den lebendigen Geist
(FHA 13:418, 436)

Chorus

New world

    and it hangs like an iron vault
The heaven above us, and curse lames the
Limbs of men, and the nourishing, joy-infusing
Gifts of the earth are as chaff,
She mocks us with her gifts, our mother,
And all is semblance—

Oh, when, when will it open
    the flood over the wasteland.

Yet where is he?
That he might conjure the living spirit[.]

Where is he? *Who* is he? Are you so sure of who you are? These will be the questions that the third draft leaves us with, and without recourse.[15]

We may begin our reading of the third draft proper with the concluding lines of scene 2. They are difficult to establish with any certainty: Beißner lets four lines fall away that Sattler rescues for his reconstituted text (they appear below in italics). Sattler's text reads:

> Und will die Seele dir nicht ruhn, so geh
> Und frage sie, die Brüder in Aegyptos.
> Dort hörest du das erste Saitenspiel
> Uraniens und seiner Töne Wandel.
> *Dort wird dir vieles helle seyn und groß,*
> *Und daß wir Sterblichen, so wie wir uns*
> *Vor Augen stehn, nur Zeichen sind und Bilder,*
> *Deß wirst du nimmermehr bedauern, lieber!*
> Dort öffnen sie das Buch des Schiksaals dir.
> Geh! fürchte nichts! es kehret alles wieder,
> Und was geschehen soll, ist schon vollendet.
> (FHA 13:401, 430)

> And if your soul gives you no peace, then go
> And inquire of them, my brothers in Egypt.
> There you will hear the earnest play of
> Uranian strings, the alchemy of their tones.   ' ' A
> *There much will become luminous and grand for you,*
> *And that we mortals, such as we are when we see ourselves*
> *Face to face, are mere signs and images*
> *Is something you will no longer regret, my friend!*
> There they will open for you the Book of Fate.
> Go! Fear nothing! Everything recurs.
> And what is to occur is already accomplished.

"Mere signs and images," *Zeichen und Bilder*. Empedocles' main speech in response to Manes is full of signs and images, images of the gods of nature whom the youthful Empedocles can call by name, signs of celestial lightning and earthly flames (FHA 13:416, 434–435). The final sign is to be the plunge into the crater. Empedocles asks Manes whether he would like to join him in

---

15. There is an august philological tradition that sees the early Hegel as the model for Manes, Hegel as the critic of the "beautiful soul," not in his *Phenomenology of Spirit* but in the early essay called by editors *The Spirit of Christianity*. See JV 3:361. Whatever role Hegel may have played during the gestation of *The Death of Empedocles* and during Hölderlin's experiences in Frankfurt and Homburg generally, however, it is important to note that the *who?* question, transposed to the third draft of the play itself, cannot be answered by such autobiographical references. Doppelgänger are essentially eponymous, no matter what they may be called, and no matter who inspires them.

producing this sign. A bold sign, a strong sign. However, as we recall from chapter 2, above, the sign in tragedy = 0, which is to say that the hero is presented most originally on the stage when he or she appears not in strength but in vulnerability. The type of *image* Empedocles himself constitutes is now the capital question for Hölderlin. He will already have written about this image in "The Ground to Empedocles," before beginning the third draft. What he says there has everything to do with the "Book of Destiny" and with the very meaning of tragic destiny. We also recall the importance of written signs for the priests of Neith as they are portrayed for us in Plato's *Timaeus*. Critias recounts the tale told him by his grandfather of the same name, who accompanied Solon there. (Hölderlin may in fact have the name *Kritias*, who is the archon in the first draft of his play, from *Timaeus* and *Critias*.) The ancient Egyptian priests have to laugh at the Greeks, who are forever children. They are children because they are illiterate: they have no written histories, no alphabetic signs to record the floods of the past, so that the cultures of Atlantis and Ancient Athens are forever lost to them and they must always start from scratch. Manes, the Doppelgänger of Empedocles, steps out of the pages of *Timaeus* into the third draft of *The Death of Empedocles*.

The word *sign* appears several times in the essay that is sketched into Hölderlin's manuscript alongside the "plan for the continuation of the third version," the essay commonly known as "Becoming in Passing-away" (*Das Werden im Vergehen*), Sattler's *Das untergehende Vaterland*, "The fatherland in decline. . . ." In the opening lines of that essay we read the words *eine neue Welt*, the very words that open the final chorus of act one. In this essay, Hölderlin heralds the birth of a new world in the decline of a prior finite world, arguing that "this downfall and commencement is like the language expression sign presentation [*die Sprache Ausdruck Zeichen Darstellung*] in a living yet particular whole" (I 641; DKV 2:446). The word *image*, *Bild*, plays an important role in the essay written presumably immediately prior to this one, "The Ground to Empedocles." In the third part of that essay, the "Ground" proper, the remarkable word *Trugbild* appears—mirage, *fata morgana*, illusion. (In his reconstituted text, Sattler has merely the root *Trug*, which is very odd on its own—although Schelling uses the word.)[16] *Trugbild!*

16. *Trug* and *Täuschung*, betrayal and deception, play an important role in Schelling's 1842 *Philosophy of Mythology*. There he notes that the ancient Greeks even had a number of goddesses, Titanesses, or sprites (perhaps modeled on the Furies) dedicated to betrayal and deception, namely, the Ἀπάτη. "How deeply these Ἀπάτη were felt by the Greeks can perhaps be concluded from the happenstance that they had their own festival, called the *Apaturia*, the festival of deception" (II/2:148; cf. 623). See also Roberto Calasso's remarkable account of Ἀπάτη, the servant girl of Aphrodite, based

is the very word that Manes tosses in the face of Empedocles at the outset of the heavily revised third draft (FHA 13:405 [cf. 401], 430). Manes' accusation is that Empedocles is simply deceived about his self-proclaimed status as elect, as the favorite of the gods. Or, if not simply deceived, that he is an imposter. Yet Manes is no carping, conniving Hermocrates, no priest of the usual, power-seeking sort. We sense this in the exchanges with Empedocles in the third draft, in which Empedocles is wrathful and tempestuous, Manes cool and distant, taking the long historical perspective, urging caution. When we look back to "The Ground of Empedocles" we in fact discover that Hölderlin himself affirms Manes' principal point. There Hölderlin speaks of *Trug*, or *Trugbild*, and even of *der glückliche Betrug*, "the fortunate betrayal." The word *betrayal* will play an important role in the "Notes on Oedipus" (see chapter 9 of this volume). For the moment, we can say that what Hölderlin has in mind is this: Empedocles appears to be the perfect resolution of the problem of his time, inasmuch as he combines the supremely developed qualities of both nature and art in his person. When he is least attentive to himself and most natural, he is a thinker, organizer, builder; when he is most meditative he is as wild as fire, entirely aorgic. Empedocles, born to be a singer, unites all the qualities one could hope for—but he does so *too intensely and too individually*. His unification of these qualities is tragic, inasmuch as *no* individual can "solve the problem of destiny"—his, like all the others, can only be a "momentary unification" (I 576–577; DKV 2:233–234). Hölderlin does not state in so many words what "the problem of destiny" is, but he does insist that no individual can encompass an entire world; it is the *death* of Empedocles that solves the problem more adequately than his life, because it is only in passing away that an individual can be the avatar of a passing world. For all his exceptional qualities, then, Empedocles is bound to be a *Trug* and a *Trugbild*, his sign a null cipher, his ideal deed at the end *ein glucklicher Betrug*, "a fortunate betrayal."

Are you the One? Manes asks over and over again. His speech points or gives signs variously to the Christ, to Prometheus, to Zeus, to all the gods and idols and prophets one could imagine. His warning is that a certain *excess* is bound to cling to every claim of intimacy with the gods. Empedocles is *too* much. Again one is tempted to speculate on the relation of the German *zu* to the Greek ζα-, from δύο, meaning double, overmuch, excessive. If πύρος is fire, ζάπυρος is holocaust. It may also be that the prefix ζα- has to do with

on the effects of a woman's perfume and makeup (RC 97, 201). See ch. 11 of this volume for further discussion.

the δαι- of δαίμων, and even with what wants to be and yet does not want to be called by the name Ζεύς.[17]

One of the most tentative suggestions one may make about the third draft is that in it the voice of Empedocles becomes most fully Hölderlin's own voice. In the "Ground to Empedocles" Hölderlin says that nature appears "with all its melodies" in the "spirit and mouth" of the ancient magus Empedocles, indeed, "so intimately and warmly and personally" that he is loved by the all the people and accepted by them (FHA 13:347–348, 365–366). How Hölderlin yearns for this kind of acceptance! Yet his own fate is described in words Empedocles uses in his opening speech, words that have not yet been placed in Empedocles' spirit and mouth in the first two versions. Empedocles is speaking of the people who have banished him and of hearing—ringing in his ears—"the cold laughter of a hundred voices, when the dreamer, / The fool, went on his way weeping" (FHA 13:376, 421). "[T]hat I have to weep like a child," Hölderlin had written to Neuffer on November 12, 1798. Several lines later in the play he accuses himself of a certain coldness, and the words he uses are words his own mother had often used against a son she could not understand: "For greatly have I sinned from my youth onward / Never loved human beings in a human way, served, / Yet only blindly, as water and fire serve, / For that reason they never met me on human terms" (FHA 13:376, 422). In that same letter to Neuffer, we read, "I shy away much too much from the common and the ordinary in real life." Here *nefas* shifts from grand Promethean blasphemy and sacrilege to the singer's alienation from his community, which in turn greets him with derision. If in the second of the three parts of "The Ground to Empedocles" Hölderlin speaks of the necessity, in dramatic representation, of finding "a bolder, more foreign simulacrum and exemplar" than one's own subjectivity can be, especially when the *nefas* portrayed comes perilously close to *Innigkeit*, intimacy and intensity, it is nonetheless the case that the third version—undoubtedly the most historically conscious of the three drafts, on a grand scale and in the grand style— gives us Hölderlin as well as Empedocles. This simply confirms what the "General Ground" says, namely, that the tragic drama too must arise from "the world and the soul of the poet" (FHA 13:331, 359). It might almost have said, from "the spirit and mouth" of the poet. And if all three drafts are poems of tenderness, of languor and love, as also of a certain languishment, we recall

17. These philological musings between the Greek and the German are what lay behind the book *Daimon Life*—the title itself a pleonasm. The point here, in any case, is that the *zu*, the "too much," marks the failure of Empedocles. Yet it is a failure that is as much of destiny as of the hero's own *nefas*.

those other words from the same letter to Neuffer, near the end: "I am nothing but a pedant, if you will. Yet, if I'm right, pedants are usually cold and loveless, whereas my heart is overanxious to be a brother to every person and every thing under the moon. I almost think I am pedantic for no other reason than love."

To be sure, most of the language of the theoretical essays surrounding *The Death of Empedocles* can be reduced to the sphere of German Idealism. An exception perhaps is the word *Innigkeit,* unless it is mistranslated as "interiority." For the excess of intimacy and intensity in the figure of Empedocles is quite new and startling. It is that excess of intensity that characterizes the rhetoric of the essays themselves—their unending sentences, their need to prolong the point, to locate it everywhere on the line, and in the end to burn it in celestial fire. The excess of intensity, *Übermaß der Innigkeit,* is that which shatters all unification, or lets unification appear only as the illusion of a resolution of the problem of fate. Every resolution, if it is tragic resolution, is *scheinbar,* an apparent, semblant, radiant simulacrum of resolution. The excess of intensity and semblance prevents the absorption of Hölderlin into the philosophical systems of German Idealism, no matter how intensely he contributed to the oldest program toward such a system. *Übermaß der Innigkeit* is the prevailing mood of the tragic absolute. If Empedocles unites in himself the more aorgic and the organizing powers, if he approximates the perfect synthesis of the particular and the universal, he can do so only as downgoing. He will have to shout, as Schelling's hero shouted, "You see? I *was* the perfect unification!"

Why, then, does the ideal deed at the end, the speculative suicide of Empedocles, not avail? Why is Hölderlin unable to write it, unable to carry it out? The interpreter's *nefas* is to be too confident about a reply. Let us say that two things restrain the Empedocles of Hölderlin. First, the need to leap into the crater not out of wrath or in the spirit of rancor but in order to rejoin earth and aether in gratitude and affirmation. "From this green earth / My eye shall not pass without joy," says Empedocles at the end, having heard at long last what Rhea was telling him from the beginning. Act II, scene 3 of the first draft ends with Empedocles' asserting that he "can also go in wrath to the gods" (FHA 12:123, 220). Yet it is not so. All the "accidents" of the play—Delia, Panthea, Pausanias—have been teaching Empedocles that essential lesson. Love will hold him back. Love? Let us say, a certain desire, a certain languor. These may lie at the secret heart of nature—in the crater of the volcano itself, which embraces the watery fire of the sky and the fiery breath of the earth—or in the secret heart of a mournful and bootless humanity. Second, the undecidability of Empedocles' *identity* holds them back. The questions, common to the two earlier versions, mount to a crescendo in the third: after Manes cries *Imposter!* Empedocles asks, "What! Where? Who are you, man?"—the very question Pausanias put to Empedocles in an earlier draft. Manes, the "old man," asks Empedocles, "Are you the man? the very one? are you this?" And because Empedocles cannot answer, Manes asks again, "Oh, tell us who you are! and who am I?" And again, after Empedocles' long and magnificent swan song, Manes' simple reply is, "How is it with us? are you so sure of what you see?"

These questions infuriate Empedocles before he can give himself over to fire. They frustrate every possible ideal deed at the end. "Once you have a double on the scene," notes Roberto Calasso, "it's like entering a hall of mirrors; everything is elusive, stretching away into a perspective where nothing is ever final" (RC 229). Nothing is ever final, yet everything has already transpired. Empedocles' passing has already occurred before the leap. Poe tells us that when Doppelgänger meet, at least one of them is already dead.

HÖLDERLIN'S "TRANSLATIONS" OF SOPHOCLES

8

The heroic books, even if printed in the character of our mother tongue, will always be in a language dead to degenerate times; and we must laboriously seek the meaning of each word and line, conjecturing a larger sense than common use permits out of what wisdom and valor and generosity we have. The modern cheap and fertile press, with all its translations, has done little to bring us nearer to the heroic writers of antiquity. They seem as solitary, and the letter in which they are printed as rare and curious, as ever.

—HENRY DAVID
THOREAU, *Walden*

The German publisher's boast in 1804 that Hölderlin had been "laboring away" at his translations of Sophocles' *Oedipus the Tyrant* and *Antigone* "for ten years" seems an exaggeration—even if the publisher, Friedrich Wilmans of Frankfurt, received this information from Hölderlin's close friend, Isaak von Sinclair. Yet it is nonetheless true that Hölderlin's preoccupation with Sophocles extends far back into his life history. His first published translation of a fragment from Sophocles—specifically, the fragment containing what Nietzsche was to call "Silenic wisdom," taken from the choral song of Sophocles' *Oedipus at Colonus* (ll. 1224–1227) that begins μὴ φῦναι, "Never to have been born"—goes back to the year 1796. Yet Hölderlin's work on Sophocles stretches back much farther than that.[1]

One can readily trace Hölderlin's love of and competence in Greek literature and philosophy back to his primary and secondary school education at Maulbronn and

---

1. For a detailed account of Hölderlin's relation to Sophocles and to the task of translation, see JV 4:1–146, esp. 46–99, which contains a fine commentary, a generous selection of documents, and an excellent account of recent scholarship on these topics.

Denkendorff. Yet it will be enough here if we refer to his university studies. A friend and fellow poet at the University of Tübingen, Rudolf Magenau, reports that Hölderlin was so thoroughly absorbed in the Greek world that it made life in the world of his contemporaries difficult for him. Magenau's reminiscence of Hölderlin the university student and poet, although both condescending and star-struck, is worth quoting at length, inasmuch as it depicts a number of Hölderlinian traits that perdure:

> H[ölderlin] will surely achieve many good things. The effects of his muddled predisposition, visible in all the things he works on, are vanishing little by little, and now he is beginning to be clear and comprehensible. How Neuffer and I have had to battle against his *caprices!* He first engages in a laborious study of the material for his poems; only then does he put pen to paper. His fantasy is not without fire; it's just somewhat too wild. When he is caught up in a thought, he trembles. He has gathered together a fine store of knowledge in Greek and in philosophy.
>
> Whoever saw him loved him, and whoever got to know him remained his friend. Unlucky love, *amor capriccio*, embittered him against Tübingen from time to time, yet he wasn't deaf to his friends' admonishments and castigations. A small company of good friends, with a moderate amount of Rhine wine, galvanized his soul, and these little get-togethers he loved above all else. (CHV 3:572–573)

In the summer of 1790, as a twenty-year-old master's degree student at Tübingen, Hölderlin presented a thesis paper on *The History of the Fine Arts among the Greeks up to the End of the Periclean Age* (CHV 2:11–27). Following Winckelmann's theses quite closely, though with additional material from other sources, Hölderlin devoted considerable space to the qualities of tragedy—Sophoclean tragedy in particular:

> Nothing was more appropriate to the genius of Greece at this time than the mourning-play. Every people finds something attractive in the depiction of grand personages, passions, deeds, and situations. Yet the religion, the festivals, the freedom, the vitality, and the seriousness of the Greeks made them particularly receptive to the mourning-play as well as all the other artistic genres. Judging a piece by Aeschylus was as important to them as a political consultation. For his part, Aeschylus wrote in a manner that was appropriate to his times. Even the coldest person has to *admire* his *Prometheus*. Yet one is not so readily touched by his pieces. His mode of expression is sublime, proud, and militant, as is that of his contemporaries. . . . Sophocles soon followed in the footsteps of his teacher Aeschylus, and with such qualities that the latter had to worry about the status of his own fame. Sophocles was an Athenian, well-made in body and soul, a master in music and the art of dance. At age sixteen he portrayed to the Athenians their victory at Salamis, reciting, accompanying himself on the lyre, dancing, and performing mime. And in this way the youth won over all the spectators. As a re-

ward for his *Antigone* he received the prefecture of Samos. Finally, the respect of the Athenians for the great poet went so far that they declared him Pericles' equal in supreme service to the state. He died in his ninety-fifth year, overjoyed by a victory won by one of his mourning-plays. Just as Aeschylus wrote in the spirit of the warlike decades of his life, Sophocles wrote in the spirit of his more cultivated epoch. Altogether a mixture of proud manliness and feminine tractability: his mode of expression pure, well-pondered, and yet so warm and captivating, quite appropriate to the Periclean age. Passion everywhere guided by good taste. Sophocles occupies the space between Aeschylus and Euripides. The latter is even more tractable, more sensitive. (CHV 2:23, 25–26; FHA 16:13)

During the years 1794–1795 Hölderlin studies Sophocles' *Ajax*, incorporating Ajax's lament and his praise of Salamis into sketches for his novel *Hyperion*. Then a striking reference to *Antigone* appears in the 1797 *Fragment of Philosophical Letters*. The context is the apparent conflict between two kinds of justice, or the need to correct or supplement the law with what Aristotle in *Nicomachean Ethics* (5:10) calls *equity*. The argument could be made—and has been quite forcefully made—that the law itself is tragically flawed, inasmuch as it declares in universals, whereas human beings act as individuals and in quite particular circumstances.[2] In the *Fragment*, Hölderlin understands the lack of equity in the law as a negative sign of his overriding desire—a desire doubtless fired by Rousseau and shared with Schelling and Hegel—to achieve both for himself and for his fellow human beings a more intense, intimate, and even infinite "nexus of life." Hölderlin writes:

> If there are higher laws that determine the more infinite nexus of life [*jenen unendlichern Zusammenhang des Lebens*], if there are unwritten divine laws, the ones of which Antigone speaks when in spite of the strict public prohibition she buries her brother—and there must be such laws if that higher nexus is not a mere phantasm—I say, if there are such laws, then they are in any case insufficient [*unzulänglich*], insofar as they are represented as being *merely* for themselves and not as caught up in life [*im Leben begriffen*]. They are insufficient in the first place because, precisely to the degree that the nexus of life is more infinite, so too the activity and its element, the manner in which the activity proceeds, and the sphere within which all this is observed, encompassing the law and the particular world in which the law is being applied—all this too is bound

2. See Kevin Thomas Miles, "Razing Ethical Stakes: Tragic Transgression in Aristotle's Equitable Action" (Ph.D. dissertation, DePaul University, 1998). If Vernant and Vidal-Naquet, following Louis Gernet, are correct in viewing the historical moment of Athenian tragedy as the moment that experienced the clash of two systems of *law*—the older inchoate law of heroic times and the newer increasingly complex and codified law of the *polis*—then the tragic character of justice, caught between the universals of legislation and the particulars of life, can hardly surprise us, especially if justice is one of those "norms" that has to suffer ongoing "reappraisal." Tragedy and justice will be discussed further at the outset of ch. 9. See VV 32.

up more infinitely with the law. Thus, even if it were a universal law for all civilized peoples, the law could never be conceived at all in abstraction from a particular case. It could never be thought of at all if one were unwilling to take into account its very own peculiarity [*Eigentümlichkeit*], namely, its intimate imbrication [*innige Verbundenheit*] with the sphere in which it is applied. (CHV 2:54–55)

In the first draft of his *Death of Empedocles*, examined in the foregoing chapter, a striking paean to Sophocles appears. It is once again the figure of Antigone that is singled out for praise, even if the issue of equity and the law are no longer at the forefront. Hölderlin places the paean in the mouth of Rhea:

. . We too take joy
In great men, and one of these
Is now the very sun in the sky of Athenian women,
Sophocles! Everyone wishes herself to be a mere thought
In the mind of this splendid man;
She would gladly find sanctuary in the poet's soul
For her ever-lovely youth, before it fades.
And all inquire and consider, Who is she?
That sublime, most tender, pious heroine,
The one he called Antigone. Yet our brows brighten when
This friend of the gods strides into the theater
On the cheerful festival day.
And the delight we take in him is untroubled, though
For no other do our loving hearts lose themselves
In such painful devotion, which draws us on and on.
(CHV 1:772; FHA 12:36–37, 182)

That is hardly the end of the story, however, inasmuch as Hölderlin's development from *The Death of Empedocles* to *The Mourning-Plays of Sophocles*, while continuous, is steep. Many would accept the judgment of Hölderlin's half-brother, Carl Gock, who in his 1841 autobiography wrote that Hölderlin turned to translation simply because he was no longer up to original creative work (FHA 16:32). And it is true that from 1800 onward Hölderlin was under ever-increasing pressure to build upon his success (with *Hyperion*) as a writer, or else to surrender the pen and get a steady job. That, in addition to the stress of his disastrously truncated relationship with Susette Gontard, culminating in her sudden death in the summer of 1802, strained the poet to the breaking point. Perhaps translation (like philosophy, earlier on) served as a way of remaining on task when the work seemed to have lost its audience—or its sole audient—and the focus and the resourcefulness required for work had gone missing. Yet it may indeed be the case that Hölderlin had been heading toward Sophocles and translation for at least a decade, and it is certainly the case that neither the "translations" nor the "Notes" betray signs of surrender. True, both Hegel and Schelling, joining the chorus of early reviewers, found signs of "mental instability" in the translations, so much so that Hölderlin's former friends recommended that the translations be excluded from the first collected edition of the poet's works. Instability, perhaps; startling originality of insight and overwhelming poetic force, beyond question.

During the year 1799 Hölderlin had been struggling to establish a new literary journal, *Iduna*, hoping to engage his friends and acquaintances—especially the renowned authors among them, such as Schiller—to the project. A letter to his friend Neuffer dated Homburg, June 4, 1799, is especially revealing in this respect, and it includes a direct reference to Sophocles. Hölderlin says that his projected "poetic monthly" will contain original work along with essays in the history and criticism of literature, rhetoric, and aesthetics. He hopes to publish there his own drama, *The Death of Empedocles*, along with a number of lyric poems and elegies, and he cites the possibility of essays from various contemporary authors on "ancient and modern poets" such as Homer, Sappho, Aeschylus, Sophocles, Horace, Rousseau (the author of *La nouvelle Héloïse*), and Shakespeare. As for the specific themes to be treated, he writes: "Depiction of the peculiar character of their works, or particular sections of those works. Thus, in the *Iliad*, especially the character of Achilles; in Aeschylus, the *Prometheus*, in Sophocles, the *Antigone* and *Oedipus*" (CHV 2:764–765).

In October of that same year, 1799, the second volume of his novel *Hyperion* appeared. Two passages in it indicate something of Hölderlin's preoccupation with Sophocles. Hyperion's famous diatribe against the Germans begins with a comparison of Hyperion's hapless situation with that of the Oedipus of *Oedipus at Colonus*, who arrives on the scene at the gates of Athens as a homeless, blind suppliant (CHV 1:754). Perhaps even more striking is the passage from *Oedipus at Colonus* that Hölderlin chooses to serve as the epigraph of this second volume, a motto that must surely have struck the young Nietzsche with particular force, inasmuch as "the wisdom of Silenos" dominates Nietzsche's entire reading of Greek tragedy. Hölderlin cites lines 1124–1127 in the Greek, signing them with the name "Sophocles." In translation: "Never to have been born—that is the supreme thought for a human being; once one has entered onto the scene, to return whence one has come as quickly as possible—that is second best" (CHV 1:696). Nor is such Silenic wisdom absent from Hölderlin's *Hyperion* as such, which may be taken as a work of mourning from start to finish, mourning Diotima, a vanquished Greece, a renegade army of liberation, and gods who are themselves bereft. The following brief extracts, as samples of such mourning—inasmuch as the mood of mourning is, in Hölderlin's vision, the prevailing mood of Sophocles as well:

> Hyperion to Diotima: (. . .) Pious soul! I would want to tell you to think of me when you come upon my grave. Yet they will surely toss me into the surging sea, and I would be happy to see that happen, if my remains should sink to the bottom, where the sources of all the streams I loved are gathered, and where the storm clouds rise to soak the mountains and the valleys I loved. And the two of us? O Diotima! Diotima! when will we see one another again? (CHV 1:725)

Oddly, the first volume of the novel quite early on refers to Diotima's grave, so that the passage above, as well as the following one, seem anachronistic. Indeed, mourning seems to be pure anachrony. "Notara to Hyperion: (. . .) It is a terrible mystery, that such a life [as Diotima's] must die, and I must tell you that since I saw that happen I myself have no meaning, no belief" (CHV 1:751).

A passage we have already read in the preceding chapter locates this Sophoclean mood in the figure and fate of Empedocles: the great Sicilian, banished from Agrigent, "intimate with the soul of the world" and impelled by his lust for life, casts himself into the crater of Etna. For he has "had enough of ticking off the hours" (CHV 1:753). We will find in Hölderlin's *Mourning-Plays of Sophocles* another reference to this "ticking off" of the hours (see the discussion of the figure of Danaë in chapter 9 of this volume). Indeed, such counting of the hours is one of the crucial hints concerning Hölderlin's fascination with *Antigone* and with Greek tragedy in general. For that fascination has to do with the *time* of mourning and mortality, which even the immortals come to share. Above all, immortal Zeus, whom Hölderlin identifies as the father of time and the earth, and whom Schelling declares to be identical to the advenient god, Dionysos, will come to partake of mortality. Perhaps the following passage from *Hyperion* captures better than any other the Sophoclean mood of mourning, precisely because it touches on the sufferings of the immortals:

> Hyperion to Bellarmin: (. . .) Best friend! I am calm, for I want nothing better than what the gods have. Must not everything suffer? And the more splendid a being is, the deeper its suffering. Does not holy nature suffer? O my godhead! that you were able to mourn to the extent that you were blessed—that is some-

thing I was long unable to grasp. Yet the delight that does not suffer is sleep, and without death there is no life. (CHV 1:751)

By the summer of 1800 it is clear that Hölderlin is devoting more and more of his time and energies to Sophocles, and especially to the plays *Oedipus the Tyrant* and *Antigone*. This is the time of his poetological essay, "The lyric poem, in appearance ideal. . . ." Here Hölderlin contrasts Sophocles' two great tragedies in ways that may become clearer to us by the end of the present volume—that is to say, by the time we have studied in considerable detail the translations and the "Notes." By way of an initial hint, and one that admittedly is none too clear, Hölderlin contrasts *Oedipus* and *Antigone* in terms of the "intellectual intuition" attained in each: in *Antigone*, the intellectual intuition proceeds from the "concentrating parts" of the play, so that the play is "more lyrical" in character; in *Oedipus*, the intellectual intuition is "more objective," the separation involved in it proceeding from the ancillary parts (*Nebentheile*) of the play, more objectively, more after the manner of epic poetry, indeed, advancing from what is supremely separable—that is, from Zeus himself (CHV 2:107). The sense may be that the intellectual intuition produced by both tragedies is achieved at the moment of caesura in each. In *Antigone*, as we shall see, the caesura falls *after* the midpoint of the play, in the "compressed" or perhaps "concentrating" parts of the play, where Antigone herself—about to march to her death—becomes "more lyrical." By contrast, both the caesura and the intellectual intuition of *Oedipus the Tyrant* occur well *before* the midpoint of the tragedy, in those initial (ancillary?) scenes that set Oedipus apart, separating him out, as it were, for his apparently self-inflicted catastrophe. Yet only *apparently* self-inflicted, inasmuch as objective fate has dictated what is to befall in this saga, or "epic," as though the episodes are arbitrarily set in motion by Zeus, the distant father of time and the earth.

Certainly, none of this is clear to Hölderlin in the summer of 1800, and it may never be clear to us. If this early comparison of the two plays leaves us baffled, let us return to the more prosaic theme of the chronology of Hölderlin's work on the translations, leaving for later chapters a closer examination of the caesura and its effects.

The Labors of Translation

The precise chronology of Hölderlin's labors to translate *The Mourning-Plays of Sophocles* is unknown. It is surely no exaggeration, however, when on June 2, 1801, Hölderlin writes to Schiller that he has occupied himself with

Greek literature "for years now, practically without interruption" (CHV 2:904). True, he is at that moment trying to convince Schiller to intervene on his behalf at the University of Jena, where he hopes to be appointed to a lectureship in Greek language and literature. More in the literature than the language, to be sure: he tells Niethammer that he would prefer to liberate students from slavish preoccupation with the letter, so that they may devote themselves to the "characters in the great poetic works" of the Greek authors (CHV 2:907). Once again this emphasis on character and characters! His famous letter to Casimir von Böhlendorff at the end of that year, written immediately before his departure for Bordeaux, contrasts the "holy pathos" of the Greeks with the "Junonian sobriety" of the modern Western world in general and Germany in particular. One must learn not only from the foreign; one must also study what comes naturally—and natally, so to speak—to one. And yet even at the end of a life-long cultivation of the foreign and the native, one may remain as poverty-stricken as one was at the outset. No fire from heaven touches us in our besotted time, he complains to Böhlendorff, not in our more tender relationships, and not even on the funeral pyre: "That is what is tragic about us: we depart from the land of the living boxed in repose in some sort of container; we never let the flames consume us, never commit ourselves to those flames which we cannot bring under our control" (CHV 2:913).

If, as "The Ground to Empedocles" tells us, the tragic ode begins in supernal fire, so also, we must assume, do Hölderlin's translations of the tragedies of Sophocles begin in that element, and perdure there. An anonymous writer for *La Nouvelle Revue Germanique* tells us in 1831, twenty-seven years after the publication of Hölderlin's *Mourning-Plays of Sophocles,* that Hölderlin prepared the translations principally during the six months of his employment as a tutor in the household of Consul Meyer in Bordeaux: "*C'est là qu'il traduisit, avec un rare talent, les* Tragédies de Sophocle" (FHA 16:31). D. E. Sattler grants this memorious witness more credence than we perhaps should: all we can say with confidence is that during the years 1802–1803, while Schelling was lecturing in Jena on the philosophy of art, Hölderlin was working much more than intermittently on the translation of these plays of Sophocles. Indeed, the translations seem to have been his major creative project during these years. And if that project was carried out at least in part in the south of France, to which (it should be noted) Hölderlin traveled on foot, then it was carried out in proximity to heavenly fire. Solar fire and flame seem to be its very element—*liquid* fire, perhaps in the form of *magma*, the watery, fiery, gaseous earths of Etna, which incorporate all four traditional Empedoclean elements. Perhaps the sea of brazen *aether*, which is the Empedoclean

257

element par excellence, embraces the elemental earth and sky, underworld and chaos, sun and star, and is the liquid fire that surges in all that lives.[3] Hölderlin writes of the fiery element in his second letter to Casimir von Böhlendorff, composed in the early autumn of 1802 after his return (also on foot) from Bordeaux to Stuttgart and Nürtingen (via Paris and Strasbourg). He returns to his homeland only to receive the shattering news of the death of Susette Gontard. The scorched earth has become a more mournful planet, and the poet himself is strangely adrift, an unhappy wanderer on the plains of doom:

> I have not written you in a long time, have in the meantime been in France and have seen the sad and lonely earth; the shepherds of southern France and isolated beauties, men and women who have grown up in the anxiety of patriotic doubt and in hunger.
>
> I was seized constantly by the overwhelming element, the fire of the sky and the repose of the human beings, their life in nature, and their rather limited and contented character; and I may say of myself what one says about heroes, to wit, that Apollo has struck me. . . .
>
> The athletic quality of southerly humanity, seen in the ruins of the antique spirit, made me more familiar with the authentic essence of the Greeks; I learned about the nature they confronted and about their wisdom, their bodies, the way they grew up in their climate, and the rule by which they protected their headstrong genius from the violence of the element.
>
> This determined their national trait, their way of taking on natures that were foreign to them and communicating themselves to them.[4] That is the reason why they have their own individuality, which comes to the fore so vitally to the extent that supreme intellect in the Greek sense is the power of reflection; this becomes comprehensible to us when we grasp the heroic body of the Greek; it is tenderness, like our national trait. (CHV 2:920–921; 3:550–551)

The sense of this last phrase is difficult to capture, inasmuch as Hölderlin usually *contrasts* rather than *equates* the foreign Greek to the native German. Here he seems to be saying that the athletic Greek and the tender German ("tender" perhaps in the sense of Schiller's "sentimental" as opposed to "naive"?) are identical. Michael Knaupp suggests that the word *sobriety* may be missing from the end of the sentence; that is, that whereas tenderness is the Greek trait, sobriety is the German. Presumably, Hölderlin would be repeating the thesis of his *first* letter to Böhlendorff, dated December 4, 1801, that whereas heavenly fire is the national gift of the ancient Greeks, Junonian sobriety of representation is the German national gift. However, if Hölderlin indeed means what he writes here, the sense might be that "tenderness,"

---

3. See especially the third and final version of *The Death of Empedocles*, lines 449–458.
4. "National trait" here translates *Popularität*, following the suggestion of Michael Knaupp (CHV 3:551).

Zärtlichkeit, expressed (however surprisingly to us) in the agonistic, athletic Greek body, is—or ought to be cultivated as—a national characteristic of the Germans as well. Yet perhaps one should not be so surprised: what is characteristic of Achilles, the greatest of the Greek warriors, is in Hölderlin's view less his wrath—which is what the muse of *The Iliad* has always sung—than his "melancholy tenderness" (CHV 2:65). *Hölderlin's* Achilles is the godly youth who weeps for his lost Briseïs and cries out to his mother for succor. For love, as we recall from the *Fragment,* is "tender discovery": *Da hingegen die Liebe gerne zart entdekt* (CHV 2:60). The southerly, solar, athletic, but also reposeful and even "contented" body of the Greek and the Provençal may be characterized precisely by forces of love—by tenderness. And the German? Jochen Schmidt's way of reading *Popularität* as "the capacity for openness and communication vis-à-vis others" (DKV 3:922) makes this identification of the Greek and the German possible. For such tenderness or openness, in Hölderlin's view, is the essence of both religious and political community. After a paragraph break, Hölderlin's letter to Böhlendorff continues as follows: "Viewing this antique world made an impression on me that helped me to understand better not only the Greeks but also what is supreme about art in general; for even in supreme movement and in the phenomenalizing of concepts and of everything that is seriously intended, everything is preserved and stands for itself, so that assuredness in this sense is the supreme art of depiction" (CHV 2:920–921). The letter closes with the hope that modern poets will sing "naturally," in a way appropriate to their own nations and national gifts, with authenticity and originality—a hope that has to sustain, however tenuously, Hölderlin's translations from the ancient Greek into his own Hesperian German.

D. E. Sattler argues that the *first* letter to Böhlendorff, written on the eve of Hölderlin's departure for Bordeaux, marks the real starting point of Hölderlin's work on the translations. Conceding that we cannot date Hölderlin's *intention* to translate them with any certainty, he argues nevertheless for the opening days of the year 1802 as the date of commencement for the actual work. For up to that time Hölderlin seems to have been occupied with other matters. Although he appears to have given up work on his own tragedy, *The Death of Empedocles,* early in 1800, he continued to work on his poetological essays, and by July of 1800 was sketching out numerous odes and elegies. By winter he was translating Pindar. In the spring and summer of 1801 he was working on the great hymns for which he is most renowned. There was talk of their being published by Cotta at Easter of 1802, and throughout the autumn of 1801 Hölderlin prepared final copies of many of his odes, elegies, and hymns in a neat hand for this proposed publication. By January 28, 1802, when he arrived in Bordeaux, all these other projects had either been completed or had gone awry. The path to Sophocles was open.

All the editors of the sundry editions of Hölderlin's works in fact agree that the Sophocles translations were the poet's principal project in Bordeaux during the winter and spring of 1802, and also back in Germany after his return to Stuttgart and Nürtingen in mid-June of that same year. By October of 1802 the translations were far enough along that Hölderlin could ask his friend Sinclair to begin casting about for a publisher. Hölderlin pursued leads in Berlin, Leipzig, and Jena. He mailed the manuscript to Friedrich Wilmans in Frankfurt on December 8, 1803, explaining that the long delay was due to the need to revise the translation of *Antigone*. The language of his translation, he explained, was "not lively enough," and the "Notes" did not yet adequately express his convictions concerning Greek art in general and the meaning of these two plays in particular. Wilmans sent Hölderlin a number of proposed samples of type and the poet chose Walbaum-Antiqua, a rather modern "Latin" font. Wilmans then had the translations set in type by Johann Peter Bayrhoffer of Frankfurt. Bayrhoffer, perhaps under time pressure from Wilmans, set the two volumes hurriedly. In late March or early April Hölderlin completed the second set of corrections—the first set had come back to him full of errors. Because Wilmans was in a hurry to present the book at the Leipzig book fair, however, he paid little or no heed to Hölderlin's many corrections to the second set of proofs. No one would pay the book's errors much mind, said the publisher, and in any case they wouldn't blame the author for them, so why should Hölderlin worry? Hölderlin's reply—and his revenge—came late. Toward the very end of his long life and his protracted illness, Hölderlin responded to a visitor's query concerning the Sophocles translations, "I tried to translate *Oedipus*, but my publisher was an _____." Hölderlin repeated the unprintable epithet—no doubt related to what in chapter 1 was called *Afterdienst*—a number of times in rapid succession (StA 5:454; FHA 16:32).

The crucial matter, of course, is the way in which Hölderlin actually set about translating Sophocles. According to Jochen Schmidt, Hölderlin used the Juntina edition (which Schmidt designates "Brubachiana 1555," after its German printer, Braubach, and the year of the particular edition in Hölderlin's possession) for all of *Antigone*, which he translated second, but a more modern and more philologically reliable edition for two-thirds of *Oedipus*, which Hölderlin translated first. Presumably, a more modern edition of Sophocles' Greek text was available to him in Bordeaux at the residence of

Consul Meyer. Back in Germany, Hölderlin was forced to rely entirely on the Juntina (Brubachiana 1555) edition in his own modest library, although he did possess the quarto-sized edition, containing the *scholia*, or detailed commentaries on the plays (DKV 2:1324).

Friedrich Beißner identifies four principal stages in Hölderlin's work on the translations, without, however, claiming to be able to assign to them a specific chronology: first, a relatively free formulation of the meaning of the Greek phrases, whereby the individual Greek word appears to count for little; second, a version that tries to follow quite faithfully the Greek prosody and rhythms; third, the "procedure of attentive listening" (*die "hinhörende Verfahrungsart"*), applied after the manner of Hölderlin's translations of Pindar, which preserve to the greatest possible extent the *word order* of the Greek original; and fourth, a late revision, especially of *Antigone*, but also of *Oedipus*, in the autumn of 1803, during which Hölderlin takes ever greater risks, translating in an increasingly "lively" (*lebendigeren*) fashion, in order to capture the force of the Greek for his modern Hesperian readers and would-be theatergoers (StA 5:451). D. E. Sattler confirms that internal evidence (to repeat, the availability to Hölderlin of a more modern edition of Sophocles in Bordeaux and his unfortunate dependence on the Juntina [Brubachiana 1555] edition by the time he is back in Nürtingen) indicates that by May 1802 Hölderlin has drafted at least two-thirds of the *Oedipus*, although he may have begun the *Antigone* translation only once he was back in Germany.[5] Perhaps the most telling of the variations in Hölderlin's procedure cited by Sattler is the fact that, following a differential calculus for the two tragedies, Hölderlin opts to *begin* the acts of *Antigone* with the choral odes, whereas the acts of *Oedipus* *end* with those odes. Much could be said about this difference in light of Hölderlin's argument concerning the need to achieve equilibrium in the two plays in very different ways, and the need to protect the *beginning* of *Oedipus the Tyrant* and the *end* of *Antigone* by means of the carefully inserted caesurae, or counterrhythmic interruptions. It may pertain to the more lyrical nature of *Antigone* that the choral odes *introduce* the acts, as though in processional, whereas the more objective and epic-like drama of *Oedipus the Tyrant* places the odes at the conclusion of each episode. (See chapters 9 and 10 of this volume for further discussion.)

Let us try now to summarize the principal features of Hölderlin's labors on the Sophoclean tragedies. For the most part, Hölderlin used the Juntina

5. For details on these matters, including the positioning of particular choral odes and the apportioning of entire scenes and acts, see FHA 16:63–64. These positionings and apportionings are the major indices for Sattler's determination of the progress of the translations as such.

text of Sophocles' plays, published in Frankfurt in 1555, as the basis for his translations of *Oedipus the Tyrant* and *Antigone*. The Juntina was the text that Hölderlin happened to own and to which he therefore most often had recourse. However, there are a number of indications that he used other more current and more authoritative versions of the Greek text whenever he had access to a library that was better stocked than his own. This occurred early on in his work on the translations in Bordeaux and is especially important for the first two-thirds of *Oedipus the Tyrant* and for the choruses of the two tragedies. The bulk of the translating and revising work, done at his mother's house in Nürtingen and at his friend Sinclair's house in Bad Homburg vor der Höhe, was, to repeat, based on the philologically unfortunate—but affordable—Juntina edition.[6]

6. Beißner speculates that the more modern edition that was from time to time available to Hölderlin was that of Thomas Burgess of Oxford (StA 5:452); Sattler argues that Hölderlin had access to a French edition published in Greek and Latin in Paris in 1871 (FHA 16:12). Presumably, Consul Meyer's library in Bordeaux would have contained a more modern and dependable edition of Sophocles, and it may have been the very edition (Paris, 1871) that Sattler cites. The Juntina edition is nevertheless the one that Sattler chooses as the basis for his indispensable edition of *Die Trauerspiele des Sophokles*. Indispensable it is—and yet one must still refer to the Stuttgart edition of Hölderlin's works, that is, the first historical-critical edition, edited by Friedrich Beißner, as well as to the handy—and affordable—Hanser edition by Michael Knaupp, who assisted Sattler on the Frankfurter edition. Perhaps the most important edition for contemporary readers of Hölderlin's Sophocles translations, however, is that by Jochen Schmidt for the Deutscher Klassiker Verlag, which contains a far more detailed commentary on the translations than any of the other editions, including the two historical-critical editions. True, one often finds that Schmidt (Jochen, not Dennis!) is excessively disparaging of Hölderlin's knowledge of Greek, and that he consistently underestimates both the poet's capabilities and his poetic will to transmute both the Greek and the German. Schmidt cites Norbert von Hellingrath, one of the early-twentieth-century editors of Hölderlin's works, to the effect that whereas our poet seems to have had extraordinary expertise in the *literature* of Greeks he had very little mastery of the rules of Greek *syntax*. Schmidt sometimes seems to take schoolmasterly delight in this disparity, gleefully touting up the hundreds of "corruptions" in the Brubachiana 1555 text and the numberless "calamitous mistranslations" made by the poet. Schmidt writes: "Hölderlin either followed this edition [i.e., the Juntina, or Brubachiana 1555], and so arrived at a false or sometimes even meaningless translation, or he tried to read a sense into those parts of the text that he could not understand—inasmuch as precisely *in themselves* they make no sense—with the result that he wandered away from translation, engaging in sheer speculation, and thus erred even farther" (DKV 2:1326). Add to Hölderlin's shaky knowledge of Greek grammar the parlous textual basis of the Juntina or Brubachiana edition and the very project of Hölderlin's translations appears about to tumble. There are several problems with Schmidt's analysis, however, one of them being that Schmidt often scolds Hölderlin for errors and confusions that almost certainly are intentional transgressions or risks on the poet's part. The merits of these supposed errors—instances of an admittedly unheard-of poetic license—are no doubt infinitely debatable. In general, however, one wants to remind Schmidt of the warning expressed by Henry David Thoreau in *Walden* to all those who suppose that knowledge of Greek grammar and literary mastery should and most often do go hand-in-hand: "Indeed, there is hardly the professor in our colleges, who, if he has mastered the difficulties of the language, has proportionally mastered the difficulties of the wit and poetry of a Greek poet, and has any sympathy to impart to the alert and heroic reader." Nevertheless, at the end of the arduous day, one is grateful to Jochen Schmidt: no other editor has taken the extraordinary trouble he has taken to offer a truly critical edition of Hölderlin's translations and a detailed commentary on their Greek basis. For the quotation from Thoreau, see Henry David Thoreau, *Walden*, ed. William Harding, Variorum Ed. (New York: Washington Square Press, 1968), 79.

There is no extant manuscript for *The Mourning-Plays of Sophocles*, although there may have been several manuscripts that were preserved until Hölderlin's death in 1843. In June of 1822 Hölderlin's half-brother Carl Gock instructed Carl Ziller to examine Hölderlin's papers in Nürtingen. The papers that were *not* destined for the collected edition of Hölderlin's works were to be sent to the home of Hölderlin's nephew Breunlin. These were "mostly translations of *Sophocles* and fragments of notes from courses" (FHA 16:30). These papers have disappeared. The poet Eduard Mörike, himself a student at the Tübinger Stift from 1823 to 1826, claims to have seen in the Nürtingen house much later, in 1843, "a large basket of manuscripts," among them "translations of Sophocles (published in part), Euripides, and Pindar" (CHV 3:673–674; StA 5:452). Yet none of these manuscripts survives. The original is therefore the 1804 edition published by Wilmans.[7] The 1804 edition is highly problematic, yet it is the sole available textual basis for Hölderlin's translations—themselves based largely, as already indicated, on the philologically problematic Juntina or Brubachiana 1555 edition.

Granted all the misfortunes suffered by the texts of both Sophocles and Hölderlin—*libri habent sua fata*—it is difficult to avoid the conclusion of the editor of the Stuttgart historical-critical edition of Hölderlin's works, Friedrich Beißner, who argues that Hölderlin's *Trauerspiele des Sophokles* demands of its editors and commentators a more than modest amount of *conjecture* (StA 5:455). Apropos of conjecture, then, two final questions. Should one feel duty-bound to instruct the beginning student of Greek that Hölderlin's translations of Sophocles are not "translations" in any simple or accepted sense? Or should one instead take the opportunity afforded us by Hölderlin's labors to ask about the simple and accepted sense of translation, and about the very task of the translator? This second question will be taken up at the end of the present chapter.

The Reviews

Reviewers of Hölderlin's Sophocles translations dashed the poet's hopes for the fruits of his labors. D. E. Sattler, Christoph Jamme, and Frank Völkel reprint virtually all these reviews, and they make for dismal reading. Hölderlin himself had warned his publisher that the translations tried to correct the errors that prior translations had made, errors that arose principally from the fact that translators so often had to make concessions to the reading public's

7. A facsimile of this 1804 edition is available from Stroemfeld/Roter Stern Verlag (Basel and Frankfurt am Main, 1986).

limited range of experience. Hölderlin's versions, in contrast to more traditional renderings, were "more lively," *lebendiger,* insofar as they emphasized the "Oriental" aspects of ancient Greek culture, which prior renderings had refused to acknowledge. Precisely what Hölderlin means by *das Orientalische* has been widely discussed in the critical literature; obviously, it includes those aspects of Greek religion, myth, and literature that borrow heavily from ancient Near Eastern cultures. Less obviously, it may be that these "more Oriental" aspects of the Greeks are precisely what a good portion of nineteenth- and twentieth-century classical studies—from Jacob Bernays and Erwin Rohde through Jane Ellen Harrison, Gilbert Murray, W. K. C. Guthrie, E. R. Dodds, Jean-Pierre Vernant, and Walter Burkert—have taught us to expect and accept. Be that as it may, the Winckelmannian and Voßian conception of a pristine and purely Occidental Greek antiquity did not succumb so easily.

Many reviewers faulted Hölderlin for his insufficient mastery of Greek syntax, and classicists today—as noted earlier—continue to find fault with his Greek, no doubt with some justice. The problem, to repeat, is that Hölderlin's relation to Greek is so foreign to us that it is often difficult to know whether he is simply misinformed or whether he is deliberately stretching and twisting the Sophoclean text. It is easy enough to discover where the Juntina text leads him astray, and Jochen Schmidt performs a genuine service to readers of the Deutscher Klassiker Verlag edition when he does this, but everything else is more difficult to ascertain. For example, present-day editors join a nineteenth-century reviewer in faulting Hölderlin for his translation of τύραννος as "tyrant." They explain, patiently, that a *tyrannos* is simply a king. Yet is Hölderlin misinformed about this commonly known word, or is he trying to tell us something about Oedipus's rage and obsession, that is, about the tyranny of consciousness and of the need-to-know that is driving him to his blindness and ruin—and his mother and spouse to her death? Would it not be ironic if righteous reviewers and ambitious editors were suffering under that very same Oedipal tyranny? While one must try to avoid hero-worship and wild overestimation of Hölderlin's capabilities, one must also avoid underestimating the poet, since underestimation seems to be the native gift of the scholar and critic in our Hesperian age.

Even Hölderlin's friends, Schelling and Hegel among them, were convinced that the Sophocles translations showed signs of mental instability and emotional debility. On July 11, 1803, Schelling wrote Hegel that the "saddest sight" he had seen during his visit to Swabia was that of a Hölderlin *am Geist ganz zerrüttet,* "altogether mentally unhinged," no doubt still capable of some work—namely, of translating from the Greek—but only of a very limited sort.

"Otherwise his mental disturbance is complete" (FHA 16:17). One year later Schelling finds Hölderlin "somewhat better," yet he confirms that the poet's ongoing "mental deterioration" is perfectly depicted in the recently published Sophocles translations (FHA 16:20).

What his friends suspect, strangers and enemies gleefully declare. Heinrich Voß the Younger, son of the famous translator of Homer, asks, "Is the man crazy, or is he just faking it, and is his translation a hidden satire on lousy translators?" (ibid.; cf. JV 4:79–88). Voß reads some passages aloud to his friends Schiller and Goethe, and they all, he says, share a good laugh. (Some commentators partial to Goethe note that Schiller laughed harder.) Voß finds countless errors in the scansion of the lines, uncovers acts of "unruly boldness," spots "weird designations," and in general grows faint in the face of Hölderlin's "unstable modes of expression." Not only that. Hölderlin also uses some "provincialisms," and even "words of low origin," a euphemism for slang. In general, Hölderlin's expressions are "excessively plastic" and "too coarsely sensual." Hölderlin would have done better if he had used a lexicon, referred to published commentaries, and stayed off the streets. Hölderlin would have done better if he had been less lively, more deadly dull.

And then the errors, the downright mistakes, the mind-boggling bloopers! Voß counts 55 in *Oedipus* and 117 in *Antigone*, on which Hölderlin worked even harder (FHA 16:123–124). (Over the years, editors and critics have improved and have found lots more.) You'd think you were listening to a loony on his way to the bin, cries Voß, even though the "Notes" tell you that all this has been done *consciously*. "Obviously, these are all unheard-of characterizations of thoughts that have never been heard of and will never be heard of again," concludes Voß. Another reviewer, J. G. Gurlitt, agrees: even the "Notes" to the two mourning-plays "reach supreme heights of modern aesthetic nonsense" (FHA 16:27; JV 4:88–89). "You can easily skip a page while you're reading," Gurlitt growls, "and not realize that you've lost the sense, because here there isn't any." "Ridiculous and pedantic," cries G. Merkel (FHA 16:29; JV 4:89–92), and Voß concludes: "How Herr Hölderlin got so high we really don't know; if he just happened to fall upstairs, then we earnestly beg him to come back down and join the rest of us" (FHA 16:25). One can also fall into the heights, Hölderlin once said (CHV 2:580), but his critics preferred gravity.

The affirmative reviews were far fewer, but they are attached to names we remember. Achim von Arnim, in February 1828, refers to the "Notes" in this way: "And now, when he expresses himself concerning the tragic, he liberates himself marvelously from all the petty hair-splitting of philosophy; with simple words he penetrates to wondrous depths" (FHA 16:31). Bettina Brentano von Arnim writes in her epistolary novel *Die Günderode* (1840):

> St. Clair [i.e., Sinclair] gave me the *Oedipus*, which Hölderlin translated from the Greek, telling me that one could understand so little of it, or that one maliciously wanted to understand so little of it, that one could declare the language riddled with traces of insanity, but he said that this only goes to show how little the Germans understand the splendors of which their tongue is capable.—Encouraged by him, I have now studied this *Oedipus*, and I tell you true, it led me down a trail of universal suffering, yet not because of the language, which strides musically, apprehending with its organ every expression of violence. This suffering organ, and it alone, so moves the soul that we are forced to lament with Oedipus, lament deep and deeply.[8]

Bettina von Arnim's rare affirmation goes to join Wilhelm Waiblinger's. To be sure, Waiblinger is ambivalent about the Sophocles translations, "which contain much that is marvelous and much that is mad" (JV 4:96). Yet when Waiblinger receives from Hölderlin's landlord the poem we have come to know as *In lieblicher Bläue*, he says of it—as of the man who produced it— "When it is comprehensible, it speaks always of suffering; of Oedipus; of Greece" (CHV 3:656). Among the lines of this late poem, composed probably during the year 1807 or 1808, after Hölderlin's release from the Autenrieth Clinic, are the following ones, so reminiscent of the sufferings of both Oedipus and Antigone, and now of Hölderlin himself:

> When someone looks into the mirror, a man, and in it sees his image, as though painted there; it resembles the man. This image of the man has eyes, as opposed to the moon, which has light. King Oedipus has an eye too many perhaps. The sufferings of this man, they seem indescribable, unspeakable, inexpressible. If the play portrays such a thing, that is the reason why. Yet how is it with me when I think of you now? The end of something sweeps me away, as though in streams, something that reaches as far as Asia. Naturally, this suffering, Oedipus has it. Naturally, that is what it is all about. (CHV 1:909)

8. Bettina Brentano von Arnim, *Die Günderode* (Frankfurt am Main: Insel, 1983), 161; cf. FHA 16:32; cf. JV 4:98. A contemporary "positive review" appears in the introduction to David Constantine's recent translation of Hölderlin's *Mourning-Plays of Sophocles*, under the title, *Hölderlin's Sophocles: Oedipus and Antigone* (Tarset, Northumberland, England: Bloodaxe Books, 2001), 7–13. Although Constantine's translation came to my attention only after my work on the present volume was drawing to a close, I am happy with so many of his judgments. Himself a poet, Constantine refers to Hölderlin's as "a language truly poetic, strange and beautiful, the true language of elsewhere, poetry at its best" (7); he is also right, I believe, when he claims that the language of *Oedipus the Tyrant* is "odder," "more difficult," and even "more foreign" than that of *Antigone*, and that this is surprising in view of Hölderlin's efforts to make the latter "livelier" than the former (10); finally, Constantine sees Hölderlin as not only "the most passionate of poets, but also among the most calculating" (12), although invariably a poet who puts himself "ever more at risk," exposing himself and his language of elsewhere ever more intensely to madness, rage, and violence (11).

Hölderlin intended from the outset that his translations of Sophocles' *Oedipus the Tyrant* and *Antigone* be performed on the stage: his fervent hope was that Goethe, urged on by the philosopher Schelling and the poet Schiller, would see to their production at the theater of the Weimar court. That hope, of course, was never fulfilled. To be sure, the translations have been performed a number of times in Germany: Beißner lists some eighteen performances between the years 1921 and 1951, a number that surely has been augmented in the past five decades. Bert Brecht prepared a stage version of Hölderlin's translation of *Antigone* that premiered in Chur in 1948. Philippe Lacoue-Labarthe's French versions were performed in Strasbourg in 1978 and 1979 and were at least prepared for the stage at the Avignon Theater Festival in 1998–1999. Of special note is Carl Orff's opera *Antigonae*, which premiered in Salzburg in 1949, presenting the entire Hölderlinian text without alteration or abbreviation.[9] Never has an opera been so thoroughly dominated by its text—which is in no sense a libretto. Orff does not set the Hölderlinian text to melodies; rather, he accentuates the rhythms of the text. The dialogues are largely chanted in recitative, the choruses declaimed. The orchestra is almost entirely percussive, stony, brittle, glassy (no pun intended), abrupt. Orff sets the Hölderlinian rhythms (including, of course, the counterrhythmic interruptions or caesurae) masterfully, producing a score that one would call Spartan if it were not so entirely Theban. The Salzburg production was repeated in the Prinzregententheater of Munich in 1951 and 1952, with the same cast, and with Solti again conducting. The effect of Orff's *Antigonae* on its Munich audience is nowhere better described than in Heinrich Wiegand Petzet's memoir of Heidegger.[10] Petzet begins by describing the mood of the audience, still very much in the throes of postwar depression and disorientation:

> The musician Orff succeeded at something far removed from any sort of extrinsic 'operatic treatment': it was a work that conjured up almost perfectly a world

9. A digitally remastered recording of the January 12, 1951, performance in Munich's Prinzregententheater by the Bayerische Staatsoper, directed by Georg Solti, is available from Orfeo under the catalogue number C 407 952 I. Skeptics will need to hear it only once; students of opera dozens of times. The only dissenting voice I have heard thus far is that of Philippe Lacoue-Labarthe, who calls Orff's work "a monument to vulgarity." See Lacoue-Labarthe, *Métaphrasis* (Paris: Presses Universitaires de France, 1998), 4; cited henceforth by page number in the body of my text. Perhaps Lacoue-Labarthe succumbs to the desire to ridicule the opera because of its composer's highly problematic political background—yet as Jacques Barzun demonstrated long ago in the case of Wagner (as opposed to Berlioz), and as Adorno demonstrated *volens nolens* with his analyses of Brahms (as opposed to Mahler), music resists reduction to social-political agendas of every stripe.

10. See Heinrich Wiegand Petzet, *Auf einen Stern zugehen: Begegnungen mit Martin Heidegger 1929 bis 1976* (Frankfurt am Main: Societäts-Verlag, 1983), 168–172, esp. 170, for what follows. Petzet's hagiography often achieves unintended comic effects, and Heidegger's congratulation of Orff is one of them. Yet those hagiographic excesses do not harm the substance of the story, which is moving.

that had foundered in the past. It did so by uniting sounds that were at first alienating, harsh, and often almost aggressive with the power of the poetic word. No one could distance himself or herself from the message that became visible and audible in those words. . . . A sense of the religious significance that the performance of tragedies must have had for the ancients gripped those who were present with ever-increasing force.

Heidegger was among those present in 1952—present and gripped. Hölderlin's wish that the translations be performed was fulfilled late, but with a power and intensity that take the breath away.

Absolute Intensity and the Task of the Translator

Perhaps one insists too much on the novelty of Hölderlin's reading of Sophocles. The truth is that his reading, while incomparably radical, bears a relation to many other more familiar interpretations. For example, David Grene, in his succinct introduction to the University of Chicago translations of *Oedipus the King, Oedipus at Colonus,* and *Antigone,* proffers a reading that is not so far removed from that of Hölderlin. Grene stresses what he calls "the generic side of tragedy," *generic* not in the pejorative sense, but in the Schellingian sense of the *mythic* background common to the plays. All three Theban plays, in his view, deal with the legendary tyrants, Oedipus and Creon, hence with the question of tyranny or "despotic authority" in general (C 7–8). More broadly still, suggests Grene, what captivates Sophocles is "the generic aspect of human dilemmas" (ibid.). The word *dilemma* is important here. For it is never a question of a clear-cut fault, flaw, sin, or crime in tragedy; rather, the heroes of the tragedies act and suffer in a shadowy realm beyond justice and all just deserts. Furthermore, if Oedipus and Creon alike represent the tyrant, Sophocles handles the plots of their respective tragedies with growing profundity: "if the character is generic, the situation is deepening" (ibid.). Grene's interpretation, like that of many others, emphasizes the importance of Creon in *Antigone,* not in order to deny the significance of the title figure, but to exhibit the close relation of *Antigone* to the *Oedipus* plays. What is "sacred" for Sophocles is the core of the legend: what touches on the holy is not any particular personage attached to the legend but the pattern of the mythic conflict itself.

If one accepts this "generic" reading, the question arises: What, in Hölderlin's view, is the generic import of tragedy? That is to say, is there a central axis of myth or legend about which all the tragedies of Sophocles revolve? Is there a central question about which all the tragedies of antiquity turn? What is sacred, or holy, for Hölderlin's Sophocles? The answer to the second and third questions is, in Hölderlin's view, clearly in the affirmative, although more than that is difficult to ascertain. The "generic" question for Hölderlin would have to do with the unification and violent separation of human beings and gods, the appearance of the god in the figure of death, and the character of *suffering* that every word of the tragic dialogues and choral songs embodies—all of these themes broaching the holy. Can more than this be said? Something about the more enhanced tenderness, perhaps? Yes, but only with the appropriate caution, and, in the present instance, only in the course of the detailed studies of the following chapters.

Hölderlin's translations of Sophocles may not be entirely novel, but there is a poetic and thoughtful intensity about them that is impossible to exaggerate. We get an idea of how radical Hölderlin's reading of Sophocles is when we notice the reasons for which Hölderlin's contemporary and friend, Schelling, praises the great Greek tragedian. Like Heidegger after him, Schelling praises Sophocles for having epitomized Greek ethicality, *Sittlichkeit*. Schelling elaborates what he means by Sophoclean ethicality: the complete subordination of human being to the gods, the sense of limit and measure in all ethical matters, the repudiation of pride and ὕβρις, and the rejection of all blasphemous violence—these are, according to Schelling's 1802–1803 lectures on aesthetics, Sophocles' ethical achievements (5:417; cf. 702). It is not too much to say, however, that Hölderlin challenges the validity of every one of these ethical principles—or, rather, he shows us Sophocles himself challenging them. Hölderlin's Sophocles, "wandering amid unthinkable things," challenges the notion of subordination, steps beyond every measured limit, and asserts the absolute necessity of what others call blasphemy and excessive pride. Sophoclean *excesses* are what the following chapters must sound, as they go to read Hölderlin's renderings of *Oedipus the Tyrant* and *Antigone*.

Yet what about the task of translation in general? In one of his essays on early Greek thinking, Heidegger remarks that before a translator begins to translate a thought-provoking text he or she must be translated to the foreign shore of what is to be thought.[11] How is that to occur? Not by wishful thinking, not by hoping that some sort of pure intuition of the original, foreign language will magically appear once one has reached a point of oblivion concerning what is one's own ("Ach! I'm forgetting all my English!"). Yet also not by

11. See, for example, Heidegger, "Der Spruch des Anaximander," in *Holzwege*, 303; translated as "The Anaximander Fragment" in Heidegger, *Early Greek Thinking*, 2nd ed. (San Francisco: HarperCollins, 1984), 19.

relying on the dozens of dictionaries and other philological tools one has consulted, however crucial they may be from the beginning of the task all the way to its completion. Heidegger himself finds it hard to specify the precise labors of thinking that are requisite here. It is much easier to say how and when these labors fall short: during their seminar on Heraclitus, Eugen Fink can never truly satisfy Heidegger's demands in this regard, so that when Heidegger is detained one day and cannot attend the session Fink can scarcely hide his elation.[12] During the course of that seminar, Heidegger never tires of saying how much has intervened between the thinking of the early Greeks and his and Fink's own efforts. In Heidegger's view, Hegel is perhaps the decisive intervention, although one could also think of Schelling and Hölderlin, and also of Nietzsche. One can scarcely come to terms with the ways in which the various projects of the intervening thinkers shape our own approach to the Greeks, even (or perhaps especially) when we try to bracket out their influence on us. It is clear that Hölderlin, who is himself a Hesperian, that is, one who is closer to the Hesperides (the land of evening, or "West," the isles of the blessed, or the realm of the dead) than to ancient Greece, is intimate with the world of Sophocles—yet how does that happen? And whose world is it, after all? When all is said and done, we do not know. How, then, can we say anything at all about "the task of the translator," even if the translator in the present instance is Hölderlin?

Walter Benjamin's essay of that title may not help any more than Heidegger's more *ad hoc*—yet equally cryptic—remarks.[13] Hölderlin's translations of Sophocles are precisely the texts Benjamin cites whenever it is a question of the outer limits of translation. No poetic text in the original is there in order to communicate anything: that is Benjamin's uncompromising starting point, which is soon followed by the inevitable conclusion. If translation aims to communicate something of an original to a different language group, it devotes itself to what is inessential in the original. What is essential in an original is its survival over historical time and cultural space, the achievement of a greater nexus of life (a paraphrase of Hölderlin on Benjamin's part) for the work. Translation would then be the relationship of two entire languages, not merely two works, to one another (52–53). Yet, again, not as copies (*Abbilder*)

12. Martin Heidegger and Eugen Fink, *Heraklit* (Frankfurt am Main: V. Klostermann, 1970), 165; see D. F. Krell, "Hegel Heidegger Heraclitus," in *Heraclitean Fragments*, ed. John Sallis and Kenneth Maly (University: University of Alabama Press, 1980), 22–42.
13. Walter Benjamin, "Die Aufgabe des Übersetzers," in *Illuminationen: Ausgewählte Schriften* (Frankfurt am Main: Suhrkamp, 1977), 50–62; translated as "The Task of the Translator (1921)" in *Selected Writings, 1913–1926*, ed. Marcus Bullock and Michael W. Jennings (Cambridge, Mass.: Harvard University Press, 1996). I will cite the German text by page number in the body of my text.

of one another, inasmuch as both languages are constantly developing and shifting. (Perhaps even a "dead" language can be said to undergo transformation, though the very definition of "dead" denies this: Benjamin does not take up this possibility of the development of a "dead" language—a possibility that might resemble what Aristotle says about a father's excellent chance of being unhappy even after his death, in the event of his children's ill-fortune.) The relatedness of the two languages, for its part, does not lie in their similarity; rather, it lies in the happenstance that languages pertain to a general "intentionality" of language—*die reine Sprache*, "pure language," or "pure speech," perhaps once again on the model of Hölderlin's *das reine Wort* (54). The original and the translation do not achieve proximity in such intentionality: if the import of a poem relates to its language as the pulp of a piece of fruit relates to its skin, the relation of the translated poem to its language will be that of loose drapery—a royal robe, but "hanging in broad folds" (56). This is true not only for the products of second-rate poets (Benjamin cites Luther, Voß [the Elder?], and Schlegel [August Wilhelm?]), but also those of "the greatest, such as Hölderlin and Stefan George" (56–57). The task of the translator consists in finding the intention or intentionality that heads in the direction of the target language, that is to say, the language "from out of which and in which an echo of the original can be roused" (57). The translator, standing not within but outside the dense forest that is his or her "own" language, declaims the original into that forest, in the hope that an echo of the original will reverberate in the target language—one echo instigating another, so to speak. The goal cannot be to approximate the original language, inasmuch as one does not approximate even one's own language. Hence the necessity for the most rigorous discipline in order to acquire what others assume to be a national gift freely given, the native talent, the innate second nature, a birthright. For Benjamin, however, an even greater task is to assist in the integration of all languages. "For there is a philosophical *ingenium* whose most proper quality is the longing [*Sehnsucht*] for that language which is announcing itself in the translation" (ibid.). As in Schelling, so in Benjamin: pure language is the language for which both the original and the target language languish—what Benjamin will soon call, misleadingly enough, *die Lehre*, "teaching," "doctrine," "lore." A literal translation, one that tries to conform to the syntax of the original, can only be a bad translation: "For the nineteenth century, Hölderlin's translations of Sophocles loomed right before their eyes as monstrous examples of literalness" (58). Benjamin will soon deny that this appearance of a slavish adherence to Greek syntax in Hölderlin's German is in fact characteristic of Hölderlin's translations. For what Hölderlin does is to break up the grammar and syntax of his own language in an effort to hear an echo of the original—or, again, in the effort to rejoin the intentionality of language as such, to hear pure language. The translator must break his or her own language into unfamiliar shards in the effort to restore the shattered original, and this by paying heed to "the manner of intending," *die Art des Meinens,* in one's own language, the "target" language. A successful translation will therefore never "read like the original," as we are so fond of saying. It will instead seek to "redeem" what is banished in the original. To do this it will break down the already rotting barriers of its own language, thus extending the boundaries of the language, enlarging its capacities, as though in order to prepare a sanctuary that may accommodate the banished. If this seems too dramatic a figure, Benjamin offers a more gentle and more precise turn of phrase: "In the way that the tangent touches the circle, fleetingly and at one point alone, and in the way that this touching—though not the point—prescribes the law according to which the tangent pursues its straight line on into infinity, the translation touches the sense of the original, fleetingly and at one infinitesimal point, in order then to pursue its own most proper trajectory in accord with the law of fidelity and in the freedom of linguistic motion" (60). Christina M. Smerick rightly praises the geometric metaphor Benjamin finds to describe the relationship between an original and its translation:

> [I]f the original is a circle, then translation is a tangent line touching that circle at but one point. Rather than attempting to mimic or reproduce the circle itself, which would be the impossible attempt fully to convey the meaning of a work, the tangent line brushes against it at a crucial place while continuing on into infinity. So too the translation does not mimic or reproduce the original, but rather touches upon the sense of the work lightly and at an "infinitely small point" in order to continue on its own course. That small point is the point of literal fidelity, which Hölderlin demonstrates so gracefully in his translation of *Antigone.* The infinite journey indicates the freedom in, and of, translation. What is most beautiful in this image is that point of contact. It symbolizes the effect not so much of the translation upon the original (the taking of meaning from the original and subsequent conversion into the second language) but of the original on the translation. This point resonates along the infinite line of translation. Its membership, if you will, as a point among infinite other points on that line changes the line itself.[14]

Benjamin himself cites Rudolf Pannwitz in order to demonstrate his point—the point on the periphery of the circle touched by pure, tangential translation. Pannwitz's words and his syntax perform what they constate, so

14. Christina M. Smerick, "Between the Garden and the Gathering: The Intertwining of Philosophy with Theology in Walter Benjamin." Ph.D. dissertation, DePaul University, 2003), 162–163.

that it is a mistake to "translate" them into something more comprehensible than the following:

> our transposings [*übertragungen*] even the best of them start with a false premise they want to germanize the hindu greek english instead of hinduizing greekifying putting a little english on the german. they have a much more noteworthy respect for the usages of their own language than for the spirit of the foreign work.... the translator's fundamental error is that he clings to the contingent state of his own language instead of letting that language be powerfully moved by the foreign tongue. especially when he is translating a quite distant language he must press back to the ultimate elements of that language itself where word image tone become one he must expand and deepen his own language by means of the foreign language one has no conception of the extent to which this is possible the extent to which every language can be transformed language distinguishing itself from language in practically the same way that dialect distinguishes itself from dialect though this occurs when one takes language not lightly but altogether seriously. (61)

Smerick concludes by noting that in the contact of tangent (one's own language, the "target" language) and circumference (the foreign, "original" language) it is the tangent that changes, not the circle. The alteration, expansion, and deepening of one's own language by the original, foreign language is precisely that which enables the line of the tangent to proceed to infinity— approaching, perhaps as the asymptote of the parabola, the pure language that, in Smerick's words, "resides in the secret heart of all utterances."[15]

As he nears the end of his own "Task," Benjamin once again refers to Hölderlin, this time more extensively: "Hölderlin's translations, especially the two Sophoclean tragedies, confirm this matter [namely, of the fleeting contact of original and translation] and every other essential aspect. The harmony of the languages in these translations is so profound that the sense is touched as though by the mere breeze that blows through a wind chime. Hölderlin's translations are primal images of the very form of translation" (61). For that very reason, however, a danger resides in them, "the monstrous and original danger of all translation" (62). The danger is that "the gates of such an expanded and thoroughly governed [*durchwalteten*] language slam shut and lock the translator in silence" (ibid.). Benjamin notes that these translations are Hölderlin's final works, suggesting that in them Hölderlin suffers Antigone's fate, if not the fate of the defeated Sphinx herself. "In them, the sense plunges from abyss to abyss, until it threatens to lose itself in the bottomless depths of language" (ibid.).

However, in the dramatic peroration of his text Benjamin adds that there is a possible foothold. No text other than that of sacred scripture can grant a

15. Ibid., 163.

foothold. In the sacred text, sense or meaning has ceased to be the watershed for the streams of language and revelation. Wherever the text, in its literalness, pertains immediately (that is, without a mediating sense) to "the true language," that is, to "truth" or to "doctrine" (*Lehre*), it is straightforwardly translatable. Translatable, that is to say, for the sake of language as such, if not for communication. Here, literalness and freedom of translation ought to work upon the model of an interlinear translation—seamlessly. "For to some degree·all great writings, but supremely so the sacred ones, contain between the lines their virtual translation" (ibid.). Benjamin's concluding sentence: "The interlinear version of the sacred text is the primal image or ideal of all translation" (ibid.).

Nothing might seem more foreign to the notion of the tragic absolute than this appeal to sacred teachings, or hieratic lore, and the atavistic notion of a "true language." Yet in a very real sense Hölderlin regards the Sophoclean text as a holy text, precisely as many Athenians themselves did. As we will see in chapter 9, Karl Reinhardt too emphasizes this religious dimension of Hölderlin's translations. As long as the hieratic sense of "truth" and "the true language" is thought in a way that deprives it of all authority and authoritarianism—though every institution of Judaism, Christianity, Islam, and every other "world religion" will struggle to maintain and expand that authority—Benjamin's essay can be helpful to us. Perhaps it is not too much to say that Benjamin's *Lehre*, his sacred lore, is absolutely ironically (and absolutely tragically) equivalent to Schelling's absolute mythology. The "purity" of its "truth," found nowhere else than in "pure language," is nothing other than the true task and the pure tribulation of the finite translator: his or her languishing—and anguishing—in the face of the *monstrous* task of translation.[16]

16. See the wonderful commentary by Carol Jacobs, *In the Language of Walter Benjamin* (Baltimore: Johns Hopkins University Press, 1999), "The Monstrosity of Translation," 75–90. In the spirit of the final lines of her chapter, which offers a monstrous demonstration of an interlinear "translation" of the opening of the Gospel of John, I offer the following interlinear translation of l. 926 of *Oedipus the Tyrant* (DKV 2:823; l. 910 in L), which is itself a line of sacred Sophoclean text. First, the Greek text; second, the translation by David Grene in C; third, the translation by F. Storr, B. A., in L; fourth, Hölderlin's translation; and fifth, a translation of Hölderlin's translation. The chorus, which now sounds very much like a priest of Apollo, speaks:

1. ἔρρει δὲ τὰ θεῖα.
2. God's service perishes.
3. Faith grows cold.
4. *Unglücklich aber gehet das Göttliche.*
5. Yet divinity wanders in misfortune.

With regard to Benjamin's figure of tangent line and circle for the target and original languages of translation, one must note that according to Benjamin the tangent proceeds into infinity after touching a foreign original. Hölderlin's account would be far more modest. He knows that curvilinear

As we proceed through the following chapters, let us remember that in Hölderlin's view one must go to Sophoclean tragedy as one goes to bear witness to the uncanny and altogether monstrous holy. If Schelling and Benjamin call it languor, Hölderlin will call it *Leiden*, "passion," "affliction," "suffering," *passio*.

Translating "Theatrality"

Bearing witness to the holy? Yes, but in a theater, not in a temple—even if, or precisely because, the theater has gone silent. In "The Wine God" (CHV 1:317), and in the first draft of "Bread and Wine" (CHV 1:378), Hölderlin laments the loss: *Warum schweigen auch sie, die alten heilgen Theater?* "Why have they too turned silent, the ancient holy theaters?" In the face of such stony silence, Hölderlin resolves to translate (for) the tragic theater, the theater of unpleasure. At the outset of Aeschylus's *Prometheus Bound* (l. 69; cf. 304), Hephaistos speaks of the unpleasant pleasure we experience in the tragic theater: ὁρᾷς θέαμα δυσθέατων ὄμμασιν, "You are watching a play that plays hard on the eyes."

Perhaps it is only philosophers who would think it an insult to say that a

---

and straight-line motion, the two planetary motions about which Kepler theorized, do not leave one another untouched. The centripetal pull of gravity prevents any straight-line motion from occurring in the universe; it also bends all circles and spheres out of shape. These facts impressed the young Hölderlin. For him, all planets and we ourselves proceed "in an excentric orbit," that is to say, in an elliptical orbit (an ἔκκεντρος κύκλος, Hipparchos called it) where neither straight line nor well-centered circle prevail. In the *Thalia* fragment of *Hyperion*, written in the summer of 1794, Hölderlin notes the elliptical development of a human life: two centers, or foci, determine its development, namely, the unicity that is granted it by its natural organization, on the one hand, and the education and formation that are applied to it, on the other. "The excentric orbit that the human being follows, both in general and in the particular, proceeding from one point (the more or less pure unicity) to the other point (the more or less completed formation), always seems, *in its essential directions*, to be equal to itself" (CHV 1:489). Perhaps the *seems* needs to be emphasized, however, inasmuch as *Hyperion* is all about the way in which the School of Destiny, which forms us, most often runs roughshod over the School of Nature. In the preface to the penultimate draft of *Hyperion*, Hölderlin is more succinct: "We follow the path of an excentric orbit; there is no other possible path from childhood to our completion" (CHV 1:558). In a late letter, from the year 1804, Hölderlin writes of "the excentric enthusiasm" of his Hesperian times, an enthusiasm he hopes he has resisted for the sake of achieving "Greek unicity" (CHV 2:930). He has already, during the previous year, written of Tiresias, the overseer of nature, entering on the scene of Greek tragedy in order to tear human beings away from the midpoint of their lives, snatching them off into "the excentric sphere of the dead" (CHV 2:311). This excentric sphere—the elliptical kingdom of the dead—will occupy us in the following chapters. For the moment, let us merely observe that for Hölderlin no line of text or life proceeds to infinity. Its orbit is elliptical. Ellipsis in Greek means shortfall. The sole infinity in Hölderlin is the infinite approximation of the asymptote. No perfect circles, no perfect originals, no hotline to the infinite, no lore. Translation for Hölderlin would therefore have to be something quite different from interlinearity—unless it were the monstrous kind of interlinearity demonstrated above and, more forcefully, in Carol Jacobs's fine chapter. On *die exzentrische Bahn*, see Wolfgang Schadewalt, "Das Bild der exzentrischen Bahn bei Hölderlin," *Hölderlin-Jahrbuch* (1952): 1–16.

poet and thinker of Hölderlin's stature is above all a great *director*. Philosophers prefer Plato to Pasolini, Bergson to Bergman. Yet Philippe Lacoue-Labarthe is undoubtedly right when he celebrates Hölderlin as a dramaturge who works at his craft with "an extreme precision" (*Métaphrasis*, 3). By contrast, Heidegger is one of those who feel they can ignore with impunity Hölderlin's devotion to the theater and to drama. In Lacoue-Labarthe's view, Heidegger's neglect of Hölderlin the dramaturge and theoretician of theater may be largely responsible for the lopsided reception of Hölderlin in the French and English-speaking worlds (4–5). This is not meant to detract in any way from the renown of the great hymns and elegies; it is said in order to affirm that there is another Hölderlin waiting to be discovered.

"Theatrality" is not "theatricality." Nothing is less theatrical, for example, than Tiresias in both *Oedipus the Tyrant* and *Antigone*. In each play the blind seer is led onto the stage in order to pronounce facts and destinies familiar to all—known to both the figures on the proscenium and the spectators in the theater. As we shall see, however, these scenes with Tiresias are at the very heart of Hölderlin's Sophoclean theater. What, then, is theatrality? Lacoue-Labarthe suggests convincingly that around 1800 Hölderlin manages to integrate his practices of poetry and philosophy by combining them in the project of μετάφρασις. That is to say, by the time he is working on the third draft of *The Death of Empedocles* and developing his plan to *translate* all of Sophocles' tragedies it becomes clear to him that "the tragic is . . . nothing other than philosophy itself" (14). Indeed, the tragic may be identified with what Kant views as the metaphysical drive in human beings as such—tragedy is *der Trieb der Vernunft*, the compulsion of reason itself (14–15). If Dame Philosophy is a tyrant, she herself is tragically driven.

Hölderlin turns to Empedocles of Acragas, not in search of some exotic backdrop and not out of nostalgia, not in order to restore the Golden Age of Greek theater; rather, he does so for the sake of *modern* theater—that is to say, for the theater of his own times. It is not simply that he wishes his own dramatic works to be performed at the court theater of Weimar. He clearly believes that by taking up the themes and characters of antiquity, whether of the philosopher Empedocles or the playwright Sophocles, he will be inviting his Hesperian contemporaries to "return to the foundation of theatrality" (47). Moreover, says Lacoue-Labarthe, what causes Hölderlin finally to surrender the project of *The Death of Empedocles* is his discovery—long in coming—that what the three drafts lack is precisely theatrality. The three versions of Hölderlin's drama reflect a mere *idea* of tragedy, argues Lacoue-Labarthe, the "speculative scenario" of a failed Platonic philosopher-king (48, 51). The re-

sult of Hölderlin's labors is not a piece of theater but "an exercise in elo-
quence," "an oratorio without music" (52). Hence the turn to Sophocles.

If we ask what it is that Lacoue-Labarthe takes "the tragic" as such to be,
the answer can be stated only quite cryptically at first: "The essence of the
tragic, for Hölderlin, rests on the absolute paradox of theophany" (30). He
adds, after a paragraph break: "Greek theophany is death" (ibid.). Whatever
the tragic conflict of a given tragedy may be, the absolute paradox of theophany—that is, of the god's coming to presence in the very figure of death—
demands that there be absolutely no resolution or conciliation. Indeed, tragedy is "without issue, produces nothing—no meaning, if you will" (70).
Lacoue-Labarthe emphasizes the themes of (1) the double infidelity of god
and mortal, (2) space and time, experienced as conditions of limit, or finitude,
(3) the categorical turning away of divinity as such, along with the mourning
(*Trauer*) that such a turning enjoins in mortals, and (4) the conception of divinity itself in terms of finite temporality (35–40). No matter how cryptic
these four motifs may seem at this point, they will serve as spurs to the discussion in the remaining chapters of the present book. Each of the four culminates in the matter Hölderlin calls *caesura*, the counterrhythmic interruption that occurs as Tiresias's intervention in the plays. "The caesura is the
condition of the possibility of manifestation, of the (re)presentation [*Darstellung*] of the tragic," writes Lacoue-Labarthe (73). He adds, "That is the law,
or if you prefer, the principle of its theatrality" (ibid.). Tiresias, to repeat, is the
avatar of such presentation, or representation, even if—or precisely because—
he interrupts the action of the plot and slows the momentum of the scenes.
Tiresias, the utterly untheatrical seer, halts the action in precisely the same
way that the inimical power of nature stops a human life, which is to say, tragically. Nature tears a human life away from the midpoint of its everyday preoccupations and sweeps it off into what Hölderlin will call "the excentric
sphere of the dead," a sphere to be discussed in greater detail in the following
chapters.

In the interim, we may relate Lacoue-Labarthe's equation of theophany
and death to Jean-Pierre Vernant's account of the masked god, Dionysos, as
the god of appearances and the divine sponsor of tragedy. At the outset and
conclusion of his article, "The Masked Dionysus of Euripides' *Bacchae*," Vernant demonstrates that what Lacoue-Labarthe calls *theatrality* may also be
seen in Euripides' great final (or penultimate) contribution to the theater of
classical Athens (VV 381–383; 411–412). For here too the matter of theatrical representation as such is bound up with the epiphany of the god, who, as
we noted above, appears in baffling disguise. As far as King Pentheus is con-

cerned, of course, the redoubled disguises of the god culminate in the figure of death. The ambiguous mask of Dionysos in the play therefore reveals something about both the appearing god and the speculative—and even ontotheological—character of the tragedy. Vernant writes:

> The poet sets him [i.e., Dionysos] on stage as the god who himself stages his own epiphany there, in the theater, revealing himself not only to the protagonists in the drama but also to the spectators seated on the tiered steps, by manifesting his divine presence through the unfolding of the tragic drama—drama that is, moreover, specifically placed under his religious patronage. It is as if, throughout the spectacle, even as he appears on stage beside the other characters in the play, Dionysus was also operating at another level, behind the scene, putting the plot together and directing it toward *dénouement*. (VV 381–382)

Something of the ontotheological import of *The Bacchae* is reflected in the fact that, whereas the characters of the play see in the theatrical mask of the god nothing but the sign of the god's emissary or "missionary" in Thebes, the spectators know that the Lydian foreigner is actually the disguised god himself, come to reward his followers but to wreak vengeance on those who have not acknowledged him. Vernant underscores the ambiguity of the mask and thus the ambiguity of theatrality as such. Worn simultaneously by the Lydian stranger and the god, the mask exhibits

> both the affinities and the contrast between on the one hand the *tragic* mask that sets the seal upon the presence of a particular character, giving him a firm identity, and on the other the *religious* mask whose fascinating gaze establishes an imperious, obsessive, and overwhelming presence, the presence of a being that is not where it seems to be, a being that is also elsewhere, perhaps inside one, perhaps nowhere. It is the presence of one who is absent. It is a "smiling" mask (ll. 434, 1021), unlike the usual tragic masks, a mask that is consequently different from all the rest, a mask displaced, disconcerting, and that, seen there on the theater stage, is an echo that calls to mind the enigmatic face of some of the religious masks of the god used in the civic religion. (VV 382–383)

At the end of the chapter, Vernant returns to the question of theatrality—that is, to repeat, the question of the epiphany of the godhead in tragic representation as the figure of death. He notes that Euripides' Dionysos is a god who is "as tragic as human existence" itself (VV 411). The only way one can come to understand the masked god is "to enter into his game oneself" (ibid.). "And only a tragic poet is capable of doing that, having reflected on his art, conscious of the special skills at his command, since he is past master at casting the spells of dramatic illusion" (ibid.). Such Dionysian spells produce the most bizarre effects, at once pleasureful and terrifying. "Transposed to the stage, the magic ploys of the god undergo a transmutation. They harmonize with the techniques of the dramatist and the enchantment of his poetry and thus, be they most terrible or most sweet, they contribute to the pleasure of the dramatic spectacle" (VV 411–412). Vernant stresses the fact that Dionysos challenges the city of Athens with "practices that, either openly or covertly, present aspects of eccentricity" (VV 402). *Eccentricity*, taken literally as *excentricity*, is the very word Hölderlin will use to designate the sphere of the dead to which tragedy transports us. It is therefore almost as though Vernant is writing with the hand of Hölderlin when he observes of the Dionysian mask, with its gaping, staring eyes, that its gaze is hollow, vacuous, "indicating the absence of a god who is somewhere else but who tears one out of oneself, makes one lose one's bearings in one's everyday, familiar life, and who takes possession of one just as if this empty mask were now pressed to one's own face, covering and transforming it."[17]

Within the excentric, decentered, and riven sphere that tragedy opens up, Dionysian or tragic (re)presentation will give us whatever is left of an essentially masked divinity itself—in the figure of death. *Unglücklich aber gehet das Göttliche*, says Sophocles in Hölderlin's translation of *Oedipus the Tyrant*. Divinity limps. Such is the essence of theatrality for Hölderlin, and the remaining chapters of the present book will go in search of it.

---

17. VV 396; see also "Features of the Mask," VV 189–206, esp. 204–205. Dionysos is so omnipresent in Vernant's account of tragedy that even his chapter on Aeschylus contains the following sentence: "It is in this respect that Greek tragedy derives from Dionysus, the god of confusion and transgression" (VV 264). Dionysos is thus the god of theatrality.

A SMALL NUMBER OF HOUSES
IN THE TRAGIC UNIVERSE

9

Fortune-blessed are those in times
that taste no ill;
For once a house is stirred by the
celestial ones
It is not lacking in madness, not
lacking
In times to come, when the house
Increases and multiplies.

　　　　—SOPHOCLES/HÖLDERLIN,
　　　　Antigone, ll. 604–608

ἰὼ, ἰώ, δῶμα δῶμα

Alas, alas! the house, the house!

　　　　—AESCHYLUS,
　　　　Agamemnon, l. 410

Tragedy, according to Aristotle, is no small matter. It is big, as big as a house. Tragedy has size and grandeur, its elevated status deriving from its plot and characters, its action and diction. Tragedy is serious. It gives serious pleasure, provoking fears and evoking ecstasies of compassion, then blowing them all away. No form of embodied presentation is as important for serious individuals and for a serious city as tragedy is. And yet the stories enacted in the tragedies have their source in a very small number of houses—very special houses. Tragedy therefore ought to be a parochial matter, involving as it does only a handful of families, which have very particular and very peculiar stories to tell.

Yet Plato was exercised enough to construct his entire polity—not merely in one of its particulars but from top to bottom—in opposition to tragedy. Aristotle in turn was concerned enough to rescue the art of tragedy for philosophy, as though much if not all of his ethics and politics could be best viewed through its prism, and as though perhaps even physics and the philosophy beyond physics (μετὰ τὰ φυσικά) were somehow bound up with that art. Centuries later, Hölderlin found his own voice in Greek tragedy. His novel *Hyperion* and mourning-play *The Death of Empedocles* became steps *toward* Sophoclean tragedy, not departures from or progressions beyond it. It was as though, for Hölderlin, all the world—and every mortal and every god in it—depended on that small number of plays that told of an even smaller number of households.

It is already much too much to want to write about both Aristotle and Hölderlin. The present chapter will therefore restrict its inquiry to a few lines of Aristotle's *Poetics* and several passages from Hölderlin's "Notes" to his translations of Sophocles' *Oedipus the Tyrant* and *Antigone.*[1]

At the Center of Aristotle's Thought: *The Poetics*

In chapters 13 and 14 of his *Poetics* Aristotle identifies the types of events that excellent tragedies portray. These events have to do with domestic economy and household management in a very broad sense. How the tragic poet manages the presentation of the events themselves, husbanding their portrayal on the proscenium and in the orchestra, will decide whether or not the pleasure that is peculiar to tragedy will eventuate in the spectators. The οἶκος governs everything here: in two pages of text Aristotle uses cognates of this word five times.

Tragic events involve the change of fortune in an ἐπιεικής, that is, a "decent," just, and equitable human being, one who is perhaps not entirely noble, serious, and elevated—not fully divine, but certainly superior to us. Some grave error in judgment and action drives the hero or heroine from happiness to misery. The "proper pleasure" of tragedy requires such a reversal. "Proper" here means the pleasure that most perfectly defines tragedy, the pleasure that is "at home" in tragedy (1453b 11: ἡδονὴν ἀπὸ τραγῳδίας . . . τὴν οἰκείαν). Were the change of fortune to go from misery to happiness, we would find ourselves moving out of the household of tragedy into that of comedy (1453a 36: τῆς κομῳδίας οἰκεία).

Euripides, the "most tragic of the poets," never made this mistake. Even if he often failed to "manage well" in other respects (1453a 29: μὴ εὖ οἰκονομεῖ), Euripides always remained within the walls of tragedy. He did so by selecting only those houses for his dramas in which the events and reversals

---

1. For the Greek text of Aristotle's *Poetics,* see the Oxford Classical Text *Aristotelis De arte poetica liber,* ed. Rudolf Kassel (Oxford: Oxford University Press, 1965); I have also used English translations by Richard Janko (Indianapolis: Hackett Publishing, 1987) and Ingram Bywater, in Richard McKeon, ed., *The Basic Works of Aristotle* (New York: Random House, 1966), 1455–1487, along with the French translation by Michel Magnien, *Poétique* (Paris: Livre de Poche, n.d.).

of fortune were inherently tragic. For the tragic is a matter of special families or family lines (γένη, perhaps what Heidegger, following Trakl, calls *Geschlechter*, and what Gabriel García Márquez, on the final page of *One Hundred Years of Solitude*, calls *estirpes*, and Henry David Thoreau *stirps*)[2] and special houses or households (οἰκεῖαι), such as the family of Oedipus—that is to say, the House of Labdacus, son of Cadmus and Harmony—and those like it.

Those like it are few. Rare though they may be, however, these tragic families are essential to the art, presumably inasmuch as they reveal something catastrophic about the city and its citizens, and possibly about nature and human nature, perhaps about all being. For if these special families and rare households were mere exceptions to the rule, if they were merely quirky or kinky, no one would pay them any mind and their stories would be pointless eccentricities. Kinky families may provide the storylines for burlesque and comedy, but surely not for tragedy. No, such tragic families and houses are memorable for serious reasons; they are remembered as having suffered serious setbacks, and for a long time now. The chorus of Aeschylus's *Seven against Thebes* cries, "Oh, the calamities of this house [ὦ πόνοι δόμων], so new, yet blended with ancient evils [νέοι παλαιοῖσι συμμιγεῖς κακοῖς]!" (ll. 739–741).

Why and how do the poets remember them? Schelling has already informed us of the answer he finds in Aristotle: "At first the poets told the stories they picked up wherever by great good luck they found them," says Aristotle; in Aristotle's own day, however, the "finest tragedies" were "constructed around a few households" (1453a 18–19: νῦν δὲ περὶ ὀλίγας οἰκίας). In other words, chance, τύχη, originally played a role in the availability of these myths, fables, and sagas, although by Aristotle's time poetic τέχνη made the selection of those households on the basis of insight. True, the oligarchy of households in the present instance was a disastrous one, and the insight that guided their selection must itself have rested on a familiarity with disaster. For these were families and houses "which happen to have had dreadful things done to them, or to have done them themselves" (21–22). Here we encounter a second moment of τύχη—actually, the first moment in the order of the things themselves, the moment when the deeds themselves were done. Here, in line 21, the troubling word συμβέβηκεν, troubling especially for physics and metaphysics, refers to those dreadful, horrifying, and uncanny things (δεινά) that were either suffered or committed (22: ἢ παθεῖν δεινὰ ἢ

---

2. The English word *stirp* is now archaic. Thoreau uses it in the sense intended here in *Walden*. See the Variorium ed. (cited in note 6 of ch. 8, above), 199, l. 4 f.b. For a use of γένος in the sense of "House," see Sophocles, *Oedipus at Colonus*, l. 965.

ποιῆσαι) in those rare and special houses where, by chance, the poets first found their stories.

Aristotle repeats the same set of claims at the end of chapter 14. There he is describing the most suitable kinds of incidents for a tragic plot, finding them precisely in the family home, where loving relationships (what Hölderlin will call "the more tender relationships," *zärtere Verhältnisse*) ought to prevail. When enemies fight or strangers quarrel no one is surprised; neither dread nor compassion is aroused in such cases. "But when suffering happens within loving relationships [1453b 19: ἐν ταῖς φιλίαις ἐγγένεται τὰ πάθη], such as brother against brother, son against father, mother against son or son against mother . . . this is what we are looking for."

This is what we are *looking for*? If so, then what we are looking for is what Empedocles sees as the origin of all strife and what the treatise on friendship in the *Nicomachean Ethics* decries as the most horrid of crimes, to wit, a child raising its hand against the father (1160a 5). (One might have thought that raising one's hand against a *mother*, who is the very excess of loving, especially where her own children are concerned, is still more horrifying [1159a 27, 1161b 27, 1166a 9, 1168a 25]; in either case, however, the crimes in question are matters of house and home, where *philia* ought to have been engendered.) Tragic art, the highest and most serious of poetic arts, superior to epic, dithyramb, comedy, and all the rest, searches out those households in which *philia* has gone missing and strife is on a spree. Why? The short answer, which presumably was enough to satisfy Euripides, is that the *pleasure* that is at home in tragedy requires such households for the solicitation, arousal, refinement, distillation, and purgation of pity, fear, and all such emotions.[3]

The longer answer is that the pleasure elicited by embodied presentations of the sufferings of the rarest households produces serious art, art that is replete with the pleasures of music and μίμησις, art that is vivid, concentrated, and in every way *grand*—the art that presumably teaches us most about the world and our place in it. Precisely in the rarest households we learn some-

---

3. Jacob Bernays, in his classic work on catharsis, emphasizes the importance of *Lustgefühle* (that is, of the hedonic) in tragedy, and specifically in tragic catharsis. He underscores Aristotle's insistence that even if Euripides got everything else wrong he was still the most cathartic—and hence the most tragic—of poets. Not until the end of his monograph on catharsis, however, does Bernays broach the theme of the present chapter, which is the paradox of a small number of houses in the tragic universe. We will therefore have to return to his extraordinary text. On Euripides as the most tragic and most cathartic of poets, see Jacob Bernays, *Grundzüge der verlorenen Abhandlung des Aristoteles über die Wirkung der Tragödie*, ed. Karlfried Gründer (Hildesheim: Georg Olms Verlag, 1970 [orig. publ. 1857]), 8–9, and esp. 41, cited henceforth in the body of my text by page number.

thing serious about the universe of being, insofar as that universe enjoins or permits suffering:

> It is for this reason, as was said a moment ago, that the tragedies are not about a great number of families [1454a 9–10: οὐ περὶ πολλὰ γένη]. The poets went in search [10: ζητοῦντες] of these families in order to render such situations in their plots; they found them, not by means of their art, but by good fortune [10–11: οὐκ ἀπὸ τέχνης ἀλλ᾽ ἀπὸ τύχης εὗρον]. They saw themselves constrained to return always and again to those same households, the ones that happened to suffer these same passions [12–13: ἀναγκάζονται οὖν ἐπὶ ταύτας τὰς οἰκίας ἀπαντᾶν ὅσαις τὰ τοιαῦτα συμβέβηκε πάθη].

Accident (τὸ συμβεβηκός, *accidens*), fortune or chance (τύχη), and necessity (ἀνάγκη) are brought together here in a way that should give philosophers pause: *by chance* the poets found their way to those families in which *by accident* dreadful things occurred; yet the dreadful character of those sufferings themselves derived from some dire *necessity* at work in the families concerned, so that συμβεβηκός here seems to have the double (and well-nigh contradictory) sense of a pure *contingency* that in itself (or at least in and for this household) was *absolutely essential*, or at least *unavoidable*, such that, finally, *by necessity*, and on the very basis of their know-how (τέχνη), the poets had to go back to these accident-prone or star-crossed families again and again for their plots. Indeed, there is something eminently Greek in this apparent confusion of contingency and necessity. Eteocles speaks of a defender of Thebes trying his luck and taking his chances with necessity: ἐξιστορῆσαι μοῖραν ἐν χρείᾳ τύχης, "He would seek out his fate in the necessity of contingency" (Aeschylus, *Seven against Thebes*, l. 506). It is no accident that Aeschylus, like Sophocles and Euripides after him, had to revert again and again to the royal house of Thebes for his fables.

Let us back up a bit, however. So many things in the universe of being lend themselves to embodied enactment or *mimēsis:* the music of flute, lyre, and voice, and in voice language, harmony, and rhythm; all the forms of mime and dance, all the rhythms and gestures that body forth the entire human panoply of characters, passions, and actions; and, to end a list that could go on, all the genres of literature, whether dithyramb, epic, or comedy. Further, embodied enactment is the natural source of the pleasure we experience in learning—and all human beings, as we know from watching our children, desire to know and to learn. Yet if so many things in the wide universe offer themselves to *mimēsis,* whence in all the world the need for that small number of contingent, dreadful, necessitous, and above all "chancy" houses?

Let us back up a bit farther and return to basic definitions. "Tragedy, then, is the embodied presentation of an action that is serious" (1449b 24–25: μίμησις πράξεως σπουδαίας). Serious; not playful but elevated in character; noble. Serious and complete, "as having magnitude" (μέγεθος). It is otiose to argue whether magnitude is meant mathematically or dynamically here, as extension or grandeur. For tragedy becomes grand when it surrenders its petty plots, its merely improvised sketches and satires (1449a 19). The language of grand tragedy is "embellished" or "refined," as each of its parts requires, and the events of tragedy are acted out, not narrated. Finally, tragedy moves us to pity and fear, "purifying us of all such emotions" (1449b 27–28: τὴν τῶν τοιούτων παθημάτων κάθαρσιν). Tragedy embodies— and bodies forth in—the deeds of serious characters (1448a 2: σπουδαίους), elevated personages of excellence and virtue (3: ἀρετή); or, at least, tragedy depicts its characters in such a way that they appear to be better than we are (4: βελτίονας, 12: βελτίους). The persons who are born into that small number of special households which lend tragedy its incidents and accidents are "better" than the norm, and they prove it by killing their fathers and sleeping with their mothers, or by serving up their brother's children to him on a platter, or by sacrificing their own children in order to assure the success of a military adventure, so that they in turn may be killed by their wives, who for their part will be killed by . . . and so on and on.

Why and how take pleasure in such dire embodied enactments? Aristotle hints at the answer when he tells us that the pleasures of *mimēsis*, by which the human animal learns whatever it does learn, are extreme pleasures—or, rather, pleasures taken in extremes. They are "best felt in the perfect embodiment of the forms of the most repugnant animals or of cadavers" (1448b 11–12: οἷον θηρίων τε μορφὰς τῶν ἀτιμοτάτων καὶ νεκρῶν). Mimetic pleasure, which is most intense in the extreme repugnance felt toward the objects of its embodiments, perhaps kindles the secret joy of all learning and the very ἔρως of νοῦς—as almost every folk tale, *Märchen*, or nursery rhyme we recite to our children attests. The repugnance of the deeds and the sufferings of our betters, and especially the catastrophic reversal of fortune our betters undergo, may be precisely what makes poetry more philosophical and more serious (1451b 5–6: φιλοσοφώτερον καὶ σπουδαιότερον) than scholarly inquiries such as the one in which we are now engaged. Whereas scholarly ἱστορίαι merely recount a succession of past events (τὸ γενόμενα), tragic dramas, delving back even farther into the past—indeed, all the way back into its quasi-mythical, heroic period—enact in an embodied way what *may* happen (τὸν δὲ οἷα ἂν γένοιτο), or, as a recent French translation puts it, *ce à quoi l'on peut s'attendre* (117). Tragic dramas thus speak to the universal or general (7: τὰ καθόλου) with regard to verisimilitude and necessity (9: τὸ εἰκὸς ἢ τὸ ἀναγκαῖον), even though the contingencies depicted in them are attributed to particular contingent characters. In other words, a small number of quite singular characters in a small number of very special households apparently reveal—if only in uncanny and unhomelike hints—what the universal condition of humankind may be. Which would suggest how desperately all philosophy *needs* tragedy.

Is such a reading tenable? Can one really take the battered, tattered text of Περὶ ποιητικῆς as a prism and examine Aristotle's entire philosophical position through it? To see science through the optics of art, but art through the optics of life: such was Nietzsche's project. Would it be legitimate to make one further cut, add one more facet to the prism, and attribute that prism not only to Nietzsche but also to Aristotle? To see science through the optics of art, art through the optics of life—and life through the optics of tragedy? Nietzsche never thought otherwise. Neither did that other renowned student of Professor Friedrich Ritschl, Jacob Bernays.

At the end of his remarkable work on catharsis, cited several pages above, Bernays demonstrates Euripides' "most tragic" quality by showing that precisely this poet is "most cathartic" (41). This identification of catharsis and tragedy sends Bernays along a path that leads to the very paradox of "a small number of houses in the tragic universe." For in his inquiry into the homeopathic nature of catharsis Bernays is driven to put the question of the nature and scope of tragic pleasure. Tragic pleasure, like every pleasure, is *ecstatic.* "For all types of *pathos* are essentially ecstatic; through them the human being is set *outside itself*" (44). There is thus a sort of ecstatic *Urpathos* that characterizes humankind—not merely those few catastrophic humans who live in a small number of houses but virtually every citizen who attends the tragedy and observes the fate of the catastrophic ones. Moreover, this *Urpathos* is essentially (as Nietzsche will later say) powerful and pleasurable. No matter how severe the pain or profound the mournfulness, a certain sweetness accompanies them; there is a certain honey that wells up in anger, a certain delight at the very bottom of deep despondency. How to define that sweetness? It arises in each case, according to Bernays's account of Aristotle's *Rhetoric,* from the twofold action of a sudden agitation, shuddering, and even shattering (φρίττειν, *frisson, Erschütterung*), followed by an equally sudden restoration of equanimity in the soul. The "solicitation" of affect that occurs in tragedy is therefore essentially ecstatic and hedonic, no matter how dire the affect itself may be. The human personality—and, if Schelling is right, the divine personality as well—is expanded or dilated in an experience of the affect, and a certain pleasure rises to envelop the object that looms and threatens us from the stage. The model for this twofold operation, according to Bernays, is ecstatic possession by the god Dionysos, with Maenadic-Bacchantic possession in turn resting on the "power of motion and frenzied song" at work "in the universe," *im Weltall* (47).

Music and dance, at work in the universe? Catharsis, according to Bernays, has to do with the depiction of human destiny and even the destiny of the world as such in sound and in motion. It is as though Bernays has been reading Schelling's *Philosophy of Art*. Aristotle's achievement is to have seen the workings of fear and pity as exposing nothing less than the eurhythmic *Urform* of the human character as such and as a whole: no matter how conspicuously the *individuality* of the person or personage on the stage who inspires pity and fear may come to the fore, that individuality must remain in proximity to the *Urform*. The individual thus becomes comprehensible "for the entire human race," *für das ganze Menschengeschlecht* (49). When compassion, or "pity," achieves the upper hand in the cathartic struggle between fear and pity, so that the profoundly moved spectator stops rotating on the axis of his or her own fears and surrenders to the centrifugal force elicited by the players on the proscenium, he or she witnesses "the frightening, sublime laws of the universe" (50). The shattering affect "loosens" the spectator, opens him or her to a confrontation with universal fate; his or her ecstatic shudder and ensuing calm "in the face of the universe" turn out to be supremely pleasurable. Whether such pleasure can be subsumed under the more general categories of pleasure in learning and delight in recognition, or whether the reverse is true, namely, that all recognition and learning share in some sense in the ecstasy of agitation and restoration of tranquillity in the psyche, so that tragedy would be the primal scene of human cognition, as it were, Bernays does not speculate. In any case, tragedy makes palpable our mortal fate. Even though Aristotle is reluctant to discuss the Μοῖρα, the sisters of destiny or fate, unless in the form of τύχη (which, however, Bernays does not mention), he does show us how tragedy causes the spectator to confront "the rule of the universal law of the world," *dem Walten des allgemeinen Weltgesetzes* (ibid.). In the final sentence of his extraordinary work, Bernays bends back to modify the beginning of his monograph, which may have been excessively critical of Lessing's "moral" interpretation of catharsis. Bernays cites Goethe's words,

Im Erstarren such' ich nicht mein Heil,
Das Schaudern ist der Menschheit bester Theil.

> I seek not my salvation in a frozen heart,
> Shuddering is humanity's very best part. (52)

With the tragic shudder and its attendant shattering and reestablishment of equanimity, its attendant *pleasure*, the suffering members of a small number of houses initiate the rest of us into the far-flung tragic universe.[4]

So much for Bernays's Aristotle, the Aristotle of *The Poetics*, read hedonically-cathartically. Yet what about Aristotle generally, Aristotle as The Philosopher of the tradition, Aristotle in every nook and cranny of his philosophy? No doubt, certain sites in the Aristotelian corpus would be more accommodating than others to the reading proposed here. For example, as we saw in the foregoing chapter, Kevin Thomas Miles argues that the need for what is translated as *equity* in *Nicomachean Ethics* (5:10) exposes the tragic character of all justice. For the law must declare in universals, but universals never speak to the particulars that justice must respect—unless they do so in and as tragedy, which, we recall, speaks to the universal precisely in the deeds and fates of contingent individuals. "Equity," ἐπιείκεια (we have already seen the word in Aristotle's description of the "decent" or equitable human being who must serve as the tragic hero), is that "fittingness" or "suitability" of what is "meet and just" that must supplement the law if there is to be justice. Aristotle writes:

> What creates the problem is that it is the equitable that is just—not the legally just, but a correction of legal justice. The reason is that all law is universal, but about some things it is not possible to make a universal statement that will be correct. In those cases, then, in which it is necessary to speak universally, but not possible to do so correctly, the law takes the usual case, though it is not ignorant of the possibility of error. And it is none the less correct; for the error is not in the law nor in the legislator but in the nature of the thing, since the matter of practical affairs is of this kind from the start. (*Nic. Eth.* 5:10; 1137b 10–20)

The error is in the nature of the thing—not as a fly in the ointment but as a flaw in being. The logic of the supplement is never more relentless in its es-

---

4. For an incisive discussion of Aristotle on κάθαρσις, including the "debate" between Aristotle and Lessing, see Max Kommerell, *Lessing und Aristoteles: Untersuchung über die Theorie der Tragödie,* 5th ed. (Frankfurt am Main: V. Klostermann, 1984 [orig. publ. 1940]), esp. 50–62 and ch. 1. Kommerell sees clearly that the issue of catharsis has to do with both pleasure (of a peculiar sort) and shattering, *Erschütterung*, and that this very conjunction banishes the tragic from the realm of what is traditionally conceived of as "aesthetic." Yet tragic experience ought to be at the very heart of the aesthetic. Kommerell concludes, in italics: "*At the very commencement of European aesthetics, the concept of the aesthetic is thereby canceled and surpassed* [aufgehoben]" (58). See also the excellent essay on Hölderlin's caesura and Aristotle's concepts of enigma, metaphor, and catharsis by Elizabeth B. Sikes, "The Enigmatic Burden of Metaphor in Hölderlin's Poetics of Tragedy," in *"Es bleibt aber eine Spur / Doch eines Wortes": Zur späten Hymnik und Tragödientheorie Friedrich Hölderlins,* ed. Christoph Jamme and Anja Lemke (Paderborn: Wilhelm Fink Verlag, 2004), 379–399.

sentially tragic character than it is in the supplementation of legal justice by equity. As we also recall from the previous chapter, it is precisely Hölderlin who describes the difficulty so well when he refers to Sophocles' *Antigone* and to the more intrinsic "nexus of life" that must unite universal and particular.

Not only justice and equity, but many other matters in the *Nicomachean Ethics* may also strike us as essentially tragic: the insufficiency of virtue or excellence for happiness, the residual need for prosperity and great good luck in the virtuous life, the inevitable acknowledgment of death and transience in Solon's affirmation, "He *was* happy," the incapacity of φρόνησις to offer anything like assurance of right or fitting action, the imprecision of ethical deliberation and moral theory, the dispersion of "the good," the identification of "the better" as always "the more difficult," the wish of friends that they may spend their days and lives together—as a *wish*, and, to end a list that could go on, the very fact that the good is what we *aim at* rather than possess. In a word, and it is Martha Nussbaum's word, the entire *fragility* of goodness.[5]

By contrast, it is doubtless difficult if not impossible—prior to Nietzsche—to regard Aristotelian circular motion, whether in the heavens or in the mind, as essentially tragic. Yet precisely how such eternal circuits are to be thought as proper to finite, embodied human existence on this earth is a grand (and perhaps tragic) aporia.[6] If ideas or forms, thought as the being of things,

---

5. See Martha Nussbaum, *The Fragility of Goodness: Luck and Ethics in Greek Tragedy and Philosophy* (New York: Cambridge University Press, 1986). Roberto Calasso comments on Solon's affirmation, reported by both Herodotus and Aristotle, as follows. Solon is visiting Croesus, who wants to impress the Athenian not only with his wealth but with his happiness. Solon counters that an anonymous old Athenian who dies in battle has a better chance at happiness than the flourishing Croesus. Solon "is explaining the Greek paradox as far as happiness is concerned: that one arrives at it only in death. Happiness is an element of life which, before it can come into being, demands that life disappear. If happiness is a quality that sums up the whole man, then it must wait until a man's life is complete in death. [¶] This paradox doesn't exist in isolation. On the contrary, it is only one of the many paradoxes of wholeness to which the Greeks were so sensitive. Their basis can be found in the language itself: τέλος, the Greek word par excellence, means at once 'perfection,' 'completion,' 'death'. . . . Never has such an effective circumlocution been found for telling a truth that, if told straight, would be too brutal, and perhaps not even true anymore: that happiness does not exist" (RC 160). See the opening lines of Sophocles' *Women of Trachis* for the classic formulation of the dilemma of happiness and death. In the play itself, Herakles' wife, Deianeira, speculates, after so many years of her husband's absence, that he may have "attained his life's goal," ὡς ἢ τελευτὴν τοῦ βίου μέλλει τελεῖν, which is to say, that he may be dead (l. 79). Oedipus, while at Colonus (l. 1473), speaks to his daughters of his βίου τελευτή, the goal or end of his life; soon thereafter (ll. 1530–1531), Theseus confirms Oedipus's passage to the goal or end of his life, τέλος τοῦ ζῆν (cf. l. 1551: τὸν τελευταῖον βίον). The word takes on a more ominous sense when Clytaimestra prays to Zeus, Zeus the Accomplisher, Ζεῦ Ζεῦ τέλειε, begging him to help her accomplish her plans, τὰς ἐμὰς εὐχὰς τέλει, since we know that she is planning to "accomplish" Agamemnon at his bath (ll. 973–974, 1107). In turn, such "accomplishment" is Orestes' plan for her, which he too expresses as τελεῖται (Aeschylus, *Choephoroi*, l. 384).

6. See Aristotle, *Physics* 8:9, *Metaphysics* Λ:6, *On the Soul* 1:3, and elsewhere; and Jacques Derrida, "Ousia and Gramme," in *Margins of Philosophy*, tr. Alan Bass (Chicago: University of Chicago Press, 1982), 29–67, esp. 52–53: "This is what will not budge from Aristotle to Hegel. The prime mover, as 'pure act,' . . . is pure presence. As such, it animates all movement by means of the desire it

cannot be separated from the things, as Aristotle insists they cannot, then Aristotle's own anti-Platonism militates against the putative separability of the thinking soul—which is in a way all things—from the body. (We will later hear Hölderlin refer to "the divinely wrestling body.") That would bring us closer to a tragic conception of being, perhaps closer than Aristotle himself may have desired—although in this he and we would be constrained, as it were, by the things themselves (*Met.* 1:9). Thus the question raised of old, raised now and always, "is always the subject of doubt"; as a dubious matter, the question of being (τὶ τὸ ὄν . . .) invariably broaches the tragic. For "if nothing is by accident perishable" (*Met.* 10:10), then perishing belongs to the essence, and not to accident. To the essence of *perishable things alone,* one has always replied. Yet the aura of those perishable things—the aura of deleterious time, chance, and accident in all our houses—radiates outward to the putatively perfect circles of the universe of being, contaminating even them with tragedy. While eternal being, utterly unmoved, moves perishable beings as the object of their desire as well as their thought (*Met.* 12:7), it must surely hope that nothing comes to shatter the narcissistic circle of its autonoesis and autoerotics. Yet that very hope shows that Aristotle's god, his unmoved mover, never feels the delight of loving, which in Aristotle's own view is the superior delight. For loving, not being loved, is the dream of the finest friend and the most energetic mother. Indeed, as Schelling would have affirmed, the *hope* for autonomy is evidence of rupture itself: Io's interruption of Prometheus's wretched solitude, Semele's and Danaë's and Alkmene's interruption of Zeus's putatively absolute sway. Such ruptures, whether of love or (other forms of) suffering, preside over the very birth of tragedy. Schelling's word for these scissions driven by love and desire, we remember, is *Sehnsucht.*

Arguably, there are an infinite number of places in the Aristotelian corpus as a whole where the optics of tragedy enable us to see Aristotle's problems

---

inspires. It is the good, and the supremely desirable. Desire is the desire of presence. Like movement, Hegel calls the *telos* that puts movement in motion, and that orients becoming toward itself, the absolute concept or subject. The transformation of parousia into *self*-presence, and the transformation of the supreme being into a subject thinking itself, and assembling itself near itself in knowledge, does not interrupt the fundamental tradition of Aristotelianism. The concept as absolute subjectivity itself thinks itself, is for itself and near itself, has no exterior, and it assembles, erasing them, its time and its difference in self-presence. This may be put in Aristotle's language: νόησις νοήσεως, the thought of thought, the pure act, the prime mover, the lord who, himself thinking himself, is subjugated to no objectivity, no exteriority, remaining immobile in the infinite movement of the circle and of the return to self." It will not be possible to show here how the structure of the trace, writing, *différance,* and ellipsis in Derrida's view disturbs the continuity of the metaphysical tradition. Such a disturbance reveals a deeper continuity in our traditions than that represented by metaphysics, namely, the continuity of *tragic thinking,* extending perhaps from the time of Gilgamesh to our own era. To be sure, that continuity is all about what Hölderlin will call *caesura,* or counterrhythmic interruption.

and achievements in a new light. While it may not be the usual way to read and teach Aristotle, the prism of tragedy reveals possibilities for thinking through a number of classic problems of philosophy in an unfamiliar way. Here, then, is a cursory list of sites—a dozen of them, seven from the *Organon*, five from the *Physics*—almost at random, simply as a beginning and a mere indication.

1. In the *Organon*, the problematic relation of οὐσία to "individuals" in a "primary" or "secondary" sense, the apparently inevitable slippage between any given *this* and the genus to which it belongs, creates a situation in which we form impressions that are "not strictly true" (*Cat.* 5). For philosophers, but also for lovers, such slippage can be tragic.

2. The "awkward results" of the reign of necessity, which operates in the "fullness of time," also point to a tragic situation. For necessity does not seem to admit of any alternatives in human destinies, alternatives that could be introduced by "deliberation and action" (*De int.* 9).

3. The nondemonstrability of "basic premises" and "basic truths," about which "it is hard to be sure" (*Post. Anal.* 1:3, 9), would surely be tragic for one who desperately wants to know. Such as the philosopher. Likewise:

4. The possible untruth of valid argumentation (*Post. Anal.* 1:19).

5. The unavailability of being (τὸ ὄν) to genus-species differentiation, and the concomitant inexhaustibility of being. As Aristotle puts it, laconically, "One can always ask why" (*Post. Anal.* 2:7).

6. The risky induction of primary principles: "It is like a rout in battle stopped first by one man making a stand" (*Post. Anal.* 2:19). A clear case of heroism, no doubt, but perhaps a tragic heroism.

7. The impossibility of a radically reflexive or perfectly autonomous knowledge: "Demonstration cannot be the originative source of demonstration" (ibid. 2:19).

8. In the *Physics*, we learn that matter ("a mother, as it were") *desires* the form, "as the female desires the male and the ugly the beautiful—only the ugly or the female not *per se* but *per accidens*" (1:9). Yet this is a disconcerting reduction of matter to desire and of desire to that bipolar "accident" we saw a moment ago, "accident" precisely with a view to desire for necessitous form.

9. The supposition that "art imitates nature," or that art "partly completes what nature cannot bring to a finish, and partly imitates her," inasmuch as in both art and nature "mistakes are possible," shows us that even self-doctoring doctors suffer not only from illness and demise but also from professional incompetence and malpractice (2:2, 8).

10. If τέχνη is mimetic of φύσις, one must wonder whether the most

imitative of arts, namely, the poetic art, and in poetic art the elevated art of tragic drama, imitates nothing less than φύσει ὄντα, the entire universe of nature (ibid.). Or, thinking φύσις with Heidegger, whether the pure upsurgence into radiant presencing of all being as such may in some sense be tragic.[7]

11. Nature is the scene not only of causality, which is the object of philosophy as such, but also of chance, which is "inscrutable to human beings": "it is with reason that good fortune is regarded as unstable; for chance is unstable, as none of the things which result from it can be invariable or normal," except for the happenstance that chance normally and even invariably plays a role in both ethical and natural life (ibid.), which are precisely for that reason tragic.

12. The identification of *time* as "the cause of decay, since it is the number of change, and change removes what is" (4:12), may itself be the most tragic of Aristotle's physical and metaphysical insights. Whereas time may seem to be as much the cause of coming to be as of passing away, it is more properly described as the cause of oblivion, senescence, decrepitude, destruction, and demise (4:13). Which is a little bit like peripety. Sometimes it seems as though sheer succession—time tearing ahead and tearing us away with it—suffices for tragedy.

Such a list, although a mere beginning, a mere indication, truncated and presented here without sufficient reflection and patience, may nevertheless encourage us to take Aristotle's *Poetics* as more central to the Aristotelian corpus than it is usually considered to be. If such a list fails to overcome our skepticism, however, what now follows will seem even more fantastic. For even if we succeed in reading *Aristotle* as a tragic philosopher, can we make of *Hölderlin* a tragic Aristotelian?

Divine Betrayal: Hölderlin's "Notes on Oedipus"

There are only two references to Aristotle in Hölderlin's works, one explicit, the other a mere allusion having more to do with Sophocles than Aristotle. The direct reference apparently has nothing to do with tragedy, although it does seem to arise from an experience of having read the *Poetics*. We will take up the allusion to Aristotle later, in the context of the *Anmerkungen* or "Notes" to Sophocles' *Antigone*, where it appears. For the moment, let us

---

7. In "The Anaximander Fragment," Heidegger suggests that the experience of being that is captured in the words διδόναι δίκην . . . τῆς ἀδικίας, "they let order belong by the surmounting of disorder," is neither pessimistic nor optimistic. "It is tragic." See Heidegger, *Holzwege*, 330; *Early Greek Thinking*, 44 (both cited in note 11 of ch. 8, above).

examine the sole explicit Hölderlinian reference to Aristotle. It appears in a poem sketched in 1789 but left incomplete, an ode to the *Sacra via* of poetry, the "sacred way" of poetry as a way of life. The poem is called *Die heilige Bahn* (CHV 1: 67–68), and two of its stanzas envisage Aristotle:

> Ha! wie den Richtstuhl Purpur umfließt
> Und der Smaragd wie blendend er glänzt
> Und auf dem Stuhl, mit dem großen Scepter
> Aristoteles hinwärts blikend
>
> Mit hellem scharfem Aug' auf des Lieds
> Feurigen Lauf. . . .
>
> Ha! how the royal purple flows over the seat of judgment
> And the emerald—how blindingly it gleams,
> And on the seat, wielding the great scepter,
> Aristotle gazing ahead
>
> With his bright keen eye on the hymn's
> Fiery course. . . .

If Aristotle holds the scepter and sits in judgment of poetry, it seems strange that Hölderlin's mourning play, *The Death of Empedocles,* and his translations of Sophocles' tragedies, along with the "Notes," should ignore him. It seems stranger still that Hölderlin's theoretical essays on tragedy should report nothing of Aristotle's views. It is therefore perhaps perverse to argue for a certain proximity in their approaches—perverse, even though no one can doubt the overwhelming force of Aristotle's *Poetics* for all criticism that comes after it, including that of Hölderlin. One might present another list, it too quite hastily composed, of places in Hölderlin's "Notes" where a kind of tragic Aristotelianism seems to prevail. Such a list may seem entirely opaque as first, yet it might serve as an invitation to begin. Five brief points, then, by way of a beginning.[8]

1. Hölderlin's "lawful calculus" (*gesetzliches Kalkul*) appears to be quite close to Aristotle's ubiquitous yet poorly defined διάνοια. Especially in chapter 19 of *The Poetics* Aristotle affirms what Hölderlin will define as *das Idealische,* namely, tragedy's having to do with *ideas,* with thinking and language. The plot and incidents of tragedy are also matters of "the idea," and are there-

---

8. See Jacques Taminiaux, "L'ombre d'Aristote dans les *Remarques* de Hölderlin sur *Oedipe* et *Antigone,*" which is ch. 4 of his book *Le théâtre des philosophes* (Grenoble: Jérôme Millon, 1995), 239–301. In spite of a rich and detailed discussion, Taminiaux does not discuss the paradox of a small number of houses in the tragic universe. Philippe Lacoue-Labarthe does not press the point either, although he is vocal about the proximity of Aristotle and Hölderlin. Hölderlin's move to Sophocles, he says, "is *also* the passage to Aristotle" (*Métaphrasis,* 57).

fore essentially dianoetic. Would not Hölderlin affirm that intense focus on the *idea* is what the school of poetry needs in our own Hesperian time? Would he not affirm that even though no calculus can ever calculate the content of a play, the *idea*—in an intellectual intuition of the higher nexus of life—must dictate the sequence and the speed of the drama's embodied presentations?

2. As obvious as it may seem, one must ponder the possibility that Hölderlin's famous caesura or counterrhythmic interruption may be read also in terms of Aristotle's τὸ δέσις and τὸ λύσις, the tying and loosening of the knots, the complication and resolution of the plot. For even though the term *caesura* is borrowed from versification, Hölderlin applies it to the faculties of human knowing and feeling as well as to the events and actions of the tragic plot. Would not Hölderlin affirm that the caesura is a protracted instant or elongated point within which we can see how and why matters are tearing ahead so relentlessly and so perilously?[9] Or, if the caesura cannot be described in terms of τὸ δέσις or τὸ λύσις as such, must we not still think the counterrhythmic interruption as enabling a kind of retrograde motion, or looping forward and back, in our view upon the rapid progression of scenes?[10]

3. The progression itself, which effects what Hölderlin calls "tragic transport," ought to be related to what Aristotle's treatise on time in *Physics* (4:10–14) calls "the sudden," ἐξαίφνης. The "Notes on Oedipus" refer to "the precipitous changes of scene," *der reißende Wechsel der Vorstellungen,* and the "excentric rapidity" of the rhythm in the sequence of scenes, *exzentrischer Rapidität.* The tragic hero or heroine is "torn away" from his or her familiar life to the land of the dead; the audience too is suddenly "seized" and caught up in a kind of terrible enthusiasm. The dominant words here are *rapider, Rapidität, entrücken, reissen, hingerissen.* If Aristotle's analysis of time serves as the very thesaurus for Heidegger's *existential* analysis of Dasein and its *ecstatic* tempo-

---

9. On *der verlängerte Punct,* see CHV 2:86, "Wenn der Dichter einmal des Geistes mächtig . . ."; see also Krell, *Lunar Voices* (cited in note 8 of ch. 2, above), ch. 2.

10. Taminiaux brings the caesura into connection with what Aristotle (*Poetics* 51a 5) calls the εὐσύνοψις, or encompassing overview, which enables us to see the unity of the plot; the caesura opens a view upon the σύστασις of the acts that constitute the plot as having a beginning, middle, and end. See Taminiaux, 289–290. For Hölderlin, the counterrhythmic interruption enables us to see not merely the particular representations that constitute the play but the play as a whole *as* representation. Often at the moment of deepest involvement we achieve the vision of the play as a play. The power of this notion of caesura is not restricted to Hölderlin, of course. Indeed, it may well be that the best testimony to the power of the concept of caesura in contexts other than that of Hölderlin (admittedly, after Walter Benjamin's "Goethe's *Wahlverwandtschaften*") comes from Max Kommerell's treatment of the structure of *Faust II* in terms of its caesurae. For the cuts or interruptions within the scenes of *Faust,* according to Kommerell, set "the tempo of meditation [*Besinnung*]" for our reading of the entire work: the caesurae "open up for us, between the worlds, the self's catching its breath in the truth of its inner state." See Kommerell, *Geist und Buchstabe der Dichtung* (cited in note 11 of ch. 7, above), 65. Kommerell's remarkable book will be cited hereinafter by page number in the body of my text.

rality, Hölderlin's use of that same language becomes all the more intriguing. If the lawful calculus must try to regulate the speed of the representations in a tragedy, that is because not only κάθαρσις but also the ecstasies of disclosure as such and in general—the upsurgence of *truth* in the play—are matters of ἐξαίφνης. Indeed, they have been so since Plato's Seventh Letter and Plotinus's *Enneads*, on through Schelling's and Hölderlin's ideas concerning intellectual intuition and tragic unification. Similarly, Hölderlin's notions of *Metapher* (μεταφορά, taken quite literally as transport) and *Umkehr* (both as the categorial reversal of space and time and one's reversion to one's place of birth) need to be thought in terms not only of Aristotelian diction (and of metaphor in particular) but also of the μεταβολή and περιπατεία of fortunes that guide the selection, order, and velocity of incidents in the plot.[11]

4. Hölderlin's notions of ecstatic removal to the excentric sphere of the dead (*Entrükung in die exzentrische Sphäre der Todten*) and of the limitless unification (*das gränzenlose Eineswerden*) and boundless separation (*gränzenloses Scheiden*) of gods and mortals need to be discussed in terms of the peculiar pleasure (ἡδονή) that Aristotle espies in tragedy. This is the uncanny pleasure (discussed a moment ago in the context of Bernays's work) that is bound up with the universally discussed yet ever mysterious κάθαρσις of emotions. Nothing seems farther removed from Hölderlin's understanding of tragedy than pleasure. Yet it may be that Aristotle's insistence on the word ἡδονή will prove particularly instructive for Hölderlin's lawful calculus and his location of the caesura. Moreover, tragic ἡδονή may not be far removed from what Hölderlin calls suffering or passion (*Leiden*), especially when it comes to the sufferings of the father of time and the earth, that is to say, Zeus. Zeus, pain, and pleasure? Zeus and catharsis? Let us see.

5. Finally, in order now to truncate the list, what Hölderlin calls the "deadly factical" word in Greek tragedy ("Das *griechischtragische Wort ist tödtlichfaktisch*") may provide a bridge connecting discussions of peripety and diction (λέξις), the latter considered in chapters 19–22 of the *Poetics*. The factical word, which is deadly for us Hesperians more in the sense of deadening, or mortifying ("*mehr tödtendfaktisches*"), may be the key to understanding

---

11. Dennis Schmidt, *On Germans*, 57, relates the suddenness of peripety, or reversal of fortune, in tragedy to the suddenness of death. He writes: "What becomes visible here is the expanse of the human condition—the possibilities belonging to *praxis*—an expanse so great that it is capable, at any given moment, of converting its situation into its other. In the end, all life belongs to the possibility of this conversion insofar as life, at any given moment, is convertible into death. This inevitable conversion of the whole of life which every life suffers is the reason that death plays a preeminent role in the conception of tragedy" (59). On peripety as the essence of what Hölderlin calls *Transport*, see Taminiaux, 286–289.

why and how we are to experience the choruses and dialogues of the plays as the bodily organs of a suffering godhead.

Admittedly, none of these five points speaks directly to our central paradox—that the smallest number of houses introduce us to an entire universe of tragedy. We may take it as a given that Hölderlin is at home in the tragic universe, that even his gods are destined to experience tragedy. This we know not only from the late hymns but also from the early novel *Hyperion,* and also especially from the three versions of *The Death of Empedocles.* For the historical Empedocles, himself the author of books on both nature and catharsis, is the tragic thinker of the vanished godhead. However, do Hölderlin's thoughts on Greek and Hesperian tragedy, on the tragedy of space, time, history, and divinity, relate in any specific way to those exceptional houses to which Aristotle directs our attention?

Nothing seems less likely than a Hölderlinian preoccupation with a small number of houses. For nothing short of universal mortality and immortality is his subject—gods and humans, nature and art, life and history viewed as a whole. None of the accidental references to "houses" in Hölderlin's "Notes" will fool us, neither Oedipus's words to Jocasta, quoted by Hölderlin in the notes to *Oedipus the Tyrant* (CHV 2:313), nor Antigone's reply to Creon, quoted by Hölderlin in the notes to *Antigone* (CHV 2:370). When Jocasta receives the good news from the Corinthian messenger that King Polybus has died—obviously not at the hand of Oedipus—she sends a servant to call her husband. As Oedipus exits their home he cries:

O liebstes, du, des Weibs Jokastas Haupt!
Was riefest du heraus mich aus den Häußern? (ll. 972–973)

O my most beloved, you, countenance of my wife Jocasta!
Why do you call me out of the places where we dwell?

When Creon challenges Antigone to defend her forbidden deed, she replies:

Darum, *mein* Zeus berichtete mirs nicht,
Noch hier im Haus das Recht der Todesgötter etc. (ll. 466–468)

For the reason that *my* Zeus did not report to me
That here in my house the right of the gods of the dead etc.

Apart from these merely occasional references to the house of Oedipus and Antigone, there is no specific reference to the House of Labdacus in the "Notes," not to that house or to any other. No, Hölderlin's focus, to repeat, is "the power of nature, which tragically . . . removes the human being from its sphere of life" (CHV 2:310–311). The human being "as such," we are tempted to say, no matter which house is his or hers, no matter how rare the family into which he or she is born.

And yet. The second division of the notes on *Oedipus* does become concerned with the confusion of houses in Oedipus's fate. It is the confusion that arises between Thebes and Corinth, Laius and Polybus, Jocasta and Merope (or Periboea, as the sources in myth call her), that causes Oedipus to interpret the oracle "too infinitely," which here means "suspiciously in detail." The young king's passion to know his origins swells with the confusion within and among a very small number of houses. Similarly, when much later in the play Oedipus is "seduced back into life" by Jocasta and the good news of Polybus's peaceable passing, it is precisely the dreamhouse that Jocasta—Oedipus's mother and spouse—has constructed for Oedipus that captures Hölderlin's attention. True, Hölderlin leaves without comment those remarkable lines in which Jocasta tries to reassure Oedipus that incest with one's mother is every mortal son's dream (ll. 1000–1015). Yet Hölderlin does stress that this scene with Oedipus and Jocasta (the scene one might call "the shadow caesura" of the drama) occupies the *midpoint* of the tragedy. Indeed, he sets in spaced type (here set in italic) those *early* words of Tiresias—in the speech that constitutes the proper caesura of the play—that highlight the role Jocasta plays in the penumbra of the house of Oedipus:

> Kund wird er seyn, bei seinen Kindern wohnend,
> Als Bruder und als Vater, und vom Weib, das ihn
> Gebahr, Sohn und Gemahl, *in Einem Bette mit*
> *Dem Vater und sein Mörder.* (ll. 463–466)

> He will come to know of his dwelling with his children
> As brother and father, and of the woman that
> Gave birth to him, son and husband, *in one bed with*
> *The father and his murderer.*

Odd are both the way in which Hölderlin emphasizes the line (although that emphasis tallies with the words stressed in the previous quotation, namely, "the murder / Of Laius") and the way in which the line itself shifts back and forth between the errors of Oedipus and Jocasta: she, the heart and hearth of the home, who will hang herself from the roofbeam of the house, is the one with whom Oedipus is not merely dwelling but the one with whom he is in bed. For her part, Jocasta is in bed not with *her* father, as Hölderlin's translation might lead us to suspect, but with *the* father, Oedipus's father, and with that father's murderer, Oedipus himself. David Grene translates, "He shall be proved father and brother both / to his own children in his house; to her / that gave him birth, a son and husband both; / a fellow sower in his father's bed / with that same father that he murdered" (C ll. 458–459). The meaning is clear, although the lines of poetry and of generation alike are gnarled here, and have to be unraveled.[12]

Finally, from the long series of quotations by which Hölderlin hopes to exhibit the "mad questioning" (*das geisteskranke Fragen*) of Oedipus, we note the two final passages, in which Oedipus's search for a dependable mother and a stable house becomes startlingly clear. Both passages are directed—in a deadly factical manner, as it turns out—at Jocasta:

> Sei gutes Muths! käm' ich von dreien Müttern
> Dreifach ein Knecht, es machte dich nicht schlimmer. (ll. 1084–1087)

> Be of good cheer! even if I came from three mothers
> Thrice a slave, you would not be worse off.

> . . . Ich aber will, als Sohn des Glüks mich haltend,
> Des Wohlbegabten, nicht verunehrt werden.
> Denn diß ist meine Mutter. Und klein und groß
> Umfiengen mich die mitgebornen Monde. . . . (ll. 1100–1107)

> . . . Yet will I account myself a son of Fortune,
> Replete with gifts, and not to be dishonored.
> For this is my mother. And small and tall
> My sibling moons surrounded me.

---

12. Jean-Pierre Vernant comments on these difficult lines as follows: "What he has done without knowing it and with no evil intent or criminal volition is, notwithstanding, the most terrible crime against the sacred order that governs human life. Like birds that eat the flesh of birds, to borrow Aeschylus's expression, he has twice satiated himself with his own flesh, first by shedding the blood of his father and then by becoming united with the blood of his mother" (VV 122). Vernant later makes the analysis more specific—and dizzyingly complex: "Even before he knows anything of his true origins Oedipus describes himself, from the point of view of his relationship to Laius, as sharing the same bed and having a *homosporon* wife. On his lips the word means that he is impregnating with his seed the same woman that Laius has impregnated before him; but in line 460 Tiresias gives the word its true meaning: he tells Oedipus that he will discover himself to be both the murderer of his father and his *homosporos*, his co-impregnator. *Homosporos* usually has a different meaning, namely: born of the same seed, blood relative. And indeed, without knowing it, Oedipus is of the same blood as both Laius and Iocasta. The fact that Oedipus and his own sons are equal is expressed in a series of brutally forceful images: the father has sowed the seed for his sons in the very spot where he himself was sown; Iocasta is a wife, but not a wife; rather, a mother whose furrow has produced in a double harvest both the father and the children; Oedipus has sown his seed in the woman who gave him birth, in whom he himself was seeded, and from these same furrows, the 'equal' furrows, he has obtained his own children. But it is Tiresias who lends the full weight to this terminology expressing equality when he addresses Oedipus as follows: Misfortunes will come that 'will make you the equal of yourself by making you the equal of your children.' The identification of Oedipus with his own father and his own children, the assimilation of mother and wife in the person of Iocasta make Oedipus the equal of himself, that is, turn him into an *agos* [a defilement], an *apolis* [outcast] incommensurable and without equality with other men, who, believing himself to be the equal of a god, in the end finds himself to be the equal of nothing at all" (VV 136–137).

However, in the face of these bizarre words, heard from the mouth of furious Oedipus, we should hesitate: it is clear that we have gone too far too fast. Let us backtrack a bit, back to the companionship of Hölderlin and Aristotle and to our central paradox.

Perhaps the most telling of the ties between Hölderlin and Aristotle is the fact that for both of them Sophocles' *Oedipus the Tyrant* is the exemplary Greek tragedy. Further, Hölderlin's fascination with *Oedipus* and *Antigone* surely has to do with that *family*, that *household*, in which "raging curiosity" and "mournful calm" alternate. For the moment, that most telling of ties will be the only one discussed at any length. The following account begins with the *Anmerkungen zum Oedipus* and then proceeds directly to the *Anmerkungen zur Antigonä*.[13]

If Hölderlin admires "the μηχανή of the ancients," desiring to enhance the craft of poetry in the German lands by attending to the skill or *Geschik* of the Greeks, it may not be too far-fetched to think of his "lawful calculus" as a meditation on Aristotelian διάνοια—inasmuch as "reasoning" has to do equally with the contrivances of plot, the mechanics of poetic diction, and the intricate flying machines of metaphor.[14] Hölderlin is quick to admit that the "particular content" of any given tragedy cannot be reduced to a calculus. Neither the content nor "the living meaning" of any given play can be calculated in advance. The lawful calculus of tragedy is further complicated by the fact that it involves an entire "system of sensibility," that is to say, "the whole human being" viewed under the influence of "the element" (presumably, the element of tragedy) in all its essential respects.[15] Tragedy presents us with a

---

13. The "Notes" are to be found after the respective translations in Knaupp's edition at CHV 2:309–316 and CHV 2:369–376. For selections from the "Notes," related documents, insightful commentary, and a review of the secondary literature, see JV 4:46–146, esp. 46–73. Because the "Notes" involve so few pages, and because my own reading will proceed rather directly through these dense pieces, I will cite page numbers only rarely. While I am grateful for Thomas Pfau's translation of these pieces, I have worked only with the German text. See Friedrich Hölderlin, *Essays and Letters on Theory*, ed. and tr. Thomas Pfau (Albany: State University of New York Press, 1988).

14. Taminiaux (285) convincingly identifies μηχανή with the general Aristotelian emphasis on the τέχνη of poetry in the *Poetics*.

15. Yet what *is* the element of tragedy? Is it the element of action? Is it the more aorgic realm of nature and the body? Is it the warring of the elements as described by Empedocles (DK A37, B26, ll. 3–7, and B53)? Is it the element of fire, fire from heaven, as Hölderlin refers to it in his letter of December 4, 1801, to Böhlendorff (CHV 2:921)? As far as I am aware, Hölderlin refers to "element" only once in the *Anmerkungen*, so that its interpretation remains difficult. See, however, his use of the word in the "Fragment" (CHV 2:53, l. 19), where the human being is cited as acting within the nexus of his element—where element suggests nature, life, and, if one may say so, *world*. Perhaps the meaning of the word is similar to that quite expansive sense in the *Grund zum Empedokles*, where Hölderlin writes that it seemed to the people of Acragas that Empedocles "walked among them as the spirit of the element in human shape, dwelling among mortals" (CHV 1:875). Lacoue-Labarthe is right to claim that Hölderlin's phrase "under the influence of the element" designates both nature and divinity, both "necessity and power" (*Métaphrasis*, 68).

succession—but also and especially an *equilibrium*—of presentations, sensations, and reasonings (*Räsonnement*, perhaps, again, to be understood in terms of διάνοια, if not of ἀπόδειξις). The lawful calculus enables "tragic *transport*," which is "properly empty and utterly unbound." Empty of what? Perhaps, once again, of any particular content. Utterly unbound? Perhaps, once again, more infinite and undetermined, thinking the infinite as Anaximandrian ἄπειρον, as Hölderlin so often does. Yet Hölderlin himself (DKV 2:796, l. 211) uses the word *Ungebundesten* to translate Sophocles' ἀδάμαστ', the adamantine arrowheads of Apollo, which the chorus hopes the god of healing will direct against Ares. However, no one is more aware than Hölderlin that Apollo's golden bow is "sacredly treacherous," *heiligfalsch* (l. 209), inasmuch as plague-ridden Thebes has been struck by none other than Apollo—the ostensible healer. As Roberto Calasso reminds us, one of Apollo's epithets is Σμινθεύς, "mouse," "mouse-killer," "vermin," or, as Calasso prefers, "Apollo of the Rat, harbinger of the plague" (RC 143). To be caught up in tragic transport is to be struck by Apollo—and perhaps by the wine god as well.

At all events, tragic transport is what Hölderlin means by *metaphor*. He thinks of metaphor as a mode of transport(ation), the μεταφορά, as others of his texts suggest (CHV 2:80, 102; 3:398). The tragic has its significance in its "ideal character," and is the bearer—or metaphor—of an "intellectual intuition." The editors of the Hanser edition of Hölderlin's collected works offer a useful summary statement concerning "intellectual intuition":

> *Intellectuale* [or *intellectuelle*] *Anschauung:* a spiritual-intellectual envisaging, the supreme form of knowing in the Neoplatonic doctrine of spirit (νοῦς); excluded from theory of knowledge by Kant as impossible for the human understanding, treated by Reinhold in the context of a general theory of the faculty of representation, appropriated by Fichte as the supreme act of the (absolute) ego for the grounding of the "doctrine of science" ['*Wissenshaftslehre*'], and finally taken up by Schelling as the constitutive act of the ego. For Hölderlin it is an intuition— the intuition that "all is one"—that exceeds theoretical and practical consciousness alike.[16]

16. The editors refer us to two of Hölderlin's letters, one to Schiller dated September 4, 1795, the other to Niethammer dated February 24, 1796 (CHV 2:595–596, 614–615). The letter to Schiller, cited in ch. 7 of this volume, is particularly illuminating: Hölderlin speaks of intellectual intuition as an aesthetic notion—intellectual, inasmuch as it is an intuition in which the unification of subject and object becomes possible, aesthetic, inasmuch as such unification is not a matter of theory. The very possibility of unification is one of infinite approximation, as in squaring the circle: one would have to be immortal to achieve it. See also the important statements in "Seyn, Urtheil, Modalität," CHV 2:50, and "Hermokrates an Cephalus," CHV 2:50–51. Once one sees the extent to which Hölderlin's view of intellectual intuition differs from that of Fichte and the young Schelling, one can be less fearful of attributing such intuition to Hölderlin. Taminiaux proves to be fearful of such an attribution through-

Schelling offers us a more detailed account in his 1800 *System* (3:369). He envisages "a knowing whose object is not *independent* of it, hence, *a knowing that is at the same time the producing of its object*—an intuition that is universally and freely productive, and in which producing and produced are one and the same." He continues:

> Such an intuition—in contrast to sensuous intuition, which does not appear as the producing of its object, and in which therefore the *intuiting itself* differs from what is intuited—is called *intellectual intuition.*
>
> Such an intuition is the *ego,* because *through the knowing of the ego by itself* the *ego itself* (the object) first originates. For, inasmuch as the ego (as object) is nothing else than this *knowing of oneself,* the ego originates precisely through the sole happenstance *that* it knows about itself; hence the *ego itself* is a knowing that at the same time produces itself (as object).
>
> Intellectual intuition is the organ of all transcendental thinking. (3:369)

Schelling later in the same treatise transforms intellectual intuition into an aesthetic act: "Aesthetic intuition is intellectual intuition become objective" (3:625). Clearly, in both Schelling's and Hölderlin's theoretical works, ancient Greek tragedy appears to be forced to respond to the modern philosophical quandary of the subject-object split. Tragedy, as the bearer of an intellectual-aesthetic intuition, would expose the unity of a world or the nexus of a life in which subject and object are either not yet or no longer separated. Hölderlin, in the same poetological sketch (from late autumn or early winter, 1799) in which the concept of metaphor is extensively deployed, *Das lyrische dem Schein nach idealische Gedicht,* defines the unity of subject and object in terms of "the unity with everything that lives" (CHV 2:104). Such unity is not theoretically ascertainable, however, and cannot be broached by epistemology. While it may be closer to practical philosophy, at least in Fichte's and Schelling's conceptions of it, such unity properly pertains to aesthetics in the broadest sense—a sense that would embrace both major parts of Kant's third *Critique,* along with the Transcendental Aesthetic of his first *Critique.* For the unity

---

out his fourth chapter, and it misleads him into thinking that the "Notes" to Sophocles' plays constitute a radical departure from the earlier poetological essays, in which intellectual intuition plays a major role. However, Hölderlin never thought of intellectual intuition as a tool of absolute idealism. He thought of it as Max Kommerell thinks of it, namely, in terms of tragedy. Tragedy is a revelatory genre, unveiling and disclosing within an intellectual intuition *that is precisely not a concept,* inasmuch as "among the poetic forms it corresponds to the mythic state of life" (331). In the mythic state, "one perceives the particular in the whole, the whole in the particular, which is also where the Hölderlinian concept of *Innigkeit* is to be placed, as an amicable dwelling-within-one-another of the extremes" (ibid.). As for the word *innig,* it must be translated not as "interior" (which is the hobgoblin that makes the commentators fear intellectual intuition so much), but in the way Kommerell translates it, to wit, as *überinnig* (356), hyperintense. *Innigkeit* is excess, and so is the intellectual intuition that dwells—or tries to set up its household—in excess.

Hölderlin is seeking has to do with *life*. Viewed negatively, intellectual intuition arises from "the impossibility of an absolute separation and individualization" (CHV 2:104). Viewed positively, the unity established in intellectual intuition asserts its "rights" when it partakes of "its entire measure of life" (CHV 2:105). Yet precisely in this most positive moment the negative reasserts its prerogative. Once again the element of *excess*, of the *too much*, rises to unsettle all dominion. Subject and object are, in intellectual intuition, "too unified" (*zu einig*), precisely in the way that Empedocles proved to be "too intense, too singular" (*zu innig, zu einzig*) for his historical age. Something akin to Empedoclean "Strife" (Νεῖκος) disrupts the sphere of intellectual intuition. Aesthetics will not succeed where theory and practice alike failed: Hölderlin's preferred analogies for the attainment and the disruption of intellectual intuition are the quadrature of the circle and the infinite approximation of the asymptote. Aesthetics gets us as close as we can get to an experience of unity—and then repels us. Hölderlin attributes "the ideal beginning of the actual separation" of subject and object to "the necessary *arbitrariness of Zeus*," or, more neutrally, inasmuch as *Willkür* means both, to the necessary *will* of Zeus.[17] In either case, it almost seems that what Aeschylus's *Prometheus Bound* asserts of Zeus is true, namely, that the father of the gods is himself a member of one of those rare and factious households of ancient Greece that open their door to tragedy. Be that as it may, however, and no matter how we are to understand it, intellectual intuition *is* in Hölderlin's view *tragic* thinking.

In this early text, as we saw in the previous chapters, Hölderlin distinguishes Sophocles' *Antigone* from *Oedipus the Tyrant* in terms of the type of intellectual intuition achieved in each. If the intellectual intuition is "more subjective," and if the separation of subject and object arises from the "concentrating parts" of the play, as it does in *Antigone*, with its highly compacted final scenes between Antigone and Creon, the style of the tragedy is lyrical. If the separation of subject and object is more objective, that is, if it proceeds from the supreme possibility of separation, which is Zeus himself, as in the case of *Oedipus*, then the tragedy is eminently tragic. In *Oedipus* the sweeping succession of incidents separates all the characters radically from the divine.

---

17. Taminiaux (277) prefers to translate *Willkür* as freedom, citing §43 of Kant's *Critique of Judgment*, in which Kant speaks of artistic production as essentially free. As far as it goes, and it goes halfway, *Willkür* as freedom must surely be attributable to Zeus—who is the source of radical separation. Yet Zeus, as the son of Kronos, also stands for the more aorgic power of nature, which acts *arbitrarily*. *Willkür* is therefore both freedom and arbitrary necessity—as Schelling too would insist. Moreover, when Zeus enters the cell of Danaë, he himself, as we shall see, becomes subject to the power of nature. He becomes subject, above all, to *time*.

Thebes is besieged by plague not only because the temples of Apollo at Delphi and Abae are sick but also because some dread illness—namely, the *mortal* illness—has spread to the gods and to the father of time himself. However, let us return to the "Notes on Oedipus."

Oedipus—the most famous scion of the Theban house that embraces Cadmus, Pentheus, and Dionysos (the New Zeus) himself—struggles to achieve consciousness through an intellectual intuition. Yet what he achieves in the nexus of life is violent disruption. The rhythmic sequence of embodied presentations in which he strives for unification and consciousness of self will itself be subjected to an early counterrhythmic interruption, the dramatic equivalent of poetic caesura, which will prevent the play from tearing ahead too quickly, in excentric rapidity, to its violent conclusion. Slowing down the process of dissolution will not stop it, however. In *Antigone*, by contrast, the final scenes are compressed by the initial ones, so that the equilibrium of the piece inclines toward the end, with the consequence that the end must be "protected from" the beginning by the insertion of a caesura. Here too, however, protection of the end will not stop or fundamentally alter it: Creon's entire family will join Antigone in downgoing; she will precede them only in the order of time.

In both tragedies, the appearance of Tiresias marks the moment of caesura, or counterrhythmic interruption, if only because Tiresias is the mediator between the immortals under the aegis of Zeus and the mortals under the reign of nature's more aorgic power, represented by Kronos the Titan. The more aorgic power of nature is the power that will eventually transport mortals to the underworld. Tiresias therefore has as much to do with Kronos as with Zeus, who, after all, are father and son. Of Tiresias, Hölderlin writes: "He intervenes in the course of destiny, as overseer over the power of nature, which tragically snatches the human being from its life-sphere, from the midpoint of its inner life, and transports it to another world, tearing it away into the excentric sphere of the dead" (CHV 2:310–311). The midpoint of the plays must accordingly be calculated both formally (in terms of the problem of the excentric or decentered equilibrium of the sequence of scenes in the plays) and materially (in terms of the unified life of the hero or heroine in essential yet tenuous equilibrium with his or her world). Even if the transport (*Entrükung*) or tearing (*Reißen*) of the hero out of the midpoint of life into the sphere of death *seems* to have nothing to do with Aristotelian notions of pleasure or purification (ἡδονή, κάθαρσις), it remains true that the upsurgence of the more aorgic and elemental nature does serve as something of a corrective to the hyperorganized human order of the city. For if what *Hyper-*

ion calls "the School of Destiny" has deprived Hyperion and the rest of us Hesperians of all the pleasures that nature has to offer, will not "the School of Nature" compensate all the more violently, all the more aorgically?

Something about that "special house" of Oedipus comes to the fore in Hölderlin's detailed analysis of the play in section 2 of the *Anmerkungen* (CHV 2: 311–315). Ironically, it is Oedipus's "marvelous, furious curiosity," which interprets the quite general pronouncement of the Delphic oracle "too infinitely," here meaning all-too-particularly, that is his undoing. Oedipus's ὀργή, his fury, perhaps not unrelated to the wrath of Schelling's goddess, is a family story: as he begins to break through the barriers of his unknowing with regard to his origins and his crimes, Oedipus is "as though intoxicated in his regal harmonic form," at least at first, until in the end he can "no longer bear what he knows." His suspicion of Creon at the outset of the play, along with the way in which his interrogations of both Creon and Jocasta elicit from them the answers that will obsess him, betray how insecure Oedipus is under the burden of his "unbounded thought, freighted with mournful secrets." Angry excess, or "unmeasure," soon destroys Oedipus's splendid harmony, an excess that is "gleefully destructive" and that blindly obeys the imperious time that rushes ahead to doom. Oedipus the tyrant is tyrannized.[18]

18. Taminiaux (290, 292) is quite right to emphasize that Oedipus becomes increasingly *tyrannized* by his need to know, and that the tyranny begins (as Hölderlin suggests) when Oedipus overinterprets Creon's account of the words of the Delphic Oracle. As I argued in the preceding chapter, Hölderlin's choice of a title, *Oedipus the Tyrant*, seems to have resulted not from a mistranslation of τύραννος but from his having thought about Oedipus's fury to know his origins. Hölderlin's choice of the cognate is corroborated in our own time by three detailed analyses by Jean-Pierre Vernant. Vernant argues, first, that Oedipus's entire character is built around the opposition τύραννος-φαρμακός, that is, his exceptionally kingly and even quasi-divine status and his role of lowly scapegoat. Oedipus's very name suggests either the one who *knows* the foot or the one whose foot is deformed. As the one who knows the answer to the *riddle* of the foot (i.e., the riddle of the sphinx), Oedipus is *tyrannos* (VV 123–124). Vernant argues, second, that Oedipus's banishment in his infancy, his having been exposed to death by his mother and father, is in fact a very common trait in tales of the great tyrants: "Like the hero, the tyrant accedes to royalty via an indirect route, bypassing the legitimate line; like him, his qualifications for power are his actions and his exploits. He reigns by virtue not of his blood but of his own qualities; he is the son of his works and also of Τύχη. The supreme power that he has succeeded in winning outside the ordinary norms places him, for better or worse, above other men and above the law" (VV 127). Vernant argues, third, that Oedipus's expulsion from Thebes at the end of the play mirrors the Athenian practice of ostracism. Oedipus is both a godlike king and a pariah by the end of the play, both tyrant and scapegoat, and he more than anyone in Greek literature demonstrates the near-identity of these highest and lowest of types: "If Sophocles chooses the pair τύραννος-φαρμακός to illustrate what we have called the theme of reversal, it is because the two figures appear symmetrical and in some respects interchangeable in their opposition. Both are presented as *individuals* responsible for the *collective* salvation of the group" (VV 132). It would not be terribly difficult to translate Vernant's arguments into the language with which Hölderlin defines Empedocles' and Oedipus's excessive qualities—*zu innig, zu einzig*—vis-à-vis their respective historical times. In and to their respective cities, they can appear only as *tyrants*.

Something else about that "special house" of Oedipus becomes clear immediately after the formal midpoint of the play, in a second counterrhythmic interruption, one that is pervaded by an uncanny, penumbral calm. In the eleventh of the play's seventeen scenes, Jocasta interrupts the stormy sweep of disaster with a mother's tranquil, lucid, and utterly remarkable words to her son, who is about to destroy himself. Jocasta almost succeeds in soothing her son-and-spouse's *second* nightmare, which is the nightmare about *her*. Her words instill in Oedipus a "mournful calm" (*traurige Ruhe*), a "stupor" or veritable *embarras*. We hear the "powerful man" deceive himself, piteously, about his parentage—for the last time. Hölderlin does not cite her words in his *Anmerkungen*, nor does he refer to such a thing as a "shadow caesura," but how magnificently he has translated Jocasta's shadowy words in the body of the play! He finds a language that gives us contemporary readers the entire Oedipus Complex in so sovereign and tranquil a form that it seems to preempt all psychoanalysis (CHV 2:287):

Jokasta.

Was fürchtet der Mensch, der mit dem Glük
Es hält? Von nichts giebts eine Ahnung deutlich.
Dahin zu leben, so wie einer kann,
Das ist das Beste. Fürchte du die Hochzeit
Mit deiner Mutter nicht! denn öfters hat
Ein Sterblicher der eignen Mutter schon
Im Traume beigewohnt: doch wenn wie nichts
Diß gilt, er trägt am leichtesten das Leben.

For what does a human being have to fear if his luck
Holds? There is no clear presentiment of anything at all.
To live straight ahead, as well as you can,
That is best. Do not fear wedding
Your mother! For oftentimes
In dreams a mortal has slept with
His own mother: yet when he takes this as counting for
Nothing at all, he can most readily bear life.

Hölderlin has already used the phrase *Im Traume*, "In dreams," fourteen lines earlier. If in Jocasta's mouth the phrase translates ὀνείρασιν, in Oedipus's it translates Polybus's languishing (πόθῳ) for his lost adopted son:

Oedipus.

. . . wenn er anders
Im Traume nicht umkam, von mir. So mag er
Gestorben seyn, von mir. . . . (Ibid.)

305

> ... unless
> In dreams he died of me. In this way
> He may have died on account of me. ...

Dreams of longing and languishing play a vital role for both father and son, and perhaps even for mother-and-wife and son-and-husband, in the special economies of tragedy and psychoanalysis. Indeed, there are moments when one is convinced that Freud in fact *studied* the play, perhaps in Hölderlin's more aorgic translation, and that he merely extrapolated from this very rare and special household in the direction of the universal—as Aristotle, Hölderlin, Bernays, and Nietzsche before him had done.

If Oedipus "desperately wrestles in order to come to himself," he is at this point in the play (well after the caesura, now in the course of a shadow caesura) "tempted back into life once again." On the far side of the excentric midpoint or shifting fulcrum of the play, at least in Pier Paolo Pasolini's film version of *Oedipus Rex*, Oedipus and Jocasta join hands as young lovers. Pasolini's script to his magnificent film reads at this point as follows:

> Jocasta draws close to him, and presses his hand in hers. In that moment, he would seem almost to have triumphed over destiny.
>
> JOCASTA: *You see? Don't think any more on these atrocities which have obsessed you these last few days* ...
>
> OEDIPUS: *Yes, but there is one thing more which terrifies me* ... *The idea of making love to my mother* ... *This still horrifies me* ...
>
> JOCASTA: *But why? Why? We are at the mercy of fate, and no one can ever foresee what is going to happen next! The wisest course is to pin our faith on fortune, and live as we can* ... *And why does the idea of making love to your mother hold such terror for you? Why? Think how many men must have made love to their mothers in their dreams!*
>
> These words drip into the silent assembly as a revelation. The councilors look with shocked expressions at Jocasta and Oedipus; but there are some amongst them who are smiling: a faint, derisive smile born of the realization that here is something very much out of the ordinary, a scandal in fact.
>
> JOCASTA: *Who has not dreamt of making love to his mother? And does he live in horror of his dream? Of course not, unless he wants to clutter his life with useless suffering.*[19]

There are grounds on Hölderlin's own terms for seeing this shadow caesura as a more striking interruption of the rapid flow of the scenes than the

---

19. Pier Paolo Pasolini, *Oedipus Rex*, tr. John Mathews (London: Lorrimer Publishing, 1971), 92, 144. In the final cut of the film, Pasolini the Director excises almost all of the dialogue presented here, reducing the scene (which is shot in the penumbra of a palace garden) to a brief exchange between mother and son. He seals the scene with a shot of their entwined hands, joined as the hands of lovers.

earlier counterrhythmic confrontation with Tiresias. More striking because it is the *final* slowdown in the terminal rush of scenes, final perhaps because Jocasta herself embodies that feminine element which Tiresias too, at least in his prehistory, mysteriously incorporates as his particular insight. Even after the shadow caesura, however, the rush continues to the inexorable end. Life is soon hanging from the roofbeam, as Oedipus strives "almost shamelessly" to gain control over himself. Hölderlin calls this almost shameless effort by Oedipus the "foolishly savage rummaging [*das närrischwilde Nachsuchen*] for a consciousness"; soon he will call it an "insane questioning after a consciousness." If it is intellectual intuition that Oedipus is after, the vision that will make him one with the expanding rings of his living world, only the blind Tiresias and the hanged Jocasta can show him the excentric path to it. From the instant of his birth, or at least from the moment his heels are pierced and his toes sewn together, Oedipus is caught up in utterly violent relationships, trapped in "the more violent nexus" (*in gewaltsamerem Zusammenhang*) precisely where he had hoped for tenderness. Jocasta herself will be tangled in the knots of her hair, her feet dangling over the floor of the house; she will be "hanging together," as it were, before her son-and-spouse, in the very special room of their very special abode.

Yet let us push the paradox a little farther, as Hölderlin does. In the third section of his "Notes," he reflects on the monstrous union of god and human being, of external nature and inmost humanity, in *wrath*, where boundless unity purifies itself by means of boundless scission. Perhaps this monstrous unification or coupling (*sich paaren*) of god and human in wrath (*Zorn*), followed directly by boundless separation (*gränzenloses Scheiden*), both the coupling and the divorce being essential to tragic transport, is what Hölderlin takes catharsis to be. He does call the boundless separation a *sich reinigen*, a purifying of oneself (CHV 2:315, l. 14).[20]

At all events, without apparent rhyme or reason, Hölderlin now makes an allusion to Aristotle. He cites the tenth-century Byzantine lexicon, the *Suda*, on Aristotle, implying perhaps (as Heidegger too will later imply) that Sophocles is the true Aristotle, or that Aristotle is truly tragic. Hölderlin cites the phrase from the *Suda* without translating it, and without diacritical marks: Της φυσεως γραμματευς ην τον καλαμον αποβρεχων ευνουν. "He [Aristotle, according to the *Suda*, but here apparently Sophocles] is the gramma-

---

20. See Taminiaux (294–295), for whom the boundless separation of god and mortal is the very concept of catharsis. Recall also the role of wrath (*Zorn*) in the Age of Chaos as Schelling interprets it in his 1811 version of *The Ages of the World*. There the divine essence itself undergoes boundless scission.

tologist of nature, writing with his pen dipped in pure mind." Perhaps more than the identification of Aristotle and Sophocles, or more than the replacement of the former by the latter, is at stake here, however; perhaps it is here a matter of a boundless pairing—and an equally boundless separation—of the more aorgic realm of nature (τῆς φύσεως) and of the human being, whether philosopher or tragedian, who tries to comprehend through the agency of the written word (γραμματεύς . . . εὐνοῦν) both the more violent and the more tender relations in the baffling nexus of life. Such boundless couplings and separations—one thinks of the intermittent couplings of Apollo and Dionysos cited by Nietzsche at the outset of *The Birth of Tragedy*—take place in those much maligned and admittedly maddening yet undeniably very special houses visited by Greek tragedy.

In the famous concluding lines of section 3 of the *Anmerkungen zum Oedipus*, it is the betrayal of the gods—and betrayal *by* the gods—that Hölderlin exhorts us to remember. Such betrayal occurs in a time of vanity and futility (*in müßiger Zeit*), a time of pestilence and confusion of meaning, a time out of work, a time that reminds Hölderlin as much of his own age as it does of the tragic age of the Greeks. In order that the course of the world show no gaps (see also CHV 2:73–74, *Das untergehende Vaterland . . .*), and in order *"that the memory of the celestial ones not be extinguished altogether,"* such memory *"communicates itself in the all-oblivious form of infidelity,* inasmuch as divine infidelity is the most readily retained" (CHV 2:315–316). It is not easy to see or say what such mutual betrayal between god and mortal may be, their monstrous and furious union now ruined by boundless separation, their hasty, unwritten covenant now revoked simultaneously by both sides, their sole prophet now an angel and an agent of death. We will continue to encounter such betrayal in *Antigone*, even if the *Anmerkungen zur Antigonä* no longer mention *göttliche Untreue*. These moments of oblivion and betrayal are instants of reversal (*Umkehr*). In the "Notes on Antigone," Hölderlin will think this reversal in national-political terms, or, better, in *natal*-political terms, as the fatherland in tumult. At the present moment, in the context of *Oedipus the Tyrant*, he thinks of it in terms of the abandoned temples and barren altars of plague-ridden Thebes. "What should I sing?" asks the leader of the chorus, who is foundering in desperation, announcing that he will no longer go to the erstwhile sacred places (CHV 2:284):

Unglücklich aber gehet das Göttliche.

Yet divinity wanders in misfortune.

Divinity suffers the same misfortune as the wrathful and violent Oedipus, who now, after the vaguely adumbrated excentric midpoint of mournful calm has passed, dreams that his mother is Lady Luck, Τύχη, the maid of the moon, otherwise known as Chance and Hazard (CHV 2:292). Let these uncanny lines from the shadow caesura be repeated:

Was soll, das breche. . . .
Ich aber will, als Sohn des Glüks mich haltend,
Des wohlbegabten, nicht verunehrt werden.
Denn diß ist meine Mutter. Und klein und groß
Umfiengen mich die mitgebornen Monde.
Und so erzeugt, will ich nicht ausgehn, so,
So daß ich nicht, ganz, weß ich bin, ausforschte.

Whatever is to be, let it break upon me. . . .
Yet will I account myself a son of Fortune,
Replete with gifts, and not to be dishonored.
For this is my mother. And small and tall
My sibling moons surrounded me.
And, thus engendered, I will not be extinguished, no,
Not thus; not until I have searched out whose I am.[21]

In this ambiguous universe of lunar voices, of chance encounters with the dark side and the new, what happens in a very particular family touches on solar space and initiates solar and lunar time. "For in the extremity of suffering nothing subsists other than the conditions of time or space" (CHV 2:316). The human being, caught up in the moment of everydayness and all its "interests," forgets himself or herself; the god, who is nothing other than time, forgets itself. All are unfaithful. All forget the unity with the world that

---

21. Jean-Pierre Vernant comments on this passage as follows: "Installed in his role of solver of riddles and king dispensing justice, convinced that the gods inspire him, and proclaiming himself the son of Τύχη, Good Luck, how could Oedipus possibly understand that he is a riddle to himself the meaning of which he will only guess when he discovers himself to be the opposite of what he thinks he is: not the son of Τύχη at all but her victim, not the dispenser of justice but the criminal, not the king saving his city but the abominable defilement by which it is being destroyed? So it is that, at the moment when he realizes that he is responsible for having forged his misfortune with his own hands, he accuses the deity of having plotted and contrived everything in advance, of having delighted in tricking him from the start to the finish of the drama, the better to destroy him" (see VV 45; cf. a similar passage, 126). However, as Vernant himself emphasizes elsewhere, there is something undeniably true about Oedipus's suspicions against Apollo, and in a situation of disastrous ambiguity little is left for him other than blasphemy: "Tragedy expresses this weakness inherent in action, this internal inadequacy of the agent, by showing the gods working behind men's backs from beginning to end of the drama, to bring everything to its conclusion. Even when, by exercising choice, he makes a decision, the hero almost always does the opposite of what he thinks he is doing" (VV 83). Perhaps this is what it means to be a child of Τύχη: "When life strips off all her finery, what remains is fortune. Everything that happens is a constant collision of tossed dice" (RC 353).

intellectual intuition, through the mediation of the poetic word, promises. Yet all now also suffer the sudden disruption or ecstatic displacement of a turning, a "categorial reversal," in which all our ends refuse to rhyme with our beginnings; as the god shudders, shivers, sinks into oblivion, the human being is swept along in a sequence of events that break the very back of space and time. Hölderlin adds: "Thus stands Haemon in the *Antigone*. Thus Oedipus himself in the middle of the tragedy of *Oedipus*." Haemon? He wanted to found a special house of his own with the daughter-sister of Oedipus. Oedipus in the middle? That is the point of mournful calm, the shadowy, piteous point at which Jocasta tells him to keep on dreaming, dreaming is best.

In the Figure of Death: Hölderlin's "Notes on Antigone"

Oneiric, naive language *is* the language of Sophocles, Hölderlin tells us in the "Notes on Antigone." Sophocles speaks and writes the language of a human understanding "wandering amid unthinkable things." The "Notes on Antigone," after outlining a more technical account of the calculable law of the caesura, pick up where the "Notes on Oedipus" left off, with the categorial turning of time. If the caesura comes quite late in *Antigone*, once again with the appearance of Tiresias, the highest flight or supreme moment of the play comes earlier, immediately after the midpoint (occupied by Haemon) and the fourth choral song.[22] That song juxtaposes Eros and Hades, "the spirit of love and peace" and "the all-silencing god of death." Antigone's subsequent dialogue with the chorus invokes the fate of Niobe (at line 852: "*Ich habe gehört*"). Both here and in the fifth choral song, superlatives of juxtaposition are achieved, superlatives of beauty and horror, sacrilege and divine visitation. With regard to these superlatives, Hölderlin writes:

> When the soul labors secretly, it is of enormous help to it that at the point of supreme consciousness it eludes the grasp of consciousness. And before the present god can actually seize the soul, the soul goes to encounter the god with bold words, often the very words of blasphemy. And in this way it preserves the sacred, the living possibility of spirit. (CHV 2:371)

As we shall see, Sophocles brings Niobe, Danaë, Lycurgus, and the Greek Cleopatra together in this moment of human genius and virtuosity, a moment

22. Perhaps the shadow caesura of *Antigone* (which would be a *foreshadowing* caesura) occurs when at the midpoint of the drama Creon chides his son as "Weaker than woman!" His choice of words suggests that Haemon is a hysteric, that he has, or is attached to, a wandering womb. That insult is one of the worst and one of the last out of Creon's mouth, and from here (though after the caesura proper, which is Creon's confrontation with Tiresias) the play rushes to its conclusion in Antigone's—and Haemon's—tomb.

that hovers between the sacred and sacrilege, between blasphemy and openness to the god. That moment is entirely "orgic" and is thus ready to be swept back into the more aorgic realm of nature. These special women and men who are cited in the fifth choral ode defy the gods and bring disaster on themselves and their children, but they also introduce the gods to their own divine disaster—to the lunar and solar disaster that the gods themselves are.[23] Danaë, for example, reveals to Zeus, the father of time and the earth, who he *is*. Danaë's own father, Acrisius, imprisoned his only daughter in a dungeon, for she had already been seduced by his twin brother Proetus. The oracle had told Acrisius that Danaë's future son, Perseus, would kill Acrisius, very much in the way that Io's father, and Zeus himself, had been warned about Io's race or stock, which many generations down the line would produce Zeus-destroying Herakles. Somewhere down the line, it seems, the gods of love always have to appear—even to themselves—in the guise of death. At all events, Danaë, surprised by Zeus in her cell, does not merely serve as the passive receptacle for Zeus's golden shower; she retains her kinship with Ananke by showing him what time is, what time it is, and whose time it is. She shows him *nolens volens* what Aristotle calls the superior delight, the delight in loving; she also shows him what such loving and being loved entail. How do we know this? Hölderlin deliberately "mistranslates" Sophocles' lines in order to enable us moderns to better understand what is happening, he says, but in so mistranslating he gives an extraordinary twist to Zeus's willful, arbitrary nature (CHV 2:353):

Sie zählete dem Vater der Zeit
Die Stundenschläge, die goldnen.

She counted off for the father of time
The strokes of the hours, the golden.

Danaë did something *for* the god? She *counted* for him? Well, he was there with her, and for reasons that were not arbitrary.

23. On this entire matter, see Bernhard Böschenstein, "*Frucht des Gewitters*": *Zu Hölderlins Dionysos als Gott der Revolution* (Frankfurt am Main: Insel Verlag, 1989), esp. 65–66 and 204. Böschenstein lays particular emphasis on the *suffering* of Danaë, as *leidend, mitfühlend*, with Lycurgus taking over the role of the rebel. Böschenstein's work serves as necessary corrective to my own, which, as we will soon see, tends to emphasize a secret mastery in Danaë's ticking off of the hours, a mastery-in-suffering that in some odd way grants her superiority over the very king of the gods—over the father of time and the earth. As both Renate and Bernhard Böschenstein assured me in a private communication, my reading tends to efface the difference between the Olympian gods and the Titanic demigods. Yet I see that effacement as the reassertion of Zeus's paternal side: Zeus remains the son of Kronos, son of Ouranos, and the time of Chaos continues to shine through in him. "For as you begin, so you shall remain," as the *Rhein* hymn says. (During the days in which I was completing this book, Renate Böschenstein died in Geneva. I am grateful for her work and for Bernhard Böschenstein's continued engagement in Hölderlin studies.)

Instead of being the unwilling recipient of the father's golden shower, Danaë becomes a figure of λόγος. She is the one who *counts*, in both senses of the word. She counts the sequence of events, metes out destinies according to the lawful calculus of time, foreshadows the counterrhythmic interruption that can only forestall (so that Zeus and we may see it better) but not quash calamity. Hölderlin's mistranslation is in fact uncannily close to the Greek: καὶ Ζευὸς ταμιεύεσκει. Ταμιεύω means to serve as a treasurer, not in the sense of collecting and hoarding gold within a thesaurus, but in the sense of dealing out and dispensing. *She* dispenses, *to* and *for* the father. Danaë teaches the father what his very own golden flow, γονὰς χρυσορύτος, means, and she teaches him by keeping time. Indeed, there is much counting or ticking off of the hours in the poetry and prose of Hölderlin, and it all has to do with mortality. Recall *Hyperion* on "the great Sicilian," Empedocles, "who, when he had had enough of counting off the hours [*des Stundenzählens satt*]," went to the crater's rim (CHV 1:753). The Frankfurt Plan for *The Death of Empedokles* cites "the time of succession" as that which binds and chafes Empedocles (CHV 1:763). "To the Germans," from the *Stuttgarter Foliobuch*, tells us that we "see and count off the number of our years [*Unserer Jahre Zahl sehen und zählen wir*]" (CHV 1:267). Finally, the "Elegy" of 1800 invokes the "all-too-sober kingdom" of the dead, where the defunct count off the hours in the frozen, desiccated wilderness ("*Wo die langsame Zeit bei Frost und Dürre sie zählen*") (CHV 1:289). Neither Antigone nor Danaë is therefore alone.

Hölderlin notes that when the names of the gods are spoken *seriously* (im Ernste), σπουδαῖος, Zeus must be taken as meaning the father of time and the earth. Yet the genitive is as much subjective as objective, inasmuch as Zeus *belongs to* time, *belongs to* the earth. Hölderlin explains: "For it is his [Zeus's] character to be in contrast to the eternal tendency, that is, to reverse the *striving from this world into another world* in such a way that it becomes *a striving from another world into this one*" (CHV 2:372). A god striving to enter *this* world? Well, he was there with her, and for reasons that were not arbitrary. Perhaps an unheard-of fidelity underlies all of Zeus's flamboyant escapades and betrayals? Perhaps a faith undergirds all his infidelities? Perhaps a truth that is a troth will accompany him to the death, his own death? Even before he writes *Hyperion*, we recall, Hölderlin is fascinated by this striving of the absolute to enter into the world of mortals, to become the tragic absolute. In an early draft of the novel, discussed in chapter 2 of this volume, a sage tells Hyperion about the moment when the "originally infinite essence" first comes to suffer some sort of resistance and restriction. That is the moment when Resource (Πόρος) and Penury (Πενία) mate and engender Eros. It is the moment of Aphrodite's birth, the birth of beauty. It is also the moment of the birth of *consciousness*, which is "inhibited force"; consciousness needs its confinements and barriers, its longings and languishings, in order to *be*. Consciousness and finitude are one and the same: time embraces them both. And the intentionality of finite, time-bound consciousness, which is always consciousness-of, is beauty. For the father of time and the earth, and for all his children, the sole noematic and objective correlative is Aphrodite. Yet the time of Aphrodite is *suffered*.

The categorial *reversal* of time, along with the reversal of the eternal tendency in the direction of an earthbound, temporal tendency, may best be understood through a reading of the myth of Plato's *Statesman* (269d 5–274e 3), that is, the myth of the Golden Age, when human beings were still under the guidance of Kronos and Zeus. This is of course the myth that accompanies Hölderlin throughout the gestation-period of *Hyperion*, precisely as it accompanies Schelling through his *Ages of the World* and "Divinities of Samothrace." Zeus/Kronos's categorial reversal of time takes us back to the earth and to the pretemporal or prototemporal Chaos of mortal bodies. For the human body initiates the time of what *Der Rhein* calls *uralte Verwirrung*, "primeval confusion," what the *Statesman* calls τῆς παλαιᾶς ἀναρμοστίας, "the ancient disharmonies" (273d 1). If "golden" refers to the beams of the sun, the sun of the Golden Age, and if the light of the sun pertains to the great sky gods Ouranos, Kronos, and Zeus, those beams—so dangerous and so searing when they grow excessive—must nonetheless be refracted by a lunar reckoning. "That happens always and only when time is counted in suffering [*wenn die Zeit im Leiden gezählt wird*], because then our heart of hearts follows with much greater compassion the course of time, and thus comprehends the simple passing of the hours—but this is nothing like an intellectual deduction of the future on the basis of the present" (CHV 2:372).

These remarkable lines, in search of a more appropriate relation to time for both mortals and the father of time, suggest that the infidelity of gods and mortals alike induces suffering. Danaë gives Zeus the time of day, the time of night, the time of his life. Zeus comes to suffer for this privilege. Presumably, he could have quit the dungeon, that smallest of small houses, at any time. Yet he was there with her, and for reasons that were not arbitrary. We may reassure ourselves that it was his choice, his *will*, his *liberum arbitrium*, to be there and to stay for a time; but it was in any case a time *she* would count, she in her very special house. If he proved fickle, if he persisted in moving house, it was always only in order—like Old Faithful itself—to learn, through suffering, about time and fidelity. "Learn through suffering," πάθει μάθος, is Aeschylus's maxim for mortals (*Agamemnon*, l. 77), along with "wisdom through groans," σωφρονεῖν ὑπὸ στέναι (*Eumenides*, l. 519). Yet the suffering and the groans pertain to Zeus as well. Myth has it that all of Zeus's mortal women were children of Niobe, and that he was seeking from them a son who would protect him and his fellow gods from the dire fate that Prometheus had predicted for them all in the necessitous course of time.

From here, of course, one would have to proceed to the (impossibly difficult) third section of the "Notes on Antigone." One would have to make sense of so many (impossibly difficult) things: above all, of the god who becomes present in the figure of death (*in der Gestalt des Todes*), of the "deadly factical" nature of the word in Greek tragedy, as opposed to the "mortifyingly factical" word of our own presumably "more humane" era, in which a "more genuine Zeus" reigns; of the course of nature, so inimical to human beings, a course itself now "*compelled more decisively back to the earth*," precisely in the way that Zeus himself is driven toward the earth rather than away from it; of the Hesperian fatherland and its need to grasp, understand, and depict clearly, along with its peculiarly dismal form of suffering, to wit, its lack of destiny; and, finally, of *Antigone* as a republican play, in the sense of a celebration of the French Republic, which is caught up in tumult and listing awkwardly to port (*aus linkischem Gesichtspunkt*), yet which even so is the hope of all who live in more benighted lands. All this is too demanding.

Let me therefore work my way toward a conclusion. In the fifth choral song of *Antigone*, immediately prior to the caesura (the dialogue between Tiresias and Creon), Hölderlin sees the conflict between Antigone and Creon presented in the purest possible form: here the two characters differ "solely with regard to time." Their conflict and suffering arise from the unalterable turning of time (*wie . . . sich die Zeit wendet*), a turning that first strikes us when Haemon rushes off the stage, heading for his botched patricide but successful suicide, and that we later comprehend when Creon survives Antigone. Creon differs from her by grace of time alone (*nur der Zeit nach verschieden*), she the loser simply because she presides over the beginning, he the winner— in the sense of *Winner Take Nothing*—simply because his time succeeds upon hers, as upon that of his own son. Sometimes it seems as though sheer succession—time tearing ahead and tearing us away with it—suffices for tragedy.

Meanwhile, the fifth choral song places Creon in the assembly of Lycurgus (hence of Pentheus) and Oedipus. It places Antigone in the family-line of Niobe, Danaë, Cleopatra, Semele, Io, and Persephone. Whereas in *Oedipus the Tyrant* the words of both chorus and dialogue are only *mediately* factical, inasmuch as the word, in proper Greek fashion, first becomes deadly when it seizes "the more sensuous body," *Antigone* points toward a later Western, more Hesperian age, in which the word becomes *immediate*, attacking "the more spiritual body." "The Greek tragic word is factically deadly, because the human body that it seizes is actually killed."[24] In our own Hesperian time, by contrast, "because we stand under the more genuine Zeus," who does not merely dwell between earth and the savage world of the dead but, as we only now said, compels the course of nature (which is always hazardous to humankind) more decisively back to the earth, the materials and modes of tragedy shift. If the principal tendency of Greek tragedy is to get hold of itself (*sich fassen zu können*), so that it may not perish utterly in the flames of passion (in what the first letter to Böhlendorff calls "the fire of heaven" [CHV 2:912]), Hesperian art struggles for aptness of depiction and skill of representation, inasmuch as its weakness is its lack of destiny, *das Schiksaallose*, δύσμορον, to wit, the misfortune of having somehow bypassed its promise. Admittedly, Hölderlin's use of *Schiksaal* seems especially here to cross paths with *Geschik*, skill of representation. To repeat the same point in other words, the factically deadly word, the word that seizes the body in rage, "actual murder through words," is eminently Greek; by contrast, in modernity, in the land of evening, the word seems rather to mortify, to kill the spirit through repeated poisonous draughts. *Oedipus at Colonus*, which induces awe by means of its words uttered from an inspired mouth, seems more suited to the Hesperian age than to the athletically Greek age, the tragic age, whereas the truly Greek tragedy, *Oedipus the Tyrant*, seizes the body, hanging or enucleating its nexus of characters.[25]

24. Judith Butler writes: "Indeed, words exercise a certain power here that is not immediately clear. They act, they exercise performative force of a certain kind, sometimes they are clearly violent in their consequences, as words that either constitute or beget violence. Indeed, sometimes it seems that the words act in illocutionary ways, enacting the very deed that they name in the very moment of the naming. For Hölderlin, this constitutes something of the murderous force of the word in Sophocles." Judith Butler, *Antigone's Claim: Kinship between Life and Death* (New York: Columbia University Press, 2000), 63.

25. It will be clear from the above that I disagree with the judgment of Philippe Lacoue-Labarthe, followed in this regard by Françoise Dastur, and now also by Dennis Schmidt, that in Hölderlin's view *Antigone* is the "most Greek" of tragedies. I believe that all the evidence, early and late, shows that in Hölderlin's view *Oedipus the Tyrant* is the most profoundly Greek of Greek tragedies. Perhaps Lacoue-Labarthe and Dastur are confusing the *character* and *fate* of the personages Oedipus and Antigone with the plays themselves. Oedipus does crave *consciousness*, and to that extent he does seem to be a Hesperian character. Likewise, to the extent that the time of Creon follows upon that of Antigone, who upholds the law of chthonic divinities, she seems to be an utterly Greek character, whereas Creon seems to be more Hesperian. Yet the properly Hesperian play is *Oedipus at Colonus*, and the properly Greek play is *Oedipus the Tyrant*, whose word is mediate but murderously factical, at least when one takes Jocasta's death seriously. One should not confuse a character (even a *title* character) with the play as such. True, Oedipus is mad for a consciousness, hence seems to be a Hesperian, but his and Jocasta's fates are deadly, factically Greek. *Antigone* hovers between these two Oedipus plays, and is as Greek as Greek can be, though listing toward modernity. At all events, the

At this point in the long third and final section of the "Notes," Hölderlin turns from the suffering of heroes to the suffering of gods, and especially of the father of the gods, who betrays one mortal woman after another but never escapes from the house of Niobe. Zeus's pleasure and pain—his captivation and captivity—enable him to plight his troth and then to hear the hours, *his* hours, *his* golden flow, being counted off by a mortal. Zeus goes down for the count. He can become present only in and as his brother Hades, the very figure of death, *in der Gestalt des Todes*. In *The Marriage of Cadmus and Harmony*, Roberto Calasso invokes that dramatic moment when Hades leaves the underworld in order to beg Zeus for a *living* queen to take back to the underworld. Zeus is unnerved by the request, sensing that a whole way of life is coming to an end in that request. Calasso calls this moment "the Eleusinian crisis." He writes:

> The Eleusinian crisis came about when the Olympians developed a new fascination for death. Zeus gave his daughter Kore to Hades, Demeter gave herself to a mortal. To find out more about death, the gods had to turn to men, death being the one thing men knew rather more about than they did. And, to get help from men, both Dionysus and Demeter had to prostitute themselves. A god surrendering himself to a mortal is like a man surrendering himself to death: every dead man has to bring a coin with him, to pay his way to Hades. Gods don't use money, so they give their bodies. After all, from the Olympians' point of view, men are already dead, because death lurks within them. (RC 214)

Hades is, of course, the object of Antigone's devotion. Antigone herself seems to be the Kore betrayed by Zeus and delivered over to his brother. One must concede that "divine infidelity" has as such dropped out of Hölderlin's discussion, and this is surprising, inasmuch as Antigone seems to be a victim of divine manipulation as much as her brothers and her brother-and-father were: the fourth and fifth choral songs identify Antigone as a girl torn between the gods of love and death. She is the sister-daughter who finds her brother-and-lover in death. One must therefore wonder whether divine betrayal is not even more readily remembered in *Antigone* than in *Oedipus the Tyrant*. This will be the theme of the following two chapters. But now, briefly, to the sufferings and betrayals of the gods themselves in general.

In *Antigone* the gods' names are systematically translated by Hölderlin in a "livelier" fashion, that is, more earnestly. Hölderlin began to do this in *Oedi-*

---

matter is complex and needs to be examined from several points of view. It behooves us to refrain from using the Greek-Hesperian distinction as coordinates for mapping the great Greek tragedies, which are themselves greatly nuanced. See Philippe Lacoue-Labarthe, "La césure du spéculatif," in *L'imitation des modernes: Typographies II* (Paris: Galilée, 1986), 52–53; Lacoue-Labarthe, *Métaphrasis*, 15, 46; see also Dastur in *Hölderlin: le retournement natal* (cited in note 10 of ch. 2, above), 26, 66, 93–96. See, finally, Dennis Schmidt, 151–152.

pus, designating Hades as "hell," the sphinx as "songstress," and Apollo as "the god of the plague," all of these names redolent of a certain infidelity, indeed, of an infernal betrayal. Yet in *Antigone*, on which Hölderlin worked especially diligently in 1803, the gods' names are almost always transliterated or transposed into expressions of meaning.[26] As we have heard, Zeus is often transliterated as "lord" or "father" of time and the earth. Ares is "spirit of battle," Nike "victory." Δίκη is "conscience" (*Gewissen*), Olympus "the heaven of my fathers." The Erinyes are "rage," "the mockers," and "the women who judge." Eros is "the spirit of love and peace," Aphrodite "divine beauty," Persephone "a wrathfully compassionate light" (*zornigmitleidig . . . ein Licht*). Bacchus is "the god of joy," Iacchus "the jubilant lord" (CHV 3:439–440). Hades is "the future site of the dead," "the world of the dead," "the god of hell," "the god of the dead," or quite simply, "the Beyond." Finally, Deo, or Demeter, thought as the languishing mother of the ravished and vanished maid, is "the impenetrable" (*Undurchdringliches*).

Many of these transliterations appear in the sixth choral song of *Antigone* (CHV 2:359–360), which opens with the apostrophe *Nahmenschöpfer*, πολυώνυμε, "Creator of names," or "God of many names," as Elizabeth Wyckoff has it. The god in question is the New Zeus, Dionysos, ostensibly the jubilant lord, the god of joy. Yet is Dionysian polynomy related to suffering, betrayal, oblivion, and categorial reversal? Could it be that all these names, and every tragedy, invoke the sufferings of the god Deo-Urania-Dionysos? Could it be that every strange house and every strange family of tragedy is the house of Semele and Zeus, the house of the moon, the house of the wine god?

> Jezt auch kommet ein Wehn und regt die Gipfel des Hains auf,
>   Sieh! und das Schattenbild unserer Erde, der Mond
> Kommet geheim nun auch; die Schwärmerische, die Nacht kommt
>   Voll mit Sternen und wohl wenig bekümmert um uns
> Glänzt die Erstaunende dort, die Fremdlingin unter den Menschen
>   Über Gebirgshöhn traurig und prächtig herauf. (CHV 1:314; 372–373)

> Now too a wind stirs and excites the peaks of the grove;
>   Look! the silhouette of our Earth, the moon
> Comes stealthily now too: the enthusiast, Night, comes
>   Full of stars and very little concerned about us
> Shining there, the astonishing woman, a stranger to us humans,
>   Above the mountaintops, mournfully, splendidly.

---

26. This may in fact be a part of that "emphasis on the Oriental" that the Greek world wanted to deny but that Hölderlin insisted on emphasizing (CHV 2:925). Indeed, one of the ways of defining the special households of tragedy more precisely has always been to note their thoroughgoing "Orientalism."

Among these lively translations of the names of the gods, perhaps the two most uncanny ones are those of Persephone and Demeter. Persephone, who is both dark and light, is *zornigmitleidig*, as furious as Oedipus and as compassionate as Jocasta. Perhaps *Persephone* is a name for the monstrous coupling and separation of gods and mortals, a name for the intense pleasures of catharsis as such? She is surely that for the Schelling of "Samothrace." And she is surely that for the narrator of *Hyperion*, who invokes "the goddess of death [*die Todesgöttin*], the nameless one, whom they call Destiny [*Schiksaal*]" (CHV 1:710). And the mother of Persephone, Demeter? Why are the Eleusinian plains of Demeter, or Mother Earth, where the polynomial gods gather, more vitally translated as "the impenetrable"? Has not the famous second choral song already defined human beings as the creatures who tirelessly plow the earth, irrigating and irritating her surface? Δηοῦς ἐν κόλποις, "Gathering in the bosom of the goddess," sings Sophocles' chorus, whereas Hölderlin reads and translates that bosom as *Undurchdringliches*. Κόλπος is the bosom or lap upon which a child or a domestic animal lies; for Aristophanes, in *The Birds*, τὰ ὑπὸ κόλπου means all that is bound up with Aphrodite; in medical literature the phrase means the vagina or the hollow of the womb; in poetry it is a metaphor for the tomb, "the body concealed in the loins of the earth," impenetrable at last. The Great Goddess, she of the brazen wheels, is surely that for Schelling as well.[27]

If not outright betrayal and infidelity, Dionysian polynomy and treachery (Euripides' Dionysos to Pentheus: "Would you like to *see* the women in the mountains?") do seem to retain something of categorial reversal. As Creon, bereft, slips off into the Hesperian west, to a more humane though more dismal time, a time of "firm opinion born of divine destiny," and as the readings of the play *Antigone* become more overtly political, depicting a conflict of persons who have been stylized or formalized—by Hegel, among others—to represent a certain status or role, only an echo of Greek tragedy proper remains. Hölderlin calls the characters of Greek tragedy "ideal configurations in the struggle for truth." The dialogues and choruses of Hesperian tragedy become more relentless (*unaufhaltsamer*) and more allusive (*deutend*), while those of Greek tragedy as such remain more violent (*gewaltsamer*) and more gripping

---

27. Perhaps the "impenetrability" of Demeter is to be understood more generally. Vernant, discussing tragic action in general, and making no reference to Demeter, says the following: "From a tragic point of view, then, there are two aspects to action. It involves on the one hand reflection, weighing up the pros and cons, foreseeing as accurately as possible the means and the ends; on the other, placing one's stake on what is unknown and incomprehensible, *risking oneself on a terrain that remains impenetrable*, entering into a game with supernatural forces, not knowing whether, as they join with one, they will bring success or doom" (VV 45; emphasis mine).

(*haltend*). Yet in both cases the dialogues and choruses of tragedy "give to infinite strife the direction or the force to be the *suffering organs* [leidende Organe] of the divinely wrestling body [*des göttlichringenden Körpers*]" (CHV 2:374). The polynomial words of tragedy, whether factically murderous or relentlessly mortifying, are *organs*. We should understand these organs as organizational factors, attuned to διάνοια, yet solicited by the more aorgic realm of nature. These dianoetic organs, the dialogues and choruses of any given tragic drama, flesh out the body of the suffering godhead, Dionysos. The words dare not go missing, "because even in the tragically infinite configuration the god cannot communicate himself to the body absolutely immediately." Rather, the god must be "comprehendingly grasped" or "*captured* by the intellect" (*verständlich* gefaßt); or, better, the god must be "appropriated in a living way" (*lebendig zugeeignet*). How does such appropriation take place? The factical word permeates the play from beginning to end, not so much in any particular utterance, but in the very nexus (*Zusammenhang*) of characters and incidents, under the influence of a certain form of reasoning (*Vernunftform*). The latter may not be the διάνοια to which we are accustomed; nor will it be the familiar and reassuring intellectual intuition of the philosophers. It will "take shape in the frightful muse of a tragic time" (CHV 2:375).

We have already heard something about that higher nexus in the Hölderlinian-Aristotelian context of the aporia of law, equity, and justice. Yet what about the nexus of the godhead, of the suffering organs of the god's body? What are we to make of the incapacity of the god to communicate himself to the human body absolutely immediately, an incapacity that must have become obvious to Danaë? What can such an incapacity mean in our more humane time, the time of a more appropriate human and mortal temporality? If it belongs to the essence of Zeus to reverse the tendency toward eternity to an earthbound drive, does a more appropriate and genuine Zeus become less like himself, reverting to the sky, or does he become more authentically earthbound than ever? One may of course interpret the mystery Christologically, as the problem of an incarnate son who has need of a mediating word, a holy spirit. However, in a more violent time, a time of incessant interruption and seizure (and I leave it to my readers to weigh on Hölderlinian scales our own age), one may be cast back to the dungeon in which Danaë ticks off the hours for the struggling father of time. His wrestling body does not have every organ it needs; Zeus needs her to dispense his gold. She is the *Es* of *Es gibt Zeit*.

Well, he was there with her, and for reasons that were not arbitrary.

Presumably, Zeus dreams of Danaë in the way Oedipus dreams of Jocasta, the way the chorus of Theban elders dreams of Antigone, the way Empedocles dreams of Panthea and Pausanias, and the way Dionysos dreams and fumes above the smoldering grave of impenetrable Semele. And what way is that? Let us agree, *faute de mieux*, to call it *excessive*. *Zu innig, zu einzig*, "too intense, too singular," as Hölderlin says of Empedocles; *zu unendlich*, "too infinite," as he says of Oedipus. Here the word *zu* carries the force—the excessive force—of life itself: ζωή, Ζεύς, Ζάς, ζα-.[28]

An obsessive reading such as this one—rummaging through a few houses in the universe of tragic being—clearly must respond to the diametrically opposed hermeneutical difficulties of reading Aristotle and Hölderlin. The Aristotelian corpus seems so familiar that we manipulate its concepts and texts with scarcely a thought, Hölderlin's writings so utterly strange that we grasp at straws, accepting almost any clue that promises to get us from one line to the next. Aristotle assures us that chance must be subaltern to both mind and nature. Chance nevertheless disrupts both νοῦς and φύσις, as though in counterrhythmic interruption of entelechy. The subaltern position of chance only aggravates its impact on a universe where neither mind nor nature was clever enough to exclude it at the outset from the realm of Chaos. (Recall, however, that even Plato's δημιουργός was not so clever, and Schelling's essence—not even close.) If nature built houses, says Aristotle, she would proceed precisely in the way intelligent art proceeds. Nature builds no houses, though she helps to form families and households. Some of these, perchance, build very special houses, houses in which, as Aristotle also says, "mistakes are possible" (199a 35). They are the houses that spawn tragedy.

In a more violent time, a time such as our own, in which the bodies of mortals are once again factically seized, divinity and humanity collide in rage, then draw boundlessly apart. Humanity mourns and languishes. Never was a word of blasphemy more necessary than in these sycophantic times, when pious prattle reigns supreme among the scheming mortals. Yet the prattle comes to nothing. For the father of time and the earth has already inherited the mantle of mortality from his own children; from hence his time too will be for the human body, human time, and human words. In a more "humane"

---

28. See Krell, *Daimon Life* (cited in note 17 of ch. 2, above), 14–16, on the "excessive" prefix ζα-. I did not know at the time *Daimon Life* was written that the sacred mountain of Naxos is called Ζάς. Otherwise I would have added a note on this fact—along with an entire chapter on Minoan-Mycenean and Cycladic mountain cults, the cults of the goddess. The *suffering* Zeus is bound up with these mountain cults: the final lines of Sophocles' *Women of Trachis* identify excessive life as Zeus when they assert that no matter how painful the trials and death of Herakles may be, "There is nothing in all this that is not Zeus."

time, divinity appears to have flown, and there is a certain nostalgia for its return. Yet that departure and return will always already have taken place—and
nowhere else than here on the earth. The entire romanza of divine departure
and return amounts to what Max Kommerell calls the "ferment of discord,"
the ferment of sky, earth, time, and mortality.[29] It happens over and over
again. In Françoise Dastur's unforgettable words, "The fire of spirit will
mount toward the heights, but love and pain [*l'amour et la douleur*], which are
the lot of mortals, bend that flame back to the earth [*courbent la flamme vers la
terre*]."[30]

Once installed, forever enthralled, divinity on earth learns mortality,
achieves the supreme consciousness that is finitude. The suffering god—not
altogether without organs, yet never with all the organs it needs—will be in-
eluctably *en famille*. Whenever gods need families and households, however,
someone somewhere tolls a bell, sounds a knell, counts the strokes of the
hours for all divinity. Yet it is not as though the gods or any other living creature had a choice. We may rest assured that whether in golden orgasmic ecstasy or in the throes of death, divinity zeroes in on a small number of houses.
Divinity never quits those very special mortal houses, does not survive that
small number of houses in the tragic universe. At least, that is what the fables
of the tragedians and the thoughts of the thinkers, if not the systems of the
philosophers, have always told us.

29. Kommerell, *Geist und Buchstabe*, 348. For the expression, "ferment of time," *Gärung der Zeit*,
see 327.

30. Dastur, *Hölderlin: le retournement natal*, 51.

HÖLDERLIN'S TRAGIC
HEROINES

10

And it will never come to shame,
That powerful pleading
On the eyelids of the bride; it was
Companion to Becoming, in the
  beginning,
When vast alliances were struck.

—SOPHOCLES/HÖLDERLIN,
Antigone, ll. 824–828

In the foregoing chapter we considered the Aristotelian paradox according to which the great tragedians invariably turned to a very small number of houses or families for their plots, adopting and adapting over and over again particular myths that seemed to express something universal about the mortal destiny. Perhaps it was natural enough that the women of these houses—for example, in the House of Oedipus, Jocasta, the mother and wife of Oedipus, and Antigone, his sister and daughter—exerted a particular pull on the poets. In the lost pseudo-Hesiodic *Catalogue of Women,* which must have been the richest source for the genealogies of the heroic households, Jocasta and Antigone would surely have occupied a special place—if only because of the complication they introduce into genealogical succession.

Jocasta assumes a puzzling position in what one might call the "shadow caesura" of *Oedipus the Tyrant,* that is, the second counterrhythmic interruption that slows down the pace of the drama immediately after its midpoint. (The caesura proper comes early on in the play, as the fourth of its seventeen scenes, when Tiresias confronts Oedipus with the complete tale of his destiny.) Jocasta slows the tempo and alters the rhythm of the scenes even more dramatically than Tiresias does. For Jocasta, in the "shadow caesura," is herself the shadow that haunts the House of Oedipus. She is a tragic heroine not merely because she dies but because she holds the key to Oedipus's mad search for an origin.

Equally striking is the character Antigone, especially after the fourth choral ode (the hymn to Eros) forces us to inquire into Antigone's *desire.* Whereas Antigone identifies herself with the figure of Niobe mourning her dead children—dead precisely because of their mother's hubris and blasphemy—the chorus of Theban elders compares her to the figure of Danaë. Danaë's name means either "parched," which would accord with her imprisonment, or "she who judges," which would make her a more formidable character than we—or Zeus—may have expected.[1] The Theban elders mention Danaë at the very moment when Antigone is about to march off to her imprisonment and death. As though by way of consolation for Antigone's being buried alive, unwed and unwept, the chorus of old men tells her that Danaë too, though of noble birth, was cast into a dungeon; they go on to rejoice that Zeus penetrated her cell and dignified her with his shower of gold—a consolation for old Theban men, no doubt, if not much comfort to Antigone, unless Antigone, like Danaë, is a more daimonic figure than she seems. To be sure, the comparison with Danaë makes us wonder whether and how Antigone will be "visited" in her tomb, and what her relations with both the sky god and the chthonic divinities might be. Add to this the fact that Hölderlin's most daring and deliberate mistranslation of Sophocles' text occurs precisely here, in the story of Danaë, and there is at least a prima facie case for saying that Hölderlin's heroines—his Jocasta, Antigone, Niobe, and Danaë—call for study and reflection. The case is strengthened when we recall that in the "Notes" on *Oedipus* and *Antigone* Hölderlin's obsession is the coupling or pairing (*sich paaren*) of god and human, followed by a boundless parting, which is conceived of in the "Notes on Oedipus" as the mutual betrayal of god and mortal. In the "Notes on Antigone," Hölderlin stresses the fact that in *Antigone* Zeus is compelled to alter his usual itinerary: he does not abandon the earth for the sky but turns decisively back to the earth. In search of Danaë? In order to "visit" Antigone? And if this pairing of god and mortal is to be taken so literally, what about Jocasta? The reply would be that even if Jocasta does not mate

1. On the name Danaë, see Robert Graves, *The Greek Myths,* 2 vols. (Baltimore: Penguin Books, 1955), 2:388.

with a god as such, her coupling with Oedipus occurs at one of the outermost limits of human coupling, a limit that in many cultures defines both the sacred and the profane, worship and sacrilege, the essence of the best and the heart of calamity.

What do the gods—and, for that matter, the mortals—desire of these women?

What do the women themselves desire?

How do these convergent or divergent desires drive tragedy?

Those are the questions of the present chapter. In an effort to respond to them, I will turn to Sophocles' great tragedies in their incomparable renderings by Hölderlin. Yet I want the reading to be informed by three commentaries, even at the risk of excessive delay and dispersion. Let me turn to three very demanding interpretations by, respectively, Max Kommerell, Karl Reinhardt, and Nicole Loraux.[2]

Three Commentaries: Kommerell, Reinhardt, Loraux

Kommerell does not directly address Hölderlin's Sophocles translations, although his final chapter, on Hölderlin's *Death of Empedocles*, extends well beyond its *topos*.[3] Yet the relevance of Kommerell's book is still more striking than that. For even the earlier essays on Goethe and Kleist are germane to the question of tragic heroines. Kommerell reads the final scene of *Faust II*, for example, as "a justification of Eros" (124), a scene in which the patriarchal God is no longer permitted to speak (47). (Faust's sole protection against the devil, says Kommerell, consists in his not inquiring after God [127].) Faust is saved not by faith but by Gretchen's love. What looks like grace (*Gnade*) in

2. A fourth commentary, by Jacques Lacan, exceeded the bounds of this chapter; see now ch. 11. Finally, a fifth commentary was to have been that of Carol Jacobs, "Dusting Antigone," in *Modern Language Notes* 111 (1996): 889–917. Jacobs reads Hegel and Luce Irigaray on Antigone as "the irony of the community" and shows how unstable that irony is. When Antigone gathers the dust to bury her brother, serving him more like a mother than a sister, albeit a "mother of the dust," she makes no mark in the earth. Precisely in this way, argues Jacobs, the text of *Antigone* offers no incisions or inscriptions for a definitive reading, whether idealist or feminist: "Antigone's unimaginable place as mother leaves no room for a clear oppositional struggle, for she who would bury Polyneices and give him meaning and form also produces or rather has already produced the dispersal of that form-giving, as mother of the dust, as carrion feeding bird, as prefiguration of intelligible interpretability gone awry. No one can gather these together into a single completed shape either of opposition or of resolution" (910). The range of commentaries we are offering here will present no oppositional struggles; nor are they written in stone, or even in earth, unless as dust. Finally, I had the pleasure of reading Judith Butler, *Antigone's Claim*, only after this chapter was finished. Butler comments briefly on Jacobs, though she does not see Jacobs's claims as a challenge to her own (83–84 n. 3).

3. Max Kommerell, *Geist und Buchstabe der Dichtung*, is cited here by page number in the body of my text. It was Professor Carlo Petzold of Tübingen who first put Kommerell's book into my hands, and I am grateful to his memory for that—and for many other things as well.

the last act is the effect of Gretchen's having loved Faust, or, to say it in the here altogether appropriate passive voice, Faust's *Geliebtwerden*, his having been loved. Kommerell emphasizes the essential passivity of Faust in this respect. The Faustian active agent, the Hesperian knower and doer, typically a bester buster boaster (as Joyce says of Blazes Boylan, another well-known Hesperian), owes his salvation to utter passivity. Neither faith nor works nor charity nor science amount to a cent here; in fact, all four constitute a hindrance to Eros, though not a decisive one. For at long last Faust succeeds in living not by self-assertion but by self-surrender, indeed, by pleasure taken in emotional potlatch, *Selbstgenuß in der Selbstverschwendung* (129). The conclusion of Part II of *Faust: A Tragedy* is in fact Goethe's most buoyant comedy. Yet the joke is on neither Faust nor Homunculus, who is the seed of man searching high and low for a body while Faust searches for the phantom of Helen: the joke is on God, who must undergo the Classical Walpurgisnacht like everyone and everything else that lives. If there is tragedy here, as Kommerell suggests and as Schelling and Hölderlin would confirm, it is a tragedy of the disembodied absolute.[4]

This brings us to Kommerell's commentary on Heinrich von Kleist's *Amphitryon*, which in turn will take us to Antigone and Danaë. In Kleist's play the joke is on Jupiter-Zeus and Molière, from whom Kleist takes the story. For under Kleist's hand the divine bedroom farce turns a more somber hue. Comedy becomes mystery, and mystery divine tragedy.[5]

The story? Jupiter, disguised in the form of Alkmene's husband Amphitryon, spends the night with Alkmene. Unsatisfied with mere conquest, however, the king and father of the gods, the father of the earth and time, then interrogates the woman so that he might gloat. Who pleases Alkmene more, he

---

4. Roberto Calasso emphasizes what few have noticed, namely, that Helen is most likely a phantom during that decade in which the Greek and Trojan heroes decimate one another and so fulfill Zeus's plan of depopulating the earth of its heroes. "For ten years the war had raged around an absent woman" (RC 129). Helen, the unique and irreplaceable woman, is always a simulacrum of Helen, not only for Faust but also for Paris and Menelaus: "Helen is the power of the phantom, the simulacrum—and the simulacrum is that place where absence is sovereign" (RC 123). Her body remains in Egypt, while her aura, haunting the halls and the walls of Troy, both amazes and destroys. When she walks around the wooden horse that contains the bravest of the Achaean heroes, she calls out to them, and each man seems to hear the voice of his best beloved. Odysseus, in order to keep Anticlus from crying out in response, must strangle him (RC 362). Helen works from the inside. And yet, years later, back in Sparta, she will sit beside her husband and tell Telemachos stories about Troy as if she had never betrayed anyone, as if she had never been there. Perhaps she wasn't. Perhaps, disembodied, she was (with) the absolute. Yet in this case, the absolute would be absolute hell. The chorus of Aeschylus's *Agamemnon* brings Helen's name into relation with the words ἑλέναυς, ἕλανδρος, and ἑλέπτολις, all of which suggest that the phantasmatic Helen must be written with a double-ell: Hellen is a little bit less than Hellenic, a little bit more like Hell'n. See *Agamemnon*, ll. 687–698.

5. For the following, see *Kleists Werke in einem Band*, ed. Gerhard Stenzel (Salzburg: Bergland Klassiker Verlag, n.d.), cited by page number or by act and scene in the body of my text.

begs to know, who satisfies her better—her mere mortal of a husband or the king of the gods in all his glory? Unfortunately for the god, Alkmene hesitates before replying. That instant of hesitation is enough to instigate the god's tragedy. Zeus is forced to discover that he can win Alkmene's *Zärtlichkeit*, her *tendresse*, only by actually becoming the mortal he merely pretended to be. In act 2, scene 5, Alkmene declares that if she could make time go backward she would bolt her door against all the gods and obliterate the name of Zeus. Jupiter-Zeus mutters to himself as an aside (*für sich*), "Accursed be the delusion [*der Wahn*] that tricked me into coming here [*mich hierhergelockt*]!" It is as though behind the girdle of Aphrodite, Atē and Anankē lie concealed—even when a mortal dons that girdle. To Alkmene Zeus says, with reference to himself, the king of the gods:

Du wolltest ihm, mein frommes Kind,
Sein ungeheures Dasein nicht versüßen?
Ihm deine Brust verweigern, wenn sein Haupt,
Das weltenordnende, sie sucht,
Auf seinen [ihrem] Flaumen auszuruhen? Ach, Alkmene!
Auch der Olymp ist öde ohne Liebe.
Was gibt der Erdenvölker Anbetung,
Gestürzt in Staub, der Brust, der lechzenden?
E r will geliebt sein, nicht ihr Wahn von ihm.

Would you not want, my pious child,
To sweeten his monstrous existence?
Would you deny him your breast when his head,
Which sets worlds in order, seeks it,
To find repose on that skin of down? O Alkmene!
Olympus too is desolate without love.
What does the worship of earthlings, prostrate in the dust,
Profit one whose breast is parched?
He would be loved, not their illusion of him.

Parched of breast, Zeus seeks Alkmene's breast, as though the original nectar were her astral milk. Yet he seeks it in disguise, will not come clean. When a parched Zeus persists in pretending to be Amphitryon, that is, persists in perpetrating the illusion mortals have of him, the jig is up. Although the play ends as a comedy or farce—and Goethe expresses his displeasure over the ending presumably for this reason—Zeus's end in fact comes much earlier in the piece. The last word of the play is Alkmene's *Ach!* Yet the god has already uttered that same word of lamentation long since: *Ach, Alkmene!* he gasps. The irony is exquisite: Alkmene confesses that Amphitryon was never more amphitryonic than on that divine night when she lay with god, but with this concession the god cannot be content—he needs to hear his own name uttered by her lips. If Jupiter-Zeus was merely Amphitryon-plus to her, Amphitryon potentiated, the god can only gnash his immortal molars (264). One might almost surmise that the father of the gods is jealous, though of what or whom we are too perplexed to say. It is as though the faithful Alkmene has cuckolded him by her fidelity, precisely by sleeping with Amphitryon-plus, the exponential god himself. One can imagine Kleist's Jupiter-Zeus stung by the subversive words of Iago to Othello (3.3, ll. 180–183):

> That cuckold lives in bliss
> Who, certain of his fate, loves not his wronger;
> But O, what damnèd minutes tells he o'er
> Who dotes, yet doubts, suspects, yet fondly loves!

In short, the cunning god, having gone to the uncanny woman, gets his mortal comeuppance; he is entangled in his own snare, the snare of his self-contradiction, or in her snare, it is hard to say which. Some would call it the snare of desire, others the snare of languor and languishment. In the end, Jupiter-Zeus begs Alkmene to take pity on him (265). Pity? As in "fear and pity"? If so, then the god invites the mortal woman to attend (to) his tragedy, hoping perhaps that she will undergo a catharsis that will at least resemble a second coming; for god the father, however, the outcome of the tragedy will be something larger than a little death. One recalls Hölderlin's "mistranslation" of Sophocles' lines on Danaë, whom the god also visited:

> Sie zählete dem Vater der Zeit
> Die Stundenschläge, die goldnen. (ll. 987–988; DKV 2:896)

> She counted off for the Father of Time
> The strokes of the hours, the golden.

Ask not for whom the bell tolls. For even if every night hence Alkmene should languish for the god in Amphitryon, that languor, *Ach!* avails Jupiter-Zeus nothing. Even when "the minutes told o'er" are not "damnèd" but celestial, golden suns in an azure sky and silver moons in the night's porphyry, Othello's reply to Iago remains unchanged: "O misery!" So it is in the present instance, as the victorious god suffers the defeat called *die schmachtende Sehnsucht*. It is Schelling who informs us of the final irony of the story: when Zeus lies with Alkmene she conceives Herakles—the descendant of Io whom Prometheus prophesies will destroy Zeus (II/2:335). Aeschylus's *Prometheus Bound* (ll. 871–873) makes this very clear: Zeus tries to be Amphitryon-squared in order to generate a son who will protect him from the son he is at that instant engendering in Alkmene. In Kleist's ironically titled *Amphitryon*, where the leading character, Alkmene, is so silent, so discreet, while the two Amphitryons compete noisily for her, one hierarchy is destroyed and another established. Destroyed, says Kommerell, is the erstwhile superiority of creator over created, or immortal over mortal; instaurated is the superiority of woman—unnamed in the title—over man. A double tragedy, some would aver. From here it would be but one step to the theme of the "dangers of surrender," and thus to Kleist's *Penthesilea*.

Roberto Calasso, in *The Marriage of Cadmus and Harmony*, helps us to draw the clear consequences of this unexpected development for Zeus Pater. All begins well for the mature Zeus, although we recall his hair-raising infancy. Zeus shares the bed of Hera, who can do things not even Aphrodite dares (RC 24). Yet over and over again Zeus is tempted by "that minimal difference" in the mortal women he craves, Io, Europa, Danaë, and the rest (ibid.). With the reign of Zeus the epoch of conviviality between immortals and mortals ends, the epoch in which gods and humans sit at the same table. With Zeus commences the epoch of rape, "the sudden, obsessive invasion" (RC 54). Yet if violence seems to replace compassion, that violence, in its very obsession, recoils on the perpetrator. If the Olympians may be said to glisten like an enamel surface, then with rape the "bright enamel of divine apparition is scarred by sudden cracks" (RC 59). What the violent Zeus craves from Alkmene and all the others is χάρις, free and spirited consent in the embrace; what he gets is yet another victim—a victim, moreover, who threatens him with the gravest harm: "Thus Zeus's womanizing takes on a new light. Each affair might conceal the supreme danger. Every time he approached a woman, Zeus knew he might be about to provoke his own downfall" (RC 93). How? Precisely by engendering the son that would (as Necessity had decreed) topple the father. Yet Zeus has already engendered Apollo and Dionysos by less-than-immortal mothers. "Over the never-ending Olympian banquet, a father and son are watching each other, while between them, invisible to all but themselves, sparkles the serrated sickle Kronos used to slice off the testicles of his father, Uranus" (ibid.). Mortal women thus introduce Zeus to mortality. Calasso concludes: "The most archaic form of the amorous chase, still close to the realm of perennial metamorphosis, was thus only a hairbreadth away from the most modern of dangers, that of the dawning of a post-Olympian era" (RC 136). Finally, what Kleist is able to show in *Amphitryon* is that Alkmene is dangerous, not because of the Herakles she will bear, but because of the grace, the χάρις, she withholds from the god. Her slightest hesitation is all the sickle that the god ever had to fear.

Max Kommerell's last chapter is on Hölderlin's three *Empedocles* drafts, considered in chapter 7 of this volume. Yet Kommerell touches on the theme of the heroine even here, and this first excursus will have to go on a moment longer. Well into the chapter, Kommerell argues that the most profound insights of Hölderlin's *Empedocles*, including the doctrine of eternal return, have to be placed in the mouths of others, specifically, Panthea and Manes, who become the successors of *Hyperion's* Diotima. Panthea-Diotima is called, we remember, the woman who interprets both the world and the interpreter. What does that mean? It means that at least five of Hölderlin's own deepest insights are placed in the mouth of a woman. First, says Kommerell, she is the one who is *open to transition* and who resists all absolute positions and positings. Such resistance and openness make Hölderlin's poetry as such possible. Second, she is the one who undergoes the *mourning of lovers*, the one who understands the fact that separateness or apartness (*Geschiedenheit*) is the origin of all suffering. Such isolation is experienced in missing the lover, in memorializing the lover, and in the mythic and phantasmatic restoration of the lover (320). Third, she is the one who understands intimately the god's passion for humanity, recognizing that without humankind the god's existence is merely "latent" (324). "For the inequality in rank between gods and humans is remarkably counterbalanced by the fact that the gods are defenseless" (325). It is not so much that human beings blaspheme and thus usurp the place of divinity; it is that human life, when it is beautiful, drives the god wild. If there is sacrilege here, the fault lies not with the mortals. Human beings assert themselves the only way they can, namely, by prevailing over the tender defenselessness (*die zarte Wehrlosigkeit*) of the gods—the very gods who threaten to pulverize humanity (ibid.). Fourth, she knows that the ferment of time (*die Gärung der Zeit*) will eventually sour the freedom of Zeus. The vaunted *Willkür des Zeus*, if it can be thought of at all as freedom and not serendipity, dissolves when the god meets the human beings who make him forget himself (329). Herein lies the intensity (*die Innigkeit*) that no "interiority" will ever succeed in translating. Danaë and her sisters teach the god the daimonic meaning of time; in so doing, they expose what Kommerell calls "the god's self-contradiction" (334). Fifth, and finally, woman is the one who understands what Empedocles, Hölderlin, and Nietzsche mean when they utter the inspired word that death is to become a festival (340). She understands that the sole actuality of infinity occurs in the boundless parting or scission (*Scheidung*) that so occupies both Schelling and Hölderlin. She is, in a word, Kathleen Ferrier singing Mahler's *Der Abschied* as thankfulness to the Earth. The god appears to her in and as the figure of imminent death; yet it is she who lets him know that time counts. Zeus becomes Dionysos-Hades in her arms, forever in pursuit of that great light, Persephone. None of this will be altered in any fundamental way, concludes Kommerell, when the god receives the designation *Christos* (350).

Karl Reinhardt's essay "Hölderlin and Sophocles" was written in response to a performance of Carl Orff's extraordinary opera, *Antigonae*, discussed briefly in chapter 8 of this volume. Reinhardt's sole specific reference to the opera, significantly, occurs during his discussion of the figure of Danaë. Before proceeding to that reference, however, some general remarks are in order.[6]

Reinhardt notes that Hölderlin's translations of Sophocles are anything but what our literary-humanistic tradition assumes translation to be. *The Mourning-Plays of Sophocles* is not a mere secondary work of Hölderlin's, "not a *parergon*, but one of his major works" (386). Further, Hölderlin's reading of Sophocles arises out of *Innigkeit*, a word we have already heard Kommerell emphasizing, meaning the intensity and intimacy that result from confrontation not with a literary object but—as Benjamin would concur—with a *religious* text. Intimacy arises from the nearness of divinity and a corresponding surrender of subjectivity (382). Intensity results from the fact that the nearness of divinity in the present case has little to do with traditional piety. It is neither chilly pietism nor chiliastic frenzy but *hymn*—in Hölderlin's sense of that word.

In terms of the plot and characters of *Antigone*, notes Reinhardt, Hölderlin's reading involves a reversal (or, more radically, a dismantling) of the usual (i.e., Hegelian) assignment of roles: not Creon but Antigone herself is identified as *antitheos*, that is, as an opponent of the gods, whereas Creon is seen as the one who honors the established god of law and shows piety in the face of destiny. Antigone represents a revolutionary, ecstatic, or prophetic relation to divinity; she is, like Empedocles in antiquity and Rousseau in modernity, a fool of the gods (384).[7] Not a harmless fool, however. If, as we shall see in the following chapter, her intensity has to do with the death drives, and if she is a fool to the death, Antigone incorporates in Reinhardt's view "the revolutionary, explosive, liberating, and dangerously daring" (385). She is, in effect, a moment within the time and times that are tearing ahead, *ein Moment der*

6. Karl Reinhardt, "Hölderlin und Sophokles," in Karl Reinhardt, *Tradition und Geist: Gesammelte Essays zur Dichtung*, ed. Carl Becker (Göttingen: Vandenhoek and Ruprecht, 1960), 381–397, cited in what follows by page number in parentheses. Note that Lacan, in the *Ethics of Psychoanalysis*, comments with enthusiasm on Reinhardt's *Sophocles* (Oxford: Basil Blackwell, 1979).

7. Lacoue-Labarthe concurs: "Tragic personages, starting with Antigone, are fools." See *Métaphrasis*, 62.

"reißenden Zeit" (387), in the direction of the excentric realm of the dead. In Hölderlin's view, time as such is the theme of tragic poetry. "For him, time is the ecstatic, that in which being [*das Sein*] reveals itself" (ibid.). And that also means *historical* time. Because our own Hesperian age is entirely different from and even opposed to the ancient Greek era, that is, because we live in a time of anxious expectation and awkward false starts, as opposed to a time of fulfillment and completion, the Sophoclean text must be transposed rather than merely translated. A key decision in such transposition is to let the *Oriental* character of Greek tragedy, which the Greeks themselves sought to repress, come to expression. The Oriental, while related to the Christian tradition, is above all "the primal home of the Dionysian" (389). *Oriental* therefore means "more original, stronger, more abundant, inspired and free, more unbounded, more 'foreign' and 'unconventional,' more nonclassical and nonapollonian, more immediate, Dionysian, naive, ecstatic, and closer to god—primal word and primal celebration" (ibid.). Hölderlin's hymns, at least from 1800 onward, speak this language of the Orient, and in his translations of Sophocles too, especially *Antigone*, such language prevails (390).

The most striking example of this Orientalizing tendency of the translation, introduced by Hölderlin for the sake of the Hesperian ear, is the alteration of the chorus's lines concerning Danaë. The chorus wishes not only to draw a parallel between Antigone's having been condemned to a live burial and Danaë's imprisonment by a father who feared her progeny but also to offer Antigone hope and consolation by means of the parallel. How? Zeus visits Danaë in her cell in the form of golden rain and Danaë conceives and later gives birth to Perseus—the sort of son (like Alkmene's Herakles) that every father rightly fears. Danaë comes from a noble family line, the chorus says, and she is entrusted by Zeus with his gold-flowing seed. The hymn to Eros has already been sung, so that we know what sort of consolation the chorus has in mind. It is this consolation that Hölderlin's alteration of Sophocles is going to radicalize.

Hölderlin treats Zeus's name "seriously," transliterating it as the father of time or father of the earth. "Seriously" means, according to Reinhardt (393), preparing for the return of the god. Reinhardt cites Hölderlin's lines from the "Notes on Antigone" that identify Sophocles' "gold-flowing becoming" as "beams of light, which also pertain to Zeus insofar as the designated time, by means of such beams, becomes more calculable" (ibid.; DKV 2:916). Reinhardt continues: "Time always becomes more calculable, however, when it is counted in suffering, because then the heart follows the flow of time with much greater empathy and thus grasps the simple passing of the hours" (ibid.). Reinhardt asks how Hölderlin's retranslation or transposition makes the myth "more demonstrable" for Hesperian ears and minds. Here, to repeat it once again, is the transformation of Sophocles' lines, *from* "entrusted by Zeus with the gold-flowing seed" *to* "She counted off for the Father of Time / The strokes of the hours, the golden." Reinhardt notes that the strokes of the hours, sounding from a church tower—say, from Melville's "The Bell-Tower"—are a deliberate anachronism. Yet the calculability of these strokes *in suffering* Reinhardt takes to mean "holding out in time—and in solitude" (394). He is clearly thinking of the sufferings of Danaë, alone in her cell. Reinhardt cites a number of references in Hölderlin's poems to this counting of the days and hours; the bulk of these references suggest the "stagnation" of time.[8] Reinhardt concludes: "Thus Hölderlin's Danaë, who counts off for the father of time 'the strokes of the hours, the golden,' is an image of tragic heroism, devoted to the time-god [*ein Sinnbild tragischen, dem Zeitgott hingegebenen Heroismus*], or, as Hölderlin says, 'remaining firm in the face of ongoing time'" (394–395).

Reinhardt takes Hölderlin's transformation of the Danaë myth to be esoteric, if not the result of a misunderstanding of the Greek text. "And yet!" he exclaims: Hölderlin's transformation causes the strophe in question to be even more fraught with tension and possible reversal than Sophocles may have intended. Reinhardt notes that these two final lines, in Carl Orff's opera, are recited in a sudden *pianissimo*.[9] The contrast, of course, is between Danaë's iron bars and the golden strokes of the hours. With this image of human existence as a prison, says Reinhardt, "the intensity is complete" (395).

Yet what if we were to push Reinhardt's reading in a direction he would doubtless find even more esoteric? What if the return of Zeus to time and the earth were not some grand second coming but, as Hölderlin says, and as Kleist intimates, a more decisive turn toward the earth within the god's own destiny? What if the suffering in question were not Danaë's, but the godhead's? Reinhardt says that Danaë is a tragic heroine who holds out in time and in solitude. That she does—until the god appears. What happens then?

8. Among Reinhardt's references, the most telling are these: a reference to the first version of *Der Tod des Empedokles* (DKV 2:347), to *Emilie vor ihrem Brauttag* (DKV 2:588), and to the poems "Elegie" (DKV 1:266) and "Diotima" (DKV 1:172). Surely, the most important reference is to Empedocles' "ticking off of the hours," in the second volume of *Hyperion* (DKV 2:166).

9. I do not have the score of the opera before me, but in the 1951 recording that I possess I do not hear the tenors' singing of the final two lines as a suddenly introduced *pianissimo*. Nevertheless, when the tenors do take over the chant from the bass singers, there *is* a noticeable alteration in the tone of the passage. *Pianissimo* would be the way to describe Antigone's lines immediately prior to the choral ode—among the most effective and affecting lines of the opera. Listeners may refer to the recording by Georg Solti (cited in note 9 of ch. 8, above).

Reinhardt fails to note the irony—or the sacrilege—involved in Danaë's counting the strokes of the hours to and for the father of time. Is Danaë telling the father what he already knows? Or is a more esoteric reading of this coupling of god and mortal possible and even necessary? Like Antigone, Danaë is *antitheos*. She knows the god in a way that lies outside of established and lawful attachments. In her deed too, as in that of Niobe or Lycurgus or Pentheus, there is a touch of hubris, *nefas*, or blasphemy, and a hint of human or divine betrayal. Danaë in some way turns the tables on the desirous father of time; she, like Kleist's Alkmene, in all her innocence assumes and destroys the father's prerogatives. Precisely Reinhardt's *religious* interpretation requires us to ask how this turning of the tables—or of the tricks, or of the hourglass of existence—transpires, and what its consequences are.

We have pushed Reinhardt so hard, however, that we have advanced to our own reading of Hölderlin's Sophocles. Let us slow down once again, however, and present the final commentary, that of Nicole Loraux.[10]

So many aspects of Loraux's little book deserve analysis in their own right; for the most part, however, we must restrict ourselves here to matters germane to Jocasta and Antigone. "For the most part," because certain methodological decisions of Loraux's remind us of decisions made by Hölderlin—above all, her realization that in both the performance and the reading of the tragedies "everything comes to us through words," or is "entrusted to the power of words" (vii; 33; 64–65). That is to say, women's deaths in tragedy are almost always *reported* deaths, grisly in word, invisible in deed, and for that reason overwhelming in the imagination, whether one is seeing the play or reading the text. Moreover, the "controlled pleasure" of the spectator and the "intense pleasure" of the listener, the very pleasures that are enigmatically bound up with the cathartic effect of tragedy, derive in part from the drastic *accounts* of these deaths (ibid.). One is reminded of what Hölderlin refers to as the mediate yet factical force of words, whether in stichomythia or in the choral odes. The fact that women's deaths can be entrusted solely to words does have a sociological basis: "It was in the depths of her house that a Greek woman was supposed to live out her existence as a young girl, as wife, and as mother; and it was shut up in her house, far from the gaze of others, that she had to end her life" (ix). Yet the somewhat muted and controlled pleasure produced by these reported deaths, which are painted in the goriest of verbal colors for the imagination of the spectator-listeners, also has to do with feminine

---

10. Nicole Loraux, *Tragic Ways of Killing a Woman*, tr. Anthony Forster (Cambridge, Mass.: Harvard University Press, 1987), referred to in the body of my text by page number.

beauty; here Loraux's thesis meets and generally supports Lacan's account, which we will examine in chapter 11, no matter how suspicious Loraux may be about accepting psychoanalysis "bag and baggage" (61).

Loraux focuses throughout her book on the throats of women and girls, who meet their deaths by either the sacrificial sword or the noose. The throat is a synecdoche for the entire neck, gorge, and bosom—the very heart of feminine beauty. Whether a virgin dies by the sword or a wife by the rope, whether death comes as a result of the split throat (σφαγή) or the bruised and distended neck (αἴρεσθαι), what Plato's *Timaeus* calls the "narrow isthmus" separating the head from the torso is the privileged site of feminine beauty *and* vulnerability. Beauty and vulnerability—yet also dangerous seductiveness. Loraux recalls Baudelaire's words about beauty "lending itself to conjecture," a conjecture that is intensified by the fact that the tragic deaths of women are reported deaths (x). Both Jocasta and Antigone die by strangulation and suffocation, each by her own hand, Jocasta within sight of her degraded marriage bed, Antigone shrouded by the silent darkness of her chaste tomb. Both deaths are reported rather than seen. Indeed, Jocasta's is reported twice, at first briefly ("One word is enough"), and then in titillating detail ("How? Tell us, how?") (4). Antigone's is in yet another sense a double death: condemned to death and sacrificed as a virgin, she then hangs herself, as though executing her nuptials with Hades in order to frustrate the sacrifice to civic law—or to tyrannical decree—ordered by Creon. Jocasta and Antigone thus join ranks with an illustrious line of suicides by hanging, a line that goes back to Minoan Crete: Roberto Calasso lists Telephassa, Argiope, Pasiphaë, Ariadne, and Phaedra, and immediately notes that these names "evoke a broad, pure, shining face that lights things up at a distance, that lights up all of us, like the moon" (RC 9). These lunar women who enrage gods and mortals alike by their shimmering beauty all end in the noose. Calasso writes:

> In the rapture of her sea crossing on the back of a white bull, Europa conceals within herself, like still undiscovered powers, the destinies of her love-crazed granddaughters Phaedra and Ariadne, who would one day hang themselves out of shame and desperation. And down among the celestial roots of this story tree we come across the wanderings of the mad heifer, the ancestral Io, who again holds within herself the image of another mad heifer, mother of Phaedra and Ariadne: Pasiphaë. And she too hanged herself in shame. . . . Pasiphaë, who hanged herself, Ariadne, who was preparing to hang herself, and her sister, Phaedra, who would hang herself some time later. . . . The bull didn't experience the ultimate perpendicular death of hanging, the being lifted away from this earth. (RC 10–11, 18)

Suicide by hanging is an ignominious death and is anything but heroic; it is therefore forced off the tragic stage. Death by hanging is, as Loraux notes, a "hideous death," a death without form, style, or plan (ἀσχήμων), a final defilement terminating a life already defiled (8–9). The word *defilement* betrays the intertwining of suicide and seduction: women hang themselves in their veils and girdles, in their headbands and by their own hair, which are among the cunning instruments or natural ensnarements of seduction; the *martial* sword is set aside, reserved for men and virgins (10), and is replaced by the *marital* weapon, as it were. [11] Jocasta hangs from the Sapphic roofbeam of the marital chamber (θάλαμος). Her body sways (αἰώρα) as though in ghastly mimicry of the Minoan swing goddess, suspended lifelessly between heaven and earth. She seems to be flying like a bird, both soaring and immobile at once, both dancing and dead.[12] All of this, to repeat, is in reported speech alone: "The staging in Sophocles even follows a standard sequence—a silent exit, a choral chant, and then the announcement by a messenger that, out of sight, the woman has killed herself" (20–21). Such staging represents both an innovation in and a preservation of traditional roles: neither Jocasta nor Antigone nor Creon's queen Eurydice—the last-named woman dealing "a final blow to Creon's doubtful manliness" by using a sword to end her life—dies without *éclat*, and yet the manner of their deaths follows rather strict conventions (54). "Women's glory in tragedy," Loraux insists, is "an ambiguous glory" (28). Why ambiguous? Because in the matter of femininity, "tragedy is two-faced" (30). Why two-faced? "We should accept that tragedy constantly disturbs the norm in the interest of the deviant, but at the same time we must be aware that under the deviant the norm is often silently present" (ibid.; cf. 60).

Antigone nevertheless embodies something of an anomaly for Loraux.

---

11. Euripides, in *The Phoenician Women*, handles Jocasta's death quite differently: she dies by the sword, sharing in her sons' martial gore and glory—she dies as a *mother* rather than as a defiled *spouse* (26). As for the instruments of seduction, recall Phaedra placing the noose around her neck precisely in order to ensnare Hippolytus. Phaedra's is the ultimate μῆτις of feminine death, inasmuch as her desire for Hippolytus has already put the noose around her neck: "Bitter indeed is woman's destiny! / I have failed. What trick is there now, what cunning plea, / to loose the knot around my neck?" For Phaedra, only a second knot can undo the knot of desire. Euripides, C ll. 669–671.

12. Loraux, 18. Antigone too is a soaring bird, as Carol Jacobs points out. When Antigone returns to her brother's corpse to find the first dusting undone, she shrieks like a mother bird returning to an empty nest. "In the figure of the bird, Antigone shrieks, echoing in advance the birds of augury, shrieks of a kinship that leaves obscure the difference between foretelling and predation, intelligibility and frenzy, and these with motherhood: In the family of Oedipus where the son is husband and the mother wife, why should it take us by surprise that the sister is mother?" (908). And, as Loraux has already noted and will note once again, when Antigone goes to hang herself she does so in the womanly noose (βρόχος) that is also a snare. See also Jacobs, 906.

Whereas the heroine ought to offer "the pure blood of virgins" to the sacrificial sword, she hangs herself as though she were wife or hetaera or mother. Hers is therefore a "mixed death" and a "striking exception" to the rule (31). Loraux elaborates:

> Although Creon thought he had taken care not to engage his own personal responsibility and that of the state, he actually condemned Antigone to Hades, a young life offered as a victim to the gods below. Buried alive, the daughter of Oedipus was doomed to die by suffocation, and in making a noose of her virgin's veil she brought on suffocation by other means. She gained twice, by contriving her own death, and by condemning Creon to the defilement that he wanted to avoid. But the significance of this hanging is not exhausted in the gesture by which Antigone, faithful to the logic of Sophoclean heroines, chose to die by her own will and so to change execution into suicide. By killing herself in the manner of very feminine women, the girl found in her death a femininity that in her lifetime she had denied with all her being; she also found something like a marriage. (31–32)

Loraux promises to return to the issue of Antigone's lethal marriage, which, she says, is in fact the key to every interpretation of her. By way of anticipation one may say that the "middle third" of the play, commencing with the hymn to Eros, alters Antigone—or our perception of her—in a fundamental way. There is doubtless a certain continuity in the sacrificing of virgins, whether the victim is Antigone or Iphigenia: "When the victim is a virgin, the sacrifice is tragically ironic in that it resembles, all too closely, a marriage"; indeed, such sacrificed virgins are universally pronounced "brides for Hades" (37). All such sacrificial victims are, like Euripides' Polyxena, brides without a groom and virgins no longer virginal (39, 80: νύμφη ἄνυμφος, παρθένος ἀπάρθενος). The most drastic form of the sacrificial metonymy is blood flow at the throat: when the virgin's throat is cut (not on stage, but only in reports), the stain of her blood transforms her from virgin to woman and wife—"as though a throat-cutting equaled a defloration" (41). Antigone, to be sure, does not die this way. Either she retains her virginity or, equally as likely, she has already lost it through her elopement with Acheron. Yet in either case we find ourselves at the throat and neck of the victim. Our reading of Loraux must therefore not end before it recounts her most remarkable analysis of "regions of the body" in tragedy, including both the upper and the nether throats.

The initial point is perhaps also the most telling. When Greek womanhood acquires a body, and it does so in tragedy, it attains that body only in order to surrender its life. When it comes to the Greek imaginary, writes Loraux, "the rule of the game is that what you win you instantly lose" (49). Woman's weak point (although it is the weak point of countless virile warriors in *Iliad* as well) is the throat (δέρη), whether her death is by sword or rope (52). Clytaimestra's δέρη narrowly escapes noose after noose (Aeschylus, *Agamemnon*, ll. 875–876), only to be split by her son Orestes' sword (*Eumenides*, l. 592). Loraux comments: "There is a conclusion of this analysis that we cannot avoid: death lurks in the throats of women, hidden in their beauty, which the texts never evoke more freely than at the precise moment when their lives are threatened and in the balance. . . . The Euripidean fantasy of the knife on the throat reveals tragedy's concept of feminine seduction, which is especially dangerous for the woman, who is its too vulnerable agent" (53). The sacrificial throat, the σφαγή, in fact extends from the larynx to the sternum and includes the chest and the breasts—it is the bosom, or *la gorge*, as drawn in our own Hesperian age by Félicien Rops.[13] Loraux calls this, as we have heard, the site of feminine beauty, and she is not alone in doing so; yet she also indicates that the signs of beauty— breasts, cheeks, and hair—are the very places where a woman strikes herself when mourning irrupts (88 n. 38). It is always the throat, moreover, that is exposed when women face the ultimate threat, as we recall from the murder of the beautiful widow in Kazantzakis's *Alexis Zorba*. Clytaimestra's murder offers the most telling ancient example. As though to refute Electra's charge that her mother was never what that word implies, Clytaimestra bares her breast to her son's sword. "Feel shame, son, before this breast!" αἴδεσσαι, τέκνον, μαστόν (Aeschylus, *Choephoroi*, ll. 896–897). Orestes' resolve slackens. The only thought that stiffens it again—his own repeated words attest to this—is that of his mother's adultery with Aegisthus. By steeping his mind in swirling images of her infidelity, Orestes summons up the rage to kill her. In order to account for all this, Loraux shifts her ground, turning from a reading of the texts of tragedy to an analysis of the "gynecological thinking of the Greeks" (61). Woman is precisely the creature who is "caught between two mouths, between two necks, where vagaries of the womb suddenly choke the voice in a woman's throat, and where many a young girl old enough to be a νύμφη hangs herself to escape the threat of the terrifying suffocation inside her body."[14] Jocasta, rather than Clytaimestra, would be the very figure of these two mouths or throats, so exces-

13. For an illustration of Rops's work, see Krell, *Purest of Bastards* (cited in note 15 of ch. 4, above), 56–60, 98–102. Can the analyses in those chapters, on the ultimate site of vulnerability for the logocentric tradition, that is, the voice in the throat, be brought to bear on Loraux's account of the most vulnerable site for the tragic woman? Only if one weaves together her themes of bloodletting, hanging, and the *spoken words* of tragedy.

14. Loraux, 61. Concerning those two necks, namely, the throat as such and the cervix of the womb, one might tell a long story, as long as the entire history of anatomy and physiology. See Charles Singer, *A Short History of Anatomy and Physiology from the Greeks to Harvey* (New York: Dover, 1957), 6–7, 45, 94, 112–113, 120; cf. 164–165. Representations of the womb in Western physiology from ancient Egypt through Vesalius show the organ as a second neck and head within the torso of the female

sively open in her life that she feels the need for the dire constriction that will close her life. Vagaries of the womb? Who can match such a description better than the mother of Oedipus and the grandmother of their daughter?

Even though tragedy itself "wants no part of this gynecological imagery, or at least does not want to talk of it explicitly" (ibid.), Loraux does not hesitate to point to what psychoanalysis refers to as "genitofugal displacement."[15] Loraux cuts short her account of psychoanalysis, however, hastening to add that nothing in her own work is meant as a contribution to "the sterile opposition between feminism and misogyny" (62). Indeed, if the attitude of Euripides toward women cannot be decided, that of Sophocles, who is a "master of ambiguity" (63), certainly remains mysterious.

Loraux's book ends with a reflection on the Greek imaginary, which attains a certain pleasure in hearing about (though not seeing) things that one can only call atavistic, namely, the sacrificial deaths of virgins and the ignominious suicides of beautiful women. For only if one can speculate on what the spectators "gain from thinking, in the mode of fiction, things that in everyday life cannot and must not be thought" (64) can one pursue the question of tragic pleasure and purification—the classic question of catharsis (65). Yet if that is too vast a question for Loraux's book, it is also one we have merely touched on earlier by citing Aristotle on the pleasures of revulsion. Let us keep Kommerell, Reinhardt, and Loraux in mind as we proceed—finally!—to the texts of Sophocles and Hölderlin themselves.

Jocasta's Shadow, Antigone's Ἄτη, Niobe's Tears, Danaë's Gold

It is as though Pier Paolo Pasolini, before producing his extraordinary film, Oedipus Rex, read Hölderlin's every fragment on tragedy, including the aborted "introduction" to The Mourning-Plays of Sophocles (DKV 2:561). For in that "introduction," as we noted earlier in these chapters, Hölderlin begins to develop the paradox of the sign (das Zeichen) in tragedy: when the tragic

---

body. Note especially the hieroglyph sa, similar to the ankh, or crux ansata, as a simulacrum of the cervix and womb, or neck and head, of woman. Of particular interest to Loraux would be the binding or constricting—by a cincture or noose—of the place where the inferior neck and head are joined, as though in anticipation of one of the tragic ways of killing a woman, to wit, suicide by hanging.

15. Loraux refers to Freud's Dora case, but one might also refer to Sandor Ferenczi, Schriften zur Psychoanalyse, ed. Thure von Uexküll and Ilse Grubrich-Simitis, vol. 2 (Frankfurt am Main: S. Fischer Verlag, 1982), 317–400, esp. 326, 328–329, and 351; English translation, Thalassa: A Theory of Genitality, tr. Henry Alden Bunker (New York: W. W. Norton, 1968), 11, 14, and 38. Once again, the long story of the etiology of hysteria, from Plato to Foucault, emphasizes the rising of the gorge and blockage of breath, as the restless womb wanders upward—in genitofugal displacement—from its proper place. See Krell, "Female Parts in Timaeus," Arion: A Journal of Humanities and the Classics, nos. 2, 3 (Fall 1975): 400–421.

"original" appears in all its strength, it enters on the scene as debility (*Schwäche*). The sign itself is nonsignifying (*unbedeutend*) when it best exposes "the concealed ground of every nature." In other words, when tragedy comes down on us with all its force, its sign = 0. Pasolini says that the proper sign of *Oedipus the King* is Jocasta, inasmuch as she is "a non-sign" in the language of the play—unreadable, beyond interpretation, a sign that is not read.[16] In one of the most uncanny early scenes of the film, set in Bologna in the 1930s, Pasolini has the young mother who will become Jocasta gaze into the camera: the woman, who has no eyebrows, who is all eye and mask and mascara, wears a vague smile at first; then, in a most minute and gradual transformation, her face becomes the very mask of tragedy, only to revert to that slight smile. We have no idea what that look means, even as it devastates us. The look = 0. Yet no one who sees Pasolini's film ever forgets it.

Jocasta's appearance on the Sophoclean stage produces what I have been calling a "shadow caesura," the final counterrhythmic interruption in the play's dramatic action before the catastrophe. Whose catastrophe? Hers, of course. True, Oedipus loses his sight at the sight of her dead, but Jocasta loses her life. If the word in Greek tragedy is in fact deadly, *tödlichfaktisch*, as Hölderlin says (DKV 2:918), then Jocasta is the properly Greek heroine, in all her strength and original mystery, in all her vulnerability and fragility. For indeed—and this is her strength—we never know exactly what Jocasta knows or when she knows it, whereas we are quite attuned to the fluctuating degrees of Oedipus's ignorance and insight. What we do come to know with regard to Jocasta—and this is her weakness—is that there are limits to what she too can take.

When Tiresias, in the proper caesura of the play, taunts Oedipus, he seems to be aping Manes' taunting of Empedocles: *Weißt du, woher du bist?* (l. 420; DKV 2:804). "Do you know where you are from?" The blind seer, half-man, half-woman, evokes Jocasta as the unknown origin, the inscrutable original whose sign = 0; her debility will defeat her, but her strength will blast her son and consort. She enters on the stage for the first time as the chorus is telling Creon and Oedipus that their quarrel should be played out under the eyes of this woman who is now emerging from the house (l. 640; DKV 2:813). She is soon able to quell Oedipus's wrath against Creon, if only because, as he himself proclaims, she is the person he honors most in the world (l. 714; DKV 2:816). She is full of contradictions from the start. For example, she tells Oedipus to respect Creon's oath of innocence, yet she herself is openly contemptuous of oaths, oracles, and prophecies, which she will soon

---

16. Pasolini, *Oedipus Rex*, 13.

tell Oedipus too to scorn. Indeed, she is the perfect embodiment of what the chorus is complaining about, namely, the decline of worship in Thebes and the withering away of the force of the oracles throughout Greece. Nevertheless, this same Jocasta makes sacrifice and utters a prayer to Apollo in order that her husband may find calm. Of course, once the messenger arrives with the good news of Polybus's death—good news, for it means that Oedipus cannot have murdered his father—Jocasta reverts to her earlier expressions of contempt for the oracles.

Yet her contradictions do not stop there; they are nothing short of murderous. She blames her infant's purported death on Laius, yet according to the later revelations of the old servant (l. 1188; DKV 2:835) she is the one who hands the baby over for exposure. The shadow of infanticide thus haunts this penumbral character and her son throughout the play: in spite of her outspoken contempt for the oracles we begin to wonder whether it was in fact she who convinced Laius of the danger embodied in the newborn, she who after the oracle's warning moved to have the child killed. We can begin to wonder this because Jocasta is the zero-cipher, the blank screen onto which our every anxiety and all our paranoia can be projected flawlessly. What Sophocles composes dianoetically, we spectators experience paranoetically.

Part of what we desire to know but are afraid to ask is what transpires in the bedroom of a mother and her son. One ancient source is explicit about this. As it describes Oedipus's crimes against both father and mother, the third choral ode of Aeschylus's *Seven against Thebes* adds an uncanny remark concerning Oedipus and Jocasta in bed. One would sooner expect to hear such a remark from Euripides or Sophocles than from the stern Aeschylus. The poet tells us that a certain frenzy, a certain frenetic extreme—indeed, some form of madness and utter distraction of mind—distorts the love-making of these two: παράνοια συνᾶγε νυμφίους φρενώλης, "Tumultuous madness unites these lovers" (ll. 756–757). One thinks of Pasolini's Oedipus, furiously pecking at his mother's neck and face, as though he is trapped in the oral phase and paranoid about the phases to come. One thinks too of Pasolini's Jocasta, who has worked through all the phases and who laughs dementedly in the face of what she already knows yet dares not know and therefore does not really know; she too is paranoid about what once was, what now is, and what is to come.[17]

17. Something of Jocasta's paranoia is clarified in Jean-Pierre Vernant's extraordinary account of the House of Labdacus—not a House to satisfy even the least demanding of women. In the chapter entitled "The Lame Tyrant," Vernant indicates that Labdacus himself was lame, his son Laius "clumsy" and "one-sided," and his grandson Oedipus a cripple. Vernant writes: "Labdacus, the lame

During their exchange in act 3, it is Oedipus who seems to know the truth, as Jocasta, remarkably innocent, even demure, supplies him with all the details he needs for his demise. In act 4, the shadow caesura, her contempt for the priests and seers passes over into scorn for the incest taboo—or, if not scorn, her astonishingly blasé attitude concerning what some consider the very pillar of exogamous civilization. Every boy dreams of sleeping with his mother, she says. Get over it. (See once again ll. 995–1002; DKV 2:827.) As the shadow lengthens in the course of act 4 of Sophocles' play, Jocasta seems to know everything; indeed, she now seems always to have known it all, in spite of her earlier "innocence." Her sole concern in act 4 is to frustrate Oedipus's discovery of what she herself knows without knowing:

Wer sprach, von welchem? kehr dich nicht daran!
Und was man sagt, bedenke nicht zu viel es. (ll. 1075–1076; DKV 2:830)

Who was speaking? and about what? do not concern yourself!
And whatever they say, think not overmuch about it.

If you care about life, she says, halt your search. And if you care about me, whom you honor above all in the world, she says, halt your search. "I am sick enough" (l. 1080; DKV 2:831). In their final bitter exchange, the one that in effect kills her—for she *is* killed by Oedipus's cruel words, mediately, but factically-mortally—Oedipus tells her that her blue blood will not be sullied no matter how vulgar his own lineage may prove to be. With this insult to her love he cuts himself off from her. He cuts the cord, as it

---

one, dies when his son [Laius] is still a baby, only one year old. The legitimate lineage is broken as the normal link between father and son is cut. The throne is occupied by a stranger, Lucus. Young Laius is not only pushed aside but is sent away, expelled from Thebes. He takes refuge with Pelops. [¶] When Laius, the left-hander, grows up, he proves to be unbalanced and one-sided both in his sexual relations and his relations with his host. His erotic behavior is rendered deviant by his excessive homosexuality and by the violence to which he subjects the young Chrysippus, Pelops' son, thereby breaking the rules of symmetry and reciprocity that should obtain both between lovers and between guest and host. Chrysippus kills himself. Pelops pronounces a curse against Laius, condemning his race to infertility: the *genos* of the Labdacids is not to be perpetuated. [¶] Laius returns to Thebes, is re-established on the throne and marries Iocasta. . . . Then he receives a warning from an oracle. He must not have a child. His lineage is condemned to sterility and his race bound to disappear. If he disobeys and engenders a son, this 'legitimate' son, instead of resembling his father and carrying on the direct line, will destroy it and sleep with his mother. The *gnesios*, the well-born son, will turn out to be worse than a *nothos* [i.e., a bastard], beyond even bastardy: he will be a monster. [¶] Laius's sexual relations with his wife are deviant, in the homosexual manner, to avoid producing children. But on one evening of drunkenness, he forgets to take care: he plants a child in the furrow of his wife. This son, at once legitimate yet cursed, is expelled at birth from Thebes, left out on the open slopes of Mount Cithaeron, to die of exposure" (VV 212). The story goes on, but becomes now more familiar. After reading it we are inclined to exclaim: No wonder Jocasta welcomes Oedipus to Thebes and to her bed—after her trying tenure with Laius! Yet if her son alone should be the instance of her pleasure, would this not occasion a distraction of mind, a certain frenzy, an upsurgence of paranoia?

were, and leaves her hanging by it, the catachresis of generation that spells her death. The final exchange, in the translation by Hölderlin (DKV 2:831; ll. 1081–1091):

> OEDIPUS: Take courage! if I came from three mothers,
> Three times a slave, it would not make you any worse.
> JOCASTA: It would. Obey me, I beg you, do not do it!
> OEDIPUS: I cannot but do it, I have to know quite precisely.
> JOCASTA: I intend your good and tell you what is best.
> OEDIPUS: This best of yours has long been torturing me.
> JOCASTA: Wretched one! if only you would never know who you are!
> OEDIPUS: Will someone go and bring me the shepherd?
> Let this one enjoy her rich family!
> JOCASTA: Oh! Miserable wretch! that is the one thing I can still
> Say to you, nothing else, not now, not ever!

In the ensuing scene, the old servant tells Oedipus that the woman within the walls of the house would in fact have one more thing to tell him, to wit, that it was she who handed the child over to be exposed on the mountain. Hölderlin translates Oedipus's question into an eerie present tense (ll. 1189–1192; DKV 2:835–836):

> OEDIPUS: Then she is the one who gives it to you?
> SERVANT: Yes, my king.
> OEDIPUS: To do what with it?
> SERVANT: That I might take its life.
> OEDIPUS: Because she was unhappy to give birth?
> SERVANT: Out of fear of evil predictions.
> OEDIPUS: And what were they?
> JOCASTA: It would kill its parents; that was what they said.

"Its parents," in the plural: τοὺς τεκόντας, so that both father and mother have to fear and have to act. "How could a mother do such a thing?" is the prior question, according to most translations of τεκοῦσα τλήμων . . ., "How could she have turned over the fruit of her own body to death?" Hölderlin supplies a possible motive for Jocasta's action, a surmise based on a more literal—perhaps more intensely Oedipal—reading of τεκοῦσα: "Because she was unhappy to give birth?" Oedipus, whose questions are increasingly terse, going from four words to two to one word, as though these questions were feet a human being has to stand on, concludes the exchange with an apparent reference to the murder of Laius, but it might just as well be to the imminent murder of Jocasta (ll. 1200–1202; DKV 2:836):

Man sagt, ich sei gezeugt, wovon ich nicht
Gesollt, und wohne bei, wo ich nicht sollt', und da,
Wo ich es nicht gedurft, hab' ich getötet.

They say I was engendered where I ought
Not, that I am sleeping where I ought not, and that there
Where I dare not, I killed.

Interpreters of *Oedipus the Tyrant* seldom note the fact that when Oedipus dashes off in search of Jocasta it is not in order to rescue her from her fate, a fate the chorus fears she has already fulfilled, but to kill her. He calls for a sword, pursues her, breaks down two doors to get to her, cursing the woman that bore him and bedded him, she the twice-plowed field and he the double harvest. This second murder of a parent, foretold at Delphi ("It would kill its parents; that was what they said"), is stayed only by an accident of time: Jocasta beats him to it, killing herself by her own hand, αὐτὴ πρὸς αὐτῆς, *sie selber durch sich selbst*.[18] If Oedipus puts out his eyes at the sight of her, it is so that he cannot see the crime he himself desired and in a way accomplished, in mediating-factical word if not in deed, and accomplished well—for hers is the ignominious death by hanging, not the glorious death of the sword. Perhaps that is why in the "Notes on Oedipus" Hölderlin refers to the scene of their final exchange not only as one of Oedipus's being "tempted back into life," and of his desperate struggle to come to consciousness, but also as the scene of his "absolutely destructive [*niedertretende*] almost shameless striving to gain control of himself" (DKV 2:853). If Oedipus is remorseful, it is only *après coup*. He puts out his eyes so that when he goes to Hades he will not have to see his father *and* his mother, both of whom he has wrathfully dispatched (l. 1389; DKV 2:843).

We have thereby established Jocasta as a properly Greek tragic heroine, precisely as the one who factically dies. Yet we will have to return to her at the end—that wretched mother and glorious queen, the original and powerfully present woman whose strength is vulnerability and whose sign = 0. Yet let us now abandon Jocasta for her daughter, or granddaughter.

18. *Oedipus the Tyrant*, l. 1257; DKV 2:838. Sophocles loves this expression: he uses exactly the same words, barring the gender difference, with regard to Ajax in the tragedy of that name—Ajax falls on his own sword, αὐτὸς πρὸς αὐτοῦ (l. 906). Aeschylus loves the phrase as well. When Orestes seeks to evade the blame for the matricide he is about to commit, he uses a related phrase: σύ τοι σεαυτήν, "You have done this to yourself!" (*Choephoroi*, l. 923). Yet the sophism does not work: the Erinyes will know the one they must pursue. Finally, when in *Prometheus Bound* Io asks the suffering Titan who will finally wrest the scepter from Zeus's hand, Prometheus—having already seen Zeus's lust for Io—renders the ultimate paradox of divinity: πρὸς αὐτὸς αὑτῷ, "He will do it to himself," ἐπ'αὐτὸς αὑτῷ, "He will act on himself," that is to say, against his own interests (ll. 762, 921).

Concerning Antigone, no one will ever have written or said enough, certainly not about her desire, which Hölderlin's lines so powerfully communicate. Let us therefore focus on this "middle third" of the play—not that one has to wait all that long for Antigone's peculiarly erotic character to come to the fore. Concerning her brother, she says early on to Ismene: *Lieb werd' ich bei ihm liegen, bei dem Lieben* (l. 75; DKV 2:863). "Lovingly will I lie with him, with my beloved." And later to Creon: *Zum Hasse nicht, zur Liebe bin ich* (l. 544; DKV 2:879). "Not for hate, for love am I." The heroine of *Antigone*, the bluest of the blue angels, will always have been about a peculiar love. As we have seen, the readings by Kommerell (at least in tendency), Reinhardt, and Loraux revolve about the famous fourth choral ode, the hymn to Eros. (In general, one is tempted to say concerning these choral songs that if there are "shadow caesurae" in *Antigone* they occur in and as the hymns, which in contrast to the choral songs of *Oedipus the Tyrant* open rather than close the scenes in Hölderlin's texts.[19]) It is thus the erotic Antigone, the beautiful child Antigone, the little girl with clout, who intrigues the contemporary reader.

If we may anticipate Lacan's reading of *Antigone*, to be taken up at length in the following chapter, we can say that Hölderlin seems to be particularly attuned to an Antigone who moves beyond the pleasure principle (though taking it with her as she goes) to the death drives. One of Hölderlin's most daring Hesperian moves (see, e.g., ll. 606, 635, and 645; DKV 2:883–884) is to translate Ἄτη, "doom," consistently as *Wahnsinn*, "madness," although *Wahnsinn* sometimes also translates μανία. Hölderlin is not reluctant to double up on madness. If Antigone's situation can be described as ἐκτὸς ἄτας, "beyond Ἄτη," somehow *beyond* doom, *beyond* madness, Hölderlin translates that situation as the excessive "cost" of *ein gesetztes Denken*, the "price" of a thinking that is well-established and steeped in laws. Yet the beyond of madness is also that infatuation with which a treacherous god infects a mortal who has for whatever reason offended divinity. In the present case, as so often in the tragedies, this god is Apollo, the purifier/polluter:

Das Schlimme schein' oft trefflich
Vor einem, so bald ein Gott
Zu Wahn den Sinn hintreibet.
Er treibet's aber die wenigste Zeit
Gescheuet, ohne Wahnsinn. (ll. 645–649; DKV 2:884)

19. On the choruses in Hölderlin's renderings of Sophocles, see Manfred Lossau, "Hölderlins Sophokleschöre," *Hölderlin Jahrbuch* (1996–1997): 255–265. Lossau shows how Hölderlin restructures the formal contours of Sophocles' choral odes in order to achieve a more "affective" and even "Oriental" impact (265).

What is wicked often seems suitable
To one, as soon as a god
Drives his wits to madness [πρὸς ἄταν].
Only for the briefest span of time
Does he act wisely, without madness [ἐκτὸς ἄταν].

Hölderlin's translation of ἵμερος, "desire," in the fourth choral ode, as *das Mächtigbittende*, "powerful pleading," is quite striking; it supports an erotic reading of the play, as long as that reading is aware of the alliance of eros and death from the beginning:

Und nie zu Schanden wird es,
Das Mächtigbittende,
Am Augenlide der hochzeitlichen
Jungfrau, im Anbeginne dem Werden großer
Verständigungen gesellet. (ll. 825–829; DKV 2:890)

And it will never come to shame,
That powerful pleading
On the eyelids of the bride; it was
Companion to Becoming, in the beginning,
When vast alliances were struck.

Mindful of both Eros-Himeros and the alliance with death, Schelling's πόθος, let us now return to the story of Danaë as Karl Reinhardt was recounting it—up to the point when we decided to "push" his account.

What happens when Zeus enters Danaë's prison cell? What draws the father of time *into* time, the father of the earth *back to* earth? Even the son of a Swabian Pietist mother knows to call it *desire*. We remember that as a secondary school pupil Hölderlin was already aware that the Greek gods were infinitely susceptible to beauty, and to beautiful mortality in particular. As a result, writes the schoolboy, in delightful understatement, the gods regularly "descended to earth for the sake of beauty" (DKV 2:474). Danaë was among those who had sufficient allure to instigate divine desire. "Allure" is admittedly too shallow a word for the terrible power of beauty, that *éclat* which we never confront with disinterested delight (*pace* Kant and Schopenhauer) but which always perturbs us and sometimes paralyzes us, offering us a foretaste of death. For what does the radical erotization and temporalization of gods and humans alike imply? It implies the tragic insight that all who have their hours counted off for them are bounded and hounded by a terrifying alterity, an otherness that they can only *suffer*. Elizabeth Sikes puts it incomparably well:

Our common mortality binds us to one another; consciousness of that mortality makes us human. Such consciousness also enables human beings to love, for it is knowledge of mortality that makes us love life with the fierceness of Antigone, irrecusably, with a depth and intensity (*Innigkeit*) that makes us love others who may or may not survive us. And when the capacity to love reveals mortality, as is the case with Antigone, the suffering entailed—inherent in all πάθη—has the countenance of Aphrodite. This is the Beautiful, because it marks an infinite movement toward the other whom we know will ultimately pass away, cannot remain. In life's passing away, the infinite striving toward life is revealed; recognition of both the passing and the striving engenders love. . . . Love and time are known in passing, in the movement of the moment, in downfall and in becoming, with which even the gods must reckon when, like Zeus, they fall for a mortal woman.[20]

Does the heroine have a special prerogative among mortals, and even among the immortal gods, whom the heroine demonstrates to be as mortal as herself? She does, at least in the visions of Sophocles and Hölderlin, although Ganymede certainly has a right to demur. At all events, Diotima's instruction would be that when it comes to Eros and Himeros we are all—mortals and immortals alike—children of penury. Sophocles says of Eros, in Hölderlin's grand reinscription:

Fast auch Unsterblicher Herz zerbricht
Dir und entschlafender Menschen, und es ist,
Wer's an sich hat, nicht bei sich. (ll. 17–19; DKV 2:890)

The heart of immortals too well-nigh shatters before you,
And the heart of dimly stirring humanity, and it is as though
Whoever has got it is not altogether there.

Among those who are not "altogether there" are the omnipresent immortals. For Hölderlin it is fundamentally a question of the coupling or mating (*sich paaren*) of god and human. Others may desperately try to take this coupling merely metaphorically; yet the Greeks invented metaphor in response to the ravishing encroachments of the godhead. Hölderlin's central intuition becomes clear in his translation of the chorus's lines in act 4, with the fifth choral ode. At the risk of belaboring the point, I want to look at these lines on Danaë once again, this time in their larger context:

Der Leib auch Danaes mußte,
Statt himmlischen Lichts, in Geduld
Das eiserne Gitter haben.

20. Elizabeth Sikes, "Translation of Κάθαρσις, Κάθαρσις as Translation: The Post-Kantian Revolution of the Tragic in Hölderlin and Nietzsche" (Ph.D. dissertation, DePaul University, forthcoming in 2005), ch. 2, which I have been fortunate to see in manuscript.

Im Dunkel lag sie
In der Totenkammer, in Fesseln;
Obgleich an Geschlecht edel, o Kind!
Sie zählete dem Vater der Zeit
Die Stundenschläge, die goldnen. (ll. 981–988; DKV 2:896)

Danaë's body too was forced
To accept with patience, instead of celestial light,
Bars of iron.
In the dark she lay
In the sepulcher, in fetters;
Although she was of noble lineage, o child!
She counted off for the father of time
The strokes of the hours, the golden.

The final three lines form a syntactical and semantic unity, though a tensed one, if we do not take the exclamation point after *Kind!* to mark the end of the sentence. It marks the end of the apostrophe, but the sentence begins with an *Obgleich*, "although," so that we have to anticipate an antithesis. After the words "noble lineage" have fallen, we can expect to be returned to Danaë's wretched state. Such an expectation tends to support Karl Reinhardt's more conservative reading of the lines: *even though* Danaë was of aristocratic lineage, as is Antigone, she had to suffer; presumably, she had to suffer not only the patient acceptance of solitude but also the god's visitation. The theme of Danaë's (and not Zeus's) suffering would therefore be a constant in the hymn. Yet the two last lines are the lines that Hölderlin tweaks for our Hesperian ear, and the question is how the alteration is to affect us.

Perhaps a contrast with Hölderlin's treatment of a line in the fourth choral ode will help. Here, as we have only now seen, Hölderlin introduces an "almost" into the line that says that even immortal hearts shatter when Eros strikes them: *Fast auch Unsterblicher Herz zerbricht*, writes Hölderlin, whereas Sophocles says, "And no immortal whomsoever [οὔτ' ἀθανάτων . . . οὐδεὶς] can escape from you" (*Antigone*, l. 787). In the fifth choral song, with Zeus's entry into Danaë's cell, Zeus's heart shatters quite beyond the "almost." For Danaë hits the father of time where he is presumably most at home—in time. Zeus brings the time of the sky, of the planets and stars in their courses, to earth. Does nothing happen to that celestial time upon entry, or reentry, into the thickening mortal atmosphere? What is the father of time and the earth doing? More tellingly, what is happening to him? As we have already suggested in the foregoing chapter, Danaë does not merely hoard the golden rain; rather, she counts the strokes of the hours, strokes that are themselves golden. Hölderlin here seems to be closer to the Greek text than all the editors who chide him for his inadequate Greek. Ταμιεύω, as already indicated, does not mean to store in a treasury, or a womb, but to dispense. Danaë *dispenses* the hours to the father of time. Danaë *gives* to the all-giving father. Yet in so giving, she *measures* the allotted time—the time allotted *to him*.

Is it too fanciful to see in Danaë's measured donation or dispensation of time Zeus's μοῖρα? We know that Zeus, like Danaë's own father, Acrisius, and like Laius, the father of Oedipus, is plagued by the thought of progeny, that is, of the grandson who will deal with him as handily as Zeus himself dealt with Kronos, and Kronos with Ouranos. Yet in spite of Zeus's Acrisius Complex, the father of the gods leaps into the breach every chance he gets. Zeus repeatedly takes his chances with the beautiful. What Danaë teaches the father of time is that to be the father *of* time is to be *within* time and subject *to* time. With every deft movement of her body—and it is Hölderlin who introduces her body into Sophocles' text, a body imprisoned, in irons, and in the dark—she erases the once clearly drawn line between immortals and mortals, the line that organized Greek wisdom from Homer through Plato and Aristotle. One can almost hear her murmuring in the dark the following unheard-of words, as though they were the abacus on which the hours were being counted off, one paratactic word falling after the other like the relentless ticking of a clock: "Immortal mortals, mortal immortals, each living the death of the other and dying its life."[21]

Is it too hazardous to allow Danaë's body to remind us once again of another passage in Hölderlin's "Notes on Antigone," one of the strangest passages in this strangest of texts, in which Hölderlin calls the lines of the tragic choral ode "*suffering organs* of the divinely wrestling body [leidende Organe des göttlichringenden Körpers]"? (DKV 2:919). May we extend Hölderlin's *athletic* analysis of tragedy—*Ajax* as fencing, *Oedipus the Tyrant* as boxing, *Antigone* as a footrace to the point of exhaustion, that is, to the point where the athletes gasp for breath and clasp the body of another runner for support—to the particular kind of ἀγών in which Zeus and Danaë are engaged? Why do we fear to attribute to Hölderlin such a body? Do we really believe that Diotima taught him nothing? or that Danaë taught the father nothing? What does she ever and always teach him? That only for a brief span of time can god and mortal step beyond his or her doom, and that each time he or she desires, each time there is languor, that step is already taken. That is why in our own time the Orthodox priests of Crete and across Greece in general threatened to blow up any movie theater that would dare to show Martin

21. Heraclitus, DK B62.

Scorsese's film of Kazantzakis's *Last Temptation of Christ,* whereas Mel Gibson's sadism never ruffled the curates' feathers.

Perhaps this elevation of Danaë (and thereby of Antigone) to quasi-divine status—to be sure, however, an elevation that succeeds only if the divinity in question is subject to time, Eros, Himeros, and Pothos—gains in credibility when we turn to the figure of Niobe. Antigone herself (in lines 852ff.; DKV 2:891) invokes Niobe before the chorus conjures up the figure of Danaë. When the chorus responds to her invocation of Niobe by mentioning Niobe's divine status, Antigone accuses them of mocking her, as though it had not been she herself who raised Niobe's ghost. It is a ghost of snow-laden mountain crags washed by tears: "Flowing down her throat, laving it, snow-bright tears from her lashes" (ll. 859–860; ibid.). Antigone anticipates the tears she will weep in her own mountain hollow.

As we remember, the figure of Niobe is important for Schelling's lectures on aesthetics and for the first draft of *The Ages of the World,* and precisely with regard to the matter of death. Yet the importance of Niobe for Hölderlin soars to new heights, and it takes an unexpected turn in the direction of Niobe's hubris. It is high time we recalled the myth in some detail. Phrygian—that is to say, *Oriental*—Niobe, the daughter of Tantalos, married Amphion, King of Thebes, and bore him seven sons and seven daughters. One day the haughty queen mocked Leto, the mother of Apollo and Artemis, for having given birth to only two children. Yet this one instance of *nefas,* or blasphemy, was insufficient for her. The prophetess Mante, daughter of Tiresias, urged the Theban women to burn incense to Leto and beg forgiveness for their queen's rash remarks. Niobe discovered the women at sacrifice and berated them: "She . . . furiously asked why Leto, a woman of obscure parentage, with a mannish daughter and a womanish son, should be preferred to her, Niobe, grandchild of Zeus and Atlas, the dread of the Phrygians, and a queen of Cadmus's royal house? Though fate or ill-luck might carry off two or three of her children, would she not still remain the richer?"[22] The Theban women tried frantically to placate the twice-injured Leto, but Apollo and Artemis promptly strung their bows and slaughtered Niobe's children. Niobe wept for nine days and nine nights but could find no one to bury them—Zeus, supporting Leto, had turned the Thebans to stone. Niobe returned to her home in the Phrygian Orient, becoming a recluse on Mount Sipylus, where there is a statue dedicated to the Hittite Mother Goddess. Zeus eventually pitied Niobe and turned her into a statue on that same mountain. Each spring the

22. Graves, 1:259.

statue weeps tears, perhaps because it is in reality a snowy crag: when the sun's rays burn the snow cap—"Niobe," according to Robert Graves, means "snowy"—the mountain appears to be weeping.

Among the aspects of the story that must have captured Hölderlin's fancy is Niobe's Oriental provenance, representing the more aorgic and Titanic realms of antique nature (= Chaos) and ancient culture. Yet it is Niobe's insulting the mother of Apollo and Artemis that must have most intrigued him: Niobe is one of those who go to meet divinity with a curse in their mouths and blasphemy on their lips, in order, says Hölderlin, to preserve the life of spirit (DKV 2:916). Niobe, like Antigone, and like Electra, to whom Sophocles also relates Niobe (*Electra*, l. 150), is *antitheos*. Moreover, Niobe's lineage is certainly as divine as Leto's, so that one has to admit that her haughtiness is not entirely without grounds. Indeed, in her origins and in her end she dwells in the vicinity of the Great Goddess, she of the brazen wheels. Sophocles' Theban chorus emphasizes this, and here again Hölderlin must have been struck by the proximity—and even imbrication—of immortal and mortal in the figure of Niobe. "God's child and god she was," sings the chorus, whereas "we are born to death" (ll. 832–833 in the Greek text). Hölderlin translates these lines (ll. 862–863; DKV 2:892) as follows:

Doch heilig gesprochen, heilig gezeuget
Ist die, wir aber Erd' und irdisch gezeuget.

And yet, proclaimed holy, engendered in holy fashion
Is she. But we of earth are engendered in an earthly way.

Niobe is both θεός and θεογεννής, whereas the old men of Thebes are βροτοί and θνητογενεῖς, creatures who if they partook would choke on ambrosia, ephemera who are born to die. The divine figure of Niobe is the one that the old men now apply to Antigone. They celebrate her having gone "like a god" to her fate, "in living and dying alike" (ll. 835–836 in the Greek). In Hölderlin's version (ll. 865–866; ibid.):

Du habst, Gott gleichen gleich, empfangen ein Los,
Lebendig und dann gestorben.

To you it has been allotted to be like the likes of God,
Living, and then having died.

Antigone, though not a goddess, is proclaimed ἰσοθέοις, which is something more than "godlike." Indeed, it is more like "equal to the gods," isomorphic with divinity. Equal to them *in both living and dying*, or in "having died." Antigone's elevation is due to her divine mortality.

What, then, is heroic about Hölderlin's heroines, Jocasta, Antigone, Niobe, and Danaë? If they are god-creators and god-destroyers—and they are—they do not thereby elevate themselves to immortal status. They, of all people, do not dream of shuffling off the mortal coil. In Hölderlin's view, to be human, whether as man or as woman, is to be finite. Yet what he is perpetually discovering, from *Hyperion* through *The Mourning-Plays of Sophocles*, is that divinity itself is finite—indeed, godhead is finitude itself. Only as a configuration of death, *in der Gestalt des Todes*, does the god appear. Nowadays, at the funerals of those who die young, preachers admit that faith cannot explain why death has come in so untimely a manner. They go on to preach hope in a god of resurrection. Yet all who are present feel that the sole unchallengeable divinity, present in all its power and numinosity, is right under the preacher's nose. They, at least, believe in this coffin, have faith in this palpable death in a box. For an instant, at least, the pyre burns for them. Danaë and all her sisters teach the father of time and the earth that he can appear in full potency only as the figure of death. Danaë and Niobe are more severe than the meek Alkmene, but they all teach the same lesson. At the same time, for all their severity, Hölderlin's heroines are not battleaxes. They drop all the phallic weaponry; their signs = 0, if only because "love is happy to uncover tenderly" (DKV 2:521). The desire of the other, of the other mother, prevails since the beginning of becoming, when those vast alliances were struck. That tender desire adheres to the death drive precisely when it clings most desperately to life.

Return to Jocasta

As Antigone processes to her living death, advancing beyond her dying life, she explains that her brother is irreplaceable because the womb that bore them both is already in Hades. She is thinking of Jocasta, who is both her mother and, on her father's side, her grandmother. Let us then, by way of conclusion, return to this grandest of mothers, haunted all her life by the dire predictions of seers and prophets, hounded to death by her son and husband, as the oracle said she would be. Jocasta tries to curb Oedipus's "foolishly savage search for a consciousness" (DKV 2:853) and seeks to assuage his anxiety concerning the desire of the other mother—the "of" here indicating the objective and subjective genitive alike—which she herself embodies. Everything about

Jocasta is dogged by desire, precisely because she is hounded by finitude. Hölderlin has the chorus say:

> Aber des Schicksals ist furchtbar die Kraft.
> Der Regen nicht, der Schlachtgeist
> Und der Turm nicht, und die meerumrauschten
> Fliehn sie, die schwarzen Schiffe. (ll. 989–992; DKV 2:896)

> Yet the force of destiny is frightful.
> Not the rain, not the spirit of battle,
> Not the tower can flee it, nor,
> Tossed by the sea, the darkling ships.[23]

What can account for Oedipus's tempestuous violence against Jocasta? Why his factically deadly words to her, words that pierce her throat like daggers? Why in the end does Oedipus wield the sword, and only after his mother's death by hanging, the fibulae of her chiton? Why does he repeat the gesture of undressing his wife—whom he now knows to be otherwise—in order to garner the weapons of his enucleation? Oedipus has all along been furiously searching for a consciousness, says Hölderlin. Perhaps what he desires is the naked surface of *her* extinguished consciousness. His deceased wifemother's consciousness. What would that be? Perhaps he wants to put on her knowledge with her power, before the indifferent beak can let him drop a second time—the unexpected reversal of Leda and her divine swan?

According to the Homeric myth of Oedipus, the Erinyes, or Furies, torment Oedipus for having murdered his mother.[24] Why this desire to murder? Oedipus wants to be present at the origin, wants to be giving birth to himself; he wants to hand himself over to himself, and not be handed over to some servant who will carry him off to desolation and death on Mount Cithaeron. Son, like mother, wants to prove all the oracles—and even the sphinx, the source of his fame—bankrupt. He wants to undo what was done in his own house prior to his birth. He wants to challenge the "it was" of time, which Nietzsche calls the source of all rancor and resentment.[25] Like Zeus, the father of time, Oedipus wants to annihilate time. He wants, Lacan will say, the

---

23. Why "rain"? Jochen Schmidt explains in some detail that the Brubachiana 1555 text is corrupt here (DKV 2:1445–1446), and that modern editions have the word *wealth* rather than *rain*. One might speculate, however, that if Hölderlin was forced to deal with "rain," it could only have been the golden shower of the previous lines that he had in mind. And, after all, if Ares, the spirit of battle himself, cannot flee μοῖρα, why should the father of time and the earth be any exception? The first line of Sophocles' antistrophe is so powerful: ἀλλ' ἁ μοιριδία τις δύναμις δεινά. "Many things are frightful, but nothing is more frightful than . . . whatever pertains to fate."

24. Graves, 2:12.

25. See Friedrich Nietzsche, "Von der Erlösung," in Part 2 of *Also sprach Zarathustra*, KSA 4:180–181.

ex nihilo, the secret of all creation and generation. He wants what Schelling calls the pristine, remote, elevated age of the world, the storied yet uncounted and unrecounted time that preceded all the times of the world. He pursues that desire the only way it can be pursued, namely, through annihilation—Sadically, if not sadistically. Oedipus wants the blood of menstruation and birth on his own hands, wants to reclaim the blood—his own—that is on Jocasta's hands. He would terminate the nightmare of a desire that even in the conjugal bed is the always already alienated desire of the (m)other. His envy cries out of him: Why must *she* always be the One? How much more satisfying to mock in the way that Creon mocks Haemon: "Weaker than woman! You worm of the womb!" (l. 745; cf. l. 680). Yet what if one *is* such a worm? What if both Creon and Oedipus, and not merely the women, are themselves creatures compressed between two mouths?

Jocasta towers, even when she hangs suspended from the roofbeam, her feet dancing above the floor, sky and earth now held in boundless separation. Her secrets are gone with her. We understand nothing. She remains the null-cipher, no matter how ravishing Pasolini's Oedipus reveals her to be when his final embrace—about the knees—causes her chiton to slip from her body. As she dangles by the cord of shame, naked to the riveted, unseeing eyes of us all, she deigns by the slightest margin not to kill us. She is the sign that is not read and must not be touched. She is as maddening as the Ἄτη she herself transgresses for a brief span of time—a span, it is true, that encompasses her entire adult life—and then passes on to a passionate daughter. Daughter, mother, grandmother—all instructresses in that most demanding initiation . . . into mortality.

ANTIGONE'S CLOUT

11

Sophokles.

Viele versuchten umsonst das
Freudigste freudig zu sagen
Hier spricht endlich es mir, hier in der
Trauer sich aus.

Sophocles

Many tried in vain joyfully to say
what is most joyous
Here it finally speaks to me, here, in
mourning.

—F. HÖLDERLIN *(CHV*
1:271; ca. 1800)

Have you been acting in conformity
with your desire?

—J. LACAN, *The Ethics of*
Psychoanalysis

Jacques Lacan's astonishing work *The Ethics of Psychoanalysis* brings *the* matter of psychoanalysis, the matter or "thing" called *desire*, to a conclusion—or perhaps to a certain impasse—with its reading of Sophocles' *Antigone.*[1] Lacan, reading *Antigone* at the culmination of his seminar on ethics, stops punishing his audience of analysts at least for an instant and confesses himself flummoxed. By whom or by what? By Antigone's desire, and also by the desire of Antigone's mother, Jocasta. If Jocasta *is* her mother. For, on the father's side, at least, Jocasta is Antigone's grandmother—her father's mother as well as her own. At all events, what can one say of *Jocasta's* desire? Lacan confesses his bewilderment to his listeners, a group he usually prefers to slap around, a group that, like the bulls in a Castilian *corrida*, always needs more punishment in order to help it focus. Here is Lacan's confession—let me start with that, it is so delicious, it will

---

1. Lacan's *Ethics of Psychoanalysis* is cited in note 9 of ch. 6, above. I cite both the French and the English in what follows by page number in the body of the text. The relevant chapters are 19–21, although the conceptuality of the entire book—from its meditation on catharsis and the Cathars to its readings of the ethics of Aristotle, Kant, and Sade, and from the "thing" of desire to the impossible creation *ex nihilo*—comes to bear on the reading of Antigone.

have been my only moment of revenge: "Think about it hard. What happens to her [Antigone's] desire? Shouldn't it be the desire of the Other and be linked to the desire of the mother? . . . The desire of the mother is the origin of everything. The desire of the mother is . . . the founding desire of the whole structure" (329/283). At the end of this chapter I shall have to return once again to the mother, or to the grandmother, Jocasta.

I cannot read Lacan and have never understood him. In this I am only following his instruction. He tells us, for example in "L'instance de la lettre," that he prefers his texts to be difficult for his readers.[2] Difficult to enter, one might add, and impossible to exit. He is writing, after all, for psychoanalysts; if he castigates them, it is only to remind them of the boundless hubris of their shared profession:

—So, you think you're a psychoanalyst? You analyze the soul, do you? You plumb the depths of the most brilliant and most wretched companions of our history? You'll tell us all about the souls of Dante and Michelangelo? You'll smooth for us the rough edges of Shakespeare's heart? You'll make Sade feel better about himself?

Lacan slams his listening and reading audience against the blackboard— for they are in a lecture hall, not on a couch—and explains to them, not very patiently, that they aren't ready yet, that they are overreaching themselves. If the analysand, or patient, is not smug but miserable, then complacency does not become the analyst. Psychology, especially American ego psychology, which culminates in Dr. Phil—and by that I do not mean a degree from Oxbridge—always feels good about itself. Lacan's only recourse is to punish. It may therefore be the case that the most-discussed structures of his doctrine—the real, the symbolic, and the imaginary—along with his daunting algorithms of the subject of desire, are nothing more than hits upside the head, clouts meant not to enlighten but to darken and obscure the clean, well-lighted place that is the analyst's world. Before the analyst can be permitted to respond to the demand of the analysand, he or she must suffer the insight that the demand is always, "in sum, profoundly unconscious" (9/1). *Obliged,* inasmuch as Lacan is talking about an *ethics* of psychoanalysis. And precisely because the unconscious is structured as a language (42/32), the signifying chain works its befuddling effects and endless ruses on the demand of even the most benign and innocent of patients.

I will not be able to discuss Lacan's seminar in its entirety, for it treats of so many classic topics in ethics, from happiness to duty to moral masochism,

2. Lacan, *Écrits*, 493.

and touches on so many classic texts of ethics, from *Nicomachean Ethics* to the second *Critique* and *The Metaphysics of Morals* to *Juliette*. Masochism is perhaps the *telos* of the course. That is what Lacan tells us at the end of his introduction to "our program" (24/14–15), alluding to Freud's 1924 "Economic Problem of Masochism." That economic problem, we remember, has to do with *Triebvermischung*, that is, the bedeviling interpenetration of the pleasure principle, the death drives, and the reality-probe.[3] The reading of *Antigone* occurs very near the end of Lacan's course, in its penultimate section. It may be safe to say—"safe" if we disregard for the moment the absurdity of applying twentieth-century psychoanalytic categories to a figure of antiquity—that Antigone will either make or break the economy of masochism. "Moral masochism" and perhaps even "the death drives" seem almost facile phrases when applied to her.[4]

The present chapter is divided into three parts: first, a summary of Lacan's reading of *Antigone* in the second-to-last section of the seminar, which he calls "The Essence of Tragedy" (283–333/243–283), along with reminiscences of some of the principal features of Hölderlin's translation of and "Notes" on Sophocles' *Antigone;* second, a summary of the final section of Lacan's work, "The Tragic Dimension of the Psychoanalytic Experience" (335–375/291–325), once again with some Hölderlinian reminiscences; and third, a return to Sophocles' play and all its "unthinkable things," in order to see how Lacan and Hölderlin might inflect (or infect) our experience of the play.

---

3. Freud, *Studienausgabe* 3:344–345; 354.

4. Jean-Pierre Vernant's crankiest chapter is surely his response to Freud. See Vernant, "Oedipus without the Complex," in VV 85–111. For reasons one can affirm, and I am affirming them here, Vernant is allergic to the ahistorical way in which Freud and others use Greek tragedy without being sufficiently informed about the social, political, and religious practices of fifth-century Athens. Nevertheless, one feels constrained to reply to Vernant, if only by way of indirection. One may accept Vernant and Vidal-Naquet's claim, following Louis Gernet, that Greek tragedy has its "historical moment" in ancient Athens and nowhere else—indeed, in the century that separates Solon's disgust in the face of the first dramatic representations from Aristotle's desire to salvage tragedy for philosophy—and yet be plagued all the more by the question as to how and why tragedy continues to speak to foreign peoples in distant times, all the way down to Freud's, Lacan's, and our own. Whether we latecomers understand anything at all about that historical moment, we certainly find ourselves fascinated by it and unable to leave it to the experts. In the end, the call from fifth-century Athens is more compelling than even the most abysmal ignorance. Schelling and Hölderlin were not the first to hear that call. Nor were Corneille, Racine, Kleist, Klopstock, Schiller, and Goethe. Nor will Freud and Lacan be the last. One will not mistake either Freud or Lacan for a classics scholar; no classics scholar in our time needs to tell us this. Yet the level of "culture" in these two great psychoanalysts is truly astonishing. Furthermore, to employ Vernant's own vocabulary, *questions* and *problems* concerning the *riddles* of Greek tragedy—in all its *ambiguity*—are raised in many walks of life and in multiple modes of inquiry, so that there is never really any need to be cranky. What Vernant himself calls the "transhistorical" impact of tragedy, citing Marx, belies his own overdrawn complaint concerning psychoanalysis. See "The Tragic Subject: Historicity and Transhistoricity," esp. VV 237 and 242.

Lacan on the Essence of Tragedy

The penultimate section of Lacan's course comprises three chapters: 19, "Antigone's Splendor," 20, "The Articulations of the Piece," and 21, "Antigone in the Between-Two-Deaths." "Antigone's Splendor," which is to say, her *éclat*, has to do with the beauty and power of this figure—arguably the most famous of Greek antiquity. Yet Lacan begins in the most traditional way possible, by affirming catharsis as the essence of tragedy. His audience will no doubt immediately think of what Breuer and Freud, in their *Studies on Hysteria*, called *Abreaktion* and the "cathartic method." Yet Lacan insists that his audience also read Aristotle—both the *Poetics* and the *Politics*. The former defines catharsis as purification, by means of pity and fear, of all such emotions. *Nota bene:* not the purgation of pity and fear but the purification of every strong emotion through the distillation and refinement of compassion and terror. Lacan emphasizes above all the preposition διά in the phrase δι' ἐλέου καὶ φόβου (*Poetics*, 1449b 27–28). He reminds us of his earlier treatment of the Cathars in the course, as well as of the Hippocratic uses of catharsis. However, he chooses as the principal site of his exposé the eighth book of Aristotle's *Politics*, which offers an account of *music*. Lacan thereby follows—if not Schelling's 1802–1803 *Philosophy of Art*—Jacob Bernays's 1857 text on catharsis. As we recall, whereas the first and second chapters of Bernays's book develop the classic account of catharsis in terms of the medical concept of purgation, the remarkable fourth chapter (unfortunately not well known in the English-speaking world, because untranslated) considers the effects of music as a stimulus of enthusiasm and ecstasy. In general, one suspects that Lacan's reading of tragedy owes a great deal to the remarkable text by this uncle of Freud's wife, Martha Bernays; it would not be difficult to show that Nietzsche too is indebted to Jacob Bernays—indeed, Karlfried Gründer has already shown this.[5] For Bernays takes the ecstatic process of catharsis to be what enables human beings to experience what we have heard him call "the frightfully sublime laws of the universe" (182).

The Aristotelian phrase "all such emotions," τοιούτων παθημάτων, enables Lacan to raise the question of the proper place of desire as such in tragedy. Antigone's desire is Lacan's particular object, the goad of his own desire. "In effect, *Antigone* reveals to us the line of sight that defines desire" (290/247). Why? Because Antigone, the heroine of Sophocles' play, has

---

5. See Gründer's Introduction to Bernays's text, viii–ix. Among the places where Nietzsche cites Bernays are the following: KSA 7:71, 504; KSB 2:103, 105, 204, 287, 322; 4:97; 8:589.

"clout," *éclat.* ("Radiance" and "splendor" are no doubt more graceful ways to translate *éclat,* and I have been able to find no etymological connection between the English *clout* and the French *éclat;* yet for the moment I ask my readers to bear with the word-play and to accept Antigone's "clout.") She has it due to a double circumstance, namely, her youthful beauty and her uninhibited death drive. What would her death drive be without the glowing, stunning, even maddening beauty that seems to cry out for life and more life? And what would that beauty be if we did not mourn from the outset the imminent destruction of such radiance? The beauty of this personage both nourishes and frustrates our desire, drawing it on while inhibiting it. Lacan would surely admire what Rilke says about the beautiful—namely, that it terrifies us by deigning by the slimmest margin not to destroy us. Perhaps what we mourn when the beautiful confronts or affronts us is *our own* imminent undoing? *Coup de foudre!* is never a victorious cry, but a lament. Recall Rilke's lines from the first Duino elegy. Lacan might have remembered them from his reading of Heidegger's Nietzsche lectures on "The Will to Power as Art," even if he does not cite them:

> . . . Denn das Schöne ist nichts
> als des Schrecklichen Anfang, den wir noch grade ertragen,
> und wir bewundern es so, weil es gelassen verschmäht,
> uns zu zerstören. Ein jeder Engel ist schrecklich.[6]

> . . . For the beautiful is nothing
> but the onset of the terrifying, an onset we but barely endure;
> and it amazes us so, since with equanimity it disdains
> to destroy us. Every angel terrifies.

The angel in question is not simply a victim, however; she is her own lightning-rod, if one may break or stretch the metaphor; she is her own Angel of Death. Antigone, "this terribly self-willed victim," disconcerts us (290/247). It is necessary to speak of Antigone's beauty "in the superlative," Hölderlin notes, because her beauty consists in her "heroic virtuosity" (DKV 2:915). The heroic virtuoso, however, is superlatively good at dying. One wonders whether Lacan or Rilke (if not Hölderlin) may have seen one of Nietzsche's earliest jottings on Greek tragedy, from the autumn of 1869: "The charm [*Anmuth*] of the terrifying—the 'frightful graces': truly known to the ancients alone" (KSA 7:37). As a beautiful young girl who walks into her

---

6. R. M. Rilke, *Werke in drei Bänden* (Frankfurt am Main: Insel Verlag, 1966), 1:441. Heidegger cites Rilke in the first of his lecture courses on Nietzsche, "The Will to Power as Art." See Heidegger, *Nietzsche,* 2 vols. (Pfullingen: G. Neske, 1961), 1:137; in English, see Martin Heidegger, *Nietzsche,* 2 vols. (San Francisco: HarperCollins, 1991), 1:116.

tomb, Antigone is, in Lacan's estimation, a cathartic image, an image that purges the imaginary (290/248). To be sure, we may have been led to believe that the imaginary is inexhaustible in its capacity to lead us by the nose. Such is the radiance and radiation, such is the clout of this image, however, that it blows every other image of beauty away. It does so by revealing a second death for Antigone. It is her second death, according to Lacan, that we must struggle to experience and to understand. Lacan takes the notion of a second death from Sade, defining it as "the point at which the very cycle of natural transformations is annihilated" (291/248). Sade's heroes respond to beauty by desiring that it suffer beyond death, well beyond the first death, into the infinity that is so successfully represented by the Christian hell. Priests and bishops are always among the Marquis's heroes. One of those heroes, from *One Hundred and Twenty Days*, celebrates the "infamy" that he hopes will "dismember nature and deracinate the universe."[7] Yet the second death is not foreign to antiquity. For both Creon and Antigone fundamentally confuse the domains of life and death. Creon wants to inflict further damage on Polyneices, who is already dead: every dog or bird who tears at the corpse is elaborating Creon's desire for a second death for Polyneices. Antigone too, though in a much less obvious way, one that hides behind the mask of family loyalty and traditional religious piety, is driven by the passion of a second death—for herself. It is not merely her fate but her desire to be buried alive in a tomb; she does not shy from such a death but rushes to embrace it as though that first death will never be enough (291/248–249; cf. 302/259–260).[8]

According to Lacan, the effect of beauty on desire, which is the effect of blindness, somehow lures or traps the subject in such a way that its desire is tempered or even extinguished—disrupting the normal relation to existent objects in a manner that would have pleased the Kant of the third *Critique*. Clearly, Lacan is at this moment interested in *our* response to the beauty of Antigone, which is captured in the responses of the chorus of "old Theban men." Lacan thus seems to be expanding on the view of Schiller: if the chorus

---

7. Sade, *Les cent vingt journées de Sodome*, 336.

8. In this, Antigone is reminiscent of the most fanatical of the followers of Orpheus. Plutarch (here aided by Roberto Calasso) tells the story of the Athenian Timarchus at the cave of Trophonius in Lebadeia, a story in which a "second death" plays a crucial role: "Timarchus had imagined he was going toward Hades. But now he realized that Hades had been turned inside out into the sky, become a shadowy cone between the moon and the earth. . . . They [the souls of the dead] were trying to land on that woman's face, the moon, despite the fact that it grew more and more terrifying the nearer they got. . . . Yet it was there that salvation lay, and they had come so close. Had they managed to set foot on this outpost of Persephone, they would one day have undergone a second death, more gradual and more delicate than the first. One day Persephone would have separated their minds, νοῦς, from their souls, the way Apollo could prize the armor from a warrior's shoulders" (RC 277–278).

speaks to all who are present in the theater, it also desires in the name of us all. The chorus of old Theban men? *C'est vous!* exclaims Lacan. That is to say, we spectators are "the people who are moved" by the play (294/252), moved, though not conciliated. Lacan will soon say that the chorus members—and we—are *deranged* by the action of the play. It is as though we were all in the position of Ajax, stirred by Athena into a delusional rage, ἄτη κακῇ (l. 123). In *Ajax*, Sophocles identifies such delusion with θεία μανία (l. 611), a being displaced by "divine madness," which readers of Plato's *Phaedrus* doubtless hoped would be a more constructive affair. The beauty effect is a blindness effect—a delusional stroke. The spectators of *Antigone* are struck by it, but so, arguably, is the heroine herself.

In his chapter on the "articulations" of Sophocles' play, Lacan counterposes Creon to Antigone. Creon remains caught up in the interests of the state, hence in the traditional hierarchical system of goods. His "error" induces his own tragedy—indeed, twice over. First, he refuses to grant death to the dead and life to the living by confusing Antigone with her brother. Then, after the intervention of Tiresias, he hurries off to bury Polyneices before rescuing the living Antigone—thus destroying the lives of his son and his wife. Creon makes mistakes, juggles the goods, bungles the job. Perhaps (although Lacan makes nothing of this) his primary mistake involves some confusion of desire concerning his son and his son's bride. Creon: "I am no man and she the man instead / if she can have this conquest without pain" (C ll. 483–484). By contrast, Antigone transcends all ἁμαρτία and every definable system of goods. The traditional interpretation, represented most influentially by Hegel, finds her asserting the good of the chthonic divinities over the good of the sky gods, or the good of the unwritten Δίκη of familial law over that of civil law. Yet what does Antigone want when she wants the "justice" of the chthonic divinities? Lacan's answer is trenchant, and it removes Antigone from every system of goods. "We no longer know anything at all about what the gods are," he says (301/259), echoing what Hölderlin says of the modern, Hesperian age, in which gods and mortals are caught up in mutual oblivion and betrayal. Even if we are immured in "creationism," our thinking is and must be "rigorously atheistic" (303/261): we take our point of departure from the *ex nihilo*, that is, from the nothing. We can thus relate to only two aspects of traditional religiosity: first, the feeling of abandonment, captured in the phrase "Father, why hast thou forsaken me?" and second, the founding phantasm of Sade, which is eternal suffering—the exquisite pain of the *Inferno*—in the second death. Here, to repeat, the beauty-blindness-effect is essential, whether it be the beauty of the crucifix, which has been the object of so much mystical devotion in the past, or the blinding beauty of Sade's boys and girls. Indeed, Sade's victims are not only beautiful but also graceful, in their "final flower" (304/261). The infinitely gentle Hölderlin too, it must be said, finds the effect of beauty to consist in a certain suffering, a certain excess, a certain blindness. More on this later.

Lacan now begins to work his way toward his principal insight concerning Antigone, to wit, that as a heroine she sustains a special relationship to the gods. She is made not for hate but for love, as she herself says (305/262; 1. 523). Lacan will eventually say that her fate is to be "used" by the gods. It will be this notion of the "divine use" of Antigone that brings his interpretation into the greatest possible proximity to that of Hölderlin—a proximity with a difference, however. The key to such proximity is Antigone's relation to her ἄτη, or doom. The chorus defines ἄτη as that which a mortal can escape, or stand outside of, or be beyond, for only a brief amount of time (ibid.). Why or how is one only "briefly" able to transgress the line of doom? We do not know. The chorus tells us (1. 624) only that the time is short: "Only for a brief span of time [ὀλίγιστον γρόνον (= χρόνον)] is a human being beyond doom [ἐκτὸς ἄτας]." Yet what about the crossing over, the transgressing itself?

Once again we may appeal to Roberto Calasso for assistance. For Calasso both chides contemporary psychology for its tendency to reduce the daimonic realm of Greek antiquity to the categories of modern subjectivity, thus missing the impact of the Greek experience altogether, and offers a differently nuanced account of ἄτη from the one Lacan unleashes on us. Like Lacan and Hölderlin, Calasso regards Antigone as *antitheos*. She is one of a long line of women who make trouble for her city—Ariadne for Knossos, Helen for Sparta, Antigone for Thebes. "Antigone betrays the law of her city to make a gesture of mercy toward a dead man who does not belong to that city" (RC 69). At the same time, however, Calasso sees precisely in this betrayal of the city a moment of grandeur—as though *nefas* were essential to the life of the human spirit. Any exceptional human deed requires something like daimonic possession, whether for good or ill:

No psychology since has ever gone beyond this; all we have done is invent, for those powers that act upon us, longer, more numerous, more awkward names, which are less effective, less closely aligned to the glean of our experience, whether that be pleasure or terror. The moderns are proud above all of their responsibility but in being so they presume to respond with a voice that they are not even sure is theirs. The Homeric heroes knew nothing of that cumbersome word *responsibility*, nor would they have believed in it if they had. For them, it was as if every crime were committed in a state of mental infirmity. But such infirmity meant that a god was present and at work. What we consider infirmity they saw as "divine infatuation" (ἄτη). They knew that this invisible incursion brought ruin: so much so that the word ἄτη would gradually come to mean "ruin." But they also knew, and it was Sophocles who said it, that "mortal life can never have anything great about it except through ἄτη." (RC 94)

Remarkably, the lines of Sophocles that Calasso is translating (in the final words of the passage) are the very lines that Lacan stresses in his interpretation, namely, lines 613–614, which conclude with the first reference to the "outside of" or "beyond" of ἄτη. Human life can never be exceptional unless it steps outside of or beyond the limit of its doom. Yet it belongs to the nature of that limit, we hear ten lines later, that it can be transgressed "only very briefly." What Lacan will attempt is a reading of *Antigone* that initiates modern psychology to the blinding beauty of the double-edged Sophoclean text, in which ἄτη is both ruinous and grand.

In the tragedies of Aeschylus and Sophocles (leaving Euripides out of account for the moment) ἄτη is both omnipresent and variegated. When Pelasgos, King of Argos, describes his predicament—turn the suppliant women away and offend the god of hospitality, receive them and risk war with the sons of Aigyptos—he does so in terms of the bottomless and impassable sea of doom, ἄτης δ' ἄβυσσον πέλαγος οὐ μάλ' εὔπορον (Aeschylus, *Suppliant Maidens*, l. 470). King Agamemnon pictures doom as a windstorm that blows over Troy, ἄτης φύελλαι, himself unaware that the fallout from that storm is hovering over his own homecoming in Argos (Aeschylus, *Agamemnon*, l. 819). The Persian women of Aeschylus's tragedy (ll. 93–100) retain for the word ἄτη the sense of ensnarement—indeed, the ensnarement of mortals by a god:

> The deceptions woven by a god—
> What mortal man can escape them?
> Who is so fleet of foot that with a leap
> He can find rescue?
>
> For alluringly she draws
> The mortal into her nets, this Ἄτη,
> Whose weft no mortal
> Can escape.

The chorus of Sophocles' *Electra* chides that heroine for allowing herself to get mixed up in the doom of her household, οἰκείας εἰς ἄτας (l. 215). It urges her "not to generate doom out of doom," μὴ τίκτειν σ' ἄταν ἄταις (l. 235; cf. 1002), knowing as it does that ἄτη bears a special relation to reproduction and birth. Oedipus, having already referred to "ill-intending doom," δύσφρονος ἄτας, tells the chorus that his two daughters, or two sister-daughters, are children of doom, παῖδε, δύο δ' ἄτα (Sophocles, *Oedipus at Colonus*, ll. 202, 531). The chorus of Aeschylus's *Agamemnon* says that persuasion itself, Πειθώ, at least in the case of Paris persuading Helen, is a child born from the womb of Ἄτη (ll. 385–386). For her part, Cassandra speaks of doom as a site of concealment, a place of ambush, ἄτης λαθραίου (l. 1230). Foreseeing her own doom at the hands of Clytaimestra, the prophetess identifies herself with both the foresight and the doom: "Another prophetess of doom [ἄλλην τιν' Ἄτην] will inherit my riches!" she cries (l. 1268; cf. 1433). The chorus of *Agamemnon* concludes that the House of Atreus is joined in doom, laminated and glued together, "collated" with doom, as it were, κεκόλληται γένος πρὸς ἄτᾳ (l. 1566).

Doom therefore has to do with blood crimes and their cleansing. Yet if the crimes persist in working their dire effects, the cleansing of them is a sometime thing. Although at the outset of Aeschylus's *Choephoroi* the cupbearers are confident that the goddess Ἄτη will punish all murderers, that she merely defers that punishment until the crime, like a noxious plant, ripens to the full (ll. 68–69), they are less confident at the end. After listing the three murders that have plagued the House of Atreus (omitting Agamemnon's sacrifice of Iphigeneia, however), the chorus cries, "When will it end, when will it abate / And cease to rage, this ἄτη?" (ll. 1075–1076). Without a doubt, ἄτη is precisely what catharsis hopes to cleanse—catharsis not of the spectators, in Aristotle's sense, but of the characters in the play, in Goethe's sense. "Only when the horror [of blood guilt] is routed from the hearth, / Only then will ἄτη be cleansed [καθαρμοῖσιν]" (ll. 967–968). However, to repeat, when will it end? When will guilt be routed from the hearths of that small number of houses which includes Antigone's own House of Labdacus? And if ἄτη nestles in the heart of Antigone herself?

Curiously, one of the marks of Antigone's peculiar relation to her own doom is the "exceptional cruelty" she shows toward Ismene. Her cruelty marks her as inhumane, well-nigh inhuman. The chorus (l. 471) says she is "the stubborn daughter of a stubborn father," yet her inflexibility derives from a divine source. Lacan points out that the adjective used here is ὠμός, meaning "raw," in the sense of the raw meat devoured by the Titans and the Maenads. Hölderlin translates: "One sees the raw kinship of a raw father / In the child." Antigone is thus reminiscent of the worshipers of Dionysos as Zagreus, Dionysos fragmented, the god consumed in ritual ὠμοφαγία. Although Lacan himself does not refer us to it, it may be helpful for us to recall the early

363

note of Nietzsche on Dionysos Zagreus, which identifies ὠμηστής and Ζαγρεύς with the ritual eating of "the dead Zeus." The note reads as follows:

Ζόννυξος (= Διόνυσος im Lesbisch-aeolischen Dialekt.
　　　　Ursprünglich wohl Διόνυσος). Dies führt auf einen Stamm νεκ
　　　　also νεκύς, νεκρός usw.—neco.
Dionysus ist Hades nach Heraclit.
Kuretenkult des Zeus ursprünglich.
Ζόννυξος ist "d e r t o d t e Z e u s" oder der "tödtende Zeus"—Zeusjäger =
Ζαγρεύς und ὠμηστής. (P I 15a; KSA 7:82; 1870)

In translation:

Ζόννυξος (= Διόνυσος in the Aeolian dialect of Lesbos.
　　　　Originally it must have been Διόνυσος). This takes us to the stem
　　　　νεκ thus νεκύς, νεκρός etc.—neco.
Dionysus is Hades, according to Heraclitus.
The Kouretes-cult of Zeus at the origin.
Ζόννυξος is "t h e d e a d Z e u s" or the "killing Zeus"—Zeus hunter =
Ζαγρεύς and ὠμηστής.

Nietzsche is here pursuing the origin of the name *Dionysos,* believing he can find it in the Greek words for "the corpse," νεκύς, and "the dead one," νεκρός. (The Latin *neco* means to murder, assassinate, annihilate.) According to Heraclitus (DK B15), ὡυτός δε Ἀίδης καὶ Διόνυσος, "Dionysos and Hades are the same." Concerning the cult of the Curetes, and what it tells us about the nature of Zeus, we recall from chapter 5 the account of W. K. C. Guthrie. He informs us that the Curetes worship Zeus not on the plane of power but on the plane of weakness. For the Cretan Zeus is not the god of the thunderbolt but the defenseless infant concealed in a cave on Mount Ida or Mount Dikte, where the infant either barely survives or is slaughtered by those same Curetes. Yet in the eighth book of his *Politics,* as we have also heard, Aristotle tells us that the enthusiastic, ecstatic music of these "protectors" of Zeus produces the effect of κάθαρσις, and catharsis is the very purpose of tragedy. Not only Hades and Dionysos are the same, however: so are Zeus and Dionysos, even if we normally conceive of Zeus as the father and Dionysos as the son. Finally, the reference to Zagreus is to the fragmented Dionysos (or the murdered Zeus), torn apart and consumed by the Titans. The word ὠμηστής (cf. ὠμοφαγία) means the devouring of raw flesh, the flesh of the youthful god, as practiced by the Maenads and by other ancient— and contemporary Christian?—cults.

The devouring of raw divinity, omophagy, may be the primordial ritual, the one that absorbs even the ritual of sacred marriage, hierogamy. As Roberto Calasso points out, the recurrent references to the sacrificing of young girls conjoins elements that we moderns would like to keep far apart, namely, the sacred marriage of immortal with mortal and the bloody sacrifice of the mortal to the immortal in ritual eating. The two rites meet in the body fluid known as saliva:

> Hierogamy and sacrifice have in common taking possession of a body, by either invading it or eating it. But, as Prometheus would have it, to assimilate a body men had to kill it and eat its dead flesh. In the meantime the smoke would envelop the gods. And, in reply, the gods would envelop bodies like a cloud and suck out their juices drenched in eros. Saliva becomes the sacrificial element par excellence, the only one in which the two sides of sacrifice—expulsion and communion—converge. We expel saliva, as something impure, but we also mix it with other like substances and assimilate them, in eros. (RC 292–293)

Lacan would no doubt have something to say about this convergence of desires in saliva, this fluid concealed in the mouth. And he would also be intrigued by the festival of Apaturia, discussed in chapter 7 of this volume, which celebrates concealment as such. The following passage is one of the strangest in Calasso's extraordinary book—one can scarcely find a context for it. Yet if desire is of the essence for Lacan's ethics of psychoanalysis—and it is—we are led to this passage by the nose. It has to do with shame, concealment, body fluids, and a suppressed misogyny in the worship of the mother and daughter. But it begins with crime and punishment:

> After slaughtering their men, the women of Lemnos were struck by a kind of revenge the gods had never used before nor would again: they began to smell. And in this revenge we glimpse the grievance that Greece nursed against womankind. Greek men thought of women as of a perfume that is too strong, a perfume that breaks down to become a suffocating stench, a sorcery, "sparkling with desire, laden with aromas, glorious" [Anacreon, fr. 125], but stupefying, something that must be shaken off. It is an attitude betrayed by small gestures, like that passage in the Pseudo-Lucian where we hear of a man climbing out of bed, "saturated with femininity," and immediately wanting to dive into cold water. When it comes to women, Greek sensibility brings together both fear and repugnance: on the one hand, there is the horror at the woman without her makeup who "gets up in the morning uglier than a monkey" [Pseudo-Lucian]; on the other, there is the suspicion that makeup is being used as a weapon of ἀπάτη, of irresistible deceit. Makeup and female smells combine to generate a softness that bewitches and exhausts. Better for men the sweat and dust of the gymnasium. "Boys' sweat has a finer smell than anything in a woman's makeup box" [Achilles Tatius]. (RC 79)

These are matters that presumably have to do more with Jocasta than with Antigone, with the hanged matron than with the virgin under the sword. Yet if there is a kind of hierogamy with Antigone—Antigone as Persephone— then there is omophagy as well. But let us return to the raw Antigone.

Raw daughter of a raw father, Antigone inherits all the cares and troubles of the House of Labdacus. She seems alienated utterly from her desire— hence that "exceptional cruelty" and that almost inhuman scorn. Earlier on in his lecture course, in his chapter on "the function of the beautiful," Lacan develops this sense of alienation by means of a notion quite reminiscent of Nietzsche's central genealogical concept of *ressentiment*, from the second and third treatises of the *Genealogy of Morals*. For Lacan, it is a matter of showing how every hierarchy of goods involves what he calls "life envy," *Lebensneid*. Such envy arises out of the mystery of "the thing," untouchable desire itself. "In the irreducible margin as well as at the limit of its own good, the subject exposes itself to the never entirely resolved mystery of the nature of its desire" (278/237). Desire is of " 'the good that mustn't be touched,' " so that all we have of it is the prohibition. *Jouissance* is of the Other; hence *Lebensneid*. Life envy, obviously, would be a condition with twice the scope and double the impact of *Penisneid*:

> *Lebensneid* is not an ordinary jealousy, it is the jealousy borne in a subject in its relation to an other, insofar as this other is held to enjoy a certain form of *jouissance* or superabundant vitality that the subject perceives as something that it cannot apprehend by means of even the most elementary of affective movements. Isn't it strange, isn't it very odd, that a being admits to being jealous of something in the other to the point of hatred and the need to destroy, jealous of something that it is incapable of apprehending in any way, by any intuitive path?[9]

Lacan later refers to Sophocles' word μέριμνα, a word he is first tempted to translate as *ressentiment*. Yet the word *ressentiment* is too psychological,

9. Lacan, 278/237. I cite this passage at length because it seems the key to the mysterious and horrifying theme of racial and ethnic hatred and genocide. See D. F. Krell, "National Erotism (Derdiedas Responsibilities)," in *Ethics and Responsibility in the Phenomenological Tradition*, ed. Richard Rojcewicz (Pittsburgh: Duquesne University Press, 1992), 33–56. Nor does it seem too far-fetched to relate the concept of *Lebensneid* to the φθόνος that motivates the classical Athenian practice of ostracism. Jean-Pierre Vernant, again following the lead of Louis Gernet, defines this "popular feeling" that led to the expulsion year after year of the most gifted citizens—without hearing or trial— as "a mixture of envy and religious distrust of anyone who rose too high or was too successful" (VV 134). Vernant cites Solon's dictum, "a city can perish from its too great men," and Aristotle's advice to choral directors (in Book III of the *Politics*) not to admit to the chorus a singer the beauty of whose voice "would surpass the whole rest of the chorus put together" (VV 135). Finally, Roberto Calasso adds a decisive word about the φθόνος that infects even the gods: "That happiness is an early symptom of misfortune, that 'inherent' within happiness is the power to bring on misfortune, above all through the agency of resentment (φθόνος), whether of men or gods, is a vision that was to persist among the Greeks when almost all others had faded" (RC 262).

whereas μέριμνα is something in between subject and object, something that "compels Antigone toward the frontiers of *Atè*" (306/264). The word μέριμνα means "care, thought, solicitude," "pursuit, ambition," but also "anxious mind" and "memory." It derives from the Sanskrit *smárati* and yields the Latin *memor*, "to remember." (Lacan notes the relation of μέριμνα to μνήμη, "memory.") Remarkably, μέριμνα is one of the words Heidegger refers to in section 42 of *Being and Time* as an early word for *Sorge*, or care, the existential-ontological determination of human existence as such.[10] Heidegger underestimates the antiquity of the word, however, taking it as having originated in the Stoa, whereas it is a word of Pindar and the tragedians. In Aeschylus's *Seven against Thebes* (1. 843), μέριμνα expresses the chorus's "anxiety concerning the city." Nevertheless, μέριμνα, which Aeschylus's *Agamemnon* calls "nocturnal," νυκτηρεφές (1. 460), retains something of *ressentiment* and the spirit of revenge: in *Eumenides* (1. 360), the chorus of Erinyes speaks of the murderous "trouble" or "care" (μέριμνα) that it is their "earnest task" to prosecute. Remarkably, the Erinyes use Heidegger's second-favorite root-word for *Sorge*, namely, μελέτη (μελεταῖς) in the very next line in order to describe their avenging "toil." At all events, Antigone, like all her house, is driven by *Kummer* and *Bekümmerung*, "trouble" or "worry," as the Marburg Heidegger would have said. Though such care or trouble is the human trouble, Antigone bears it with a special aura, as though she has partaken of divine flesh—or as though divine flesh has partaken of her. Precisely because of her trouble, however, the girl has existential-ontological clout.

Another mark of Antigone's exceptional position with regard to her doom is her crying out like a mother bird the second time she goes to her brother's corpse. As we noted in the foregoing chapter, Carol Jacobs has written incisively about this maternal Antigone—whose desire of Polyneices is precisely that of a mother. Lacan too alludes to the bird as a universal figure of mourning. In our literature, that figure is perhaps best portrayed in Whitman's "Out of the Cradle Endlessly Rocking," where both bird and sea murmur the low and delicious word that is Antigone's word:

The aria sinking,
All else continuing, the stars shining,
The winds blowing, the notes of the bird continuous echoing,
With angry moans the fierce old mother incessantly moaning,
... Lisp'd to me the low and delicious word death,
And again, death, death, death, death.[11]

10. Martin Heidegger, *Sein und Zeit*, 12th ed. (Tübingen: Max Niemeyer, 1972), 199 n. 1.
11. Whitman, 251–252.

To be sure, for Whitman too that low and delicious word terminates the aria of Eros, which sings of desire, not death.

The middle third of Sophocles' play, that is, the scenes that begin with the chorus's hymn to Eros and end with Antigone's final exit, move through the zone of beauty and desire. "It is when passing through that zone that the beam of desire is both reflected and refracted till it ends up giving us that most strange and most profound of effects, which is the effect of the beautiful on desire" (291/248). It is the effect suffered by the divine essence, as Schelling analyzes it, caught between centrifugal and centripetal forces, drawn out of itself and inhibited at once. Lacan's reading of *Antigone* will be as far-removed as possible from the usual reading of the contest "Antigone vs. Creon," which, to repeat, is the reading of Hegel, the reading we were taught in our high school world literature classes.[12] Whereas traditional discussions of Creon's transgression regale us with pious platitudes about the unwritten law, justice, and ethics, discussions of Antigone's transgression leave us puzzled and restive. Concerning Creon's transgression of the law—the unwritten laws of the chthonic gods—we have already heard Lacan say that we no longer know a thing about the gods. How then can we know the meaning of transgression? "What then is this famous sphere into which we must not

---

12. In general, Judith Butler resists the Hegelian reading of *Antigone*, resists it with a vengeance. Yet one aspect of her account needs to be corrected. Butler attributes Hegel's notorious mistranslation of lines 982–983, "*Weil wir leiden, anerkennen wir, daß wir gefehlt,*" "Because we are suffering, we acknowledge that we have been remiss," to Hölderlin's 1804 translation: see 34 and her note at 90 n. 5; cf. Hegel, *Phänomenologie des Geistes* (cited in note 1 of ch. 6, above), 336. Yet in the 1804 version of *Antigonä*, which is his own final (and only extant) version, Hölderlin translates these lines as follows: *Doch wenn nun dieses schön ist vor den Göttern, / So leiden wir und bitten ab, was wir / Gesündigt. Wenn aber diese fehlen, / So mögen sie nicht größer Unglück leiden, / Als sie bewirken offenbar an mir.* "Yet if this is beautiful to the gods, / Then we shall suffer and do penance / For the way we have sinned. If it is they who are remiss, however, / Then may they suffer no greater misfortune / Than they are openly committing against me." Hegel may in fact be quoting an early translation of Sophocles' Antigone on which he worked during his student years, spent in Stuttgart and in Tübingen. There is some speculation that Hegel and Hölderlin may have worked together on such a translation when they were in the Tübinger Stift. H. S. Harris, in *Hegel's Development: Toward the Sunlight* (cited in note 1 of ch. 1, above), citing Karl Rosenkranz, *Georg Wilhelm Friedrich Hegels Leben* (Darmstadt: Wissenschaftliche Buchgesellschaft, 1963 [orig. publ. in Berlin, 1844]), reports that the translations of *Antigone* on which Hegel worked during the Tübingen years have disappeared. Harris notes: "Hegel worked on Sophocles for several years both at Stuttgart and at Tübingen. Rosenkranz speaks of 'the surviving translations' of the *Antigone*, which indicates that Hegel translated parts of the play several times. At Tübingen, probably under the influence of Hölderlin, he attempted metrical versions of passages from Sophocles, which were not very satisfactory" (48 n. 1). At all events, the translation that appears in Hegel's *Phenomenology* has no demonstrable connection with Hölderlin. In a sense, Hegel is not quoting either Hölderlin or Sophocles at all: he is tweaking the line in order to suggest that Antigone is unequivocally conscious of her guilt—for that is the role she is forced to play in the "ethical" drama that Hegel's *Phenomenology of Spirit* prescribes for her. My thanks to Christoph Jamme for helping to clarify the false attribution.

cross? We are told that it is the place where the unwritten laws, the will, or, better yet, the Δίκη of the gods rules" (301/259). Lacan's agnosticism captures Nietzsche's response to the Hegelian interpretation—through the medium of Euripides: just as Euripides, according to Nietzsche, could no longer understand what Aeschylus was about, that is, what Aeschylus intended tragedy to effect, so we can no longer understand Hegel's petty-bourgeois confidence in a tidy and readily resolvable conflict between the neophyte ethical community and the dialectically transcended family. If Antigone is the tragic heroine of the play that takes its name from her, the question has to be: What is *her* transgression, beyond her refusal to obey a tyrannical edict? The issue from start to finish, according to Lacan, is Antigone's transgression, not her victimization. Antigone's transgression has to do with her obsessive pursuit of her own doom, with her death drive, which propels the young woman—at least for a brief span of time—beyond the limit of Ἄτη. Even the sixth choral song, at the close of the play, the hymn to Dionysos, is not a celebration of human liberation or of Antigone's victory over unjust laws, nor even of her sacrifice to the unwritten laws, but the sign that a limit has been transgressed (312/268–269). Antigone herself, according to Lacan, "pushes to the limit the realization of something that might be called the pure and simple desire of death as such. She incarnates that desire" (328–329/282). What is clear about Antigone's desire, clear to both the chorus of old Theban men and the Hesperian analyst of Paris, is what the latter calls "the beyond of Ἄτη" (305/262–263). What is this "beyond"? It is the forbidden space and impossible place of the aftermath of one's own death. Antigone dares to step across the limit that any given human life "can only briefly cross" (ibid.). When the old men of Thebes say, "No fool is fool enough to love death" (C l. 220), or as Hölderlin's translation has it, "No one here is such a fool that he would gladly die" (DKV 2:868; l. 228), they miss the very essence of Antigone. It is almost as though Antigone uses the obstreperous but oh-so-vulnerable Creon to achieve her own end, which is . . . her own end.

Lacan's twenty-first chapter, "Antigone in the Between-Two-Deaths," focuses on the middle third of the play, with which we are now concerned. It is the third that particularly fascinates Lacan, as it fascinated Hölderlin before him. Both thinkers feel the clout of this virgin who is caught up in her passion and her *passio*. Lacan: "The violent illumination, the glow of beauty, coincides with the moment of transgression or of realization of Antigone's Ἄτη. . . . The beauty effect is a blindness effect" (327/281). Here we confront Antigone's position at the limit, or beyond it—ἐκτὸς ἄτας, as the chorus says more than once. To a certain extent, Antigone bears the traits that, according to Karl Reinhardt, all Sophoclean tragic heroes bear: they are μονούμενοι, loners, ἄφιλος, friendless, already dead (316–317/271–272). Philoctetes is in this respect the ultimate Sophoclean hero, "wretched, alone, isolated, and friendless in the worst possible way," δύστηνον, μόνον, ἐρῆμον ὧδε κἄφιλον κακούμενον (*Philoctetes*, ll. 227–228; cf. 1018). Yet Antigone too is alone and over the edge; her soul, she tells us, has long been dead (315/270; l. 559). Lacan cites the Oedipus of *Oedipus the Tyrant* as the only possible exception in Sophocles' oeuvre, inasmuch as the play begins with Oedipus triumphant; yet one must remember that long before a bemused Oedipus steps onto the stage he too is over the edge—or, as Lacan prefers to put it, "at the end of the road, his race run," *au bout de course*. Indeed, if at the outset of the drama Oedipus's race has not already been run, it is because long ago the infant's feet were mutilated. Be that as it may, Antigone now bursts onto the stage, "borne along by a passion" and incorporating the very essence of "the-race-is-run" (297/254). To be sure, she is an anamorphic image of this passion for death, that is, an image that cannot be seen head-on but has to be viewed on the oblique—like the skull that takes shape beneath the two central figures of Holbein's "The Ambassadors" only when we move to the side and almost out of sight of it. Lacan's attempt to envisage Antigone's desire from the side, as it were, from the very limits of perceivability, arises from his general view of the house of cards that every tragedy is: "What occurs [in tragic action] concerns forms of subsidence, the piling up of different layers of the presence of heroes in time. That is what remains undetermined: in the collapse of the house of cards represented by tragedy, one thing may pile up before another, and what one finds at the end when one turns the whole thing around is that it may appear in different ways" (308–309/265). One can safely say that what Hölderlin too is doing in his translations is turning the whole Sophoclean "thing" around in order to show the sundry facets of heroes—and heroines—in time.

Ἄτη, "doom," the impossible site of Antigone's own death drive, is therefore at least this much: a limit of and for perception. Ἄτη "concerns the Other, the field of the Other. . . . It is the place where Antigone is situated" (323/277). Situated only briefly, to be sure, between two deaths. Why two deaths? Whose deaths? Her own, no doubt, both of them, inasmuch as she is already mortified (*tödtendfaktisch*) from the moment she enters on the scene. Indeed, there is something Sadean about her predilection for the things of the netherworld, as though she were already dwelling there with the shades of her mother, father, and brothers. (One should not be confused by the later play

Oedipus at Colonus: in *Antigone,* composed first of the three Theban plays, in 441 as opposed to 405 B.C.E., Oedipus is clearly and repeatedly—from the first scene on—declared to be already in Hades.) Antigone seems as much a shade as Prudencio Aguilár, in Gabriel García Márquez's *Cien años de soledad*—Aguilár, who begins to love his murderer, José Arcadio Buendía, and to seek out his company, "so terrifying [was] the nearness of that other death which exists within death."[13] Yet it is also tempting, within Lacan's framework, to think of Antigone between the deaths of Jocasta (who, as the mother, represents for Lacanian psychoanalysis precisely this "field of the Other") and Oedipus (who, as both father and brother, is also "otherwise"). For those two deaths, which can be interpreted variously as the deaths of her mother and grandmother, as well as of her brother and father, dictate the well-known logic of Antigone's peculiar devotion to her brother Polyneices: because both the womb that bore Antigone, Ismene, Eteocles, and Polyneices and the seed that engendered the four of them are alike in Hades, her brother is irreplaceable. The word ἀδελφός, "brother," as Lacan rightly remarks, contains a reference to the womb (324/279). And what a womb! So open for so long to so many influences! Jocasta, as we said earlier, may have wanted to constrict it at the end. For, to repeat, Jocasta is both the siblings' mother and—at least when viewed through the strange refraction that is Oedipus—their grandmother. Antigone thus hovers between two generations, owing nature at least two deaths. Further, the concealed reference to the womb in "brother" also points to Oedipus, who—when viewed through the strange refraction that is their (grand) mother—is also Antigone's brother. Oedipus is the brother who spawns the "other" brothers; he too owes more than one death to nature. By harping on Polyneices, Antigone seems to be languishing for the brother who is in fact her father, her fraternal father—her oldest brother, *the eldest possible brother*—who is already dead. When Antigone says, "My brother, you found your fate when you found your bride" (C l. 869), or, in Hölderlin's rendition, "Alas! alas! my brother! / Fallen in a treacherous wedding!" (DKV 2:893; l. 900), interpreters universally assert that the brother she is addressing is Polyneices, whose wife Argeia, the daughter of King Adrastus of Argos, urged Polyneices to plot against Thebes. Yet in the lines immediately antecedent to these Antigone is invoking Jocasta's "husband-son, my father." Indeed, her entire speech, which betrays her "darkest thought," is uttered in reply to the chorus's having reminded her of her *father's* suffering. The sudden shift to her "brother" would therefore be disconcerting, or at least disorienting, were it not

13. Gabriel García Márquez, *Cien años de soledad,* 73/84.

for the fact that in this exceptional family a father can be a brother as well, especially if he is a brother who found his fate when he found his bride. With regard to Antigone's strange logic, which has fascinated interpreters at least since Goethe, one might wonder whether this confusion of brother and father, hence of mother and grandmother, in this most peculiar of households is the key—though Lacan does not push matters this far. When she argues for the irreplaceability of brothers alone (DKV 2:894; ll. 939ff.), is it not because Oedipus preempts all "other" brothers, all "other" siblings? And when Antigone devotes herself to her "brother," does she not do so as the incarnation of her own mother's desire for Oedipus—Oedipus the riddler, the destroyer of the sphinx, the unnatural-antinatural boy who knows human nature and who rescues his mother from an unsatisfying marriage? (Laius, we remember, was interested in other things.) Is not Oedipus the incestuous object of the desires of both Antigone and Jocasta, no matter how many swollen feet he may be standing on—four in the morning, two at noon, and three in the evening? Antigone's words in *Oedipus at Colonus* (ll. 1697–1703), spoken after her fraternal father's death and transfiguration, are quite revealing in this respect:

> Does languor [πόθος], then, survive terrible things?
> For what was far from lovely I loved,
> As long as I held him in my arms [ἐν χεροῖν].
> O Father! O Friend! [ὦ πάτηρ, ὦ φίλος].
> Now forever concealed in earth's darkness,
> Even out of reach you are not unloved by me [οὐδέ γ' ἀπὼν ἀφίλητος ἐμοί
> ποτε],
> And not unloved by my sister.

Early on in *Antigone's Claim*, Judith Butler asks: "Can we assume that Antigone has no confusion about who is her brother, and who is her father, that Antigone is not, as it were, living the equivocations that unravel the purity and universality of those structuralist rules [of kinship]?" (18). She replies that Antigone "is one for whom symbolic positions have become incoherent, confounding as she does brother and father" (22). Antigone is one who "puts the reigning regimes of [kinship] representation into crisis" (24), one who "represents a kind of thinking that counters the symbolic" (54), and one who "is caught in a web of relations that produce no coherent position within kinship" (57), even and especially when she pronounces the sacred name of her one and only brother:

When she claims that she acts according to a law that gives her most precious brother precedence, and she appears to mean "Polyneices" by that description, she means more than she intends, for that brother could be Oedipus and it could be Eteocles, and there is nothing in the nomenclature of kinship that can successfully restrict its scope of referentiality to the single person, Polyneices. The chorus at one point seeks to remind her that she has more than one brother, but she continues to insist on the singularity and non-reproducibility of this term of kinship. In effect, she seeks to restrict the reproducibility of the word "brother" and to link it exclusively to the person of Polyneices, but she can do this only by displaying incoherence and inconsistency. . . . Thus she is unable to capture the radical singularity of her brother through a term that, by definition, must be transposable and reproducible in order to signify at all. Language thus disperses the desire she seeks to bind to him, cursing her, as it were, with a promiscuity she cannot contain. (77)

In a word, writes Butler, "Antigone says 'brother,' but does she mean 'father'?" (67). Whether Antigone craves brother or father, whether she is driven to her death as the daughter-sister of Oedipus or the (grand) daughter of Jocasta, she too is in some sense like all her brothers—and also like their mother—already defunct, dead twice over. If the name *Antigone* truly means "in place of a mother," as Robert Graves suggests and as Carol Jacobs elaborates, then it is as a moribund mother of the moribund.[14]

It is this already-dead character of Antigone and her forebears that forces her to remain, as Lacan puts it, on the surface of things, between two deaths: "What is, is, and it is to this, to this surface, that the unshakable, unyielding position of Antigone is fixed" (325/279). Her race, like that of Polyneices, has

14. Graves, 2:380; Jacobs, 891. If Antigone is more mother than sister, however, it is only in radical displacement and suspension. Jacobs writes: "She is there on the one hand 'before or against the production of seed,' 'against generation,' and 'in place of a mother'—not because she saves her mother's son, but because she is able to produce both the male and herself as incomplete and in suspension" (907). Judith Butler, I believe, fails to note Lacan's question concerning the desire of the mother; she focuses instead throughout her work on the role of the *symbolic*—hence of the father, the phallus, and the superego—in Lacan's reading. While Butler's interpretation has the merit of recalling Lacan's debt to the structuralism of Claude Lévi-Strauss, and the further merit of advocating a radical rethinking of the social norms of kinship (30), it underestimates the disruptive effect Lacan's reading of *Antigone* has on the Lacanian system itself, and thus fails to realize the radical potential of the Lacanian reading for the very rethinking she most wants to promote. For the ethical strength of the entire book, *The Ethics of Psychoanalysis*, is its self-reflexivity, radical recoil, and ultimate vulnerability. For Lacan, the image of Antigone purges the imaginary, causes fatal slippage in the signifying chain of all symbolic adventures—including the psychoanalytic—and opens itself without subterfuge to the real of mortality. In *this* work of Lacan it is simply not the case that "the symbolic place of the mother . . . is taken over by the symbolic place of the father" (4). Rather, the question of the desire of the mother—as an *unanswered* question—causes the entire symbolic structure to totter. And because Butler does not pursue The *Ethics of Psychoanalysis* into its final section, on ethics proper, she does not see the "theological impulse" (21) in Lacanian psychoanalysis and the "universalizing function" of its utterances (41) absolutely stymied. In the end, as we shall see, Lacan does not preach from the Book of Psychoanalysis; he is instead hungry for it and has to eat it—and choke on it.

already been run—run on the bare surface of existence. It does not matter what Polyneices did in his life; his crimes are irrelevant; the diachronic depths of historical drama and biography count for nothing. Antigone is attached to his bare being, his unadorned having been, his naked corpse strewn across the surface of earth, his now quite *impossible* being—and this is "precisely the limit or the *ex nihilo* to which she keeps" (ibid.). Lacan identifies this limit marked by the phantasmatic creation-out-of-nothing with the simple name of the dead brother. Yet the limit appears in what Derrida calls the testamentary character of all names and dates, which is to say, the testamentary character of language in general.[15] Antigone's attachment to her brother "is nothing more than the cut [*coupure*] that the very presence of language inaugurates in the life of man" (ibid.). Such a cut, of course, is what Lacanian analysis, in its resistance to all humanism—that is, to every attempt to grasp humankind as a unified whole—is all about: "From our point of view man is in the process of decomposition, as if as a result of a spectral analysis, an example of which I have engaged in here by moving along the joint between the imaginary and the symbolic in which we seek out the relationship of human beings to the signifier, and the 'splitting' it engenders in them" (319/273–274). Antigone adheres to the surface of signification, and yet her adherence to such a surface is the plunge into an abyss. For it is a fixation, and fixity is always illusory. All Antigone needs to do is utter the words *my brother* and she thinks that signification is achieved, the signifying cut annealed, language fixed, and the meaning of life secured—in a tomb, as it were.

With regard to the testamentary nature of names and of language in general, that is, the way in which words mark the absence and even the death of things themselves, one may adduce a word or two on language and particularly on issues of translation. For when Lacan is most outrageous in his demands on the Greek language his translations have Hölderlin's renderings as their best allies. It is in fact uncanny how often, and in what decisive places, Lacan and Hölderlin read—and translate—eye to eye. Lacan agrees with Hölderlin (without citing him, or without saying whether or not he has ever had access to Hölderlin's translations) that in line 359 of the famous ode to humankind, πολλὰ τὰ δεινά, the second choral song of the play, there should be no full-stop or semi-colon between the words παντα πόρος ἄπορος, "resourceful without resource." That is to say, the force of the paradox or oxymoron is not that human beings are so skilled that nothing can stop them but

---

15. For a discussion of the sources in Derrida, see "A Mournful Logic," in Krell, *Purest of Bastards* (cited in note 15 of ch. 4, above), 9–14.

that, as Hölderlin believes, they are stymied—for all their cleverness—by death. The now accepted Greek text reads, in a standard translation: "He can always help himself. / He faces no future helpless. There's only death / that he cannot find an escape from. He has contrived / refuge from illnesses once beyond all cure" (C 11; T 202–203, ll. 360–364). Death alone, according to the accepted text, interrupts Sophocles' celebration of human ingenuity. Lacan, however, objects that Sophocles is talking about *homme*, not *Prudhomme;* that is to say, Sophocles is not spouting "platitudes" about man being the master of all things (320/274–275). Lacan would therefore be much happier with Hölderlin's rendering. Hölderlin, no doubt following a problematic Greek text (see Jochen Schmidt's commentary at DKV 2:1414, commenting on lines 375–376 at DKV 2:873), translates as follows: "*Allbewandert, / Unbewandert. Zu nichts kommt er.*" "Well-traveled, / Going nowhere. He comes to nothing." The words παντοπόρος ἄπορος thus anticipate the subsequent words about an incorrigible nothingness, simply by transposing the semi-colon to a position *after* ἄπορος. Heidegger, let it be remembered, does the same thing. He transliterates the famous phrase as follows: *Überall hinausfahrend unterwegs, erfahrungslos ohne Ausweg kommt er zum Nichts.*[16] "Everywhere setting off, getting under way, without experience or a way out, he comes to the nothing." Lacan, for his part, transl(iter)ates this most famous passage of the second choral ode as follows: "'He [namely, the human being] advances toward nothing that is likely to happen; he advances and he is παντοπόρος, "crafty," ἄπορος, always "screwed" [*toujours couillionné*]. He doesn't bungle a single thing. He always manages to cause everything to come crashing down on his head'" (321/275). Further, whereas contemporary translations of Sophocles universally have humankind successfully defending itself against fearful diseases (again, see Jochen Schmidt's attempt to "correct" Hölderlin, at DKV 2:1415, commenting on lines 379–380 at DKV 2:874), both Hölderlin and Lacan are less certain. Hölderlin has: *Der Toten künftigen Ort nur / Zu fliehen weiß er nicht, / Und die Flucht unbeholfener Seuchen / Zu überdenken.* ("The advancing site of the dead / He does not know how to flee, / Nor how he might devise / Flight from intractable epidemics.") Whereas the currently accepted Greek text and modern translations wax confident ("He has contrived / refuge from illnesses once beyond cure"), Lacan intensifies Hölderlin's doubts about the good doctors. He insists that "the only way" to translate Sophocles here is to have the chorus say that because human beings cannot cope with death they "escape *into* impossible sicknesses" (ibid.). In other words, illness is a

---

16. Martin Heidegger, *Einführung in die Metaphysik* (Tübingen: M. Niemeyer, 1953), 116.

temporary refuge from the death drive, better, a makeshift shelter provided by the death drive itself, and not a chance for the medical industry (including its psychoanalytic branch) to roll up its sleeves and brag that it is ready for anything, immortality is right around the corner. But to return to the principal theme, which is Antigone's second death.

Antigone declares that if she should die before her time it would be a gain (l. 461). She says to Ismene, "Take heart. You live. My life died long ago, / And that has made me fit to help the dead" (ll. 559–560). Creon later confirms her point of view: when Ismene addresses her sister, who is standing right there beside the two of them, Creon says, "Don't speak to her. For she is here no more" (l. 567). Antigone insists throughout that she longs to join her brother and lover in death. "Acheron is my mate," she says (l. 815). She is a creature of the δαιμόνιον, of the in-between: "Alive to the place of corpses, an alien still, / never at home with the living nor with the dead" (ll. 850–851). Hölderlin's rendering sharpens the dilemma: *Nicht unter Sterblichen, nicht unter Toten*, "Not among mortals," that is, not among those who are about to die, "not among the dead," that is, not among those who have demonstrated their mortality for the last time. Antigone complains to the chorus, but her complaint is more like a pledge: "Ill-fated past the rest, / shall I descend, before my course is run" (l. 896). In short, Antigone is always already attached to the sepulcher and to funeral rites, as well as to the names and dates on the surface of grave markers—that is her "thing." She is dedicated to the corpse, rapt to the cadaver, which Heidegger, in *Being and Time*, says is neither of the things like Dasein nor of the things unlike Dasein, even though that distinction was supposed to have been the universal axis of fundamental ontology.[17] Antigone has been ἐκτὸς ἄτας from the beginning. She lives in perpetual prolepsis, having already shattered the limit. Living dead, she processes like a dead woman into her tomb. Immured in stone, she seems at home. The name Niobe has already crossed Antigone's lips: Antigone sees herself as an avatar of Niobe, transformed into stone in high mountains, where snowmelt and time alone touch her. She is now finally at the end of the trail, at the end of the road, her race run.

---

17. See Krell, *Daimon Life* (cited in note 17 of ch. 2, above), 56, where the theme is *life*, not the corpse, and 60–63, where the theme is the *cadaver*. In section 47 of *Being and Time*, Heidegger insists that not even the anatomist turns to the cadaver as an item of equipment, as something handy or at hand in objective presence. The significance of the failure of this distinction (*daseinsmäßig / nicht daseinsmäßig*) in the face of the cadaver cannot be exaggerated: the fate of Heidegger's fundamental ontology of Dasein hangs in the balance. So too does the possibility—within fundamental ontology—of an ethical relation to the other as envisaged by Emmanuel Lévinas.

Even though Lacan is careful not to characterize her actions in terms of ἁμαρτία, and even though he is sympathetic to Antigone's insistence that she is not meddling in chthonic matters, it is clear that Antigone arrogates to herself the authority of the gods of the dead. "Antigone *appropriates* the god," writes Lacoue-Labarthe.[18] That is why no simple opposition to Creon is possible. Here Lacan approaches Hölderlin's quite radical view, which takes Antigone to be not the spokesperson of the gods but herself an *antitheos*. And while it is not likely that Lacan would have been familiar with Schelling's work, it may be permissible to insert a word concerning Schelling's analysis of the *antitheos* here, in order to deepen the significance of Hölderlin's designation of Antigone as running counter to the divine. In his 1842 *Philosophy of Mythology* (II/2:223), Schelling defines τὸ ἀντίθεον as *das Widergöttliche*, the counterdivine. What Schelling takes this to mean is that the divine itself is caught up in two contradictory wills or forces: even if her innermost essence is to will dilation and expansiveness—to move to the periphery and make herself accessible to her creatures—she must at the same time will her own contraction and self-preservation. For the contractive force assures being (*Sein*). Even if what she most wants is to be expansive, to be *able* to be (*seinkönnend*), the centripetal drive of being cannot be overcome. The *antitheos* is what one might call τύχη, chance or accident, as it applies to the divine essence as such. For Schelling, this would be the key to the tragic absolute as such. He sees it, ironically, or presciently, as the principal characteristic of the doctrine of the ancient Zarathustra. Lacan sees it in the perfect melding of the erotic and death drives in Sophocles' *Antigone*.

Nothing can be less certain, says Lacan, than Antigone's piety—Antigone, who stakes a claim on divine Δίκη for her criminal brother's sake. Thus her appeal to Zeus too is problematic, because ultimately negative. The fact that Antigone's transgression cannot be reduced to her defiance of Creon's edict and her defense of the unwritten divine law is what lends force to Antigone's insistence that—traditional interpretations to the contrary notwithstanding—it was not Zeus who either sanctioned Creon's decree or ordered her to disobey that decree by burying her brother (324/286). Hölderlin too is concerned with Antigone's rejection of Zeus as the source of her deed as well as of Creon's decree. Hölderlin cites his own translation of Antigone's lines in his "Notes," as though in order to draw attention to these lines, perhaps as an alteration of the Sophoclean text for the sake of our Hes-

---

18. Lacoue-Labarthe, *Métaphrasis*, 24; cf. 25, 63.

perian ears, although he does not comment on the lines. His translation adds one of the few emphatic expressions to his text, although, admittedly, the emphasis does not erase the ambiguity from Antigone's motivation. In response to Creon's question as to how she dared break the law, she replies: *Darum. Mein Zeus berichtete mirs nicht* ("For this reason. *My* Zeus did not report it to me" [DKV 2:877, 914]). Hölderlin, like Lacan, is prepared to take the question of Antigone's transgression—what Hölderlin would call her *nefas*—quite seriously, though he too would never reduce this transgression to an error of judgment or a flaw of character, a regrettable ἁμαρτία.

Lacan, it must be said, is not entirely consistent about Antigone's transgression—her trespass into the space of her own death. At the conclusion of his extended analysis of *Antigone*, he runs the risk of collapsing back into the traditional interpretation by emphasizing Antigone's defiance of Creon: he identifies her desire, in its "radically destructive character," with her embrace of Polyneices, her criminal brother. "Between the two of them, Antigone chooses to be purely and simply the guardian of the being of the criminal as such" (329/283). Yet this is too close to the biography and historical drama of Polyneices about which Lacan has warned us earlier on; if Antigone "perpetuates, eternalizes, immortalizes" that Ἄτη which is her doom (ibid.), it is not because of Polyneices' crime against the state, but because of her obsession with his naked (in)existence. Not her defiance but her desire is the issue. Antigone's transgression has to do with her own impossible crossing over into the realm of the dead, that is, with what Hölderlin envisages as tragedy's seizing a human being at the midpoint of his or her life and absconding with that life to "the excentric realm of the dead" (DKV 2:851). Lacan interprets the seizure of and by Antigone as a symptom of the language of desire. Antigone transgresses by fixating the signifying chain, by insisting on the surface of things, reading—or perhaps incising—the name and the dates of Polyneices over and over again:

—He is what he is, he is my brother. I bury my brother, we are of the same womb, we are already dead. We are what we are, my brother and I. Call us "Belligerence."

Or perhaps she fixates on another name, another set of dates, another brother:

—He is what he is, he is my brother. I bury my brother, we are of the same womb, we are already dead. We are what we are, my brother and I. Call us "Swell-foot."

The chorus, accompanying Antigone toward the tomb of her living death, driven mad by the radiant vision of her, caught up in ἵμερος ἐναργής, "manifest desire," cites the myths of Danaë, Lycurgus, and Cleopatra, daughter of the North Wind. A lot could be gained in interpreting these myths, says Lacan. He is of course correct, as we have seen: if one reinterprets the myth of Danaë in accord with Hölderlin's translation of the fifth choral ode, nothing less than a reversal of the positions of mortal and immortal occurs, as Danaë counts off for the father of time, Zeus himself, the golden hours. For Lacan, the myths are a burden that by his own admission he cannot lighten. Nevertheless, he has the key insight concerning the import of these myths, and it is a Hölderlinian insight: "They all concern the relationship of mortals to the gods" (328/282). In what way? They depict "dramatic destinies that are all on the boundary between life and death, the boundary of the still-living corpse" (311/268). Hence the *uncanny* nature of the fifth choral ode, sung as Antigone prepares to walk into the chilly embrace of her tomb. These myths invoke that naked surface, that bare being, mentioned a moment ago, which has to do with language and imperfect signification. Antigone is αὐτόνομος by virtue of the fact that the human being, "miraculously," is the bearer of language, that is to say, of "the signifying cut that confers on the human being the indomitable power of being what it is in the face of everything that may oppose it" (328/282). Even if Antigone fixates, even if she is deluded, she maintains her rapport with language. Lacan's signifying cut—that splitting (yet also elevating) of humanity in language—is reminiscent of Max Kommerell's insight into the counterbalancing of immortal power and mortal vulnerability, an insight that also entails a radical displacement of mortal and immortal destinies. For Kommerell, developing Hölderlin's radical insight, identifies the "tender defenselessness" of the gods in the face of beautiful mortals—whom, of course, the gods *could* pulverize at any instant. "Tender defenselessness" is the gods' downfall, the *antitheos* at the heart of every god. Such is the tragedy of divine desire; such is the tragic absolute.

It may be that Xenophanes of Colophon had an inkling of that tragedy and that he tried to ward it off.[19] His critique of the anthropomorphism endemic in Homer and Hesiod's portrayal of the Olympian gods rests on his accusation that "they have attributed to the gods everything that is a shame [ὀνείδεα] and a reproach among human beings" (DK B11; 168). In his effort to reassert the power and dignity of the immortals, Xenophanes says of Zeus: "Always he remains in the same place, moving not at all; nor is it fitting for

---

19. For the following, see G. S. Kirk and J. E. Raven, *The Presocratic Philosophers: A Critical History with a Selection of Texts* (Cambridge: Cambridge University Press, 1966), 167–171; fragments cited according to Diels-Kranz (DK), with Kirk and Raven's page numbers indicated in the body of the text within parentheses.

him to go to different places at different times, but without toil [ἀπάνευθε πόνοιο] he shakes all things by the thought of his mind" (B26 and 25; 169). To this one may compare Aeschylus's depiction of Zeus in *The Suppliant Maidens*: "He hurls mortals in destruction from their high-towered expectations, but puts forth no force: everything with regard to the gods is without toil [πᾶν ἄπονον δαιμωνίων]. Sitting, he [Zeus] nevertheless at once accomplishes his thought, somehow, from his holy resting-place" (ll. 96–103, 171). Zeus does not toil when it comes to exertions of his strength and sovereignty. Yet even if he does not move in order to work his effects and exercise his powers, is he never moved? Kirk and Raven comment on this, indirectly, by invoking the concept of Ἄτη: "That thought or intelligence can affect things outside the thinker, without the agency of limbs, is a development—but a very bold one—of the Homeric idea that a god can accomplish his end merely by implanting, for example, Infatuation (Ἄτη) in a mortal" (170). Infatuation, "for example." Yet what if this is the one example that backfires on divinity? What if desire moves in both directions, invading even the lapidary Zeus of Xenophanes? It would no longer be a matter of the immortals not needing *Sittlichkeit*, or ethicality, as Schelling says; it would be a matter of their not being able to resist what settles on the cheek of a young girl. Indeed, if one may be allowed to add one further word of Schelling's, the infatuation we are speaking of here may gain another dimension—that of inevitable recoil. In his 1842 *Philosophy of Mythology* (II/2:336), Schelling defines Ἄτη as "thoughtlessness personified," *Unbesonnenheit, Unbedachtheit*. It is almost as though Schelling is thinking ahead to Hannah Arendt's warning that thoughtlessness is all it takes to produce the most horrific effects on earth.[20] Ἄτη is called the oldest daughter of Zeus, says Schelling, πρέσβα Διὸς θυγάτηρ, in order to signify that there never was a time when such infatuating doom was not present in the divine family. Yet there is something Antigone-like about the goddess called Doom: she has tender feet, which can never touch the ground. That is why she hovers above the heads of human beings as she studies on the ways she might ensnare them and harm them. Doom—a tenderfoot? Does thoughtlessness, like infatuation, recoil upon divinity itself? Thoughtless infatuation as the downfall of the gods? Divine desire as the tragedy of the divine?

Lacan does not go so far, if only because of his stringent agnosticism. Yet even though he feels unequal to the task of commenting on the three mythi-

---

20. Hannah Arendt, "Thinking and Moral Considerations," *Social Research* 38, no. 3 (Autumn 1971): 7–37.

cal figures of the fifth choral ode, and even though he seems to sense nothing of the radical displacement of gods as well as mortals in that "thing" called desire, Lacan feels the pressure in the fifth choral hymn mounting. Indeed, he says, that pressure "mounts higher and higher toward I don't know what sort of explosion of divine delirium," at which point "Tiresias, the blind one, appears" (311–312/268). Lacan here feels the impact of the device that determines Hölderlin's entire approach to Sophoclean drama, namely, the caesura. According to Hölderlin, Sophocles' *Antigone* is marked by the late appearance of its counterrhythmic interruption. Tiresias, by appearing when he does, after the fifth choral ode, resists for an extended interval the momentum that has built up since the initial scenes of the play; his interruption protects the end of the play from being crushed, as it were, by the momentum of the prior scenes. Tiresias rescues the final moments of the play by establishing a kind of equilibrium in the whole, establishing it not at the midpoint of the drama, which is Haemon's confrontation with Creon, but roughly in its final fifth, or final quarter, in the eighth of its ten scenes. By slowing the action so late in the game, so late in Antigone's race to the end, Tiresias enables the spectators to see quite clearly the mistake Creon has made and to feel the clout of Antigone's death drive. This in turn enables them to see the sequence of representations in the play *as* representation—in other words, to see the play as a whole.

It will not do to abandon Lacan's commentary on *Antigone* without repeating his final question to the play and its heroine, but also to us, his berated and battered readers. "Think about it hard. What happens to her desire? Shouldn't it be the desire of the Other and be linked to the desire of the mother? . . . The desire of the mother is the origin of everything. The desire of the mother is . . . the founding desire of the whole structure."[21] Lacan's final question, if nothing else, forces us to return ever and again to Jocasta. Jocasta, the (grand) mother, "the fierce old mother incessantly moaning." The question forces us to raise old ghosts, themselves lusting after a second death, ghosts who warn both Orestes and Hamlet, "Taint not thy mind, nor let thy soul contrive / Against thy mother aught: leave her to heaven, / And to those thorns that in her bosom lodge, / To prick and sting her" (*Hamlet*, 1:5). Leave the mother above all to her second death, the death associated with her desire and her pleasure. Is this what the divine Antigone does—though only in the

---

21. Lacan, *Ethics of Psychoanalysis*, 329/283. Patrick Guyomard has clearly recognized the importance of Lacan's admission: Guyomard's discussion, while starkly critical of Lacan's insistence on the mother, is insightful and very much worth study. See Patrick Guyomard, *La jouissance du tragique: Antigone, Lacan et le désir de l'analyste* (Paris: Aubier, 1992), 60, and throughout.

wings, where no one can see? Does she battle her (grand) mother, who always insists on life and more life, and then hasten to submit to the dead mother's fate, which is the love of her defunct father-brother? Lacan stresses that what is decisive in the case of Antigone is not so much her defiance of the state but her troubled relation to the gods: "it is clear that the question raised at the end concerns what I shall call the divine use of Antigone" (331/286). Such "divine use" reminds us once again of the figure of Danaë, both used by the god and, in some unheard-of sense, abusing him, or perhaps *disabusing* him—in any case, thoroughly readjusting "the relationship of mortals to the gods" (328/282). What is important about Danaë, and also about Antigone, is her transgression, not her victimization.[22]

Divine use, as it turns out, at least in Hölderlin, pales before divine defenselessness. This would be Hölderlin's principal *contribution* to Lacan's reading, his way of urging the reading to become still more radical. For it would, precisely in its reading of the Danaë myth, take us back to the befuddling question of the desire of the mother. What is *her* use of the god? And if every mother's son and every mother's daughter is implicated here, what is *her* use of *us*?

Lacan on the Tragic Dimension of Psychoanalytic Experience

If Freud's wish for psychoanalysis is that it transform neurotic misery into normal unhappiness, Lacan's is that the analyst learn to be as wretched as everyone else. He wants ethics to move beyond Aristotelian εὐδαιμονία and Kantian duty in the direction of something far more daunting. He wants to universalize the maxim of mortal distress. He wants Dr. Phil weeping helplessly on Oprah's formidable couch. Lacan's is the ethics of the universal thump, as Melville recounts it in the opening chapter of *Moby-Dick:* "Who aint a slave? Tell me that. Well, then, however the old sea-captains may order

22. It is perhaps surprising that Freud, who is usually criticized for having plundered Greek tragedy for his "complexes" without having understood it, confirms Hölderlin's principal insight into the transgression and blasphemy that tragedy entails. In his essay of 1905–1906, "Psychopathic Personages on the Stage" (*Studienausgabe*, 10:164–165), he notes the origin of tragedy in sacrificial cult— the destruction of goat and scapegoat—and the "rebellion against the divine world order" that first produces heroic suffering. Tragedy commences as "struggle against the divine." Tragic heroes and heroines "are in the first place rebels against God or some divinity, and out of the feeling of misery typical of the weaker party who goes to confront the might of the god some sort of pleasure is to be drawn. It is to be drawn by means of the masochistic satisfaction and even direct enjoyment found in those personalities that are emphatically described as having grandeur." For Freud's daring interpretation of the chorus as the "primal horde" hypocritically projecting onto the hero or heroine the guilt deriving from its murder of the father-god, see ch. 4, section 7, of *Totem and Taboo* (9:438–439). I am grateful to Professor Iris Därmann for first directing me to Freud's *Bühne*.

me about—however they may thump and punch me about, I have the satisfaction of knowing that it is all right; that everybody else is one way or other
served in much the same way—either in a physical or metaphysical point of
view, that is; and so the universal thump is passed round, and all hands should
rub each other's shoulder-blades, and be content."[23] The only thing that
Lacan would alter in this Melvillean ethics would be the final remonstration.
Be content? No, be wretched—honor the transference at least to that extent.

What impact does Antigone—both the figure and the play—have on the
ethical dimension of psychoanalysis? Lacan tells us, at the end of the *Antigone*
commentary, that prior to the ethics developed by Socrates, Plato, and Aristotle, Sophocles presents us with human beings "on the paths of solitude, sit-
uating the hero for us in a zone where death encroaches on life, setting the
hero in rapport with what I have called here the second death" (331/285). We
are familiar with those funny stories about Lacan greedily insisting on being
paid. Yet he tells us that the psychoanalyst always pays, pays with his or her
words—the words of interpretation—and with his or her person, of which the
transference divests her or him (337/291). There will always be a judgment,
perhaps a Last Judgment, about the efficacy of psychoanalysis, and that judgment will fall hard on the one who cannot fulfill the impossible demand.
What is *demanded* of the psychoanalyst, to repeat, is the production of happiness (339/292–293). That is the demand made on political constitutions and
on all systems of the good since Plato and Aristotle. Regrettably, nothing like
a fulfillment of the demand is possible for psychoanalysis, in spite of—or precisely because of—its focus on genitality and sexuality. Sublimation alone
comes close to fulfilling that promise. Hence the psychoanalyst's desire to pull
the sublime rabbit out of the crumpled hat of sublimation and figure out what
sort of beast it is.

Satisfaction without repression is what sublimation promises, the perfection of metonymy, as for example in the Apocalyptic figure of the eating of
the book.[24] Or in the eschatological figure of the Last Judgment (340/294).
The analysand's demand that one *realize* one's desire can be met as long as the
analyst knows that *realization* is of *the real* and that the real is the encroach-
ment of death on life (341/294). Moreover, there is a second death, as Sade

---

23. Melville, *Moby-Dick* (cited in the Introduction, above), 25.
24. Revelation 10:9–10: "And I went to the angel / and said to him / 'Give me the little book
[*Büchlin*].' And he said to me / 'Take it and swallow it / and it will cramp your belly [*dich im Bauch
krimmen*]. / But in your mouth it will be as sweet as honey.' And I took the little book from the angel's
hand / and swallowed it / and it was sweet in my mouth like honey. / And when I had eaten it / my
belly cramped." (After Luther.)

fancies, a suffering beyond death. This "second death" may remind us of Kafka's and Blanchot's notion of the *impossibility* of death. That *impossibility*, however, would be nothing like a victory over death. Such a second death would be an absolute limit: no salvation here, no resurrection. A season in hell is always recommended for the would-be analyst, a perpetuation of suffering forever the order of the day. Or, at the very least, protracted sojourns in an underworld of bloodless shades—the subsoil of myth and legend. Lacan does not wear his "culture" on his sleeve but on the shield and lance of his own drive *to know*. Yet how does one come to *know* the death drive? Answer: by experiencing the ruptures and raptures of the signifying chain of language, which is marked by the splitting of signification.

Precisely this is the function of the beautiful, namely, "to indicate the place of rapport between the human being and his or her own death, and to indicate it solely by means of incandescence [*éblouissement*]" (342/295). Something radiant—even if that something should be an old pair of shoes, espied by Heidegger or by one's life partner (343/297). It is not a matter of the Kantian "ideal beauty" here, but of the transition from life to death—which, to be sure, may well have to do with the "ideal appearance of beauty," which, as Kant teaches, comes to the fore invariably in the *Gestalt* of the human body (345/298; cf. KU §17). At all events, the transition from life to death is "punctual," or "temporal"; in spite of the appearance of narcissism, the transition in question has to do also with the second death, inasmuch as the second death is "the signifier of one's desire" (ibid.). Once again Lacan invokes the old men of Thebes: their ἵμερος ἐναργής, "manifest desire," points to "the central mirage," where desire is desire of nothing. The second death, where the beautiful shimmers and bedazzles us, exhibits the place where the human being experiences its "lack in being" and "its failure to see that place" (ibid.). An uncanny exhibition, no doubt, reminiscent of Novalis's (non)absolute method. For here the *Gestalt* of the ideal beauty in the human body and the *Gestalt* of divine death—in which alone the god comes to presence—coalesce.

In some strange way, the god of shame, Αἰδώς, related to the phallus as signifier, makes a claim on the virginal and veiled Antigone.[25] Shame—better, concealment—comes to the fore in Antigone's drive to death, and espe-

---

25. See Jacques Lacan, *Écrits*, 692: "The phallus is the signifier of this *Aufhebung* which it itself inaugurates (initiates) by its disappearance. That is why the demon of Αἰδώς (*Scham*) comes to the fore at the very moment in which, during the ancient mystery, the phallus is unveiled (cf. the famous painting of the Villa of Pompeii)." See also Jacques Lacan and the École Freudienne, *Feminine Sexuality*, ed. Juliet Mitchell and Jacqueline Rose (London: Macmillan, 1982), 82.

cially in her suicide, the precipitation of her own death, which occurs "in a crisis of μανία" (346/299). Αἰδώς is here Ἅιδης, the domain and the god of the dead. Lacan too refers to Heraclitus's saying, "Dionysos and Hades are the same" (DK B15). The shameful parts are (to be) as invisible as death. This in fact accounts for the phantasm of the phallus as the signifier par excellence, inasmuch as the phallus works its effects only under the condition of *Penisneid* in the female and castration anxiety in the male. Perhaps *Lebensneid* is a way of saying both at once. If Αἰδώς may be translated at all as "shame," perhaps it must be in the sense Nietzsche gives it in a note from the final weeks of the year 1870: "*Shame:* the feeling that we stand under the spell of illusion *even though* we see through it*" (KSA 7:119). Nietzsche continues: "We have to *live* with this sensation, pursuing our mundane plans. That is the tribute we have to pay to the principle of individuation. Our intercourse with human beings has this delicate membrane about it—at least in the case of the tragic human being" (ibid.). Such would be "the central mirage," in which beauty, desire, and suffering fade into and out of one another, as adumbrations of the death drive. Even though one might expect that nothing could be farther from Hölderlin's world, we recall his description of the lines of dialogue and choral song in Greek tragedy as "leidende Organe *des göttlichringenden Körpers,*" which one may now translate as "the suffering organs of a *body wrestling with divinity*" (CHV 2:374). Such suffering is Antigone's lot.

If the analysand insists on knowing the sovereign good for man, the Silenic psychoanalyst knows that there isn't one, that the problematic of desire must replace that of the hierarchy of goods (347/200). The patient's demands are (in) vain, and are regressive, as are the demands of the philosophers. The analyst knows that for all the generations of mortals past, present, and future, there has been and will have been only ἄτη, a congenital source of unhappiness. The only thing the psychoanalyst has to offer—though now he or she sounds very much like a philosopher—is what he or she has, namely, his or her own desire, as an *averted* desire. The analyst will insist on distance (348/300–301). Avoiding the fraudulent trafficking in systems of goods, including all systems of genital oblativity, the analyst will have to acknowledge a certain helplessness (351/304). He or she will have to indicate repeatedly "the fundamental rapport with death" that marks human beings; that very helplessness will have to help the patient to confront "the reality of the human condition" (ibid.). In addition to the word *Hilflosigkeit,* "helplessness," Lacan offers the words *anxiety* and *distress,* along with the phrase *expecting aid from no quarter.* To be sure, the psychoanalyst, like Kalchas the Seer and Tiresias, is the human being who "had known," pluperfectly and imperfectly at once, the human being who wants to know now, and who will always want to know more (352/304). Oedipus too, mad to know, occupies a zone beyond death, the zone of the phantasm expressed in the words of the chorus of *Oedipus at Colonus*, "Never to have been born is best," μὴ φύναι (353/305; l. 1224). These are the words that Hölderlin affixed as the epigram to the second volume of his *Hyperion*. Nietzsche read that volume when he was sixteen; Lacan, presumably, later in life.

What does Oedipus, son of Laius and father of Antigone, know? He knows that the father, the *real* father, is *le Grand Fouteur*. If E. T. A. Hoffmann's Nathanael wants to glorify and sentimentalize his dead father, he may do so in a phantasm, by grace of a split in the father image. Yet when he deals with the *real* father, it will turn out to be the Doppelgänger, Coppelius/Coppola, David Lynch's "Bob." The ultimate function of the well-read superego, says Lacan, is to hate God, to reproach him for having botched things so badly (355/308). This reproach may be no more than a Late Hesperian way of putting into our mouths Hölderlin's conviction that true spirituality requires our going to meet the godhead with words of blasphemy. The mutual betrayal of god and mortal is not some fault, not some nefarious deed on the part of mortals, but the essence of the tragic absolute. Freud's myth of the murdered father, and the entire ambivalence of lovehate toward the father that the sons (and daughters?) incorporate, are but responses to the μὴ φύναι: Silenic wisdom, in Lacan's words, confronts our *véritable être-pour-la-mort*; in Heidegger's words, our *Sein-zum-Tode* (357/309). In Hölderlin, the ambivalence of love-hate, or life-death, assumes univocity for an instant, an instant of caesura, when, as he says, divinity itself becomes present *in der Gestalt des Todes*, in the figure of death.

In the final chapter of his book, "The Paradoxes of Ethics," Lacan poses *the* ethical question of psychoanalysis. Get ready to hang your head in shame, for the question is: "Have you been acting in conformity with your desire?" (359/311). The American ego psychologists have developed a new bumper sticker in response to this fearsome Lacanian interrogation: "What have *you* done for your desire today?" Yet the impossible demand that we act in conformity with our desire will not take us very far—at least, those of us who lack Antigone's clout. The field of ethics is by its nature *excentrique*, writes Lacan, once again borrowing a word from Hölderlin, so that it is difficult to know how to conclude, except elliptically. What Hölderlin calls the "excentric orbit" of a human life has to do with his tragic view of humankind from early on in his work, from his preparations for *Hyperion* to the very end, with the translations of Sophocles. All we can be sure of in the case of psychoanalysis is that one must reject Aristotle's ethics of the master, the ethics of the city and of power, inasmuch as every human action has its hidden side, its "shame," such that taking the measure of it is difficult indeed (360/312). To be sure, the psychoanalyst retains an element of the protophilosophical γνῶθι σεαυτόν. Yet Lacan reiterates that such self-knowledge is outside the realm of the good and all systems of goods, that it opens up instead the dimension of "the tragic experience of life" (361/313). The tragic dimension of psychoanalysis is therefore nothing less than the life-experience of the psychoanalyst whole and entire. The triumph of death, or of being-for-death, which is formulated in the μὴ φύναι of *Oedipus at Colonus*, is the selfsame negativity that is expressed in the human subjection to the signifier, a subjection suffered by both analysand and analyst (362/313). The phallus may process comically or hide tragically, but in any case it frustrates signification. Hence there is something tragicomic in the Last Judgment of psychoanalysis, with the "of" here enjoining both the subjective and the objective genitives, something tragicomic in the thunderous question it poses, "Have you been acting in conformity with the desire that inhabits you?" It is a question for gods and beasts, Aristotle would say, signifying as it does the world of the unthinkable (*le monde de l'impensable*) for human beings (363/314). Recall, however, that in Hölderlin's view this is precisely the world in which Sophocles wanders, "amid unthinkable things." With his Oedipus, with his Antigone.

Have you been acting in conformity with your desire? Such a question oscillates between the unconditional *Thou shalt* of Kant's categorical imperative and the Sadean phantasm of a jouissance erected into an imperative (364/315–316). Yet as long as the subject is constituted in its relation to the signifier, there will be rupture, division, scission, and inevitable ambivalence, which is where desire builds its nest (365/316). Above the nest, a little sign says, "House of Languish." If the sole culpability, for an ethics of psychoanalysis, is that of having fallen back from or ceded on one's desire (*d'avoir cédé sur le désir*), one can rest assured that the price for such concessions will be paid. Neurosis is real. We may hope for a holiday on the sands of Entre-Deux-Mèrs, sipping its crisp white wine, but we are toiling *entre-deux-morts*, between two deaths. Lacan notes that as the subject falls back and cedes on his or her desire, the subject himself or herself senses a betrayal (*trahison*), which may be either permissible or nefarious, either *faste* or *néfaste* (370/321). These expressions are so close to those of Hölderlin—to *Trug*, *Betrug*, and the *nefas*—that it is hard to imagine that Lacan could have gleaned them elsewhere. The betrayal is whispered to us by our daimon, which says, "Sublimate as much as you like, you will have to pay something for it. This something is jouissance" (371/322).

Yet the final words of Lacan's seminar on ethics have to do with the eminently sublimated passion of the analyst, the passion *to know*. Antigone teaches us that the laws of heaven and earth and underworld are the laws of desire. One must eat in order to live. And one will desire in order to die. Yet one can spend a lifetime eating books, and one has to do so, especially if one desires to break into the hubristic profession that analyzes the soul in all its good and ill. Good and ill? Lacan sounds like Schelling when he declares, "What is important is not knowing whether man is good or bad in his origin; what is important is knowing what the book will give us once it is altogether eaten" (375/325).

Antigone between Two Deaths, Two Births

Without being able to say precisely how Hölderlin and Lacan shape the following reading, I want to risk the proposition that Antigone grows younger and more blindingly beautiful as the play proceeds. It is as though she were a creature of that Golden Age presided over by Zeus and Kronos, the age recounted in the myth of Plato's *Statesman*. She advances from a harsh and brittle maturity to a tender adolescence, and from thence to a helpless infancy and gestation—until she finally disappears into the body of the grand mother. Between two deaths, she is also, as Heidegger and Arendt would say, *gebürtig*, between two births. She begins as the decisive and even callous activist who chides her timid sister, while Ismene can only reply by indicating the paradoxical nature of Antigone's passion: "You have a hot heart [θερμὴν . . . καρδίαν] for chilly things" (l. 88). As Carol Jacobs demonstrates so well, this mature Antigone who scolds her sister and "dusts" her brother, and who then screeches like a mother bird returning to a ravaged nest, is indeed more a mother than a sister. She is in fact the ancient crone who has washed the bodies of all the members of the House of Oedipus and prepared them for burial. At the midpoint of the play, by the time she has regressed to a more tender age, she will appear as the bride-to-be of Haemon, whose name plays on the promise of a young woman's marriage. By the time of the fourth choral ode, the hymn to Eros, she will be the demure girl on whose blushing cheek the god of love settles. The glow of that cheek will disquiet mortal and immortal alike, all the more so as it grows more callow. Shades of Alkmene! Shades of

Danaë! Throughout their exchanges with Antigone, the old men of Thebes call her παῖς, "child." In their eyes the condemned one grows ever more vulnerable, ever more fragile and resourceless. Antigone seems to shrink—if not in stature (327/281), then certainly in boldness. Her little legs will hardly support her as she takes those first halting steps toward the tomb. Once ensconced there, in that great mother gone to stone, she attaches herself by a gauzy umbilical cord—by the cloth of her clout—to the wall of the womb-tomb, the σῶμα-σῆμα of mortal signification. She dangles and dwindles there as her mother before her had done, that is to say, as her grand mother before her had done. And when Haemon coughs up his own jetting blood and spatters her cheek, it is the blood of the marriage she never wanted, the blood of a second birth in a second death. A word, then, at the end, about the grand mother, rehearsing matters we have already heard but still do not understand.

Jocasta, after hearing Oedipus's dire insult to her, rushes to her chamber. The chorus is worried about her. They urge Oedipus to investigate. Instead, he takes up his sword and tears down doors. Soon enough he finds her, albeit no longer fit to kill. She is swaying softly to no music, dancing in silent solitude, her bare feet a foot or two above the floor. Jocasta absconds with her secrets—her fears both of and for her children, her love and hatred of her husbands and her son. In her last retrospect, they must all have appeared to her to have been lame—Labdacus, Laius, and even the best of them, her son Oedipus, "swell-foot." Jocasta remains discreet, however, forever the null-cipher, the zero of tragedy, precisely through her laughter (Pasolini has her laughing in the uncanniest places throughout the film) and her moments of devastating sadness and terror (that long look into the camera). Her desire, the desire of the grand mother, will never illuminate for us poor mortals the desire of her grand daughter or of her wretched son and husband. Jocasta might as well be entombed with Antigone, Antigone with Jocasta, entombed and enwombed. Darkness and stillness and aloneness—the three inexpugnable sources of what Freud calls the uncanny—embrace them both. No music, no strain of analysis, shatters the silence of daughters, the taciturnity of mothers.

By this time we do not ask, concerning Antigone, *What is her desire?* or even *What is her drive?* We ask, *What is the real?*

Like Persephone, Antigone has made a "love pact" with "the king of the night" (RC 210). She betakes her living body to a place where no living body has been before. *Eros,* accompanying her living body, penetrates the realm of *Thanatos.* Antigone is the origin of *Triebvermischung.* Between two deaths, she incorporates what Melville so appreciates in Hawthorne, namely, "the blackness of darkness." Yet Antigone illuminates the way ahead—our own way, which is also the way of gods and heroes. Between two births, she radiates the splendor of the living. She takes our breath away, then gives it back, deigning for unknown reasons not to kill us.

Readers and spectators of Sophocles' *Antigone* desire both irradiations. We desire both the clout that is her sweet vestment, the noose of her cloth still redolent of her sweet body, and the clout that is the knowledge of her bitter, bloody doom. We see the representations *as* representation. We accept the reality principle. We want to know what time it is. And yet we still want her to bestow on us the golden hours. She grants both of our desires, this superlatively shining girl, and that is why she will haunt us in every recess of our being-toward-the-end. In her beauty and in her disaster, she is the perfect embodiment of Dionysos, the masked god, invoked by Yeats in "The Phases of the Moon": "twice born, twice buried," she must wax before the full moon, only to dwindle before the new moon, which is no moon at all but the blackness of darkness. In the face of both the full and the new, between two births and two deaths, Antigone waxes and wanes like a god, which is to say, "helpless as a worm."[26]

26. William Butler Yeats, *A Vision* (New York: Collier Books, 1966), 60.

NIETZSCHEAN
REMINISCENCES

12

I stood before her, and heard and saw the peace of heaven, and in the midst of sobbing Chaos appeared to me Urania.

—F. HÖLDERLIN,
Hyperion (ca. 1797)

Urania is not merely Urania; rather, she has concealed Dionysos within herself.

—F. W. J. SCHELLING,
Philosophie der Mythologie (1842)

The interpenetration of sorrow and joy in the essence of the world is that on which we live. We are mere husks about that immortal kernel.

—F. NIETZSCHE, *KSA*
7:213 (1871)

In this final chapter it will not be a matter of trying to show how either Schelling or Hölderlin "influences" Nietzsche.[1] Not that such an attempt would be uninteresting—especially in the case of Hölderlin. Nietzsche's secondary school composition on his "favorite poet," considered below, is evidence enough of how early and how profound such influence is. If one were to postulate only one such possible influence, one might ask where Nietzsche first heard the wisdom of Silenos: "Never to have been born is best; next best is to die as soon as you may."[2] To be sure, at Schulpforta, while

1. Nor will I be offering here an account of Nietzsche's extraordinary contribution to the theory of tragedy. For a thoughtful account of the larger issues surrounding Nietzsche's *Birth of Tragedy*, including the historical background to the work, see ch. 5 of Dennis Schmidt's *On Germans and Other Greeks* (cited in the Introduction, above). I also remain indebted to John Sallis, *Crossings: Nietzsche and the Space of Tragedy* (Chicago: University of Chicago Press, 1991). Of course, the bibliography of excellent books on Nietzsche's classic work is vast, though I will stop listing them here.

2. Traditional Nietzsche scholarship has Nietzsche encountering the wisdom of Silenos for the first time in "fragment 6" of Aristotle's *Eudemian Ethics*. I have not found such a reference in Nietzsche's works. It is far more likely that he first encountered such wisdom in the μὴ φύναι of Sophocles' *Oedipus at Colonus* or in volume two of Hölderlin's *Hyperion*. True, in the *Eudemian Ethics* we do find an extraordinary elaboration of Silenic wisdom at the outset of Book I, ch. 5, a passage I cannot refrain from reproducing here: "About many other things it is difficult to judge well, but most difficult about that on which judgment seems to all easiest and the knowledge of it in the power of any man—viz. what of all that is found in living is desirable, and what, if attained, would satisfy our desire. For there are many consequences of life that make men fling away life, such as disease, excessive pain, storms, so that it is clear that, if one were given the power of choice, not to be born at all would, as far at least as these reasons go, have been desirable. Further, the life we lead as children is not desirable, for no one

studying *Oedipus at Colonos* in an advanced Greek class. Yet Nietzsche may also have come across these lines of Sophocles' while privately reading Hölderlin's *Hyperion*. Here the wisdom of Silenos stands as a kind of sphinx-riddle, serving as the epigram or exergue to volume two of Hölderlin's novel—whence the direct line of Dionysian descent from *Hyperion* to the *Birth of Tragedy from the Spirit of Music*. One may be surprised to learn that *Hyperion* is a tragic, Silenic work. One forgets that in it Diotima dies. One also forgets that in it the absolute dies.

At all events, not "influence." Perhaps, instead, a kind of "confluence." Why should one want these two poet-thinkers, Hölderlin and Nietzsche, to mingle, and to do so in the company of Schelling, the *Wunderkind* of German Idealism? Why refuse to distinguish too sharply between the three of them? Merely in order to consolidate one's heroes? Perhaps. Yet perhaps also because even in postmodernity our position between antiquity and modernity is still so troubling, and because Schelling, Hölderlin, and Nietzsche alike are experts in this trouble.

Not a Single New Goddess?

Nietzsche, the philosopher of Dionysos, writes so little about Schelling, and when he does write about him it is almost always in disparagement. Schelling is clearly one of those Tübingen theologians who "beat the bushes" in search of a new power or faculty of the mind, preferably a "faculty of faculties," one that would allow the Romantics to flee the harsh structures and strictures of Kantian Critique. Above all, the faculty of "intellectual intuition" seems to enable Schelling to beat those same bushes in order to flush out a new god—a new god who is all-too-reminiscent of the old one.[3] "—Fichte,

---

in his senses would consent to return again to this. Further, many incidents involving neither pleasure nor pain or involving pleasure but not of a noble kind are such that, as far as they are concerned, nonexistence is preferable to life. And generally, if one were to bring together all that all men do and experience but not willingly because not for its own sake, and were to add to this an existence of infinite duration, one would none the more on account of these experiences choose existence rather than nonexistence." This is, of course, the beginning—and not the end—of Aristotle's inquiry into εὐδαιμονία; yet one should occasionally remind oneself of the Silenic gloom that all ethics is called upon to dispel. See *Eudemian Ethics*, tr. J. Solomon, in *The Complete Works of Aristotle: The Revised Oxford Translation*, vol. 2, ed. Jonathan Barnes, Bollingen Series (Princeton, N.J.: Princeton University Press, 1984), 1924–1925.

3. On the Tübingen theologians and "intellectual intuition," see *Beyond Good and Evil*, aphorism 11, KSA 5:25; cf. 14:731, commenting on 1[17], and 11:445. For the remainder of what follows, see the references in KSA 15:348. Jason Wirth reminds me that Karl Löwith was among the first to note the proximity of Schelling and Nietzsche: see Löwith, *Nietzsches Philosophie der ewigen Wiederkehr*, 4th ed. (Hamburg: F. Meiner Verlag, 1986 [originally published in 1935]), 154. One must also note Heinz Heimsoeth, *Die sechs grossen Themen der abendländischen Metaphysik*, 5th ed. (Darmstadt: Wissenschaftliche Buchgesellschaft, 1965), 170ff.

Schelling, Hegel, Schleiermacher, Feuerbach, Strauß—all theologians" (KSA 11:152, 262). When Nietzsche juxtaposes Kant and Schelling for the purpose of ascertaining "the various *degrees* of enjoyment of what is 'true,'" we suspect that Schelling will surely suffer by the comparison, especially when he is aligned with Seneca, Sir Walter Scott, and Hafez, as opposed to Machiavelli, Stendhal, and Plato (KSA 11:237). To be sure, Kant himself is guilty of wreaking havoc on future philosophy with his concept of "appearances" and his discourse on "faculties" or "powers." Kant is the one who enables "the Schelling swindle" to get its start (KSA 11:273). It is Schelling, along with Hegel, who seduces the young Wagner, tempting him away from absolute music to "the Idea" (KSA 6:36). And what is true of Wagner is all the more true of the Wagnerians: the writing style of the latter strikes Nietzsche as "the most extravagant nonsense since Schelling" (KSA 13:507).

Yet Nietzsche finds Schopenhauer too harsh in his polemic against Schelling and Hegel, these paragons of Romanticism—too harsh, because Schopenhauer himself is a mere "veil-maker," *es sind Alles blosse Schleiermacher* (KSA 6:361; cf. 11:604–605). That said, Schelling is surely among those who are responsible for the German educational culture, which in *Daybreak* Nietzsche attacks as sometimes repulsive, sometimes piteous: "For one thing, the addiction to appearances of moral *excitation,* along with the demand for glittering generalities without backbone and the willful intention to see everything more beautifully . . . —unfortunately, more 'beautifully' according to a wretchedly vague taste, which prides itself nonetheless on being of Greek descent" (KSA 3:163). Who will be surprised, however, to learn that a certain ambivalence concerning Schelling occasionally enables the inveterate Romantic to appear in a slightly more favorable light? For example, no Englishman dare raise his voice against Schelling, whereas the latter is encouraged to express his contempt for Locke (*Beyond Good and Evil,* aphorism 252; KSA 5:195). Schelling serves as proof that Nietzsche manifests a certain fidelity to German culture, however troubled the marriage. In the autumn of 1870 the still youthful Nietzsche attacks Max Müller for having taken the side of the English moralists against the German thinkers Kant, Hegel, and Schelling. "Insolent!" cries the new Basel professor. "Insolent! And ignorant!" (KSA 7:109). Much later, in 1885–1886, as he is sketching out the first part of a proposed book on eternal recurrence, Nietzsche notes that his book will argue "against Schelling, for example" (KSA 12:130). Yet the context of the note suggests that Schelling himself somehow stands at or near the culmination of a long development in Christian morality itself, one that leads inevitably to its demise:

Christianity perishing of its own morality. "God is truth," "God is love," "the just God,"—the grandest event—"God is dead"—, indistinctly felt. The German attempt to transform Christianity into a Gnosis turned out to be productive of the most profound mistrust: the "untruthful" character of that attempt has been most strongly felt (against [or toward: *gegen*] Schelling, for example). (KSA 12:129–130)

There is *almost* a suggestion here that Schelling too may have sensed something of the mendacious character of Christianity, that the long development of "the grandest event" may have in some way touched even this late Gnostic, this veil-maker, this absolute mythologist.

Nietzschean reminiscences of Schelling? The title of the chapter seems to suggest either that Schelling can remember forward to Nietzsche or that some more positive reminiscence of Schelling lies hidden in Nietzsche's work. Perhaps there *is* something like a forward-looking remembrance. Perhaps every thinker looks forward to those few who will pick up the thread of his or her thinking—not as the "unthought" of that thinking, but as the very thread that Ariadne ravels and allows to trail behind her. Perhaps too there is something in Nietzsche's work that demands of us a more sympathetic and protracted response to Schelling than the response Nietzsche appears to offer.

Does Schelling give Nietzsche nothing to think about? He certainly offers him some things to *laugh* about. For example, during an otherwise sober discussion in his *Introduction to the Philosophy of Revelation* of Aristotelian νόησις νοήσεως, "thought thinking itself," which becomes the concluding *in hoc signo vincis* of Hegel's *Logic*, Schelling suddenly enters a long footnote. The note makes the ironic concession that "it is hard to accept that God's felicity, as described by Aristotle, consists in his philosophizing for all eternity after the manner of Hegel" (II/3:106 n. 1). In another text from the same year, *Introduction to the Philosophy of Mythology*, Schelling asserts the prevalence and even primacy of polytheism for all of written history; in order to assuage the aggrieved monotheists he notes that the very doctrine of *one* god is in fact polytheism, inasmuch as monotheism merely has *not yet heard of* the other gods (II/1:127). Monotheism is a polytheism that has not yet advanced beyond narcissism.

Yet Schelling's potential importance for Nietzsche goes beyond laughter—or, rather, it extends as far as the golden laughter of Dionysos himself. In the tenth through thirteenth of his Berlin lectures of 1842, published as the monumental *Philosophy of Mythology*, lectures delivered before a distinguished audience in the capital city of Brandenburg-Prussia, Schelling finally tells the story that has long been outstanding in his philosophy of mythology up to that point—the story of Dionysos, which begins in Arabia. (Distinguished audience? Yes, for the most part distinguished, although there are a number of eccentric characters present, for example, a hairy Russian radical by the name of Bakunin and an equally hairy German named Engels, a wizened crank with the unlikely name of Schopenhauer, and a witty, dapper, anxiety-ridden Dane by the name of Kierkegaard. Jacob Burckhardt, who will be Nietzsche's most distinguished colleague at Basel, is in the audience as well. Some twenty-seven years down the road he will no doubt tell Nietzsche of this Arabian Dionysos.) Schelling takes up Herodotus's account of Dionysos in the Near East only after he has told tales of Serduscht, Zoroaster, or Zarathustra (Burckhardt will tell Nietzsche about that, too) and of the cult of temple prostitution in Babylon. The cult of Mylitta requires that every married woman in the great Babylonian cities at least one time in her life sit on the steps of the temple. When a stranger to the city, a foreigner, tosses a few coins into her lap, she must go with him. Why? Schelling's account, going far beyond what a scandalized Herodotus can offer, is ingenious: a new god, he explains, a stranger to the city, is coming; this new god will replace the stern star-god of the fathers; the new god, the *coming* and *becoming* god, will in fact be "the first feminine divinity" (II/2:238). S/he is "the feminine *becoming* of consciousness" in the old god himself (II/2:239). In other words, it is not so much that the new god will simply replace the father; rather, s/he will radically remake and transform the father. And what a remake! The resultant new god will be marked by "supremely sensuous naiveté, candor, and lewd licentiousness" (II/2:241). In order to break faith with the jealous old god whom up to now they have been serving, the women are called upon to break faith with their jealous husbands—to do what Mylitta herself has to do, namely, assert her femininity in the face of the unforgiving father. It is a kind of brazen infidelity to the old in honor of the new, the strange, the foreign. If Herodotus is shocked, he is supposed to be. Some would call the women's actions *nefarious,* "unspeakable," but the ongoing life of consciousness necessitates their challenge. Indeed, says Schelling, wherever in the world the new god(dess) arrives, it arrives in the company of feminine divinities. These divinities grant liberation from prior confinements, introduce a carnivalesque excess, and release unbridled lust (II/2:246). Always tumult, always an orgasmic swooning, in the face of the new consciousness.

Yet even if consciousness is now androgynous—and it is—the new god should not be called hermaphroditic, if only because the old god has lost too much of Hermes in the process. She can scarcely recognize herself in the looking-glass (II/2:253). Although Schelling does not mention Euripides'

Pentheus, one recalls the severe young king—after his transformation *by* the new god *into* the new god—suddenly primping, mincing, and prancing. It is a painful spectacle to behold, as it is painful for the women to embrace whatever happens along. Sacrifice *is* painful.

This cross-dressing in honor of the god(dess) fascinates Schelling, and he devotes several moments of his lecture course to it, no doubt much to the discomfiture of those members of his audience who are not eccentrics. In one of the rare references back to the material treated in "The Divinities of Samothrace," Schelling refers to the figure of Ἀφρόδιτος, the male Aphrodite (II/2:249). This, we recall, is Pentheus's nightmare. The tales the king has heard concerning the new prophet from the East, to wit, that the charms of Aphrodite shine in his eyes (χάριτας Ἀφροδίτης ἔχων [l. 236]), is borne out when he confronts him: the new prophet or god is shapely, like a woman (οὐκ ἄμορφος . . . ὡς ἐς γυναῖκας [ll. 453–454]), and all the new god's thoughts dwell on possible victories for Aphrodite (τὴν Ἀφροδίτην καλλονῇ θηρώμενος [l. 459]). Centuries later, during the Christian era, Clement of Alexandria will mock Dionysos as χοιροψάλης, "the one who touches the vulva," making it vibrate "like the strings of a lyre" (RC 44). The new god *is* this inherent and essential confusion of genders and sexualities. S/he is δυάς, the twofold, the double who unleashes and unlatches, loosens and dissolves all the constraints. In the most barbarous and extreme nations of the East—and that will always mean Babylon—s/he insists on the castration of hundreds of boys. (Schelling does not yet refer back to the Great Goddess of *The Ages of the World*, she of the brazen wheels, though she is much on his mind, perhaps even when he discusses the compromise solution, circumcision, demanded by the Hebrew Elohim.)[4] Castration too is merely the cultic imitation of that essential transition of consciousness "from manliness to femininity" in divinity itself.

What is missing from Schelling's account here, at least for hundreds of pages, is precisely what makes the 1811 *Weltalter* text and the 1815 "Divinities of Samothrace" so compelling, namely, the account of a *languor* so powerful that it reduces the glory and majesty of all the gods to penury. The words *Sehnsucht* and *Schmachten*, Nietzsche and all the eccentrics in the audience

---

4. The Elohim demand circumcision of Abraham and his tribe—circumcision being already a common practice in the ancient Near East: the prepuce is "brought as tribute to the primal god [*dem Urgott*]" (II/1:164). Schelling makes no reference back to the Great Goddess here in his "Introduction" to the philosophy of mythology. Yet he does record with evident delight the heresy of Cardinal Bembi, who refers to the Virgin Mother as "the goddess" (II/1:259). Perhaps it was Cardinal Bembi who inspired the final scene of *Faust II*, where the Virgin Mother is celebrated as *Göttern ebenbürtig* and even as *Göttin*, the "goddess" who is "equal in birth to the gods."

would be quick to point out, although they are crucial in Schelling's vocabulary during the years 1809 to 1815, do not appear up to this point in the elderly Schelling's lectures on mythology. Indeed, they will not appear until the very end of the course. They have generally been replaced by the more optimistic words *Wille*, the will that is identified as masculine, and *Seinkönnen*, "the ability to be," a surprising neologism, which is now the ontological earmark of the god who develops in the feminine direction, moving out of his former self-centeredness to the periphery. (*Seinkönnen?* There must have been yet another eccentric character in Schelling's Berlin audience, short and stocky, in Black Forest costume, even though he promised to stay in the provinces.)[5] Yet what is present in the 1842 lectures on mythology is remarkable enough. What Schelling is discussing here is the *materialization* of divinity, inasmuch as *mater* and *materia* "are, at bottom, but one word" (II/2:193). No matter how "uncanny" the becoming-womanly of the masculine god may be, it is essential to all theogony.

The Old Testament too has its Queen of Heaven, *Melaekaeth haschamaim:* Schelling cites Jeremiah 7:18 and 44:17–19 and 25.[6] Although her ancient names are many—Mylitta, Astarte, Urania—her process is one. Or *almost* one. For the materialization of the god "could also be represented as the unmanning or emasculating of the first exclusively ruling god" (II/2:194). When Kronos tosses Ouranos's severed member into the sea, Aphrodite arises from the foam. Even church fathers such as Clement of Alexandria testify to a sudden release in the tension of the stern Titanic father, his unexpected inclination toward tenderness, defining it as a θηλύνεσθαι τῷ θεῷ, a becoming female in the god. The sudden release in tension somehow, inexplicably, "produces" the mother, who is sometimes called Mitra. The latter is merely one more name for Astarte—in Farsi, *mader*, the mother. The Phoenicians, we re-

5. In his *Philosophie der Mythologie*, Schelling develops a remarkable account of this "ability to be." At first it has to do with the feminine development of the primal godhead, then with human being as such. Human being is *jenes Seynkönnende, das in der ganzen Natur außer sich war*, "that ability to be which within the totality of nature was *outside* itself." In other words, human being, like the godhead, is both ability-to-be and ecstatic (II/2:141). Both divinity and humanity "comport themselves as feminine," that is, as *anders-Seyn*, being otherwise. "Consciousness itself, so to speak, is androgynous" (II/2:156).

6. Jeremiah bewails the ancient custom by which the women of Judea bake cakes and offer potions to Melecheth of the Sky for the sake of a good harvest. Luther comments that Melecheth is to be understood as "the impact, or the forces, or the weather, or storms of the sky," which is to say, "rain, dew, snow, frost, ice, cold, heat, light, shine [*schein*], and, in sum, every sort of weather." The women have since ancient times sworn an oath to perform such sacrifice, and they compel their men to obey— to help prepare the fires of sacrifice. The appeal to Melecheth of the Sky has in Christian times, concludes Luther, become a prayer to St. Urban (for good weather in the vineyard) and St. Alexius (against thunder and lightning), and suchlike. Luther does not translate *Melecheth des Himels* as "Queen" of Heaven, but merely lists those putatively masculine effects of the stormy sky god.

call, are responsible for transporting the Cabirian cult to Samothrace. They also take their Mylitta to an island that will be named after her, Melite, or Malta. Her cult, whether on Samothrace or Malta, will always be about the sudden relaxation of a certain hostile tension in the father; the result of this slackening in tension, the escape or deliverance from a situation of strife and conflict, is what we call *matter*. Schelling elaborates:

> Hence, Urania is in mythology the first abjection [*Niederwerfung*] of the principle that at one time found itself in the vertical position [*im Zustand der Aufrichtung*]. I can best express it by calling it the first καταβολή. In mythology, it is the selfsame moment in nature that we have to think as the proper inception of nature, the transition to her, when everything that was originally spirit gradually set about becoming material, releasing a matter that only then became accessible to the higher demiurgic potency; it is the moment when the ground of the world is laid, which is to say, when that which itself is first of all established and comes into existence comes to be relatively nonexistent, comes to be ground. It becomes the ground of the world proper, if by *world* we understand the collectivity of manifold things that differ from one another and are hierarchically ordered—in short, the world of articulated being [*des getheilten Seyns*]. For, prior to that, there was only undivided being. (II/2:201–202)

All must worship at the temple of the material mother, who, no matter how matronly—or Mitranly—she may be, is the maiden who carries the water, the ὑδροφόρος Κόρη (II/2:203). "For precisely this first womanly divinity was everywhere thought to be related to the *moist* element" (II/2:202). (Among the eccentric characters in the audience, whom Schelling always addresses as *Herren*, a woman of small stature but strong character insinuates herself; eminently tender under that tough exterior, however, she will tell Burckhardt to tell Nietzsche to tell Zarathustra to come down from his mountain to the sea.) Only when the stern father is coaxed away from the center and onto the periphery (II/2:207), only when he grants the right of succession to his feminine progeny and accepts that what is past is past (II/2:208), only when he undergoes the *Krisis* of consciousness that Urania represents (II/2:210), only when he experiences a *love* for the creatures who circulate on the periphery (II/2:211), will the eon of merely *relative* monotheism pass. If Mithras is *Deus Sol Invictus*, the unconquered sun that Michelangelo paints into his "Last Judgment" as the backdrop to the stern judge, Mithras will have to learn to live with himself as Mitra, the maid of the moon. She is perhaps the mother of God in Michelangelo's mural, who looks demurely or abashedly to the side as her son the judge rises in ire or desire. Or she may be "Rachel," the "woman in green," who is the only figure in the painting who seems to be ignoring the Apocalypse in order to gesture toward some one or some thing beyond the margins of the mural. Perhaps she is gesturing toward Melecheth, the Queen of Heaven?

Semele-Selene, the mother of Dionysos, is precisely that lunar figure of the new god, the god(dess) to come. Dionysos is forever a god of arrival, or of not-yet-having-arrived. "Dionysos, that second god, is throughout the entire mythological process the one who is coming, the one who is entirely caught up in coming [*ein kommender, ein im Kommen begriffener*]" (II/2:254). It is to Friedrich Creuzer's credit, says Schelling, that the omnipresence of Dionysos in mythology has finally been recognized (II/2:277). Indeed, Schelling confirms Creuzer's belief that the lore surrounding Dionysos contains at least one of the keys to Greek mythology. That key is first found, as we have seen, in Herodotus's Arabia, in the Orient. For, as the first historian reports, the Arabs "take Dionysos and Urania alone to be god" (Schelling, at II/2:254, cites *The Histories*, 3:8). "To be god"—in the singular. Because Dionysos is always caught up in becoming, and because Urania is always giving birth to the new god, the coming god, Urania and Dionysos, are one.[7] "Urania is not merely Urania; rather, she has concealed Dionysos within herself. If the Arabs call Dionysos Orotalt, and Urania Alilat, the first is Ulod-Allat, namely, the child Allah, and the second is Allah herself, the goddess" (II/2:256). Her other related name is Ἀίττα, which is nothing other than "the woman in childbirth," *die Gebärerin*. In *Twilight of the Idols*, Nietzsche will invoke the pangs of the woman in childbirth as the essence of the Dionysian experience.

It is precisely the arduous process by which Urania and Dionysos have become one that Schelling recounts in his lectures on the philosophy of mythology, and this is where Nietzsche has something to learn from him.

---

7. Herodotus, in ch. 8 of Book III, reports: "No nation regards the sanctity of a pledge more seriously than the Arabs. When two men wish to make a solemn compact, they get the service of a third, who stands between them and with a sharp stone cuts the palms of their hands near the base of the thumb; then he takes a little tuft of wool from their clothes, dips it in the blood and smears the blood on seven stones which lie between them, invoking as he does so the names of Dionysus and Urania; then the person who is giving the pledge commends the stranger—or the fellow citizen, as the case may be—to his friends, who in their turn consider themselves equally bound to honor it. Of the gods, the only one the Arabs recognize is Dionysus-and-Urania; the way they cut their hair—all round in a circle, with the temples shaved—is, they say, in imitation of Dionysus. Dionysus in their language is Orotalt, and Urania Alilat." Herodotus, *The Histories*, tr. Aubrey de Sélincourt, rev. A. R. Burn (Harmondsworth: Penguin, 1972), 205–206. Translation revised in conformity with Schelling's reading of the Greek: Διόνυσον δὲ θεῶν μοῦνον καὶ τὴν Οὐρανίην ἡγέονται εἶναι. Obviously, for Schelling, the word μοῦνον takes on great significance. For the Greek text see the Loeb Classical Library edition of Herodotus, tr. A. D. Godley (London: Heinemann, 1928), 2:10–11, citing Book III, ch. 8, of *The Histories*.

Mylitta is a sanctuary or dwelling place beyond being, that is, beyond the being of the former god. She is, to repeat, ability-to-be, *Seinkönnen*. As καταβολή, she helps divinity to materialize, helps it to matter. Mythology is therefore the philosophy of nature conducted at a higher level (II/2:258). It is that physics with wings cited so many pages earlier in the present book, although such physics also possesses gravity. For the materialized god learns a new passivity. By means of a certain evasion or deliverance, s/he has moved to the periphery and become accessible to his/her creatures. Earlier on in its life, divinity was "absolutely excluded from consciousness" (II/2:259). That was what it meant to be absolute. Now, in the moment of birth, s/he sees the light of day. *Deus* is now Δυάς, irreducibly twofold. Kronos is unmanned by Rhea's stratagem and Zeus's agility, although the agile infant must flee to Crete, where he undergoes a second long gestation (II/2:261). Zeus's own story, as later historians of myth will confirm, begins to look more and more like the story of Dionysos, and the story of Dionysos more and more like the story of his mother. Dionysos begins his life as a δαίμων in Plato's sense (II/2:275). He is a middle essence or middling creature, *ein Mittelwesen*, midway between sky and earth, immortals and mortals, and halfway between male and female. By the end of mythology, both he and his mother Semele will be fully divine. Yet the story of Dionysos's rise to consciousness is painful: suffering will mark not only his mother's but also his father's side of the family. For Dionysos, consciousness is something to which one is condemned, something for which one is destined; the god has no free relation to it, at least not at first. Consciousness can only mean confusion and massive overstimulation, the inclination in Dionysos and in all his followers to madness and delusion (II/2:276). Paradoxically, however, Dionysos is as old as mythology itself. For mythology begins with downgoing, is essentially polytheistic and, if one may say so, "materialistic." Viewed from the perspective of theogony as such, Dionysos is as old as Urania, as old as humankind's escape from Zabism, the fixated religion of the fixed stars, the stern religion of a stern father—Roberto Calasso refers to that escape as liberation from "millennia of astral submission" (RC 100). Even when Schelling's lectures wander off into other territories—with the long discussion of Herakles, for example—the kinship with Dionysos is always central (II/2:334, 340). Both Herakles and Dionysos are daimonic creatures, though their way of achieving full immortality differs: Herakles mounts and ignites his own funeral pyre in order to consume all his mortality in flames, whereas Dionysos has already been purified by Semele's fiery death—the death that comes not with Dionysos's birth but with his very conception

(II/2:345). Semele dies *in der Umarmung des Zeus,* writes Schelling, "in Zeus's embrace," which has to remind us of Etna's furious embrace of Empedocles. Irigaray would call it not an embrace but an embrazier.[8]

After a long disquisition on the mythologies of Egypt, India, and China, Schelling returns to Hellenic mythology in his twenty-fifth lecture. From this point on it is simply a matter of understanding the Olympian brotherhood of Zeus, Poseidon, and Hades, as successors to Kronos. The implacable Hades remains self-centered, refuses to go to the periphery, even when he stoops to rape. Hades is "the *Kronos* in Kronos" (II/2:579), perhaps in the way that rhythm is the *music* in music. Stormy Poseidon remains bitter and brackish— the salt sea is not the principle of moisture but τὸ Κρόνου δάκρυον, "the tears of Kronos" (II/2:581). Poseidon does not become the lord of liquid nature, κύριος τῆς ὑγρᾶς φύσεως, inasmuch as this is an honor reserved for the new god, but remains confined to the underworld of the deep. Poseidon and Hades alike remain "children of terror, anxiety, melancholy [*Unmuth*], and despair" (II/2:582). They belong to the past of god; they *are* the past (II/2:208, 238, 584: *die Vergangenheit*) as such. Zeus alone, and even Zeus only when his story coalesces with that of Dionysos, is the new god of the present. Schelling speaks of a perdurant present in Zeus, yet he notes the Stygian traces in Zeus himself (II/2:584). Nietzsche will elaborate on these Stygian traces by pointing to "the character of the original Zeus," the Zeus of the Prometheus myth, as "an enemy of human beings" (KSA 7:138).

As his lectures draw to a close, Schelling pays renewed attention to the female figures of mythology, about which the entire course has in fact revolved. He speculates that Hesiodic χάος is precisely what Plato's *Timaeus* means by χώρα, traditionally understood as space and elementality in one, the mother and matrix (Schelling writes *Unterlage,* no doubt translating ὑποδοχή, the Timaean "receptacle") of all sensible things (II/2:596). Indeed, he derives the very name of the earth (Γαῖα, γέα, γῆ) from the verb γάω, related to χωρέω, meaning to make room for, to accede to, perhaps even to evade—by way of a dance step. Gaia is the footfall of rhythm. If she is peripheral, that is because she dances the round-dance. She is of the essence, and is to be thought together with χώρα and χάος as an essentially twofold, Janus-faced figure (II/2:616). One of the two faces of Janus is beardless and womanly—it is the face of the moon, Selene-Semele (II/2:602). Janus "himself" is

8. Luce Irigaray, *L'Oubli de l'air* (cited in note 2 of ch. 2, above), 99: *elle embras(s)e tout.* In the English translation, see 107: "embraces/emblazes."

the Chaos out of which gods are born and back into which they die (II/2:614). Hesiod names the feminine figures first, "remarkably," adds Schelling, so that the story that remains to be told at the very end, after the story of the Kronide sons, Hades, Poseidon, and Zeus, is that of Hestia (the Latin Vesta), Demeter, and Hera. Even though Hera is linked with Zeus, so that we would expect her to assume preeminence, the story will instead turn about Demeter, Persephone, and Dionysos—the mother, the maid, and the Maenadic. Demeter, says Schelling, is "the hinge" (II/2:628).

He derives the Δη- of Δημήτηρ not from Gaia, but from the δαί-μονες: Demeter is the "knowing, spiritual mother, liberated from the material" (II/2:630). Nietzsche would of course indicate that this description is an insult to Demeter, and that it represents a regression on her part and a repression on Schelling's part. Nietzsche would be more comfortable with Hölderlin's inhospitable translation of Demeter as "the impenetrable."[9] At all events, Demeter, and not Hera, is the proper mate of Zeus. For her part, Demeter bears Persephone by Zeus, not by Poseidon.[10] When Persephone is snatched

---

9. Recall that Hölderlin translates Demeter's name as *Undurchdringliches*, all that is impenetrable, as though to contrast her with the surface of the earth, which men scrape with their plows, and to invoke the impenetrable mysteries of Eleusis (CHV 3:440; DKV 2:904, 1456). Impenetrable though she may be, however, she is associated with Dionysos—as bread is associated with wine. Jean-Pierre Vernant writes: "For the god is to what is liquid and potable all that the goddess is to what is solid and edible. The one by inventing wheat and bread, the other by inventing (*The Bacchae*, l. 279) the vine and wine, together brought to humankind the means to pass from a wild life to a civilized one. All the same, there is a difference between wheat and wine. Wheat is entirely on the side of civilization, but wine is ambiguous. When it is neat, it conceals a force of extreme wildness, a burning fire; when diluted and consumed in accordance with the rules, it brings to civilized life an extra, as it were supernatural, dimension; joy in the feast, with evil forgotten. It is a drug (*pharmakon*) that makes pain fade away; it is the ornament, the crown, the living, happy brilliance of the banquet (ll. 380–383), the joy of celebration" (VV 399–400). Against Vernant, and for Schelling, one may want to insist that both wheat and wine are subject to fermentation and leavening. When the temple prostitute transforms Enkidu into a human being, she feeds him leavened bread instead of grass, wine instead of water, and she leavens his sex with hers. Vernant would no doubt reply that it remains true that the ambiguity of wine is stark: "Like wine, Dionysus is double: most terrible yet infinitely sweet. His presence, which is a bewildering intrusion of otherness into the human world, may take two forms, be manifested in two different ways. On the one hand it may bring blessed union with the god, in the heart of nature, with every constraint lifted—an escape from the limitations of the everyday world and oneself. That is the experience extolled in the *parodos:* purity, holiness, joy, sweet felicity. On the other hand, it may precipitate one into chaos in the confusion of a bloodthirsty, murderous madness in which the 'same' and the 'other' merge and one mistakes one's nearest and dearest, one's own child, one's second self for a wild beast that one tears apart with one's bare hands: ghastly impurity, inexpiable crime, misfortune without end, without relief (l. 1360)" (VV 400). Yet let the note on Dionysian liquidity end with praise. Roberto Calasso gives the ferment of wine the edge over that of bread: "No other god, let alone Athena with her sober olive, or Demeter with her nourishing bread, had ever had anything that could vie with that liquor. It was exactly what had been missing from life, what life had been waiting for: intoxication" (RC 36).

10. In the eighth lecture hour of the *Philosophie der Mythologie*, Schelling discusses Persephone at considerable length. Mythology, which is the very becoming of Zeus, depends on the departure of Persephone from the side of Demeter. Persephone, that bright light (*zornigmitleidig . . . ein Licht*, says

from Demeter's side by Hades, the daimonic mother is "left behind as the consciousness that is empty and unfulfilled—become, as it were, pure desire, obsession [*Sucht*], and hunger" (II/2:631). At long last we reach the stage of mythology at which the 1815 "Divinities of Samothrace" begins. "Demeter is the figure by which Hellenic mythology receives its utterly peculiar character," continues Schelling in 1842. "Without Demeter there would be no Greek panoply" (ibid.). For the first time in these lectures, the word *Sehnsucht* appears, "languor," just as the word *Zorn*, "wrath," will soon appear. "To be sure, in the beginning, with the initial feeling of emptiness and unfulfillment, the wrathful [*zürnende*] and mournful [*trauernde*] Demeter rages against all the gods, on account of the rape of her daughter—the entire panoply that was established with Zeus can offer her no replacement for her *god*. Hence her hope in the return of her daughter; hence her languishing [*Sehnsucht*] after the one she has lost" (II/2:632). Demeter's languishing for her god—who is either her daughter or the simulacrum of the daughter in the father, the simulacrum that both wants to be and does not want to be named Zeus—marks the end of exoteric mythology in Greece. What remains is mystery, that is, the mystery religions, especially the esoteric doctrines of Eleusis. All we know about them is that the mysteries try to reconcile Demeter for her loss or losses, to assuage her grief and calm her wrath. "Yet how can this yearning [*Sehnen*] of Demeter be stilled, her mourning be alleviated, her rancor be quelled by acts of goodness?" (II/2:633). Mythology cannot tell us this. Its surmise is that Dionysos, thrice transformed, will come to Demeter. For Demeter is *die Gebärende*, the goddess in childbirth. The mystery is called *Kunft*, or *Advent*. The *third* Dionysos will advene; Demeter will smile again. Nietzsche too, especially in section 10 of *The Birth of Tragedy from the Spirit of Music*, will remember this smile on the face of Demeter (KSA 1:72; cf. 7:144, 154, 179).

Schelling recognizes that the Olympian panoply, under the reign of Zeus, "is actually the panoply of Dionysos" (II/2:642). Dionysos is the god who enters history and releases all the tension of the father. Dionysos is Λύσιος, the hero or demigod who unties the knots, liberating mortals too from Titanic forces. He is—Schelling is on the cusp of writing—the Savior, the Son of Man, or at least the brother of that Son. What holds Schelling back from writing the ultimate syncretic sentence is the *uncanniness* of Dionysos: for precisely *how* Dionysos releases all the tension of the father, whether by the grape, by love, or by the sickle, and precisely what role the feminine plays in

---

Hölderlin [CHV 3:439–440]), "the girl whose name cannot be uttered," says Euripides (RC 204), is "the suffering Dyas," devoted from the outset to downgoing. See II/2:167ff.

this release—these matters are mysterious to the point of uncanniness. It is no surprise, therefore, that the two references to the "uncanny" that will serve Freud as the essential definition of uncanny phenomena appear in these very pages of the *Philosophy of Mythology*.[11]

Homer's Apollo, the shining god himself, must be understood as a pendant to Dionysos: the two share deeds, adventures, and music (especially the Lydian music of mourning); both possess destructive as well as beneficent qualities; and both haunt the woods of Parnassos and the shrine of Delphi (II/2:668). Yet, to repeat, what lies beyond is mystery. And the mistress of mystery is Demeter, "Deo," the impenetrable.

Now that Apollo has been mentioned, however, one has to remember the philosopher whom Schelling calls most daimonic and most Dionysian, namely, Socrates (II/2:284). Nietzsche, who always seems to be engaged in a battle or contest with Socrates, but who more than anyone else recognizes the importance of "the music-practicing Socrates," would have several nettlesome questions to put to Schelling. The principal question would have to do with Schelling's refusal to persist in his own intuition in *The Ages of the World* that the feminine essence infiltrates divinity *from the outset*. The feminine is the

---

11. As indicated in note 14 of ch. 4 of this volume, Freud cites Schelling's *Philosophy of Mythology* in his 1919 essay "The Uncanny" (*Studienausgabe* 4:248, 250, and 264). The second reference to Schelling's text (specifically, to II/2:658) has to do with the *Unheimlichkeit* in which the early Greek sculptors formed the facial features of the gods. Their intention was to conceal something about the gods, not letting it show through, by adding something superhuman or subhuman—in any case, something foreign—to those features, "trying to surround them with a certain uncanniness." The first and third references (both of them to II/2:648) are the essential ones, however. Schelling is here referring to "the uncanny principle" as such, which tries to conceal something in mystery. His argument involves Homer, and it is very close to Nietzsche's view of Homer in *The Birth of Tragedy* (see, for example, sections 2 and 4). Schelling writes: "The world of the Homeric deities silently encloses a mystery within itself; it is, as it were, erected over a mystery, over an abyss, which it bestrews with flowers. . . . That is why Greece has a Homer—because it has mysteries, because it succeeded in vanquishing completely that principle of the past which prevailed in Oriental systems, internalizing what was exterior in them, that is to say, turning it back into a secret, a mystery (which is the place whence it had originally come). The clear skies that shine over the Homeric poems could first vault across Greece after the darkling and darkening rule of that uncanny principle which prevails in earlier religions was compelled to become mystery. (One calls *uncanny* everything in secret, everything in concealment that was to remain in latency and yet has come to the fore.)" This parenthetical phrase serves Freud as the essential clue to the meaning of the uncanny, as "that species of the terrifying which goes back to things well known, long familiar" (4:244). An entirely new inquiry—a Freudian reminiscence, as it were—would have to ask whether the split in the father imago suffered by E. T. A. Hoffmann's hero Nathanael, as well as his identification with the puppet Olimpia, which he loves to the point of dissolution and death (4:255–256 n. 1), are not repetitions in another key of the myths Schelling, Hölderlin, and Nietzsche are pursuing. Above all, one would have to ask whether Freud's dismantling of that Doppelgänger we call *the soul* to "an uncanny herald of death" (4:258), very much like Hölderlin's god, *in der Gestalt des Todes*, lies at the heart of the tragic absolute. For Schelling's mythology, Hölderlin's understanding of Sophoclean tragedy, and Nietzsche's Dionysos hover about the core of the impenetrable mystery Freud calls *primal repression*, Urverdrängung.

most primordial, self-centered, centripetal, wrathful moment of divinity. She will always have to have come first. In his philosophy of *nature* Schelling recognizes the female sex as the basis of all reproduction in nature: we recall from chapter 2 of this volume that wherever sexlessness seems to prevail, there is the female. The centrality of Demeter should have taught him the same about mythology and theogony. The vaunted masculinity of a flaunted—even if *relative*—monotheism is something that Schelling should have been able to overcome. This is not to say that Nietzsche himself is never confused by Ariadne, that he himself is never "a little bit lost there," as the most eccentric member of Schelling's audience once said. Other Nietzschean questions and reminiscences, however, would involve the *sufferings* of Dionysos and Semele, as of Gaia and Rhea and all their progeny, including Zeus. For those sufferings never seem to subside. Can it ever be a question of the materialization of what is primordially spiritual? Never in that order! Never such a hierarchy! Schelling's fundamental intuition concerning Demeter and the pangs of the woman in childbirth—*Die Qual der Gebärerin* being the title of one of the *Dionysos-Dithyramben*, and, in a sense, the title of all of them—is thus not at all about the coming of the *third* or the *second* god, unless the second always comes *first*. It is an intellectual intuition of the shared mortality of mortals and immortals—of the death of all gods and of God. It is the tragic absolute.

There are times when Schelling comes close to embracing the tragic absolute. Nietzsche would have enjoyed Schelling's long meditation on Jehovah's remark *after* the Fall of Adam and Eve: "The human being has become one of us." That is to say, precisely as *fallen*, the human being approaches divinity (II/2:167). Nietzsche would also have wanted to remember for his *Thus Spoke Zarathustra* Schelling's analysis of δεισιδαιμονία. One might translate that term as *Gottesangst*, but only if one thinks of it as anxiety *for* the god. Not fear *of* the lord, but fear *for* the lord (II/2:300). Desdemona, fearing that she will lose her lord, holds desperately onto him at the moment of extreme peril; ultimately, hers is a fear, not of what will become of her, but of what will happen to him after he destroys her. Faith may waver and wane in δεισιδαιμονία, but only because a certain worry, a worry about the absolute, waxes. Near the outset of his *Philosophy of Mythology*, Schelling notes that one usually calls God *das Absolute*. Yet only what is fully accomplished, or fully gathered up and harbored in its end (*das Voll-Endete*), can be absolute. Because God has no beginning and no end, however, because s/he is process and development—and mythology is nothing other than the story of that unfolding—s/he cannot be said to be *id quod omnibus numeris absolutum est* (II/2:43). If monotheism has primacy over polytheism, says Schelling, it is only as the dicotyledonous seed awaiting germination and growth.[12]

Yet there can be no doubt that Schelling has faith in the germination and growth of divinity—and that the fruit of this growth will be Christianity in one form or another. Nietzsche would therefore intervene at the moment when Schelling, resisting the force of all the material he has amassed in his lectures on mythology, tries to rescue Christianity from the fate of "paganism," a word that can be spoken only from within the deluded exceptionalism of Christianity. Schelling does note the vanity of the entire god-building process of mythology: Kronos senses that he will perish—the intimation of his downgoing produces the anxiety that causes him to double up and fend off all alterity, especially the alterity represented in his own children. Prometheus knows that Zeus will perish, that the reign of the new god is as tenuous as that of the father. The prophet knows that the Messiah is not a king but a servant who will suffer and die (II/2:316, 347). The feeling that the entire development of god is vain arises from the sense of transience, *Vergänglichkeit*, that pervades all this past, *Vergangenheit*. "*That* is precisely the tragic, the trait of profound despondency that permeates all pagan culture: in the midst of total dependence on the gods, whom human beings are compelled to serve by an intractable delusion, the feeling of the finitude of these very gods is also a constant companion" (II/2:346).

Nietzsche would merely encourage Schelling to liberate himself from the final delusion concerning the ostensible exception that calls itself Christianity. "Two thousand years, and not a single new god!" That should have been the rallying cry of the author of a philosophical compendium of mythology. If Schelling seems to be weaving new veils for the old god, however, it may be because he finds new life in her.

---

12. A persistent theme throughout Schelling's late philosophy of mythology and revelation is the precedence of monotheism in the history of consciousness and culture. Polytheism ensues only after Babel, whereas monotheism prevails "in the time before the separation of nations" (II/1:83, 119). Yet the initial monotheism is *relative*, inasmuch as the split between the designations *Elohim* and *Jehovah* indicates a polytheism at the heart of monotheism. According to Genesis, Jehovah is known only to the second generation of human beings—second or *third*, since Cain and Abel are not mentioned in the genealogy (II/1:148). "Without the second God," writes Schelling, referring to Jehovah as opposed to the Elohim, "without the solicitation to polytheism, there would have been no progress to genuine monotheism" (II/1:164). The primal, relative monotheism is prehistorical, whereas polytheism stretches as far back as history itself (II/1:180–181), and as far back as *consciousness* as such. The ground of mythology "is already laid in the first actual consciousness," which is essentially polytheistic; mythology is both the primal *history* of consciousness and a *suprahistorical* and *necessary process* of consciousness itself (II/1:192–193).

"Against the Oncoming Night"

If Nietzschean reminiscences of Hölderlin are now our goal, we should perhaps start quite close to the beginning of Nietzsche's scholarly life, with his secondary-school paper on the little-known poet. The letter appears here in its entirety.[13]

A Letter to My Friend
in Which I Recommend that He Read My Favorite Poet

19 October 1861   by F. W. Nietzsche

My dear friend,

A few remarks in your last letter concerning Hölderlin surprised me considerably, and I am moved to plead the case of my favorite poet against you. I want to begin by bringing before your eyes once again your harsh and unjust words; it may well be that you already have a better opinion of him. You wrote: "How Hölderlin can be your favorite poet is a complete mystery to me. The impression made on me, at least, by his vague, half-insane locutions, the expressions of a lacerated and broken mind, can only be described as sad and sometimes repulsive. Turgid blather, sometimes the thoughts of a madhouse, wild rages against Germany, deification of the pagan world, here naturalism there pantheism, and then polytheism, all mixed up—this is what characterizes his poems, even if they are expressed in highly successful Greek meters." In highly successful Greek meters! My God! That is the extent of your praise? These verses (speaking only of their external form) that have flowed from the purest and most gentle heart [Gemüth], these verses in all their naturalness and originality overshadowing the art and formal agility of Plato, these verses rising on the afflatus of the most sublime breaths of air or losing themselves in the most tender sounds of melancholy, these verses you can praise with no other phrase than the vapid, everyday expression "highly successful"? And, truth to tell, that is not the gravest of your injustices. Turgid blather, and sometimes the thoughts of a madhouse! These snide remarks of yours betray nothing other than the fact that you are possessed of a vulgar prejudice against Hölderlin, and above all that you have only vague, fanciful notions concerning his works, quite simply because you have neglected to read his poems and his other productions. And, by the bye, you seem to believe that he wrote no more than poems. Thus it is clear that you do not know his *Empedocles*, this extremely significant dramatic fragment, in whose melancholy tones resounds the future of the hapless poet, the living grave of years spent insane—yet not, as you believe, in turgid blather, but in the purest Sophoclean language and in an infinite plenitude of profound thoughts. Nor are you aware of *Hyperion*, which, in the sonorous movement of its prose and in the sublimity and

---

13. "Brief an meinen Freund, in dem ich ihm meinen Lieblingsdichter zum Lesen empfehle," in Friedrich Nietzsche, *Jugendschriften 1861–1864*, ed. Hans Joachim Mette (Munich: Deutscher Taschenbuch Verlag, 1994 [first published by C. H. Beck Verlag, 1933–1940]), 1–5.

beauty of the personages who come to the fore there, has made an impression on me that I can only compare to the pounding surf of a stormy sea. Indeed, this prose is music: sounds that flow and melt, interrupted by painful dissonances, finally evaporating in gloomy, uncanny threnodies.—But what I have said so far touches principally on the external form alone. Allow me now to add a few words about the cornucopia of thoughts that you seem to regard as confusion and lack of clarity. Even though your scolding strikes home in the case of some of the poems from the period of his madness, and even though the profundity of some of his poems even prior to that period struggles against the oncoming night of madness, by far the greater number of poems stand as the most precious pearls of our poetry. I merely refer you to such poems as "The Return to My Homeland," "The Fettered Stream," "Sunset," and "The Blind Singer," and I will copy out for you here the final strophe of his "Evening Fantasy," in which the most profound melancholy and longing for tranquillity are expressed.

—In the evening sky a springtime blossoms;
　Numberless bloom the roses and tranquil shines
　　The golden world; O take me there,
　　Porphyry clouds! and may up above

In light and air my love and my sorrow evaporate! —
　Yet, scattered by a foolish plea, the magic
　　Flees. It grows dark, and I am
　　Alone under the sky. As always.

Come now, soft slumber! The heart craves
　Too much, but in the end, O youth, you will smolder!
　　You restless one, you dreamer!
　　Peaceful and cheerful, then, will be my old age.

In other poems, especially "Remembrance" and "The Journey," the poet elevates us to supreme ideality, and with him we feel that this was his native element. Finally, one must mention a whole series of poems in which he tells the German nation some bitter truths, often very well grounded truths. Even in *Hyperion* he flings sharp and cutting words against German "barbarism." Nevertheless, this revulsion in the face of reality can go hand-in-hand with the greatest love of country, which Hölderlin in truth possessed to a high degree. Yet he hated the mere functionaries, the Philistines, among the Germans.

In the never-completed mourning-play *Empedocles*, the poet unfolds for us his own nature. Empedocles' death is a death resulting from divine pride and contempt for humankind, from a surfeit of the earth and a hunger for the gods. Whenever I read it in its entirety, this work in particular always shatters me; a divine height is achieved in this *Empedocles*. By contrast, in *Hyperion*, although an aura of transfiguration seems to surround it, all is lack of satisfaction and fulfillment. The personages that the poet conjures up are "airy images that surround us with sounds and tones arousing nostalgia, enchanting us, but also awakening in us an unsatisfied languor." To be sure, nowhere else does the longing for Greece manifest itself in purer tones, nowhere else do we see so clearly the affinity of soul with Schiller and with Hegel, his intimate friend.

Up to now I have barely scratched the surface, dear friend, but I will have to leave it to you to paint a complete portrait of the hapless poet from the few traits I have sketched here for you. If I do not refute the objections that you raise with regard to his contradictory views concerning religion, you will have to accept the fact that my all-too-meager knowledge of philosophy is responsible; a closer examination of his views demands such knowledge to a considerable degree. Perhaps you yourself will undertake to study this issue, which may shed light on the causes of his mental illness, although it is hardly likely that his illness is rooted in this matter alone.

You will surely forgive me if in my enthusiasm I have at times had recourse to hard words against you; I only wish—and this you must take as the purpose of my letter—that you be moved to acknowledge and to evaluate without prejudice this poet whose name the majority of his nation scarcely knows.

Your friend,

F. W. Nietzsche

Nietzsche's German teacher at Schulpforta, Herr Koberstein, gave him a B– grade for the "letter," and encouraged his pupil to devote his energies to a "healthier" and "more German" poet. Nowadays we would give Nietzsche a much better grade, especially because of the recognition of *Der Tod des Empedokles*, both for its high ideality—its *shattering* ideality—and its more than "highly successful" Sophoclean rhythms. If the present book affirms the affinity of soul between Hölderlin and *Schelling* rather than Hegel, that is no doubt due to its all-too-meager knowledge of philosophy. And if by "religion" Nietzsche is referring to Hölderlin's "Notes" on Sophocles, then one must also confess to sharing Nietzsche's feelings of inadequacy. Yet the reminiscences of Hölderlin in Nietzsche, and of Nietzsche in Hölderlin, must engage us further, no matter how meager our preparation for them.

Κάθαρσις and Ἔκστασις in Absolute Music, Absolute Rhythm

Nietzsche's 1870 lecture course at Basel on Sophocles' *Oedipus Tyrannos* is notable for many reasons, the principal one being that it shows us how early most of the major ideas of *The Birth of Tragedy from the Spirit of Music* had taken shape.[14] No doubt, many of these ideas, especially those concerning the role of the chorus in tragedy, are borrowed from Schiller, expressly so, and not

---

14. Nietzsche's *Philologica* have been published in five volumes in the new *Kritische Gesamtausgabe der Werke, zweite Abteilung*. The Basel lecture course that I am citing here (henceforth in the body of my text) appears in the *Werke*, ed. Fritz Bornmann and Mario Carpitella (Berlin: Walter de Gruyter, 1993), II/3:1–57.

from Hölderlin.[15] Nietzsche begins the course by rejecting the "moral-aesthetic" interpretation of Greek tragedy, which wants guilt and punishment to be distributed in perfect proportion to each hero and heroine. Such a moralizing interpretation—and here Nietzsche rejoins Bernays's critique of Lessing—makes catharsis incomprehensible. For the moralizing interpretation could only produce "a feeling of triumph in the just, moderate, passionless human being," that is to say, in the moralizing esthete who represents, in effect, "the Phariseeism of the Philistine" (II/3:8). Catharsis of affects would yield to "the snail's feeling of security as it sits in its house and lugs that house around with itself" (II/3:9).

Even if Nietzsche seldom writes about κάθαρσις in his published texts, his meditation on tragedy circles about it constantly. When viewed through modern eyes, and discussed in modern words, it is clear that all the events in a Greek tragedy belong in one modern tragic act, namely, the fifth (II/3:20). Indeed, one may say that—*Oedipus Tyrannos* apart, or perhaps even there—the peripety of every tragedy comes *before* the beginning of the play. The clash between mortals and the force that rules their fates has always already occurred; on the tragic stage the last act alone is being played out. Further, as we have heard Nicole Loraux affirm, whereas moderns prefer to *look at* the events of a plot, the ancient Greeks prefer to *listen to* them. Moreover, what they listen to is not principally the words of the dialogue but the music of the chorus. There is a tension, then, between πάθος and δρᾶν in each tragic performance: because the principal need of the Greeks is to *hear the pathos* in the music, drama is restricted to a bare minimum. Greek tragedy is therefore (*pace* Aristotle) not about complication of plot; it is about *Vertiefung*, a deepening of the πάθος (II/3:29; cf. KSA 7:27). Viewed in the retrospect of modern drama, classical drama develops surprisingly slowly—one actor, then two, then another, as though by concession. By Euripides' time, of course, and certainly by Aristotle's, all that has changed: music and dance have become subservient to plot, and Aristotle can insist on the logic of the plot without risking ridicule (II/3:22–23). Nietzsche counters that it is not peripety that arouses the emotions of the ancient spectator but the Dionysian music, the dithyramb: no series of incidents in the plot could produce the "ecstatic excitation" of music, an excitation that is "related to ascetic self-alienation by the infliction of pain and terror" (II/3:11). This very early assertion of Nietzsche's shoots an arrow toward one of his last preoccupations, to wit, the meaning of the ascetic ideal

15. See Friedrich Schiller, "On the Use of the Chorus in Tragedy," the introductory essay to *The Bride of Messina*, in *Werke*, 2 vols., ed. Paul Stapf, Tempel-Klassiker (Munich: Emil Vollmer Verlag, n.d.), 1:1039–1047, esp. 1042–1046. I will cite Schiller by volume and page in my text.

in Western life—the subject of the third treatise of his *Genealogy of Morals*. There too, to be sure, Nietzsche is aware of how deep the roots of the ascetic ideal run. Here, at the outset of his career of thought, Dionysian ecstasy is seen as being at least "related" to that ideal. Initiates in the cult of Bacchus are "shattered [*erschüttert*] by terrifying images," their souls transposed or transported outside themselves (II/3:12). The affects themselves are transformed and even interchanged in the state of ecstasy: "Pains arouse pleasure, terrors awaken joy" (ibid.). The key to such transport is the music as such. As folk music, it is song and dance, but accompanied by instrumental music, "which emphasizes the purely musical impact [*die rein musikalische Wirkung*]" of the dithyramb (II/3:15). What one senses throughout the lecture course is that Nietzsche is already beginning to lose faith in the capacity of Wagnerian music drama, to say nothing of opera as usually practiced, to produce these effects. His tendency, as we shall see, is toward absolute music and absolute rhythm.[16]

Such music is complex, and so are its effects. The dithyrambic style of the choral songs not only impels the listener in the direction of ecstasy but also creates a moment of lucidity and reflectiveness. Here is perhaps the earliest sign of the paradox of the Dionysian as such, a paradox (closely related to the paradoxical effects of Hölderlin's caesura) fully developed in "The Dionysian Worldview" and *The Birth of Tragedy*. Dionysiac possession, which shatters the bonds of individuation, does not obscure consciousness, but clarifies it. Nietzsche highlights a number of Schiller's theses on the role of the chorus, and this emphasis on reflection and lucidity is one of them. "Tragedy, which presents the most profound conflicts of life and thought, cannot do without reflection," Nietzsche asserts (II/3:25–26). "Reflection must preserve its place in tragedy," says Schiller (1:1044). The chorus in tragedy *motiviert die Besonnenheit*, "motivates lucidity," he adds (1:1046), and even induces *Ruhe*, "calm" (1:1045). *Besonnenheit* is the very word that Nietzsche uses to describe the Dionysian dream of the Maenad troupes as described by the messenger in Euripides' *The Bacchae*. At the heart of Dionysos, the epitome of Apollo.

What the chorus therefore produces by means of the *combination* of "bold lyrical freedom" and "the sensuous power of its music" is an elevation of the dramatic poem—the entire play—as such. Nietzsche and Schiller alike (II/3:25–26, 39, 44; 1:1045) stress the *purification* of the drama through the choral ode: "*der Chor reinigt also das tragische Gedicht*," writes Schiller (ibid.). It

16. See the wide-ranging meditation on rhythm and melody with regard to Nietzsche and Theodor Reik (among others), in Philippe Lacoue-Labarthe, "The Echo of the Subject," in *Le Sujet de la philosophie: Typographies I* (Paris: Aubier-Flammarion, 1979), 217–303.

does this by separating off reflection from the plot, creating that "living wall" between proscenium and spectator that we know as the chorus. In reading both Nietzsche and Schiller, we begin to think of Hölderlin's caesura in a new way: the caesura would be a moment of musical, counterrhythmic reflection inserted into the plot structure itself, and Tiresias would be the oldest of the old Theban men—the most distinguished coryphaeus, crowned with ivy and poised for the dance.

The seventh section of Nietzsche's 1870 lecture course is especially noteworthy. It recounts later attempts in the history of Western music to rediscover and recapture the force of Greek music as practiced in tragedy. Italian Humanism and the Renaissance are especially important in this history. Vicenzo Galilei rejects polyphony in order that listeners may hear the solo voice, thus preserving the meaning of the sung text in a clear *melos;* Jacopo Corsi devotes his full attention to *dramatic* music; Jacopo Peri, himself a singer, develops a mode of song somewhere between the spoken and the sung word—his *stilo rappresentativo* being the prototype for *recitativo.*[17] Claudio Monteverdi completes this development, not only by developing the solo and the duet for singers, however, but also by enriching the orchestra. In effect, absolute music, at first overcome in order to grant priority to the voice, returns in order to complement and expand the voice's effects: from Monteverdi on, *Tonkunst* becomes sufficiently inventive to reflect "the entire life of feeling, from the most cheerful dance to the most dismal pain" (II/3:32). Even though music is made to serve spectacle in the history of opera—even in Mozart, who nonetheless believes he still has the upper hand—absolute music is all the while learning to express human emotion. The lesson is an old one. As Nietzsche has already told his students at the outset of his discussion of music in tragedy, whereas the overbearing and loquacious intellectualism of "Socratism" reduces the role of the Dionysian in tragedy to the point where tragedy ultimately expires, "the dithyramb undergoes a new form of development outside of tragedy, from which it has been ejected" (II/3:17). Nietzsche says little about this new form of dithyramb, and merely mentions the names Philoxenos of Kythera (435/434–380/79 B.C.E.) and Timotheos of Miletos (ca. 450–360 B.C.E.), both of them controversial representatives of "the new music" and composers of innovative dithyrambs, who were "supported by a richly developed instrumental music" (ibid.). Nietzsche then mentions, with-

---

17. Nietzsche discusses *stilo rappresentativo* more fully in section 19 of *The Birth of Tragedy,* KSA 1:120–129.

out further recorded comment, the final *rondo* movement, *Allegro con brio,* of Beethoven's Seventh.

A number of Nietzsche's observations concerning Sophocles may conclude this account of Nietzsche's 1870 lectures. First, the *thinking* or *reflection* that Sophocles introduces into his choral odes—and this will change with Euripides—are "still in accord with instinct," that is, with the profound creativity of culture during the tragic age of the Greeks (II/3:37). "Instinct" does not mean that Sophocles is a traditionalist. He is less bound to the structure of tetralogy, for example, than his mentor Aeschylus is. If Aeschylus's tetralogies are like a bas-relief on a curved surface, so that some episodes of the story are visible to us at any given moment while others are no longer or not yet present, Sophocles' plays are like free-standing sculptures (II/3:38). The implication is not merely that each play is independent from the others in the tetralogy but that, because of the element of *reflection* in them, we can, as it were, walk about them and marvel at them from every angle. Nowhere is the statue metaphor more fitting than in the role of the chorus. The Sophoclean chorus, which is responsible for the element of reflection, is no longer a protagonist in any sense. "It introduces calm [*Ruhe*] into the artwork, hindering our unconditioned abduction [*Fortgerissenwerden*] by the strong effects of the [choral] virtuosos: as Schiller says, we are not to get mixed up in this matter" (II/3:39). Once again Nietzsche speaks of the cleansing (*das Reinigen*) of the dramatic poem as a whole by "the element of thought," or "reflection" (II/3:39, 44). Even though Sophocles' plays are "infinitely more harsh" in their subject-matter than anything in either Aeschylus or Euripides, Sophocles himself is called the mild one, the sweet one, by his contemporaries: γλυκὺς, μέλισσα. The harshness or bitterness Nietzsche has in mind is precisely that tendency to unspeakable blasphemy and sacrilege (*nefas*) that Hölderlin sees as essential to Sophoclean tragedy. In Nietzsche's view too, blasphemy plays an important role in the contrast between Aeschylus and Sophocles. For the former, "there is no *necessity* for blasphemy on the part of the individual," in spite of the primal belief that a curse may hang over the heads of an entire clan of mortals generation after generation. The implication is that with Sophocles the necessity of blasphemy is fully developed, and not as a mere "inclination" or "proclivity" of mortals. This brings Nietzsche as close as he will come to Hölderlin's radical view of Sophocles. A note from late 1870 or early 1871 says, "Pain as appearance—difficult problem! The sole means of theodicy. *Blasphemy* as *becoming*" (KSA 7:203). Yet the twenty-five-year-old Nietzsche stops just short of Hölderlin's radicality:

The worldview is tragic only in Sophocles. The fact that *one does not deserve* one's destiny seemed to him tragic: the enigmatic nature of human life, truly terrifying, was his tragic muse. The κάθαρσις comes on the scene as a necessary feeling of consonance in a world of dissonances. *Suffering*, the origin of tragedy, achieves with Sophocles its transfiguration: it is grasped as something that makes one holy. One recalls the way in which Oedipus at Colonus is mystically transported, an event that is full of blessings [i.e., for the future of Athens]. The distance between the human and the divine is beyond measure: the most profound obeisance and resignation are called for. The true virtue is σωφροσύνη, not an active virtue, but only a negative one. Heroic humanity is the noblest humanity, devoid of virtue; its destiny demonstrates an infinite chasm [vis-à-vis the divine]. There is scarcely *guilt;* only a lack of knowledge concerning the worth of human life.[18]

Thus far the 1870 lecture course on *Oedipus Tyrannos*. When we peruse Nietzsche's notebooks from the period surrounding *The Birth of Tragedy from the Spirit of Music*, we see further signs of his fascination with absolute music and absolute rhythm. In the autumn of 1869 Nietzsche, here strongly influenced by Schopenhauer, writes:

What does music do? It dissolves an intuition into will. [¶] It contains the universal forms of all the states in which we crave something: it is the symbolism of drives through and through, and as such it is thoroughly comprehensible to everyone in its simplest forms (beat, rhythm). [¶] It is therefore always more universal than any particular plot. It is therefore more comprehensible to us than any given plot: music is thus the key to the drama. . . . The Greek music drama is a preliminary stage of absolute music, a form within that entire process. (KSA 7:23–24; cf. 59)

Because absolute music is a late development, however, the earliest poets seek a musical equivalent—that is to say, a "lyrical-musical expression"—in mythology. Precisely in the way that Schelling's "absolute mythology" and his sense of sound and rhythm are intertwined, so too Nietzsche sees in myth and music together the Apollonian and Dionysian roots of tragedy. To be sure, Greek music remains occasional music; the word, whether spoken or sung, maintains precedence (KSA 7:24). In the beginning, at the birth of tragedy, it is a question of *"song cycles for chorus, tied together by a narrative"* (KSA 7:28). When the Greek music drama disintegrates, absolute music and "family

18. KGA II/3:40. Compare, however, those remarkable paragraphs in section 9 of *The Birth of Tragedy* on Sophocles and the essential role of blasphemy, *Frevel*, in the advance of civilization. Here once again Nietzsche writes of the essential harshness or acerbity (*das Herbe*) of Sophoclean tragedy. See KSA 1:69–70. Unfortunately, in these same paragraphs, Nietzsche is tempted into comparing this Sophoclean harshness with an "Aryan" and "masculine" trait, contrasting it with the "Semitic" and "feminine."

drama" go their separate ways (KSA 7:25–26). Nevertheless, Nietzsche goes to considerable lengths to establish music as the origin of tragedy. In so doing he confirms Novalis's thesis (examined in chapter 2 of this volume) that the tragic can and does appear across many genres of literature and life. Nietzsche writes, in the winter of 1869–1870:

> It is nonsense to speak of a unity of drama, lyric, and epic in the ancient epic songs. For here one is taking the tragic to be the dramatic: whereas the sundry forms of the dramatic are merely forms of *mime*.
>
> The shattering outcome, φόβος and ἔλεος, have nothing to do with drama, and they pertain to tragedy *not* because it is drama. Every story can have these qualities, especially the musical lyric. . . . Every art demands a "being outside oneself," an ἔκστασις; the step to drama occurs from here, since here [in drama] we do not return to ourselves but, in our ἔκστασις, remain lodged in a foreign being. We act as though enchanted. Hence the profound astonishment when we watch a drama: the floor is shaken, our belief in the indissolubility of the individual [is shaken].
>
> With lyric poetry too we are astonished, when we sense that the feelings which are deepest in us are coming back at us, tossed back to us by other individuals.

This is what ties the theme of absolute music to κάθαρσις: the experience of ecstasies of terror and compassion, described by Bernays in 1857 and by Hölderlin in 1804, as the shattering that removes us from the midpoint of our lives and transports us to an alien realm, is in Nietzsche's view a fundamentally musical experience. Bernays himself writes of music and dance transporting us to a confrontation with the fundamental laws of the universe; Hölderlin elaborates the lawful calculus of the rhythm of scenes and the counterrhythm of the caesura for the sake of "intimacy" and "intensity," *Innigkeit*, not as interiority but as ecstasy. Nietzsche seeks the same: a note on Schiller ends with the equation "*Musik Innigkeit*" (KSA 7:302); a note on the "mothers of existence" ends with the remark that "the true Helen" is music (KSA 7:314).

Nietzsche's reflections culminate in a long note sketched between the end of 1870 and April of 1871.[19] The note, an early draft of section 6 of *The Birth of Tragedy from the Spirit of Music*, speculates on the eminence of music in the genesis of poetic language. Whereas music may spin off images, these remain mere byplays, *Beispiele*, and do not capture the essence of music. One can talk of *Pastorale* only because the symphony has not yet been purged of "the schematism of fiction" (KSA 7:317), and in any case such schemata say noth-

19. KSA 7:185–192. Cf. the long note at 7:359–369, which focuses more on Schopenhauer's treatment of music and word.

ing about the Dionysian source of the music itself. Not that music is misused or even abused in opera. For abuse is simply *an impossibility*. "Music *can never* become a means, no matter how much it is squeezed and twisted and tortured: as tone, or as the rattle of a drum, reduced to its simplest and most primitive level, music overwhelms poetry and makes it a subordinate mirror-image" (KSA 7:186). Thus Mozart will have been right all along. When opera tries to make the music conform to the words and gestures of those gaudy marionettes on the stage, the result is simply bad music. Music is the heart of the artwork, the libretto and the stage-setting its frame, its *parergon*. When music is heard, the eye moistens, blurs, loses its focus (*umflort sich das Auge*), and the action on the stage fades before an imagination on fire with its own images: Dionysos is the most distant but most demanding drummer (KSA 7:188). So-called "dramatic" music is therefore either a slave to convention, a mere memorandum for a sluggish audience, or a clown full of surprises—a gilded gewgaw for drowsy emperors. All the more astonishing, therefore, is the miracle of ancient Greek folk lyric as practiced by Archilochus. What the miracle produces is a *shared vision of the god*, and out of this shared vision comes the choral ode of Greek tragedy. Out of the choral ode, in turn, comes the plot of drama. And the plot is always one or other mask of the fragmented god:

> The process of the *gradual revelation of the vision*—spreading from the individual to the chorus—appears once again as the *struggles and victories of Dionysos*, and it is visualized right before the eyes of the chorus. Now we gaze into the profound necessity of the transmitted fact that in the most ancient times the suffering and the victory of Dionysos constituted the sole content of tragedy. Indeed, we now immediately grasp the fact that every other hero of tragedy must be understood as the mere representative of Dionysos—as it were, a mask of Dionysos. (KSA 7:191–192; cf. 221–222)

And Dionysos himself? What Schelling affirms, Nietzsche here confirms: "Sorrow, languor, lack [*Das Leid, die Sehnsucht, der Mangel*] as the primal font of things" (KSA 7:202).

What is striking about *Hölderlin's* reading of Oedipus, we recall, is that the ἁμαρτία and ὕβρις of the tragic hero, what Hölderlin calls *nefas*, are larger than Oedipus, and have to do with the coupling of god and mortal—a coupling followed by radical separation. Thus Oedipus and Jocasta in some way reduplicate on the human scene the divine scene of Zeus and Danaë, or Zeus and Semele, or Dionysos and Ariadne. These furious couplings, in all their natural power, tear humankind out of the sphere of life and sweep it off to the sphere of the dead. These couplings, with their too-intense unification, enjoin boundless separation. They seem to produce κάθαρσις by means of compassion, "pity to the point of total exhaustion," as Hölderlin writes, coming here as close to Aristotle as he ever comes. Yet Hölderlin's entire effort is to show not what the healthy restoration of the audience might look like, but how god and mortal meet and mate and separate in a world of pestilence and confusion, in a time of toil and destitution: they meet and mate and divorce, says Hölderlin, "*in the all-oblivious form of infidelity*" (CHV 2:316). "For," he adds laconically, "divine infidelity is most readily retained" (ibid.). If Nietzsche's notes from the autumn of 1870 contain that famous *urdeutschen* notion, "All gods must die" (KSA 7:107), they are no more triumphant in tone than Hölderlin's "Notes" of 1804; the entire story of the sufferings and wanderings of Dionysos revolves about the identical mystery for both thinkers—joined in this respect by Schelling.

In the "Notes on Antigone," Hölderlin has more to say concerning the mutual infidelity of god and man. Here it is less a matter of anger, more of wild and untamed nature. Here *Zorn* translates ὀργή, what Hölderlin elsewhere calls the "more aorgic" power of nature. Antigone represents the split between sky and earth, between Titanic powers and human interests, between the dead and the living. At her most profound, Antigone embodies that striving of Zeus to enter this world, the world of our earth and all its consequences. Zeus struggles to enter the cell of Danaë so that this mortal woman can count off for him, the father of time, the strokes of the golden hours. Here the coupling of god and human would be experienced by both mortal and god as passion and pain. "For time is always more calculable when it is counted off in suffering [*im Leiden*]" (CHV 2:372). To these sufferings Nietzsche gives the name Zagreus, Dionysos in pieces.

Hölderlin proposes that the very text of the tragedy to be performed, the lines of dialogue in rhythmic alternation with the choral songs, manifest the sufferings of the godhead as well as of the mortal hero or heroine. As we have heard several times now, he calls these lines of poetry "the *suffering organs* [leidende Organe] of the divinely wrestling body" (CHV 2:374). The precise way in which the suffering body of god or mortal, suffering in and as time, is experienced tells us whether we are in the presence of a Greek or of a more modern, more Hesperian tragedy. Central to that experience is the effect of the dramatic word, which in any case is always bound up with death. Hölderlin distinguishes between Greek and Hesperian tragedy by noting that the word in Greek tragedy kills directly, "athletically," as it were, even if by mediation. In Greek tragedy the word is *tödtlichfaktisch,* "factically deadly" (CHV 2:373). Perhaps it is possible to think this "athletic" word in Nietzsche's sense as the *musical* word—when, for example, the pain of a laceration *sings* exquisitely. By contrast, when tragedy is made more accessible to us moderns in a turn or reversal to our native, Hesperian land, the word performs *tödtendfaktisch* (CHV 2:374). Whereas the word in Greek tragedy is more violent and murderous, the word in Hesperian tragedy, especially in dialogue, is "more relentless," "more incessant," *unaufhaltsamer.* Hence the present participle, suggesting continuous action: *tödtendfaktisch,* "killingly factical," "murderously factical." Philippe Lacoue-Labarthe finds an astonishing word for this: he translates the "murderously factical" as *meurtissant,* or *le meurtrissure.*[20] The latter is the bruise that is visible on a cadaver that has suffered a blow or a puncture wound, a bruise or contusion upon the livid corpse. Lacoue-Labarthe associates such contusions with "spiritual wounds" or "lacerations of the mind," and he further associates these lacerations with madness, mystical absorption, and exile amid unthinkable things. Under the influence of Nietzsche's analysis of the ascetic ideal that pervades modernity but also has some relation to Dionysian self-alienation, and perhaps also under the influence of Benjamin's *Trauerspiel* book, one may be tempted to translate Hölderlin's term for the action of the word in Hesperian tragedy as *mortification.* If Greek tragedy kills directly, tragedy in our time, which is a time of a dire lack of destiny, δύσμορον (cf. *Oedipus at Colonos,* l. 332), kills through mortification. If Zeus is more "humane" in the Hesperian age, that is because he possesses traits that one must call "human, all-too-human," working his effects through guilt and what Hölderlin in the *Frankfurt Aphorisms* calls "monkish morality." In our dismal time, Zeus suffers less from the deed than from guilt. And he is met, not with truly spiritual words, which Hölderlin identifies as words of blasphemy, but with wheedling and cajoling words. We moderns, like bartering Bartolomeo in Michelangelo's "Last Judgment," seek to strike bargains.

A final word on Hölderlin's *Anmerkungen zur Antigonä* as a future reminiscence of Nietzsche. Hölderlin does not falter but confronts in a startling way the deadly nature of divinity in both Greek and Hesperian tragedy. He begins the third and final section of the "Notes" by underscoring what the "Notes on Oedipus" had already intimated: tragic presentation rests on the "becoming altogether one" of god and mortal, followed by their sacred separation (*heilig sich scheidend*). The god becomes present "in the figure of death [*in der Gestalt des Todes*]" (CHV 2:373). Lacoue-Labarthe is right to insist that

---

20. Lacoue-Labarthe, *Métaphrasis,* 21, for this and the following.

Hölderlin's remarkable words—as strange to us today, no matter how many times we hear them, as they were in his own time—mean something more than a negative theology or a theology of the *deus absconditus*, something much more than a post-Lutheran, post-Hegelian theology of the death of god. In the following words the full lesson of Danaë is drawn:

> There is nothing other than time, time "itself," which "is" nihilating. God himself *is* not. Pure *passage*, the prophets say. Which is to say not only that he is *finite*, "existing," but also, still more unthinkable, that insofar as he is existing merely as passage itself, that is, as existence, he does not exist. That is his *condition*.... This is what tragedy presents: nonrevelation, that is, the *condition* of god. Which is precisely our own, and nothing more. A-theology without a common measure.[21]

This is the *condition* that Schelling descries in the inassimilable *ground* of god's essence, and is scarcely able to say or write. This is the condition of god's presence, as *Gestalt des Todes*, to mortals. Their death, shared, though not as a common measure. No reconciliation, no mediation.

So many elements of Hölderlin's "Notes" on Sophocles remain unremembered here, yet the appearance of the god in the figure of death surely invites us now to take up, if only briefly, the Nietzschean reminiscence of the death of God. If one were to develop one further idea from *The Birth of Tragedy from the Spirit of Music* in the direction of Hölderlin's "Notes," it would be the central idea of section 10, expressed also in the notebooks examined earlier, namely, the idea that every tragedy sings the sufferings of the godhead, so that Dionysos is the sole hero of Greek tragedy. If, as Hölderlin avers, the tragic poem is only extrinsically heroic, that in substance it is *idealisch*, "ideational," Nietzsche replies that the "ideality" of tragedy rests on the consolidation of everything "individual" (inasmuch as everything "individual" is comic rather than tragic) under the mask of Dionysos Zagreus, the fragmented god. "From the smile of this Dionysos come the Olympian gods, from his tears humankind" (KSA 1:72). Even the third Dionysos would be precisely that redoubled, duplicitous, daimonic nature—the δυάς—in which the divine and the human are excessively joined and excessively sundered. Oedipus, Jocasta, and Antigone suffer as embodiments of the tragic absolute, insofar as one can say that the absolute is always fragmented, always Dionysos.

Nietzsche rejoins Hölderlin when he poses this question to Winckelmann: What is the nature of Greek cheerfulness, *Heiterkeit*? He expands on this question in his "Attempt at a Self-Criticism" by asking whether pes-

21. Lacoue-Labarthe, *Métaphrasis*, 34, 40–41.

simism has to be what it is for us "moderns," namely, a symptom of decline (KSA 1:12). More positively, is there a "pessimism of strength"? Is there "an intellectual predilection for what is hard, terrifying, wicked, and problematic in existence, but a predilection out of well-being, superabundant life, and *plenitude* of existence"? (ibid.). After sixteen years, the riddle of the tragic mythos, the riddle of Dionysos, has become only more puzzling to Nietzsche. If modernity is characterized chiefly by devotion to science, modernity will have begun in Socrates or even before Socrates, perhaps in an Aeschylean-Empedoclean turn. Modernity will also be characterized as morality, a morality that we may describe in Hölderlinian fashion as *tödtendfaktisch*, killingly factical, utterly mortifying. Antiquity, for its part, is marked by divine μανία, by the wisdom of the tragic mythos, by the revelation of Silenos. According to Nietzsche, all modern ideas—optimism, belief in progress, rationality, and utility—pale before the art of Greek tragedy. He is sometimes unable to resist the temptation to depict such art in the terms of the very morality he wants to resist: "The world—in every moment the *accomplished* redemption of the god—as the eternally changing, eternally novel vision of the one who suffers most, is most beset by contraries, is richest in contradictions, the one who is able to redeem himself only in *radiant appearance* [Schein]" (ibid.). Nietzsche regrets having confused in his early work this ancient pessimism of strength with "the most modern things" (KSA 1:20), things such as the Wagner of the collective artwork. He regrets the language of consolation and redemption—even as he repeats it sixteen years later. He wishes that the language of *Zarathustra* had been available to him, wishes he were more poet than genealogist, wishes that he had *sung*, or even better, that he had obeyed Zarathustra's injunction and fashioned a new lyre. Yet the fact that the god is *redeemed* rather than redeemer, and redeemed *in the world*, the world of *suffering*, sets Nietzsche in proximity to Novalis, Schelling, and Hölderlin in their most radical moments.

To all this one would be right to object: Where here is there any talk of the absolute, whether in the ascendant or in demise? Before advancing any farther into Nietzsche's analysis of the absolute importance of Greek tragedy, one ought to try to respond to this objection. A typical Nietzschean reference to the absolute appears in the second aphorism of the first part of *Human, All-Too-Human.* Here Nietzsche denies the existence of eternal, "absolute" truths. Several pages later in *Human,* the word *absolute* appears again, as it does scores of times in Nietzsche's oeuvre. One has to concede, of course, that Nietzsche is in no sense a philosopher of the absolute in Hegel's sense. Yet would it not be enlightening to see his work, from *The Birth of*

Tragedy, through *Thus Spoke Zarathustra* and *Beyond Good and Evil* (especially the final pages on "Dionysos philosophos"), up to *Twilight of the Idols*, as an extended essay in tragic thinking—a thinking that elevates tragedy to absolute significance and thinks the absolute as tragic? Such a tragic absolute, however, is inextricably bound up with absolute music. And absolute music? Let us speculate a moment longer on the new lyre.

We know that when Nietzsche returned to Naumburg from the front of the Franco-Prussian War in mid-September of 1870 he devoted himself entirely to the study of Greek prosody, rhythm, and meter. That winter semester, in Basel, he taught courses in this area and prepared articles for publication—articles that never appeared. If one looks beyond the immediate scholarly purpose of these articles and studies—namely, the effort to refute the prevailing scholarly accounts of Greek prosody, which are, in Nietzsche's view, excessively influenced by modern modes of prosody and unaware of the vast gulf that separates the modern from the ancient Greek sense of rhythm—one senses something of Nietzsche's desire to focus on music, even absolute music, as the origin of tragedy. The philosophical reason for this is not difficult to descry. As we have already seen, it has to do with the combination of music and word in tragedy as such. Nietzsche's suspicion is that if tragedy is born of music, it dies of the word. To put it most strongly: if Socratism is older than Socrates, that is because the death of tragedy has to do with the very introduction of the spoken or sung word into the music of the dithyramb. Or, if the dithyramb is always sung, that is, is always an affair of words, then the death of tragedy is determined in and by its very commencement. Absolute music is itself the tragic absolute. Something like that is suggested by the following note, jotted by Nietzsche into a notebook during the winter or spring of 1869–1870 (KSA 7:67–68): "The ancient dithyramb purely Dionysian: actually transmogrified into music. Now Apollonian art is added to it: it invents the actors and members of the chorus, it imitates the rapture, creates scenes for it, tries to come to preeminence with the entire artistic apparatus at its disposal: above all with the word, with dialectic. It transforms the music into a maid-servant, into a ἥδυσμα." If in the beginning was the word, that word eventually poisons tragedy, killing it factically. From dithyramb to embellishment, from Dionysos to dialectic: Nietzsche's note tells the story so quickly that it enables us to see the problem of the word as such. Eventually, the word causes tragedy to dwindle in importance—it becomes something legible: "*Against Aristotle*, who takes ὄψις and μέλος to be mere ἡδύσματα in tragedy: in that very step he sanctions the drama as a thing to be read" (KSA 7:78, 128). To be sure, the lyre is not as helpless as all that. A note from late 1870 pays heed to "the monstrous, *mimic* power of music—on the basis of a monstrous *absolute* development of art," especially in the direction of poetry (KSA 7:117). Yet the musical element remains "imprisoned" in poetry, and Nietzsche envisages a higher form of culture for which Greek tragedy would merely be the precursor: he feels himself to be the legatee of a long tradition that has as its goal not the rebirth of music drama, but the liberation of music from the tyranny of the word (KSA 7:118). It is therefore not entirely strange to find Nietzsche doting on Wagner not for the sake of the collective artwork but in hopes of "the further development of the symphony," as though even *Tristan* were a symphony to which the myth is superadded (KSA 7:228–229). Perhaps Nietzsche is already dreaming of the Wagner who spends his last days working on a symphony in C, already dreaming of a Sibelius whose final symphony will be the same. If in antiquity Aeschylus is accused of having profaned the mysteries, Nietzsche sees a certain "symbolic" truth in the accusation, if indeed music and a wordless mysticism and mystery must develop hand-in-hand (KSA 7:118, 123).

There can be little question but that the struggle between μύθος and music, word and tone, meter and rhythm, Apollo and Dionysos, is being carried out in sections 16–25 of *The Birth of Tragedy from the Spirit of Music*. We will have to be satisfied with a brief reference to these reflections, a reference to the moment when Nietzsche writes about *dissonance* in music. For the moment of dissonance—brazen dissonance, one might say—is the moment of the common origin of the gods of word and music. This is the point (in section 24 of *The Birth of Tragedy from the Spirit of Music*) at which Nietzsche reminisces on Schellingian matters and maters, even if one must say that his reminiscence remembers more than Schelling may have been thinking, or that Schelling may have been trying to remember ahead to Nietzsche—in short, that the following is what Schelling may have been trying to say in the first half of the first draft of *The Ages of the World*: "The pleasure produced by the tragic myth shares its home with the pleasureful sensation of dissonance in music. The Dionysian, with the primal pleasure that it experiences even in its pain, is the womb that gives birth to both music and the tragic myth" (KSA §24, 1:152). "Dionysian" here, of course, means the mother(s) of being—Urania, Kybele, Deo-Demeter, Persephone, Semele.

At the outer reaches of Nietzsche's thought at this very early time, very early yet already well beyond Wagner's collective artwork and all forms of opera, we confront questions concerning pure music and pure rhythm in their relation to the human body. For example, precisely when the beat falls, at the emphatic moment, the foot of the dancer touches the ground (KGA

II/3:102). Musical time, the beat, or *Takt*, is πούς, the "foot"; the elements of *Takt* are χρόνοι ποδικοί or σημεῖα ποδός; the effect of the entire measure of beats is *rhythm* (ibid.; cf. 156). Nietzsche agrees with Schelling that the ancient Greeks possess a highly developed and complex sense of rhythm: μεταβολή, or "alternation," he says, is their principal means of expression (II/3:135). Pulse and pace, heart and footfall, are the two major sources, or "organs," of the beat. The beat is an experience of ecstatic temporality, in the sense of Aristotle's account of "the sudden" as "removal," the tragic rapture of time as such:

> When we hear [a rhythm], a gap is needed, a very brief pause. Here the tone *dies away*. The whole process is that of a tonal wave that is coming to rest. [¶] The most rapid motion of a pendulum comes in the first half of its fall, the strongest tone at the beginning of the tonal wave. It is a force that consumes itself. [¶] Whether it is a breath or a stroke, the sound will always be most forceful at the beginning. (II/3:163)

When one speaks of "absolute music," and even "absolute rhythm," however, misunderstandings may arise. Nietzsche is indeed searching for the χρόνον πρῶτον that would be the atomic, irreducible σημεῖον upon which every rhythm is constructed (II/3:147–148); he appears to find it in what we call the sixteenth note, calculated upon the ratio of two paces for every beat of the pulse (II/3:258–259; 292–293). In spite of this search for "absolute rhythm," however, Nietzsche emphasizes throughout his investigations that no rhythm or beat consists of absolutely identical units and intervals. "Important are the *composite rhythms*, . . . the same sort of beat, yet different κατὰ διαίρεσιν. . . . *Identity of beats* is not a universal principle. The μεταβολαί [alter(n)ations] occur quite often. . . . Infinite mimicry: music has no absolute character[.] Insofar as it is imitative, it has no identical beats (at least not necessarily)" (II/3:192). And even more sharply:

> *Identity of beat*. Considered with mathematical precision, two beats are *never* alike: the more soulfully [*je geistiger*] the performer is disposed, the more minutely the beat individualizes itself, first, in its duration (ἀγωγῇ), then in its *ictus* (in accord with its declamation), and, third, in the duration of its component parts. This individuality waxes with the sequences and periods. Architectonic rigidity is the death of performance. (II/3:205)

The force of musical rhythm is such that it can encompass and even regulate to some extent the sundry rhythms of the body, affecting pulse as well as footfall. "Suddenly, everything moves in accord with a new law: not that the older rhythms no longer prevail; they still rule, but they are differently determined. The physiological grounding and explanation of rhythm (and its power). [¶] The ancient essence of music is to be reconstrued: the mime dance, ἁρμονία, ῥυθμός."[22]

It seems a long way from these highly technical considerations of rhythm and beat in dance, music, and poetry to the pangs of the woman in childbirth. Yet once the body has been discovered—and Nietzsche discovers it early on—it sets its own beat. Nietzsche's thought in this respect is like ancient Greek rhythms: it is *agile*. And its agility takes it unfailingly to Greek tragedy and to the essence of Dionysos as the matrix for these matters. Nietzsche's fascination with the question of woman in his early notes on tragedy, and also with the nature of sensuality and sexual difference, surely has something to do with the ecstasies of absolute music. When he proclaims "tragic insight" the "mother of art," it is not as though he has simply draped his thought in a familiar metaphor (KSA 7:204). In general, one detects in this apparently most misogynistic of thinkers, one whose most withering critiques invariably involve a reference to effeminacy, a certain nostalgia for possibilities that a masculinist civilization has irretrievably lost. His question is why, "in spite of Helen, in spite of Dionysos," our civilization does not develop in a womanly direction—that is, in the direction of a profound respect for the night and for nature (KSA 7:146; cf. 170–179). He notes the awe felt by the ancient Greeks in the face of the *wisdom* of woman, citing the names Diotima, Pythia, Sibylla, and Antigone—each of these as important to him as it is to Schelling and Hölderlin before him. Such too is the wisdom of Oedipus, the murderer of his father and mate of his mother: like the Persian magus born of incest, Oedipus plunges the sphinx into the abyss when he solves the riddle of nature (KSA 7:141). Yet each time the riddle is posed, the beautiful body of the sphinx rises out of the abyss and "seduces us back into existence" (KSA 7:144; cf. 156), like Jocasta tempting Oedipus back into life during the shadow caesura. The "smile of nature," Demeter's smile, defeats all pessimism and all wisdom alike:

> Tragedy is beautiful insofar as the drive that produces what is terrifying in life, here as an artistic drive, appears with a smile, like a child at play. In this lies what is touching and affecting in tragedy as such: we see before us the horrific drive to art and to play. The same is true of music: it is an image of the will in a still more universal sense than tragedy.
>
> In the other arts, the appearances smile at us. In drama and music the will itself. The more profoundly we are convinced of the accursed nature of this drive

---

22. KGA II/3:322. Compare with this that famous aphorism on rhythm in *The Gay Science*, no. 84, "The Origins of Poesy"; KSA 3:439–442.

[*Unseligkeit dieses Triebes*], the more profoundly we are affected by its play. (KSA 7:145)

Sophocles is for Nietzsche too, as he is for Hölderlin and Schelling, the master of such play, precisely as the poet of *"the sufferings of the agonal individual"* (KSA 7:397). If there is no surface without terrifying depths, at least in the life of the Greeks of the tragic age, it is Sophocles who best mirrors depth and surface at once. The Apollonian language of his characters, in dialogue, bestows on the characters themselves a certain simplicity and transparency—they always *dance* well, says Nietzsche (KSA 7:159). The spirit of the music to which they dance, especially in the choral odes, betrays the true nature of the characters of the play. Characters such as Oedipus "are themselves abysses" (ibid.). What hides in their depths? Nothing less than the secret of an "unheard-of suffering" that produces "a strong sensation of joy" (KSA 7:216–217). Again and again in Nietzsche's notes from 1869 and 1870 one finds Oedipus joined with Empedocles and the erotic, music-practicing Socrates, a trio at the very heart of Hölderlin's drive to write a mourning-play: Hölderlin, like Nietzsche, moves from Socrates to Empedocles to Oedipus in order to gaze into the abyss of absolute separation, the abyss of the tragic absolute.[23]

The Tragic Absolute

"Tragedy," writes Philippe Lacoue-Labarthe, "is the work of art that speaks absolutely."[24] He is speaking of Hölderlin, while thinking ahead to Nietzsche. It may be that he is also thinking of Schelling, at least when Schelling is at his most radical. Lacoue-Labarthe continues:

Tragedy is the absolute *organon* (the *opus meta physicum* par excellence, as Nietzsche will later say of Wagner's *Tristan*) because tragedy is itself presentation of the tragedy of the absolute. That is to say, tragedy is presentation of the absolute as contradiction and—indissociably with that—the necessity of its presentation or manifestation, which is dialectically its death. One of Hölderlin's notes indicates that in tragedy "the sign = 0." The sign is understood here as the sign of the absolute: it is the hero. The fact that it equals zero means to say that the hero dies as a result of what he is, namely, the sign of the absolute or, more precisely, the absolute as sign. Nothing presents better the presentation of the absolute than tragedy.

23. On *Nietzsche's* plans to write a drama on the figure of Empedocles, the tragic human being par excellence, see D. F. Krell, *Postponements: Woman, Sensuality, and Death in Nietzsche* (Bloomington: Indiana University Press, 1986), throughout, but esp. ch. 2.

24. Lacoue-Labarthe, *Métaphrasis*, 49–50 for this and the following quotation.

The tragic absolute is no longer what either tragedy or *das Absolute* is for Hegel, namely, the tragedy that an absolute spirit "eternally plays with itself"; it is no longer a drama that culminates in "the subjugation of death" and "absolute resurrection" for spirit; it is no longer a play of pacified, eviscerated *Eumenides* (HW 2:495). It is rather that sober moment in Aeschylus's *Eumenides* (l. 648) when Apollo concedes that not even Father Zeus can reverse the process of death once it has ensued. "No one is resurrected," says the god, οὔτις ἔστ' ἀνάστασις. The tragic absolute has nothing to do with the lugubrious mummery of resurrection. Nor is it a mourning-play that would abandon Greek antiquity for "the ineffable," the prophetic or the messianic, as in Benjamin.

Nietzsche never uses the expression "the tragic absolute." Yet he is quite clear about the requirements of "the tragic attitude," *die tragische Gesinnung,* which he portrays in the fourth of his *Untimely Meditations,* "Richard Wagner in Bayreuth." Such an attitude, not as a psychological state but as a collective cultural stance, should come to characterize humanity as such and as a whole. Or, if that hope seems overblown, one can at least hope, as Nietzsche emphatically puts it, *"dass die tragische Gesinnung nicht absterbe"* (KSA 1:453), that the tragic way of thinking not vanish altogether from the realm of human possibility. Indeed, its disappearance would constitute a tragedy of its own, and Nietzsche employs the very language of tragedy to depict the absence of tragedy from modern culture: "An incomparable cry of woe would echo around the globe, were humanity to lose contact altogether with the tragic attitude; by contrast, there is no more beatific pleasure [*beseligendere Lust*] than the pleasure that accompanies what we know—which is that the tragic thought has been born once again into the world" (ibid.). Much later, in *Ecce Homo,* Nietzsche makes a pledge: "I promise a *tragic* age: the supreme art in yes-saying to life, tragedy, will be born again when humanity has achieved the state of consciousness of the hardest but most necessary wars, *without having suffered on their account"* (KSA 6:313). The fulfillment of that pledge becomes less and less likely as Nietzsche's career of thinking and writing progresses. Even if we insist that the epochs of antiquity and modernity resist demarcation, we may be certain that antiquity is not gaining ground. That does not mean that Nietzsche loses the faith. In the section of *Twilight of the Idols* entitled "What I Owe the Ancients," supplemented by the note that serves as a first draft to some of this material, we find an intriguing passage on "the psychology of the orgiastic." This passage has much in common with what Schelling calls the "anorgic" power of music and what Hölderlin calls the "more aorgic" power of nature. Nietzsche is critical here of Aristotle's account of κάθαρσις, which takes pity and fear, two "depressive affects," to be the essential affects of tragedy. Nietzsche understands tragedy as a tonic—as bracing rather than depressing. (We may perhaps understand Nietzsche's *tonic* as extrapolations of both Schelling's *Ton* and Hölderlin's *Wechsel der Töne*, alter(n)ations of tone among lyric, epic, and tragic forms of poetry [CHV 2:108–109; cf. 68, 78–79, 87].) In section 4 of "What I Owe the Ancients," Nietzsche relates the "orgiastic origin" of Greek tragedy to sexuality and the pangs of childbirth. This is noteworthy, inasmuch as *The Birth of Tragedy from the Spirit of Music*, while stressing the raptures of springtime, intoxication, and dance as sources for the Dionysian, is reluctant to attribute the "Oriental" witches' brew of cruelty and sensuality to the Greek Dionysos. If Nietzsche's first published work resists the sexual character of Dionysos, precisely in the way that the young Schopenhauer, according to the third treatise of the *Genealogy*, flees from sensuality to ascetic resignation, his late work engages it directly. It is almost as though Nietzsche comes around to Schelling's thought concerning the wheel of births in incipient nature, births that represent the series of scissions that characterize the father when he finally becomes a mother. The Dionysian mysteries express the fundamental "will to life" of the Hellenes, the "eternal recurrence of life," promised and sanctified (*verheissen und geweiht*) in sexuality (KSA 6:159). Genuine life is the collective living on of life through reproduction and "the mysteries of sexuality," Nietzsche writes—again in unwitting reminiscence of Hölderlin's "more tender relations" and Schelling's Demeter:

> For the Greeks, the *sexual* symbol was therefore the honorable symbol in itself, the proper profundity of ancient piety viewed as a whole. Every particular in the act of procreation—pregnancy and birth—awakened the highest and the most solemn feelings. In the mystery doctrines, *pain* was proclaimed holy: the "contractions of the woman in childbirth" sanctify pain in general. All becoming and growing, all nurturing of the future *conditions* pain. . . . In order for the eternal joy of creation to be granted, in order for the will to life to affirm itself eternally, the "travail of the woman in childbirth" must also be granted. . . . All this is signified in the word *Dionysos:* I know of no higher symbolism than this *Greek* symbolism, that of the Dionysia. (KSA 6:159)

Sensuality and sexuality are here no longer postponed, no longer attributed to an Oriental Dionysos who waits for an Occidental, Doric Apollo to disarm or unman him. The *Greek* Dionysos, interpreted in a more lively fashion, that is, more *Orientally*, is the Dionysos of tragedy. Section 5 of "What I Owe the Ancients" analyzes Dionysian, orgiastic philosophy in the following way:

The psychology of the orgiastic, as that of an overflowing feeling of life and force, within which even pain serves as a stimulant, gave me the key to the concept of *tragic* feeling, which has been misunderstood by Aristotle and especially by our pessimists. Tragedy is so far from demonstrating anything in favor of the pessimism of the Hellenes, as Schopenhauer thought, that it rather must be taken as the decisive rejection of and *counter instance* to such pessimism. Yes-saying to life itself even in its strangest and hardest problems; the will to life, finding its happiness in the *sacrifice* of the highest types to its own inexhaustibility—*that* is what I called Dionysian, *that* is what I surmised to be the bridge to the psychology of the *tragic* poet. *Not* in order to extirpate fear and pity, not in order to purify oneself of a dangerous affect by a vehement purgation—that is the way Aristotle understood it—but in order *oneself to be*, beyond fear and pity, the eternal pleasure of becoming, the pleasure that also encompasses *pleasure in annihilation.* . . . And herewith I alight once again upon the place from which I commenced: *The Birth of Tragedy* was my first transvaluation of all values. Herewith I occupy once again that familiar ground on the basis of which my will, my *ability*, burgeons—I, the last disciple of the philosopher Dionysos, I, the teacher of eternal return. (KSA 6:160)

We may supplement these remarks with those of the long note, "What is tragic?" Here we find Nietzsche elaborating on Aristotle's pity and fear.[25] Nietzsche calls them *"depressive* affects," and notes that, had Aristotle been correct, tragedy would have proved hazardous to life. Yet tragic art is the great *stimulans* to life, enabling us to be enraptured by life (*ein Rausch am Leben*). Tragic art does not purge us of pathological, depressive affects that have long been dammed up in us. The tragic affects are not depressive but *tonic.* Perhaps this bracing tonic is what Schelling in 1795 means by *freedom* and what Hölderlin in 1804 means by tragic *transport?* In any case, Nietzsche continues:

Something that habitually arouses fear or pity disorganizes us, weakens us, discourages us:—and if one grants that Schopenhauer was right when he said that what one gets from tragedy is resignation, that is, a tranquil renunciation of happiness, hope, will to life, then one would be conceiving of an art in which art itself would be negated. Tragedy would then be a process of dissolution, the instincts of life destroying themselves in the instinct to art. . . . Tragedy would be a symptom of decline.

One can refute this theory in the most cold-blooded way, namely, by measuring with a dynamometer the effects of a tragic emotion. And what one gets as a result is something only a systematic philosopher, psychologically accustomed to lying, would be able to mistake: tragedy is a *tonic.* (KSA 13:410)

25. KSA 13:409–411; cf. *Der Wille zur Macht* (Stuttgart: Kröner Verlag, 1964; a reprint of the 2nd ed., Leipzig, 1906), no. 851, which reproduces the note only in part, however.

What a "dynamometer" looks like remains a great mystery, though one might picture it as a sort of polygraph or Geiger counter of the emotions. To be sure, Nietzsche overlooks the fact that Aristotle himself constantly invokes the *hedonic* nature of tragedy: Aristotle knows full well that tragedy is a stimulant to the life of the city and its individuals. Whether his theory of κάθαρσις, disputed over the ages, helps us to understand how the tragic affects have a bracing impact on us, and, more important, precisely how the distillation and refinement of the affects is to be understood—these are questions that will continue to provoke the very best thinking.[26]

From Hölderlin we learn that a lawful calculus, inserting a caesura into the rapid flow of representations and thus producing both equilibrium and tragic transport, somehow elicits and cultivates the affects, bringing them to a high pitch of intensity; from Nietzsche we learn at least to doubt whether the distillation and refinement of our feelings ever lead to their being purged. We recall that Jacob Bernays too insists on the hedonic character of catharsis: at the moment when pity overcomes fear in our response to a tragedy, we experience an ecstatic *Urpathos* or primal emotion. Even if, like the tragic hero, we are swept away—ecstatically, excentrically—to the land of the dead, seeing that unhappy kingdom as our future native land, the ecstasy in itself produces elation. Catastrophe, shattering us the while, succumbs to a certain equanimity, so that even φρίττειν is bittersweet. Like Schelling's god, or goddess, we feel ourselves dilating. Without losing the lucidity that characterizes the collective dream of the Dionysian troupe on the mountain meadow, we expand in languor; we do not lose sight of the absolute separation that Hölderlin sees as the end of our coupling with gods, gods who have learned finitude. Without absolute separation, no compassion; without compassion, no vision of "the frightening, sublime laws of the universe" (Bernays, 50). Without vision, no shudder—humanity's most admirable part. Without the shudder, no recognition that life is at bottom powerful and pleasurable.

Yet what can the tragic absolute mean to us moderns, us Hesperians? Earlier we spoke of Nietzsche's highly ambivalent self-identification as a genealogist of morals and subverter of modern ideals and ideas. By mentioning genealogy we arrive at the heart of the battle between the ancients and the

---

26. Readers should examine the work of Elizabeth Sikes on the relation of Aristotelian catharsis to Hölderlinian caesura, in "Translation of Κάθαρσις, Κάθαρσις as Translation" (cited in note 20 of ch. 10, above). On Nietzsche's critique of Aristotle, see the thorough and insightful treatment by Iris Därmann, " 'Was ist tragisch'?: Nietzsches Deutung der Aristotelischen Katharsis in der 'Geburt der Tragödie' und im Spätwerk," her Habilitation lecture at the Universität Lüneburg.

moderns as the apostle of Dionysos fights it. We need not tarry long with Nietzsche's evaluation of the "modern," or Hölderlin's "Hesperian." Around the "modern," all the predictable negative attributes gather: the modern is tense, restless, scornful of measure and limit, a physiological contradiction and confusion in value-estimation, a disparity between inner and outer, the chest-beatings of the proud ape that ironizes itself but is nonetheless infinitely dissatisfied with itself; the modern is Plebeian, English, motley, both a belly full of undigested information and an emetic; the modern is, in a word, *décadent*. It sounds almost as desperate as Schelling's god. Yet all these negative qualities play a positive role in the profile of the genealogist of morals himself or herself; all these hysterical modern chickens—headless and bloodied and frantic—come home to roost in genealogy. There is a passage (a very famous one) in the third treatise of the *Genealogy of Morals* in which Nietzsche paces off his own distance from antiquity and in which he sees himself as the most far-flung Hesperian, the most modern of moderns. Yet he uses the word ὕβρις—Hölderlin's *nefas* and Schelling's *Übel*—to measure out precisely that distance:

> If we measure our entire modern being upon the standard of the ancient Greeks, measure it, at least, where it is not debility but power and consciousness of power, it turns out to be sheer hubris and godlessness. . . . Hubris is today our entire attitude toward nature, our rape of nature with the help of machines and the astonishingly mindless inventiveness of our technicians and engineers; hubris is our attitude toward God, that is to say, toward any putative spider-goal and spider-ethicality suspended behind the vast spider web of causality—like Charles the Bold in battle with Louis XI we ought to say, *"je combats l'universelle araignée"*—; hubris is our attitude toward *us*, for we experiment with ourselves in a way that we would never allow with any animal, as we contentedly slit open our souls and gaze with curiosity upon our vivisection: what does the "health" of the soul mean to us! . . . We violate ourselves now, there is no doubt about it, we nutcrackers of the soul, we questioning and questionable ones, as though life were nothing other than nutcracking; precisely for that reason we must necessarily grow more questionable every day, we must become more *worthy* of question; precisely for that reason we must also perhaps become more worthy . . . to *live?* . . . (KSA 5:357–358)

One might have supposed that Hölderlin's return to his native land, his *vaterländische Umkehr*, is as far from Nietzsche, the good European, as anything could be. Yet one must remember that Hölderlin characterizes the Hesperian age as δύσμορον. Hölderlin's critique of the "School of Destiny," and especially of Germany within that school, is as harsh and as rigorous as Nietzsche's, as the latter's "Letter" to his "friend" attests. Even when the two thinkers seem farthest apart they are actually quite close. When we examine their respective views of antiquity, there are of course differences: when it comes to tragedy, Hölderlin writes everywhere of Zeus, not of Dionysos, who is reserved for the final hymns. Yet Hölderlin's Zeus, "the father of time and of the earth," is as fragile and as fragmented as Schelling's and Nietzsche's Dionysos Zagreus. Nietzsche's famous proclamation of the death of God, which seems so foreign to the enraptured Hölderlin, is perhaps matched by Hölderlin's insistence on the suffering and passion of the godhead: Zeus, the father, the power of the more aorgic nature, is bent back to this world and this earth, very much in Nietzschean fashion. Nietzsche invokes tragedy as an expression of the pessimism of strength, Hölderlin as a presentation of original weakness; yet for both thinkers strength and weakness have to do with *life*, superabundant life, incarnated in the pain of the woman in childbirth—that is the entire curriculum of Hölderlin's "School of Nature." If Nietzsche reaffirms the Teutonic saying *Alle Götter müssen sterben,* and if to our Hesperian ears this sounds like blasphemy, Hölderlin insists that the god must be encountered with words of blasphemy, nefarious words, if anything of spirit is to be retained. For both thinkers, joined in this regard by Schelling, piety is reserved for the fundamental crises of life—birth, childhood, education, eros, and death. However, does not Nietzsche define the effect of tragedy as bracing, as a tonic and a stimulant to life? How could Schelling's disconcerting description of freedom in defeat and Hölderlin's disquieting description of tragic transport as rapid removal to the realm of the dead be regarded as stimulants to life? The answer, of course, is that the boundless union and separation of god and mortal stimulates as nothing else can: divine infidelity is what we remember best. Suffering, passion, and the languor about which Schelling never ceases to write are at the heart of such stimulation. For Nietzsche, Dionysos Zagreus is the god who suffers, but also the god who devastates; for Hölderlin and Schelling alike, the fragmented god represents the power of nature and life, the more aorgic power, both fecund and faithless. Finally, for Hölderlin, Schelling, and Nietzsche, the suffering *and* the power of divinity have to do with the sensuality and sexuality that extend beyond the human scene to the very body of god. Zeus captivated, in the cell of mortal Danaë, is Zeus captured. Zeus bemused, in the arms of hesitant Alkmene, is Zeus bound. That is Schelling's and Hölderlin's gift to Nietzsche's philosophy of orgiastic tragedy, to *Dionysos philosophos.*

Schelling and Hölderlin, joined by Novalis and also by Nietzsche, all of them sons of pious Lutheran Germany, go quite far in the direction of mortal and divine sensuality. They go to confront the body that wrestles on the stage and dances in the orchestra of the tragic absolute. If in the end all these thinkers are abashed, if they discover that freedom's just another word for nothing left to lose, that divinity is either heavy metal or rust, that the god can enter on the scene only in and as the figure of death, and that to go over toward the overman is to go down and to languish, can we be certain that in any respect we have ventured as far as they did?

Appendix: Plot Summaries of *The Death of Empedocles*

First Draft

Persons

Empedocles
Pausanias, *his favorite*
Panthea, *a woman Empedocles has cured; daughter of the archon* Critias
Rhea (or Delia), *a visitor from Athens*
Hermocrates, *an old priest, enemy of Empedocles*
Critias, *archon of Agrigent*
A crowd of Agrigentian citizens
A farmer on the slopes of Etna

Act I. In the city of Agrigent (Acragas).

Act I, scene 1. Panthea and Delia (called Rhea in the ms. of the first draft up to the final scene of act I). Empedocles' intimacy with nature, especially the plant world, discussed. "The plants noticed when he passed." Empedocles' healing of Panthea; her devotion to him. Panthea's premonition of his impending suicide. Rhea (Delia) compares Panthea to Sophocles' Antigone.

I, 2. Panthea's father, the archon Critias, and Hermocrates, the elderly priest, plot against Empedocles. They declare the nature of Empedocles' *nefas*, or hubris: "Because he forgot the distinction [between gods and mortals] too much . . ."

I, 3. Empedocles' first soliloquy, his "prayer to nature," "Into my tranquillity you came . . ." (Note the antiphonal structure of strophe and antistrophe, the first affirmative in tone, the second negative.)

I, 4. Pausanias enters, interrupting Empedocles' antistrophe, puts in question Empedocles' plan to commit suicide, raises the specter of his hubris, of a possible *ressentiment* or melancholy in Empedocles' character.

I, 5. Enter Hermocrates, Critias, and a group of citizens of Agrigent. Banishment of Empedocles and Pausanias—the magus for his blasphemy and the disciple for his insolence toward the priest.

I, 6. As the others leave, Empedocles asks Critias to remain behind, urges him to take Panthea away to the sacred precincts of Elis or Delos. He reminds Critias that he has cured his daughter.

I, 7. Empedocles' second soliloquy, addressed to the absent archon, who has turned his back on him.

I, 8. Empedocles dismisses, that is, liberates his three household slaves.

I, 9. Panthea to Delia, concerning her father: "May he be accursed also of me!" Her curse reminds us of fragment B137 of Empedocles. The two women then resolve to return to Critias in order to seek a rescinding of the banishment.

Act II. On Etna, near farmers' cottages.

Act II, scene 1. Empedocles and Pausanias on the slopes of Etna, some miles from Agrigent, seeking lodging.

II, 2. A farmer refuses hospitality to the accursed ones.

II, 3. Empedocles and Pausanias at the spring. The transformation (*Verwandlung*) of Empedocles into the yes-sayer, followed by the possible slip back into ressentiment. "Soon I will be reconciled, I already am. . . . If it has to be, / I can always go to the gods in wrath." The continuing difficulty of determining the nature of his *nefas*.

II, 4. Empedocles and Pausanias are joined by Critias, Hermocrates, and the Agrigentian citizens. They offer him forgiveness, invite him to return to the city. (Presumably, Panthea and Delia have pleaded with Critias.) Empedocles scorns their offer, Pausanias delivers a bitter diatribe against Hermocrates—excoriating the role of the priest in the city. The citizens offer the crown to Empedocles. He declares that the time of kingship is past, that the minority of the people is at an end. (Note especially Empedocles' "broken" or incomplete speech, "*Von Herzen nennt man, Erde . . .* ," "From the heart one calls you, Earth. . . .")

II, 5. Empedocles and Pausanias. Pausanias's incomprehension of Empedocles' decision to persist in the plan of suicide ("Is there honor only in death?"), then his reluctant acceptance. Departure of Pausanias. Empedocles to the absent Pausanias, "Let my departure be one of gratitude. . . ."

II, 6. Empedocles' third soliloquy expresses doubts about his own motives: "Shuddering yearning! What! Is it death alone / That kindles life in me at the end?"

II, 7. Panthea and Delia, searching for Empedocles. Their gentle debate concerning his desire for death.

II, 8. Pausanias joins them. Delia casts doubt on the justification of the suicide, while Pausanias and Panthea try to defend it. Delia: "It only tears me apart . . ." (The first draft breaks off here.)

Second Draft

Persons

Empedocles
Pausanias
Panthea
Delia
Hermocrates
Mekades (formerly Critias)
Amphares, *citizen of Agrigent*
Demokles, *citizen of Agrigent*
Hylas, *citizen of Agrigent*

[Chorus of Agrigentian citizens]

Act I. The scene is partly in Agrigent, partly on Etna.

Act I, scene 1. Chorus of Agrigentian citizens in the distance; a dialogue between Mekades and Hermocrates on the people's infatuation with Empedocles. They accuse him of having made an "insolent speech" in the agora. They also accuse him of having betrayed divine secrets (an allusion to the oath of secrecy sworn by the Pythagorean Brotherhood). They discuss his mournful attitude and they plan his "sacrifice." In all of this, Mekades is more reluctant than the old priest, Hermocrates.

I, 2. Empedocles, alone: "Into my tranquillity . . ." (Note the alterations in the antistrophe.)

I, 3. Empedocles with Pausanias. Pausanias once again casts doubts concerning Empedocles' suicide, attributes the plan to his melancholy. Empedocles' prayer to sun, earth, and aether—the elements. Empedocles' presumably sarcastic account of his own Faustian subjectivity and willfulness: "Right! I know everything, I can master all." Empedocles ends his tirade by posing the desperate question, "Who am I?"

The conclusion of the *second* act is sketched: dialogue between Panthea and Delia. Delia again expresses her doubts: "Behold! The earth is splendid and hospitable. . . ."

(According to Beißner, Pausanias joins Panthea and Delia. Delia again criticizes the master: "You are all too happy, Empedocles, to sacrifice yourself. . . ." Panthea's reply invokes the nature of the hero, his superior power and genius. The gentle debate between them concludes with Panthea's lines, *"So will es der Geist / Und die reifende Zeit, / Denn Einmal bedurften / Wir Blinden des Wunders."* "Thus spirit wills it / And ripening time, / For, if it be but once, / We blind needed a miracle.")

THIRD DRAFT

Persons

Empedocles
Pausanias
Manes, *an Egyptian seer*
Strato, *an Agrigentian citizen, brother of* Empedocles
Panthea, *sister of* Empedocles
A crowd
Chorus of Agrigentians

Act I. Place unspecified, but clearly on the rim of the crater of Mount Etna.

Act I, scene 1. Empedocles, alone, wakes from sleep, celebrates his liberation from human cares. Song to Father Etna, who is perhaps the maternal Earth mediating between a feminine-gendered sun and a masculine-gendered aether (*Sonne/Aether*). Near the end of this song of departure, on the edge, Empedocles espies Pausanias.

I, 2. Pausanias enters, tells Empedocles that he has found for them a new dwelling place high on the mountain; Empedocles rejects the stirrings of his heart, tries to drive Pausanias away. Pausanias: "I do not know you anymore. . . ." Empedocles: "I am not the one who I am, Pausanias. . . ." Note especially the final speech of Empedocles in this scene, the speech of anachrony: "I should say many things, but I will keep them from you . . . ," in particular the closing words concerning "our brothers in Egypt."

I, 3. Manes and Empedocles. In the manuscript of the third draft, Manes is simply called *Der Greis*, "the old man," which is also what Hermocrates was called in the first version. Displacements of time and scene, confusion of identities between these Egyptian "brothers." The role of "Egyptianism" or "the Oriental" is much discussed in the secondary literature; on the role of Manes here and on Hermocrates (and perhaps also Critias) in the first and second drafts, see especially Plato's *Timaeus*, 21b–26a. Note the final speech of delay by Empedocles: "I shall not go yet, old man!" Ultimate confusion concerning Empedocles' calling and his very identity.

Bibliography

Aberbach, Davis. *Surviving Trauma: Loss, Literature and Psychoanalysis.* New Haven: Yale University Press, 1989.

Aeschylus. *Tragödien.* 5th ed. Ed. Bernhard Zimmermann, tr. Oskar Werner. Zürich: Artemis and Winkler, 1995.

Arendt, Hannah. "Thinking and Moral Considerations." *Social Research* 38, no. 3 (Autumn 1971): 7–37.

Aristotle. *De arte poetica liber.* Oxford Classical Text. Ed. Rudolf Kassel. Oxford: Oxford University Press, 1965. English translation by Richard Janko. Indianapolis: Hackett Publishing, 1987. See also the translation by Ingram Bywater. In *The Basic Works of Aristotle,* ed. Richard McKeon, 1455–1487. New York: Random House, 1966. French translation by Michel Magnien. *Poétique.* Paris: Livre de Poche, n.d.

———. *Eudemian Ethics.* Tr. J. Solomon. In *The Complete Works of Aristotle: The Revised Oxford Translation,* 2 vols., ed. Jonathan Barnes, vol. 2, 1922–1981. Bollingen Series. Princeton, N.J.: Princeton University Press, 1984.

Arnim, Bettina Brentano von. *Die Günderode.* Frankfurt am Main: Insel, 1983.

Arrowsmith, William. Introduction to Euripides' *The Bacchae.* In *Euripides V,* 142–153. Chicago: University of Chicago Press, 1968.

Barthes, Roland. *A Lover's Discourse: Fragments.* Tr. Richard Howard. New York: Hill and Wang, 1978.

Beck, Adolf, ed. *Hölderlin: Chronik seins Lebens.* Frankfurt am Main: Insel Verlag, 1975.

Benjamin, Walter. "Die Aufgabe des Übersetzers." In *Illuminationen: Ausgewählte Schriften,* 50–62. Frankfurt am Main: Suhrkamp, 1977. English translation, "The Task of the Translator (1921)." In *Selected Writings, 1913–1926,* ed. Marcus Bullock and Michael W. Jennings. Cambridge, Mass.: Harvard University Press, 1996.

Bernays, Jacob. *Grundzüge der verlorenen Abhandlung des Aristoteles über die Wirkung der Tragödie.* Ed. with introduction by Karlfried Gründer. Hildesheim: Georg Olms Verlag, 1970 (orig. publ. 1857).

Bertaux, Pierre. *Friedrich Hölderlin: Eine Biographie.* Frankfurt am Main: Insel Verlag, 2000.

Blanchot, Maurice. *L'Espace littéraire.* Paris: Gallimard, 1955.

Böschenstein, Bernhard. *"Frucht des Gewitters": Zu Hölderlins Dionysos als Gott der Revolution.* Frankfurt am Main: Insel Verlag, 1989.

Burkert, Walter. *Greek Religion.* Tr. John Raffan. Cambridge, Mass.: Harvard University Press, 1985.

Bibliography

Butler, Judith. *Antigone's Claim: Kinship between Life and Death.* New York: Columbia University Press, 2000.

Calasso, Roberto. *The Marriage of Cadmus and Harmony.* Tr. Tim Parks. New York: Alfred A. Knopf, Borzoi Books, 1993.

Caruth, Cathy, ed. *Trauma: Explorations in Memory.* Baltimore: Johns Hopkins University Press, 1995.

Clark, David L. "The Necessary Heritage of Darkness: Tropics of Negativity in Schelling, Derrida, and de Man." In *Intersections: Nineteenth-Century Philosophy and Contemporary Theory.* Ed. Tilottama Rajan and David L. Clark, 79–146. Albany: State University Press of New York, 1995.

Clissold, Anna Vaughn. "Schelling's Commentary on Plato's *Timaeus.*" Ph.D. dissertation, DePaul University, 1998.

Coble, Don Kelly. "Inscrutable Intelligibility: Intelligible Character and Deed in Kant, Schelling, Mach, and Musil." Ph.D. dissertation, DePaul University, 1999.

Dastur, Françoise. *Hölderlin: Le retournement natal.* La Versanne, France: Encre marine, 1997. The volume contains "Tragedy and Modernity" and "Nature and Poesy."

Derrida, Jacques. *De l'esprit: Heidegger et la question.* Paris: Galilée, 1987. English translation by Geoffrey Bennington and Rachel Bowlby. *Of Spirit: Heidegger and the Question.* Chicago: University of Chicago Press, 1989.

———. *Glas.* Paris: Galilée, 1974. Tr. John P. Leavey, Jr., and Richard Rand. Lincoln: University of Nebraska Press, 1986.

———. *De la grammatologie.* Paris: Minuit, 1967. English translation by Gayatri Chakravorty Spivak. *Of Grammatology.* Baltimore: Johns Hopkins University Press, 1976.

———. *Khôra.* Paris: Galilée, 1993.

———. "Ousia and Gramme." In *Marges—De la philosophie.* Paris: Minuit, 1972. English translation by Alan Bass. *Margins of Philosophy.* Chicago: University of Chicago Press, 1982.

Descartes, René. *Œuvres et Lettres.* Ed. André Bridoux. Paris: Gallimard/Pléiade, 1953.

Diels, Hermann, and Walther Kranz. *Die Fragmente der Vorsokratiker.* 3 vols. 6th ed. Zürich: Weidmann, 1951.

Euripides. *Ausgewählte Tragödien.* 2 vols. Ed. Bernhard Zimmermann. Tr. Ernst Buschor. Zürich: Artemis and Winkler, 1996.

Ferenczi, Sandor. *Schriften zur Psychoanalyse.* 2 vols. Ed. Thure von Uexküll and Ilse Grubrich-Simitis. Frankfurt am Main: S. Fischer Verlag, 1982.

———. *Thalassa: A Theory of Genitality.* Tr. Henry Alden Bunker. New York: W. W. Norton, 1968.

Ficino, Marsiglio. *Platonis philosophia etc.* Zweibrücken: Studiis Societatis Bipontinae, 1786.

Freud, Sigmund. *Studienausgabe.* 12 vols. Ed. Alexander Mitscherlich, Angela Richards, and James Strachey. Frankfurt am Main: S. Fischer Verlag, 1982.

García Márquez, Gabriel. *Cien años de soledad.* Buenos Aires: Editorial Sudamericana, 1967. English translation by Gregory Rabassa. *One Hundred Years of Solitude.* New York: Harper and Row; London: Jonathan Cape, 1970.

Gawoll, Hans-Jürgen. "Die Kontroverse um das sogenannte 'älteste Systemprogramm des deutschen Idealismus': Ein Forschungsbericht." *Info Philo* 1 (1996): 46–51.

Goethe, Johann Wolfgang von. *Die Leiden des jungen Werther.* Frankfurt am Main: Insel, 1997 (originally published in 1774).

————. *Naturwissenschaftliche Schriften.* 5 vols. Ed. Rudolf Steiner. Dornach, Switzerland: R. Steiner Verlag, 1982.

Graves, Robert. *The Greek Myths.* 2 vols. Baltimore: Penguin Books, 1955.

Guthrie, W. K. C. *The Greeks and Their Gods.* London: Methuen, 1968.

Guyomard, Patrick. *La jouissance du tragique: Antigone, Lacan et le désir de l'analyste.* Paris: Aubier, 1992.

Harris, H. S. *Hegel's Development: Toward the Sunlight, 1770–1801.* Oxford: Oxford University Press, 1972.

Harrison, Jane Ellen. *Prolegomena to the Study of Greek Religion.* Cleveland: Meridian Books, 1966.

Hegel, Georg Wilhelm Friedrich. *Briefe von und an Hegel.* Ed. Johannes Hoffmeister. Hamburg: Felix Meiner Verlag, 1952–1960.

————. *Gesammelte Werke.* Vol. 8: Jena *Realphilosophie* (1805–1806). Ed. Rolf-Peter Horstmann. Hamburg: F. Meiner Verlag, 1987.

————. *Phänomenologie des Geistes.* Ed. Johannes Hoffmeister. 6th ed. Hamburg: Felix Meiner Verlag, 1952.

————. *Werke in zwanzig Bänden.* Theorie Werkausgabe. Ed. Eva Moldenhauer and Karl Markus Michel. Frankfurt am Main: Suhrkamp, 1970ff.

Heidegger, Martin. *Beiträge zur Philosophie: Vom Ereignis.* Gesamtausgabe vol. 65. Frankfurt am Main: V. Klostermann, 1989.

————. *Early Greek Thinking.* 2nd ed. San Francisco: HarperCollins, 1984.

————. *Einführung in die Metaphysik.* Tübingen: M. Niemeyer, 1953.

————. *Die Grundbegriffe der Metaphysik: Welt—Endlichkeit—Einsamkeit.* Gesamtausgabe vol. 29/30. Frankfurt am Main: V. Klostermann, 1983. English translation by William McNeill and Nick Walker. *The Fundamental Concepts of Metaphysics: World, Finitude, Solitude.* Bloomington: Indiana University Press, 1995.

————. *Holzwege.* Frankfurt am Main: V. Klostermann, 1950.

————. *Nietzsche.* 2 vols. Pfullingen: G. Neske, 1961. English translation, *Nietzsche,* 4 vols. San Francisco: HarperCollins, 1991.

————. *Schellings Abhandlung über das Wesen der menschlichen Freiheit (1809).* Tübingen: M. Niemeyer, 1971.

————. *Sein und Zeit.* 12th ed. Tübingen: Max Niemeyer, 1972.

————. "Der Spruch des Anaximander." In *Holzwege.* Frankfurt am Main: Vittorio Klostermann, 1950. English translation, "The Anaximander Fragment." In Heidegger, *Early Greek Thinking,* 2nd ed. San Francisco: HarperCollins, 1984.

Heidegger, Martin, and Eugen Fink. *Heraklit.* Frankfurt am Main: V. Klostermann, 1970.

Heimsoeth, Heinz. *Die sechs grossen Themen der abendländischen Metaphysik.* 5th ed. Darmstadt: Wissenschaftliche Buchgesellschaft, 1965.

Hemingway, Ernest. *The First Forty-Nine Short Stories.* London: Jonathan Cape, 1972.

Hermand, Jost, and Michael Gilbert, eds. *German Essays on Music.* German Library. New York: Continuum, 1994.

Herodotus. *The Histories.* Tr. Aubrey de Sélincourt, rev. A. R. Burn. Harmondsworth: Penguin, 1972. See also the Loeb Classical Library edition, tr. A. D. Godley. London: Heinemann, 1928.

Hölderlin, Friedrich. *Essays and Letters on Theory.* Ed. and tr. Thomas Pfau. Albany: State University of New York Press, 1988.

―――. *Friedrich Hölderlin Sämtliche Werke*. Ed. D. E. Sattler. Basel: Stroemfeld and Roter Stern, 1988.

―――. *Friedrich Hölderlin Sämtliche Werke und Briefe*. Ed. Michael Knaupp. Munich: Carl Hanser Verlag, 1992.

―――. *Friedrich Hölderlin Sämtliche Werke und Briefe in drei Bänden*. Ed. Jochen Schmidt. Frankfurt am Main: Deutscher Klassiker Verlag, 1994.

―――. *Hölderlin Sämtliche Werke*. Ed. Friedrich Beissner. Stuttgart: Verlag W. Kohlhammer, 1952.

―――. *Hölderlin Werke und Briefe*. Ed. Friedrich Beißner and Jochen Schmidt. Frankfurt am Main: Insel Verlag, 1969.

―――. *Hölderlin's Sophocles: Oedipus and Antigone*. Tr. David Constantine. Tarset, Northumberland: Bloodaxe Books, 2001.

Hühn, Lore. "Das Schweben der Einbildungskraft: Zur Frühromantischen Überbietung Fichtes." *Deutsche Vierteljahrsschrift für Literaturwissenschaft und Geistesgeschichte* 70, no. 4 (Dec. 1996): 569–599.

Husserl, Edmund. *Analysen zur passiven Synthesis*. Husserliana 11. Ed. Margot Fleischer from lecture and research manuscripts dating from 1918 to 1926. The Hague: M. Nijhoff, 1966.

Irigaray, Luce. *L'Oubli de l'air chez Martin Heidegger*. Paris: Minuit, 1983. English translation by Mary Beth Mader. *The Forgetting of Air in Martin Heidegger*. Austin: University of Texas Press, 1999.

Jacobs, Carol. "Dusting Antigone." *Modern Language Notes* 111 (1996): 889–917.

―――. *In the Language of Walter Benjamin*. Baltimore: Johns Hopkins University Press, 1999.

Jamme, Christoph, and Anja Lemke, eds. *"Es bleibt aber eine Spur / Doch eines Wortes": Zur späten Hymnik und Tragödientheorie Friedrich Hölderlins*. Paderborn: Wilhelm Fink Verlag, 2004.

Jamme, Christoph, and Helmut Schneider, eds. *Mythologie der Vernunft: Hegels "Ältestes Systemprogramm" des deutschen Idealismus*. Frankfurt am Main: Suhrkamp, 1984.

Jamme, Christoph, and Frank Völkel, eds. *Hölderlin und der Deutsche Idealismus: Dokumente und Kommentare zu Hölderlins philosophischer Entwicklung und den philosophisch-kulturellen Kontexten seiner Zeit*. 4 vols. Stuttgart: Frommann-Holzboog Verlag, 2003. Vol. 1: *Im Tübinger Stift (1788–1793)*. Vol. 2: *Jenaer Gespräche (1794–1795)*. Vol. 3: *In dem "prosaischen Frankfurt" / Der Homburger Kreis (1796–1800)*. Vol. 4: *Von Stuttgart über wechselnde Orte wieder nach Homburg (1800–1806)*.

Joyce, James. *Ulysses*. London: Bodley Head, 1969.

Kant, Immanuel. *Kritik der praktischen Vernunft*. Ed. Joachim Kopper. Stuttgart: Reclam Verlag, 1966.

―――. *Kritik der reinen Vernunft*. Ed. Raymund Schmidt. Hamburg: Meiner Verlag, 1956.

―――. *Kritik der Urteilskraft*. Ed. Gerhard Lehmann. Stuttgart: Reclam Verlag, 1966.

Kenney, Douglas F., and Sabine Menner-Bettscheid, trs. and eds. *The Recalcitrant Art: Diotima's Letters to Hölderlin and Related Missives*. Albany: State University of New York Press, 2000.

Kirk, G. S., and J. E. Raven. *The Presocratic Philosophers: A Critical History with a Selection of Texts*. Cambridge: Cambridge University Press, 1966.

Kleist, Heinrich von. *Kleists Werke in einem Band*. Ed. Gerhard Stenzel. Salzburg: Bergland Klassiker Verlag, n.d.

Kolk, Bessel A. Van der, A. C. McFarlane, and L. Weisaeth, eds. *Traumatic Stress: The Effects of Overwhelming Experience on Mind, Body, and Society*. New York: Guilford Press, 1996.

Kommerell, Max. *Geist und Buchstabe der Dichtung: Goethe, Schiller, Kleist, Hölderlin*. 6th ed. Frankfurt am Main: V. Klostermann, 1991 (orig. publ. 1940).

———. *Lessing und Aristoteles: Untersuchung über die Theorie der Tragödie*. 5th ed. Frankfurt am Main: V. Klostermann, 1984.

Krell, D. F. *Archeticture: Ecstasies of Space, Time, and the Human Body*. Albany: State University of New York Press, 1997.

———. "The Bodies of Black Folk: From Kant and Hegel to Du Bois and Baldwin." *boundary 2: an international journal of literature and culture* 27, no. 3 (Fall 2000): 103–134.

———. *Contagion: Sexuality, Disease, and Death in German Idealism and Romanticism*. Bloomington: Indiana University Press, 1998.

———. *Daimon Life: Heidegger and Life-Philosophy*. Bloomington: Indiana University Press, 1992.

———. "Female Parts in *Timaeus*." *Arion: A Journal of Humanities and the Classics*, nos. 2, 3 (Fall 1975): 400–421.

———. "Καλυψώ: Homeric Concealments after Nietzsche, Heidegger, Derrida, and Lacan." In *The Presocratics after Heidegger*, ed. David C. Jacobs, 101–134. Albany: State University of New York Press, 1999.

———. *Lunar Voices: Of Tragedy, Poetry, Fiction, and Thought*. Chicago: University of Chicago Press, 1995.

———. "National Erotism (Derdiedas Responsibilities)." In *Ethics and Responsibility in the Phenomenological Tradition*, ed. Richard Rojcewicz. Pittsburgh: Duquesne University Press, 1992.

———. *Of Memory, Reminiscence, and Writing: On the Verge*. Bloomington: Indiana University Press, 1990.

———. *Postponements: Woman, Sensuality, and Death in Nietzsche*. Bloomington: Indiana University Press, 1986.

———. *The Purest of Bastards: Works of Mourning, Art, and Affirmation in the Thought of Jacques Derrida*. University Park: Pennsylvania State University Press, 2000.

Kristeva, Julia. *Black Sun: Depression and Melancholia*. Tr. Leon S. Roudiez. New York: Columbia University Press, 1989.

Lacan, Jacques. *Écrits*. Paris: Gallimard, 1966.

———. *Le Séminaire, livre VII: L'éthique de la psychanalyse, 1959–1960*. Ed. Jacques-Alain Miller. Paris: du Seuil, 1986. English translation with notes by Dennis Potter. *The Seminar of Jacques Lacan*, Book 7: *The Ethics of Psychoanalysis, 1959–1960*. New York: W. W. Norton, 1992.

Lacan, Jacques, and the École Fruedienne. *Feminine Sexuality*. Ed. Juliet Mitchell and Jacqueline Rose. London: Macmillan, 1982.

Lacoue-Labarthe, Philippe. "La césure du spéculatif." In *L'imitation des modernes: Typographies II*, 39–84. Paris: Galilée, 1986.

———. "The Echo of the Subject." In *Le Sujet de la philosophie: Typographies I*, 217–303. Paris: Aubier-Flammarion, 1979.

———. *Métaphrasis*. Paris: Presses Universitaires de France, 1998.

Lacoue-Labarthe, Philippe, and Jean-Luc Nancy. *L'Absolu littéraire: Théorie de la littérature du romantisme allemand*. Paris: Seuil, 1978.

Laertius, Diogenes. *Lives of Eminent Philosophers*. 2 vols. Tr. R. D. Hicks. Loeb Classical Library. Cambridge, Mass.: Harvard University Press, 1972.

Lambek, Michael, and Paul Antze. "Introduction: Forecasting Memory." In Antze and Lambek, eds., *Tense Past: Cultural Essays in Trauma and Memory*. New York: Routledge, 1996.

Langer, Lawrence L. *Holocaust Testimonies: The Ruins of Memory*. New Haven: Yale University Press, 1991.

Laplanche, Jean. *Hölderlin et la question du père*. Paris: Presses Universitaires de France, 1961.

Le Goff, Jacques. *History and Memory*. Tr. S. Rendall and E. Claman. New York: Columbia University Press, 1992.

Libeskind, Daniel. "Between the Lines: The Addition of a Jewish Museum to the Berlin Museum." *Archithese* 19 (Sept.–Oct. 1989): 62–67.

Loraux, Nicole. *Tragic Ways of Killing a Woman*. Tr. Anthony Forster. Cambridge, Mass.: Harvard University Press, 1987.

Lossau, Manfred. "Hölderlins Sophokleschöre." *Hölderlin Jahrbuch* (1996–1997): 255–265.

Löwith, Karl. *Nietzsches Philosophie der ewigen Wiederkehr*. 4th ed. Hamburg: F. Meiner Verlag, 1986 (orig. publ. 1935).

Lucretius. *De rerum natura*. Tr. W. H. D. Rouse, rev. M. F. Smith. Loeb Classical Library. Cambridge, Mass.: Harvard University Press, 1992.

Luther, Martin. *Die gantze Heilige Schrift*. 3 vols. Ed. Hans Volz, Heinz Blanke, and Friedrich Kur. Munich: Deutscher Taschenbuch Verlag, 1974.

Melville, Herman. *Moby-Dick; or, The Whale*. Ed. Alfred Kazin. Boston: Houghton Mifflin, 1956 (1851).

———. *Selected Writings*. New York: Random House/Modern Library, 1952.

Merleau-Ponty, Maurice. *La nature*. Tr. Robert Vallier. Evanston, Ill.: Northwestern University Press, 2003.

Meyer, Johann Heinrich. "Niobe mit ihren Kindern." *Propyläen* 2, no. 1 (1799): 48–91. The journal has been photomechanically reproduced by the Cotta Verlag (Stuttgart, 1965) and by the Wissenschaftliche Buchgesellschaft (Darmstadt, 1965).

———. "Raffaels Werke besonders im Vatikan." *Propyläen* 1, no. 1: 101–127; 1, no. 2: 82–163; and 3, no. 2: 75–96. The journal has been photomechanically reproduced by the Cotta Verlag (Stuttgart, 1965) and by the Wissenschaftliche Buchgesellschaft (Darmstadt, 1965).

Miles, Kevin Thomas. "Razing Ethical Stakes: Tragic Transgression in Aristotle's Equitable Action." Ph.D. dissertation, DePaul University, 1998.

Nietzsche, Friedrich. "Brief an meinen Freund, in dem ich ihm meinen Lieblingsdichter zum Lesen empfehle." In *Jugendschriften 1861–1864*, ed. Hans Joachim Mette, 1–5. Munich: Deutscher Taschenbuch Verlag, 1994 (first published by C. H. Beck Verlag, 1933–1940).

———. "Introductory Lectures on Sophocles' *Oedipus Rex*." *Kritische Gesamtausgabe der Werke, zweite Abteilung, Philologica*. 5 vols. Ed. Fritz Bornmann and Mario Carpitella, II/3:1–57. Berlin: Walter de Gruyter, 1993.

———. *Kritische Studienausgabe der Briefe*. 8 vols. Ed. Giorgio Colli and Mazzino Montinari. Berlin: Walter de Gruyter and Deutscher Taschenbuch Verlag, 1986.

———. *Kritische Studienausgabe der Werke*. 15 vols. Ed. Giorgio Colli and Mazzino Montinari. Berlin: Walter de Gruyter, 1980.

Novalis (Friedrich von Hardenberg). *Schriften*. 5 vols. Ed. Richard Samuel et al., rev. Richard Samuel and Hans-Joachim Mähl. Stuttgart: Kohlhammer Verlag, 1981. For the theoretical work, see vols. 2–3.

————. *Werke, Tagebücher und Briefe*. 3 vols. Ed. Hans-Joachim Mähl and Richard Samuel. Munich: Carl Hanser Verlag, 1987. Vol. 2 contains *Das philosophisch-theoretische Werk*.

Nussbaum, Martha. *The Fragility of Goodness: Luck and Ethics in Greek Tragedy and Philosophy*. New York: Cambridge University Press, 1986.

Orff, Carl. *Carmina Burana*. Bayerische Staatsoper, directed by Georg Solti. Orfeo C 407 952 I.

Pasolini, Pier Paolo. *Oedipus Rex*. Tr. John Mathews. London: Lorrimer Publishing, 1971.

Paul, Hermann. *Deutsches Wörterbuch*. 6th ed. Ed. Werner Betz. Tübingen: M. Niemeyer, 1966.

Pausanias. *Guide to Greece*. 2 vols. Tr. Peter Levi, S.J. Harmondsworth: Penguin Books, 1971.

Petzet, Heinrich Wiegand. *Auf einen Stern zugehen: Begegnungen mit Martin Heidegger 1929 bis 1976*. Frankfurt am Main: Societäts-Verlag, 1983.

Plato. *Opera*. 4 vols. Ed. John Burnet. Oxford Classical Texts. Oxford: Clarendon Press, 1900. See also *Sämtliche Werke in zehn Bänden*, ed. Karlheinz Hülser. Greek and German text (Les Belles Lettres and Friedrich Schleiermacher, respectively). Frankfurt am Main: Insel Verlag, 1991. For *Timaeus* and *Critias*, see also vol. 10 of the *Oeuvres complètes*, ed. Albert Rivaud. Paris: Édition "Les Belles Lettres," 1985. For the Schleiermacher translation without the Greek text, see the Rowohlt Klassiker edition of Plato's *Werke*. Hamburg: Rowohlt Verlag, 1959.

Reinhardt, Karl. "Hölderlin und Sophokles." In *Tradition und Geist: Gesammelte Essays zur Dichtung*, ed. Carl Becker. Göttingen: Vandenhoek and Ruprecht, 1960.

————. *Sophocles*. Oxford: Basil Blackwell, 1979.

Rilke, Rainer Maria. *Werke in drei Bänden*. Frankfurt am Main: Insel Verlag, 1966.

Rosenkranz, Karl. *Georg Wilhelm Friedrich Hegels Leben*. Darmstadt: Wissenschaftliche Buchgesellschaft, 1963 (orig. publ. in Berlin, 1844).

Sade, D. A. F. *Les cent vingt journées de Sodome*. Vol. 1 of *Oeuvres complètes du Marquis de Sade*, 15 vols., ed. Annie Le Brun and Jean-Jacques Pauvert. Paris: Pauvert, 1986.

Sallis, John. *Chorology: On Plato's Timaeus*. Bloomington: Indiana University Press, 2000.

————. *Crossings: Nietzsche and the Space of Tragedy*. Chicago: University of Chicago Press, 1991.

————. *On Translation*. Bloomington: Indiana University Press, 2002.

Sallis, John, and Kenneth Maly, eds. *Heraclitean Fragments*. University: University of Alabama Press, 1980.

Sartre, Jean-Paul. *L'Etre et le néant*. Paris: Gallimard, 1943. English translation by Hazel Barnes. *Being and Nothingness*. New York: Philosophical Library, 1956.

Schadewalt, Wolfgang. "Das Bild der exzentrischen Bahn bei Hölderlin." *Hölderlin-Jahrbuch* (1952): 1–16.

Schelling, Friedrich Wilhelm Joseph von. *Antiquissimi de prima malorum humanorum origine philosophematis Genes. III explicandi tentamen criticum et philosophicum* [A critical and philosophical explication of the oldest philosopheme of the third book of Genesis concerning the first origin of human evil] (1792). In *Werke 1*, ed. Wilhelm G. Jacobs, Jörg Jantzen, Walter Schieche, et al., 1:47–181. Stuttgart: Frommann-Holzboog, 1976.

————. *Ausgewählte Schriften*. 6 vols. Ed. Manfred Frank. Frankfurt am Main: Suhrkamp, 1985.

————. *Die Weltalter Fragmente: In den Urfassungen von 1811 und 1813*. Ed. Manfred Schröter. Nachlaßband to the Münchner Jubiläumsdruck. Munich: Biederstein Verlag and Leibniz Verlag, 1946.

————. *Erster Entwurf eines Systems der Naturphilosophie.* Jena: Gabler Verlag, 1799. [Vol. 3 of the *Sämmtlich Werke.* See below.] Reprinted in *Schriften von 1799–1801*, 1–268. Darmstadt: Wissenschaftliche Buchgesellschaft, 1975. The new historical-critical edition of Schelling's works headed by Hartmut Buchner is now under way, and the *Erster Entwurf* has recently appeared there. See now the *Erster Entwurf,* in the *Historisch-Kritische Ausgabe, Werke 7,* ed. Wilhelm G. Jacobs and Paul Ziche. Stuttgart: Frommann-Holzboog, 2001.

————. *Ideen zu einer Philosophie der Natur als Einleitung in das Studium dieser Wissenschaft* (1797). In *Schriften von 1794–1798*, 333–397 (introductions only). English translation of the entire work by Errol E. Harris and Peter Heath. *Ideas for a Philosophy of Nature.* Cambridge: Cambridge University Press, 1988.

————. *Sämmtliche Werke.* Ed. Karl Schelling. Stuttgart: J. G. Cotta'scher Verlag, 1859. In Division I, vol. 1 contains *Philosophische Briefe über Dogmatismus und Kriticismus.* (See now *Werke 3* of the *Historisch-Kritische Ausgabe,* ed. Hartmut Büchner, Wilhelm G. Jacobs, and Annemarie Pieper, esp. 106–112. Stuttgart: Frommann-Holzboog, 1982.) Vol. 3 contains *Erster Entwurf eines Systems der Naturphilosophie.* Vol. 5 contains *Philosophie der Kunst.* Vol. 7 contains *Abhandlung über das Wesen der menschlichen Freiheit und die damit zusammenhängenden Gegenstände* (1809), along with the *Stuttgarter Privatvorlesungen* (1810). See also the edition of the *Abhandlung* by Horst Fuhrmans. Stuttgart: Philipp Reclam Verlag, 1964. Vol. 8 contains *Die Weltalter, Erstes Buch* (1815 version). An English translation of the 1815 *Weltalter* by Jason M. Wirth appears under the title *The Ages of the World* (Albany: State University of New York Press, 2000). Vol. 8 of the *Sämmtliche Werke* also contains "Über die Gottheiten von Samothrake" (1815). In Division II, vol. 1 contains *Einleitung in die Philosophie der Mythologie* (1842). Vol. 2 contains *Philosophie der Mythologie* (1842). Vol. 3 contains *Einleitung in die Philosophie der Offenbarung; oder Begründung der positiven Philosophie* (the Berlin lectures, Winter Semester 1842–1843).

————. *System der Weltalter: Münchener Vorlesung 1827/28 in einer Nachschrift von Ernst von Lasaulx,* ed. Siegbert Peetz. Frankfurt am Main: Vittorio Klostermann, 1990. A late formulation of Schelling's never-completed, never-published magnum opus.

————. *System des transzendentalen Idealismus.* Philosophische Bibliothek Band 254. Hamburg: Felix Meiner, 1957.

————. *"Timaeus" (1794).* Ed. Hartmut Buchner. Stuttgart-Bad Cannstadt: Frommann-Holzboog, 1994.

————. *Über Mythen, historische Sagen und Philosopheme der ältesten Welt* (1794). In *Werke 1,* ed. Wilhelm G. Jacobs, Jörg Jantzen, Walter Schieche, et al., 1:195–246. Stuttgart: Frommann-Holzboog, 1976.

————. *Von der Weltseele: Eine Hypothese der höheren Physik zur Erklärung des allgemeinen Organismus* (1798). In *Schriften von 1794–1798*, 399–637. Darmstadt: Wissenschaftliche Buchgesellschaft, 1980.

Schiller, Friedrich. *Kallias oder über die Schönheit.* Ed. Klaus L. Berghahn. Stuttgart: Reclam, 1971.

————. "On the Use of the Chorus in Tragedy." Introduction to *The Bride of Messina.* In *Werke,* 2 vols., ed. Paul Stapf, Tempel-Klassiker, 1:1039–1047. Munich: Emil Vollmer Verlag, n.d.

Schmidt, Dennis. *On Germans and Other Greeks: Tragedy and Ethical Life.* Bloomington: Indiana University Press, 2001.

Schulz, Walter. Introduction to F. W. J. Schelling, *System des transzendentalen Idealismus*, Philosophische Bibliothek Band 254. Hamburg: Felix Meiner, 1957.

Sikes, Elizabeth. "The Enigmatic Burden of Metaphor in Hölderlin's Poetics of Tragedy." In *"Es bleibt aber eine Spur / Doch eines Wortes": Zur späten Hymnik und Tragödientheorie Friedrich Hölderlins*, ed. Christoph Jamme and Anja Lemke, 379–399. Paderborn: Wilhelm Fink Verlag, 2004.

———. "Translation of Κάθαρσις, Κάθαρσις as Translation: The Post-Kantian Revolution of the Tragic in Hölderlin and Nietzsche." Ph.D. dissertation, DePaul University, forthcoming in 2005.

Simmel, Georg. *Lebensanschauung: Vier metaphysische Kapitel*. Munich: Duncker und Humblot, 1918.

Singer, Charles. *A Short History of Anatomy and Physiology from the Greeks to Harvey*. New York: Dover, 1957.

Smerick, Christina M. "Between the Garden and the Gathering: The Intertwining of Philosophy with Theology in Walter Benjamin." Ph.D. dissertation, DePaul University, 2003.

Sophocles. *Sophocles*. Tr. F. Storr. 2 vols. Loeb Classical Library. Cambridge, Mass., and London: Harvard University Press and William Heinemann, 1981.

———. *Sophocles I: Oedipus the King, Oedipus at Colonus, Antigone*. In *The Complete Greek Tragedies*, ed. David Grene and Richmond Lattimore. Chicago: University of Chicago Press, 1991.

———. *Sophoclis Fabulae*. Ed. H. Lloyd-Jones and N. G. Wilson. Oxford Classical Texts. Oxford: Oxford University Press, 1990.

———. *Sophokles Dramen: Griechisch und Deutsch*. Ed. Bernhard Zimmermann. Tr. Wilhelm Willige and Karl Bayer. 4th ed. Düsseldorf: Artemis and Winkler, 2003.

Szondi, Peter. *Versuch über das Tragische*. In *Schriften I*, ed. Jean Bollack et al., 149–260. Frankfurt am Main: Suhrkamp Verlag, 1978.

Taminiaux, Jacques. *Le théâtre des philosophes*. Grenoble: Jérôme Millon, 1995.

Thoreau, Henry David. *Walden*. Variorum ed. Ed. William Harding. New York: Washington Square Press, 1968.

Trakl, Georg. *Dichtungen und Briefe*. 3rd ed. Ed. Walther Killy and Hans Szklenar. Salzburg: Otto Müller Verlag, 1974.

Vallier, Robert. "Institution: Nature, Life, and Meaning in Merleau-Ponty." Ph.D. dissertation, DePaul University, 2001.

Vernant, Jean-Pierre, and Pierre Vidal-Naquet. *Myth and Tragedy in Ancient Greece*. Tr. Janet Lloyd. New York: Zone Books, 1990.

Vidal-Naquet, Pierre. *Assassins of Memory: Essays on the Denial of the Holocaust*. Tr. Jeffrey Mehlman. New York: Columbia University Press, 1992.

Wahrig, Gerhard. *Deutsches Wörterbuch*. Gütersloh: Bertelsmann Lexikon-Verlag, 1975.

Waiblinger, Wilhelm. *Friedrich Hölderlins Leben, Dichtung und Wahnsinn*. Ed. Adolf Beck. Marbach am Neckar: Schiller-Nationalmuseum, Turmhahn-Bücherei 8/9, 1951.

Wake, Peter. "Tragedy, Speculation, and Ethicality in German Idealism." Ph.D. dissertation, DePaul University, 2004.

Wallen, Martin. *City of Health, Fields of Disease: Revolutions in the Poetry, Medicine, and Philosophy of Romanticism*. Aldershot, Hampshire, England: Ashgate, 2004.

White, Alan. *Schelling: An Introduction to the System of Freedom*. New Haven: Yale University Press, 1983.

Whitman, Walt. *Leaves of Grass*. Ed. Sculley Bradley and Harold W. Blodgett. New York: Norton, 1973.

Winckelmann, J. J. *Gedanken über die Nachahmung der griechischen Werke in der Malerei und Bildhauerkunst*. Ed. Ludwig Uhlig. Stuttgart: Reclam, 1995 (orig. publ. 1755; 2nd, exp. ed., 1756).

Wirth, Jason M. *The Conspiracy of.Life: Meditations on Schelling and His Time*. Albany: State University of New York Press, 2003.

———, ed. *Schelling Now: Contemporary Readings of Schelling*. Bloomington: Indiana University Press, 2004.

Yeats, William Butler. *The Collected Poems of W. B. Yeats*. New York: Macmillan, 1956.

———. *A Vision*. New York: Collier Books, 1966.

Young, James E. *The Texture of Memory: Holocaust Memorials and Meaning*. New Haven: Yale University Press, 1993.

Žižek, Slavoj. *The Indivisible Remainder: An Essay on Schelling and Related Matters*. London: Verso, 1996.

INDEX

the absolute
  ego, 26, 28, 60–61, 63, 218, 222, 300
  freedom, 22; 24, 26–28, 31, 40–41, 43,
    48, 61, 63, 119, 183, 187–88
  knowing, 36, 40, 43, 46, 67, 426
  the metaphysical absolute, 1–2, 17, 53
  music, 208, 393, 409–25
  past, 106–107, 118, 120, 130–35, 174
  the tragic absolute, 1–17, 21, 41–44, 70,
    183, 190, 199, 248, 274, 312, 377,
    379, 386, 405, 419, 421, 425–32
abyss, 12, 100, 125, 128, 130, 226, 273,
    374, 404, 424–25. See also der Un-
    grund
accident, τὸσυμβεβεκός, 7, 30, 62, 64,
    116, 161, 210, 219, 222–28, 232,
    235–40, 248, 284–85, 290–91, 296,
    343, 377. See also contingency
Achilles, 54, 167, 254, 259
action, activity, δρᾶν, 4, 12–13, 21, 27, 35,
    48–51, 58, 60–63, 66, 81, 85, 87–88,
    121–22, 128, 132–33, 183–84, 190,
    198, 217, 219, 221, 223, 242, 252,
    277, 280–81, 284–86, 289, 291, 294,
    299, 304, 309, 315, 318, 325, 339,
    342, 354, 360, 370, 377, 381,
    386–88, 395, 414, 416, 418
actuality, 53–54, 76, 80, 99, 104, 113, 119,
    134, 143, 201, 302, 310, 315, 329,
    406. See also the real
Aeschylus, 11, 13, 15, 56, 102, 120, 134,
    142, 165, 174, 184, 186, 193, 203,
    215–16, 218, 231, 238, 251–52,
    254, 275, 279, 280, 282, 284, 289,
    298, 302, 314, 325, 327, 337, 340,
    344, 362–63, 367, 369, 380, 413,
    420, 422, 426

aesthetic, 1–4, 17, 24–25, 30, 33–37,
    40–43, 49, 162–65, 182, 187, 198,
    212–13, 218, 223, 254, 265, 269,
    301–302, 349, 410
affirmation, 1, 7, 9, 31, 76, 130, 145, 176,
    188, 212, 225–27, 231–32, 239,
    246, 248, 265–66, 289, 294, 356,
    357, 427, 431, 433
ages of the world, die Weltalter, 4, 5, 36,
    47–48, 50, 52, 62, 79, 84, 89–90,
    98–99, 102, 104–209, 307, 313,
    349, 396, 404, 422
Αἰδώς. See shame
air, 46, 60, 66–69, 85, 143, 159–60, 163,
    216, 401, 407–408. See also element
Allemann, Beda, 7, 236
alterity. See otherness
ἁμαρτία. See flaw
Amazons, 126–27, 130, 144, 153, 164–67,
    170–71
ambiguity, 12–14, 65–66, 70, 80–82, 100,
    140, 241, 278, 309, 335, 338, 356,
    378, 402
ambivalence, 45, 67, 76, 79, 165, 218–19,
    243, 266, 386–87, 393, 429
Ananke, Ἀνάγκη, 91, 141, 284, 311, 326
Anaxagoras of Clazomenae, 131, 182, 203,
    210
Anaximander of Miletus, 269, 292, 300
androgyny, 5, 80, 140, 395, 397
angels, 57, 61, 154–55, 159–60, 163, 308,
    344, 358, 383
animals, 87, 93, 101–102, 122, 126–27,
    130, 132, 153, 155–60, 162–63,
    165–72, 181, 285, 318, 430
die Anmut, grace, charm, χάρις, 130–32,
    171, 177, 212, 272, 324, 328, 361

447

Index

Index

Index

Index

Index

Index

Index

David Farrell Krell is Professor of Philosophy at DePaul University. He is author of many books, including *Postponements; Of Memory, Reminiscence, and Writing; Daimon Life; Infectious Nietzsche;* and *Contagion,* all of which are available from Indiana University Press.

CPSIA information can be obtained
at www.ICGtesting.com
Printed in the USA
BVHW041439090119
537429BV00007B/102/P

9 780253 217530